PICTORIAL
ATLAS
OF THE
WORLD

The following flags are copyright by and used with permission
from **The Flag Research Center**, Winchester, Mass. 01890:

p.10 – Albania, Andorra, Bosnia-Herzegovina; p.11 – Bulgaria,
Croatia, Czech Republic, Estonia, Finland, Georgia;
p.12 – Latvia; p.13 – Lithuania, Macedonia; p.14 – San Marino,
Slovak Republic, Slovenia, Spain; p.15 – Azerbaijan,
Kazakhstan, Kyrgyzstan, Russia, Tajikistan, Turkmenistan,
Uzbekistan, Yugoslavia; p.18 – Afghanistan, Bahrain,
Bangladesh, Cambodia; p.19 – Iraq; p.21 – Mongolia, Nepal;
p.22 – Saudi Arabia; p.23 – United Arab Emirates; p.26 – Cape
Verde; p.27 – Congo; p.28 – Djibouti, Equatorial Guinea;
Ethiopia; p.33 – Zimbabwe; p.36 – Bermuda; p.37 – Brazil;
p.38 – Dominica, El Salvador; p.39 – Haiti; p.40 – Nicaragua;
p.44 – Kiribati; p.44/45 – Marshall Islands, Micronesia;
p.45 – Tuvalu.

2502
This edition published in 1996 by Colour Library Direct
© 1989 CLB International, Godalming, Surrey
All rights reserved
Printed in Spain
ISBN 1-85833-515-9

PICTORIAL
ATLAS
— OF THE —
WORLD

FOREWORD

In 1636 a bound collection of maps was published by Gerard Mercator and John Hondt with a frontispiece illustrating the titan Atlas bearing the world on his shoulders. As a result, the word 'atlas' entered the vocabulary as a synonym for a book of maps. In the seventeenth century only the very rich could afford the luxury of an atlas. Cartographic masterpieces by Dutch map engravers offered their patrons the first view of a world whose horizons were being swiftly broadened by maritime discovery.

Today, most households can afford an atlas even if they do not own one. Certainly, the need for and the attraction of the atlas have never been greater. Never have so many people been on the move around the world. Never have so many been concerned with the impact of world events. 'Atlas-eaters', Dylan Thomas called those who were hungry for world news. The atlas, through its coordinates of latitude and longitude, can answer the question 'Where?'. Or, perhaps, more precisely, the index to the atlas provides the answer – hence the importance of the extended index to the *Pictorial Atlas of the World*.

In an atlas, the science of map-making is married to the art of map presentation. Techniques of production are increasingly refined; sources of information are increasingly precise. Satellite imagery, photogrammetry and computerisation have transformed map production. Most of the *Pictorial Atlas of the World* consists of topographical maps. Additionally, the pictorial section provides useful and fascinating information on the world's nations and peoples.

An atlas is no substitute for a globe. The two are complementary, for not even the larger globes can include a fraction of the information that is packed into an atlas. The task of projecting the globe onto a flat surface has taxed the ingenuity of mathematicians since the Greeks first attempted to measure the circumference of the Earth. The variety of formidably-named projections employed in the *Pictorial Atlas of the World* illustrates the extended range of options available to present-day cartographers.

Atlases have a romantic appeal as well as a utilitarian value. The novelist Alan Sillitoe, in a memorable essay on maps, recalls the flights of fancy set in motion by his 'first cheap layer-tinted atlas'. To turn the pages of the *Pictorial Atlas of the World* – to contemplate the controlling features of land and sea, to reflect upon the boundaries that define the outlines and shape the destinies of countries and to respond to the magic of the infinity of place-names – is to experience a stimulus to the imagination as well as to the intellect.

William R. Mead
PROFESSOR EMERITUS OF GEOGRAPHY, UNIVERSITY COLLEGE LONDON.

MAP LEGEND

SETTLEMENT

For scales larger than 1 inch : 30 miles   Population

BIRMINGHAM   >1,000,000

GLASGOW   500,000–1,000,000

CARDIFF   250,000–500,000

LIMERICK   50,000–250,000

• **Dover**   10,000–50,000

• Lossiemouth   5,000–10,000

o Church Stretton   <5,000

CROYDON   London Borough

For scales between 1 inch : 30 miles and 1 inch : 190 miles

NEW YORK   >5,000,000

MONTRÉAL   2,500,000–5,000,000

■ **SAN DIEGO**   1,000,000–2,500,000

• **Hyderabad**   500,000–1,000,000

• Adelaide   100,000–500,000

o Key West   <100,000

For scales smaller than 1 inch : 190 miles

■ **LOS ANGELES**   >1,000,000

• **Maracaibo**   500,000–1,000,000

• Santa Fe   <500,000

Washington National capital   **Winnipeg** State, provincial capital

COMMUNICATIONS

——— Highway

--------- Highway under construction

——— Principal road

- - - - - - - Principal road under construction

——— Other main road

– – – – Track, seasonal road

→ ← Road tunnel

——— Principal railroad

– – – Principal railroad under construction

→ ← Railroad tunnel

✈ International, main airport

BOUNDARIES

▬▬▬▬ International

▬ ▬ ▬ ▬ Undefined, disputed

——— Internal, state, provincial

– – – – Armistice, ceasefire line

The representation of a boundary in this atlas does not denote its international recognition and therefore the de facto situation has been depicted.

HYDROGRAPHIC FEATURES

River, stream

Intermittent watercourse

Waterfall, rapids

Dam, barrage

Irrigation, drainage channel

Canal

Lake, reservoir

Intermittent, seasonal lake

Salt pan, mud flat

Oasis

Marsh, swamp

Reef

Depth of sea in meters

Scales larger than 1 inch : 190 miles   Scales smaller than 1 inch : 190 miles

0   200   3000   0   1000   5000

OTHER FEATURES

▲ 3798   Elevation above sea level (meters)

▼ –133   Depression below sea level (meters)

≍   Pass

Oil, gas pipeline with field

ENVIRONMENTAL TYPES

 Permanent ice and snow

 Mountain and moorland

 Tundra

 Coniferous forest

 Deciduous forest

 Tropical forest

 Prairie

 Temperate agriculture

 Mediterranean scrub

 Savannah

Desert

This representation of the environment and its associated vegetation gives an overview of the landscape. It is not intended to be definitive.

CONVERSION SCALES

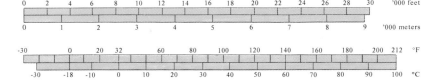

◀ *Chicago, Illinois, one of the largest cities in the United States.*

First page: Victoria Falls span the Middle Zambezi River at one of its widest points. Title Page: the well-known resort of Bled, in the Slovenian Highlands

EUROPE

*A*s the cradle of Western civilisation and the industrial revolution which now dominates the world economies, Europe may justly claim to be the historical heart of the modern world. It was in Europe that technological advances made mass-production industry possible for the first time. This led to an economic dominance over the rest of the world, which continued until the same processes were taken up by the booming population of North America and the industrial lead crossed the Atlantic.

Geographically, Europe is a highly diverse and fragmented continent without any of the vast plains, mountain ranges or deserts which characterise other land masses. In Europe everything is on a much smaller scale than elsewhere. The greatest mountain chain is the Alps, which stretch across northern Italy and on into eastern Europe, but these peaks are dwarfed by the Asian Himalayas or the South American Andes. The largest plain is that of the Ukraine, now devoted to the production of grain crops, but again this is far smaller than the North American prairies or the Mongolian grasslands.

Europe is, however, immensely diverse, with a wide variety of landscape forms being found in relatively small areas. Fertile plains jostle with mountain ranges and dense forests with productive meadows. It is the sheer diversity of the geological make-up that gives the continent its characteristic appearance. Nowhere is it possible to travel far without coming across a change in scenery.

Hidden beneath this fragmented landscape is a wide variety of mineral wealth. Pockets of every conceivable metal ore are to be found scattered across Europe. Though none occurs in the kind of mass deposit encountered on other continents, these ores have provided the raw materials for European industry for many centuries, and only now are being surpassed by bulk ores from elsewhere.

Until the immigration of racial groups from other continents in large numbers during the late 20th century, the population of Europe was remarkably homogeneous. Almost the entire population was descended from Indo-Europeans, who spread across the continent in antiquity. Earlier peoples were swamped by these new cultures, only surviving in isolated pockets, such as that of the Basques of northern Spain.

However, the populations of Europe have strong historic cultures and concepts of nationhood which transcend the rather academic classification of Indo-European. These nationalist identities are a powerful cultural impetus within Europe and sources of much pride. They may also lead to factional violence, and attempts at supra-national states have rarely survived. Among the most recent to fall before nationalist feelings is Yugoslavia, where civil war still rages after the secession of Croatia, Slovenia, Bosnia-Herzegovina and Macedonia. The colossal USSR, too, crumbled following severe economic difficulties and political unrest. The Baltic States took the opportunity of leaving the union first, followed by the other republics, which remained bound together, however, within the hastily created Commonwealth of Independent States.

The keynote of Europe is diversity. There is diversity in landscape, in geology and in human culture. Packed into the smallest of the continents are over thirty countries based around identifiable national groupings. Even within countries nationalist divisions can be found. The nation state of Italy was united little over a century ago and strong regional differences of culture, language and lifestyle are still apparent. Europe is nothing if not a continent of contrasts.

◀ Iceland - 'Land of Fire and Ice'.　　▲ Traditional costume, Bulgaria.　　▲ Dubrovnik, Croatia.　　▼ Pünderich, overlooking the Mosel, Germany.

ALBANIA

Population: 3.4 million
Area: 29,000 square kilometres
Capital: Tirana
Language: Albanian and Greek
Currency: Lek

The rugged mountain nation of Albania has been virtually cut off from the rest of Europe for decades. A province of first the Byzantine and later the Ottoman Empires, Albania gained independence as a kingdom in 1912 and as a Communist republic in 1946. Until the early 1990s, the old-style Stalinist regime retained a tight grip on running the country. In 1992, however, a non-communist regime was elected. Under Communism the nation has tried to revolutionise its economy by abandoning the traditional farming techniques which formerly employed the population and today less than half the work-force is in farming. Copper, steel and electronics are growth industries.

ANDORRA

Population: 59,000
Area: 468 square kilometres
Capital: Andorra La Vella
Language: Catalan and French
Currency: French Franc and Spanish Peseta

The independent mountain state of Andorra has retained its freedom unchanged since 1278, when the rival powers of the region agreed on a compromise. Under the 700-year-old arrangement the state is ruled jointly by Spain's Bishop of Urgel and the Count of Foix. As the estates of Foix have since passed to the French state, the President of France now undertakes this role. In practice Andorrans, govern themselves through a democratic system, though the agreement of the joint rulers is needed for all actions. Tourism and duty-free shopping bolster the modern prosperity.

AUSTRIA

Population: 7.9 million
Area: 84,000 square kilometres
Capital: Vienna
Language: German
Currency: Schilling

Until 1918 the heart of the vast Hapsburg Empire, which encompassed the Danube Basin and much of the Balkans, Austria is now a democratic republic based upon the German-speaking parts of that Empire. The capital, Vienna, has a long tradition of sophisticated culture and excellence in the arts. The economy of Austria is broadly based, though agriculture is limited by the terrain. The mountains attract large numbers of tourists who come to enjoy winter skiing and summer walking.

BELGIUM

Population: 10 million
Area: 31,000 square kilometres
Capital: Brussels
Language: Flemish, French and German
Currency: Belgian Franc

The present constitutional monarchy dates back to 1830, when the Belgian people rebelled against Dutch rule and invited a German prince to become their king. The country is governed by a two-chamber Parliament acting under the monarch. The Flemish- and French-speaking areas each enjoy a degree of regional self-government. The nation is predominantly urban, with industry and services leading the economy. The coal, steel and other metal industries dominate the scene. Agriculture contributes only a small proportion to the economy, but Belgium is now almost self-sufficient in foods.

▲ *An open-air restaurant, Brussels, Belgium.*

BOSNIA HERZEGOVINA

Population: 4.3 million
Area: 51,129 square kilometres
Capital: Sarajevo
Language: Serbo-Croatian
Currency: Din

Bosnia-Herzegovina, part of the former Yugoslavia, declared independence in April 1992 and since then has been deeply divided by civil war. Bosnia's Serbian minority, the largest ethnic Serbian group in any of the breakaway republics, boycotted the 1992 referendum on independence, with the two Serbian members of the Bosnian collective presidency resigning when the result was made known. Ancient religious and ethnic tensions soon erupted into civil war. Despite the presence of a UN peacekeeping force in Bosnia and numerous peace initiatives the war continues. Manufacturing industries include steel, aluminium and textiles. Agriculture is often at subsistence level.

▲ *Tranquil countryside, Finland.*

▼ *Old-world charm, Czech Republic.*

Above right: *The Schonbrunn Palace, Vienna, Austria.*

▼ *Nyhavn, in Copenhagen, Denmark.*

▲ *Corn harvest, Albania.*

▼ *An Orthodox priest, Cyprus.*

▲ *The Orthodox Cathedral, Tallinn, Estonia.*

▲ *Vineyards, Santenay, France.*

▲ *The mountain state of Andorra.*

BULGARIA

Population: 9 million
Area: 111,000 square kilometres
Capital: Sofia
Language: Bulgarian
Currency: Lev

Bulgaria became independent of the Ottoman Empire in 1908 and became a Communist republic following the Russian occupation in 1946. In 1989 street protests and demands for reform led the National Assembly to approve a multi-party democracy and free elections. In 1990 the Communist government resigned and in 1991 a new constitution drawn up. The river valleys have fertile soils and a climate conducive to heavy grain crops and live stock rearing. The traditional dominance of agriculture has been overtaken by a growing industrial sector.

CROATIA

Population: 4.8 million
Area: 56,538 square kilometres
Capital: Zagreb
Language: Croatian
Currency: Croatian Dinar

The former Yugoslav republic of Croatia seceded from the Yugoslav federation in October 1991. Violent internal conflict arose as long-standing tensions between Croats and ethnic Serbs erupted. Helped by Yugoslav troops, the Serbian minority tried to seize power by force. Fighting continued throughout 1991 and at the beginning of 1992 UN peacekeeping troops intervened, establishing four peacekeeping zones. At the beginning of 1993 Croatian forces launched an attack on one of these zones, an action that was widely condemned.

CYPRUS

Population: 756,000
Area: 9,000 square kilometres
Capital: Nicosia
Language: Greek and Turkish
Currency: Cypriot Pound

Settled by Greek-speakers during the Iron Age, Cyprus has during its history been ruled by the Persians, Romans, Venetians, Turks and British. In 1960 it gained its independence from Britain, but strife between Greek and Turkish communities led to the arrival of UN peacekeepers. Despite their presence, a threatened coup by the Greeks resulted in invasion in 1974 by Turkish forces. The occupied north declared itself a republic in 1983, although this has gained only Turkish recognition. Tourism and light industry play a prime economic role, although traditional agriculture remains important.

CZECH REPUBLIC

Population: 10.31 million
Area: 78,864 square kilometres
Capital: Prague
Language: Czech
Currency: Koruna

The Czech Republic occupies the western regions of what was formerly Czechoslovakia and has a predominantly urban culture with strong German influences. Once part of the Hapsburg Empire, Czechoslovakia became independent in 1918. Communists took power with Soviet aid in 1948, and an attempt at liberalisation in 1968, known as the Prague Spring, was crushed by Russian tanks. In November 1989 mass public demonstrations led to the resignation of the Communist government and the legalisation of opposition parties. Ethnic and economic tensions between Czechs and Slovacs led to the separation of the two regions in 1993. The Czech republic is a heavily industrialised nation.

DENMARK

Population: 5.1 million
Area: 43,000 square kilometres
Capital: Copenhagen
Language: Danish
Currency: Krone

The rich soil and temperate climate of Denmark have aided the traditionally-strong agricultural sector. Grains, potatoes and vegetables are grown in quantities, but it is livestock which dominates. Recently the industrial sector has grown significantly and manufacturing now outstrips agriculture in terms of economic value. The constitution is based on the monarch, who cannot act without the consent of the democratically-elected parliament.

ESTONIA

Population: 1.6 million
Area: 45,000 square kilometres
Capital: Tallinn
Language: Estonian
Currency: Kroon

In September 1991 Estonia was accepted as an independent nation for the first time since its annexation by the Soviet Union in 1939. The republic has been dominated by economic central planning from Moscow for over five decades and relies heavily on agriculture for employment and prosperity. Gas-rich shale and phosphates represent the only mineral wealth and industrial base for this small nation. Co-operation with the other Baltic states is already established and other foreign economic links are being vigorously pursued.

FINLAND

Population: 5 million
Area: 338,000 square kilometres
Capital: Helsinki
Language: Finnish
Currency: Markka

Ruled in turn by Denmark, Sweden and Russia, Finland gained independence in 1917, when the people took advantage of the chaos following the Russian Revolution to seize power. In 1940, war with Russia resulted in Finland losing much territory around Lake Ladoga to the Soviets. Modern foreign policy emphasises the need for friendly relations with Russia and with Scandinavian nations. The economy of the nation is broadly based. The vast forests provide raw material for a lumber trade. The small area of land suitable for agriculture is heavily used for raising livestock, particularly cattle in the south and reindeer in the north. Industry is concentrated on the extraction and processing of iron deposits.

FRANCE

Population: 57 million
Area: 543,000 square kilometres
Capital: Paris
Language: French
Currency: French Franc

The modern state of France is generally traced back to the accession of the Capetian dynasty to the throne of the Western Franks in 987, though Frankish power was established in the region as early as 500 A.D. The monarchy was overthrown in the Revolution of 1789, after which France was ruled by republics, emperors and kings. The Fifth Republic was established in 1958. The present constitution allows for a democratically-elected parliament, which operates under the guidance of an elected President. The economy of the nation is highly developed, with industry and services being dominant employers. Agriculture remains largely in the hands of small-scale farmers and produces quantities of grain and fruits, most notably grapes, from which the famous French wines are produced.

GEORGIA

Population: 5.4 million
Area: 67,000 square kilometres
Capital: Tbilisi
Language: Russian
Currency: Rouble

In April 1991, Georgia became an independent state, with a remarkable 98.9 percent popular vote in favour of independence. A period of political instability followed. Vast manganese deposits form the basis for the prosperous mining industry of Georgia, though coal is also found in quantity and other minerals are exploited on a smaller scale.

GERMANY

Population: 80 million
Area: 357,000 square kilometres
Capital: Berlin
Language: German
Currency: Mark

Unity and division have been the hallmarks of German history. The disparate German tribes were united under the Frankish Empire in the 9th century, but this fell apart, to be replaced by the Holy Roman Empire of the Middle Ages. Initially strong, the Empire broke up into dozens of small states and city republics. This pattern persisted until 1871 when the German states were united under Prussian rule as the German Empire. This nation remained together until 1945, when Germany lost much territory and was divided as Communist East and Democratic West Germany. In 1990 the overthrow of the Communist regime in East Germany led to reunification. The stronger West German economy is concentrating on raising the prosperity of East Germany.

GREECE

Population: 10 million
Area: 132,000 square kilometres
Capital: Athens
Language: Greek
Currency: Drachma

Home of the ancient civilisation which has had such a profound influence on all Western culture, Greece is today working to join the front runners in European economies. The magnificent history, fine climate and attractive beaches have made Greece a favourite tourist resort for generations. Tourism is now the largest single industry in terms of foreign earnings. The mountainous terrain limits agriculture, but there are extensive olive groves and citrus orchards. Industry is concentrated on food processing, textiles and leatherwork. After a period of military rule in the 1970s, Greece reverted to a democratic system of government.

HUNGARY

Population: 10 million
Area: 93,000 square kilometres
Capital: Budapest
Language: Magyar
Currency: Forint

Formerly a dominant state within the Hapsburg Empire, which ruled the Danube Basin from the Alps to the Black Sea, Hungary became independent in 1918. In 1949 a Communist government was imposed, and the 1956 nationalist rising was put down by Soviet tanks and troops. After popular protests and demands for reform, the Communist Party was disbanded in 1989, opening the way for democratic elections. Wheat, maize and potatoes are the main crops, and large numbers of cattle and pigs are raised. In recent years the role of industry in the economy has increased in importance, with metallurgy, chemicals and electronics predominating.

ICELAND

Population: 261,000
Area: 103,000 square kilometres
Capital: Reykjavik
Language: Icelandic
Currency: Icelandic Krona

Viking settlers began arriving in Iceland in the 9th century, ousting the few Irish monks already there. An independent society based on Viking social rules existed until 1264, when factional violence led to Norwegian control. In 1381, Iceland passed to the Danish crown. It recovered full self-government in 1918 and severance from Denmark in 1946. The present republic operates with two chambers under an elected President. Only two percent of land is farmed and livestock is kept in small numbers. Fishing provides the basis of the economy. Industry is very limited.

IRELAND

Population: 3.5 million
Area: 70,000 square kilometres
Capital: Dublin
Language: Gaelic and English
Currency: Irish Pound

In 1801 after centuries of growing British influence, the Irish Parliament was dissolved and the country was governed from Westminster. In 1921 the Catholic southern counties of Ireland gained independence after an armed uprising becoming the Republic of Eire in 1948, while the Protestant counties of Ulster remained part of Britain. Ongoing civil violence and terrorist activities have disrupted life in border counties and dominate Irish relations with Britain. The economy is traditionally agricultural. Large numbers of cattle produce dairy products, and sheep and pigs provide meat. Industrial activity has grown rapidly in recent years, and is now more important to the economy than agriculture. Food processing, textiles and electrical engineering are dominant.

ITALY

Population: 57 million
Area: 301,000 square kilometres
Capital: Rome
Language: Italian
Currency: Italian Lira

The various city states, kingdoms and duchies of Italy were not united until 1861, and the republic was established in 1946. The present constitution allows for two chambers, the lower elected directly and the upper elected by the historic regions. The President is elected by the two houses of parliament. There are numerous political parties representing many shades of opinion, though fascism is banned. Southern parts of the country are generally less well developed than the north. Grapes are widely grown for wine production. Industry is concentrated in northern cities where textiles, food processing and the manufacture of machinery lead the sector.

LATVIA

Population: 2.6 million
Area: 64,000 square kilometres
Capital: Riga
Language: Latvian and Russian
Currency: Rouble

The troubled history of Latvia as an independent nation began with a democratic government being installed with British military support in 1919. In 1940 Soviet power was imposed. Together with Lithuania and Estonia, Latvia became independent once again in 1991. Five decades of economic central planning has given Latvia a heritage of heavy industry, with steel, railway equipment and textiles dominating. The previous agricultural economic base has been greatly reduced.

LIECHTENSTEIN

Population: 30,000
Area: 160 square kilometres
Capital: Vaduz
Language: German
Currency: Swiss Franc

The tiny Principality of Liechtenstein dates back to 1434. In 1712 the principality passed to the Liechtenstein family, which held it from the Holy Roman Emperor. When that empire collapsed in 1806, the family retained their domains and in 1923 joined Switzerland in a customs and currency union. The present constitution places power in the hands of the Prince, though legislation needs approval of the democratically-elected parliament. The economy is based on a mixture of agriculture, light industry and commerce.

▲ *Dusk in Mykonos, Greece.*

▲ *A round tower, Co. Wicklow, Ireland.*

▼ *Luxembourg, one of Europe's smallest nations.*

▲ *The Principality of Monaco.*

▼ *The Principality of Liechtenstein.*

▲ *The Danube River, Budapest, Hungary.*

◀ *Heavy industry, Lithuania.*

▲ *A characteristic view of Malta.*

▼ *The Old City, Riga, Latvia.*

◀ *The Colosseum, Rome, Italy.*

▲ *Kinderdijk, east of Rotterdam, Netherlands.*

LITHUANIA

Population: 3.8 million
Area: 65,000 square kilometres
Capital: Vilnius
Language: Lithuanian
Currency: Coupons currently used

With a population over 80 percent ethnic Lithuanians, the republic has long desired independence. In March 1991 an overwhelming majority voted for separation from the then Soviet Union, but it was not until August 1991 that this became a reality. Traditionally an agricultural nation, Lithuania is now dominated by industry, particularly heavy engineering and textiles.

LUXEMBOURG

Population: 389,000
Area: 2,500 square kilometres
Capital: Luxembourg
Language: German and French
Currency: Luxembourg Franc

The tiny state of Luxembourg enjoyed varying degrees of self government until being conquered by France in 1795. In 1815 the current Grand Duchy came into being under the Dutch monarchy, and in 1890 full independence came. The Grand Duke is closely involved in administration with the democratically-elected parliament. The nation is part of a customs union with Belgium and Belgian currency can be used within Luxembourg. Industry is based on a thriving iron and steel business. Agriculture plays a minor role in national life.

MACEDONIA

Population: 2 million
Area: 25,713 square kilometres
Capital: Skopje
Language: Macedonian
Currency: Denar

Though Macedonia declared its independence from Yugoslavia in 1992, it was not recognised as an independent state by the international community until 1993 because of Greek objections to the use of the name 'Macedonia'. The state is land-locked, surrounded by Greece to the south, Yugoslavia to the north and by Bulgaria to the east, and throughout its history has been threatened by claims on its borders. Agriculture, particularly wheat, grapes and corn, are important to the country's economy.

MALTA

Population: 360,000

Area: 316 square kilometres
Capital: Valletta
Language: Maltese and English
Currency: Maltese Lira

During World War II Malta was a vital British naval base and came under attack by German and Italian forces. In 1942, King George VI awarded the George Cross to the people of Malta. This medal is featured on the Maltese flag, together with the colours of the Knights of Malta, who ruled between 1530 and 1798. Malta gained independence from Britain in 1964, though economic ties remain close. Malta's strategic position in the Mediterranean makes commerce, trade and ship-building lucrative industries. Tourism is the biggest single earner of foreign currency for Malta. The constitution is a multi-party democracy in which two major parties dominate.

MONACO

Population: 30,000
Area: 1.5 square kilometres
Capital: Monaco
Language: Monegasque and French
Currency: French Franc

The small Principality of Monaco has been the domain of the Grimaldi family since 1297, placing itself under French protection in 1861. The constitution allows for democratic government though the Prince retains much influence. The main economic base of Monaco is tourism, with nearly ten times as many visitors as residents in the course of a year. The scenic coastline and fine beach delight many tourists, but it is the famous casino which is the major attraction. Agriculture is virtually non-existent but the industrial sector is growing in importance.

NETHERLANDS

Population: 15 million
Area: 34,0000 square kilometres
Capital: Amsterdam and The Hague
Language: Dutch
Currency: Dutch Guilder

The nation came into being in the late 16th century, when the prosperous Protestant cities rebelled against oppressive Catholic rule from Spain. Much of the Netherlands has been reclaimed from the sea by massive projects. Much of this land is devoted to agriculture, with potatoes, sugar beet and grain being major crops. Cut flowers and flower bulbs are produced in large quantities for export, while dairy cattle graze on meadows to produce milk from which famous Dutch cheeses are made. The nation's position at the mouth of the Rhine has long ensured lucrative trade connections.

NORWAY

Population: 4.3 million
Area: 324,000 square kilometres
Capital: Oslo
Language: Norwegian
Currency: Norwegian Krone

In 1905 Norway gained independence from Sweden. The country's constitution places power in the hands of a democratically-elected parliament, though the monarch retains control of the armed forces. The mountainous terrain makes agriculture difficult and much food needs to be imported. Hydro-electric power is produced in quantity and supplies ninety-nine percent of domestic needs. Offshore oil and gas have added to the energy self-reliance of Norway. Industry is prosperous and is based on the processing of domestic metals, agricultural products and timber from the vast upland forests.

▲ *The Lofoton Islands, Norway.*

POLAND

Population: 38 million
Area: 312,000 square kilometres
Capital: Warsaw
Language: Polish
Currency: Zloty

The powerful kingdom of Poland collapsed in the late 18th century and was divided between the Prussian, Hapsburg and Russian empires. Reconstitution and independence did not occur until 1918. The German invasion of Poland in 1939 sparked World War II, and following liberation in 1945 Poland was ruled by a Communist regime imposed by the Soviet Union. Communist rule ended in 1989 after several years of opposition from the trade union Solidarity. Free elections were called for 1991, with opposition parties campaigning for the first time in decades. The Polish economy is industrially based, with iron and steel, textiles and machine manufacture being the most important. The agricultural

sector is still important, producing wheat, rye and potatoes, together with large quantities of dairy produce.

PORTUGAL

Population: 10 million
Area: 92,000 square kilometres
Capital: Lisbon
Language: Portuguese
Currency: Escudo

The coup of 1974 overthrew the dictatorship which had governed Portugal since 1933, and in 1976 introduced a democratic constitution for only the second time in Portugal's history. The present constitution, adopted in 1982, allows for an elected President who chooses the Prime Minister from the Assembly, which is elected by universal adult suffrage. Manufacturing is based on textiles and leather goods. Agriculture is based on grains and potatoes, and wine, cork and olives are important export earners.

ROMANIA

Population: 23 million
Area: 238,000 square kilometres
Capital: Bucharest
Language: Romanian and Hungarian
Currency: Leu

The overthrow of the Communist regime of President Ceausescu in 1989 was attended by street fighting and great confusion. A temporary government was elected in 1990 to draw up a new constitution based on democratic principles. Until the Communist takeover in 1947 Romania was a traditionally agricultural kingdom with little industry. The past decades have seen massive government encouragement of industry, which today is concentrated on iron and steel, chemicals and textiles. The farms continue to produce large quantities of wheat and maize, while sheep-rearing is still important.

SAN MARINO

Population: 24,000
Area: 61 square kilometres
Capital: San Marino
Language: Italian
Currency: Italian Lira

Legend has it that the 4th-century Saint Marinus founded the republic as a self-governing Christian community to escape persecution. The republic won full independence from the Pope in 1631, and in 1862 concluded a treaty with the newly-created Italian nation, securing continued independence. Agriculture is an important source of employment and wine is exported. Small scale industrial activity includes

chemicals, ceramics and paints. Much economic wealth comes from tourism and the sale of unique coins and stamps.

SLOVAK REPUBLIC OR SLOVAKIA

Population: 5.3 million
Area: 49,035 square kilometres
Capital: Bratislava
Language: Slovak, Czech
Currency: Slovak Koruna

Slovakia separated from Czechoslovakia on 1 January 1993, forming an independent state. The Czech and Slovak states had been joined in 1918, following the collapse of the Austia-Hungarian Empire. The Slovak people were proud of their heritage and were determined to assert their sovereignty. The abandonment of a Communist system has hindered the development of the country's economy and agriculture and industry are underdeveloped.

SLOVENIA

Population: 1.98 million
Area: 20,251 square kilometres
Capital: Ljubljana
Language: Slovenian
Currency: Tolar

Slovenia, formerly one of the Yugoslav republics, declared its complete independence in October 1991 and was recognised as an independent state by Germany later that year, with the EEC following suit at the beginning of 1992. The population of Slovenia is not as ethnically diverse as that of Croatia and Bosnia-Herzegovina. It is unified both by religion and by language and consequently has not suffered the violence that has marked the recent history of the other former Yugoslav republics. Metallurgy and furniture-making are the traditional industries.

SPAIN

Population: 40 million
Area: 492,000 square kilometres
Capital: Madrid
Language: Spanish and regional
Currency: Peseta

Spain regained its monarchy in 1975 after an interruption of forty-four years with the accession of King Juan Carlos. The constitution vests power in a parliament named the *Cortes*, with a lower house elected by proportional representation and a senate elected by province. The traditional agricultural economic base has now been overtaken by industry, but remains important. Wheat and barley are the major crops. Industry is dominated by motor vehicles, textiles, paper, and iron

and steel, which together account for the majority of exports.

SWEDEN

Population: 8.7 million
Area: 450,000 square kilometres
Capital: Stockholm
Language: Swedish
Currency: Swedish Krona

Sweden acquired approximately its present boundaries a thousand years ago, but has since been united with other Scandinavian nations and in the 17th century enjoyed Baltic hegemony. The present monarchy dates from 1809, when the French general Jean Bernadotte was chosen to become king on the extinction of the native line. The constitution introduced in 1975 reduced the role of monarch to ceremonial and gave power to the democratic parliament. The highly-prosperous economy is based on iron ore deposits. Over half of all manufacturing is made up of metal smelting, metal machinery and other metal products. A further quarter of the sector is composed of timber, plywood and other wood products. Agriculture is well developed, but on a small scale.

SWITZERLAND

Population: 7 million
Area: 41,000 square kilometres
Capital: Bern
Language: German, French, Italian and Romansch
Currency: Swiss Franc

A confederation of twenty-three cantons, Switzerland is famous for its neutrality. But the state had its origins in a defensive alliance in 1291, and saw many wars in its early centuries of existence. The constitution vests supreme power in the electorate which can demand laws and changes to the constitution. Each canton is self-governing, with its own parliament; the federal government being responsible for war, peace and treaties. Most crops are grown on the fertile central plain. Manufacturing is a major activity and is based on textiles, chemicals and the processing of agricultural produce. Banking and finance is a well-established sector of the economy.

COMMONWEALTH OF INDEPENDENT STATES

The Commonwealth of Independent States (CIS) came into being in 1991 when the regime that had controlled the former USSR collapsed. This loose structure handles only major central issues, while the individual nations assume other powers. There are separate listings for those republics that did not join the CIS: Estonia, Georgia, Latvia and Lithuania.

ARMENIA

Population: 3.3 million
Area: 30,000 square kilometres
Capital: Yerevan
Language: Armenian, Russian, Kurdish
Currency: Rouble

Armenia's rugged terrain allows only limited agriculture based on olive groves, cotton and sub-tropical fruits. Wide ranging mineral deposits are more promising for the economy and efficient exploitation of these in the wake of freedom from central Soviet planning may lead to prosperity.

AZERBAIJAN

Population: 7 million
Area: 87,000 square kilometres
Capital: Baku
Language: Azerbaijani, Armenian, Russian
Currency: Rouble

Recently the scene of ethnic violence between the Azerbaijani majority and the Armenian minority, this republic is rich in natural resources. Industry is based on reserves of oil, iron ore, bauxite and various precious metals. Agriculturally, the republic produces grapes and tobacco.

BELARUS

Population: 10 million
Area: 208,000 square kilometres
Capital: Minsk
Language: Russian, Polish and other languages
Currency: Rouble

Belarus has taken a lead in the development of the CIS and its institutions. The economy of the republic is based on the rich pasture land and pockets of agricultural land. The processing of the farm output accounts for much of the industry, but there are also large chemical and steel concerns.

KAZAKHSTAN

Population: 16.5 million
Area: 2,717,000 square kilometres
Capital: Alma-Ata
Language: Russian, Kazakh
Currency: Rouble

Since the collapse of the USSR, Kazakhstan has emerged as one of the Central Asian Republics of the CIS. Formerly a pastoral economy, agriculture and the mineral wealth are now exploited on a large scale.

KYRGYZSTAN

Population: 4.2 million

Area: 198,000 square kilometres
Capital: Bishbek
Language: Kirghiz-Turkish, Russian, Jagatai
Currency: Rouble

Traditionally a pastoral region, the economy of Kyrgyzstan remains firmly based on livestock. Agriculture has also become important. Much of the industry is based on processing agricultural products, though mining contributes to the economy.

MOLDOVA

Population: 4 million
Area: 34,000 square kilometres
Capital: Chisinau
Language: Romanian, Russian, Gagauzi
Currency: Rouble

Populated mainly with ethnic Romanians, Moldova is economically dominated by agriculture and the processing of farm products. Only the production of concrete and other building materials breaks the pattern.

RUSSIA

Population: 148 million
Area: 17,075,000 square kilometres
Capital: Moscow
Language: Russian, numerous other languages
Currency: Rouble

The largest of the republics within the CIS. Industry is highly developed and is a major employer. Russia's economy has led the way in throwing off central state control and embracing free market principles.

▲ *The golden domes of the Kremlin, Moscow, Russia.*

TAJIKISTAN

Population: 5 million
Area: 143,000 square kilometres
Capital: Dushandbe
Language: Tajik-Persian, Jagatai, Russian
Currency: Rouble

The republic is largely dependent on agriculture, with irrigation enabling the production of warm-climate fruits. Coal, lead and zinc mining account for most industrial activity in Tajikistan. At the end of 1992 the volatile political situation erupted and civil war broke out.

TURKMENISTAN

Population: 3.5 million
Area: 488,000 square kilometres
Capital: Ashgabat
Language: Turkish, Russian, Jagatai
Currency: Rouble

Rich oil, coal and sulphur deposits form the basis for an industrial economy, although agriculture, notably cotton, maize, fruit and vegetables, provides the majority of the employment. Turkmenistan was the first of the Central Asian Republics to declare itself free of Moscow, in August 1990.

UKRAINE

Population: 52 million
Area: 604,000 square kilometres
Capital: Kiev
Language: Ukrainian and Russian
Currency: Rouble

The traditional grain basket of eastern Europe, the Ukraine is still a highly productive agricultural region, with nearly half of the crops of the CIS coming from it. The Ukraine was one of the founder members of the CIS.

UZBEKISTAN

Population: 20 million
Area: 447,000 square kilometres
Capital: Tashkent
Language: Jagatai, Russian, Tatar
Currency: Rouble

The Uzbek economy is based on intensive agriculture producing silk, rice, sub-tropical fruits and grapes with mineral exploitation on a modest scale. Industry is limited and is largely based on the rich deposits of oil, coal and copper.

UNITED KINGDOM

Population: 57 million
Area: 243,000 square kilometres
Capital: London
Language: English, Welsh and Gaelic
Currency: Pound Sterling

The United Kingdom is a constitutional monarchy governing Britain, the northern counties of Ireland and neighbouring islands. The kingdoms of England and Scotland were united in 1603 when King James VI of Scotland inherited the English throne. The constitution allows for a single elected chamber together with a part-appointed, part-

▲ *The interior of St Peter's, the Vatican*

inherited House of Lords. Agriculture is well developed and produces about half the nation's requirements. Industry and commerce are the basis of the economic wealth.

VATICAN

Population: 700
Area: 0.3 square kilometres
Capital: Vatican City
Language: Italian and Latin
Currency: Italian Lira

The Vatican is the smallest independent state in the world and exists solely as the residence of the Pope, the head of the Roman Catholic Church. Until 1860 the Pope ruled areas of central Italy, but these were incorporated to the Kingdom of Italy, which in 1870 invaded Rome and confined the Pope to the Vatican complex. In 1929 the Vatican was recognised as an independent state in return for the Pope relinquishing claims over Rome and surrounding territory. The Vatican is the administrative headquarters of the Catholic Church.

YUGOSLAVIA, SERBIA AND MONTENEGRO

Population: 24 million
Area: 255,000 square kilometres
Capitals: Belgrade
Languages: Serbian, Croat Slovene, Macedonian and others
Currency: Yugoslavian Dinar

Yugoslavia came into being in 1918 as a confederation of southern Slavonic peoples newly independent of the Hapsburg Empire. The new constitution of 1946 made the nation a grouping of six republics, in which the Communist was the only legal political party. Attempts in 1989-90 by the central government to curb the internal government of the republics led to widespread protest. When the republics of Slovenia, Croatia, Bosnia and Macedonia seceded from Serbian dominated Yugoslavia in 1991, a bloody civil war ensued. In 1992, Serbia and Montenegro formed the federal republic of Yugoslavia.

ASIA

*A*sia is the largest and most populated continent on Earth. Just two nations, China and India, between them account for nearly two billion inhabitants. An Asian country, Bangladesh is the most densely populated on Earth, with around 730 people to each square kilometre. This compares to a mere twenty-five per square kilometre in the United States.

The incredible population statistics are made possible by the remarkably fertile soils and productive climates of Asia. Bangladesh, for example, is almost ideal for rice cultivation. The monsoon climate provides the alternate wet and dry season needed by the cereal, while the flat landscape makes the flooding and draining of fields easy to accomplish. Massive crops are produced each year. Similar conditions prevail in eastern China, where rural populations have reached saturation point in some areas.

But if Asia has been endowed with vast, life-giving resources, it also has its share of natural disasters. Earthquakes, floods and typhoons are common. Given the concentrated populations, these calamities claim horrendous death tolls among the local peoples. Many regions of Asia have a history scattered with the records of bumper crops leading to population booms, the children of which are then wiped out by disaster and famine.

Not only does Asia contain some of the densest populations in the world, it also boasts some of the emptiest regions anywhere. The vast expanses of Siberia consist of open tundra bordering the Arctic Ocean and, further south, extensive boreal forests. These great coniferous forests cover a staggering 1,100,000,000 hectares and are thought to contain about one-quarter of all the world's trees.

In central eastern Asia there are extensive grasslands on which pastoralist peoples lead traditional lives which have scarcely changed in centuries. Mongolia and neighbouring sections of both China and and the former Soviet Union are the home of ethnic Mongols, who herd cattle and horses on the open plains as their ancestors have done for millenia.

Ethnically, the population of Asia is incredibly diverse. In addition to recent immigrations of Europeans and Africans there is a wide range of indigenous peoples. In the far east, Mongoloid races form the vast majority. In the subcontinent of India Indo-Europeans and Dravidians constitute the bulk of the population. Here, as elsewhere in Asia, there are remnant populations of far older peoples. The inland uplands of Sri Lanka are home to the Veddah, who are apparently unrelated to the majority population but have affinities with the Aboriginals of Australia. Similarly enigmatic are the Ainu of Japan.

Culturally, too, the Asians present a bewildering picture to the world. Asia has been the cradle of major world religions: Buddhism, Hinduism, Confucianism and Taoism all originated in Asia, and continue to find the bulk of their adherents on that continent. Islam, originating on the Arabian peninsula, has spread across much of southern Asia as far as the Pacific Ocean.

The vast continent of Asia is rich in both agricultural and human resources. However, much of the population continues to live at subsistence level. Increases in population have kept pace with farming technology and crop increases and the per capita wealth remains low. National prosperity in most nations is devoted to finding food for their growing populations rather than in improving the standard of living. So long as this cycle of improved food production and increased population continues, the traditional lifestyles and general impoverishment of Asia looks likely to continue.

▲ The Himalayas, Nepal.

▼ Temple dancers, Bali, Indonesia.

16

◄ *Lake Kawaguchi and Mount Fujiyama, Japan.*

▼ *A natural rock formation in Dukhan, Qatar.*

◄ *The back-breaking task of planting rice, Laos.*

▼ *The bustling city of Taipei, Taiwan.*

AFGHANISTAN

Population: 18 million
Area: 652,000 square kilometres
Capital: Kabul
Language: Pustu and Dari
Currency: Afghani

Afghanistan is a country in turmoil and has been for generations. The Soviet invasion of 1979 led to the various factions uniting against the aggressor. The withdrawal of Soviet troops has seen a re-emergence of internal disputes. The mountainous republic has a long tradition of tribal independence and weak government control. The social structure remains fragmented, with most of the population belonging to distinctly different ethnic groups linked by the Islamic religion. The bulk of the population are subsistence farmers or nomadic herdsmen, the latter mainly in the south. Fruit, bread and mutton are the basis of the nation's self-produced food supply. The only mineral wealth is natural gas in the far north.

 BAHRAIN

Population: 486,000
Area: 687 square kilometres
Capital: Manama
Language: Arabic
Currency: Bahraini Dinar

In 1882 the Emirate of Bahrain handed control of its foreign affairs to Britain. In 1971 the arrangement was ended and the Emir proclaimed his nation's independence and soon after dismissed Parliament to rule the nation himself. In 1992 the Emir set up a Consultative Council. Until 1931 Bahrain was an impoverished state subsisting on pearl fishing, small scale agriculture and the profits of trade. The discovery of oil changed everything and vast wealth poured into the nation. The thirty-three islands that make up the state now support a flourishing manufacturing economy, including the production of aluminium alloys, ships and medical equipment. So many people now live in Bahrain that ninety percent of food needs to be imported and water supply is a chronic problem.

 BANGLADESH

Population: 115 million
Area: 144,000 square kilometres
Capital: Dhaka
Language: Bangla and English
Currency: Taka

In a good year Bangladesh is almost ideally suited to intensive cultivation of rice. As many as three heavy crops can be grown on the rich soils within just twelve months. As a consequence the nation is extremely densely populated by peasant farmers growing vast crops for their own consumption and for sale. Unfortunately, recurrent natural disasters, such as floods and cyclones, take a heavy toll in human life and destroy crops. The extremely high birth rate causes an ever-growing population which ensures that the agricultural wealth is fully used feeding the people rather than in improving their living conditions. Other than glass sand, mineral deposits scarcely exist and industry is negligible. The government is notoriously unstable, having suffered numerous coups and military takeovers since independence from Pakistan in 1971.

 BHUTAN

Population: 1.4 million
Area: 47,000 square kilometres
Capital: Thimphu
Language: Dzongkha, Nepali, English
Currency: Ngultrum

The mountain kingdom of Bhutan is an anomaly in India, having managed to retain its quasi-independence when Britain withdrew from the subcontinent, while other kingdoms became merged into the new state of India. Bhutan receives an annual subsidy from India in return for abiding by that country's foreign policy. Internal government is conducted by the king, with the advice of an elected assembly. The electoral system is unusual in that each family has one vote regardless of its number, and monks are separately represented. Bhutan is made up of a number of valleys isolated from each other by precipitous mountains and sheer cliffs. The different ethnic groups have scarcely mixed and they retain their identities. The basis of the economy is agriculture, with many hill tribes surviving at subsistence level. Large mineral deposits have been found but the difficult terrain has hampered exploitation.

 BRUNEI

Population: 267,000
Area: 5,700 square kilometres
Capital: Bandar Seri Begawan
Language: Malay and English
Currency: Brunei Dollar

The Sultan of Brunei is reputed to be the richest man on earth, with a personal fortune in the region of twenty-six billion US Dollars. This massive wealth is based on the oilfields of Brunei and on the fact that all national finance is conducted through the Sultan. The first oil well was drilled in 1929, and since that time fresh reserves have been continually identified. Oil production remains high and is the basis of the nation's wealth. The Sultan is currently encouraging the growth of other businesses in order to limit his people's reliance on international oil prices. The traditional industries of boat-building, silver-smithing and weaving remain in operation, and the agriculture of the tropical country continues to produce rubber, fruits and rice.

 CAMBODIA (formerly Kampuchea)

Population: 8 million
Area: 70,000 square kilometres
Capital: Phnom Penh
Language: Khmer and Chinese
Currency: Riel

In the last two decades the formerly wealthy kingdom of Kampuchea, has been plunged into a vicious maelstrom of violence, hardship and poverty. In 1970 Prince Sihanouk was ousted from power by a republican movement. When the Vietnam war spilled into Cambodia in 1975 the Communist Khmer Rouge movement took power. This new regime abolished money, expelled foreigners, closed the borders and forced city dwellers to move to the countryside. Mass executions followed any attempt at protest, and it is thought that fifteen percent of the population died in these years. Vietnamese troops imposed a new government in 1979. Nationalist resistance under both Prince Sihanouk and the Khmer Rouge began a civil war interrupted by fragile peace agreements which continues to this day. The former cash crops and industries have been destroyed and the population relies on subsistence agriculture.

 CHINA (PEOPLE'S REPUBLIC)

Population: 1.17 billion
Area: 9,572,000 square kilometres
Capital: Beijing (Peking)
Language: Mandarin and numerous dialects
Currency: Renminbi Yuan

With a civilisation dating back at least 3,500 years, China has one of the oldest cultures on earth. Despite periods of civil war and instability, there has been a constant pressure for unity among the Chinese, principally to resist the incursions of foreign barbarians. The Empire collapsed in 1912, to be replaced by the rule of several warlords. The Communist Party restored unity in 1949 under Chairman Mao and has held power since. In 1989, the pro-democracy movement was brutally suppressed by the Chinese government, an action that was condemned internationally. China's economy is based on intensive cultivation of rice, wheat and beans together with the raising of cattle, pigs and sheep. Small-scale, traditional industries are carried on within villages, but large, state-run factories in the cities produce silk, cotton and heavy industrial goods, both for internal consumption and export. Economic initiatives including the creation of special economic zones in the early 1990's have helped save the economy.

▲ *Tianzi Mountains, China.*

▼ *The ancient town of Dalï, China.*

 INDIA

Population: 890 million
Area: 3,166,000 square kilometres
Capital: New Delhi
Language: Hindi, English and various regional languages
Currency: Rupee

The most populous democracy in the world has experienced unrest in recent years with the assassination of two prime ministers and demands for independence by ethnic minorities. Despite this, however, the polyglot nation remains intact and the processes of democracy have not been overthrown. The present Indian state originated in 1947, when the provinces of British India gained independence and joined with several semi-independent monarchies to form a federal union. The economic base of the nation is agriculture, which has benefited from modern technology in recent years, ensuring that famines are a thing of the past. Rice and wheat are the main crops, though beans and sugar are also produced. Tea is grown in large quantities for export, and coffee production is increasing. Industry has grown in recent years, but remains at a low technical level and chiefly supplies local demand.

▲ Dusty hill-country Afghanistan.

▶ Tropical rain forest, Brunei.

▲ Zhang Jia Khou Pass, Great Wall, China.

▲ Ceremonial costumes, Bhutan.

▼ The 'Wailing Wall', Jerusalem, Israel.

▲ New development in oil-rich Bahrain.

▼ In the Golden Temple of Amritsar, India.

▲ Low-lying Bangladesh, veined by rivers.

▼ 14th Ramadhan Mosque, Baghdad, Iraq.

◀ Tehran, capital of Iran.

INDONESIA

Population: 183 million
Area: 1,920,000 square kilometres
Capital: Jakarta
Language: Malay, Indonesian, English and Dutch
Currency: Rupiah

The East Indies, of which area Indonesia occupies a large percentage, were previously famous as the Spice Islands, supplying mace, nutmeg, cinnamon and pepper to grace the cuisines of the world. So valuable was this trade that fierce battles were fought along the trade routes and for control of the islands themselves. In the early 17th century the Dutch gained dominance of the islands and remained the ruling power until the Japanese invasion of 1941. Independence came in 1949, since when the islands have experienced periods of both democracy and dictatorship. Spices are now negligible in the Indonesian economy. Oilfields are dominant, producing most of southern Asia's oil, backed by copper and manufactured goods. Agriculture employs many people in the production of rice, cassava and sweet potatoes for local consumption, and coffee, rubber and coconuts for export.

IRAN

Population: 60 million
Area: 1,648,000 square kilometres
Capital: Tehran
Language: Persian, Kurdish and Arabic
Currency: Rial

In 1979 a popular revolution overthrew the monarchy and established an Islamic Republic under the control of the Ayatollah Khomeni. This event marked a revival of fundamentalist Islam, which has been felt elsewhere throughout the Islamic world. The basis of the modern Iranian economy is oil, which was discovered in 1908. The industry has suffered several setbacks with the destruction of refineries and ports during the Iran-Iraq War of 1980-88, but oil remains the chief export and currency earner. Other minerals exist in some quantity but are exploited on only a modest scale. Most of the country is unsuited to agriculture due to the lack of rain, but crops include wheat and barley. Millions of sheep, cattle and goats are grazed on the sparse grasslands.

IRAQ

Population: 19 million
Area: 435,000 square kilometres
Capital: Baghdad
Language: Arabic and Kurdish
Currency: Iraqi Dinar

The economy of Iraq was severely disrupted by the Gulf War of 1990-91. The war began in August 1990 when Iraq invaded Kuwait without warning and announced the annexation of that state. International forces gathered in Saudi Arabia while attempts were made to persuade Iraq to withdraw. On 16th January allied air strikes on Iraqi positions began and in February a campaign crushed the Iraqi army and liberated Kuwait. International sanctions on Iraq crippled its economy, which before the war was based on oil exports. Internally agriculture is a major employer and large crops can be raised in the fertile Tigris-Euphrates Valley. Industry was poorly developed before hostilities. The nation is ruled by the Ba'th Party led by Saddam Hussein, the country's President.

ISRAEL

Population: 5.1 million
Area: 21,000 square kilometres
Capital: Jerusalem
Language: Hebrew, Arabic and English
Currency: Shekel

The six pointed Star of David dominates the flag of Israel, symbolising the overwhelming Jewish heritage of the nation. The state of Israel came into being in 1948 as a homeland for Jews from around the world. The demand for a Jewish state became especially strong after the persecution at the hands of the Nazis. Its creation antagonised neighbouring Arab states and the nation's history has been dominated by intermittent warfare and constant terrorist activities. Israel currently occupies large areas of territory which officially belong to neighbouring states. The nation has few mineral resources and agriculture is only possible in irrigated areas. Israel produces much of its own food and its manufacturing industries are healthy.

JAPAN

Population: 124 million
Area: 378,000 square kilometres
Capital: Tokyo
Language: Japanese
Currency: Yen

The Emperor of Japan belongs to a family that has occupied the throne for many centuries, reputedly since the sun goddess began the dynasty in around 600 BC. For many years the nation was actually ruled by powerful noblemen known as Shogun, but the Emperor regained power in 1867, and in 1947 the present democratic constitution was introduced. Since the devastation of World War II, Japan has fully revitalised its industry and is now a major economic world power. The most important industries are iron and steel, car manufacture, electronics and chemicals, in which Japan leads the world in technical expertise as well as profitable productivity. The small area of land suitable for agriculture is intensively worked to produce rice, fruit and livestock, but the nation needs to import most of its foods.

JORDAN

Population: 3.6 million
Area: 91,000 square kilometres
Capital: Amman
Language: Arabic
Currency: Jordanian Dinar

The Kingdom of Jordan is ruled by King Hussein, last surviving monarch of the four Arab kingdoms established following the collapse of the Ottoman Empire in 1918. Political parties have recently been legalised in the kingdom and martial law, imposed in 1967, was lifted in 1991. During the 1967 war with Israel, Jordan lost control of the West Bank of the River Jordan which remains under Israeli control. This entailed the loss of nearly half of the kingdom's fertile land, a serious blow to an economy dependent on agriculture. The farmland of Jordan produces large quantities of tomatoes, olives and citrus fruits. Livestock is grazed on the arid grasslands and near desert of the east. Industry is dependent on the mining and processing of phosphates and potash.

KOREA (NORTH)

Population: 22 million
Area: 121,000 square kilometres
Capital: Pyongyang
Language: Korean
Currency: Won

In 1945 the defeat of Japan in World War II led to a joint occupation of Korea by Russian and American forces. In 1948 the Russian zone declared itself the People's Democratic Republic of Korea and established a Communist state. At elections only one Communist candidate is allowed and, it is claimed, these attract the votes of over ninety-five percent of the electorate. Industry, developed during the Japanese occupation, has been enhanced by government plans and Korea now produces iron and steel in quantity and is a major shipbuilding power. Cotton spinning, hydro-electric power, cotton, silk and rayon weaving are also important industries. Agriculture is also state-run, and rice, maize and potatoes are produced in large quantities.

KOREA (SOUTH)

Population: 44 million
Area: 100,000 square kilometres
Capital: Seoul
Language: Korean
Currency: Won

Following liberation from Japan, Korea was divided into Russian and American areas. In 1948 the American zone became the Republic of Korea, with a democratic constitution. In 1950 North Korea invaded in an attempt to reunite the nation under Communism. International forces backed the South, while China supported the Communist forces. In 1953 a ceasefire was agreed but no peace treaty has ever been signed. Political life in South Korea has been unstable, with military rule and political murders. The current democratic government began in 1980. Agriculture remains important in the South Korean economy, with large quantities of rice, radishes and fruits being produced. Industry has increased dramatically in recent years and now accounts for about half of the economy. Electronics, shipbuilding, textiles and motor vehicles are among the major industries.

KUWAIT

Population: 2 million
Area: 17,000 square kilometres
Capital: Kuwait City
Language: Arabic
Currency: Kuwait Dinar

Kuwait is an hereditary Emirate on the Arabian Gulf that has been ruled by the same family since 1756. In 1899 the Emirate placed itself under British protection, only becoming fully independent again in 1961. In 1990 Kuwait was invaded and overrun by Iraqi forces which annexed the nation. British forces, together with allied troops under United Nations approval, liberated Kuwait in 1991 after fierce fighting. Kuwait's oil wells were left flaming by the war and many months later most were still on fire. The economy of Kuwait is almost entirely dependent on its vast oil reserves, which bring in large quantities of foreign money.

LAOS

Population: 4.4 million
Area: 237,000 square kilometres
Capital: Vientiane
Language: Lao and French
Currency: Kip

The modern state of Laos is unusual in having been founded by a Communist movement led by a royal prince. When the

▲ *Wadi Kum, Jordan.*

Above right: *The volcanic island of Mauritius.*

▲ *A children's orchestra, North Korea.*

▼ *Waiting for petrol, Kuwait.*

▼ *Misfat Oasis, Oman.*

▶ *Beirut, capital of Lebanon.*

▲ *Stormy skies over the Maldives.*

▲ *Angkor Wat, Cambodia.*

▼ *Rice field, Malaysia.*

▲ *On the grass plains of Mongolia.*

▶ *Agriculture in South Korea.*

French relinquished colonial control of the Lao people in 1947, a constitutional monarchy was established. The Pathet Lao rebel movement headed by Prince Souphanouvong and allied Communists from North Vietnam, began a rebellion. This culminated in 1975 with the collapse of the Royal government and the installation of a Communist state under the Pathet Lao party. The nation is predominantly agricultural, with many of the Lao raising rice in the valleys of the various rivers of Laos. The mountainous interior and poor communications have made exploitation of mineral deposits difficult and industry is at only a rudimentary level.

LEBANON

Population: 3 million
Area: 10,000 square kilometres
Capital: Beirut
Language: Arabic and French
Currency: Lebanese Pound

Lebanon is best known for the factional violence that has torn this previously-prosperous nation apart. During the 1960s the Palestinian Liberation Organisation began using bases in southern Lebanon to attack Israel. This led to great tension between the Christians and Moslems within Lebanon and civil war broke out in 1975. Israel invaded in 1982, occupying much of southern Lebanon. Syrian troops are present in many areas of the country in an attempt to enforce a ceasefire among the factions. Lebanon has a constitution with an elected National Assembly and a President, but real power remains with the factional guerillas. Lebanon is now a basically agricultural nation, having lost its banking, manufacturing and tourist industries during the civil war.

MALAYSIA

Population: 19 million
Area: 330,000 square kilometres
Capital: Kuala Lumpur
Language: Malay, Chinese and English
Currency: Ringgit

The government of Malaysia is unique in that the rulers of the nine states meet every five years to elect one of their number to be the supreme ruler, or Yang de-Pertuan Agong. Operating under the head of state is a Parliament elected from the states, in which political power is vested. The nation is among the most prosperous of Southeast Asia, having a highly diversified economy. Exports are dominated in value by manufactured goods, though agri-

culture provides employment for most people. The lush farmland not only produces food for internal consumption but also exports cash crops such as rubber, cocoa, tobacco, sugar cane and tea. There are substantial deposits of tin in the country, together with oilfields, which add to the national wealth.

MALDIVES

Population: 230,000
Area: 300 square kilometres
Capital: Malé
Language: Divehi
Currency: Rufiyaa

Scattered across the Indian Ocean, southwest of India, the Maldives number around 1,200 islands, but only 202 are inhabited. The islands were dominated by the Arabs from around 1100 and Islam is the dominant religion among the mixed population. Britain established a protectorate over the islands in 1887 and returned full independence in 1965. The Sultan was overthrown and a republic established in 1968. The stability of the islands was threatened by an attempted coup in 1988. The coral islands lack mineral wealth and only small patches of land are suitable for farming. The economy is based on fishing, tourism and the processing of coconuts and reeds into craftwork for sale abroad.

MAURITIUS

Population: 1 million
Area: 2,000 square kilometres
Capital: Port Louis
Language: English
Currency: Mauritius Rupee

Mauritius is composed of a number of islands in the Indian Ocean. The two largest islands, Mauritius itself and Rodrigues, are separated by over 500 kilometres of open ocean. The islands have an economy based on the production of sugar. Sugar cane covers most of the arable land and industry is dominated by sugar refineries. Tobacco and tea are also grown for export, while maize, beef and goat meat are produced for internal consumption. The government is a democracy based on universal suffrage, producing an assembly which elects a prime minister who appoints a cabinet.

MONGOLIA

Population: 2 million
Area: 1,567,000 square kilometres
Capital: Ulan Bator
Language: Mongol
Currency: Tugrik

During the early 13th century the Mongols, under the leadership of

Genghis Khan, conquered many peoples, creating a massive empire encompassing China, Central Asia and parts of eastern Europe. By the late 17th century, however, the Mongols had fallen under Chinese control. In 1924 the Mongols, with Soviet support, drove the Chinese out and declared an independent Mongolian nation. The new Communist government suppressed traditional Buddhist and Shamanist religions and pursued a policy of farm collectivisation and industrialisation, which has been partially successful. However, the majority of the population still leads a traditional nomadic lifestyle, caring for herds of livestock. Millions of cattle, horses, sheep and goats are driven across the vast grasslands by expert horsemen. In 1990 the Communist Party allowed free elections for the first time and retained power with a large majority.

MYANMAR
(formerly Burma)

Population: 40 million
Area: 676,000 square kilometres
Capital: Rangoon (Yangon)
Language: Burmese, Thai, English
Currency: Kyat

The history of Myanmar formerly Burma has been one of upheaval, fragmentation and unification. The process continues today, with vociferous separatist movements among the various minority populations which live in the country. Since Burma was granted its freedom by Britain in 1947 there have been numerous coups and attempted coups. The military junta which seized power in 1988 held democratic elections but power remains with the army, which numbers over 200,000. Myanmar is dominated by traditional agriculture, based on rice, cattle and pigs, which flourishes in the wet tropical climate of the region. Industrial activity is mainly concerned with processing cash crops of sugar and cotton or with manufacturing fertiliser and agricultural tools.

NEPAL

Population: 18 million
Area: 147,000 square kilometres
Capital: Kathmandu
Language: Nepali
Currency: Nepalese Rupee

The mountain kingdom of Nepal is unique in having the only flag which is not rectangular in shape. The traditional triangular banner carries a sun to represent the ruling Maharaja and a moon to symbolise the prime minister, until 1951 an hereditary post. Nepal pursued a policy of isolation until the mid 1950s, since when the economy has been slowly modernised. Many

Nepalese live in inaccessible mountain valleys where they continue to practise traditional farming techniques. Others produce cash crops of herbs and potatoes or keep cattle to produce ghee, a form of clarified butter. A valuable source of foreign currency comes from the Gurkha troops recruited in Nepal to serve in the British army. Under a constitution introduced in 1990 the Maharaja permits political parties and free elections.

OMAN

Population: 2 million
Area: 300,000 square kilometres
Capital: Muscat
Language: Arabic
Currency: Rial

Until 1937 the Sultanate of Oman was a somewhat impoverished Moslem state relying upon fishing and date production for its livelihood. In that year, however, oil was discovered and although reserves are not vast its petrochemical industry now dominates Oman's economy. The Sultan is attempting to diversify the economy by improving agriculture and the fishing industry. Copper mining in the interior is being encouraged, but further mineral exploitation is hampered by the fact that Oman's borders with both Saudi Arabia and the Yemen are in dispute. Oman has no constitution and is ruled by decrees issued by the Sultan. There is, however, a State Council composed of prominent citizens which the Sultan may call for consultation on important issues.

▲ *Honeymoon Lake, Pakistan.*

PAKISTAN

Population: 130 million
Area: 796,000 square kilometres
Capital: Islamabad
Language: Urdu, Punjabi, Sindi and English
Currency: Pakistan Rupee

The nation of Pakistan was created in 1947 by the British as an Islamic homeland after fears were expressed by the Moslems about joining a Hindu-dominated India. The population is united by its religion, but otherwise is very diverse, with occasional calls for independence by various ethnic groups. Periods of democracy have alternated with military rule, and there have been frequent charges of corruption in both types of government. The economy is based upon agriculture, which employs over half the workforce. The irrigated plains around the Indus and its tributaries produce large quantities of rice, wheat and sugar for domestic consumption and some cotton for export. Tax and economy laws favour the peasant smallholder.

 PHILIPPINES

Population: 64 million
Area: 300,000 square kilometres
Capital: Manila
Language: Filipino, Spanish, English and tribal languages
Currency: Philippine Peso

The Philippines contain over 7,000 islands, but very few of these are inhabited and most do not even have names. From about 1550 Spain gradually acquired control over the profitable Spice Islands of the Philippines and ruled until 1898, when the United States took over. Independence was achieved in 1946, and since that time a fragile democracy has been interrupted by military coups, fraudulent elections and massive corruption. The Philippines is an agricultural nation with rice, maize and coconuts as the main crops. Many coastal villages depend on fishing for income. The mining of nickel, zinc and copper lead the mining industry, while manufacturing is rapidly gaining in importance. The nation remains dependent on imported food and materials for survival.

▲ *Banaue rice terraces, Philippines.*

 QATAR

Population: 520,000
Area: 11,000 square kilometres
Capital: Doha
Language: Arabic
Currency: Qatar Riyal

The long, streaming banner of the Emirate of Qatar is based upon the red and white banner imposed by Britain in the 19th century on all Gulf states which were party to an

anti-pirate agreement. Britain controlled foreign policy until 1971, when Qatar was granted full independence. The Emir is an absolute monarch who rules by decree, but an Advisory Council of prominent citizens is consulted on major issues. Oil was first exploited during the 1950s and since then has come to dominate the economy. Oil revenue is being used to improve agriculture and fishing, with the long term aim of the country becoming self-sufficient. Industry is also being encouraged. Most of Qatar is desert, thinly populated by nomadic Bedouin tribes. Lack of water is a perennial problem.

 SAUDI ARABIA

Population: 15 million
Area: 2,200,000 square kilometres
Capital: Riyadh
Language: Arabic
Currency: Saudi Riyal

The religious kingdom of Saudi Arabia was carved out of the deserts by the aristocratic Saud family of the Wahhabi Islamic sect earlier this century, and was internationally recognised as recently as 1927. The king is also custodian of the holy mosques and the power structure is based upon Koranic law, though an assembly may be consulted by the king if he wishes. The desert kingdom began producing oil in 1937, and the economy rapidly shifted away from traditional reliance on dates and nomadic herds to concentrate on petrochemicals. There has also been some diversification into light industry and the production of plastics as a by-product of oil refining. In 1990-91 Saudi Arabia was used as a base for forces fighting to liberate Kuwait from Iraqi occupation.

 SEYCHELLES

Population: 71,000
Area: 455 square kilometres
Capital: Victoria
Language: English and French
Currency: Seychelles Rupee

When Portuguese sailors discovered the Seychelles in the 16th century they were uninhabited, and not until the 1770's was permanent colonisation begun by France. Britain acquired the islands in 1810 and independence was granted in 1976. A coup took place within a year of independence and the Seychelles are now a one-party state. Tourism is the major industry on the islands with about 100,000 people visiting each year. The idyllic coral islands and tropical climate make the Seychelles a popular holiday resort for those able to reach them. The large fishing fleet catches

▲ *Istanbul, Turkey, at dusk.*

▶ *Abu Dhabi, United Arab Emirates.*

▲ *La Digue, Seychelles.*

▲ *Sailing junks, Vietnam.*

◀ *Stilt fisherman, Sri Lanka.*

▲ *A Yemeni landscape.*

▼ *Damascus, Syria.*

▲ *The Singapore River, Singapore.*

▼ *Mecca, Saudi Arabia.*

tuna for canning and export, while coconuts and cinnamon are the main cash crops.

SINGAPORE

Population: 2.7 million
Area: 625 square kilometres
Capital: Singapore
Language: English, Chinese and Malay
Currency: Singapore Dollar

The city state of Singapore was founded by Sir Stamford Raffles in 1819 as a trading port of the British East India Company. Since then the city has flourished as a trading and manufacturing centre. Singapore passed from the Company to the British Government in the 19th century before acquiring independence in 1965. Though it has no mineral resources and virtually no farmland, Singapore is a leading economic power in Asia. Commercial and merchant banks number almost 200, and together provide the economic mainspring for much of Southeast Asia. The manufacturing base is diverse, including the processing of chemicals, foods, rubber and textiles. The state is a democracy with free elections though power is almost monopolised by a single party.

SRI LANKA

Population: 17 million
Area: 65,000 square kilometres
Capital: Colombo
Language: Sinhala, Tamil and English
Currency: Sri Lankan Rupee

Sri Lankan politics are dominated by ethnic violence between the majority Sinhalese and the Tamils, the largest minority. Many Tamils wish to form their own nation in the north of the island, and extremists undertake periodic terrorist action. Other minority groups include Europeans, Malays and the Veddah tribesmen who inhabit the forested mountains and are probably descendants of the original inhabitants. Agriculture dominates the economy, with rubber, coconuts and especially tea being grown as cash crops for export. Efforts are being made to improve rice production to reduce reliance on imported food. Industry centres on the processing of agricultural products, while precious stones are the only mineral resources of note.

SYRIA

Population: 12 million
Area: 185,000 square kilometres
Capital: Damascus
Language: Arabic
Currency: Syrian Pound

Arabs form the overwhelming bulk of the Syrian population and the Islamic religion is a strong unifying force. Government is by a democratically-elected Parliament, and the Arab Socialist Party has formed a majority since 1963, with President Assad holding executive power. Syria has been a major power in the Middle East, taking part in wars against Israel and maintaining a peace-keeping force in Lebanon. The economy is based on oil and textiles, which together make up about three-quarters of exports. Irrigated farmland in the Euphrates Valley and in the west produces quantities of wheat, and barley for domestic consumption. The southern deserts are sparsely populated by nomadic pastoralists raising livestock at subsistence level.

TAIWAN

Population: 21 million
Area: 36,000 square kilometres
Capital: Taipei
Language: Chinese dialects and Japanese
Currency: New Taiwan Dollar

When the Communist Party gained control of mainland China in 1949 the surviving nationalists fled to the island of Taiwan and set up a rival Republic of China, which is now usually referred to as Taiwan. Neither regime recognises the other as legitimate, and a continual propaganda war has been carried on. Until the Nationalist takeover, Taiwan was an agricultural island with intensively-farmed pockets of fertile land. Rice, pineapples and bananas are still produced in quantity on the few areas suitable for agriculture amid the mountainous terrain. Industrial development has been the keynote of Taiwan's economy since 1949. Light industry was encouraged first, but iron, steel and shipbuilding are now well established, together with electronics.

THAILAND

Population: 56.8 million
Area: 513 square kilometres
Capital: Bangkok
Language: Thai
Currency: Baht

The kingdom of Thailand dates back many centuries, but the present dynasty came to power in 1782, when the founder threw off Burmese control. The kingdom never succumbed to European colonialism but was overrun by Japan in World War II. The royal dynasty remains on the throne, but political power has changed hands rapidly between Parliament and army factions as coups have been common in recent years. The majority of the population lives in rural areas, where the fertile soil and ideal climate allow Thailand to produce far more food than it needs. Rice is a substantial export. The beautiful old temples and notorious nightlife of Bangkok make Thailand a popular tourist resort attracting many visitors.

▲ *Buddhist priests, Bangkok Thailand.*

TURKEY

Population: 59.5 million
Area: 779,000 square kilometre
Capital: Ankara
Language: Turkish
Currency: Turkish Lira

The Turks formerly ruled the vast Ottoman Empire, embracing the Balkans, the Near East and much of North Africa, and modern Turkey has a flag derived from that of the Empire. The modern republic was founded in 1923, when the last emperor was deposed. Democratic government has been interrupted by periods of military control, most recently in 1980-83. The interior plateau has a fertile soil and produces large quantities of grain, while the warmer coast produces heavy crops of olives, figs and citrus fruits. Flax and cotton form the basis of a flourishing textile industry. Agriculture employs over half the work-force, some at little above subsistence level. Industry is dominated by the production of iron and steel, motor vehicles and cement, and is growing under state encouragement.

UNITED ARAB EMIRATES

Population: 2 million
Area: 84,000 square kilometres
Capital: Abu Dhabi
Language: Arabic
Currency: Dirham

As the name suggests, the United Arab Emirates is a confederation of seven independent nations: Abu Dhabi, Dubai, Ash Shariqah, Ajman, Umm al Qaywayn, Al Fujayrah and Ras al Khaymah. The federation is ruled jointly by the seven Emirs, who appoint ministers to legislate and agree upon a joint budget. The federation came into being when Britain gave the Emirs full independence after a period when Britain controlled foreign policy in return for giving military protection. The bulk of the territory is desert, with little opportunity for agriculture, though fishing has potential and there is a large export trade. The economy is basically dependent on oil, which is produced in large quantities. Oil revenues are used to promote a more diversified economy and to improve living conditions.

YEMEN

Population: 13 million
Area: 531,000 square kilometres
Capital: Sana'a
Language: Arabic
Currency: Riyal and Dinar

In May 1990 the former states of Yemen and the People's Democratic Republic of Yemen merged to form a single nation. The new constitution of the united Republic of Yemen allowed for free, multi-party elections after an interim period of two years, during which complicated arrangements for fusing the armies, administrations and economies would be put into effect. The two currencies, the Riyal of the Yemen and the Dinar of the Peoples Republic remain in circulation side by side. The new nation has very little industry and most of the population is engaged in agriculture, usually at subsistence level. The arid nature of much of Yemen restricts agriculture to river valleys. Coastal villages supplement farming with fishing, with much of the catch being dried and exported.

VIETNAM

Population: 69.3 million
Area: 329,566 square kilometres
Capital: Hanoi
Language: Vietnamese
Currency: Dong

Vietnam formally came into being on 2nd July 1976 with the union of the former nations of North and South Vietnam following the Vietnam War. Just two years later Vietnam invaded Cambodia, finally withdrawing in 1988. The constitution claims that Vietnam is a proletarian dictatorship under Marxist-Leninism. In effect all power is in the hands of the Communist Party, which has followed a consistently pro-Russian stance, thus angering its neighbour China. This has led to border skirmishes in recent years. Well over half the population is directly dependent on agriculture. Over fifteen million tonnes of sweet potatoes are produced each year, but Vietnam still needs to import food. There is little heavy industry and light industry is localised and small-scale.

AFRICA

*A*frica is, in general, an underdeveloped continent, where political violence and dictatorships are common. It is also, however, a continent of great potential, with a magnificent environmental heritage and the possibility of significant improvements.

It is usual to divide Africa, for cultural and geographical reasons, into two distinct sections. The first, North Africa, includes the Islamic states that fringe the Mediterranean and northern Atlantic coasts. These nations are united by a common language and religion which is the result of their Islamic past. Most have fertile coastal regions backed by vast desert interiors inhabited only by nomadic tribesmen. Oilfields are present in most of these nations, ensuring a national wealth that pays for schemes to improve the quality of life.

The second major region is sub-Saharan Africa, which stretches from the Sahara Desert to the Cape of Good Hope. This is a more diverse region, ranging from dense rainforest through open savannah to desert conditions, but united by having a mainly Negro population and having only recently gained independence from European colonial rule. There are, however, distinct differences between the regions.

West Africa is characterised by settled farming communities of great tribal diversity, where mineral exploitation and industry is well developed compared to elsewhere in Africa. East Africa is dominated by plains originally populated by semi-nomadic pastoral tribes, where minerals are less common and farming plays a more dominant role in the economy. Southern Africa is as diverse as the entire continent, with areas of fertile farmland, dense forests and open plains to be found within a short distance of each other.

Nations bordering the Sahara are subject to periodic droughts, which bring great misery in their wake. Population booms over the past decades have led to a reliance on good crops and when these fail famine follows. Famines, like those in Ethiopia and neighbouring countries such as Somalia, have killed hundreds of thousands of people. Elsewhere in Africa famine is not such a constant threat, but chronic poverty and poor medical services cause a low life expectancy.

Though the age of European colonisation is now over, the signs of those times are still clear. The official language of most nations is still that of the colonising power. The diverse tribal tongues of most nations (some have over 200 languages) make a lingua franca essential, and it has been found most convenient to maintain that of the former ruling European power.

Most former French colonies in sub-Saharan Africa share a common currency: the Franc CFA. This currency is issued by the Banque Centrale des Etats de l'Afrique de l'Ouest and is locked into the French Franc at a rate of 50 Francs CFA to one French Franc. This arrangement has advantages for those countries within it, but also has the effect of robbing them of total discretion over their own economies which, to some extent, remain vulnerable to outside control.

Many sub-Saharan states abandoned democracy following independence. In some cases this was due to the total dominance of a single party, which then outlawed opposition but has been more normally produced by a military coup. Nearly all sub-Saharan African states have experienced dictatorship at some stage and many are still ruled without democracy though several nations have returned to multi-party civilian rule. There have been numerous accusations of human rights violations in some African states.

Most attention has been focused on South Africa, where a white minority holds total control over the nation. International pressure has been brought to bear on the nation, forcing the government to abandon the policies of apartheid that enforced this control.

The mineral wealth of Africa is vast and unexplored. Effective capital investment and improved communications would bring this wealth into the economy, but international companies are unwilling to invest heavily in nations subject to civil war or frequent coups.

Africa is undoubtedly a beautiful and potentially wealthy continent, but its endemic problems and recurring violence have locked it into a cycle of poverty which will prove difficult to break.

◀ *Sierra Leone beaches.*　　　　▲ *People of Ethiopia.*

▲ *A village in Mozambique.*

▶ *A waterfall in Cameroon.*

▼ *Harare, Zimbabwe.*

ALGERIA

Population: 26 million
Area: 2,400,000 square kilometres
Capital: Algiers
Language: Arabic
Currency: Algerian Dinar

Algeria gained its independence from France in 1962 after nearly a decade of guerilla warfare. The bulk of the population lives along the Mediterranean coast and in the Atlas Mountains, where the climate is milder and the land more fertile than in the arid Sahara which makes up most of the country. The discovery of large natural gas fields has made Algeria relatively wealthy, and some of these resources are spent on free health treatment and high quality education. Many people continue to lead a traditional Islamic lifestyle, though European influences are strong in coastal towns. In 1991, Algeria held its first multi party elections. These showed the strength of the fundamentalist Islamic opposition. Following the elections there was a period of political instability.

ANGOLA

Population: 10.6 million
Area: 1,200,000 square kilometres
Capital: Luanda
Language: Portuguese and various tribal languages
Currency: Kwanza

For most of its independent existence Angola has been racked by civil war between the communist MPLA party, which forms the central government, and the rebel UNITA organisation, which controls much of southern Angola. The long years of warfare caused much hardship and seriously disrupted the economy, making this one of the poorer African nations. However, oil production in the north and diamond mining provide a source of foreign capital which may lead to economic revival. The coastal region is the centre for industrialisation and urban life-styles. The high plateau of the interior is heavily forested and inhabited by tribes which live in a traditional way with their own languages and religions.

BENIN

Population: 5 million
Area: 112,000 square kilometres
Capital: Porto-Novo
Language: French and tribal languages
Currency: Franc CFA

The ideal of a revolutionary socialist state was recently abandoned in Benin, with the holding of free elections and the founding of several political

parties. For the vast majority of the population the change probably meant little. Traditional agricultural lifestyles dominate in the interior, where tribal culture and animist cults are common. It is thought that about ninety percent of the population practice subsistence farming. In the mountainous far north Islamic culture has filtered down from the desert regions. Only on the coast is industry to be found, and even this is heavily based on the agricultural produce of the interior, particularly sugar and palm oil. A recently-exploited oilfield off the coast is expected to help boost the economy.

BOTSWANA

Population: 1.3 million
Area: 582,000 square kilometres
Capital: Gaborone
Language: English, Setswana
Currency: Pula

Botswana is rare among African nations in having maintained its democratic constitution throughout its period of independence. The constitution granted in 1966 allowed for an Elected Assembly of thirty-eight members and a House of Chiefs comprising the twelve tribal chiefs, and this arrangement is still in place. The vast majority of the population live in traditional villages, where cattle farming is the main activity, though some crops are also sown. Industry is limited to diamond and copper mining and many young men work in South Africa for some years in order to earn money for their families at home. The vast Kalahari Desert in the southwest of the nation is inhabited by nomadic tribes.

BURKINA FASO

Population: 9.5 million
Area: 274,000 square kilometres
Capital: Ouagadougou
Language: French and tribal languages
Currency: Franc CFA

As one of the poorest and most unstable countries in Africa, Burkina Faso has experienced much hardship. Numerous coups and government changes have occurred, most recently in 1989. In 1991 a new constitution was approved. The nation is a largely artificial creation, being a former French administrative district covering the territory of several indigenous tribes. The vast majority of the population are engaged in subsistence farming in traditional tribal society. The country is periodically struck by drought and famine, being on the southern fringe of the Sahara. The recent discovery of gold and manganese deposits are unlikely to be exploited due to a

poor transport system and lack of capital. The nation depends largely on foreign aid and remains chronically depressed.

BURUNDI

Population: 5.6 million
Area: 27,000 square kilometres
Capital: Bujumbura
Language: French, Kirundi and Swahili
Currency: Burundi Franc

Sometime in the 16th century Tutsi tribes invaded the area and conquered the Hutu peoples. Even today the nation is divided into the two ethnic groups, with the Tutsi wielding power. After a period of German and Belgian rule Burundi became independent in 1962 under a Tutsi monarch. In 1966 the king was overthrown by the Tutsi-dominated army, which has since suppressed Hutu unrest and dismissed Presidents at will. Tea and coffee plantations are the mainstays of both industry and the export economy. The majority of the population, however, remains dependent on subsistence agriculture based on bananas, maize and cattle.

CAMEROON

Population: 12.6 million
Area: 475,000 square kilometres
Capital: Yaoundé
Language: English, French and tribal languages
Currency: Franc CFA

Much of the interior of Cameroon is virtually inaccessible during the rainy season, when torrential downpours wash away roads and flood large areas. This isolation is emphasised by ethnic diversity, with twenty-four languages and as many as 200 tribes. The fragmentation has slowed economic development, though the nation is relatively wealthy by African standards. The economy is based largely on agriculture, with coffee, cocoa and palm oil forming the bulk of export crops. The majority of farmland is, however, devoted to producing foods such as cassava, maize and groundnuts for local consumption. Industry is concentrated on aluminium smelting and the processing of agricultural products. Oil revenue has helped the government to invest in new projects.

CAPE VERDE

Population: 369,000
Area: 4,000 square kilometres
Capital: Praia
Language: Portugese and Creole
Currency: Cape Verde Escudo

The Cape Verde Islands have been independent only since 1975, when

▲ *Farm workers in Angola.*

▲ *A scene on the Chobe River, Botswana.*

▲ *Celebrations on the anniversary of the Algerian Revolution.*

▲ *A village in Chad.*

▼ *A domestic scene in Burkina Faso.*

▲ *Barren, drought-scarred landscape, Cape Verde.*

▲ *Riverboat merchant, Benin.*

▼ *The Central African Republic.*

▲ *Bathers in the Comoros.*

Portugal relinquished control. The islands have strong historical links with Guinea-Bissau. The government is a single-party state, though the ruling elite joined several other African nations in 1990 by announcing an intention to allow democracy. The islands are small, rugged and arid, with little opportunity for farming. Coconuts, coffee and sugar are produced in small quantities on irrigated land. Fishing is far more productive for the local population with large numbers of tuna being landed each year. The climate and scenic coastline hold out the promise of an increase in tourism.

CENTRAL AFRICAN REPUBLIC

Population: 3.13 million
Area: 622,000 square kilometres
Capital: Bangui
Language: French and tribal languages
Currency: Franc CFA

For thirteen years until 1979 this nation was ruled by Jean-Bedel Bokassa, who proclaimed himself Emperor and staged a lavish coronation ceremony. Bokassa was overthrown by the army and today the nation is a one-party state ostensibly committed to introducing democratic government. After a brief period of multi-party democracy in 1992 the President set up the Provisional National Political Council of the Republic. Though potentially rich in minerals and agriculture, the economy has been held back by political instability, by poor communications, and particularly by the lack of a coastline. Diamond, gold and uranium mining lead the small industrial sector, while the majority of the population remain employed in subsistence agriculture.

CHAD

Population: 5.9 million
Area: 1,284,000 square kilometres
Capital: N'djaména
Language: French, Arabic and tribal languages
Currency: Franc CFA

Endemic civil war has marked the history of Chad since independence from France in 1960. The fighting between various ethnic factions is based upon a struggle between the nomadic, Moslem north and the agricultural and animist south. The situation has been confused by shifting alliances and foreign intervention. Chad remains unstable and on occasion it has been necessary for French troops to intervene to restore order. The warfare has prevented exploitation of recently-discovered oilfields and deposits of gold and uranium. The population remains desperately

poor and is dependent on subsistence agriculture.

COMOROS

Population: 570,000
Area: 1,800 square kilometres
Capital: Moroni
Language: Arabic, French and Swahili
Currency: Comorian Franc

When the three Comoros islands declared themselves to be independent of France in 1975, the fourth island, Mayotte, refused to join them. The newly-independent nation has suffered three successful coups and has chronic problems of disease and poverty. The islands have, over the centuries, received influxes of African, Indonesian, Arabic and European peoples and today have a mixed population. The majority of the population engages in subsistence farming. In recent years commercial production of vanilla, cloves and coffee has been undertaken and these now account for much of the nation's exports. Though independent, the Comoros remain economically dependent on France.

▲ *The Congo's Sangha River.*

CONGO

Population: 2.7 million
Area: 341,000 square kilometres
Capital: Brazzaville
Language: French and tribal languages
Currency: Franc CFA

Formerly a French colony, the Congo was a single-party, Marxist-Leninist state until 1992 when multi-party democracy was restored. The nation is relatively wealthy by African standards, with oil reserves offshore and productive gold mines. It is also rich in minerals particularly lead, copper and zinc and there are reserves of phosphates and iron. Industry is well established around the capital and produces cement and textiles among other products. However, more than three-quarters of the population remains engaged in farming, much of it at subsistence level. The vast bulk of the population is found in the southern parts of the country, for the northern regions are covered by dense forests and unfertile land.

DJIBOUTI

Population: 557,000
Area: 23,000 square kilometres
Capital: Djibouti City
Language: Somali, Afar, French
Currency: Djibouti Franc

The state of Djibouti is dominated by disputes between Somalis and Afars. The hinterland is composed of arid grazing lands, although the bulk of the population lives in or around Djibouti City. The city has a long history as a trading centre and the economy is largely dependent on the port. Djibouti was a one-party state until 1992, when a constitution paved the way for democracy.

EGYPT

Population: 56 million
Area: 1,000,000 square kilometres
Capital: Cairo
Language: Arabic
Currency: Egyptian Pound

Egypt was conquered by the Arabs in the 7th century, and today the nation is firmly Moslem in culture and outlook. People and prosperity are concentrated in the Nile Valley, as they have been since recorded history began here in 3,000 BC. The waters of the Nile allow irrigation of the farmland which produces the bulk of the nation's food as well as export crops. Industry is well advanced in the major towns and cities. Tourism plays a major role in the economy. Egypt has a relatively stable political system though it is coming under increasing pressure from Islamic fundamentalists.

ERITREA

Population: 3.5 million
Area: 125,000 square kilometres
Capital: Asmara
Language: Arabic and tribal languages
Currency: Birr

Eritrea, a country with a diverse climate and geography, has been under Italian, British and Ethiopian rule. In 1991, after thirty years of armed struggle by the Eritrean People's Liberation Front, the country won its right to self-determination. Two years of provisional government followed, and following an internationally monitored referendum in April 1993, full independence was achieved.

EQUATORIAL GUINEA

Population: 367,000
Area: 28,000 square kilometres
Capital: Malabo
Language: Spanish and tribal languages
Currency: Franc CFA

Equatorial Guinea is divided between the mainland territory on the Mbini River and the island of Bioko. Cocoa and coffee remain important export crops, although the majority of farmland is used for subsistence agriculture, with cassava and sweet potatoes being the chief products. The wet, hot tropical climate produces vast forests in the interior and these are beginning to be exploited for their timber, which accounts for one quarter of all exports. Although over half the population lives in towns, there is virtually no industry in the nation.

ETHIOPIA

Population: 53.8 million
Area: 1,096,000 square kilometres
Capital: Addis Ababa
Language: Arabic and tribal languages
Currency: Birr

Drought, famine and civil war dogged Ethiopia for many years. Much of the country is in the hands of rebel factions, one of which recently overthrew the central government. The violence is largely due to the many ethnic groups included within the nation, many of which desire independence from strong central rule. Famine has claimed hundreds of thousands of lives and internal political unrest has undoubtedly worsened the situation. Despite this, farming is generally in good condition and in productive years can account for valuable exports of coffee and sugar. Much potentially fertile ground remains untilled due to political instability. Peace would undoubtedly help ease the plight of the Ethiopian peoples.

GABON

Population: 1.2 million
Area: 267,000 square kilometres
Capital: Libreville
Language: French and tribal languages
Currency: Franc CFA

Made up largely of the drainage basin of the Ogooue River, Gabon has numerous natural resources but lacks the finance and population to take best advantage of them. Offshore oil is being exploited, as are deposits of uranium and manganese, but the economy remains based chiefly on agriculture. The Equator runs through the centre of Gabon, and this dictates the climate and range of crops which can be produced. Most agriculture is subsistence, though sugar cane is grown in large quantities near the coast for export. The government of Gabon under a single-party state was stable from 1967 until 1990, when free elections were held and the existing system dismantled. Allegations of ballot-rigging were made.

▲ *Thatched huts in Equatorial Guinea.*

Above right: *Children in Guinea-Bissau.*

▼ *Filling water pots, Ghana.*

▲ *Women at work in Gambia.*

▲ *The mountain village of Ha Thuhlo, Lesotho.*

▶ *Landscape of Gabon.*

▼ *Kenyatta Centre, Nairobi, Kenya.*

▶ *Abidjan, Ivory Coast.*

GAMBIA

Population: 875,000
Area: 11,000 square kilometres
Capital: Banjul
Language: English and tribal languages
Currency: Dalasi

The Gambia exists because of the river from which it takes its name. The nation is made up of a narrow strip of land which follows the twists and turns of the river from Koina to the ocean. Several tribes have their territories along the river and their chiefs have an established position within the constitution. The nation is basically agricultural and has only one export of any importance. This is the groundnut, thousands of tons of which are shipped out each year. More recently the government has tried to break this hazardous dependence on a single crop. In 1982 Gambia joined with Senegal, which virtually surrounds it, to form the Confederation of Senegambia but this was dissolved in 1989.

GHANA

Population: 15 million
Area: 239,000 square kilometres
Capital: Accra
Language: English and tribal languages
Currency: Cedi

As the first black African state to become independent of a European colonial power, in 1957, Ghana has set several trends in African history. The colours of the Ghanaian flag – red, green and yellow – have been adopted by several other colonies on achieving independence, while the black star of African freedom has also become a popular motif. Ghana has experienced several coups and was ruled for many years by a Provisional Council led by Flight Lieutenant Jerry Rawlings. In 1992, democratic elections were held and Rawlings was elected President. The economy is based on cash crop agriculture, with cocoa the most important crop, though tobacco, coffee and tropical fruits are catching up. Industrial activities are based around the mining of gold, diamonds and, more recently, oil.

GUINEA

Population: 7 million
Area: 245,000 square kilometres
Capital: Conakry
Language: French and tribal languages
Currency: Syli

Guinea followed Ghana to independence one year later and adopted the same colours for its flag, though they are arranged in vertical rather than horizontal stripes. Several tribal groupings are included within Guinea, with the Fulani being the largest at around forty percent of the population. From 1984 until 1991 power rested with a military junta. Military rule was replaced by a Transitional Committee for National Rectification. The nation has a tropical climate, with a summer monsoon which brings heavy rain and high temperatures. Combined with fertile soils this climate creates ideal conditions for a variety of crops including rice, sugar cane and tropical fruits. Vast reserves of bauxite are now being mined as are iron ore deposits and diamonds.

GUINEA-BISSAU

Population: 1 million
Area: 36,000 square kilometres
Capital: Bissau
Language: Portuguese and tribal languages
Currency: Peso

For many years a one party state, Guinea-Bissau became a multi-party democracy in 1991. The fertile soil and tropical climate allow the production of large quantities of rice, rubber and groundnuts, much of which is exported. Most of the population remains dependent on subsistence agriculture and industry is virtually non-existent. Guinea-Bissau has a crushing foreign debt more than one hundred times the size of the government's annual budget. Ethnically the population is divided between the coastal Balante and the Muslim Fulani of the inland regions, though there are several smaller tribes.

IVORY COAST

Population: 13 million
Area: 322,000 square kilometres
Capital: Yamonssoukro
Language: French and tribal languages
Currency: Franc CFA

This nation takes its name from the early trade in ivory that dominated the region when it was first discovered by Europeans in the 15th century. Since then slavery, and more recently coffee, have been the mainstays of the economy. Today the rich soil of the coastal regions has been turned to support a wide variety of crops including yams, cassava and a number of tropical fruits for export. Despite this fertility the economy of the Ivory Coast is held back by massive foreign debts and limited mineral resources. The single party state which has existed for many years recently announced that it would begin a process of democratisation and free elections have been held. The former sole party still retains power, having won over ninety percent of seats in Parliament.

KENYA

Population: 27 million
Area: 582,000 square kilometres
Capital: Nairobi
Language: English, Swahili and tribal languages
Currency: Kenya Shilling

Committed until 1990 to the concept of "democracy with one party", the state of Kenya has enjoyed more stability than many other African nations since it achieved independence in 1963. This has combined with rich natural resources and a long history of international trade to make it economically viable, though not particularly wealthy. Most of the population inhabits the interior highlands, where coffee, tea and sugar are grown in large quantities for export, or the lower hills, where maize, cassava and sweet potatoes are produced for local consumption. The vast semi-arid plains are the home of gazelles, zebra and lions, which attract over half-a-million tourists each year, boosting the economy. The coastal towns have thriving commercial centres.

LESOTHO

Population: 1.8 million
Area: 30,000 square kilometres
Capital: Maseru
Language: English, Sesotho
Currency: Loti

Lesotho is one of the few African tribal kingdoms to survive into modern times. Since a coup in 1986 the king acts on the advice of the army. In the early 19th century refugees from vicious warfare in the north fled to the mountains of Lesotho and became welded into a kingdom under Moshoeshoe I, who placed himself under British protection. This wise move ensured the Sotho clans retained some form of self-government throughout the colonial era, and in 1966 became independent outside the Union of South Africa. The country has few natural resources and little agricultural land. The young men work in South Africa for long periods of time, earning enough money to support their families and keep the fragile economy of the kingdom in balance.

LIBERIA

Population: 2.8 million
Area: 111,000 square kilometres
Capital: Monrovia
Language: English and tribal languages
Currency: Liberian Dollar

The flag of Liberia is similar to that of the United States of America, indicating the origins of the nation. In 1822 an American society landed a party of freed slaves on the coast in Monrovia in an attempt to establish a haven for such people. In 1847 the nation declared itself independent and adopted a constitution similar to that of the United States. Recent years have witnessed violent upheavals, with coups and civil war raging fiercely. The situation is not yet stable. Liberia has rich mineral resources, in particular massive iron ore deposits, which make up seventy percent of exports, together with gold and diamonds. The vast bulk of the population is engaged in farming, with numerous commercial farms growing coffee, rice and sugar cane.

▲ *A lake in the Fezzan dessert, Libya.*

LIBYA

Population: 4.4 million
Area: 1,760,000 square kilometres
Capital: Tripoli
Language: Arabic
Currency: Libyan Dinar

Until recently one of the poorest Mediterranean nations, Libya is now one of the richest, following the discovery of massive oil fields in 1959. In 1969 King Idris was overthrown by an army faction led by Colonel Muammar Gadaffi, who established Libya as an Arab republic. The country has since vociferously supported Arab unity and nationalism, lending aid to various organisations such as the PLO and so earning Western enmity. The economy is based on natural oil and gas, which account for nearly all exports. Internally, however, agriculture dominates, with the most fertile lands of North Africa producing rich harvests of dates, citrus fruits and cereals. Ambitious irrigation projects are under way which aim at adding hundreds of square kilometres to the farmland.

29

MADAGASCAR

Population: 12.8 million
Area: 590,000 square kilometres
Capital: Antananarivo
Language: Malagasy and French
Currency: Malagasy Franc

The original kingdom, comprising a mixed population of Malaysians and Africans, was overrun by the French in 1897. In 1960 the island became independent as a republic, and since then has undergone several coups. The country was ruled by the Supreme Revolutionary Council and the President from 1975-1991, when anti-government unrest led to political changes. The economy is based on agriculture and the exploitation of forests, both natural and planted. The fertile soils produce heavy crops of coffee, tobacco and tropical fruits, the processing of which forms the basis of the island's small-scale industries.

MALAWI

Population: 9.4 million
Area: 118,000 square kilometres
Capital: Lilongwe
Language: Chichewa and English
Currency: Kwacha

Ruled for many years as a one-party state by Dr Kamuzu Banda, Malawi is a landlocked nation with few resources. Agriculture is the basic activity, with most of the population relying on subsistence farming for a livelihood. Tobacco and tea are grown for export, but occupy only a small part of the total agricultural land. Marble is the only major quarrying material and industry is restricted to local consumer goods. As a mountainous nation, however, Malawi has massive potential for hydro-electricity and this is now being exploited. The economy remains reliant on its migrant workers, who leave Malawi for South Africa or Zambia to work in mines and factories to earn much needed income.

MALI

Population: 8.4 million
Area: 1,240,000 square kilometres
Capital: Bamako
Language: French, Bambara and tribal languages
Currency: Franc CFA

Mali is one of the world's poorest nations, being dependent on an agriculture at the mercy of drought and semi-desert conditions. The majority of the diverse population is concentrated in the southwest, where the Senegal and Niger rivers give a semblance of reliability to the water supply for irrigation. Millet, cassava and sweet potatoes

are the chief crops for local consumption, while cotton is produced for export. The northern and eastern regions are covered by desert and are virtually uninhabited. Mineral wealth remains untapped due to poor transport and a lack of capital. The military coup of 1968 produced a stable government headed by General Traore. In 1992, the nation held its first democratic elections and General Traore was replaced by a civlian president.

MAURITANIA

Population: 2 million
Area: 1,031,000 square kilometres
Capital: Nouakchott
Language: Arabic and French
Currency: Ouguiya

The crescent and star on Mauritania's green flag indicates its Islamic heritage. The vast desert region of the north and east is the home of nomadic herdsmen, but the majority of the population inhabits the Senegal Valley in the southwest. In this region millet, rice and dates are produced in large quantities for local consumption. Coastal villages land large catches of Atlantic fish, which are dried or salted locally to form the bulk of exports by value. Industry is virtually non-existent, what there is being restricted to iron-ore mining or food processing. A long-running war with Morocco over the Western Sahara territory, which ended in 1979, drained the Mauritanian economy, which is still attempting to recover. In 1992 the country held its first multi-party elections.

MOROCCO

Population: 26 million
Area: 446,000 square kilometres
Capital: Rabat
Language: Arabic, Berber, French
Currency: Dirham

The Islamic kingdom of Morocco became independent of France in 1956, though the Sultan had always enjoyed some degree of control. The Sultanate became a Kingdom in 1957. The king holds supreme authority over both secular and religious life, though the government is actually carried out by a democratically-elected Parliament. The bulk of the nation's wealth is based on its rich mineral deposits, particularly phosphates and lead ore, which are extensively mined. Most of the population remains dependent on agriculture, however, and traditional crops of cereals, fruits and tomatoes dominate. Morocco has been involved in a lengthy war in the Western Sahara, where it claims large areas of territory.

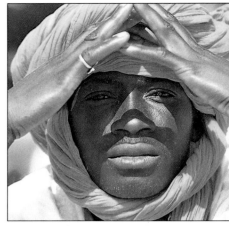

MOZAMBIQUE

Population: 16 million
Area: 783,000 square kilometres
Capital: Maputo
Language: Portuguese and tribal languages
Currency: Metical

The national flag of Mozambique features a book, a hoe and a gun; symbols which are apt for this poverty-ridden nation in southern Africa. From 1977 the Marxist Frelimo Party was the only legal political party in Mozambique, though recently opposition parties have been allowed. Opposition of a more violent kind has been maintained by the Renamo movement, which has been carrying on an armed struggle for many years. A peace treaty signed between the government and Renamo in 1992 promises to stabilise the situation. The hoe symbolises the agricultural base of the national economy, which relies on cereals, bananas and various types of nut. The long coastline on the Indian Ocean offers fine fishing opportunities.

NAMIBIA

Population: 1.5 million
Area: 825,000 square kilometres
Capital: Windhoek
Language: English, Afrikaans and tribal languages
Currency: South African Rand

The vast desert nation of Namibia gained independence from South Africa in 1990, after many years of political instability. Cuban mercenaries from Communist Angola backed the SWAPO guerilla movement, while South Africa attempted to maintain its influence by enforcing a constitution. The independence elections resulted in victory for SWAPO, but not by the margin needed for them to fulfil its goal of one-party rule. The political struggle was made more bitter by the vast mineral wealth of Namibia, which provides one the highest average incomes on the continent. Diamonds and uranium form the basis of the mineral industry. Most of the people are engaged in stock ranching of either cattle or sheep, which together outnumber humans in Namibia by six to one.

NIGER

Population: 8 million
Area: 1,268,000 square kilometres
Capital: Niamey
Language: French, Hausa and tribal languages
Currency: Franc CFA

Only around the southwestern borders is Niger a productive agricultural country. Here the Niger River provides water for irrigation

▲ *A typical Senegalese, Senegal.*

▲ *Fertile river banks, Morocco.*

▼ *Terraced hillsides, Rwanda.*

▲ *Tanandava, Madagascar.*

▲ *Djenné, Mali.*

▲ *A young girl, Mauritania.*

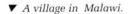
◀ *Lumber workers, Lagos, Nigeria.*

▼ *A village in Malawi.*

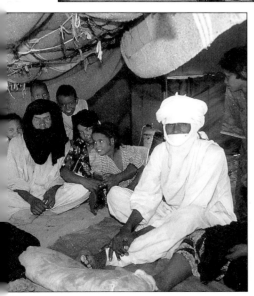

▲ *Refugees in Niger.*

▲ *Oranjemund, Nambia.*

and drinking. The bulk of the population is concentrated in this region, where they farm at a subsistence level. The capital, Niamey, stands on the banks of the Niger River and has some small-scale industry. Elsewhere through southern Niger a number of oases permit farming, but away from the Niger River the land is generally devoted to grazing livestock. In the north, the Sahara makes even grazing virtually impossible. In 1974 the government was overthrown by a military coup, and the nation was ruled by a supreme military council. In 1992 a new constitution was adopted.

NIGERIA

Population: 89.6 million
Area: 923,000 square kilometres
Capital: Abuja
Language: English, Hausa and tribal languages
Currency: Naira

Great confusion exists about Nigeria, its population and resources, due to decades of political instability and civil war. The population was reckoned in 1963 to be 55,670,000. Recent massive growths in population are known to have taken place, but estimates of the present number range from 90- to 120 million. Equally uncertain are the country's economic figures. The rich agricultural soil supports thriving farming communities, which produce crops of millet, cassava and yams for local consumption. Export crops include cocoa and groundnuts. Industrial activity has been boosted by rich oil reserves, but no accurate picture of this sector is possible. The political troubles intensified in 1983 with a military coup, followed by another in 1985. Though a return to democratic civilian government has been promised, it has still to come into being.

RWANDA

Population: 7.3 million
Area: 26,000 square kilometres
Capital: Kigali
Language: Kinyarwanda and French
Currency: Rwanda Franc

The independence celebrations of Rwanda in 1962 were nearly marred when it was realised that the intended national flag was almost identical to that already chosen by Mali. A large 'R' was hurriedly added and the events went ahead as planned. Independence from Belgium came in the wake of a savage internal struggle between the agricultural Hutu and the pastoral Watutsi. The latter had held power

for centuries but were overthrown in the fighting, many fleeing to neighbouring countries. Rwanda is a densely-populated agricultural country producing sweet potatoes and cassava for local use and coffee for sale abroad. The coup of 1973 brought the military to power, and today there is only one political party allowed in the country.

SAO TOME AND PRINCIPE

Population: 126,000
Area: 845 square kilometres
Capital: Sao Tome
Language: Portuguese and Fang
Currency: Dobra

As with many African nations, Sao Tome plans to abandon the one-party form of government for democracy. The move was agreed in 1990, but in the Presidential elections of 1991 there was, as usual, only one candidate. The economy of the islands is heavily dependent on two agricultural crops, cocoa and copra, and fluctuations in the international markets have great effects in Sao Tome and Principe. The government has recently tried to diversify crop production, but has had more success in building up a fishing industry to exploit the vast tuna shoals of the Gulf of Guinea. The flag of the republic features two black stars to symbolise the two islands and carries the green and yellow colours common to many African nations.

▲ *Sao Tome, capital of Sao Tome and Principe.*

SENEGAL

Population: 7.7 million
Area: 196,000 square kilometres
Capital: Dakar
Language: French, Wolof and tribal languages
Currency: Franc CFA

In 1960 Senegal became independent of France as part of the Mali Confederacy. After only a few months Senegal withdrew, adding a green star to the Mali flag to proclaim its independence. The nation was a one-party state for some years, but is now a democracy despite several coup attempts. The groundnut, or peanut, was introduced in the 1600s as a cheap food for slaves being transported to the Caribbean, and it remains the country's most important crop. Cotton is also grown for export and attempts at diversifying into other areas have been made. The nation has a good transportation system and this has encouraged modest industrialisation, though this is still largely confined to Dakar.

SIERRA LEONE

Population: 4.4 million
Area: 73,000 square kilometres
Capital: Freetown
Language: English, Krio and tribal languages
Currency: Leone

Freetown was founded as a settlement for freed slaves by the British in 1787, but the area was not formally taken over as a colony until 1808. When independence came in 1961 Sierra Leone adopted a flag showing blue for the ocean, white for unity and green for agriculture. The nation is now a one-party state under the leadership of the army which deposed the president in 1992. The vast majority of the population engages in subsistence farming. A small amount of both coffee and cocoa is exported, but the nation's economy is based on the mining of bauxite, diamonds and molybdenite. Local government, is based on tribal units. Each chief is supported by a Council of Elders which is responsible for law and order in the area and which has powers to raise and spend taxes.

SOMALIA

Population: 7.9 million
Area: 638,000 square kilometres
Capital: Mogadishu
Language: Somali, Arabic, English and Italian
Currency: Somali Shilling

The Somali people are a widely-scattered nation of herdsmen whose members range widely across the arid grazing lands of the Horn of Africa. Somalia came into being when British Somaliland merged with Italian Somalia and became independent. In 1969 General Barre seized power in a coup. A long-running civil war caused Barre to flee the nation in 1991. Severe famine and continuing civil war left the country in crisis and in 1992, UN-approved troops intervened. The internal troubles have prevented exploitation of the iron ore and gypsum and the development of industry. Over three-quarters of the Somalis lead a traditional lifestyle based on cattle, goats, sheep and camels. A few engage in agriculture along the river banks, but this activity is continually under threat from drought.

SOUTH AFRICA

Population: 32 million
Area: 1,123,000 square kilometres
Capital: Pretoria
Language: Afrikaans, English and tribal languages
Currency: Rand

Conflict between the white minority and various factions among the black majority have overshadowed South African history in recent years. In 1991 the government announced the end of *Apartheid*, a policy of separate racial development. In 1994 the country held its first non-racial elections, with the ANC winning the largest proportion of the vote. South Africa is the wealthiest nation in Africa. Its prosperity is founded on the efficient exploitation of a vast mineral wealth and large agricultural potential. Gold is mined in staggering quantity – 600 tonnes in 1990 – and is the most valuable of several mining exports. Industry is well developed, with food processing, metal smelting and machinery manufacture being the most productive. The massive economic base of South Africa makes several neighbouring nations dependent upon it and attracts large numbers of migrant workers.

▲ *A Sudanese group, near Jonglei Canal, Sudan.*

SUDAN

Population: 30 million
Area: 2,505,000 square kilometres
Capital: Khartoum
Language: Arabic, English, tribal languages
Currency: Sudanese Pound

In 1989 the army overthrew the government and pledged itself to ending the bitter civil war between the Arabic and Islamic north, and the south, where black Africans practising tribal religions form the majority. Despite this pledge the war continues to bring misery to millions of Sudanese. The war, combined with government control of the economy, led to drastic food shortages in 1991-1992. The nation is mainly desert or arid grassland, where cattle, goats and sheep are grazed. Agriculture is concentrated along the Nile and in the south, where irrigation is possible. Cotton and sugar are grown for export as is gum arabic in the forested southwest. Land devoted to producing food is vulnerable to the periodic droughts of the region. The large mineral reserves are undeveloped due to political instability.

▲ *The coronation of Mswati III, Swaziland.*

SWAZILAND

Population: 826,000
Area: 17,000 square kilometres
Capital: Mbabane
Language: siSwati and English
Currency: Lilangeni

Sandwiched between Mozambique and South Africa, the Kingdom of Swaziland gained independence from Britain in 1968. Since 1973 the king has ruled without Parliament, though the new king, Mswati III, has allowed an advisory college to be elected. The flag depicts the traditional shield and spears with which the Swazi successfully defended themselves against Zulu aggression in the early 19th century. Today, Swaziland is a predominantly agricultural country with the bulk of the population being engaged in subsistence agriculture. European settlers operate large-scale farms producing sugar cane, citrus fruits and cotton for export. Industry is limited to the mining of asbestos, coal and iron ore, chiefly for export.

TANZANIA

Population: 25.8 million
Area: 945,000 square kilometres
Capital: Dodoma
Language: English, Swahili and tribal languages
Currency: Tanzanian Shilling

The republic of Tanzania is made up of over 100 tribes, each with its own language and customs. From 1977 this diverse population was kept together by a government based on a single political party, the leader of which, Ali Mwinyi, won the 1990 presidential election. In 1992 a law was passed introducing multi-party democracy. The nation came into being in 1964, when the African majority on Zanzibar overthrew the Islamic Sultan and joined mainland Tanganyika to form a new republic. Most of the population is engaged in agriculture. Crops such as coconuts, cardamoms and cocoa have been introduced in an attempt to gain export sales. Deposits of several metal ores have recently been found but remain unexploited.

TOGO

Population: 3.7 million
Area: 57,000 square kilometres
Capital: Lomé
Language: French and tribal languages
Currency: Franc CFA

A white star for hope dominates the flag of Togo. This former German colony passed through French control after World War I before achieving independence in 1960. The first decade of freedom was marred by internal violence, but since 1969 power has been centralised in the hands of a single party under military control. Vast reserves of phosphates, bauxite and iron ore have provided a mineral backbone to the Togo economy since exploitation began in 1953. Most of the population is engaged in agriculture on the pockets of fertile land among the inland hills. Maize and cassava are the bulk crops for local consumption, though coffee, cocoa and cotton are produced for export. The short coastline is dotted with fishing villages which reap rich harvests in the tropical waters.

TUNISIA

Population: 8.4 million
Area: 163,000 square kilometres
Capital: Tunis
Language: Arabic and French
Currency: Tunisian Dinar

The Tunisian flag has been in use since 1835 when this was a province of the Turkish Empire, and it retains the crescent, star and red field of the Turkish flag. After a period as a French protectorate, Tunisia became an independent kingdom in 1956 and a republic the following year. Oil fields exist in Tunisia, but are not rich enough to dominate the economy in the same way as in other Arab countries. Mining of lead, iron and zinc ores is also an important source of mineral wealth. Tunisia remains, however, an agricultural nation, with nearly half the working population occupied on farms, mostly in the northern half of the country. Tomatoes, olives and citrus fruits are among the most important crops. Fishing is an important employment along the coast.

▲ *A crowded market, Togo.*

▲ *Mogadishu, Somalia.*

▲ *Typical Tunisian architecture.*

▼ *Ngorongoro Conservation Area, Tanzania.*

▲ *Kampala, Uganda's capital.*

▼ *Vineyards, South Africa.*

UGANDA

Population: 17 million
Area: 236,000 square kilometres
Capital: Kampala
Language: English, Swahili and tribal languages
Currency: Uganda Shilling

Uganda has experienced several coups and foreign invasions since independence, giving rise to numerous regimes, the most notorious being that of Idi Amin in the 1970s. The nation is made up of numerous tribes, each with its own language and culture. The political troubles have prevented the development of an industrial economy, though there is some copper mining. By contrast, agriculture is well developed and Uganda can feed itself while still producing cotton, sugar cane and coffee for export. Fishing on Lake Victoria is also a major occupation. Uganda was a British protectorate from 1894 to 1961. English is still widely spoken and the bulk of the population is Christian.

ZAIRE

Population: 41 million
Area: 2,345,000 square kilometres
Capital: Kinshasa
Language: French, Lingala, Swahili and tribal languages
Currency: Zaire

The flag of Zaire is based on the emblem of the Popular Movement of the Revolution, once the only legal political party in the country. The party held power from 1978 until 1990, when the transition to multi-party democracy began. The vast interior of Zaire is largely covered by the Congo Basin, in which flourishes dense rain forest. Much of this area has never been properly explored and remains home to tribes leading traditional lifestyles. Best known are the pygmies, but several hundred other peoples maintain their languages and cultures. Government control is limited to regions along the Congo River and the more open regions. Here mineral mining is the mainstay of the economy, with exploitation of rich deposits of copper, oil and cobalt being predominant.

ZAMBIA

Population: 8.7 million
Area: 752,000 square kilometres
Capital: Lusaka
Language: English and tribal languages
Currency: Kwacha

The Zambian economy is almost entirely dependent on copper, over half-a-million tonnes of which are produced each year. The nation is therefore vulnerable to changes on the international commodities market. The bulk of the population is employed in agriculture, much of it subsistence. Maize and livestock are the main agricultural products, though some sugar cane is produced for export. The development of more sophisticated agriculture is hampered by the tsetse fly and occasional droughts. Independence came to Zambia in 1964, and it was ruled by the United National Independence Party of Kenneth Kaunda until 1991, when multi-party elections were held.

▲ *Kapenta drying racks, Zambia.*

▲ *Plantation worker harvesting tea, Zaire.*

 ## ZIMBABWE

Population: 9.9 million
Area: 390,000 square kilometres
Capital: Harare
Language: English, Shona and Sindebele
Currency: Zimbabwe Dollar

Zimbabwe came into being in 1980, when the former white-ruled Rhodesia became a democracy under black rule. President Mugabe moved the nation towards Marxism. The new nation was named after enigmatic stone ruins discovered in the region, which indicated an advanced civilisation that had vanished some centuries earlier. The country has a balanced economy, with mining, industry and agriculture all playing their part. Mining is based on the exploitation of gold, nickel and coal deposits. Agriculture is largely conducted by subsistence farmers producing maize and sorghum. Larger scale farms produce tobacco for export and fruits. The extensive industrial scene is dominated by the processing of mining and agricultural products.

The AMERICAS

*T*he Americas are continents of contrast, where wealth and poverty, wilderness and man-made landscapes can be found in the greatest diversity and extremes.

Stretching from the Arctic Ocean to the chill, stormy waters off Cape Horn, the Americas embrace the full range of climatic zones, from frozen tundra to tropical heat and then to bare, frozen plains again. Nor is the physical geology any less diverse. The vast prairies of Central North America are flat and featureless and the Amazon Basin is a vast, alluvial depression where no land is more than a few metres above sea level. But in the Andes and Rockies the Americas can also boast one of the longest and most rugged mountain chains in the world. Heights reach almost 7,000 metres in the southern Andes and top 6,000 metres in Alaska.

Associated with climatic and geographical variation are those of ecology and habitat. The tropical regions of South and Central America are the site of the largest and most diverse rain forests in the world. These forests cover vast areas of land and contain more species of plants and animals than the rest of the world put together. The sheer beauty and diversity of the rain forests are staggering. Yet it is in the Americas that destruction of the rainforests is at its most widespread. The vast boreal forests of the far north are less under threat, though they are heavily exploited for timber and pulp. Elsewhere, a combination of semi-aridity and suitable temperature produce vast grasslands on which graze huge herds of animals.

The human impact on the Americas has been immense. North America is generally more prosperous and has felt the influence of man more widely than either Central or South America. The open prairies have been emptied of the millions of bison and are now ploughed to produce massive crops of grain to feed the world. Those areas unsuited to grain agriculture are grazed by cattle and sheep, banishing the native fauna to special reserves.

The mineral wealth of the north has been exploited and is still being extracted on a massive scale. Gold, silver, copper and other metals are gouged from the ground in huge quantities by large international companies.

These changes have resulted in a highly developed and prosperous economy for the peoples of North America. Large cities have sprung up across the United States and Canada, with populations numbering into the millions. Roads, railways and flightpaths provide good communications across the northern continent, allowing free trade and transport links further to aid prosperity.

By contrast, much of Central and South America is relatively untouched by human progress and living conditions are generally poorer. Though large areas of rainforest are being destroyed, areas still stand untouched by anything except the activities of hunter-gatherer societies which have co-existed with the forests for millenia. Industry and mining are poorly developed and the bulk of the population rely on farming for a livelihood. Often the farmers operate at subsistence level, barely producing enough for their own needs. Many of the peoples of the interior have little contact with European-style civilisation. Both in the high Andes and in the dense forests there exist settlements that continue to live as their ancestors have done for generations. Technology and beliefs are much as they have always been, preserving cultures in tune with their surroundings, but giving poor life expectancy and low standards of living.

Many of the nations are poverty stricken and have fragile economies. Though the dominant and more prosperous nations give aid and help, the tiny island republics of the Caribbean remain devoid of natural resources and have economies based on the growing of bananas or coconuts and on tourism.

Taken together the Americas provide a startling contrast of landscapes, natural ecologies and human activities. If they are continents of wealth, plenty and beauty, they are also lands where poverty, deprivation and squalor are equally common.

◀ *A hillside dwelling, Colombia.*

▲ Lake and mountain scenery, Colorado, USA.

▶ Prickly Bay Beach, Grenada.

▲ Caracas, capital of Venezuela.

ANTIGUA AND BARBUDA

Population: 64,000
Area: 440 square kilometres
Capital: St John's
Language: English
Currency: East Caribbean Dollar

This nation of three islands takes its name from the two populated islands, the third being Redonda. The islands were discovered by Christopher Columbus in 1493 but Spanish attempts at colonisation failed, as did those of France. Only when British settlers arrived to grow sugar cane in the late 17th century did a permanent settlement result. The sugar crop was abandoned in the 1970s in favour of more diversified agriculture, with cotton and fruit ranking high. The wealth of the nation, however, lies in tourism. This is a paradise for those seeking a relaxing holiday. The government is a democracy based on universal suffrage, with the Queen of Great Britain as Head of State.

ARGENTINA

Population: 33 million
Area: 2,766,000 square kilometres
Capital: Buenos Aires
Language: Spanish
Currency: Austral

As one of the largest and richest countries in South America, Argentina has the potential to become a dominant influence in that region. Internal political troubles, however, have held back the massive growth which is still possible. The most recent military rule began in a coup of 1976, and collapsed after defeat in the Falklands War against Britain in 1982. The new government has attempted to bring together in harmony the mixed population. The largest ethnic groups are the native Indian peoples, the descendants of Spanish settlers, and more recent European arrivals. Sunflower oil and wheat are both produced in quantity, but the largest exports are beef and lamb. Mining is a major contributor to national wealth, with coal, gold, silver and copper all being worked in quantity.

BAHAMAS

Population: 264,000
Area: 14,000 square kilometres
Capital: Nassau
Language: English
Currency: Bahamian Dollar

There may be as many as 1,700 islands and cays in the Bahamas, but only 700 are of any size, and a mere thirty are permanently inhabited. The low-lying coral islands support only a thin soil, a fact which has long hampered a more dynamic economy. The agricultural base of the islands remains sugar cane, though livestock and egg production for local consumption are important. Fishing the shallow tropical waters is a thriving industry and modern techniques of fish farming are boosting the catch. The business community is much larger than might be expected, due to the liberal tax laws which have turned the islands into a tax haven for foreign businessmen. The balmy climate and open beaches have made the islands a centre for tourism, which brings large quantities of foreign currency into the islands.

BARBADOS

Population: 259,000
Area: 430 square kilometres
Capital: Bridgetown
Language: English
Currency: Barbados Dollar

The trident dominates the flag of Barbados, symbolising the wealth of the sea. This is apt for the island has long depended on the sea for its livelihood. The delectable flying fish of the island's waters are a noted delicacy, and during the season hundreds of boats put out in search of these creatures and the high prices they fetch. Recent tourist promotions have boosted the economy, with outsiders flocking to Barbados in search of the warm sea and wide beaches. The island is densely populated, ranking high in the world's population density league, though most of the people live in the countryside. The traditional sugar cane crop, part of which is turned to rum, remains important to the local economy. The country has a democratic constitution with the Queen of Great Britain as Head of State.

BELIZE

Population: 196,000
Area: 23,000 square kilometres
Capital: Belmopan
Language: English and Spanish
Currency: Belize Dollar

The small nation of Belize gained its independence from Great Britain in 1981. A British military garrison remains, however, to provide protection against Guatemala, which claims Belize for its own, as the latter's army consists of a single battalion and two small naval craft. Belize has a democratic government operating under a Prime Minister and a two-chamber legislature. Only the coastal region is heavily populated, with the interior being blanketed in dense forests which are, as yet, unexploited. The mainstay of the economy is agriculture, which accounts for over half of export values. Sugar cane is the chief crop, followed by citrus fruits which are processed into juice concentrates for export. Maize, rice and livestock are raised for local consumption, making Belize self-sufficient in food.

BERMUDA

Population: 60,000
Area: 53 square kilometres
Capital: Hamilton
Language: English
Currency: Bermuda Dollar

The islands of Bermuda lie on the Western Atlantic some 800 kilometres from the North American coast. Only about twenty of the 150 islands are inhabited, the rest being isolated islets and rocky outcrops. The economy is almost entirely reliant on tourism and insurance for survival. Over half a million tourists come to Bermuda each year to enjoy the balmy climate and excellent swimming waters. Several major insurance companies are based here to take advantage of favourable local laws. The islands are officially a colony of the United Kingdom, with a Governer General being appointed by the Crown. However, the democratically-elected parliment is free to take what action it wishes in all matters other than foreign affairs, defence and the police. The Governer General is responsible for these matters.

▲ A musician performing at a festival, Bolivia.

BOLIVIA

Population: 7.7 million
Area: 1,098,000 square kilometres
Capital: Sucre
Language: Spanish and tribal languages
Currency: Boliviano

Bolivia has been landlocked since it lost its coastline to Chile in 1884, and all exports must leave via other nations, predominantly along the

▲ Kings Landing Historical Settlement, Canada.

▼ English Harbour, Antigua.

▲ *Normans Cays and Exuma Cays, Bahamas.*

▼ *Village children in Belize.*

▲ *A landscape in southern Chile.*

Below left: *Hawkins Island, Bermuda.*

▼ *The Careenage, Bridgetown, Barbados.*

◄ *Cartago, former capital of Costa Rica.*

▼ *Buenos Aires, Argentina.*

rail link to the Chilean town of Arica. The vast bulk of these exports are minerals, with tin leading the field by a large margin. It is planned to expand the smelting capacity of Bolivia so that more tin ore can be processed before export. Silver and gold are exploited in smaller quantities, as is zinc. The agricultural output includes coffee and potatoes grown in the mountains, together with increasing quantities of sugar cane and cotton in the eastern lowlands. Coca is a traditional crop which has recently boomed as a source of cocaine. The United States is sponsoring a government programme to destroy the coca crop. Bolivia is notoriously unstable politically, having experienced fourteen presidents and a military junta since 1966.

▲ *Rio de Janeiro, Brazil.*

BRAZIL

Population: 151 million
Area: 8,511,000 square kilometres
Capital: Brasilia
Language: Portuguese and tribal languages
Currency: Cruzeiro

The present democratic constitution of Brazil came into being in 1988 after two decades of military rule. The nation is the only South American state with Portuguese as the official language, a fact which dates back to a treaty between Spain and Portugal in 1494. The southern and eastern regions are the best developed and it is here that agriculture and industry are most heavily concentrated. Coffee is by far the most important crop,

producing over three-million tonnes annually. Various other tropical crops such as sugar cane, cotton, cassava and citrus fruits are also important. Industry is based on the exploitation of crops and minerals such as quartz, thorium, zirconium and chromium. The vast Amazon Basin contains the largest rainforest in the world, with an incredible diversity of wildlife. Conservationists throughout the world are concerned as large areas of this forest are felled each year to make way for agriculture and to extract the valuable timber.

CANADA

Population: 27.7 million
Area: 9,922,000 square kilometres
Capital: Ottawa
Language: English and French
Currency: Canadian Dollar

As the second largest country in area in the world, Canada has a surprisingly small population. The reason for this is that the vast majority of Canada's land lies in the harsh northern latitudes, where tundra or boreal forest cover the ground. The population is concentrated in the southern region, where the climate is kinder and agriculture is possible. Wheat production is the basis of the agricultural economy, with nearly 900 million bushels being produced each year. Beef output is almost as important, while market gardening and fur farming are important in certain localities. Vast mineral reserves include nickel, zinc, copper and gold. The industrial scene is highly diversified, with a wide range of products being produced both for internal consumption and for export. Canada is a federal democracy with each of the provinces retaining considerable powers. Demands for provincial independence have been made, particularly by Quebec.

CHILE

Population: 13.6 million
Area: 736,000 square kilometres
Capital: Santiago
Language: Spanish
Currency: Chilean Peso

The long, narrow strip of territory which makes up Chile is defined by the Pacific Ocean on the west and the watershed of the Andes on the east. The mountainous terrain has inhibited both communications and economic development and Chile remains one of the poorer South American states. Nonetheless the nation has some potential. The north has rich mineral deposits and these are being exploited on a large scale. Agriculture is restricted to valleys

and terraced highlands. The most important crops are fruits such as apples, plums and citrus fruits. Chile has had a chequered political history, with military coups and a Marxist government featuring strongly. In 1989 the military regime handed rule over to a democratically-elected civilian government, but retained some powers for itself.

COLOMBIA

Population: 34 million
Area: 1,142,000 square kilometres
Capital: Bogota
Language: Spanish
Currency: Colombian Peso

When Colombia won its independence from Spain in 1819 it included modern Panama, Venezuela and Ecuador within its frontiers. These states broke away in 1830 and 1903, while an internal revolution stripped the remaining areas of power and centralised it in Bogota. Earlier political violence appears to have ended and the government now concentrates on improving the economy and trying to curb drug trafficking. The nation is perhaps best known for its coffee, which remains an important crop. Rubber is also cultivated, but the dominant food crops are potatoes and rice. The coca crop forms the basis of a flourishing cocaine trade and the government is engaged in a bitter struggle with drug barons to stamp out the industry. Minerals are found in abundance in Colombia, with gold and silver being the most important. The mountains produce half the world's emeralds, which are exported in quantity.

COSTA RICA

Population: 3.1 million
Area: 51,000 square kilometres
Capital: San Jose
Language: Spanish
Currency: Costa Rican Colon

Named 'The Rich Coast' when first discovered by Spain in the 16th century, Costa Rica has continued to support a thriving economy despite periodic disturbances. The nation is unusual in that its constitution forbids the raising of an army for any reason. However, the para-military Civil Guard undertakes many duties usually carried out by the army in other nations. Agriculture forms the basis of the economy, with the traditional crops of coffee and bananas still dominating. A burgeoning industrial sector concentrates on processing local products. Since a civil war in 1948 government has been relatively stable and the constitution of 1949 is still in force.

37

CUBA

Population: 10.8 million
Area: 115,000 square kilometres
Capital: Havana
Language: Spanish
Currency: Cuban Peso

It is ironic that the Cuban flag is based on that of the United States, with a triangle added to symbolise Freemasonry, for the present regime is openly hostile to the United States and has a Communist system. The present flag dates to 1849 and remained unchanged when Fidel Castro seized power in 1959. Since then Castro has pursued a Marxist-Leninist programme and has lent support to similar movements in Third World nations. Agriculture remains the basis of the Cuban economy, with the traditional sugar cane being the chief crop. Tobacco growing is also important, as is cotton. Fishing is a major export earner, with numerous small craft putting out to fish the surrounding waters. Mining and associated processes make up the bulk of the industrial sector, with iron and nickel leading the production tables.

DOMINICA

Population: 108,821
Area: 750 square kilometres
Capital: Roseau
Language: English and French
Currency: East Caribbean Dollar

The tiny nation state of Dominica is a democratic republic within the Commonwealth and is one of the poorer Caribbean states. The economy is heavily reliant on agriculture. Bananas and coconuts are the principal crops, both of which are vulnerable to international price fluctuations. The crops are periodically devastated by hurricanes, bringing disaster to the country. Fishing promises to increase significantly and remove the dangerous reliance on agriculture. Tourism is also growing as visitors come to enjoy the sun on the broad sandy beaches of the island. The inland mountains have a diverse wildlife population, including a unique species of parrot, the Sisserou, which features on the national flag.

DOMINICAN REPUBLIC

Population: 7.5 million
Area: 48,000 square kilometres
Capital: Santo Domingo
Language: Spanish
Currency: Dominica Peso

The capital city of the Dominican Republic is the oldest European city in the Americas, having been been founded by Bartholomew

Columbus in 1496. During the bitter colonial struggles of the 18th century the western area of Hispaniola was captured by France, but the eastern section remained under Spanish control and this now forms the Dominican Republic. The nation became independent in 1844, since when the nation has experienced political instability and periods of occupation by United States troops. The economy remains dependent on sugar cane, with sugar refining the main industry. Sugar accounts for about a quarter of all exports, though coffee and cocoa also earn foreign cash. Minerals being exploited include bauxite, gold and silver.

ECUADOR

Population: 10.6 million
Area: approx 300,000 square kilometres
Capital: Quito
Language: Spanish and Quechua
Currency: Sucre

Perched high in the Andes, the capital of Ecuador, Quito, has witnessed much political instability since independence from Colombia in 1830. The past forty years have seen fifteen changes of government and confused party loyalties continue to complicate the power structure. There have been continual disputes with Peru over the border territories in the rainforest, and this quarrel erupted into war in 1981, when the present border was grudgingly accepted. The discovery of oil in the rainforest region has helped boost the underdeveloped economy but has added fuel to the dispute with Peru. The mountains and coastal regions are the centre of agriculture, much of which is carried out at subsistence level by the Quechua Indians. Foreign cash is earned by the export of coffee, bananas and cocoa.

EL SALVADOR

Population: 5.5 million
Area: 21,000 square kilometres
Capital: San Salvador
Language: Spanish
Currency: Salvadoran Colon

Civil war and terrorism have dominated the political scene of El Salvador for over a decade. Despite this the nation is densely populated, and nearly every piece of fertile land is now under cultivation. Coffee and sugar are the main cash crops for export but large quantities of maize, beans and sorghum are produced for local consumption. There are few mineral resources and industry is based on food processing and the supply of internal requirements for clothing and other similar items. The interior forests are being exploited for

▲ A rural scene in Ecuador.

◄ Punta Cana, Dominican Republic.

► A diver at Acapulco, Mexico.

▼ Scotts Head Peninsula Dominica.

▲ Cigar maker in Havana, Cuba.

▲ An agricultural scene, Haiti.

▼ Women washing clothes, Guatemala.

► Cutting cane, El Salvador.

▲ *A coconut palm plantation, Guyana.*

▲ *Tegucigalpa, capital of Honduras.*

commercial gain, principally for timber and tropical gums. The majority of the population is descended from the original Spanish settlers and indigenous tribesmen, the mixed-blood mestizos forming the large majority of the people.

 GRENADA

Population: 91,000
Area: 344 square kilometres
Capital: St George's
Language: English and French
Currency: Eastern Caribbean Dollar

Since independence from Britain in 1974 Grenada has remained within the Commonwealth but has experienced violent changes of government. In 1979 the democratic government was overthrown by a Marxist coup, which was followed by an army takeover in 1983 and an almost immediate invasion by United States troops at the request of neighbouring nations worried by the turn of events. Democracy was soon restored. The economy is based on agriculture and tourism, which together account for almost all foreign earnings. The local agriculture has traditionally specialised in tropical spices, with nutmeg – which features on Grenada's flag – and mace remaining valuable crops.

 GUATEMALA

Population: 9.7 million
Area: 109,000 square kilometres
Capital: Guatemala City
Language: Spanish and Mayan
Currency: Quetzal

As with most Central American states, Guatemala has experienced periods of revolution, civil war and dictatorship. A constitution introduced in 1986 restored democracy and free elections were held in 1990. The ancient Mayan civilisation dominated the region before the arrival of Spanish colonists, and Mayan is still spoken by the Indian population. Most of the people are of Spanish descent or have adopted Spanish culture. The nation relies on agricultural produce for export earnings. Coffee alone accounts for nearly half of exports by value, with cotton, bananas and sugar making up much of the remainder. The bulk of the population is concentrated in the farming regions of the south.

 GUYANA

Population: 748,000
Area: 214,000 square kilometres
Capital: Georgetown
Language: English
Currency: Guyana Dollar

The original inhabitants of Guyana, the local Indian tribes now make up

barely ten per cent of the population and live mainly in the southern highlands. The fertile coastal region is densely populated by the descendants of settlers and slaves of African, Indonesian, European and Chinese racial origins. These racial divides are reflected in the nation's politics, with parties often basing their support on the interests of sections of the population. The wealth of the nation lies in the agriculture of the coastal plain, where sugar cane and rice are grown in large quantities. Tropical fruits are also important crops and much is exported. The exploitation of minerals, particularly bauxite and diamonds, adds to the export drive.

 HAITI

Population: 6.8 million
Area: 28,000 square kilometres
Capital: Port-au-Prince
Language: French and Creole
Currency: Gourde

With an economy based on subsistence farming mixed with some cash crops, Haiti is one of the poorest American nations. Haitian coffee commands a high price; however, inefficient farming methods ensure that the business is of only limited profitability. Sugar and rum are also exported, but again without producing dramatic profits. The nation may have extensive mineral deposits, but these have never been confirmed. Haiti became the first black-governed republic when the slaves revolted in 1791, and won independence from France in 1804. After periods as a republic, kingdom and empire, Haiti fell under United States occupation before regaining independence in 1934. Between 1957 and 1986 the nation was ruled by the notorious Duvalier regime. The subsequent political situation has been unstable.

 HONDURAS

Population: 5.2 million
Area: 112,000 square kilometres
Capital: Tegucigalpa
Language: Spanish
Currency: Lempira

In 1821 Honduras joined with El Salvador, Guatemala, Costa Rica and Nicaragua to declare independence from Spain. Once colonial rule had been ended, however, the union fell apart and Honduras became fully independent in 1838. Since then the nation has been subject to coups and military rule alternating with periods of democracy, one of which began in 1982. The mountainous interior and continual troubles have combined to ensure that Honduras remains economically backward. The wealth

of the nation is derived from two crops, bananas and coffee, which together account for nearly all exports by value. Increasingly heavy catches of lobster and shrimp are beginning to feature in the economy. There is some small-scale mining and industrial activity.

 JAMAICA

Population: 2.4 million
Area: 11,000 square kilometres
Capital: Kingston
Language: English
Currency: Jamaican Dollar

Though comparatively wealthy by Caribbean standards, Jamaica has continued to be troubled by a degree of poverty and periodic unemployment. The democracy established on independence in 1962 remains in force. The island nation has a mixed economy better able to withstand international price fluctuations than others in the region. Agriculture is dominated by the traditional Caribbean crops of sugar cane, bananas and citrus fruits, though less usual products such as spices are also to be found. The bulk of exports, however, are created through the mining of bauxite and gypsum. A substantial influence in the local business community, and the island's culture, is tourism. Over a million visitors come to the island each year and pump large quantities of cash into the economy.

▲ *St Elizabeth, Jamaica.*

 MEXICO

Population: 84.4 million
Area: 1,972,000 square kilometres
Capital: Mexico City
Language: Spanish
Currency: Mexican Peso

Carved out of central America by invading Spaniards, Mexico was formerly the territory of the Aztecs and other tribes, who established sophisticated civilisations. The bulk of the population, known as Mestizos, is today of mixed blood though substantial minorities of both Indians and Spaniards remain. Once notorious for revolutions and bandits, Mexico has preserved its democratic constitution since 1917, and is now a relatively wealthy Central American nation. This wealth is largely based on oil reserves and a booming tourist business. Silver, iron and uranium are also important minerals. Many people live on the land, producing quantities of maize, potatoes, fruits and wheat for internal markets.

NICARAGUA

Population: 4.1 million
Area: 128,000 square kilometres
Capital: Managua
Language: Spanish and English
Currency: Cordoba

Nicaragua has a democratic constitution, but a state of emergency suppressed many civil liberties and much democracy. The cause of the move was the long-running civil war between the Sandanista government and supporters of the previous Somoza regime. In the 1990 election, the Sandanistas were voted out of office. Nicaragua has remained underdeveloped, with agriculture continuing to employ most of the population. Coffee, cotton and sugar make up the bulk of exports, though gold, silver and copper are being mined on a small scale. Crops of maize, rice and beans are raised for internal consumption, often by farmers operating at a subsistence level.

PANAMA

Population: 2.5 million
Area: 77,000 square kilometres
Capital: Panama City
Language: Spanish
Currency: Balboa

The Panama Canal has dominated Panamanian history and its economy ever since the nation came into being. Indeed, the province of Panama declared itself independent of Colombia in 1903 because the Colombian government had refused to sanction the construction of the canal. The canal eventually opened in 1914. The land flanking it was held by the United States, but was returned to Panama in 1979. The late 1980s saw a succession of Presidents as power was manipulated by General Noriega. In 1989 the United States invaded the country and removed Noriega from control Despite the economic dominance of the canal, local food processing and manufacturing industries are important. Agriculture is restricted due to the lack of fertile ground and provides less than half of the nation's food.

PARAGUAY

Population: 4.5 million
Area: 407,000 square kilometres
Capital: Asuncion
Language: Spanish and Guarani
Currency: Guarani

West of the Paraguay River is a vast region of open grasslands known as the Chaco, where the Guarani ranch cattle. The bulk of the population is of mixed Guarani and Spanish ancestry and inhabits the more fertile southeastern parts of the country. Cassava, maize and beans are produced in large quantities for local consumption, though coffee and tobacco are raised as cash crops. Industry is chiefly concerned with processing agricultural products as the mineral wealth of Paraguay is negligible. There is great potential for hydro-electricity and the largest such complex in the world stands at Itaipu. A 1989 coup overthrew General Stroessner, who had held power since 1956, replacing him with General Rodriguez. In 1992 a new constitution was approved, forbidding the re-election of the President.

PERU

Population: 22.5 million
Area: 1,285,000 square kilometres
Capital: Lima
Language: Spanish, Aymara, Quechua
Currency: Sol

Peru is unusual in that the bulk of its population is composed of indigenous Indians, with the Europeans and mixed-ancestry Mestizo in the minority. The Indians belong to the Aymara and Quechua tribal groups and generally lead traditional lifestyles in the Andes. The isolated villages and subsistence economy of the Indians have kept them outside the mainstream of Peruvian politics and national life. Along the coastal fringe coffee, cotton and sugar are produced as cash crops. Industrial activity is concentrated around the capital and is composed largely of iron and zinc works. The government of Peru has been notoriously volatile. A democratic constitution was in place from 1980 until 1992, when it was suspended by the President.

ST KITTS-NEVIS

Population: 43,000
Area: 267 square kilometres
Capital: Basseterre
Language: English
Currency: East Caribbean Dollar

The tiny state of St Kitts Nevis is populated almost entirely by the descendants of African slaves brought to the Caribbean during the 18th century, when sugar cane was the economic mainstay of the area. Sugar remains the major crop on the islands and industry concentrates on sugar refining. Cotton is the secondary crop and livestock is raised for local uses. Tourism is a welcome source of income for many of the citizens. The islands have a democratic constitution which guarantees Nevis the right to secede under certain conditions. After gaining internal self-government in 1967 the islands became fully independent in 1983.

ST LUCIA

Population: 153,000
Area: 617 square kilometres
Capital: Castries
Language: English and French
Currency: East Caribbean Dollar

When St Lucia was granted self-government in 1967 a competition was launched to design a flag, and the winning entry remains the national flag now that full independence has been achieved. The blue ground symbolises the ocean while the black triangle represents the volcanic peak of Mount Gimie and the yellow signifies the sun. Since independence in 1979 St Lucia has struggled to diversify its economy and prevent urban deprivation. Despite a move into the production of spices and citrus fruits, bananas, cocoa and coconuts remain the three dominant factors in the economy. Industry is limited to the processing of these foods. Tourism is significant with more people visiting the island each year than actually live there.

ST VINCENT AND THE GRENADINES

Population: 109,000
Area: 388 square kilometres
Capital: Kingstown
Language: English and French
Currency: East Caribbean Dollar

During the 18th century the sugar plantations of the Caribbean were a rich source of wealth, and they prompted rivalries between European powers. St Vincent was agreed to be neutral territory, but fighting between the British and French soon reached the island, which became a British colony in 1783. The islands achieved independence in 1979, since when the agricultural and tourist industries have continued to flourish. Agriculture is based upon bananas, cocoa, avocado pears and other tropical crops. Tourism attracts over 120,000 visitors each year, who come in search of the balmy climate and broad beaches lapped by warm waters. The constitution allows for a single elected chamber under the Governor General, who acts on behalf of the Queen of Great Britain.

SURINAME

Population: 404,000
Area: 163,000 square kilometres
Capital: Paramaribo
Language: Dutch, English and others
Currency: Suriname Guilder

In 1667 Britain exchanged Suriname for Manhattan in a deal with the Netherlands. Dutch rule continued until 1975, when the nation gained independence. Since that time Suriname has been troubled by volatile politics and ethnic diversity. The major population groups are Indonesians and Creoles, with mixed European and black ancestry, but significant numbers of Chinese, Javanese and blacks form minority communities. The dense inland forests are inhabited by indigenous Indian tribes. Since independence there were several coups before democracy was established in 1988. A military coup in 1990 ousted the government, and there followed a period of instability. The country has a flourishing economy based on mining for bauxite.

TRINIDAD AND TOBAGO

Population: 1.3 million
Area: 5,000 square kilometres
Capital: Port-of-Spain
Language: English
Currency: Trinidad and Tobago Dollar

The two islands which make up this nation were joined administratively by Britain in 1889, but differences remain marked. Tobago has gained the right of limited self-government after agitation against control from Trinidad. The population of Tobago is almost entirely composed of the descendants of African slaves, while Trinidad has a more mixed people. As with other Caribbean islands Trinidad and Tobago produce quantities of cocoa, sugar and other tropical products and enjoys a thriving tourist business. However, the basis of the economy is oil, with major fields existing both on Trinidad and offshore. Unemployment remains high and substantial parts of the population suffer poverty despite government attempts to alleviate the situation.

UNITED STATES OF AMERICA

Population: 250 million
Area: 9,529,000 square kilometres
Capital: Washington, D.C.
Language: English
Currency: US Dollar

The United States is a dominant world economic power. All sectors of the economy are highly developed and extremely

▲ *Nevis Peak, St Kitts-Nevis.*

▲ *Washing clothes, Nicaragua.*

▲ *Machu Picchu, Peru.*

▼ *Loading a schooner, St Vincent.*

▼ *Punta del Este, Uruguay.*

▼ *Paramaribo, Suriname.*

▲ *Englishman's Bay, Trinidad and Tobago.*

▼ *The Panama Canal, Panama.*

▲ *Petit Piton and Soufrière, St Lucia.*

▶ *Asuncion, Paraguay.*

productive. Throughout the large area occupied by the nation deposits of a wide range of minerals, including oil, coal and various metals are found. The fertile soils are extensively farmed to produce huge crops; over two billion bushels of wheat alone. Industry is highly developed with high-tech industries leading the world in developing new processes. In other fields, too, the United States leads the industries of the world with a highly diversified range of businesses producing almost every type of goods imaginable. The nation is a democratic federal union of fifty states in which individual states have some rights of self-government, but the most important powers are held by the central administration.

URUGUAY

Population: 3.1 million
Area: 176,000 square kilometres
Capital: Montevideo
Language: Spanish
Currency: Uruguayan Nuevo Peso

A province of Brazil until it won its independence in 1828 after a brief war, in which Uruguay enjoyed Argentinian support. Uruguay then adopted a flag sharing the same colours and the Sun of May symbol as Argentina. In 1989 democratic elections were held after more than a decade of military intervention in government. The chief wealth of Uruguay is its land, which supports a flourishing pastoral economy. There are about eleven million cattle

and twenty-five million sheep grazing on the rich grasslands of Uruguay, together with large numbers of farm animals. The processing of meat and leather are major industries in Uruguay, as is the spinning and weaving of wool. The nation has virtually no mineral resources and only a limited industrial base.

VENEZUELA

Population: 9.3 million
Area: 912,000 square kilometres
Capital: Caracus
Language: Spanish
Currency: Bolivar

The Republic of Venezuela came into being in 1830, when the area

broke away from Colombia just nine years after jointly winning independence from Spain. Venezuela is much more heavily dependant on industry than most other South American nations and has large and densely populated cities. Nearly ninety percent of the population lives in towns, far more than in neighbouring states. Vast oil reserves have been discovered and are being exploited. More established is the mining of bauxite, which supports an aluminium smelting business. Iron ore similarly forms the basis of a metal working industry. Agriculture has steadily declined in importance, with more than half of those employed in agriculture living at subsistence level.

AUSTRALASIA

*T*he nations of Australasia do not occupy a single continental entity, as do those of Asia, Africa or Europe. Instead they are united by cultural and ethnic traits more closely linked to the human populations than to the geographical limits of that region commonly called Australasia.

Strictly speaking, Australasia consists of the island continent of Australia, New Guinea, the Solomon Islands and possibly New Caledonia and New Zealand, though these latter are separate geological entities. The remaining islands strung across the vast spaces of the Pacific are isolated outcrops of volcanic rock or coral reefs with no geological or geographical connection unifying them.

These far flung islands and islets are, however, united by their human inhabitants. Several centuries ago, the ancestors of Polynesian and Melanesian islanders sailed across the vast, open stretches of the Pacific Ocean from Southeast Asia to colonise the remote islands of the tropical and sub-tropical regions. With them they brought taro, yams and other tropical crops with which to support themselves. Common ties of culture and religion bound these peoples together. Long voyages in open canoes were often undertaken between the various islands, preserving ties of technology and belief.

When European seamen arrived, from the 16th century onwards, they found the islands densely inhabited by peoples so similar that the entire region of Oceania came to be viewed as a cultural entity. European settlers and missionaries radically altered the society and cultures of the islands, though many features of Polynesian society remain even today.

The modern nations of Australasia are clearly divided into cultural and physical regions. The divides between the regions has as much to do with the economies and lifestyles of the peoples as with the physical location of the islands.

Dominating all is the great landmass of Australia. The Australian nation has a mixed culture based on the various immigrant groups, chiefly from Europe. To a much lesser extent Australian culture rests on the indigenous Aboriginal peoples who are now largely restricted to the Outback. The bulk of Australia is covered by arid deserts, where settlements are few and far between. The only populous centres are mining towns thriving on the exploitation of the rich mineral content of the nation's rocks.

Kinder climatic regions around the coasts are more densely populated, with farming communities producing crops according to the prevailing climate. All the major cities are on the coast, centred on the sites of historic ports. Here the population is engaged in industrial and service occupations more akin to developed western economies than to the prevailing culture of Australasia.

Sharing much of the flavour of Australia is New Zealand, with its largely European population and small indigenous element. The economy and lifestyle here is more rural than in Australia, while the temperate climate dictates the crops and livestock which can be produced.

Away from these economic giants of the region, the nations are far smaller and less developed, though the original cultures are more apparent. Nations may be as small as a single island with a population of just 7,000. The largest consist of archipelagoes spread across thousands of square kilometres of ocean, but even these never top one million in population. The cultures of the smaller nations are closely allied to the indigenous peoples. Christianity has generally replaced the violent ceremonies and beliefs of the former religions, and settlers from Europe and elsewhere often form sizeable minorities among the population.

The disparate nations of Australasia form a complex pattern of human adaptation to harsh environments. From the Australian deserts to the open ocean, Australasia is a place of extremes and superlatives. The differing cultures of European settlers and native populations are sometimes blended together and elsewhere stand in stark contrast to each other. But everywhere there is the great Pacific Ocean, dividing the nations and yet uniting them.

▲ Mount Tasman, New Zealand.

▶ A native girl on the beach, Kiribati.

◀ The world-famous Opera House, Sydney, Australia.

AUSTRALIA

Population: 17.6 million
Area: 7,682,000 square kilometres
Capital: Canberra
Language: English
Currency: Australian Dollar

The vast nation continent of Australia was the last major land-mass to be discovered by Europeans, remaining largely unknown until the 18th century. Immigration initially from the Great Britain but later from the rest of Europe, and most recently from Asia, produced the dominant social profile of modern Australia. The extensive grazing lands support large numbers of sheep and cattle, while the smaller areas of arable land produce wheat, rice and market crops. The large desert regions are rich in mineral deposits. Industry is well developed, with a wide range of consumer goods and engineering equipment being produced. The nation is a federation of six states, with the central government being responsible for the Northern Territory. It came into being on the first day of the 20th century, when former British colonies joined to form the Commonwealth of Australia.

FIJI

Population: 748,000
Area: 18,000 square kilometres
Capital: Suva
Language: English, Fijian and Hindustani
Currency: Fijian Dollar

Britain annexed the 330 islands of Fiji in 1874 and stamped out the endemic tribal warfare. Independence was granted in 1970 and a troubled history has resulted. The population is almost equally divided between native Fijians of Melanesian and Polynesian ancestry and immigrants from India, who arrived during British rule. In 1987 an Indian coalition won power in Parliament. Within months a coup organised by the native Fijians placed the army in power. A new constitution has been imposed, which places political power in the hands of the native Fijians. The economy is based on agriculture, with sugar cane, coconuts and ginger being the primary crops. Industry is concentrated on processing the crops, while mineral wealth is restricted to two small gold mines.

KIRIBATI

Population: 75,000
Area: 717 square kilometres
Capital: Tarawa
Language: English, Gilbertese
Currency: Australian Dollar

Although Kiribati is independent it has no currency of its own, and its citizens use the Australian dollar.

The islands are generally small but are spread over an immense area of the Pacific Ocean, being grouped into three coral archipelagos and one volcanic island. The islands voluntarily became British protect-orates in 1892 and regained independence in 1979. The democrat-ically-elected government consists of one chamber and a President. The agricultural economy relies almost exclusively on coconuts and copra, which make up over ninety percent of exports by value. The coconut tree grows well in the thin soil and tropical climate of Kiribati. Pigs, chickens and breadfruit are produced for local consumption, as is a local vegetable named *babai*.

MARSHALL ISLANDS

Population: 50,000
Area: 181 square kilometres
Capital: Dalap-Uliga-Darrit
Language: English and Marshallese
Currency: U.S. Dollar

The republic of the Marshall Islands, independent and a member of the United Nations since 1991, is an archipelago of 31 coral atolls in the western Pacific. The republic is made up of two strings of islands, the eastern and western. The form of a government is a republic, headed by a President. Tourism and agriculture sustain the economy.

MICRONESIA

Population: 110,000
Area: 701 square kilometres
Capital: Palikir
Language: English.
Currency: U.S. Dollar

The Federated States of Micronesia, until independence in 1991 better known as the Caroline Islands, had been under U.S. rule since World War II. During their history the islands had been controlled by Spain, Germany and Japan. Made up of more than 500 islands in the western Pacific, the primarily agricultural nation is a member of the United Nations.

NAURU

Population: 8,100
Area: 21 square kilometres
Capital: Yaren
Language: Nauruan and English
Currency: Australian Dollar

With a population among the lowest in the world, Nauru does not support its own currency, using instead the Australian dollar. The population is a mix of Polynesians and Melanesians who arrived generations ago and have merged to produce a single racial group. The island fell under German control in 1888, passed to Australia in 1914, and became independent in 1968. The constitution allows an assembly

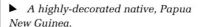
▲ *An isolated beach, Nauru.*

▶ *A highly-decorated native, Papua New Guinea.*

▲ *Lefaga Beach, Upolu, Western Samoa.*

◀ *Yasur volcano, Vanuatu.*

▼ *Mananuca Islands, Fiji.*

elected every three years under a President. Nauru retains a special link with the Commonwealth. The traditional crop of coconuts is widely grown and exported, while vegetables and livestock are kept for local consumption. Tourism is a growing business. The island nation's wealth, however, depends on phosphates mined on the island. This gives Nauru the highest per capita income in the Pacific islands and the wealth is being invested against the time when phospate deposits run out.

 NEW ZEALAND

Population: 3.5 million
Area: 268,000 square kilometres
Capital: Wellington
Language: English and Maori
Currency: New Zealand Dollar

Descendants of European immigrants form the bulk of New Zealand's population, though the native Maori form the largest minority. The exports of New Zealand have traditionally been agricultural and the pattern continues, with chilled meat, live animals, dairy products and wool far outstripping manufactured goods in value. However, industry is of growing importance internally, with iron and steel works and aluminium smelting being the largest heavy industrial works. The attractive scenery and relaxed lifestyle of the islands make New Zealand an increasingly popular tourist attraction, with nearly a million tourists visiting each year. The government is based on universal suffrage, though some seats in the Assembly are reserved for Maoris and have an exclusively Maori electorate.

 PAPUA NEW GUINEA

Population: 3.8 million
Area: 463,000 square kilometres
Capital: Port Moresby
Language: English, Motu and tribal languages
Currency: Kina

The rugged highlands of New Guinea are divided into isolated valleys covered by dense forests in which travel is difficult and communications are poor. The numerous tribes speak as many as 700 different languages, though the Motu form of pidgin English is a common *lingua franca*. Many of these tribes were untouched by the outside world, having no knowledge of whites until the 1940s, and they still lead traditional lifestyles. Agriculture for export is concentrated around the coasts and produces coffee, copra and cocoa. Gold is mined on a commercial scale and there are large copper reserves on the island of Bougainville, though an active

secessionist movement has disrupted mining. The constitution provides for a single chamber legislature.

 SOLOMON ISLANDS

Population: 339,000
Area: 28,000 square kilometres
Capital: Honiara
Language: English and tribal languages
Currency: Solomon Island Dollar

The Melanesian tribes of the Solomons retained their freedom until Britain declared a protectorate in 1893. The Japanese invaded during World War II, and Britain granted full independence in 1978. The country is governed by a Parliament elected by universal suffrage. The Head of State – the British monarch – is represented by a Governer-General. The islands are pre-dominantly agricultural, with property ownership held collectively by tribes and clans. Cocoa and coconuts are grown for export while yams, taro and sweet potatoes are consumed locally. The large fishing fleet exploits the tuna shoals of the region and the catch is canned before export. Industry is limited to processing crops for export.

 TONGA

Population: 103,000
Area: 700 square kilometres
Capital: Nuku'alofa
Language: Tongan and English
Currency: Pa'anga

The kingdom of Tonga dates back to the early 19th century, when the warlike King Tupou of the Ha'apai conquered all the island tribes. Tupou overthrew the rule of petty chiefs and established a rudimentary democracy before Britain declared a protectorate in 1899. Internal government continued under the royal family and full independence came in 1970. The present constitution is based on that of King Tupou. The Assembly consists of nine chiefs elected by the chiefs, nine representatives elected by the people and eleven privy councillors appointed by the king. The main exports are coconuts, fish and vanilla, while tourism brings in much foreign capital. Industry is virtually non-existent.

 TUVALU

Population: 9,500
Area: 24 square kilometres
Capital: Fongafale
Language: Tuvaluan and English
Currency: Australian Dollar

As with other tiny Pacific states, Tuvalu uses the Australian dollar. However, it mints its own coins with unique and attractive designs. A British protectorate from 1892 to 1978, Tuvalu has a Parliament

elected by universal suffrage and consisting of just twelve members, four of whom are ministers. There are no political parties and candidates stand as individuals. The nine islands that make up the group are coral atolls with thin soils capable of supporting little other than coconut trees. Coconuts and copra are the main exports, with vegetables being grown for local consumption. The flag is highly symbolic, with the blue field representing the Pacific Ocean, the nine stars the nine islands, and the Union Jack standing for membership of the Commonwealth.

 VANUATU

Population: 154,000
Area: 12,000 square kilometres
Capital: Vila
Language: Bislama and English
Currency: Vatu

On independence in 1980 the islands changed their name from New Hebrides to Vanuatu. The former name was given by Captain Cook because the rugged mountainous interiors reminded him of the Scottish islands, though the tropical climate is very different from that of the Scottish Hebrides. Power resides in an elected Parliament together with the tribal chiefs who sit in a separate Council. The Council advises primarily on matters of custom and tradition. Coconut, cocoa and coffee, which flourish in the hot, moist climate, are the basis of the economy. A livestock industry based on cattle is becoming established. Tropical crops such as yams and taro are grown for local markets. Industry is limited to processing export crops and freezing the local catch.

 WESTERN SAMOA

Population: 160,000
Area: 700 square kilometres
Capital: Apia
Language: Tongan and English
Currency: Pa'anga

Formerly a German colony governed from 1920 by New Zealand, Western Samoa became independent in 1962. His Highness Malietoa Tanumafili became head of state for life, but after his death future heads of state are due to be elected. Though now independent, Western Samoa maintains direct diplomatic links only within the Pacific. Elsewhere New Zealand acts on its behalf. The economy of the island is basically agricultural, with coconuts, bananas and cocoa being the most important crops. Despite the tropical climate and a marked dry season, tourism is only poorly developed. Industry is limited to the processing of agricultural products.

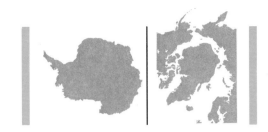

POLAR REGIONS

*T*he polar regions have an image of being blizzard-swept wastes inhabited only by penguins and polar bears. In fact the polar regions are far more than that. It is true that both the North and South Poles are ice-bound throughout the year, but the wildlife of the regions is incredibly varied. In the north polar bears, seals and whales make up the mammal population and the oceans are teeming with fish. The south, which has the advantage of a solid rock continent, is home to a variety of fauna, including penguins.

Both poles have been divided between various nations which maintain scientific bases and conduct research. As the Arctic is open ocean beneath the ice, it is technically not subject to any state. However, those nations that have Arctic coasts maintain various bases, often military, in the area and patrol it regularly.

The political situation of Antarctica is more fraught. Officially, the vast continent is divided between Australia, New Zealand, France, Norway and Britain. Other nations, however, including Chile and Argentina, claim sections of the continent. All these nations, and others, maintain scientific research stations on Antarctica. The population of these outposts varies greatly with the season and from year to year, but there are rarely more than a thousand people on the continent. English is now the recognised scientific language, but each nationality speaks its own language on the continent.

In 1959 the Antarctic Treaty was signed by nations involved on the continent, with an environmental protocol added in 1991. The treaty bans military activity and tightly regulates commercial and scientific activity in Antarctica. It is unlikely that either polar region will ever maintain a sizeable human population but both remain rich in wildlife and environmental interest. It is to be hoped that international co-operation will ensure the continued existence of these great wilderness areas.

▲ *An Eskimo in a hunting kayak, northwest Greenland.*

▶ *As temperatures drop, the sea near Signy Island starts to freeze.*

▼ *Macaroni penguins on Bird Island, South Georgia.*

▲ *Heavy-bodied walruses resting on the beaches at Round Island, Alaska.*

▼ *Probing newly-formed ice in Antarctica.*

ARCTIC OCEAN

Queen
Elizabeth
Islands

Ellesmere
Island

Lincoln Sea

Kane Basin

GREENLAND
(Denmark)

Jan Mayen
(Norway)

Banks
Island

Viscount Melville Sound

Baffin Bay

Beaufort Sea

Ostrov Vrangelya

Pt. Barrow

Chucki Sea

Amundsen Gulf

Victoria Island

Oikiqtaluk

Dudley Str.

Norwegia Sea

ICELAND

Reykjavik

Brooks Range

ALASKA
(U.S.A.)

Mackenzie Mts.

Great Bear Lake

Back

Foxe Basin

Denmark Strait

Foroyar
(Denmark)

McKINLEY
6194 ▲

Alaska Range

Yukon

L. Athabasca

Great Slave Lake

Hudson Str.

Labrador Sea

Kap Farvel

Shetland Is.
(U.K.)

Bering Str.

Gulf of Alaska

Kodiak I.

Rocky Mountains

Reindeer Lake

CANADA

Labrador

UNITED
KINGDOM

Aleutian   Islands

Aleutian Trench

Vancouver I.

L. Winnipeg

Newfoundland

DUBLIN
IRELAND

LONDON
PARIS

Bering Sea

NORTH
PACIFIC
OCEAN

Great
Plains

UNITED STATES
OF
AMERICA

Ottawa

Appalachian Mts.

NEW YORK
PHILADELPHIA
Washington

NORTH
ATLANTIC
OCEAN

PORTUGAL

Madrid
SPAIN

FRA

SAN FRANCISCO

CHICAGO

Lisboa

Acores
(Port.)

Gt. Salt Lake

LOS ANGELES

Missouri

Mississippi

Bermuda
(U.K.)

Madeira
(Port.)

Rabat

MOROCCO

Atlas Mountains

Isla de
Guadalupe
(Mex.)

Tropic of Cancer

BAHAMAS
Nassau

Ilas Canarias
(Sp.)

WESTERN
SAHARA

Al Aaiún

ALGE

Hawaiian   Islands

Gulf of Mexico

La Habana
CUBA

West Indies

MAURITANIA
Nouakchott

MALI

HAWAII
(U.S.A.)

Islas de Revillagigedo
(Mex.)

MEXICO
CIUDAD DE
MÉXICO

Port au Prince
HAITI

DOMINICAN REP.
Puerto Rico (U.S.A.)
Santo Domingo

CAPE
VERDE
IS.
Praia

Dakar
THE
GAMBIA
GUINEA
BISSAU

SEN
Banjul
Bissau

Bamako
Ouagadougou

BUR
FASO

Belmopan
BELIZE
Kingston
HONDURAS Tegucigalpa
JAMAICA

Leeward Is.

Conakry
SIERRA LEONE
Monrovia

Freetown
Yamoussoukro

GH

GUATEMALA
Guatemala
San Salvador

SALVADOR
NICARAGUA
Managua
San José
COSTA RICA

Caribbean Sea

BARBADOS

TRINIDAD
AND TOBAGO

Windward Is.

Caracas

LIBERIA

IVORY
COAST

Accra

SÃO TO
AND PRIN

P o l y n e s i a

Christmas I.

Line Islands

PANAMA

VENEZUELA

Georgetown
Paramaribo
Cayenne
FRENCH GUIANA

GUY
SUR

Equator

Phoenix Is.

KIRIBATI

Bogotá
COLOMBIA

Orinoco

Quito
ECUADOR

Islas Galápagos
(Ecuador)

Isla Fernando
de Noronha
(Brazil)

Ascension
(U.K.)

W.
SOMOA
Apia
TONGA
Nuku'alofa

Samoa
(U.S.A.)

Cook Islands
(N.Z.)

Iles Marquises
(Fr.)

French Polynesia
(Fr.)

Tahiti

Iles Tuamotu

Iles de la
Société

SOUTH
PACIFIC
OCEAN

PERU

LIMA

La Paz
BOLIVIA

Cordillera

Titicaca

BRAZIL
Planalto do
Mato Grosso

Brasília

SÃO PAULO

St. Helena
(U.K.)

Ilha da Trindade
(Brazil)

SOUTH

Tropic of Capricorn

Iles Gambier

Pitcairn I.
(U.K.) Ducie I.
(U.K.)

Isla de Pascua
(Easter I.)
(Chile)

PARAGUAY

Asunción

RÍO DE JANEIRO

ATLANTIC

OCEAN

Islas Juan
Fernández
(Chile)

ACONCAGUA
6960 ▲

Santiago

Cordillera de los Andes

URUGUAY
Montevideo

Tristan da Cunha
(U.K.)

Chatham Is.
(N.Z.)

Peru-Chile Trench

BUENOS AIRES
ARGENTINA

Gough I.
(U.K.)

Patagonia

Falkland Is.
(U.K.)

South Georgia
(U.K.)

SOUTH
ATLANTIC
OCEAN

Cabo de Hornos

Scotia Sea

South
Sandwich
Is. (U.K)

1:85,000,000 (Scale at the Equator)

G   **H**   **J**   **K**   **L**   **M**   East of Greenwich   West of Greenwich

A R C T I C   O C E A N

Severnaya Zemlya

Novosibirskiye Ostrova

Zemlya Frantsa-Iosifa
(Russia)

Karskoye
More

Lyakhovskiye
Ostrova

Vostochno
Sibirskoye
More

Gory Taymyr
Byrranga

More
Laptevykh

Novaya
Zemlya

Ostrov Vrangelya

Kolmskaya
Nizmennost

Nordkapp

Barentsevo
More

Poluostrov
Yamal

Plato
Putorana

Gydanskiy
Poluostrov

Lappland

SWEDEN

FINLAND

Helsingfors

Zapadno

Sibirskaya

Ravnina

Sredne

Sibirskoye

Ploskogor'ye

Verkhoyanskiy Khrebet

Khrebet Cherskogo

Khrebet Kolymskiy

Bering
Sea

Stockholm
Tallinn
ESTONIA
Riga
ST. PETERSBURG

Ural'skiy Khrebet

Uralskiy

København
LITHUANIA
Vilnius
Minsk
Berlin
POLAND
Warszawa
BELARUS

MOSKVA

RUSSIA

Okhotskoye
More

Aleutian Islands

Sakhalin

Praha CZECH
REP.
Kyyiv
(Kiev)
UKRAINE
MOLDOVA

Kirgiz
Step'
KAZAKHSTAN

Ulaanbaatar

Wien
Budapest
HUNG.
ROM
Chisinau
(Kishinev)
Bucuresti

Prikaspiyskaya
Nizmennost'

Ozero Balkhash

MONGOLIA

Gobi

Kuril'skiye Ostrova

Kuril Trench

Beograd
YUGO BULG.
Roma
Sofiya
Tirane
ALB.

GEORGIA
T'bilisi
ARMENIA
Yerevan
AZERBAIJAN
Baku

Caspian
Sea

Tashkent
Alma-Ata
Bishkek
KYRGYZSTAN
UZBEKISTAN

Tian Shan

BEIJING
TIANJIN

N. KOREA
Pyongyang
S. KOREA
SOUL

Sea of
Japan

JAPAN
TOKYO

N O R T H

Valletta
MALTA
GREECE
Athinai

TURKEY
Ankara

Kyzylkum
Peski
Karakumy

Tarim
Pendi

Taklimakan
Shamo

CHINA

SHANGHAI

P A C I F I C

CYPRUS
SYRIA
Levkosia
LEB.
Bayrut
Dimashq
ISRAEL
Yerushalayim
IRAQ
Baghdad
IRAN
TEHRAN

TURKMENISTAN
Ashgabat
TAJIKISTAN
Dushanbe

Hindu
Kush

AFGHANISTAN
Kabul
Islamabad

Kunlun Shan

Xizang
Gaoyuan

Huang

O C E A N

LIBYA

EGYPT

El Qahira

Amman
JOR.
Al Kuwayt
KUW.
Al Manamah
BAH.
Ar Riyad
QAT.
Ad Dawhah
U.A.E.
Abu Zabi

PAKISTAN

Thar
Desert
New
Delhi
DELHI
Kathmandu
NEPAL
BANG.
Dhaka

EVEREST

Hai

Tai-pei
TAIWAN

Tropic of Cancer

Masqat

KARACHI

INDIA
CALCUTTA

Hanoi
HONG KONG
(U.K.)

SAUDI
ARABIA

OMAN

Arabian
Sea

BOMBAY

Deccan

Bay of
Bengal

MYANMAR
Yangon

LAOS
Viangchan
THAI-
LAND
KRUNG THEP
CAM.

VIETNAM

Nan Hai

MANILA
Luzon

CHAD

SUDAN
El Khartum
N'djamena

ERITREA
San'a
YEMEN

Suqutra
(S.Yem.)

Lakshadweep
(India)

MADRAS

Andaman
Islands
(India)

Phnom Penh

PHILIPPINES

Mindanao

Marianas
Is.

Guam (USA)

M i c r o n e s i

Marshall Is.

CENTRAL
AFRICAN REP
Bangui

ETHIOPIA
Adis Abeba
SOMALIA
DJIB.

Colombo
SRI LANKA

Bandar Seri
Begawan
BRU.

Caroline Islands

Tarawa

Equator

CAMEROON
Yaounde
GABON
CONGO

UGANDA
Kampala
KENYA
Nairobi
RW.
BU.
Kigali
Bujumbura

Muqdisho

Male
MALDIVES

MALAYSIA
Kuala Lumpur

SINGAPORE

Borneo

Maluku

PAPUA
NEW
GUINEA

NAURU

Gilbert
Is.

Phoenix Is.

Congo
Basin
ZAIRE
Kinshasa
Brazzaville

TANZANIA
Dodoma
KILIMANJARO

Victoria
SEYCHELLES

Sumatera

INDONESIA

Jawa
JAKARTA

Sulawesi

Port Moresby
New
Guinea

SOLOMON ISLANDS
Honiara

Santa
Cruz
Is.

TUVALU
Fanafuti

Luanda
ANGOLA

ZAMBIA
Lusaka
MAL.
Lilongwe

COMOROS
Moroni

Timor

Laut Arafura

Coral
Sea

VANUATU
Vila

Iles
Wallice
(Fr.)

W. SAMOA
Apia

NAMIBIA
Windhoek
BOTSWANA
Gaborone
ZIMBABWE
Harare

MADAGASCAR
Antananarivo

MAURITIUS
Port Louis

Laut
Timor

Nouvelle
Caledonie
(Fr.)

FIJI
Suva

TONGA
Nuku'alofa

Kalahari
Pretoria
SWAZILAND
Maputo
Mbabne

I N D I A N   O C E A N

Reunion
(Fr.)

East Indies

Gt. Barrier Reef

Gt. Dividing Range

Tropic of Capricorn

SOUTH
AFRICA
Maseru LESOTHO

AUSTRALIA

L. Eyre

of Good Hope

Gt. Victoria Desert

Darling

Tasman Sea

C. Leeuwin

Canberra

NEW ZEALAND
Wellington

Chatham Is.
(N.Z.)

Iles Crozet
(Fr.)

Prince Edward Is.
(S.A.)

Ile Kerguelen
(Fr.)

Heard I.
(Aus.)

Tasmania

Auckland Is.
(N.Z.)

Macquarie Is.
(Aus.)

1
2
3
4
5
6

G   **H**   **J**   **K**   **L**   **M**

EUROPE

ICELAND
Horn (Nord Cap)
Akureyri
Reykjavík
ÖRÆFAJÖKULL 2119▲

NORWEGIAN SEA

Tromsø
Lofoten Vesterålen
Narvik
KEBNEKAISE 2111
Bodø
Kiruna
Gällivare
Mo i Rana

Namsos
Trondheim

Føroyar (Dan.)

Ålesund
Åndalsnes
Östersund
Umeå
Sundsvall

Bergen
Lillehammer
Shetland Islands

SWEDEN

NORWAY

Haugesund
Drammen
OSLO
Ludvika
Gävle

Stavanger
Arendal
Örebro
Uppsala

C. Wrath
Orkney Islands
Wick
Kristiansand
Skagerrak
Göteborg
STOCKHOLM

UNITED KINGDOM
Mallaig
Inverness
Jönköping
Vänern
Götaland
Vättern

Malin Hd.
BEN NEVIS Mts. 1344
Aberdeen
NORTH SEA
Ålborg
Jylland
Kalmar
Gotland (Swe.)

REPUBLIC OF IRELAND
Glasgow
Edinburgh
Londonderry
Carlisle
Newcastle upon Tyne
DENMARK
KØBENHAVN

Belfast
Galway
Isle of Man
The Pennines
Esbjerg
Odense
Malmö

Dublin
Holyhead
Liverpool
Leeds
Flensborg
Kiel
Bornholm (Dan.)

Mizen Hd.
Cork
Fishguard
SNOWDON 1085
Manchester
Nottingham
Wilhelmshaven
Rostock
Schwerin
Koszalin
Gdańsk

BIRMINGHAM
Norwich
NETHERLANDS
Groningen
HAMBURG
Szczecin

Cardiff
Bristol
s'Gravenhage
Amsterdam
Bremen
BERLIN
POLA
WARSZA

LONDON
ROTTERDAM
Utrecht
Hannover
Braunschweig
Magdeburg
Poznań
Bydgoszcz

Plymouth
Southampton
Dover
Calais
Antwerpen
Breda
Essen
Dortmund
Leipzig
Cottbus
Łódź

Land's End
Penzance
Brighton
Bruxelles
BELGIUM
Duisburg
Düsseldorf
Köln
GERMANY
Karl-Marx-Stadt
Dresden
Wrocław

English Channel
Cherbourg
Lille
Lens
Charleroi
Bonn
Weisbaden
Frankfurt am Main
PRAHA
Katowi
Kra

Channel Islands (U.K.)
Le Havre
Caen
Rouen
Amiens
LUX Luxembourg
Mannheim
Plzeň
CZECH REP.
Olomouc
Ostrava
Brno

Brest
Rennes
Le Mans
PARIS
Reims
Metz
Nancy
Karlsruhe
Stuttgart
Nürnberg
Bohemia
Ceské Budějovice
SLOVAK R

Nantes
Orléans
Troyes
FRANCE
Tours
Loire
Dijon
Basel
Strasburg
Augsburg
MÜNCHEN
Linz
WIEN
Bratislava

La Rochelle
Poitiers
Bourges
Besançon
Bern
Zürich
Innsbruck
LIECH
Salzburg
AUSTRIA
Graz
BUDAPEST

Bordeaux
Limoges
Clermont-Ferrand
Genève
SWITZERLAND
GROSSGLOCKNER
3798
HUNGA

Brive-la-Gaillarde
St.-Etienne
LYON
Lausanne
MONT BLANC 4049
BERNINA 4049
Bolzano
Ljubljana
SLOV
ZAGREB

Massif Central
Grenoble
Novara
Brescia
Verona
Trieste
CROATIA
Novi Sad

Toulouse
Valence
TORINO
MILANO
Venezia
Rijeka
LVOV

Tarbes
Béziers
Nîmes
Nice
Genova
Parma
Ferrara
Bologna
BOSNIA-HERZ.
BEOGRAD

MARSEILLE
Aix-en-Provence
MONACO
Cannes
La Spezia
San Remo
SAN MARINO
Rimini
Sarajevo

Toulon
Livorno
Firenze
Ancona
Dubrovnik
YUGO

Corse
Bastia
ITALY
Perugia
Pescara
MONT.
Igoumenit

Ajaccio
Sassari
Olbia
ROMA
Foggia
Bari
Tirane

PORTUGAL
Santarém
C. de São Vicente
Faro
Cádiz
SPAIN
MADRID
NÁPOLI
Salerno
Taranto
ALBANIA
Brindisi

La Coruña
C. Finisterre
Lugo
Cordillera Cantábrica
León
Gijón
Santander
San Sebastián
Bilbao
Vitoria
Pamplona
Sardegna
Cágliari
TYRRHENIAN SEA
C. Spartivento
Cosenza
IÓNIOI NÍSOI

Vigo
Porto
Vila Real
Burgos
Duero
Zaragoza
Lérida
ANDORRA
Gerona
BARCELONA

Coimbra
Valladolid
Salamanca
Guadalajara
Pyrénées
Perpignan

Cáceres
Tejo
Toledo
Ciudad Real
Albacete
Castellón de la Plana
Menorca
Palma
Islas Baleares (Spain)
Palermo
Messina
Catania

Lisboa
Badajoz
VALENCIA
Ibiza
Mallorca
Trápani
Reggio di Calabria
Sicilia
C. Passero

Córdoba
Jaén
Murcia
Alicante
Cartagena
MALTA
Valletta

Sevilla
Granada
Almería
C. Bon
Bizerte
'Annaba
Tunis

Tanger
Málaga
Gibraltar
EL DJAZAÏR
Bejaia
Constantine
TUNISIA

Tétouan
Melilla
Oran
MEDITERRANEAN SEA

DAR EL BEIDA
Rabat
Oujda
ALGERIA
Saïda
Sfax

Meknès
Fès
Hauts Plateaux

MOROCCO

ATLANTIC OCEAN

Bay of Biscay

English Channel

BALTIC

RUSS
Kaliningrad

50

1:12,500,000

0 100 200 300 400 500 600 700 800 KILOMETRES
0 100 200 300 400 500 STATUTE MILES

© COLOUR LIBRARY BOOKS

51

Transverse Mercator Projection

1:1,175,000

© COLOUR LIBRARY BOOKS

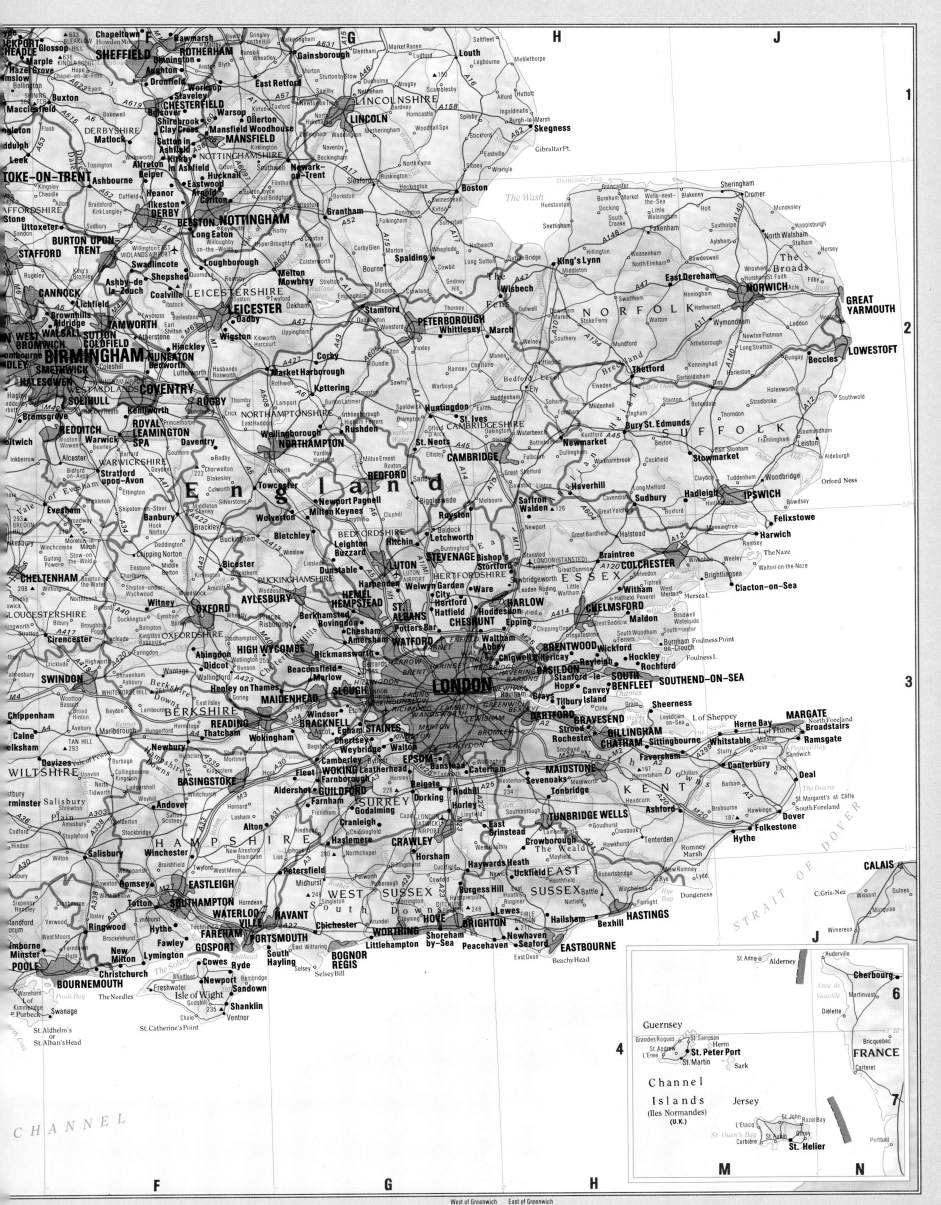

Transverse Mercator Projection

1:1,175,000

© COLOUR LIBRARY BOOKS

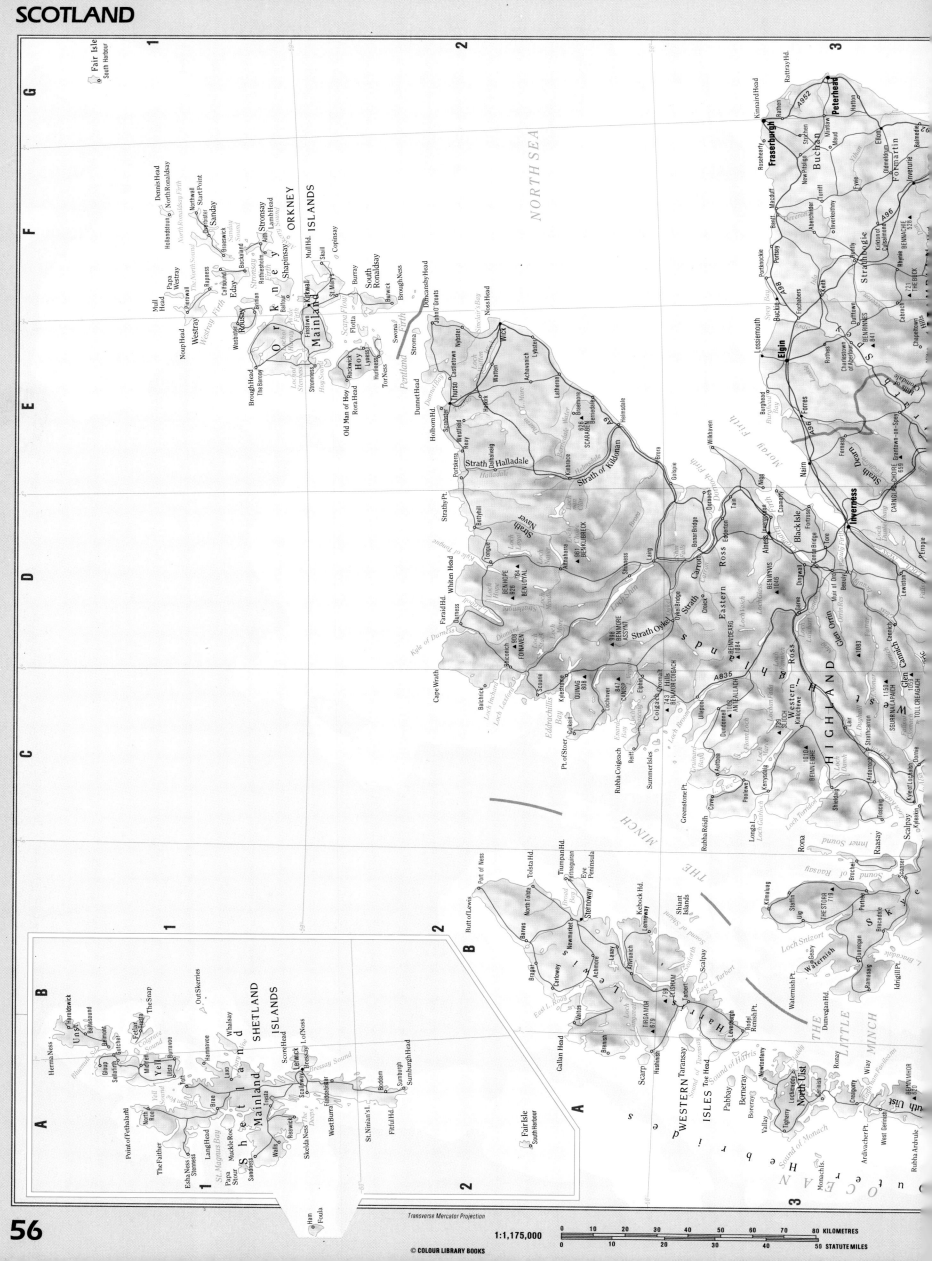

Transverse Mercator Projection

1:1,175,000

© COLOUR LIBRARY BOOKS

| 0 | 10 | 20 | 30 | 40 | 50 | 60 | 70 | 80 KILOMETRES |

| 0 | 10 | 20 | 30 | 40 | 50 STATUTE MILES |

West of Greenwich

Designed and produced by E.S.R.

IRELAND

(map of Ireland and surrounding area)

Provinces / Regions: NORTHERN IRELAND, ULSTER, CONNAUGHT, ANTRIM, DOWN, ARMAGH, TYRONE, LONDONDERRY (DERRY), DONEGAL, FERMANAGH, MONAGHAN, CAVAN, LEITRIM, SLIGO, MAYO, ROSCOMMON, LONGFORD, MEATH, LOUTH

Selected places:
BELFAST, Bangor, Newtownards, Carrickfergus, Larne, Newtownabbey, Dunmurry, Lisburn, Ballymena, Antrim, Portadown, Lurgan, Craigavon, Newry, Dundalk (Dún Dealgan), Drogheda (Droichead Átha), Coleraine, Portstewart, Portrush, LONDONDERRY (DERRY), Strabane, Omagh, Enniskillen, Letterkenny, Sligo, Ballina, Castlebar, Longford

Physical features: ATLANTIC OCEAN, IRISH (Sea), North Channel, Rathlin Sound, Donegal Bay, Clew Bay, Giant's Causeway, Antrim Mountains, Sperrin Mts., Derryveagh Mountains, Blue Stack Mts., Mourne Mountains, Iron Mountains, Nephin Beg Range, Ox Mts. (Slieve Gamph)

Scotland (inset): Kintyre, Jura, Islay, Gigha, Campbeltown, Mull of Kintyre, Mull of Oa

Lambert Conformal Conic Projection

1:1,000,000

| 0 10 20 30 40 50 60 70 80 KILOMETRES |
| 0 10 20 30 40 50 STATUTE MILES |

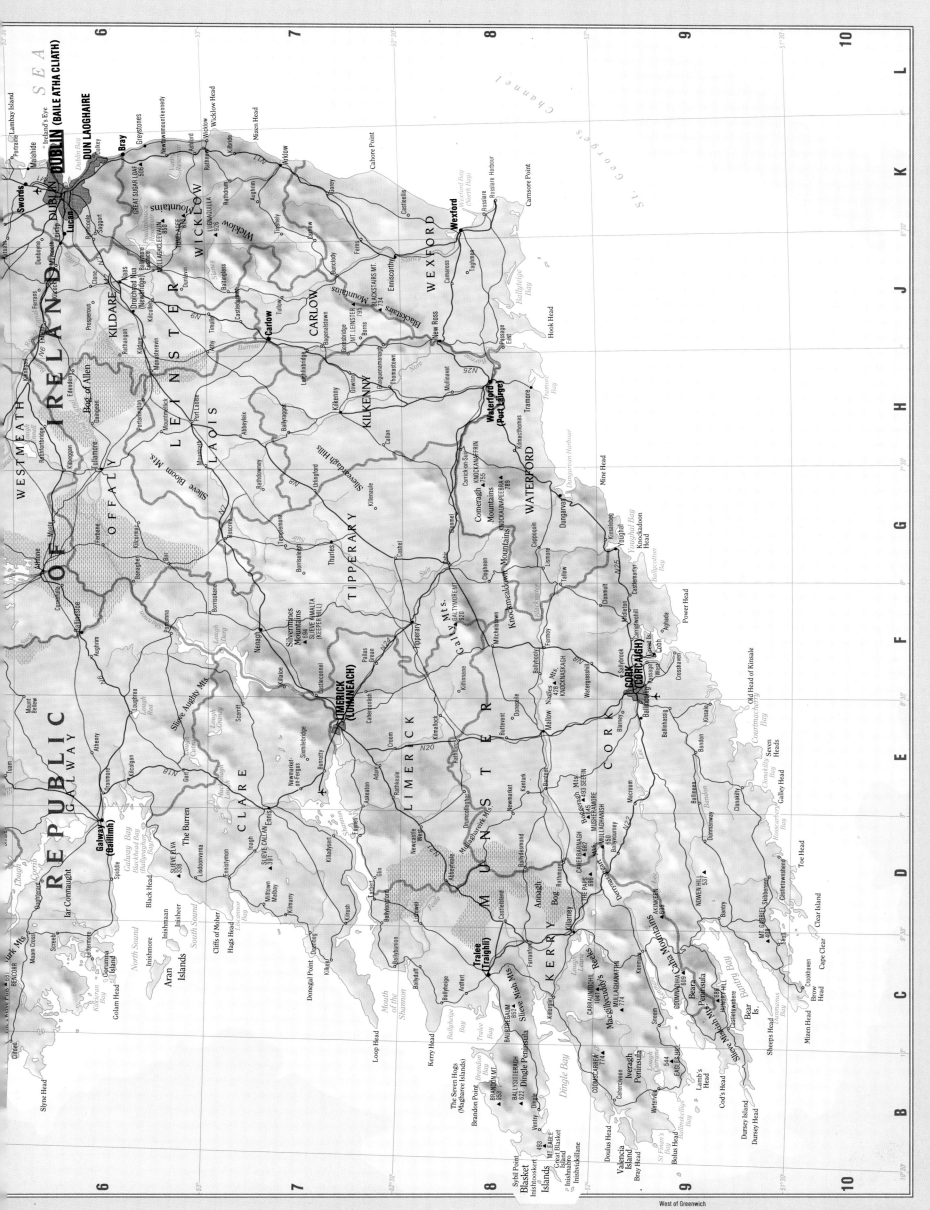

BRITISH ISLES AND CENTRAL EUROPE

1:5,000,000

© COLOUR LIBRARY BOOKS

West of Greenwich

East of Greenwich

Miller Oblated Stereographic Projection

Designed and produced by E.S.R.

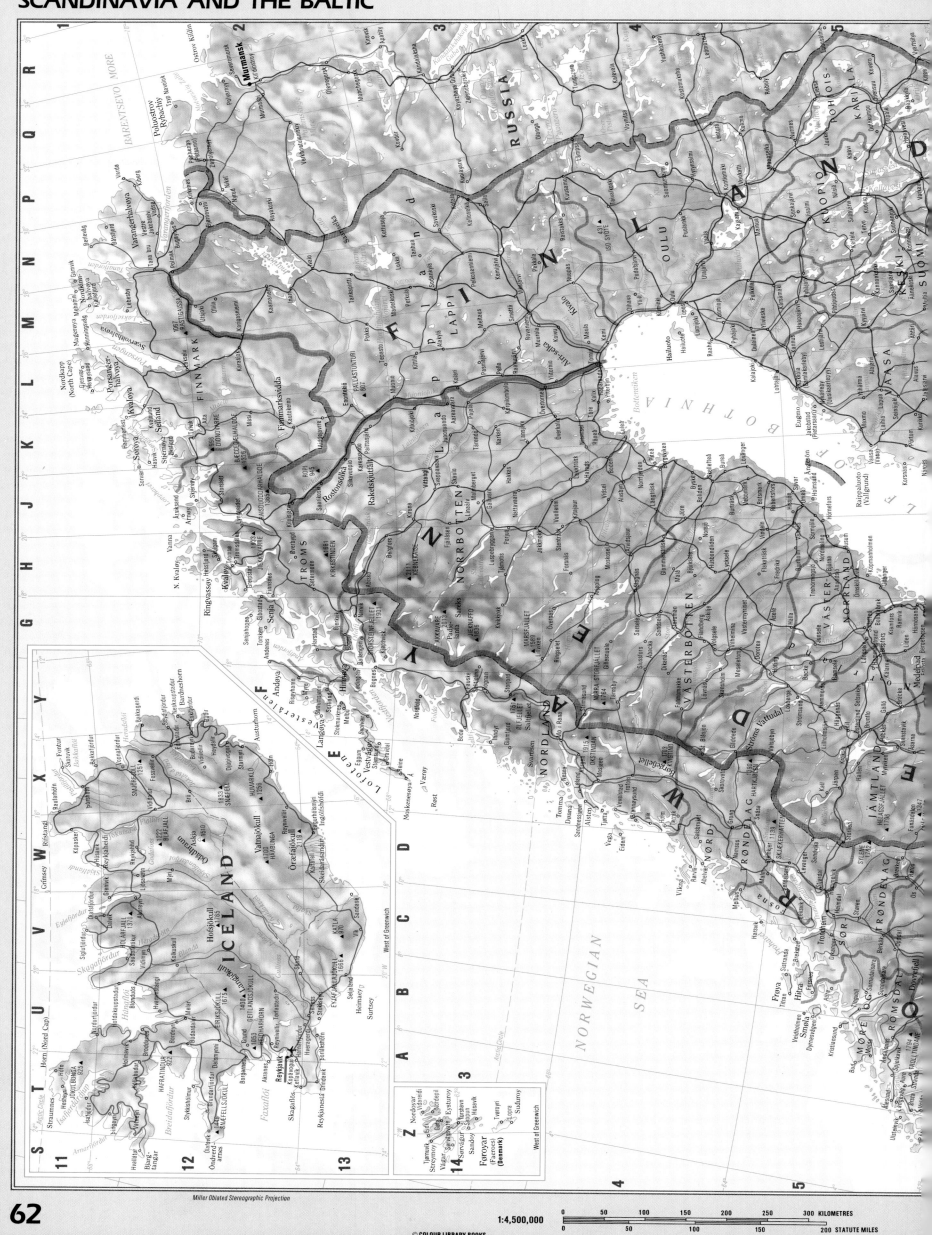

Miller Oblated Stereographic Projection

1:4,500,000

| 0 | 50 | 100 | 150 | 200 | 250 | 300 KILOMETRES |

| 0 | 50 | 100 | 150 | 200 STATUTE MILES |

© COLOUR LIBRARY BOOKS

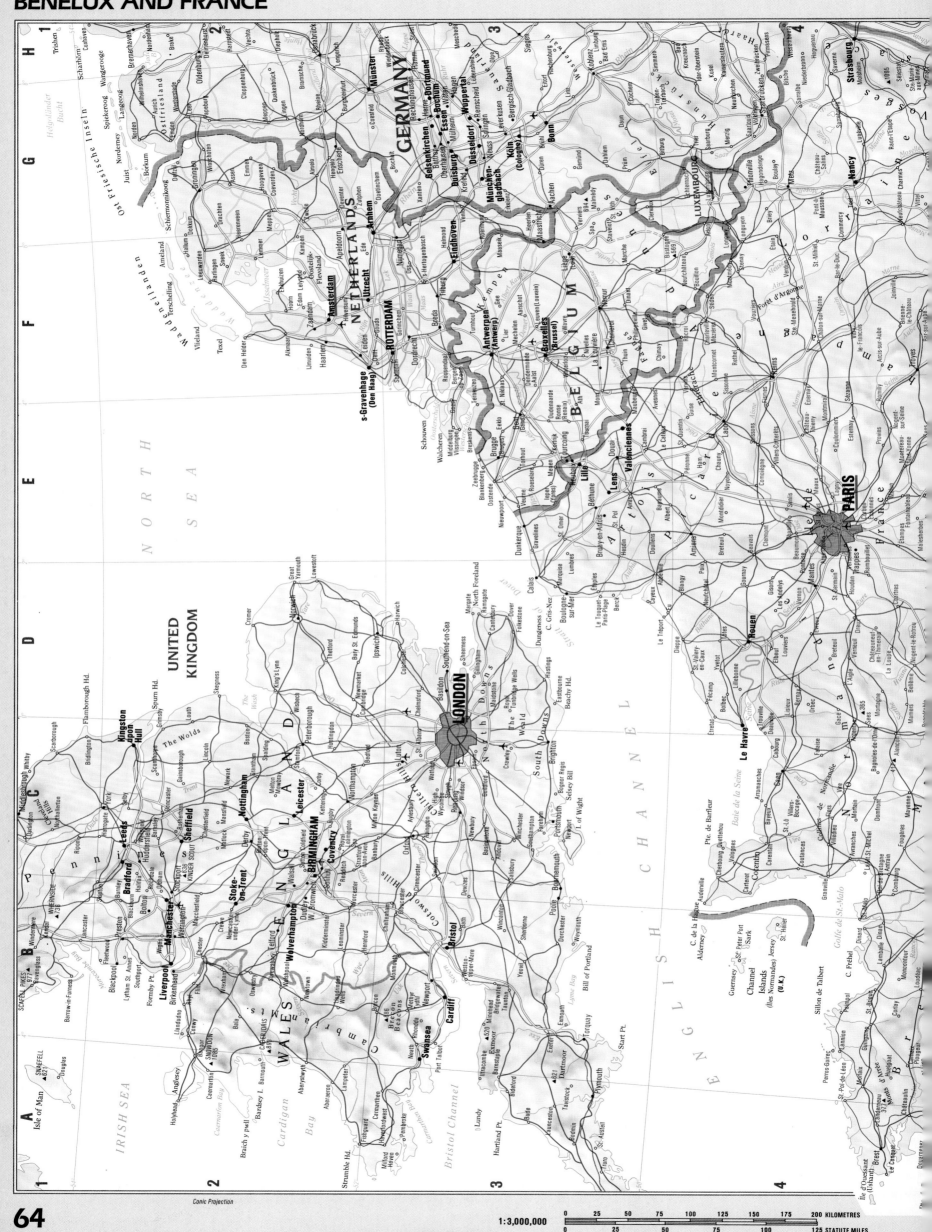

Conic Projection

1:3,000,000

0   25   50   75   100   125   150   175   200 KILOMETRES

0   25   50   75   100   125 STATUTE MILES

© COLOUR LIBRARY BOOKS

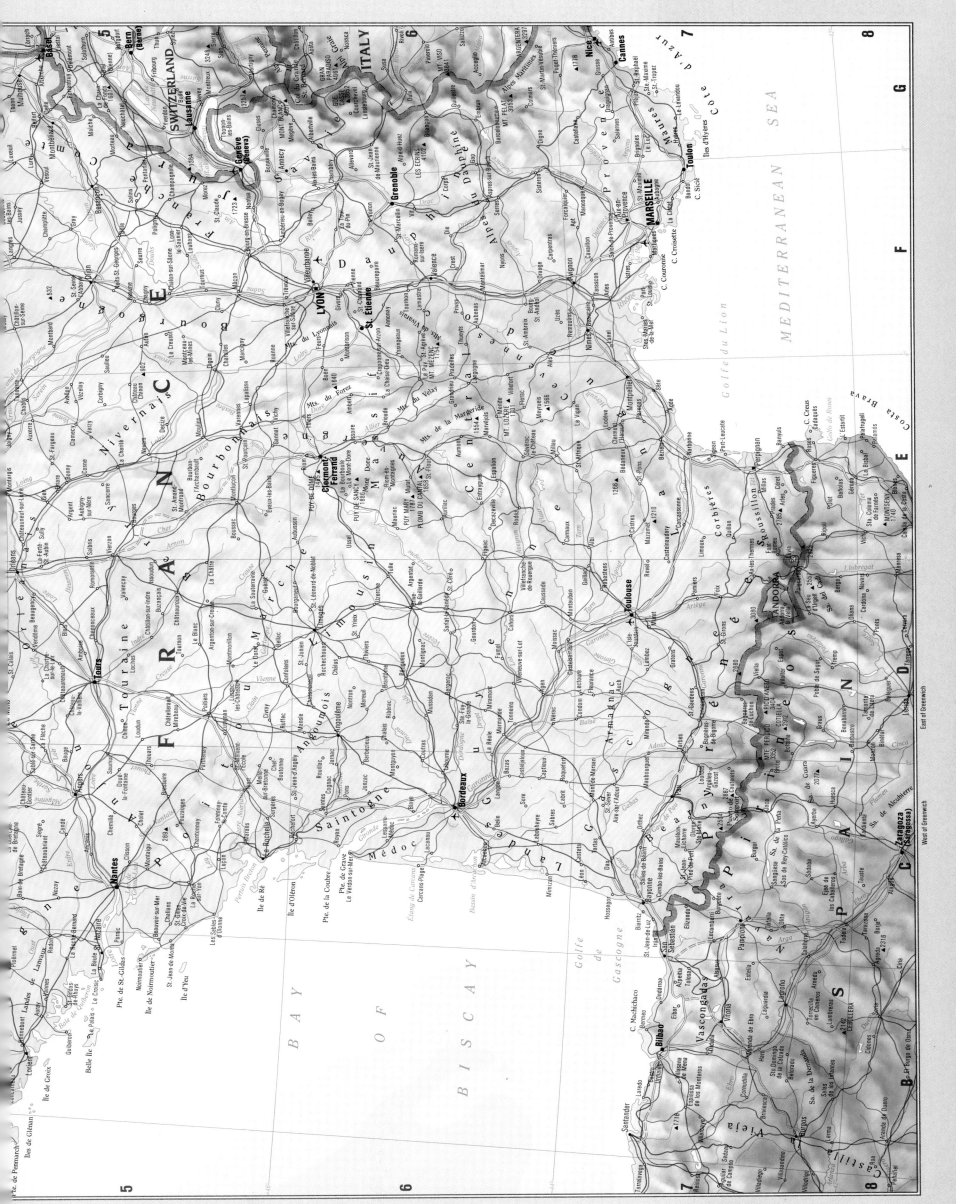

Conic Projection

1:3,000,000

© COLOUR LIBRARY BOOKS

| 0 | 25 | 50 | 75 | 100 | 125 | 150 | 175 | 200 KILOMETRES |

| 0 | 25 | 50 | 75 | 100 | 125 STATUTE MILES |

Golfo de Gascuña

F · G · H · J · K

Labrit · Roquefort · Castelsarrasin · Moissac · Carmaux · Le Vigan · Avignon · Apt · Manosque
Léon · Castets · Mont-de-Marsan · Condom · Lectoure · Montauban · Gaillac · Albi · St-Affrique · Nîmes · Beaucaire · Tarascon · Cavaillon · Salernes · Draguignan
Hossegor · Dax · St-Sever · Aire-sur-l'Adour · Auch · L'Isle-Jourdain · Rabastens · Castres · Lodève · Clermont · Montpellier · Arles · Aix-en-Provence · Brignoles · Le Luc

Armagnac · **Provence**

Biarritz · Bayonne · Mauléon · Tarbes · Toulouse · Muret · Revel · Mazamet · Béziers · Agde · Sète · St-Maximin · St-Raphaël
St-Jean-de-Luz · Orthez · Pau · Lourdes · Foix · St-Girons · Carcassonne · Narbonne · **MARSEILLE** · Toulon

FRANCE · **Languedoc** · **Roussillon**

San Sebastián · Pamplona · Jaca · Andorra · Perpignan · Golfe du Lion

Pirineos · **ANDORRA** · **Catalunya**

Zaragoza (Saragossa) · Lérida · **BARCELONA** · Hospitalet · Costa Brava

Teruel · Valencia · Golfo de Valencia · **Islas Baleares (Balearic Islands) (Spain)**

Mallorca (Majorca) · Palma · Menorca (Minorca) · Ibiza (Iviza) · Formentera · Cabrera

Alicante · Costa Blanca · Murcia · Cartagena

MEDITERRANEAN SEA

EL DJAZAÏR (ALGIERS) · Kabylie · Sétif

ALGERIA · Oran

West of Greenwich · East of Greenwich

Designed and produced by E.S.R.

67

Conic Projection

1:3,000,000

0 25 50 75 100 125 150 175 200 KILOMETRES

0 25 50 75 100 125 STATUTE MILES

© COLOUR LIBRARY BOOKS

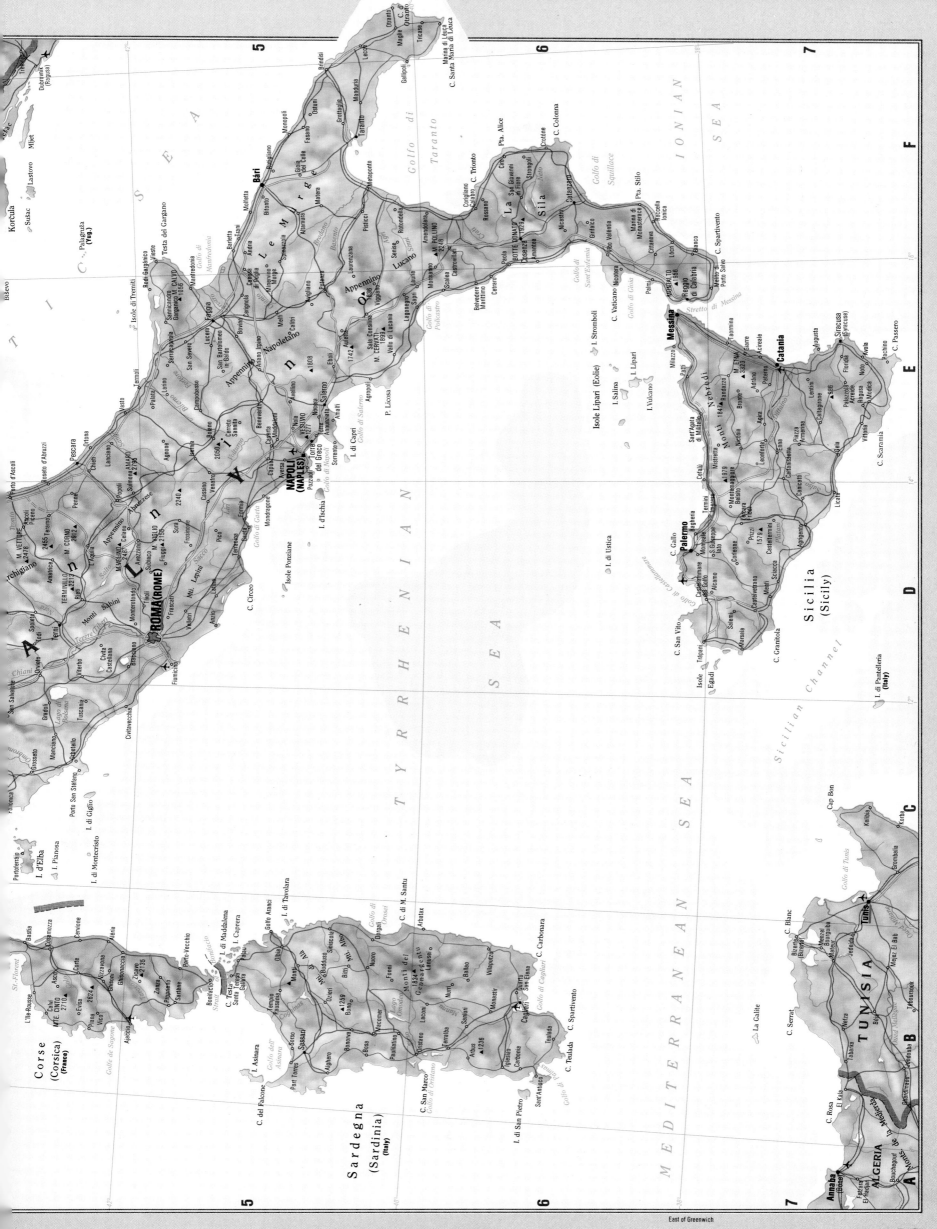

Conic Projection

1:3,000,000

© COLOUR LIBRARY BOOKS

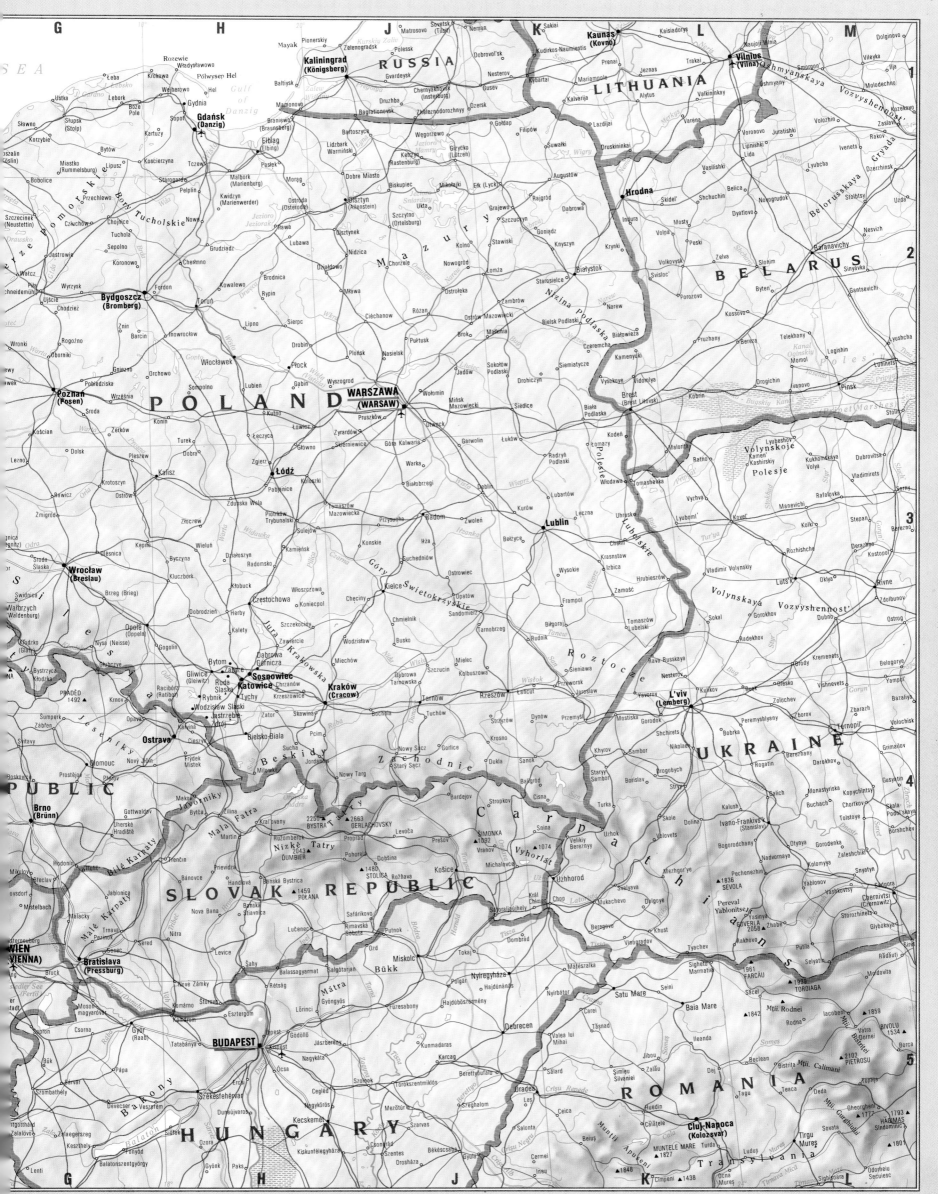

Conic Projection

1:3,000,000

© COLOUR LIBRARY BOOKS

Conic Projection

1:3,000,000

| 0 | 25 | 50 | 75 | 100 | 125 | 150 | 175 | 200 KILOMETRES |

| 0 | 25 | 50 | 75 | 100 | 125 STATUTE MILES |

Lambert Conformal Conic Projection

1:3,500,000

© COLOUR LIBRARY BOOKS

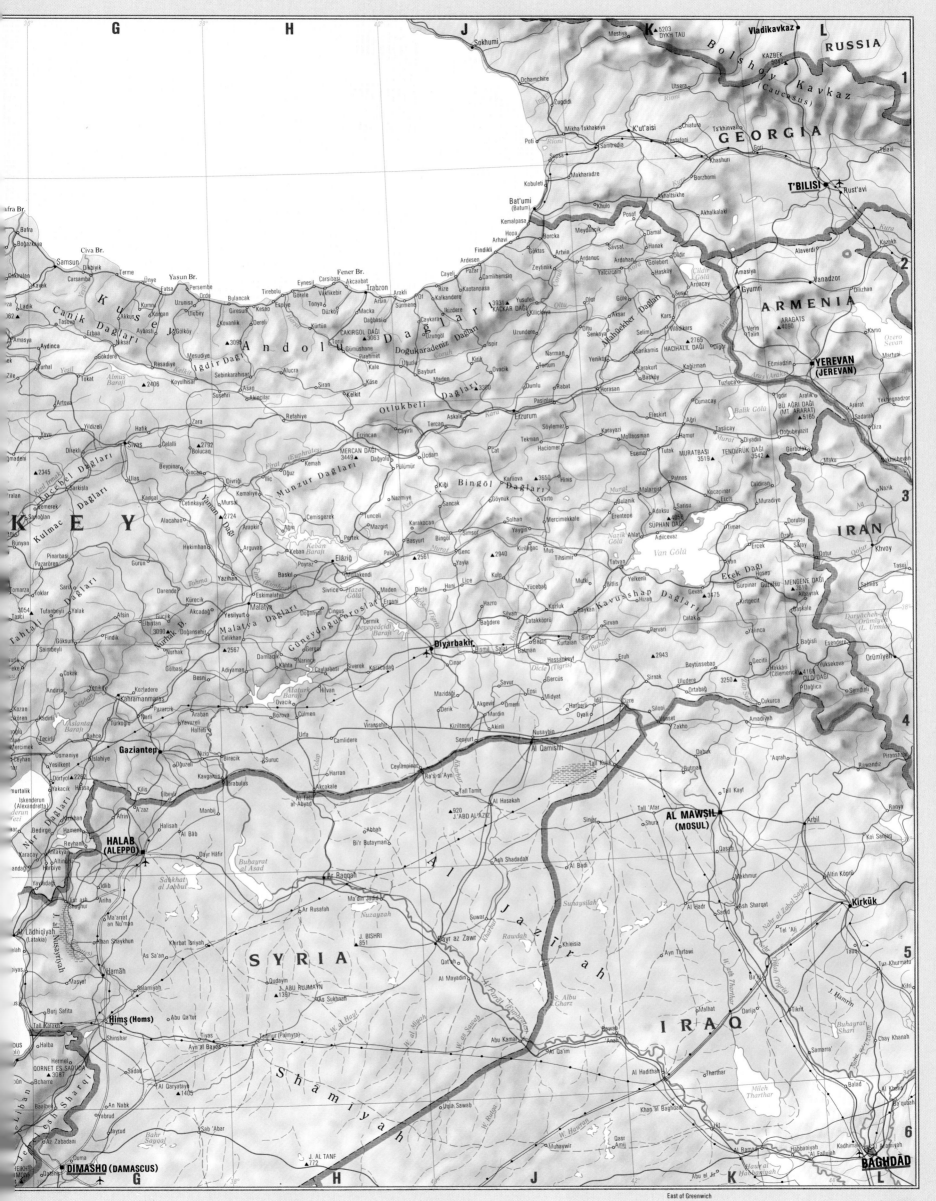

Designed and produced by E.S.R.

East of Greenwich

Miller Oblated Stereographic Projection

1:8,000,000

| 0 | 100 | 200 | 300 | 400 | 500 | 600 KILOMETRES |

| 0 | 50 | 100 | 150 | 200 | 250 | 300 | 350 | 400 STATUTE MILES |

© COLOUR LIBRARY BOOKS

East of Greenwich

Conic Projection

1:17,000,000

| 0 | 100 | 200 | 300 | 400 | 500 | 600 | 700 | 800 KILOMETRES |

| 0 | 100 | 200 | 300 | 400 | 500 STATUTE MILES |

© COLOUR LIBRARY BOOKS

L M N P Q R S T U V 3

Map Labels (geographic)

Ostrov Komsomolets
Severnaya Zemlya
Ostrov Bol'shevik

Novosibirskiye Ostrova
Ostrova De Longa
Ostrova Gennyetty
Ostrov Zhannetty
Ostrov Bennetta
O. Novaya
O. Mal. Lyakhovskiy
O. Bol. Lyakhovskiy

MORE LAPTEVYKH
VOSTOCHNO SIBIRSKOYE MORE

Ostrov Bel'kovskiy
Ostrov Kotel'nyy
Ostrov Stolbovoy

Kolymskaya Nizmennost'

Chukotskiy Poluostrov
Chukotskiy Khrebet
Uelen
Egvekinot

St. Matthew I. (U.S.A.)

BERING SEA

Poluostrov Taymyr

Gory Byrranga
Gor'y Putorana

Khrebet Cherskogo

Verkhoyanskiy Khrebet

Khrebet Kolymskiy

Koryakskiy Khrebet

Komandorskiye Ostrova

Srednee Sibirskoye Ploskogor'ye

Khatanga

Yakutsk

Khrebet Dzhugdzhur

OKHOTSKOYE MORE

Sredinnyy Khrebet
Petropavlovsk-Kamchatskiy

Srednekolymsk

IA

Yeniseysk
Krasnoyarsk
Bratsk
Angarsk
Irkutsk
Ulan-Ude

Stanovoye Nagor'ye
Stanovoy Khrebet
Aldanskoye Nagor'ye

Sakhalin

Kuril'skiye Ostrova

Chita

Yablonovyy Khrebet

Khabarovsk

Vladivostok

Hokkaidō
SAPPORO
Hakodate

Aomori

Ulaanbaatar

MONGOLIA

Da Hinggan Ling
Xiao Hinggan Ling

QIQIHAR
HARBIN
Mudanjiang

Hegang
Jiamusi
Shuangyashan
Jixi

SEA OF JAPAN

Akita
Sendai
Niigata
Fukushima

NEI MONGOL ZIZHIQU

Gobi

Manchuria
CHINA

Baicheng
CHANGCHUN
Siping
Liaoyuan
JILIN
FUSHUN
Tonghua
Benxi
SHENYANG
Liaoyang
ANSHAN

Hamhŭng

N. KOREA
PYONGYANG

SOUTH KOREA

HONSHŪ
TOKYO
YOKOHAMA
Kanazawa
NAGOYA
KYŌTO
OSAKA
KOBE
Wakayama

BAOTOU
Hohhot
Datong

Chifeng
Jinzhou
Yingkou
Dandong

SŎUL
INCH'ŎN
Suwŏn
Taejŏn

TAEGU
PUSAN
Masan

HIROSHIMA
Shimonoseki
KITA-KYŪSHŪ
Shikoku

Zhangjiakou
BEIJING
TANGSHAN
DALIAN

Yantai

Kwangju
FUKUOKA
Nagasaki
Kagoshima
Kyūshū
Miyazaki

Baoding
TIANJIN
Huanghua

BO HAI

Cangzhou
ZIBO
Weifang
QINGDAO

HUANG HAI

SHIJIAZHUANG
JINAN
TAI'AN

TAIYUAN
Handan

L M N P Q

East of Greenwich

81

Designed and produced by E.S.R.

Lambert Azimuthal Equal Area Projection

1:25,000,000

0	200	400	600	800	1000 KILOMETRES
0	100	200	300	400	500	600 STATUTE MILES

© COLOUR LIBRARY BOOKS

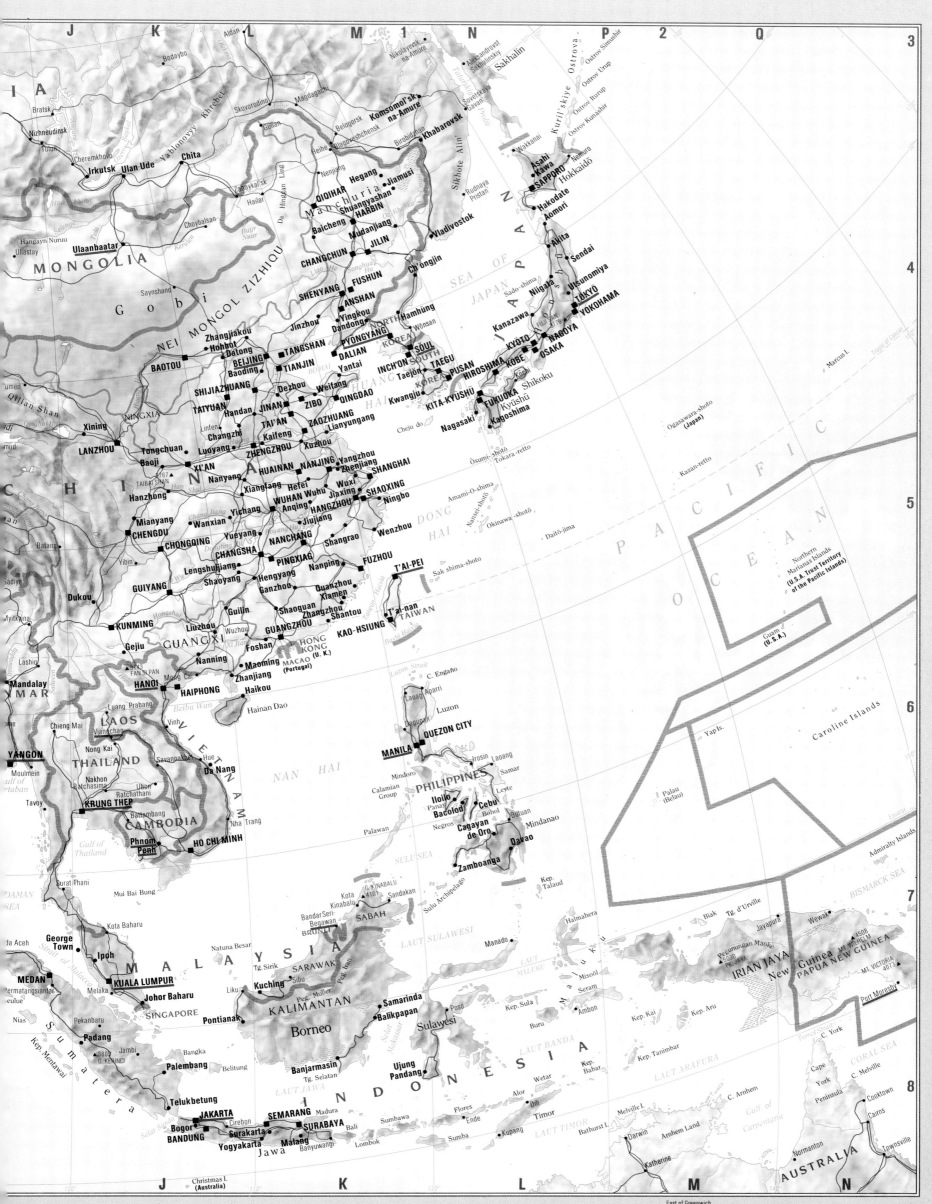

83

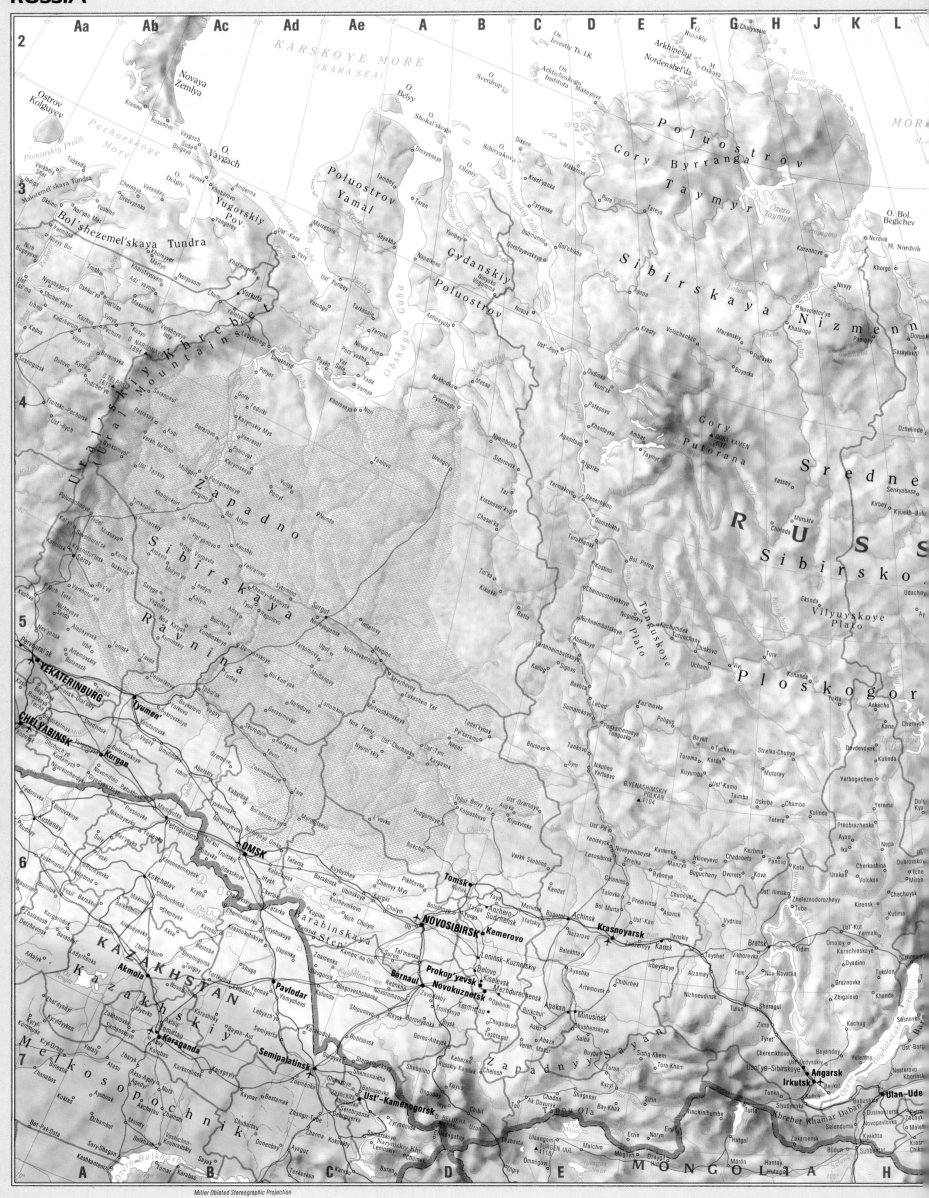

Miller Oblated Stereographic Projection

1:11,500,000

© COLOUR LIBRARY BOOKS

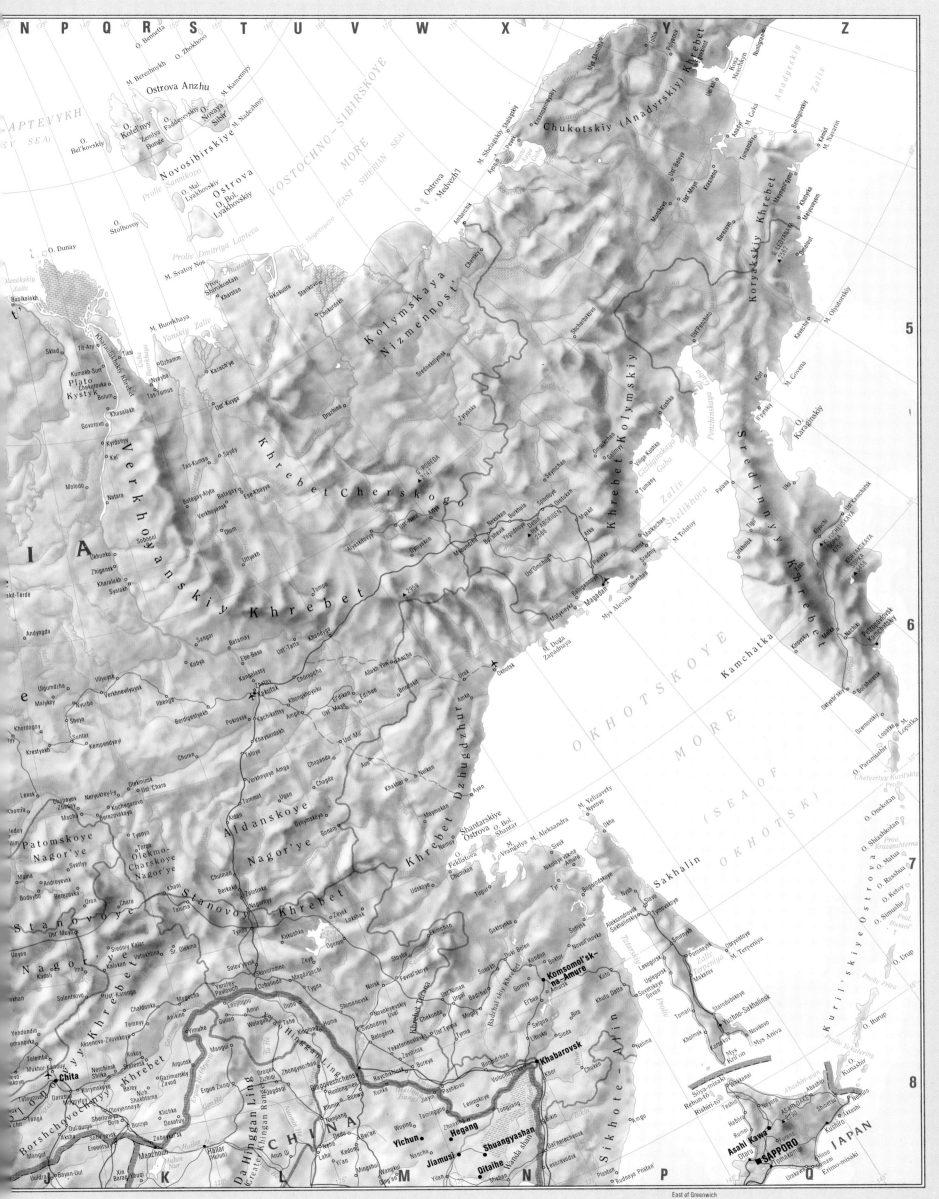

Designed and produced by E.S.R.

East of Greenwich

Miller Oblated Stereographic Projection

1:11,500,000

| 0 | 100 | 200 | 300 | 400 | 500 | 600 | 700 | 800 KILOMETRES |

| 0 | 50 | 100 | 150 | 200 | 250 | 300 | 350 | 400 | 450 | 500 STATUTE MILES |

© COLOUR LIBRARY BOOKS

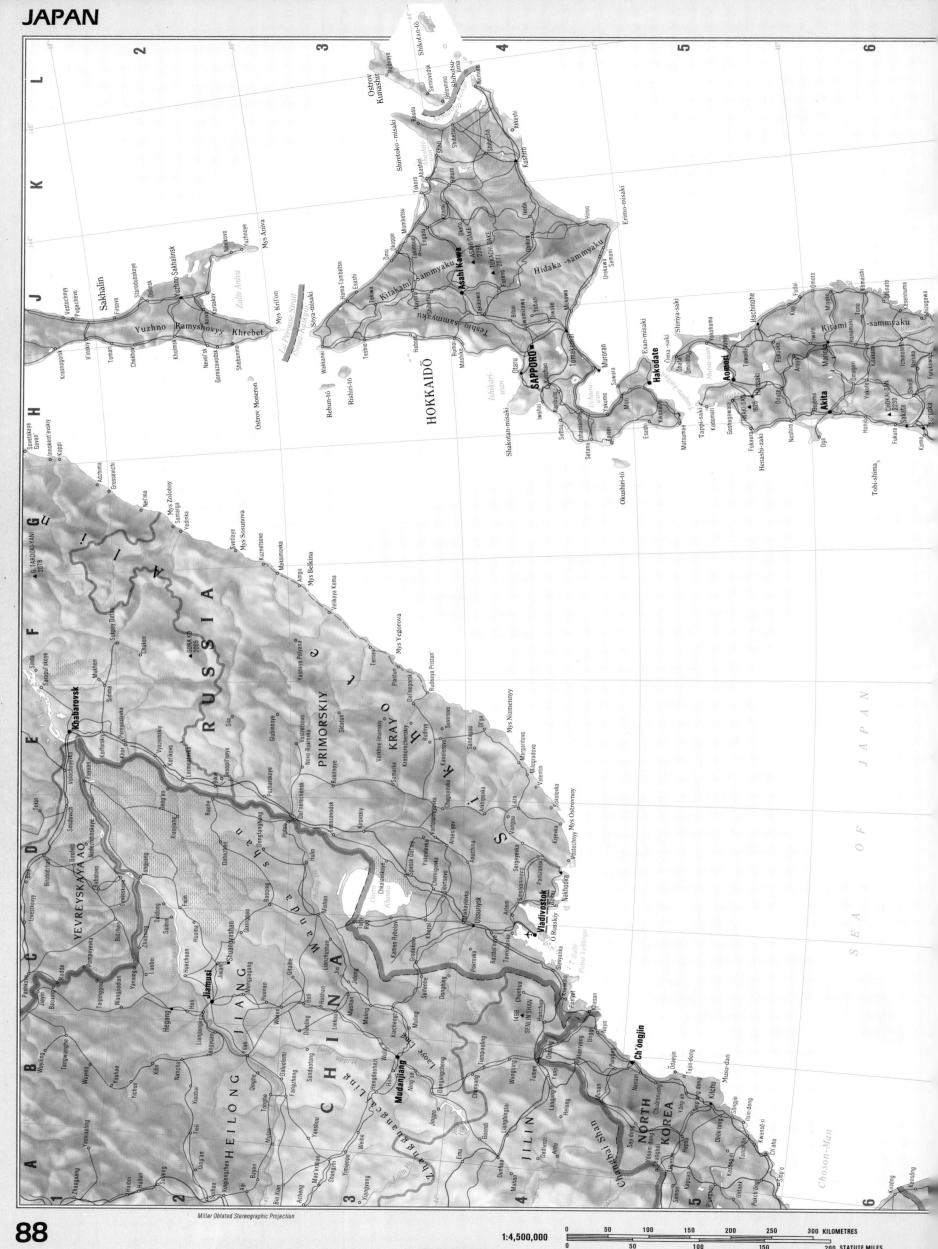

Miller Oblated Stereographic Projection

1:4,500,000

| 0 | 50 | 100 | 150 | 200 | 250 | 300 KILOMETRES |

| 0 | 50 | 100 | 150 | 200 STATUTE MILES |

© COLOUR LIBRARY BOOKS

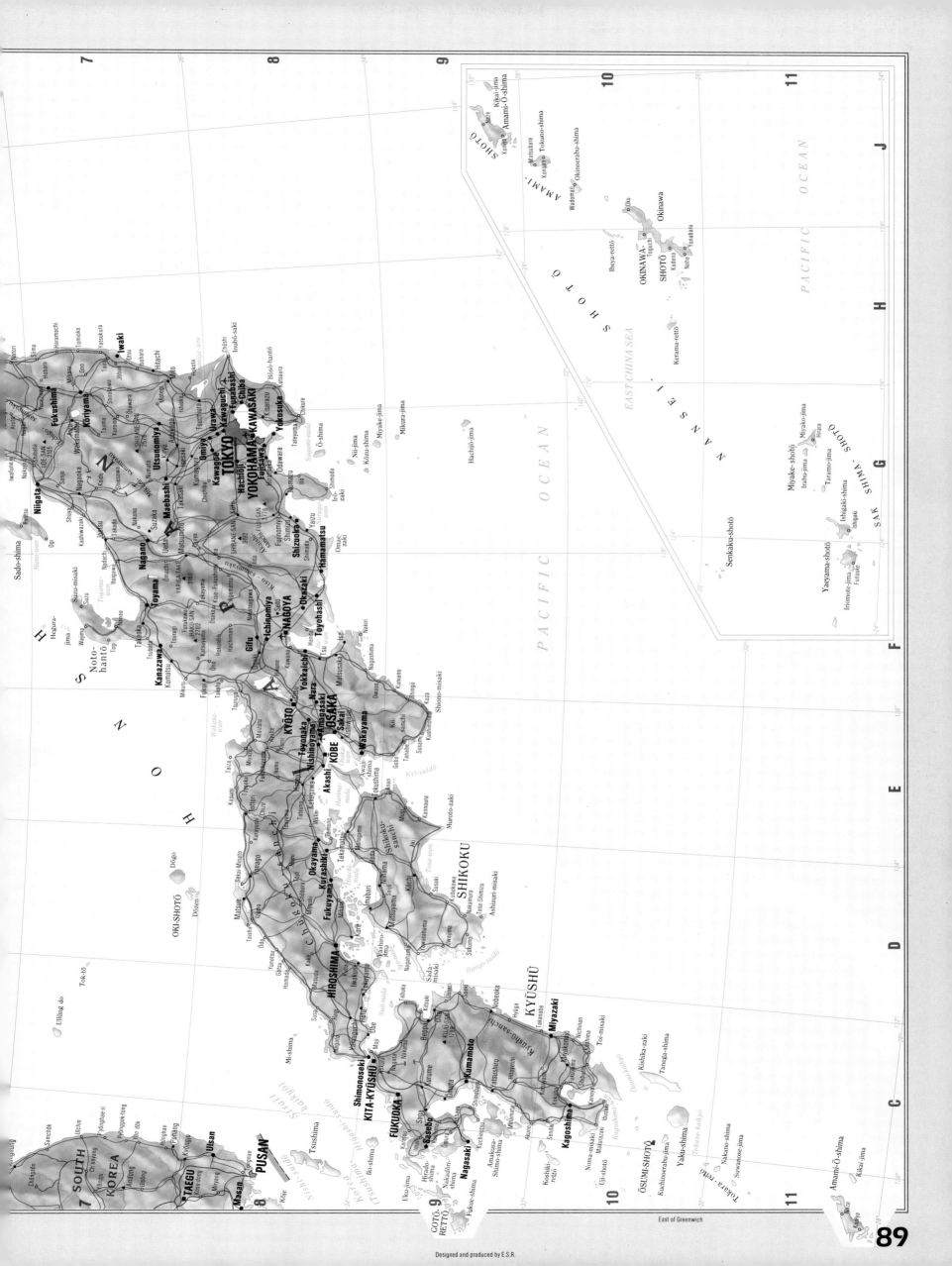

BANGLADESH

CHITTAGONG
Kutubdia
Maiskhal
Cox's Bazar

MYANMAR

MOUNT
VICTORIA
3053

Sittwe
(Akyab)
Boronga Is
Kyaukpyu
Ramree
Cheduba
Sandoway

BAY

OF

BENGAL

Cape Negrais

Mandalay

Andaman
Islands
(India)

North
Andaman

Middle
Andaman

Ritchie's
Archipelago

South
Andaman
North
Sentinel
Port Blair
Rutland

Little
Andaman

Sandy Pt.

ANDAMAN

SEA

Nicobar
Islands
(India)

Great
Nicobar

Car Nicobar

Little Nicobar

Pygmalion Pt.

YANGON (RANGOON)

Bassein
Myaungmya

THAILAND

Chieng-Mai

KRUNG THEP (BANGKOK)

Gulf

of

Thailand

Chumphon
Ko Tao

Ko Phangan
Ko Samui

Surat Thani

Nakhon
Si Thammarat

Ko Phuket
Ko Lanta
Trang
Songkhla

Pattani

CHINA

HANOI
HAIPHONG

Da Nang

Hue

CAMBODIA

Phnom
Penh

HO CHI MINH (SAIGON)

Nha Trang

Da Lat

Qui Nhon

Con Son

Parcel Islands
Xisha Qundao
(Claimed by China
and Vietnam)

NAN HAI

(SOUTH CHINA
SEA)

Nanshan Islands
Nansha Qundao
(Claimed by China, Vietnam and Philippines)

Victoria
MACAO
AOMEN
(Port.)

HONG KONG
(U.K.)

Maoming

Zhanjiang

Haikou

Hainan Dao

George Town
(Pinang)

Ipoh

KUALA LUMPUR

Johor Baharu
SINGAPORE

MEDAN

MALAYSIA

Malay
Peninsula

BRUNEI

Kota Kinabalu

SARAWAK

Kuching

KALIMANTAN

Borneo

Pontianak

Balikpa

Simeulue
Nias

Sumatra

Padang

Palembang

Tanjungkarang
Telukbetung

JAKARTA

Bogor

BANDUNG

SEMARANG
Surakarta
Yogyakarta

SURABAYA

Malang

Bali
Lomb

INDIAN

OCEAN

Jawa (Java)

LAUT JAWA

INDO

Banjarmasin

Kepulauan Riau

Equator

Mercator Projection

1:12,000,000

© COLOUR LIBRARY BOOKS

| 0 | 100 | 200 | 300 | 400 | 500 | 600 | 700 | 800 KILOMETRES |
| 0 | | 100 | 200 | 300 | | 400 | | 500 STATUTE MILES |

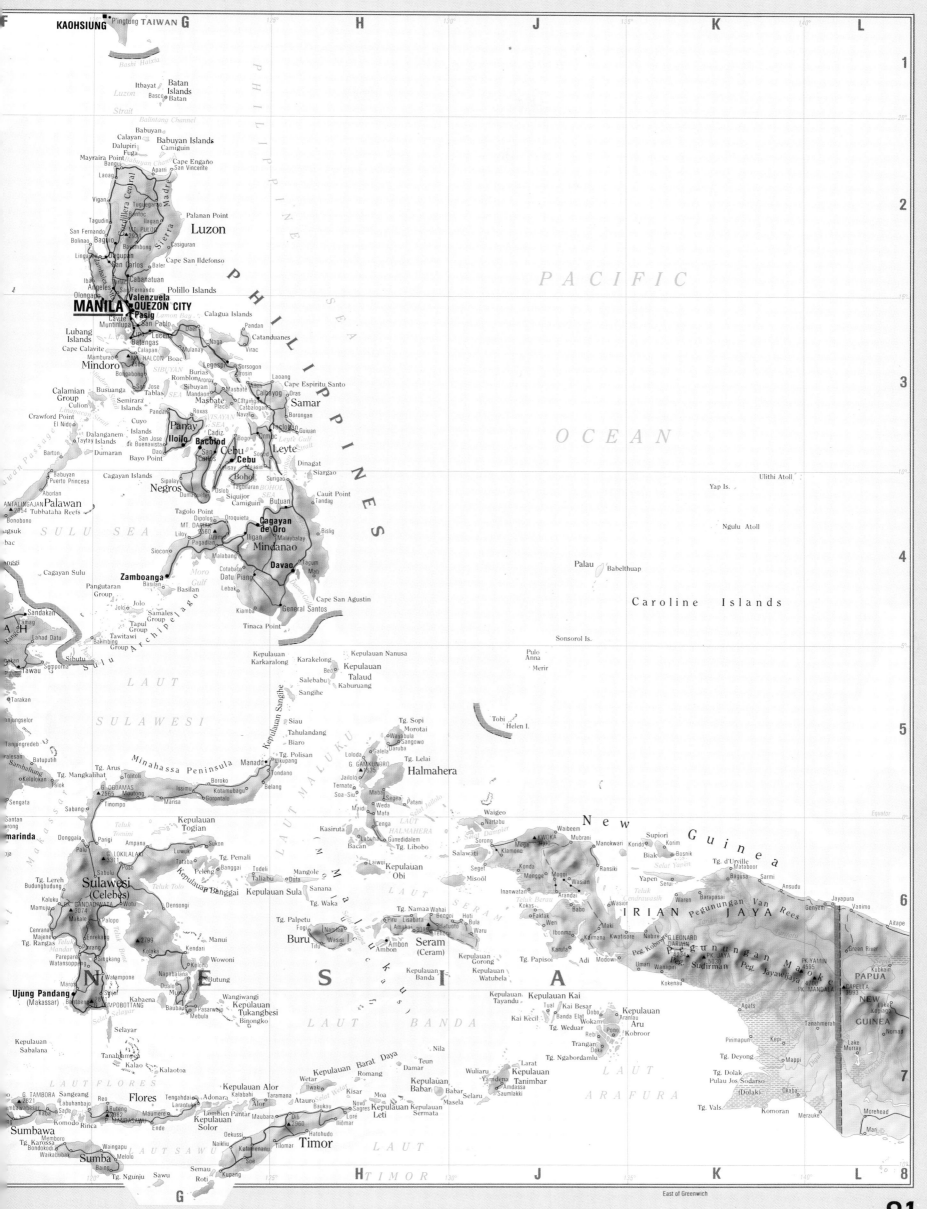

KAOHSIUNG
P'ingtung TAIWAN
Pingtung

Hashi Haixia

Itbayat Batan
Islands
Basco Batan

Luzon

Balintang Channel

Babuyan
Calayan Fuga
Dalupiri Camiguin
Mayraira Point Babuyan Islands
Bangui Cape Engaño
Laoag Aparri San Vicente

Vigan Tuguegarao
Bontoc Ilagan Palanan Point
Tagudin MT. PULOG
San Fernando 2922 Casiguran
Bolinao Baguio Cape San Ildefonso
Linga San Carlos Baler
Cabanatuan
Ibac Angeles San Fernando Polillo Islands
Olongapo
MANILA VALENZUELA QUEZON CITY
Cavite PASIG Calagua Islands
Muntinlupa San Pablo Pandan
Lubang Lucena Catanduanes
Islands Batangas Naga
Cape Calavite Calapan Mulanay Virac
Mamburao MT. HALCON Boac Legaspi
Mindoro 2585 Sorsogon
Bongabong Burias Irosin
Romblon Masbate Laoang Cape Espiritu Santo
Calamian Busuanga Sibuyan Aroroy
Group Tablas Mandaon **Samar**
Semirara Roxas Masbate Placer Catbalogan
Crawford Point Islands Pandan Calbayog Oras
El Nido Cuyo Borongan
Calamian Islands Guiuan
ANTALINGAJAN San Jose Tacloban
Dalanganem de Buenavista Iloilo **Panay** Ormoc
Islands Dao Bacolod **Leyte**
Barton Dumaran San Carlos **Cebu** Maasin
Bayo Point Cebu Dinagat
Cagayan Islands Bohol Siargao
Babuyan Sipalay Siquijor Surigao
Puerto Princesa **Negros** Dumaguete Tagbilaran Butuan Cauit Point
Palawan Tagolo Point Camiguin Tandag
ANTALINGAJAN Dipolog MT. DARAT Oroquieta
Tubbataha Reefs Liloy Ozamiz **Cagayan**
Bonobono Siocon Iligan **de Oro** Bislig
Pagadian Malaybalay
SULU SEA **Mindanao**
Cagayan Sulu Malabang Cotabato Tagum
Pangutaran Basilan Datu Piang **Davao**
Group Lebak Mati
Sandakan Jolo Kiamba
Lamag Tapul General Santos Cape San Agustin
Lahad Datu Group Tinaca Point
Tawitwi
Samales
Group **Zamboanga**
Moro Gulf

PHILIPPINE SEA

PACIFIC

OCEAN

Yap Is.

Ulithi Atoll

Ngulu Atoll

Palau Babelthuap

Caroline Islands

Sonsorol Is.

Pulo
Anna
Merir

SULAWESI

Kepulauan Nanusa
Kepulauan
Karkaralong Karakelong Beo
Salebabu Kepulauan
Talaud
Sangihe Kaburuang

Kepulauan Sangihe
Siau
Tahulandang
Biaro

Tg. Sopi Tobi
Morotai Helen I.
Wayabula
Sangowo Daruba

Tg. Arus Tg. Lelai
Minahassa Peninsula Manado Galela
G. GAMKUNORO
Tg. Mangkalihat Tolitoli Kwandang Loloda 1635
Likupang Jailolo **Halmahera**
Boroko Ternate Patani
G. OGOAMAS Mowtong Belang Soa-Siu
2565 Gorontalo Weda
Marisa Mafa
Maidi
LAUT MALUKU
Waigeo
Kepulauan Narlabu **New Guinea**
Togian Waibeem
Supiori
Teluk Kasiruta Sorong Mega Korido Korim
Tomini Gunedidalem Klamono Biak Bosnik
Tg. Pemali Bacan Salawati Konda Ransiki
Donggala Parigi Labuha Seget Yapen
Ampana Tg. Libobo Misoöl Tg. d'Urville
Luwuk Mangole Mubrani Manokwari Serui
G. LOKILALAKI Peleng Taliabu Kepulauan Waren
3311 Banggai Dofa Obi Inanwatan Wasian
Tataba Sanana Moggi
Kepulauan Napanda Mangge IRIAN
Tg. Lereh Banggai Kepulauan Sula Kwatisore
Budungbudung **Sulawesi** Tg. Palpetu Piru Kokas
(Celebes) Fogi Tg. Namaa Wahai Faklak
Kaluku G. DANDADWATA Manui Wasisi Amahai Weri
Mamuju 3074 Kendari Buru Ambon **Seram**
Cenrana Makale Wowoni (Ceram)
Majene Kepulauan
Enrekang Kolaka Gorong
Tg. Rangas Palopo 2799 Kepulauan
Parepare Singkang Watubela
Watansoppeng Napabalano Butung
Pangkajene Raha Wangiwangi
Ujung Pandang Kabaena Kepulauan Kepulauan
(Makassar) Bintan Pasarwajo Tukangbesi Banda
N Binongko
Selayar
Kepulauan Wuliaru
Sabalana Kalao
Tanahjampea Kepulauan
Kepulauan Kalaotoa Barat Daya Teun
LAUT FLORES Romang Damar
G. TAMBORA Sangeang Wetar Kisar Moa
2821 Komba Adonara Alor Atauro Nila
Labuhanbajo Reo Larantuka Maumere **Timor** Baukau
Sumbawa Sape **Flores** Kupang Dili
Bima Ruteng Lomblen Pantar

LAUT SAWU

91

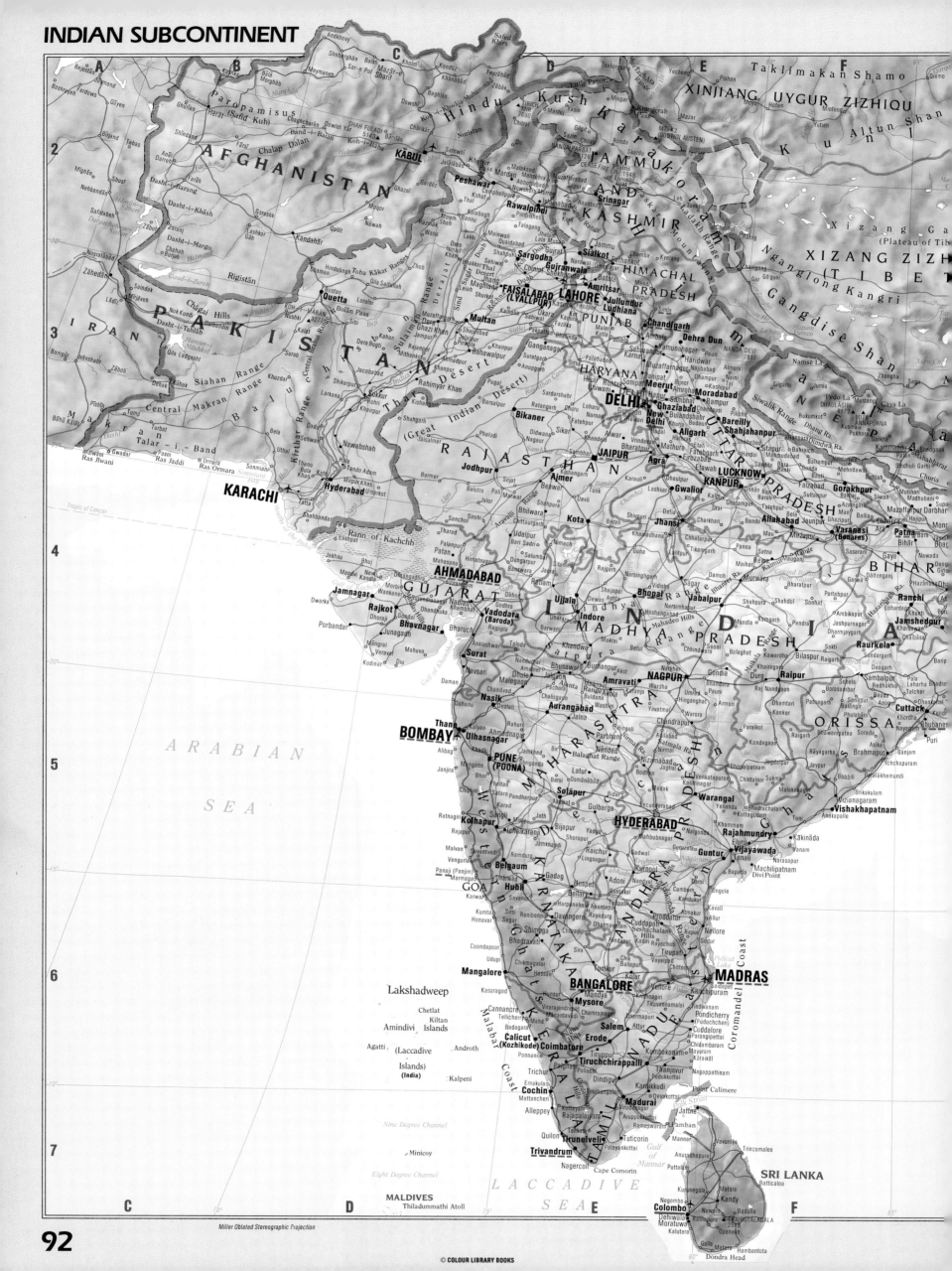

Müller Oblated Stereographic Projection

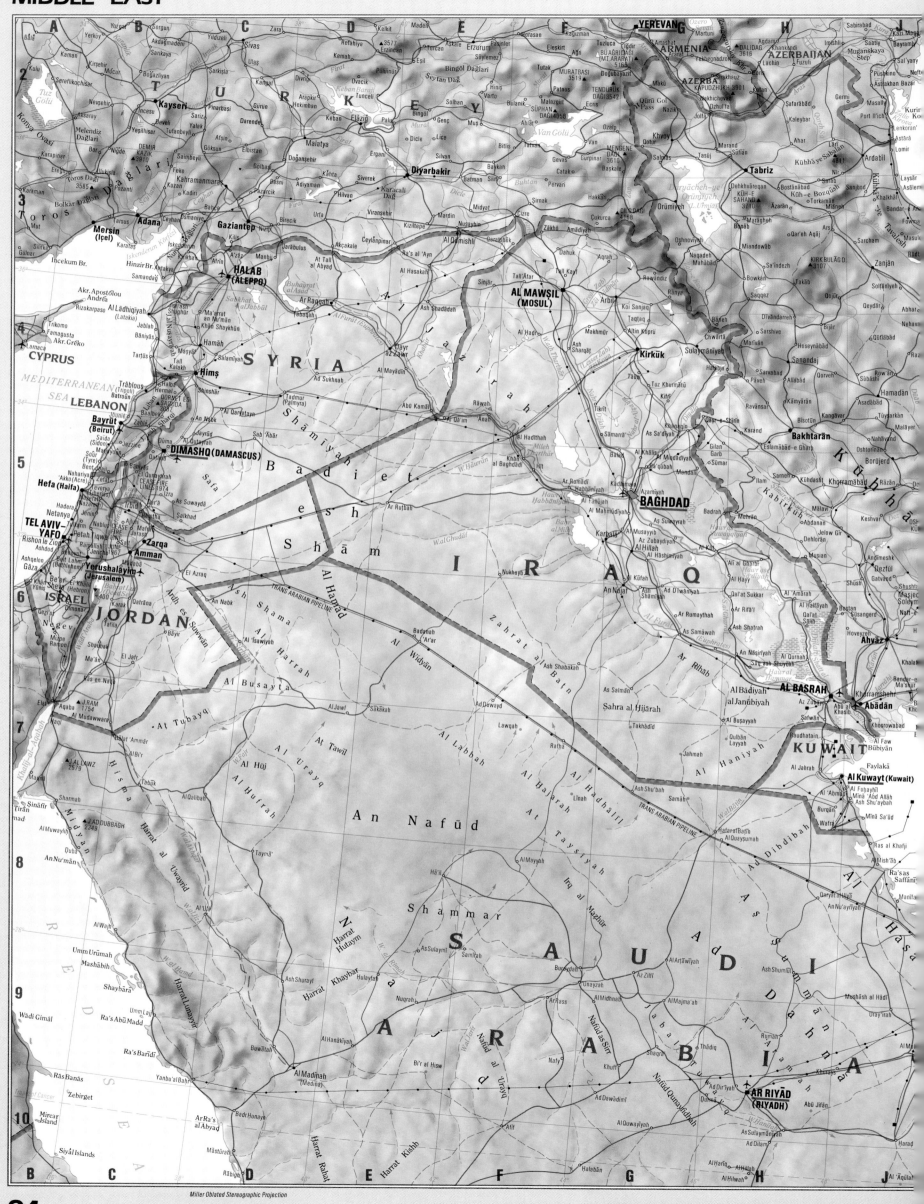

Miller Oblated Stereographic Projection

1:6,000,000

© COLOUR LIBRARY BOOKS

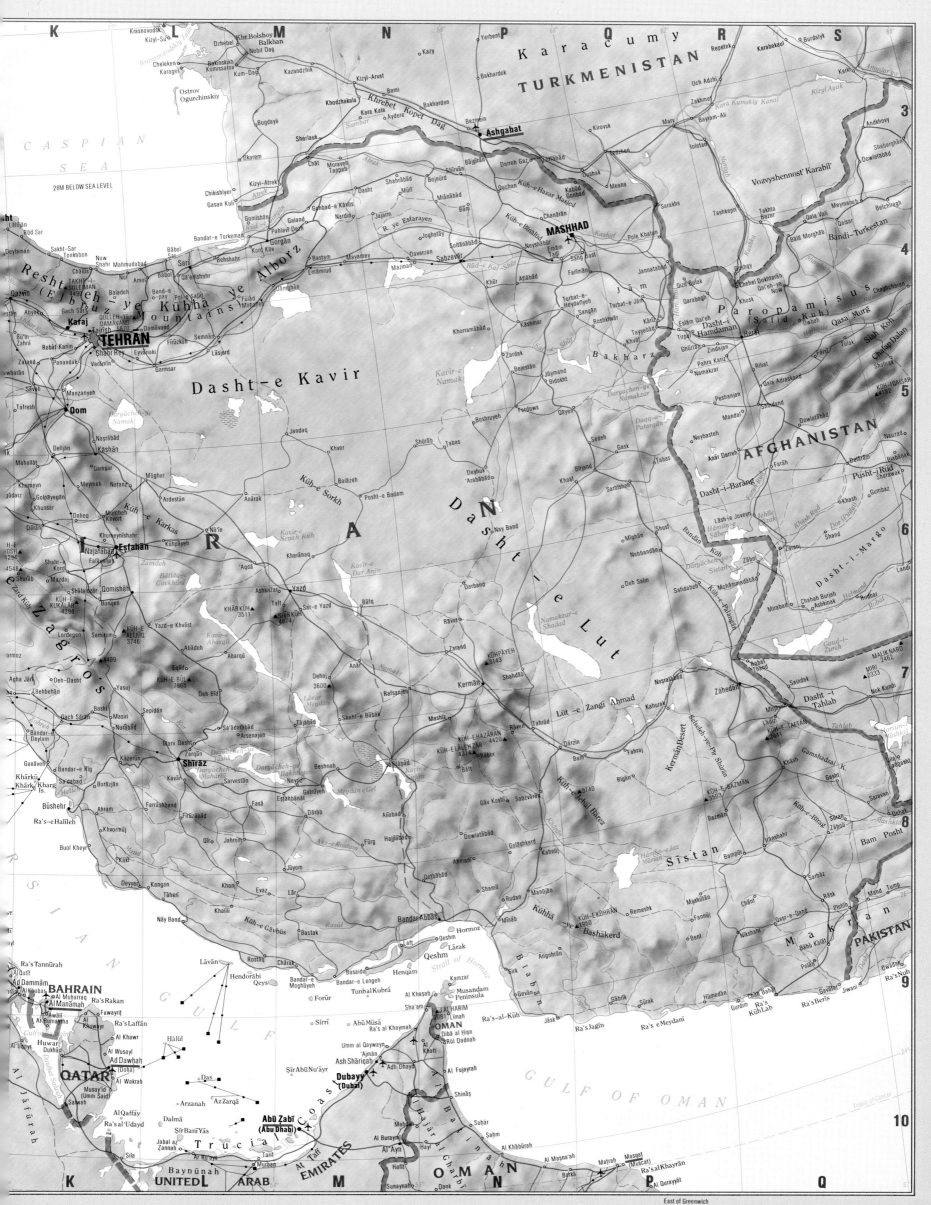

95

ARABIAN PENINSULA

Miller Oblated Stereographic Projection

© COLOUR LIBRARY BOOKS

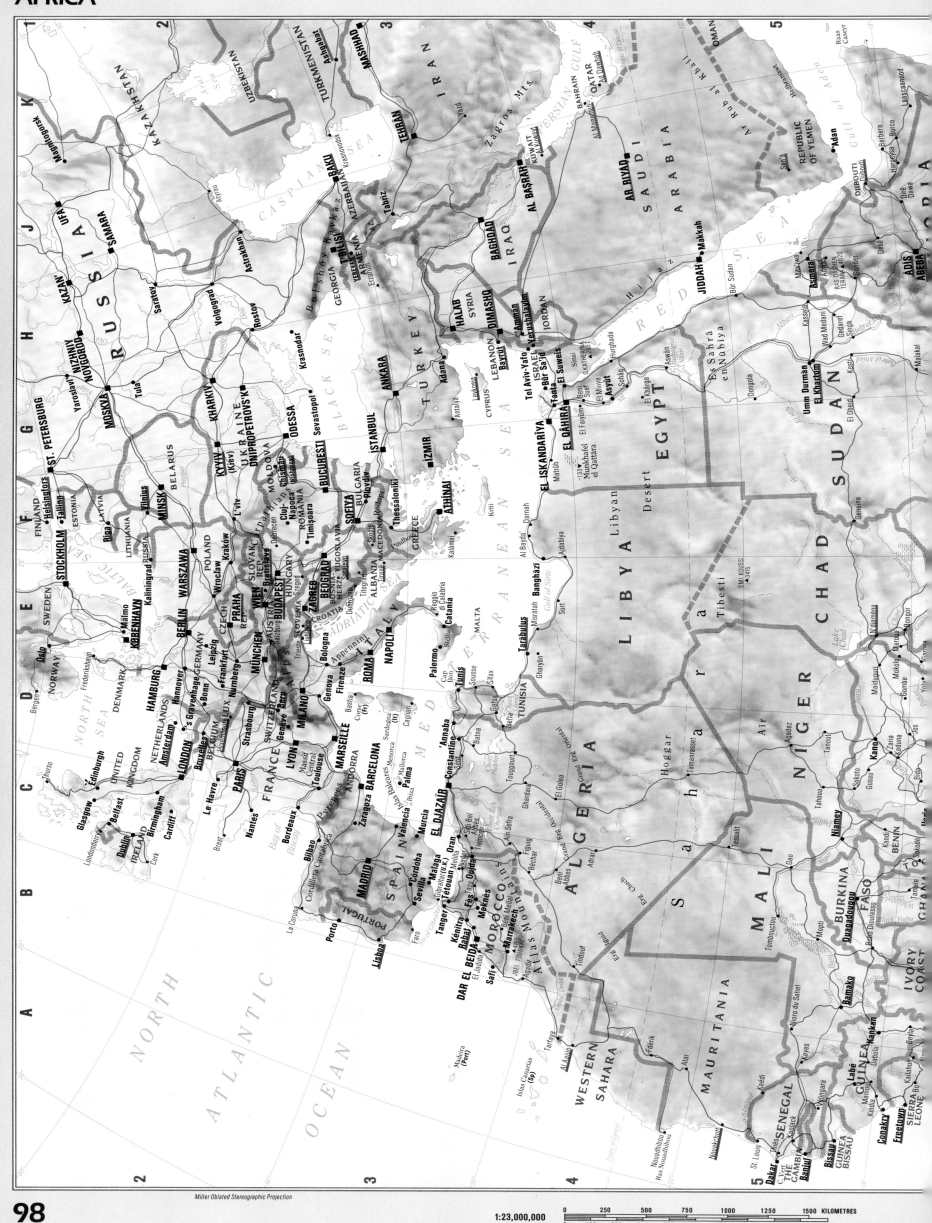

Miller Oblated Stereographic Projection

1:23,000,000

| | 250 | 500 | 750 | 1000 | 1250 | 1500 KILOMETRES |
| 0 | 100 | 200 | 300 | 400 | 500 | 600 | 700 | 800 | 900 | 1000 STATUTE MILES |

© COLOUR LIBRARY BOOKS

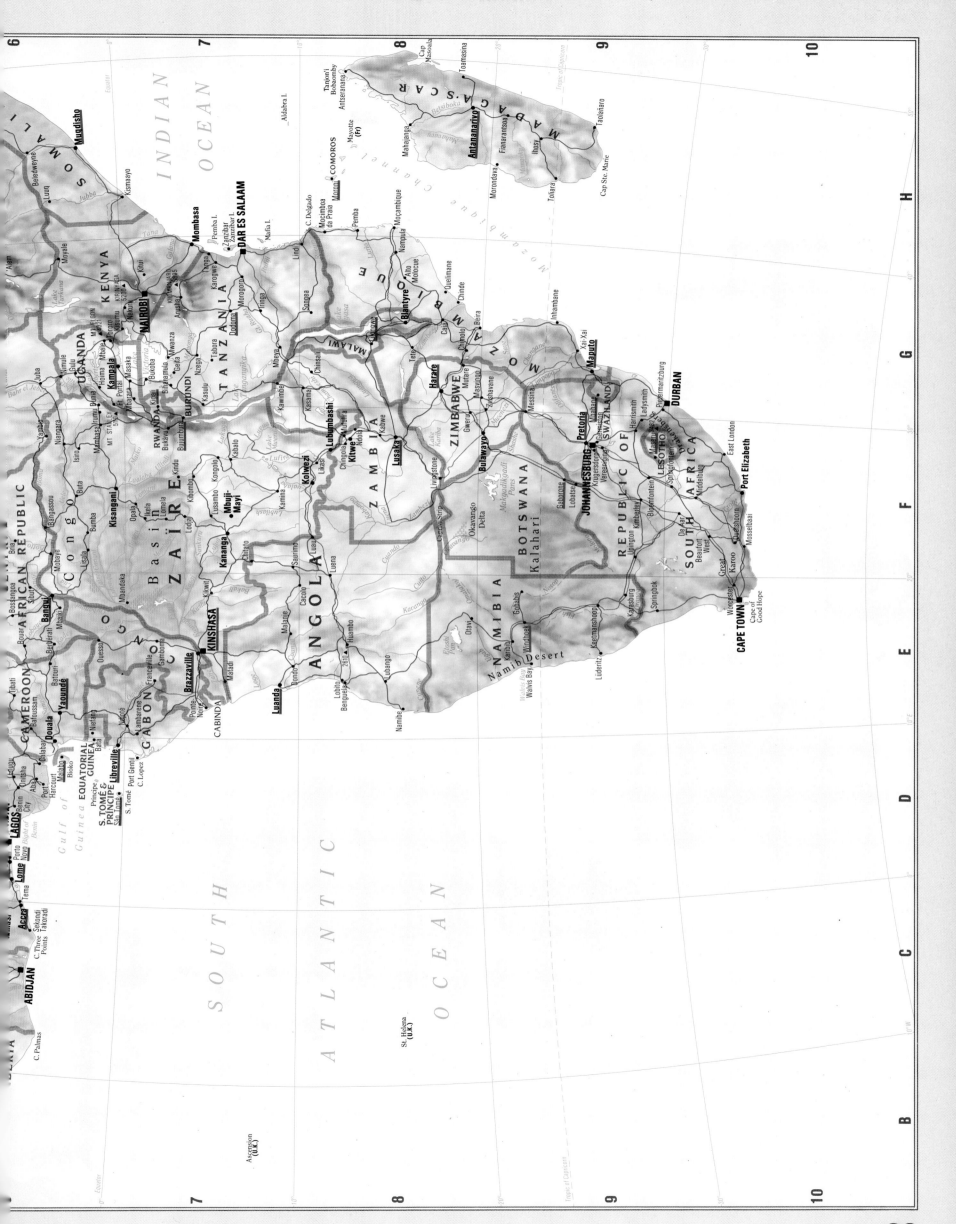

Designed and produced by E.S.R.

Miller Oblated Stereographic Projection   West of Greenwich

1:9,000,000

© COLOUR LIBRARY BOOKS

F

EL DJAZAÏR
(ALGIERS)

G

H

I

ITALY
Agrigento
Sicilia
(Sicily) Catania
Siracusa
Ragusa

Catania

J

K

GREECE

Kálamai

L

Ródhos

1

rchell
Dellys
Tizi Ouzou
Blida
Medea
Ksar El Boukhari
Bou Saâda
M'Sila

Cap Bougaroun
Bejaia
Jijel
Skikda
'Annaba
Constantine
Sétif
El Eulma
Batna
Aïn Beïda
Oum El Bouaghi
Khenchela
Tébessa

Guelma
Souk Ahras

Bizerte
Mateur
Béja
Tunis
Kelibia
Nabeul

Cap Bon

Pantelleria
(Italy)

MALTA
Valletta

Kastélli
Khaniá
Kríti
(Crete)

Iráklion
Sitia

MEDITERRANEAN SEA

X

Laghouat
Djelfa

Biskra

Kasserine

Kairouan
Sousse
Monastir
Moknine
Mahdia
Ksour Essaf

Valletta

Linosa
(Italy)

Lampedusa
(Italy)

2

Ghardaia
Ouargla

Gafsa
Nefta
Chott
El Jerid

Tozeur

Chott
Melrhir

Golfe de Gabès
Gabès
Houmt Souk
I. de Jerba
Zarzis

Sfax

al

El Oued
Touggourt

Medenine
Remada

Zuwârah
Az Zawiyah

Tarābulus
(Tripoli)
Tarhūnah

Al Khums
Zlitan
Misrâtah

Tūkrah
Shahhat
Al Bayda (Cyrene)
Al Qubbah
Darnah (Derna)
Ras al Muraysah

Tubruq

As
Sallūm
Sidi Barrani
Matrūh

TUNISIA

Ghadamis

Nalut
Yafran
Mizdah

Gharyān

Bani Walid

Surt
(Sirte)

Sabkhat
Tâwurgha

Gulf of Sirte

Ajdabiyā

Banghāzī
(Benghazi)

Qaminis

Al Jabal al Akhdar

Wādī Farīgh
Wādī Tamit
Wādī al Hamīm

Al Jaghbūb

Awjilah
Jālū

Marādah

Ed-Déffa

Munkhafed
el Qattāra
-133
(Qattâra
Depression)

Siwa

EGYPT

RIA

I Golea

Hassi Habadra

ateau
Tademaït

Aguemour

Salah

Bordj Omar Driss
(Ft. Flatters)
In Amenas

Zarzaïtine

Tan Emellel

Birāk

Al Fuqahā'
(Uled Saïdan)

Es Sahra' el
Gharbiya
(Western Desert)

L I B Y A

L i b y a n

3

Illizi
(Ft. de Polignac)

Ghât

Awbārī

Sabhā

Tāzirbū

Ramlat Rabyānah

D e s e r t

Meniet

Tassili
N'Ajjer

Murzuq

Al Khufrah
(Al Jawf)

Tropic of Cancer

In Ekker

Djanet
(Fort Charlet)

MT TAHAT
2918

Idhān Murzuq

4

Tassili
Oua-n
Ahagar

Hoggar

Toummo
(Bi'r al Wa'r)

Tamanrasset

S a h a r a

Bardai

PIC TOUSSIDE
3265

T i b e s t i

Zouar

Jef Jef
el Kebir

a

a

r

a

Ténéré du
Tafassâsset

Djado

Bilma

Grand Erg
de Bilma

Ounianga Kebir

Depression
du Mourdi

5

Aïr
(Azbine)

N I G E R

Faya-Largeau

Djourab

Fada

Ennedi

Agadez

Oum Chalouba

Ménaka

C H A D

Tahoua

Tanout

Nguigmi

Mao

Abéché

Biltine
Guéréda

Kutum
JEBEL
GURGEI
2997

SUDAN

JEBEL
MARRA
3070
3088

6

ney
Dogondoutchi

Dakoro
Madaoua
Tessaoua

Birni n' Konni
Gangara

Gourê

Zinder

N'Goun

Maïné
Soroa
Diffa

Lake Chad
(Lac Tchad)

Massakori

Yao

Moussoro

Ati

Adré
Geneina

Goz Beida
Mongororo

Mênaka

Dosso

Sabon
Birni
Isa
Kaura
Namoda

Argungu
Birnin
Kebbi
Gummi
Gusau

Maradi
Katsina

Nguru
Gashua

Gorgoram

Dikwa

Kousséri (Ft. Foureau)
Ndjamena (Ft. Lamy)

Massénya

Mongo
Abou Deïa

Melfi

Am Timan

Bitkine

Bokoro

Zalingei

BENIN

Nikki

New Bussa

Kandi

Kainji
Reservoir

Zuru
Zungeru

Sokoto

Wurno
Birni

Zoru

Kano

Funtua

Kaduna

Zaria

Kontagora

Minna
Kuta

Jos

Bauchi

Katagum

Potiskum

Maidugun

Bama

Gwoza
Mora

Maroua

Gombe

Biu

Mobi
Mokolo

Gombi

Yola

Numan
Léré

Garoua

Pala

Guider

Kaélé
Lâme

Bongor

Bousso

Kélo
Koumra
(Ft. Archambault)

Sarh

Kyabé

Gagui

Birao

CENTRAL AFRICAN
REPUBLIC

Ouanda
Djallé

7

NIGERIA

CAMEROON

Congola

Kafanchan

G

H

East of Greenwich

I

J

K

101

Designed and produced by E.S.R.

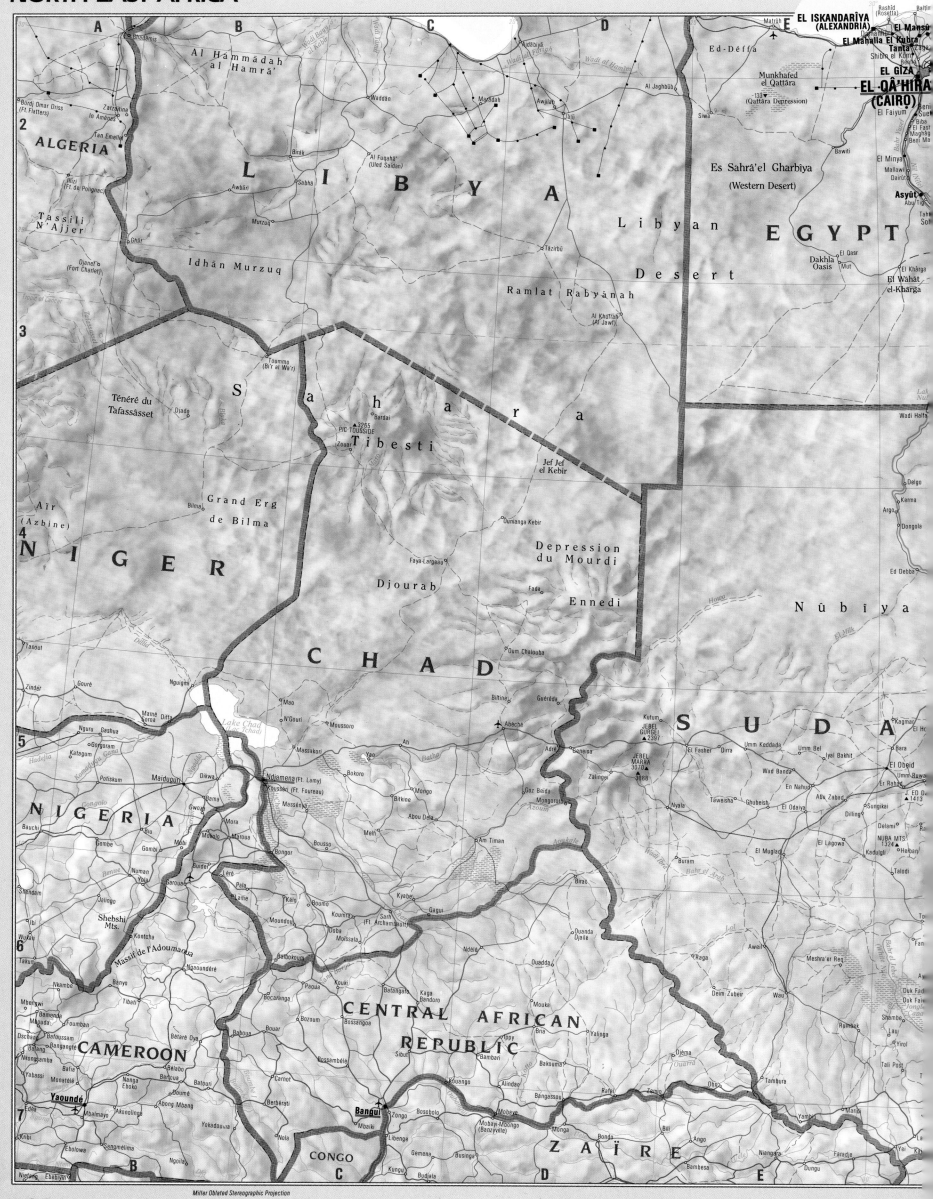

A B C D E

Rashid (Rosetta)
Baltîm
El Mansû
El Mahalla El Kubra
Tanta
Shibîn el Kôm
Zaga

El Dâmanhûr

Matrûh

Ed-Déffa

El GIZA
EL QÂHIRA (CAIRO)

El Faiyûm
Suez
Biba
El Wasta
Beni Mazâr
Beni Suef

ALGERIA

Bordj Omar Driss (Ft. Flatters)
Ghadâmis

Zarzaïtine
In Amenas

Al Hammâdah al Hamrâ'

Wadi Bayy al Kabir

Waddân

Birâk

Al Jaghbûb

Awjilah
Jâlu

Maradah

Ajdâbiyâ

Munkhafed el Qattâra
(Qattâra Depression)

Siwa

Bawiti

El Minya

Mallawi
Dairûta

Asyût

LIBYA

EGYPT

Es Sahrâ'el Gharbîya
(Western Desert)

Tan Emellel

Tassili N'Ajjer

Awbâri

Sabhâ

Al Fugahâ' (Uled Saidan)

Murzuq

Tâzirbû

Libyan

El Qasr
Mut
Dakhla Oasis

El Khârga
El Wâhât el-Kharga

Desert

Ghât

Idhân Murzuq

Illizi (Ft. de Polignac)

Djanet (Fort Charlet)

Ramlat Rabyânah

Al Khufrah (Al Jawf)

Toummo (Bi'r al Wa'r)

Sahara

Ténéré du Tafassâsset

Djado

Bilma

Bardai

PIC TOUSSIDE 3265

Zouar

Tibesti

Jef Jef el Kebir

Wadi Halfa

Delgo
Kerma

Argo
Dongola

Aïr (Azbine)

Grand Erg de Bilma

Bilma

Ounianga Kebir

Depression du Mourdi

Ed Debba

Nûbîya

NIGER

Faya-Largeau

Djourab

Fada

Ennedi

Kerma

Tanout

Zinder

Gouré

Dibbi

Nguigmi

CHAD

Oum Chalouba

Houei

El Milk

SUDA

Goz Beida

Kagmar
El Ho

Maïné Soroa

N'Gouri

Mao

Moussoro

Biltine

Guérèda

Kutum
JEBEL GURGEI 2397

El Fasher
Dirra

Umm Keddada

Umm Bel
Iyal Bakhit

El Obeid
Umm Ruwa
Er Rahad

NIGERIA

Nguru
Gashua

Gorgoram
Gana
Katagum

Hadejia

Potiskum

Maiduguri

Dikwa

Ndjamena (Ft. Lamy)

Kousséri (Ft. Foureau)

Bokoro

Yao

Ati

Batha

Abéché

Adré
Geneina

Zalingei

JEBEL MARRA 3070 3088

Nyala

Tâweisha

Ghubeish

El Odaiya

J. ED D 1413

Bauchi

Biu

Gombi

Mobi

Mukulo
Maroua

Gwoza
Bama

Mongo

Bitkine

Mongororo
Azoum

En Nahud

El Mugiad

Abu Zabad

Sungikai

Dilling

Delami

Numan
Yola

Gombe

Guider

Léré

Massénya

Abou Dela

Am Timan

Aouk

Buram

Bahr el Arab

El Lagowa

NUBA MTS 1324 Heiban
Kadugli

Shendam

Ubi
Wukari

Takum

Baroua

Pala
Lame

Kélo
Boumo

Melfi

Kyabe

Birao

Ouanda Djalle

Bahr el

Talodi

Shebshi Mts.

Kontcha

Moundou

Koumra
Sarh (Ft. Archambault)

Doba
Moïssala

Gagui

Gouré

Raga

Aweil

Meshra'er Req

Wau

Duk Fad
Duk Fai

Massif de l'Adoumaoua

Ngaoundéré

Bébodokoum

Ndélé

Ouadda

Mouka

Yalinga

Deim Zuber

Tali Post

CAMEROON

Nkambe

Banyo

Tibati

Paoua

Bozoum

Bossangoa

Bambari

Kaga Bandoro

Batangafo

Ippy

Bria

Djéma

CENTRAL AFRICAN REPUBLIC

Mbouda
Bamenda
Foumban

Dschang
Bafoussam

Bétaré Oya

Bouar

Bozo

Baboua

Sibut

Kouki

Bangassou

Rafaï

Zemio

Yampio

Mandi

Yaoundé

Bafia

Nanga Eboko

Batouri

Carnot

Berbérati

Alindao

Bangassou

Obo

Edéa
Mbalmayo
Akonolinga
Abong Mbang
Doumé
Bertoua

Yokadouma
Nola

Zongo
Bosobolo
Libenge

Mobaye
Mobayi-Mbongo (Banzyville)

MOnga

Bondo

Ango

Niangara

Dungu

Faradje

Kribi
Ebolowa
Sangmélima

Bangui

Mbaiki

Gemena
Businga

Lau

Yirol

CONGO

Nola
Ngoila
Ngolo

Niefang
Ebebiyin

CENTRAL AFRICAN REPUBLIC

ZAÏRE

Kungu
Budjala

B C D E

Miller Oblated Stereographic Projection

1:9,000,000

0 100 200 300 400 500 600 KILOMETRES
0 50 100 150 200 250 300 350 400 STATUTE MILES

© COLOUR LIBRARY BOOKS

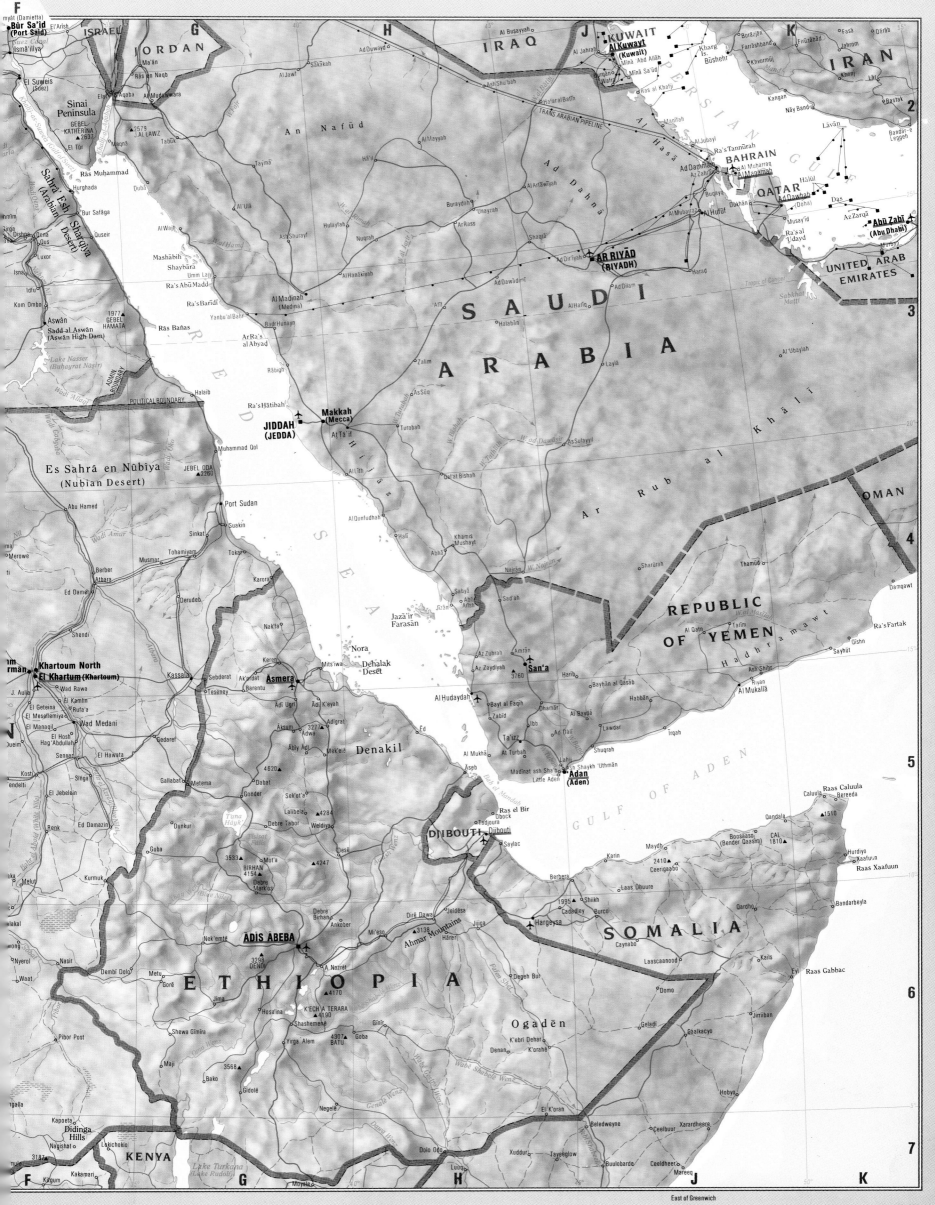

Designed and produced by E.S.R.

East of Greenwich

Miller Oblated Stereographic Projection

West of Greenwich

© COLOUR LIBRARY BOOKS

1:9,000,000

| 0 | 100 | 200 | 300 | 400 | 500 | 600 KILOMETRES |

| 0 | 50 | 100 | 150 | 200 | 250 | 300 | 350 | 400 STATUTE MILES |

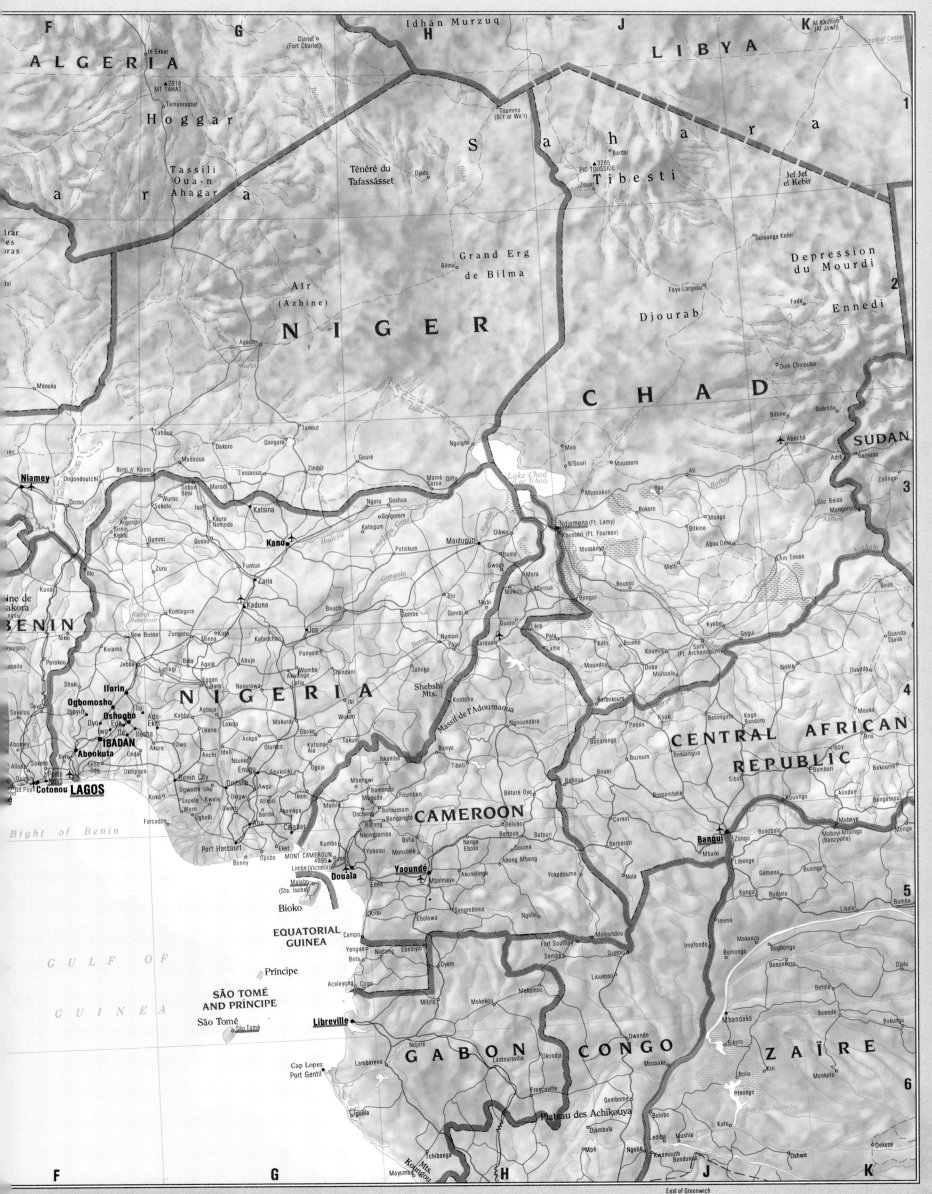

ALGERIA
Hoggar
MT TAHAT ▲2918
Tamanrasset
In Ekker
Tassili
Oua-n
Ahagar

Djanet
(Fort Charlet)
Idhān Murzuq

LIBYA

Toummo
(Bi'r al Wa'r)

Bardai
PIC TOUSSIDE ▲3265
Zouar
Tibesti

Jef Jef
el Kebir

Al Khufrah
(Al Jawf)

Tropic of Cancer

Ténéré du
Tafassâsset
Djado

Bilma

Grand Erg
de Bilma

Faya-Largeau

Oumianga Kebir

Depression
du Mourdi

Fada
Ennedi

Aïr
(Azbine)

Agadez

NIGER

Djourab

CHAD

Oum Chalouba

Ménaka

Tahoua
Tanout

Dakoro
Gangara

Gouré

Nguighi

Mao
N'Gouri
Moussoro

Ati

Biltine
Guéréda

SUDAN

Adré
Geneina

Zelingei

Niamey
Dogondoutchi
Birni n' Konni
Madaoua
Tessaoua
Zinder

Maïné
Soroa
Diffa

Lake Chad
(Lac Tchad)

Massakori
Yao

Bokoro

Mongo
Bitkine

Goz Beida
Mongororo

Azoum

Dosso
Wurno
Sokoto
Sabon
Birni
Maradi
Isa
Katsina

Nguru
Gashua
Gorgoram
Katagum

Malné

Ndjamena (Ft. Lamy)
Koussen (Ft. Foureau)

Abou Deïa

Am Timan

Birao

Kandi
Kebbi
Argungu
Birnin
Kebbi
Gummi
Gusau
Zuru
Funtua
Kano
Hadejia
Potiskum

Maiduguri
Dikwa
Bama

Massénya

Melfi

BENIN
Nikki
Kaiama
Zaria
Kaduna
Bauchi
Biu
Gombe
Gombi
Mubi

Gwoza
Makolo
Mora
Maroua
Bongor
Guider
Léré

Kyabe

Sarh
(Ft. Archambault)

Gagui

Ouanda
Djalé

Ouadda

New Bussa
Zungeru
Minna
Jos
Numan
Yola
Garoua

Pala
Kélo
Boumo
Koumra
Doba
Moïssala

Ndélé

Mouka

Perakou
Jebba
Bida
Agaie
Abuja
Lafiagi
Eggan
Baro
Panyam
Wamba
Akwanga
Lafia
Shendam
Jalingo

Kontcha
Massif de l'Adoumaqua
Moundou

Berbokoum

Bozoum
Batangafo
Kaga
Bandoro
Bria

Tippy
Bambari

Bakouma

Shaki
Ilorin
Ogbomosho
Oshogbo
Oyo
Ife
Ilesha
Ogbomosho

NIGERIA

Ibi
Wukari
Takum

Shebshi
Mts.

Ngaoundéré
Banyo
Tibati

Bocaranga
Baboua
Bouat
Bouar
Paoua
Kouki

CENTRAL AFRICAN
REPUBLIC

Kouango
Alindao
Bangassou

Abeokuta
Ibadan
Abomey
Saketé
Porto
Novo
Cotonou LAGOS
Ilaro
Ijebu
Ode
Ondo
Akure
Owo
Benin City
Ogwashi-Uku
Onitsha
Enugu
Nsukka
Idah
Oturkpo
Ogoja
Nkambe
Mbengwi
Bamenda

Foumban
Banyo
Mamfe
Bafoussam
Bangangté
Dschang

Bétaré Oya
Bertoua
Batouri
Berbérati
Carnot

Bossembélé
Bossangoa

Sibut

Baboua
Mobaye

Kouàngo
Mbaïki

Monga

Bight of Benin

Port Harcourt
Bonny
Opobo
Forcados
Warri
Ughelli
Aba
Calabar
Kumba
Nkongsamba
Yabassi
Bafia

CAMEROON

Nanga
Eboko
Doumé
Abong Mbang
Yokadouma

Nola

Bangui
Zongo
Mbaïki
Libenge
Gemena

Bosobolo

Mobayi-Mbongo
(Banzyville)

Gemena
Businga

MONT CAMEROUN
4095
Limbe (Victoria)
Malabo
(Sta. Isabel)
Bioko
Douala
Edéa
Kribi
Campo

Yaoundé
Mbalmayo
Ebolowa
Sangmélima
Ngoïla

Akonolinga

Moloundou

Sembé
Ouesso

Impfondo

Kungu
Budjala
Lisala

Bumba

EQUATORIAL
GUINEA
Bata
Yengue
Nietang
Ebebiyin
Oyem
Acalayong
Cogo

GULF OF

Principe

SÃO TOMÉ
AND PRÍNCIPE
São Tomé
São Tomé

GUINEA

Libreville

Mitzic
Makokou
Mékambo

Fort Souffay

Bimese
Makanza
Bomongo

Bikoro
Mbandaka

ZAÏRE

Basankusu

Befale
Boende

Boteko

Djolu

Cap Lopez
Port Gentil

Lambaréné
Iguéla

GABON

Lastoursville
Okondja
Koulamoutou

Franceville
Mbini

CONGO

Owando
Mossaka

Bolobo

Inonga

Kiri
Monkoto

Plateau des Achikouya

Gamboma
Djambala
Mpé
Ngabé
Kwamouth
Bendundu

Lediba
Mushie

Kutu

Oshwe

Dekese

Tchibanga
Mayumba
Mts.
Koungou
Djambala

East of Greenwich

105

Miller Oblated Stereographic Projection

1:9,000,000

© COLOUR LIBRARY BOOKS

| 0 | 100 | 200 | 300 | 400 | 500 | 600 KILOMETRES |

| 0 | 50 | 100 | 150 | 200 | 250 | 300 | 350 | 400 STATUTE MILES |

SOUTHERN AFRICA

Miller Obiated Stereographic Projection

1:9,000,000

© COLOUR LIBRARY BOOKS

| 0 | 100 | 200 | 300 | 400 | 500 | 600 KILOMETRES |
| 0 | 50 | 100 | 150 | 200 | 250 | 300 | 350 | 400 STATUTE MILES |

F

G

H

J

K

TANZANIA
Songea
Lindi
Mikindani
Mtwara
Masasi
945
C. Delgado
Makondi
Plateau
Palma
Tunduru
Mocímboa da Praia

MALAWI
Chilumba
Karonga
Mzuzu
Nkhotakota
Kasungu
Mchinji (Ft. Manning)
Lilongwe
Dowa
Salima
Chipoka
Zomba
Blantyre
Limbe
2054
CHIPERONE

Grande
Comore
Moroni
COMOROS
Moheli
Anjouan
Dzaoudzi
Mayotte
(France)

Tanjon'i Bobaomby
Antseranana
(Diégo-Suarez)
Nosy
Mitsio
Nosy Bé
Hell-Ville
Ambilobe
Vohimarina
(Vohémar)
Ambanja
Massif du
2876
Tsaratanana
Sambava
Bealanana
Andapa
Antalaha

MOZAMBIQUE
Cobue
Matala
Mecula
Marrupa
Montepuez
Balama
Ibo
Quissanga
Pemba
Mecufi
Namapa
Lurio
Memba
Nacala-a-Velha
Maaia
Moçambique

MADAGASCAR
Analalava
Antsohihy
Befandriana
Maroantsetra
C. Masoala
Mananara

Namuli
2419
Gurué
Iapala
Nampula
Mahajanga
Port-Bergé
Marovoay
Nosy Boraha
(Sainte-Marie)
Ambodifototra

INDIAN

OCEAN

J
K
55°
50°
MAURITIUS
Port Louis
Beau Basin
Curepipe
Mahébourg
Réunion
(France)
St. Denis
St. Benoit
St. Pierre
Mascarene
Islands
L

109

Bonne Projection

East of Greenwich

1:19,000,000

| 0 | 200 | 400 | 600 | 800 KILOMETRES |
| 0 | 100 | 200 | 300 | 400 | 500 STATUTE MILES |

© COLOUR LIBRARY BOOKS

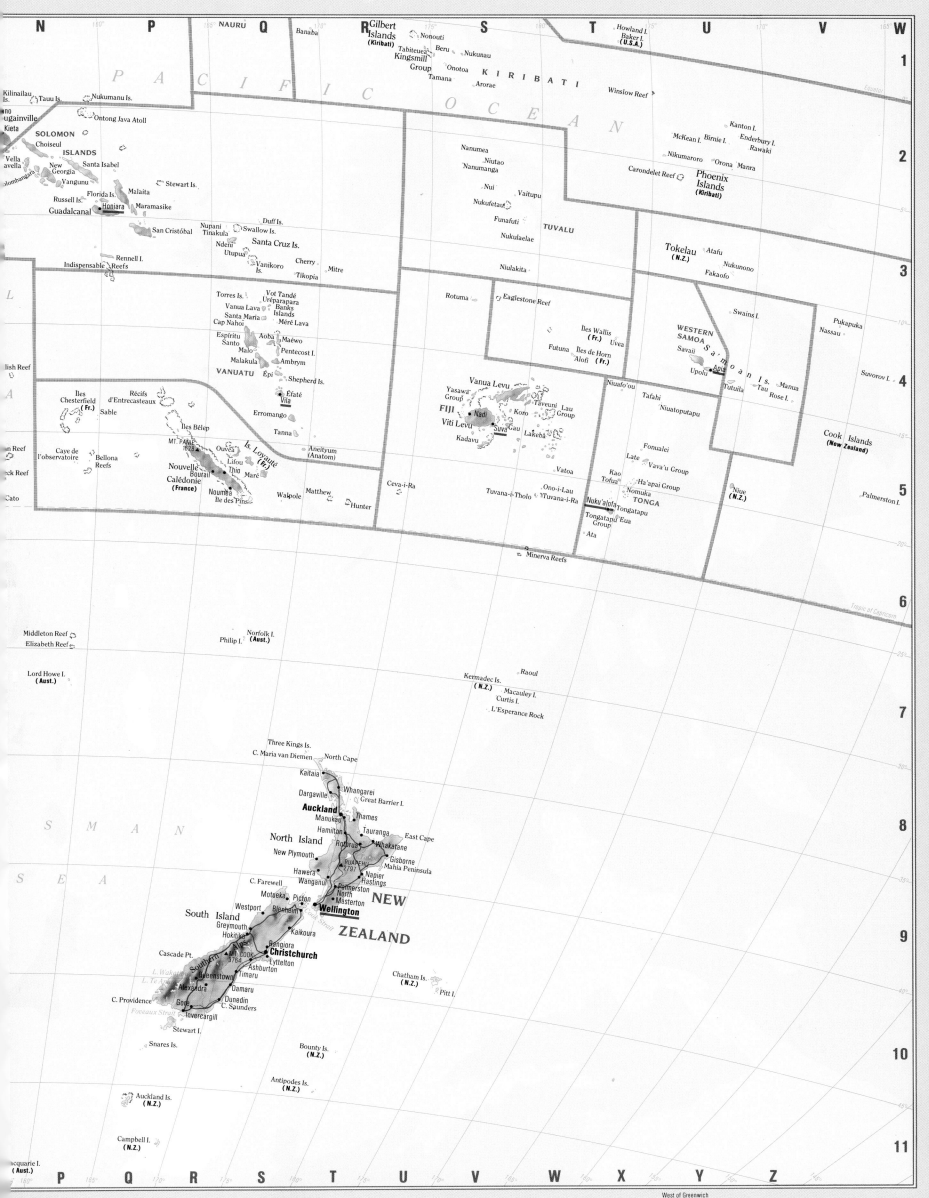

Miller Oblated Stereographic Projection

1:10,500,000

© COLOUR LIBRARY BOOKS

Designed and produced by E.S.R.

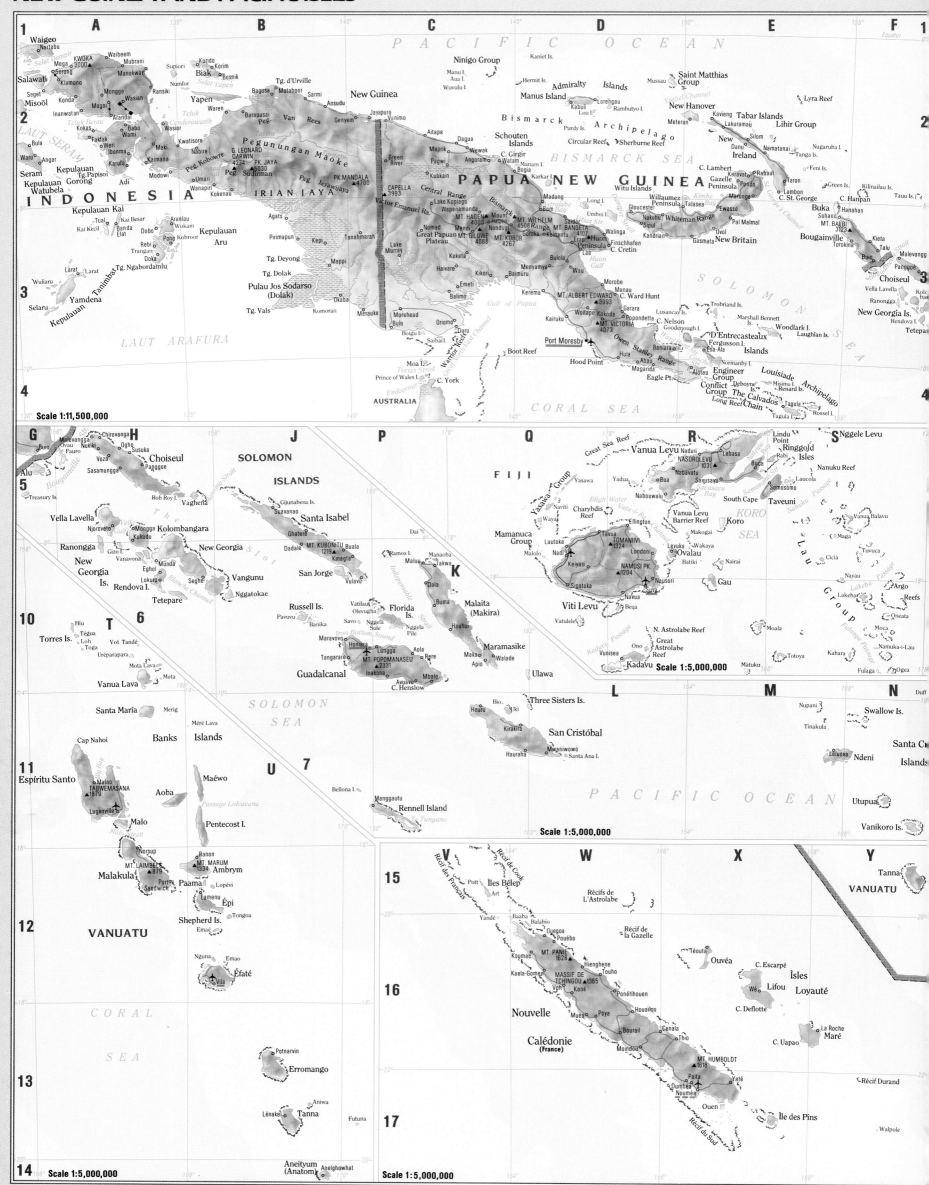

Miller Oblated Stereographic Projection

© COLOUR LIBRARY BOOKS

North Island

South Island

NEW

ZEALAND

Southern Alps

TASMAN SEA

PACIFIC OCEAN

Coromandel Peninsula

Auckland

Wellington

Christchurch

Dunedin

Stewart Island

Chatham Islands

Chatham I.

Pitt I.

East of Greenwich

1:4,500,000

0   50   100   150   200   250   300 KILOMETRES

0   50   100   150   200 STATUTE MILES

Designed and produced by E.S.R.

NORDOST

GREENLAND

ICELAND

Reykjavik

Denmark Strait

Jan Mayen (Norway)

Baffin Island

Baffin Bay

Davis Strait

Labrador

Newfoundland

Queen Elizabeth Islands

Parry Islands

Ellesmere Island

McClure Strait

Victoria Island

Prince of Wales Island

Somerset Island

Melville Pen.

Southampton Island

HUDSON BAY

Belcher Islands

Churchill

C A N A D A

Canadian Shield

BEAUFORT SEA

Banks Island

Amundsen Gulf

Great Bear Lake

Great Slave Lake

Yellowknife

Fort Smith

Fort McMurray

Edmonton

Calgary

Winnipeg

St. Paul

Minneapolis

Duluth

Mackenzie Mts.

Rocky Mountains

Cassiar Mountains

Coastal Mountains

Vancouver

Seattle

Portland

UNITED

Brooks Range

Alaska Range

Alaska

Seward Peninsula

RUSSIA

Chukchi Sea

Bering Sea

Gulf of Alaska

BERING SEA

Vancouver Island

Queen Charlotte Islands

Alexander Archipelago

MONTRÉAL

Ottawa

TORONTO

Québec

BOSTON

Halifax

Lambert Azimuthal Equal Area Projection

1:20,000,000

0 100 200 300 400 500 600 700 800 900 1000 KILOMETRES

0 100 200 300 400 500 600 STATUTE MILES

© COLOUR LIBRARY BOOKS

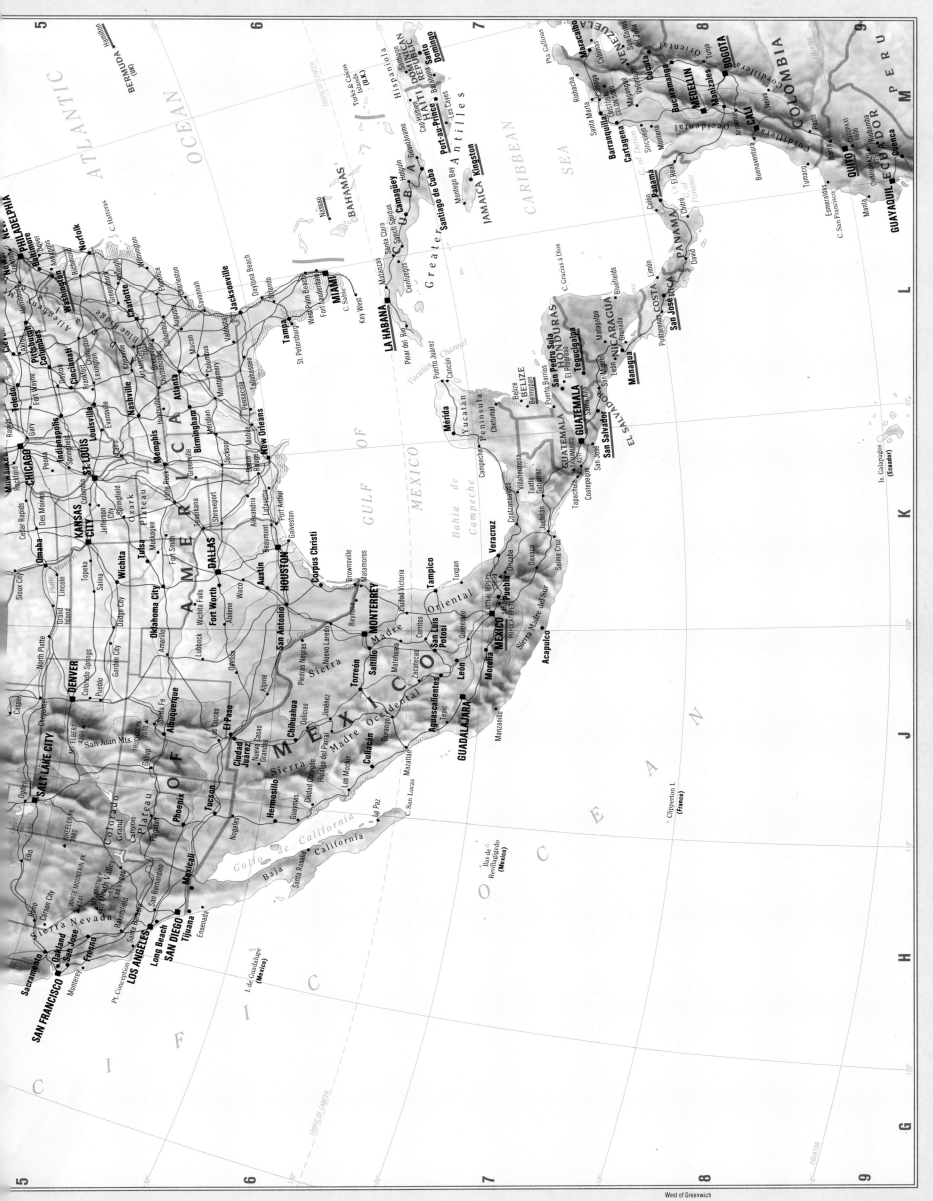

ALASKA

RUSSIA

Chukotskiy
Poluostrov

Arctic Circle

BEAUFORT
SEA

Chukchi
Sea

Pt. Hope
Point Hope

Icy C.
Pt.
Franklin
Wainwright
Pt. Barrow
Barrow

C. Krusenstern
C. Espenberg
Kotzebue

De Long Mts.

Brooks

Baird Mountains

Endicott

Range

Mts.

MT. MICHELSON
2699

Herschel I.

C. Kellett
Sachs Harb.

Amundsen

C. Dalhousie

C. Lisburne

C. Halkett

Martin Pt.
Kaktovik

Prudhoe Bay

Davidson Mts.

Richardson Mts.

Aklavik

Baillie I.

Richards I.

C. Lambton

INUVIK

Bering
Strait

C. Prince of
Wales

Seward
Peninsula

Nome

Norton Sound

Koyuk

ALASKA

(U.S.A.)

Ray Mts.

Old Crow

Inuvik
Tuktoyaktuk

Fort McPherson

Arctic Red River

Mackenzie
Bay

Melville

Parry
Pen.

Franklin B.

N. Cape
St. Lawrence I.

Gambell

BERING
SEA

Fairbanks

White Mts.

Fort Yukon

Circle

Eagle

Ogilvie Mts.

Dawson

Mackenzie

YUKON

Norman Wells

Fort Good Hope

Franklin Mts.

NC

N.O

Kuskokwim Mountains

Holy Cross

Nenana

Delta Junction

MT. HAYES
4216

MT. KIMBALL
3155

Tok

Northway
Junction

Keno Hill

Mayo

Pelly Mountains

Ross River

Carmacks

MT. SIR JAMES McBRIEN
2758

Kilbuck Mts.

Alaska

Range

MT. McKINLEY
6194
MT. FORAKER

Talkeetna

Talkeetna Mts.

Palmer

MT. MARCUS BAKER

MT. SANFORD
4950

MT. BONA
5005

McCarthy

Kluane
Cluane

Whitehorse

Carcross

St. Elias Mountains

Cassiar Mts.

MT. LOGAN
6050

Teslin

Watson Lake

MT. ST. ELIAS
5489

MT. STELLER

3239
Chugach Mts.

Cordova
Valdez

Bering Gl.

Copper Center

Gleenallen

Kenai
Peninsula
Kenai Mts.

Seward

Anchorage

Cook Inlet

Hinchinbrook

Kayak I.

Malaspina
GL.

Yakutat

Skagway

Haines

White
Pass

DEVILS PAW
2616

Dease Lake

Telegraph
Creek

Stikine Mts.

Toad River
2695
MT. ROOSEVELT

Summit
2743
CHURCHILL PK.

Sitton
Pass

Ware

Aleutian   Range

KATMAI VOL.
2047

MT. DENISON
2318

Pt. Bede

Seldovia

Kachemak B.

Knight
I.

Prince
William
Sound

GULF OF ALASKA

MT. FAIRWEATHER
4670

Chichagof
I.

Admiralty
I.

MT. RATZ
2336

Omineca Mts.

MT. ROOSEVELT

BRITI

MT. GLOTOF

Kodiak

Afognak I.

Shelikof Str.

Baranof
I.

Kruzof I.
Sitka

Kupreanof
I.

Telegraph
Creek

2755
SEVEN SISTERS

Sutwik I.

Kodiak I.

Alexander

Kulu
I.
Petersburg

Wrangell

Skeena Mts.

Hazelton

Seal C.

Chirikof I.

PACIFIC

OCEAN

C. Ommaney
Coronation I.

Archipelago

Prince
of
Wales
I.

Revillagigedo

Ketchikan

Dall I.

C. Muzon

Dixon Entrance

Prince Rupert

Terrace

BRITI

COLUM

Manson Creek

Fort St. Ja

Kemano
Kitimat

Bella Coola

MONARCH MT.
3533

MT. WADDINGTON
4042

Queen
Charlotte
Islands

Graham
I.

Porcher I.

Pitt
I.

Banks I.

Moresby
I.

Aristazabal I.

Hecate Strait

Skidegate

Bella Bella

Kunghit I.

C. St. James

Queen
Charlotte
Sound

Calvert I.

C. Scott

Port Hardy

Vancouver
Island

C. Cook

2163
VICTORIA PK.

Campb
Rive

Powell
Courtenay

Bipolar Oblique Conic Conformal Projection

Aa | Ab | Ac | Ad | Ae | Af | Ag

Attu I.
Attu
Near Islands
Agattu I.

Aleutian   Islands

Buldir I.

Kiska I.

Segula I.
Little Sitkin I.
Semisopochnoi I.

Rat Islands

Amchitka I.

Tanaga I.

Gt. Sitkin I.
KOROVIN VOL.
1533

Garefoul I.

Kanaga I.

Adak I.
Atka I.

Amatignak I.

Andreanof Islands

Seguam I.

Amlia I.

Yunaska I.

Islands of the
Four Mts.

St. Paul I.

Pribilof Is.

St. George I.

BERING

SEA

Bowers Bank

Nelson
Lagoon

Fort Randall

SHISHALDIN VOL.
7856

Unimak I.

Akutan I.

Dutch Harbor

TULIK VOL.

MAKUSHIN VOL.

Unalaska I.
7036
1253

Fox
Islands

Umnak I.

Alaska Peninsula

Meshik

VENIAMINOF
VOL.   2507

PAVLOF VOL.
2714

Akun I.

Krenitzin Is.

Sanak I.

Perryville

Kupreanof
Pt.

Shumagin
Is.

8

9

Aleutian Trench

1:12,500,000

© COLOUR LIBRARY BOOKS

1:9,000,000

0   100   200   300   400   500   600 KILOMETRES

0   50   100   150   200   250   300   350   400 STATUTE MILES

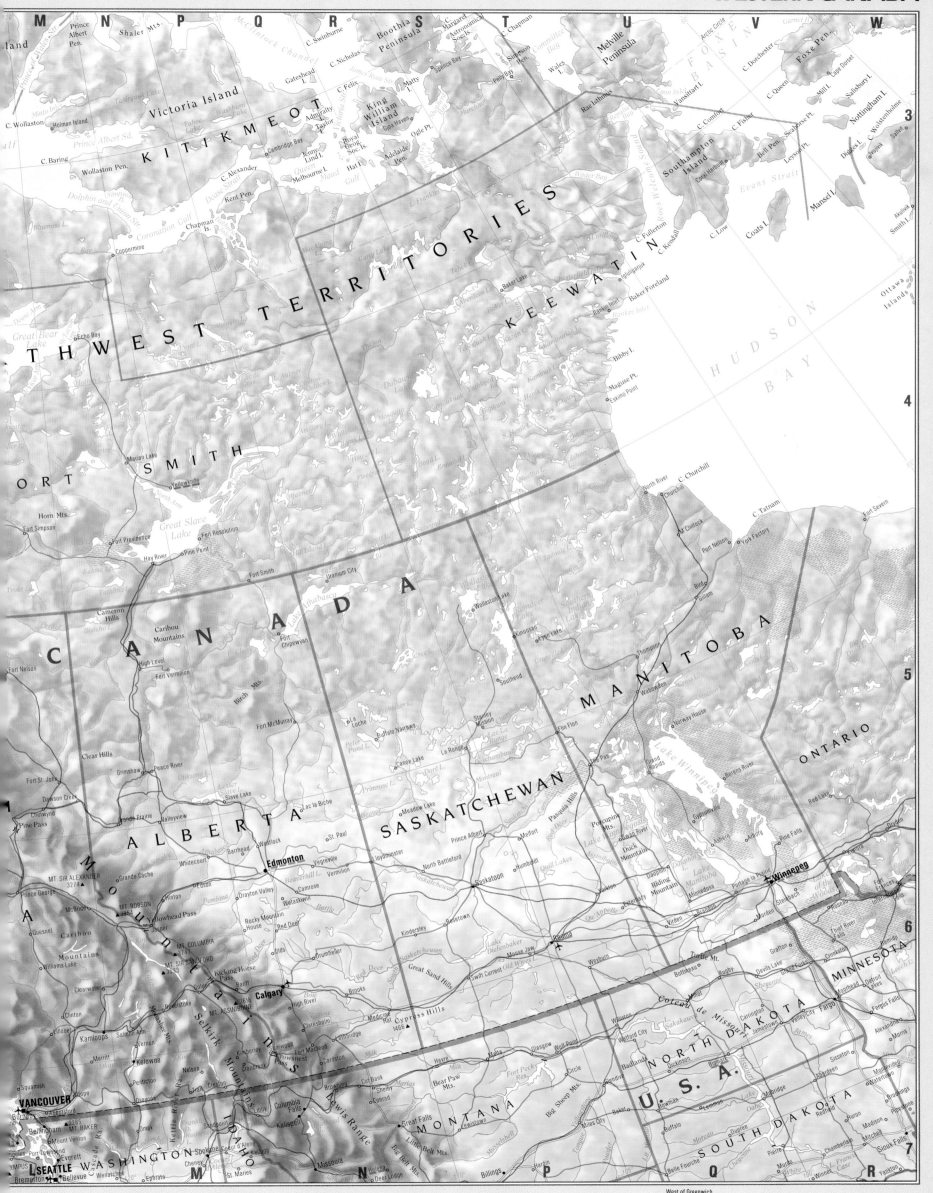

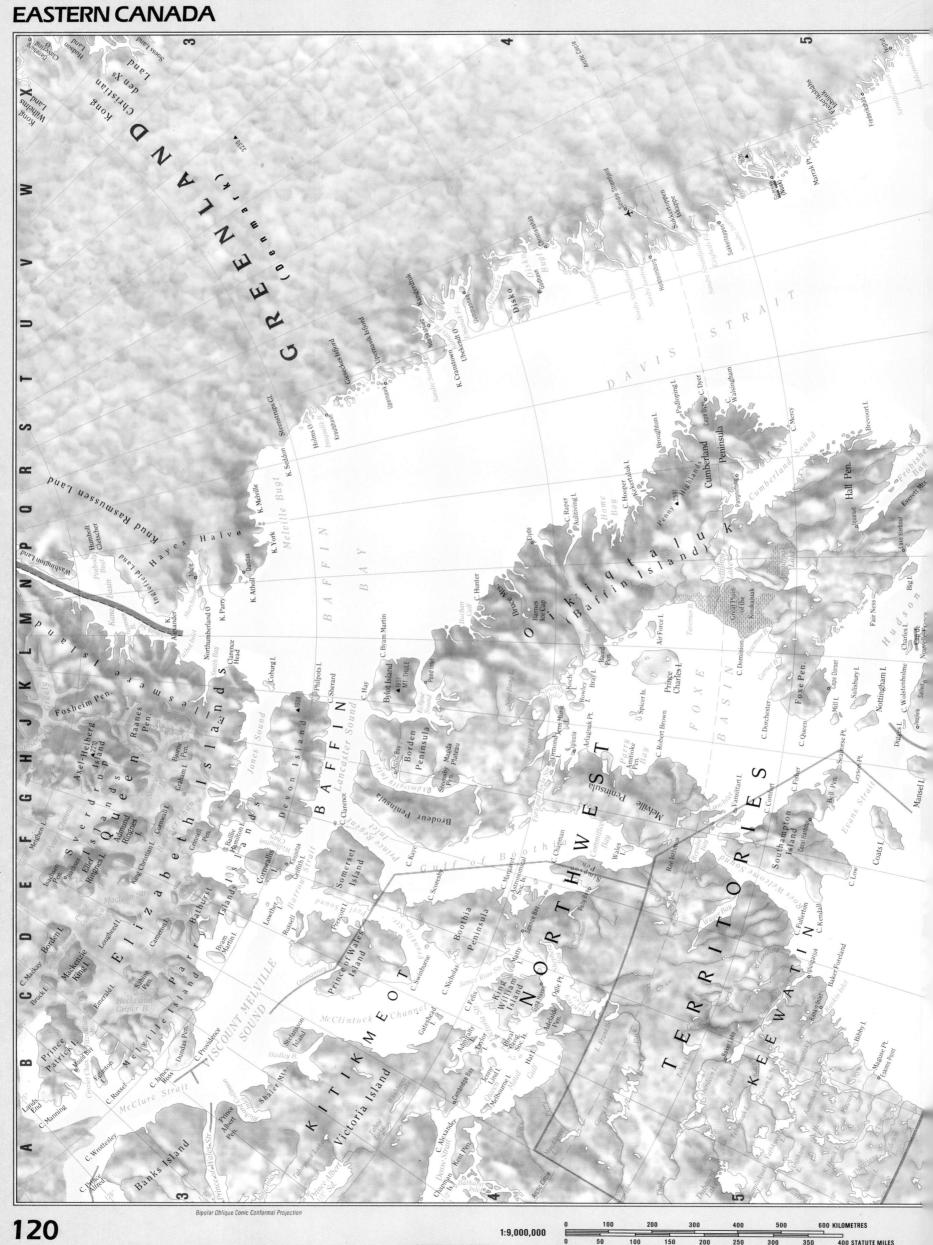

Bipolar Oblique Conic Conformal Projection

1:9,000,000

© COLOUR LIBRARY BOOKS

0	100	200	300	400	500	600 KILOMETRES
0	50	100	150	200	250	300	350	400 STATUTE MILES

West of Greenwich

Designed and produced by E.S.R.

121

Bipolar Oblique Conic Conformal Projection

1:5,000,000

© COLOUR LIBRARY BOOKS

Designed and produced by E.S.R.

West of Greenwich

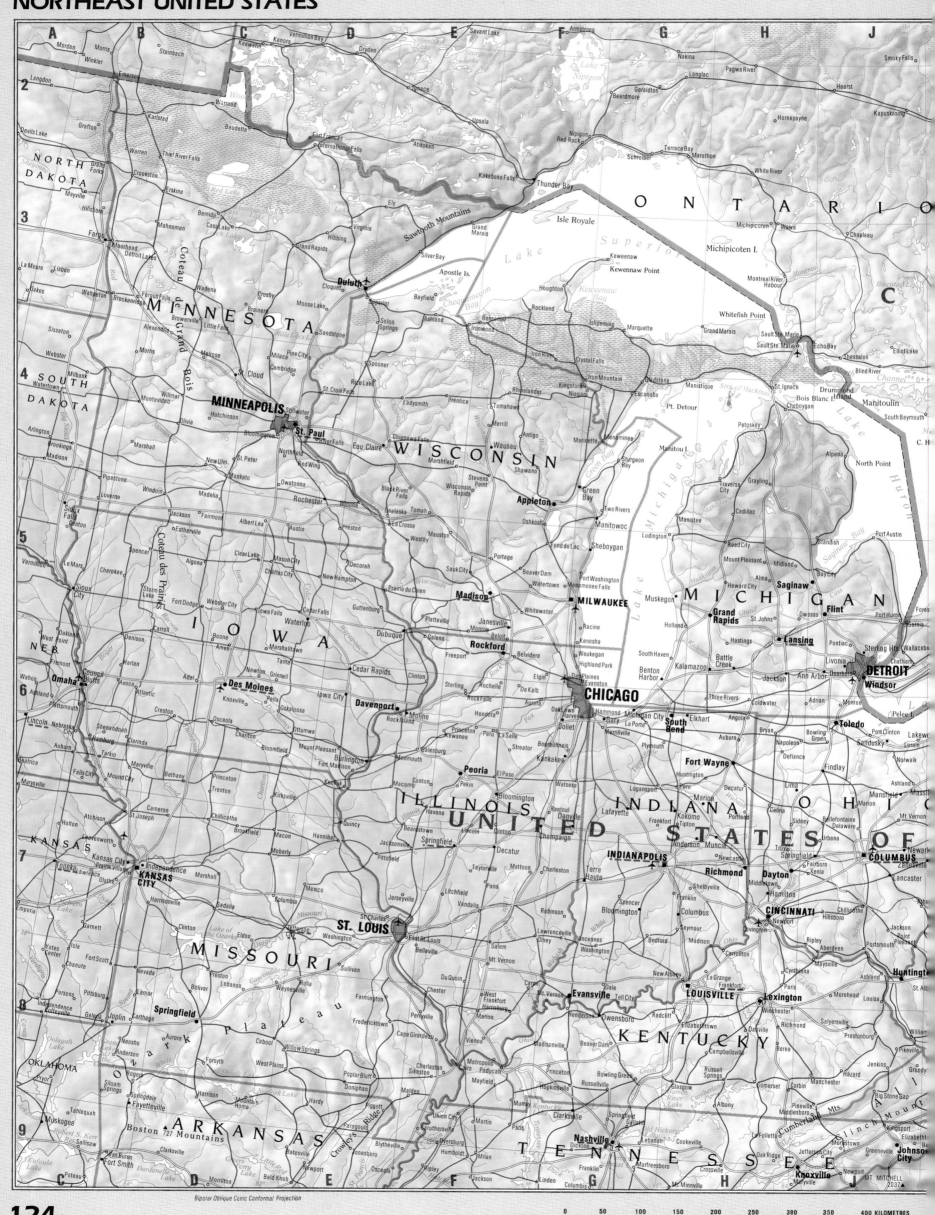

Bipolar Oblique Conic Conformal Projection

1:5,000,000

| 0 | 50 | 100 | 150 | 200 | 250 | 300 | 350 | 400 KILOMETRES |

| 0 | 50 | 100 | 150 | 200 | 250 STATUTE MILES |

© COLOUR LIBRARY BOOKS

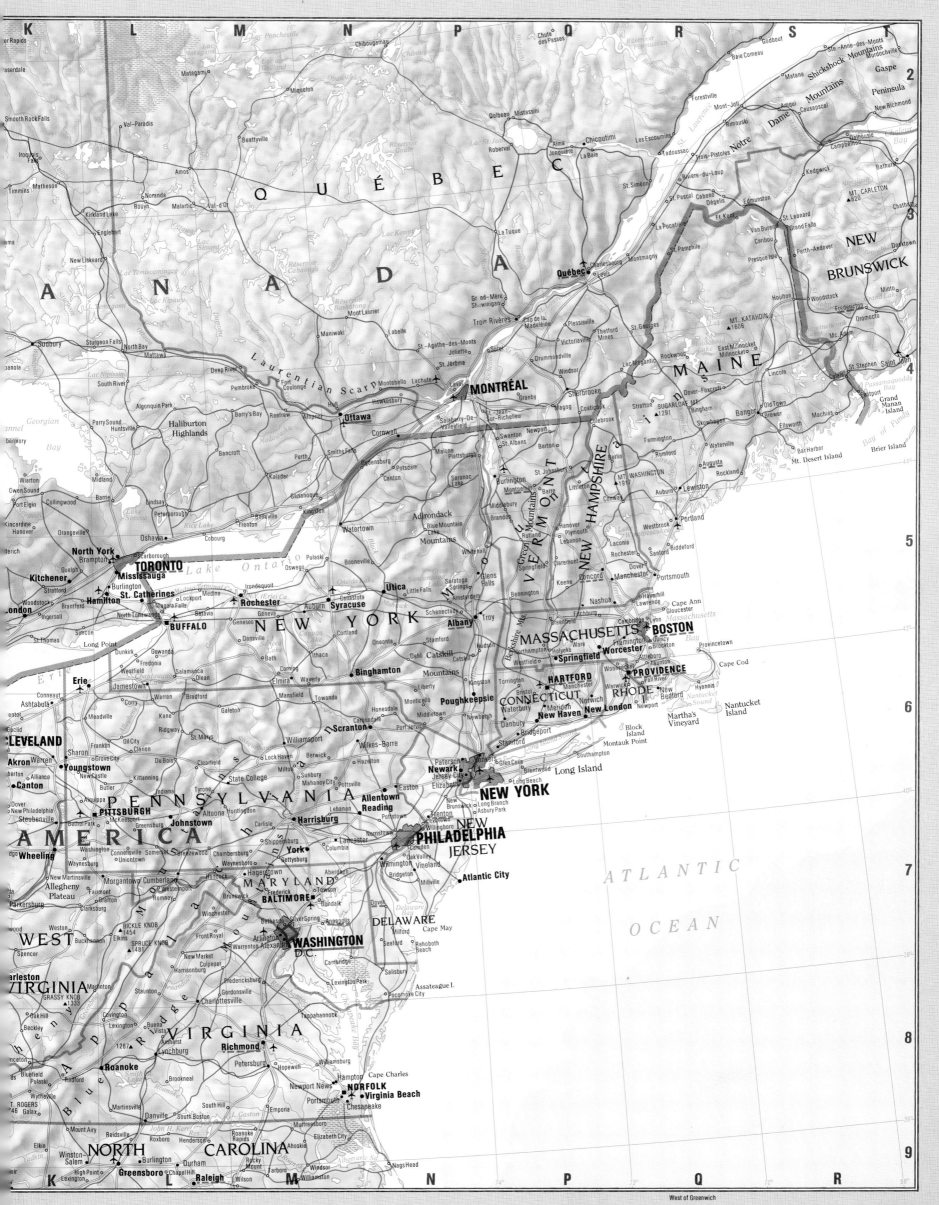

SOUTHWEST UNITED STATES

126

1:5,000,000

© COLOUR LIBRARY BOOKS

| 0 | 50 | 100 | 150 | 200 | 250 | 300 | 350 | 400 KILOMETRES |
| 0 | | 50 | 100 | | 150 | 200 | | 250 STATUTE MILES |

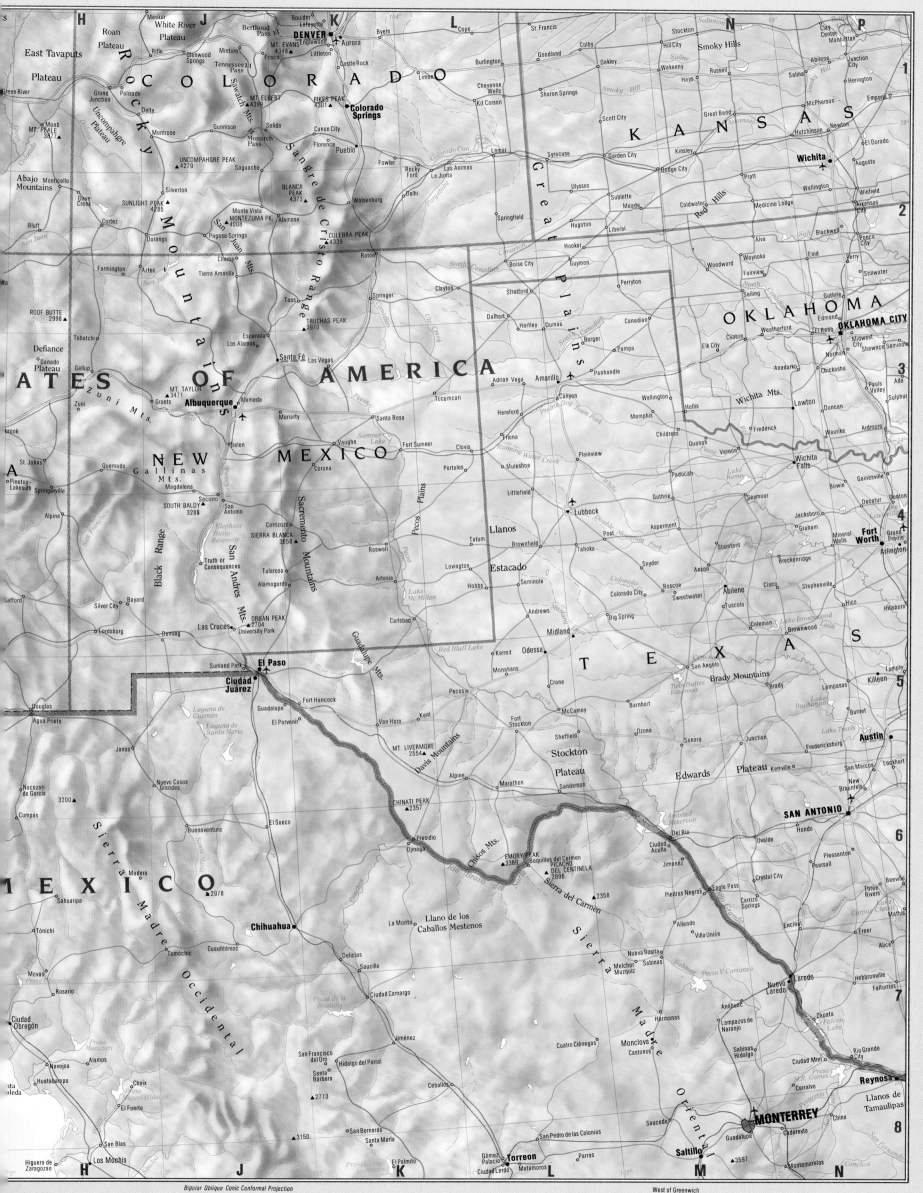

Designed and produced by E.S.R.

Bipolar Oblique Conic Conformal Projection

1:5,000,000

© COLOUR LIBRARY BOOKS

| 0 | 50 | 100 | 150 | 200 | 250 | 300 | 350 | 400 KILOMETRES |

| 0 | 50 | 100 | 150 | 200 | 250 STATUTE MILES |

Designed and produced by E.S.R.

West of Greenwich

Bipolar Oblique Conic Conformal Projection

1:6,500,000

© COLOUR LIBRARY BOOKS

| 0 | 50 | 100 | 150 | 200 | 250 | 300 | 350 | 400 KILOMETRES |

| 0 | 50 | 100 | 150 | 200 | 250 STATUTE MILES |

GULF OF MEXICO

BAHÍA DE CAMPECHE

West of Greenwich

Designed and produced by E.S.R.

CENTRAL AMERICA AND THE CARIBBEAN

GULF OF MEXICO

PACIFIC OCEAN

Tropic of Cancer

MEXICO

Yucatán

BELIZE

GUATEMALA

HONDURAS

EL SALVADOR

NICARAGUA

COSTA RICA

PANAMA

CUBA

JAMAICA

U.S.A.

FLORIDA

MIAMI

LA HABANA

Camagüey

Kingston

Little Bahama Bank

Grand Bahama

Great Abaco

Eleuthera

Andros

New Providence

Nassau

Cayman Trench

Grand Cayman (U.K.)

Little Cayman

Cayman Brac

Mérida

San Pedro Sula

GUATEMALA

San Salvador

Tegucigalpa

Managua

San José

Panamá

Golfo de Honduras

Islas de la Bahía

Mosquitia

Costa de Mosquitos

Lago de Nicaragua

Golfo de Panamá

Península de Azuero

Golfo del Darién

Serranilla Bank (Col.)

Bajo Nuevo (Col.)

Quita Sueño Bank (Col.)

Serrana Bank (U.S.A. and Col.)

I. de Providencia (Col.)

Casyo Roncador (Col.)

I. de San Andrés (Col.)

Is. del Maíz (Corn Is.) (Nic. and U.S.A.)

Swan Is. (Hond.)

Pedro Cays

CAR

132

Bipolar Oblique Conic Conformal Projection

1:7,000,000

© COLOUR LIBRARY BOOKS

| 0 | 50 | 100 | 150 | 200 | 250 | 300 | 350 | 400 KILOMETRES |

| 0 | 50 | 100 | 150 | 200 | 250 STATUTE MILES |

ATLANTIC

OCEAN

Tropic of Cancer

BAHAMAS

Cat I.
Hawknest Pt.
Conception I.
San Salvador
(Watling I.)
Rum Cay
Long I.
Clarence Town
Samana Cray
Crooked I.
South Pt.
Snub Corner
Acklins I.
Abraham's Bay
Mayaguana I.
Hogsty Reef
Little Inagua I.
Kew
Caicos Is. (U.K.)
Turks I. (U.K.)
Salt Cay
Great Inagua
Matthew Town

Cabo Lucrecia
Moa
Baracoa
Cabo Maisí
Guantánamo
Santiago de Cuba

Windward Passage

HAITI
Île de la Tortue
Port-de-Paix
Cap-Haïtien
Monte Cristi
C. Isabela
Puerto Plata
Ba. de Escocesa
C. Samaná
Gonaïves
Santiago
San Francisco de Macoris
La Vega
Ba. de Samaná
Sabana de la Mar
Golfe de la Gonâve
Île de la Gonâve
Hinche
Cordillera
PICO DUARTE 3175
Central
St Marc
San Juan
C. Engaño
C. Dame Marie
Jérémie
PORT-AU-PRINCE
Dame Marie
Massif de la Hotte 2347
LA SELLE 2660
SANTO DOMINGO
San Pedros de Macoris
Higüey
La Romana
Navassa I. (U.S.A.)
Les Cayes
Jacmel
Lago Enriquillo
Barahona
Baní
DOMINICAN REPUBLIC
I. Saona
Pedernales
Isla Beata
Cabo Beata

Antilles

San Juan
Aguadilla
Arecibo
SAN JUAN
Mayagüez
CERRO DE PUNTA 1338
Bayamon
Caguas
Ponce
Vieques
Puerto Rico (U.S.A.)
I. Mona
C. Rojo

Virgin Islands
St. Thomas (U.S.A.)
Charlotte Amalie
St. John (U.S.A.)
Road Town
Tortola (U.K.)
Virgin Gorda (U.K.)
Anegada (U.K.)
Frederiksted
St. Croix (U.S.A.)

Leeward Islands

Anguilla (U.K.)
Saint Martin (Fr.)
Sint Maarten (Neth.)
Saba (Neth.)
St Eustatius (Neth.)
Barbuda
ANTIGUA AND BARBUDA
Antigua St. John's
ST. KITTS-NEVIS
Basseterre
Montserrat (U.K.)
Plymouth

Lesser Antilles

Guadeloupe (France)
La Désirade
Basse Terre
Pointe-à-Pitre
Marie Galante (France)
Îles des Saintes
DOMINICA
Roseau
Marigot

Martinique (France)
Fort-de-France
St. Lucia Channel
ST. LUCIA
Castries
St. Vincent Passage
Kingstown
ST. VINCENT
BARBADOS
Bridgetown
The Grenadines
Carriacou
GRENADA
St. George's

I. de Aves (Bird I.) (Ven.)

CARIBBEAN SEA

Lesser Antilles

Punta Gallinas
Oranjestad
Aruba (Neth.)
Curaçao (Neth.)
Bonaire (Neth.)
Willemstad
Kralendijk
Is. Las Aves (Ven.)
Pto. Estrella
Península de Guajira
I. Blanquilla (Ven.)
Carrizal
Penín. Paraguaná
Pueblo Nuevo
Is. Los Roques (Ven.)
I. Orchila (Ven.)
Los Testigos (Ven.)
Tobago
Scarborough
Riohacha
Golfo de Venezuela
Punto Fijo
Amuay
Castilletes
Maicao
Coro
Mirimire
Isla de Margarita (Ven.)
La Asunción
Porlamar
TRINIDAD AND TOBAGO
Port of Spain
Toco
Trinidad
Santa Marta
Cabo de la Aguja
San Rafael
Capatárida
San Luis
I. La Tortuga (Ven.)
arranquilla
Ciénaga
Altagracia
Maiquetía
CARACAS
Guarenas
Cabo Codera
Cumaná
Carúpano
Penín. de Paria
Río Caribe
Guiria
Golfo de Paria
Arima
Soledad
Maracaibo
Sta. Rita
Churuguara
Pto. Cabello
Los Teques
Pto. La Cruz
Guanoco
Pt. Fortin
San Fernando
Galeota Pt.
Cartagena
Sabanalarga
Cabimas
San Felipe
Valencia
Maracay
Villa de Cura
Barcelona
2660
Maturín
Turbaco
Valledupar
Ciudad Ojeda
Carora
Lago de Valencia
San Juan de los Morros
San Mateo
Caripito
Robles la Paz
Machiques
Lagunillas
Yaritagua
Cordillera de la Costa
Anaco
Aragua de Barcelona
Caripe
Calamar
Barquisimeto
Tinaco
San Carlos
Ortiz
El Banco
Mompos
La Ceiba
Acarigua
Pariaguán
Mata Negra
Tucupita
Sincelejo
Since
El Tocuyo
Zaraza
El Tigre
Valera
Guanare
Las Mercedes
Valle de la Pascua
Barrancas
Carmen
Sierra de Perijá
Trujillo
Nueva Florida
Boca Grande
Plato
Barranca
Bobures
San Carlos del Zulia
Mérida
Cabruta
Boca del Pao
Ciudad Bolívar
José de Amacuro
Magangué
Simití
El Vigía
Cordillera de Mérida
Barinas
Calabozo
Ciudad Guayana
Pto. Ordaz
Upata
Serranía de Imataca
Ocaña
PICO BOLÍVAR 5007
San Silvestre
GUYANA
ALTO DE TAMAR 2350
Cúcuta
El Fría
Mapire
Ciudad Piar
El Callao
Port Kaituma
Bucaramanga
Pamplona
San Cristóbal
Mantecal
Cerro Bolívar
Tumeremo
El Dorado
COLOMBIA
EL VIEJO 4100
Rubio
San Antonio de Caparo
Guasdualito
San Fernando de Apure
CERRO MATO 1863
CERRO BOLÍVAR 802
San Pedro de las Bocas
Barrancabermeja
Piedecuesta
Arauca
La Urbana
Las Trincheras
La Paragua
Kartuni
Banadia
Santa María
Elorza

VENEZUELA

West of Greenwich

133

Designed and produced by E.S.R.

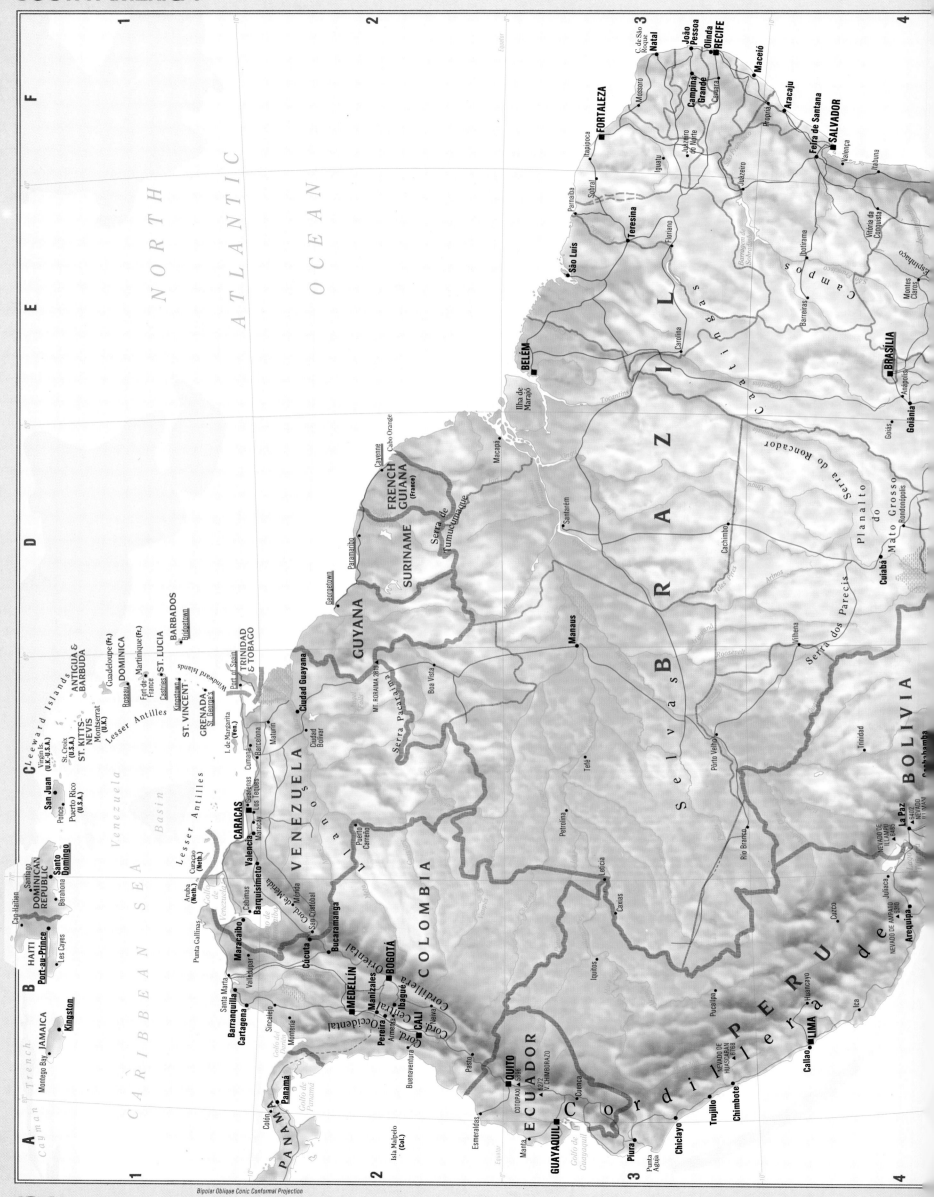

Bipolar Oblique Conic Conformal Projection

1:16,000,000

© COLOUR LIBRARY BOOKS

| 0 | 100 | 200 | 300 | 400 | 500 | 600 | 700 | 800 KILOMETRES |

| 0 | 100 | 200 | 300 | 400 | 500 STATUTE MILES |

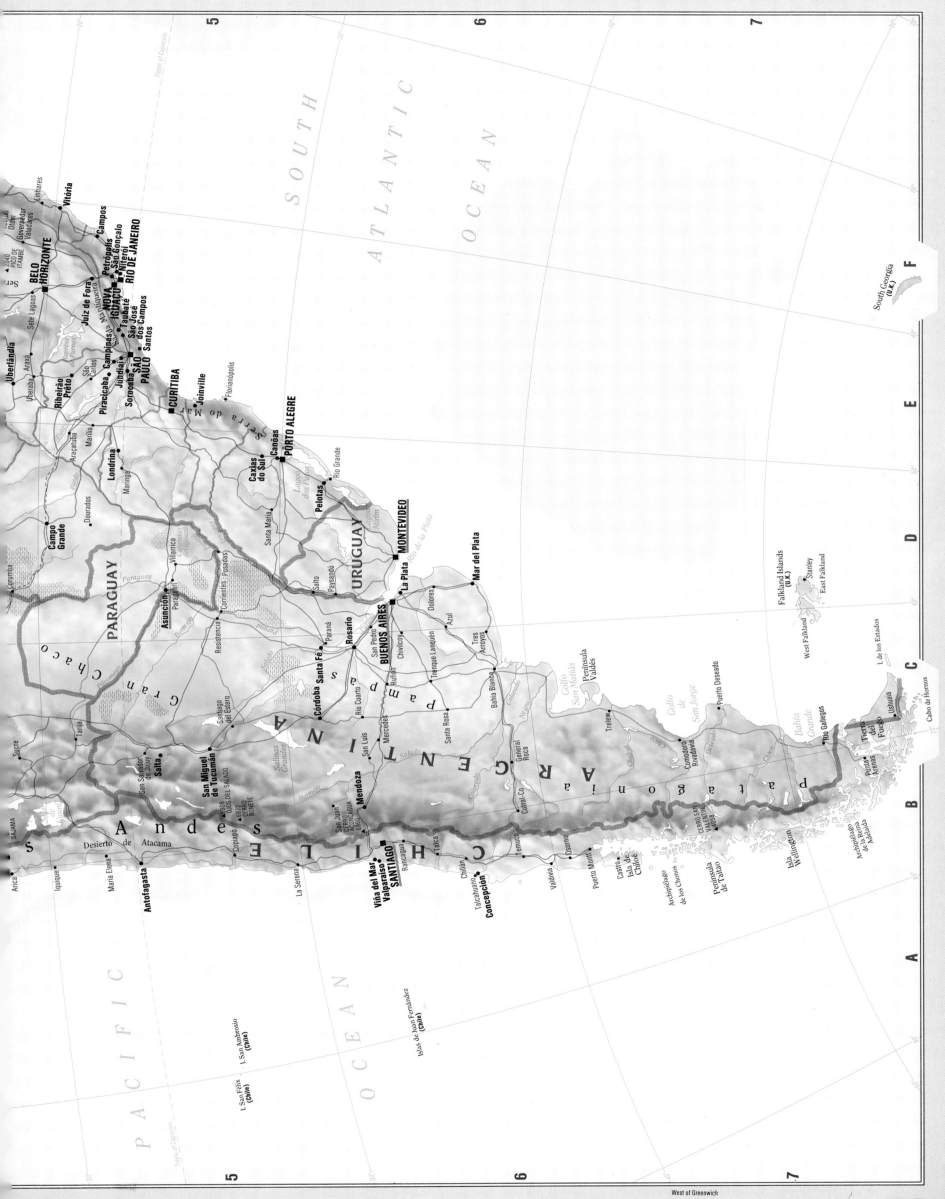

Designed and produced by E.S.R.

Bipolar Oblique Conic Conformal Projection

1:11,000,000

© COLOUR LIBRARY BOOKS

NORTH ATLANTIC OCEAN

SURINAME

FRENCH GUIANA (France)

AMAPÁ

P A R Á

B R A Z I L

Mato Grosso

MATO GROSSO DO SUL

MARANHÃO

Teresina

PIAUÍ

CEARÁ

FORTALEZA

RIO GRANDE DO NORTE

Natal

PARAÍBA

João Pessoa

Campina Grande

Olinda

RECIFE

Jaboatão

PERNAMBUCO

ALAGOAS

Maceió

SERGIPE

Aracaju

BAHIA

Feira de Santana

SALVADOR

GOIÁS

DISTRITO FEDERAL

BRASÍLIA

Goiânia

Cuiabá

MINAS GERAIS

Uberlândia

ESPÍRITO SANTO

BELÉM

São Luís

SOUTHERN SOUTH AMERICA

Bipolar Oblique Conic Conformal Projection

1:11,000,000

| 0 | 100 | 200 | 300 | 400 | 500 | 600 | 700 | 800 KILOMETRES |

| 0 | 100 | 200 | 300 | 400 | 500 STATUTE MILES |

© COLOUR LIBRARY BOOKS

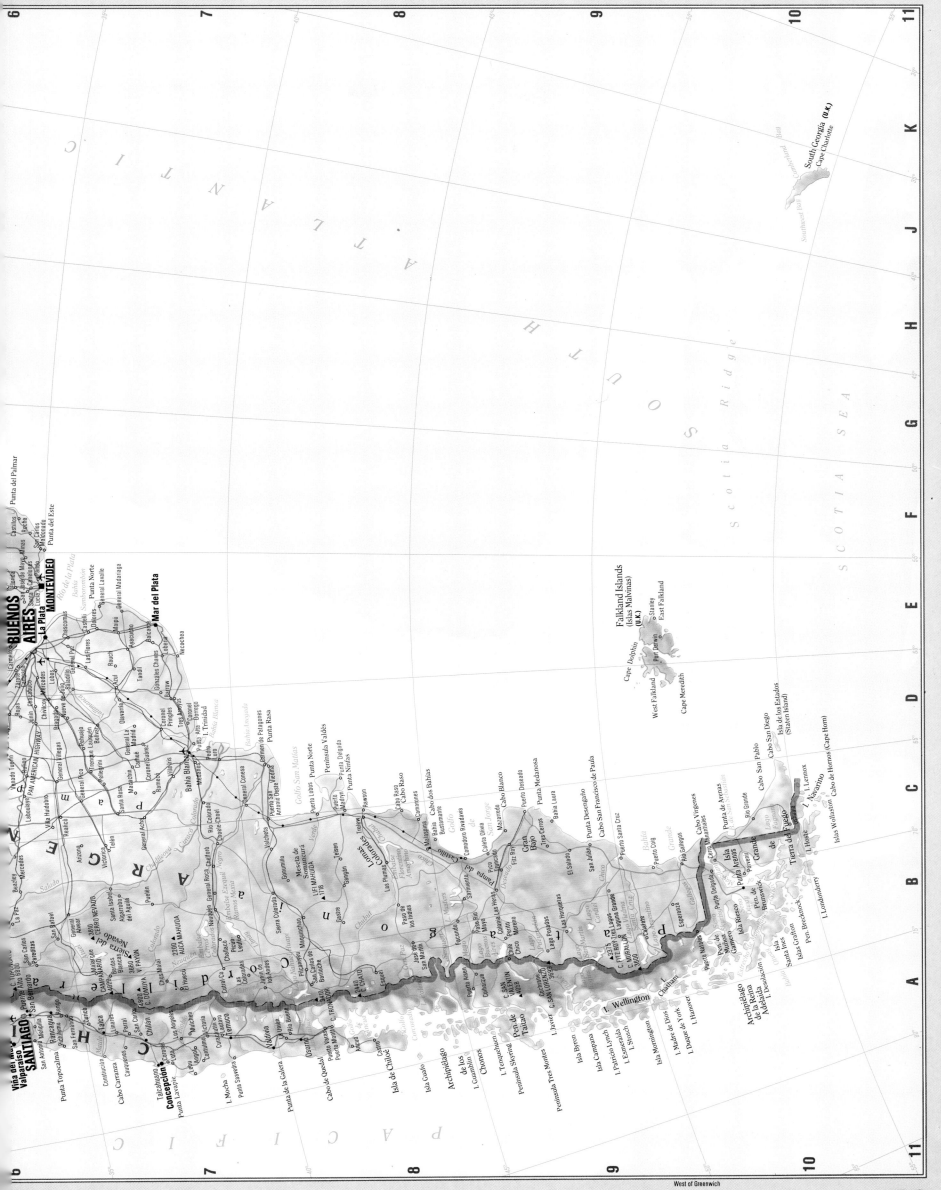

Polar Stereographic Projection

© COLOUR LIBRARY BOOKS

Scale 1:30,000,000 (Approx.)

| 0 | 250 | 500 | 750 | 1000 | 1250 | 1500 KILOMETRES |

| 0 | 250 | 500 | 750 | 1000 STATUTE MILES |

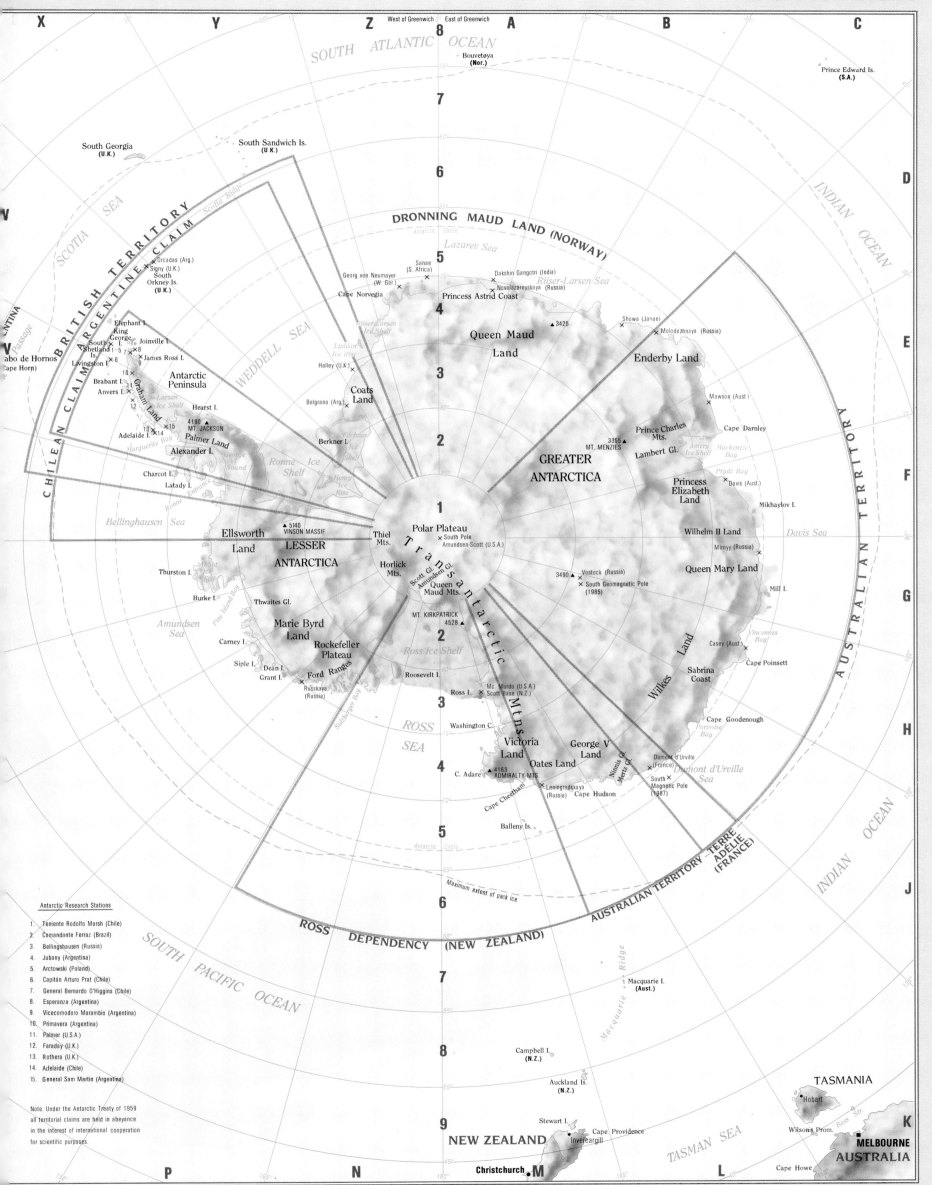

SOUTH ATLANTIC OCEAN

Bouvetøya
(Nor.)

Prince Edward Is.
(S.A.)

INDIAN OCEAN

South Georgia
(U.K.)

South Sandwich Is.
(U.K.)

DRONNING MAUD LAND (NORWAY)

Lazarev Sea

Dakshin Gangotri (India)
Sanae
(S. Africa)
Novolazarevskaya (Russia)
Georg von Neumayer (W. Ger.)

Riiser-Larsen Sea

Showa (Japan)

SCOTIA SEA

Scotia Ridge

Cape Norvegia

Princess Astrid Coast

Molodezhnaya (Russia)

Queen Maud
Land

▲ 3425

Enderby Land

BRITISH TERRITORY

ARGENTINE CLAIM

Orcadas (Arg.)
Signy (U.K.)
South Orkney Is.
(U.K.)

Mawson (Aust.)

Elephant I.
King
George I.
South Shetland 1–5
Is.
Joinville I.
James Ross I.
Livingston I.

Halley (U.K.)

Coats
Land

Prince Charles
Mts.

Cape Darnley

ARGENTINA

Antarctic
Peninsula

Brabant I.
Anvers I.

Graham Land

Belgrano (Arg.)

Berkner I.

MT. MENZIES
3355 ▲

Lambert Gl.

Amery
Ice Shelf

Mackenzie
Bay

GREATER
ANTARCTICA

cabo de Hornos
(Cape Horn)

WEDDELL SEA

Lyddan
Ice Rise

Filchner
Ice Shelf

Princess
Elizabeth
Land

Davis (Aust.)

Prydz Bay

Drake Passage

CHILEAN CLAIMS

Adelaide I.

4190 ▲
MT. JACKSON

Hearst I.

Larsen
Ice Shelf

Palmer Land

Marguerite Bay

Alexander I.

George VI
Sound

Ronne Ice Shelf

Henry
Ice Rise

Berkner I.

Wilhelm II Land

Mikhaylov I.

Davis Sea

Charcot I.

Latady I.

Ronne Entrance

Mirnyy (Russia)

Bellingshausen Sea

▲ 5140
VINSON MASSIF

Thiel
Mts.

Polar Plateau
× South Pole
Amundsen-Scott (U.S.A.)

Vostock (Russia)
3490 ▲
× South Geomagnetic Pole
(1985)

Queen Mary Land

Ellsworth
Land

LESSER
ANTARCTICA

Transantarctic

Horlick
Mts.

Scott Gl.
Amundsen Gl.
Queen
Maud Mts.

Mill I.

Thurston I.

Larot
Ice Shelf

Burke I.

Thwaites Gl.

MT. KIRKPATRICK
4528 ▲

Wilkes
Land

Sabrina
Coast

Vincennes
Bay

Casey (Aust.)

Cape Poinsett

Amundsen
Sea

Marie Byrd
Land

Rockefeller
Plateau

Ross Ice Shelf

Mts.

Carney I.

Pine Island Bay

Cape Goodenough

Porpoise
Bay

Siple I.
Grant I.
Dean I.

Ford Ranges

Russkaya
(Russia)

Roosevelt I.

Mc Murdo (U.S.A.)
Scott Base (N.Z.)

George V
Land

Nimrod Gl.
Mertz Gl.

Dumont d'Urville
(France)

Dumont d'Urville
Sea

Sulzberger Bay

Ross I.

Washington C.

Victoria
Land

Oates Land

South
Magnetic Pole
(1987)

ROSS
SEA

4163 ▲
C. Adare ADMIRALTY MTS.

Leningradskaya
(Russia)
Cape Hudson

TERRE
ADELIE
(FRANCE)

Cape Cheetham

AUSTRALIAN TERRITORY

Balleny Is.

Antarctic Circle

Maximum extent of pack ice

ROSS DEPENDENCY (NEW ZEALAND)

SOUTH PACIFIC OCEAN

Macquarie I.
(Aust.)

Macquarie Ridge

INDIAN OCEAN

Campbell I.
(N.Z.)

Auckland Is.
(N.Z.)

TASMANIA

Hobart

TASMAN SEA

Bass Str.

Wilsons Prom.

MELBOURNE
AUSTRALIA

Stewart I.
Cape Providence
Invercargill

NEW ZEALAND

Christchurch

Cape Howe

Polar Stereographic Projection

A B C D E F

West of Greenwich | East of Greenwich

1

Svalbard (Norway)

Zemlya Frantsa-Iosifa (U.S.S.R.)

Severnaya Zemlya

Novosibirskiye Ostrova

GREENLAND (Denmark)

Kolmska Nizmenn

Karskoye More

Novaya Zemlya

More Laptevykh

Lyakhovkiye Ostrova

Jan Mayen (Norway)

Barentsevo More

Nordkapp

Poluostrov Yamal

Gydanskiy Poluostrov

Gory Byrranga

Ozero Taymyr

Verkhoyanskiy

Khrebet Cherskogo

2

Norwegian Sea

Lappland

Plato Putorana

Khrebet

Arctic Circle

Denmark Strait

ICELAND

Reykjavik

SWEDEN

FINLAND

Beloye More

Uralskiy Khrebet

Pechora

Sredne Sibirskoye Ploskogor'ye

Vitim

More Laptevykh

Føroyar (Denmark)

Shetland Is. (U.K.)

NORWAY

Oslo Stockholm

Helsingfors

Tallinn

ESTONIA

ST. PETERSBURG

Ozero Ladozhskoye

Zapadno Sibirskaya Ravnina

RUSSIA

Okhotskoye More

UNITED KINGDOM

North Sea

Dublin

IRELAND

LONDON

Amsterdam
s'Gravenhage

DENMARK
København

NETH.

Berlin

POLAND
Warszawa

LATVIA
Riga

LITH.
Vilnius

Minsk

BELARUS

Kyyiv (Kiev)

Moskva

Kuybyshevskoye Vodokhranilishche

Prikaspiyskaya Nizmennost'

Kirgiz Step'

Aralskoye

Ozero Baykal

Altai

Sakhalin

Kurilskiye Ostrova

3

NORTH ATLANTIC OCEAN

Acores (Port.)

Madeira (Port.)

PORTUGAL
Lisboa

Madrid
SPAIN

FRANCE
PARIS
Bern

BEL.
Bruxelles
LUX.

GERMANY
Praha
CZECH REP.

SWITZ.
Wien
AUST.

A l p s

AND.

SLOVAK REP.
Bratislava
Budapest
HUNG.

SLOV.
CROAT.
BOS.-HERZ.
Beograd
YUGO.

MOLDOVA
Chisinău (Kishinev)

ROM.
Bucuresti

UKRAINE

Volga

Don

GEORGIA
T'bilisi

El'brus

ARMENIA
Yerevan

AZER.
Baku

Caspian Sea

Aral'skoye

KAZAKHSTAN

Tashkent
Kyzylkum
UZBEKISTAN

Karakumy

Alma-Ata
Bishkek
KYRGYZSTAN

Ozero Balkhash

Tarim Pendi

Tyan Shan

MONGOLIA

Gobi

Kunlun Shan

Ulaanbaatar

N. KOREA
Pyongyang

Sea of Japan

JAPAN

Roma

Tirane

ALB.

MACE.

Sofiya
BULG.

GREECE
Athinai

Ankara
TURKEY

Levkosia
CYPRUS

Black Sea

LEB.
Bayrut
Dimashq

SYRIA

Baghdad
IRAQ

Tehrān

Kūhhā ye Zagros

IRAN

Ashgabat
TURKMENISTAN

Dushanbe
TAJIK

Kābul
AFGHANISTAN

Hindu Kush

Islamabad

Xizang Gaoyuan

Taklimakan Shamo

Tian Shan

154

CHINA

BEIJING

TIANJIN

Huang He

S. KOREA
SŎUL

SHANGHAI

TŌKYŌ

4

CAPE VERDE
Praia

Madeira (Port.)

MOROCCO
Rabat

Ilas Canarias (Sp.)

El Djazair
TUNISIA
Tunis
Tarābulus

Valletta
MALTA

Mediterranean Sea

Al Aaiún
WESTERN SAHARA

Atlas Mountains

ALGERIA

Hoggar

LIBYA

Tibesti

EGYPT

EL QÂHIRA
-133

Yerushalayim
Amman
JOR.
ISRAEL

Al Kuwayt
KUW.
Al Manamah
BAH.
Ar Riyāḍ
Ad Dawhah
QAT.
Abu Zabi
U.A.E.

SAUDI ARABIA

Masqat

OMAN

Arabian Sea

PAKISTAN
Karachi

Thar Desert

INDIA

New Delhi
DELHI

NEPAL
Kathmandu

Thimphu
BHU.

EVEREST

Gang

BANG.
Dhaka

CALCUTTA

MYANMAR

Hanoi

T'ai-pei
TAIWAN

HONG KONG (U.K.)

Marianas Is.

Guam (U.S.A.)

WESTERN SAHARA

MAURITANIA
Nouakchott

MALI
Bamako

NIGER
Niamey

CHAD
N'djaména

El Khartum

SUDAN

ERITREA

San'a
YEMEN

Asmera

Suqutrā (S. Yem.)

Lakshadweep (India)

BOMBAY

Deccan

MADRAS

Bay of Bengal

Yangon

Víangchan
LAOS

THAI-LAND
KRUNG THEP

CAM.
Phnom Penh

VIETNAM

MANILA

PHILIPPINES

Luzon

Mindanao

Micronesia

Caroline Islands

CAPE VERDE
Praia

Dakar
SEN.
THE GAMBIA
Banjul

Bissau
GUINEA-BISSAU

Conakry
GUINEA

Freetown
SIERRA LEONE

Monrovia
LIBERIA

IVORY COAST

Ouagadougou
BUR. FASO

GHANA
Accra

TOGO
Lomé

Porto Novo
BENIN

Yamoussoukro

Lagos
NIGERIA

CENTRAL AFRICAN REP.
Bangui

CAMEROON
Yaoundé

Malabo
EQ. GUINEA
Libreville

SÃO TOMÉ AND PRÍNCIPE

GABON

CONGO
Brazzaville

Kinshasa
Luanda

ZAIRE

Congo Basin

UGANDA
Kampala

RW.
Kigali
BU.
Bujumbura

KENYA
Nairobi

Dodoma
TANZANIA

KILIMANJARO
5895

Victoria

SEYCHELLES

Colombo
SRI LANKA

MALDIVES

Malé

Andaman Islands (India)

Kuala Lumpur
MALAYSIA

SINGAPORE

Bandar Seri Begawan
BRU.

Borneo

Sulawesi

Maluku

PAPUA NEW GUINEA

Port More

5

Ascension (U.K.)

St. Helena (U.K.)

Ilha da Trindade (Brazil)

Tropic of Capricorn

SOUTH ATLANTIC OCEAN

ANGOLA

ZAMBIA
Lusaka

Harare
ZIMBABWE

NAMIBIA
Windhoek

BOTSWANA
Gaborone

Kalahari

SOUTH AFRICA
Pretoria

Maseru
LESOTHO

Mbabane
SWAZILAND

Maputo

Orange

Lilongwe
MALAWI

MOZAMBIQUE

Mozambique Channel

COMOROS
Moroni

MADAGASCAR
Antananarivo

Réunion (Fr.)

MAURITIUS
Port Louis

INDIAN OCEAN

East Indies

Sumatera

Jawa
JAKARTA

Java Trench

INDONESIA

Timor

Laut Timor

Laut Arafura

Gt. Barrier Reef

Coral Sea

AUSTRALIA

L. Eyre

Gt. Dividing Range

Darling

Gt. Victoria Desert

C. Leeuwin

Cape of Good Hope

Tristan da Cunha (U.K.)

Gough I. (U.K.)

Canberra

6

South Sandwich Is. (U.K.)

Prince Edward Is. (S.A.)

Iles Crozet (Fr.)

Ile Kerguelen (Fr.)

Heard I. (Aus.)

Tasmania

A B C D E F

CTIC   OCEAN

Queen
Elizabeth
Islands

Ellesmere
Island

Lincoln
Sea

Kane
Basin

GREENLAND
(Denmark)

Vostochno
Sibirskoye
More

Banks
Island

Viscount Melville
Sound

Baffin Bay

Oikiqtaluk

Beaufort Sea

Amundsen
Gulf

Victoria Island

Ostrov Vrangelya

Pt. Barrow

Chucki
Sea

Great Bear Lake

Foxe
Basin

Daris Str.

Denmark Strait

Arctic Circle

Khrebet Kolymskiy

Brooks Range

ALASKA
(U.S.A.)

Mackenzie Mts.

Great Slave Lake

Hudson Str.

Reykjavik
ICELAND

Anadyrskiy
Zaliv

McKINLEY
6194 ▲
Alaska Range

Yukon

L. Athabasca

Reindeer Lake

Hudson Bay

Labrador Sea

Kap Farvel

Bering
Sea

Gulf of Alaska

Kodiak I.

Rock

CANADA

L. Winnipeg

Labrador

Aleutian   Islands

Aleutian   Trench

Vancouver I.

Rocky Mountains

Great
Lakes

Newfoundland

NORTH
PACIFIC
OCEAN

Columbia

Great
Plains

UNITED STATES
OF
AMERICA

Ottawa

CHICAGO

Appalachian Mts.

NEW YORK
PHILADELPHIA
Washington

NORTH
ATLANTIC
OCEAN

Gt. Salt Lake

SAN FRANCISCO

Missouri

LOS ANGELES

Mississippi

Bermuda
(U.K.)

Açores
(Port.)

Hawaiian

Islands

Isla de
Guadalupe
(Mex.)

Gulf of Mexico

BAHAMAS
Nassau

Tropic of Cancer

HAWAII
(U.S.A.)

Islas de Revillagigedo
(Mex.)

MEXICO
CIUDAD DE
MÉXICO

La Habana

CUBA

West Indies

DOMINICAN REP.

CAPE
VERDE

Belmopan
BELIZE

Port au Prince
HAITI
Kingston
JAMAICA

Santo Dpmingo
Puerto Rico (U.S.A.)

Marshall Is.

GUATEMALA
Guatemala

HONDURAS
Tegucigalpa
EL SALVADOR
San Salvador
NICARAGUA
Managua
San José
COSTA RICA
PANAMA

Caribbean Sea

Leeward Is.

Praia

Tarawa

NAURU

Gilbert
Is.

Christmas I.

Caracas
Panamá
VENEZUELA

Windward Is.

BARBADOS
TRINIDAD
AND TOBAGO

Polynesia

Line Islands

Phoenix Is.

Bogotá
COLOMBIA

Georgetown
GUY
Paramaribo
SUR
Cayenne
FRENCH GUIANA

OLOMON ISLANDS

TUVALU

KIRIBATI

Quito
EQUADOR

Islas Galápagos
(Ecuador)

Orinoco

Equator

Isla Fernando
de Noronha
(Brazil)

Honiara
Santa
Cruz
Is.

Fanafuti

Iles Marquises
(Fr.)

PERU

Cordillera

BRAZIL
Planalto do
Mato Grosso

VANUATU
Vila
Iles Wallice
(Fr.)

W.
SAMOA
Apia
Samoa
(U.S.A.)

French Polynesia
(Fr.)

Iles Tuamotu

LIMA

Brasília

Vila
nouvelle
donie

FIJI
Suva

TONGA
Nuku'alofa

Cook Islands
(N.Z.)

Tahiti

Iles de la
Société

SOUTH
PACIFIC
OCEAN

La Paz
BOLIVIA

SÃO PAULO
Asunción

RÍO DE JANEIRO

Ilha da Trindade
(Brazil)

PARAGUAY

Tropic of Capricorn

Tonga
Trench

Iles Gambier

Pitcairn I.
(U.K.) Ducie I.
(U.K.)

Isla de Pascua
(Easter I.)
(Chile)

ACONCAGUA
6960
Cordillera de los Andes

Tasman Sea

Kermadec
Trench

Islas Juan
Fernández
(Chile)

Santiago

URUGUAY
Montevideo

BUENOS AIRES

ARGENTINA

SOUTH
ATLANTIC
OCEAN

NEW ZEALAND
Wellington

Chatham Is.
(N.Z.)

Patagonia

Auckland Is.
(N.Z.)

Falkland Is.
(U.K.)

South Georgia
(U.K.)

Macquarie Is.
(Aus.)

Cabo de Hornos

Scotia Sea

South
Sandwich
Is. (U.K.)

GLOSSARY AND ABBREVIATIONS

Language abbreviations in glossary

Afr	Afrikaans	*Dut*	Dutch	*I-C*	Indo-Chinese	*Mal*	Malay	*S-C*	Serbo-Croat
Alb	Albanian	*Fin*	Finnish	*Ice*	Icelandic	*Mlg*	Malagasy	*Som*	Somali
Ar	Arabic	*Fr*	French	*Ind*	Indonesian	*Mon*	Mongolian	*Sp*	Spanish
Ber	Berber	*Gae*	Gaelic	*It*	Italian	*Nor*	Norwegian	*Swe*	Swedish
Bul	Bulgarian	*Ger*	German	*Jap*	Japanese	*Per*	Persian	*Th*	Thai
Bur	Burmese	*Gr*	Greek	*Khm*	Khmer	*Pol*	Polish	*Tib*	Tibetan
Ch	Chinese	*Heb*	Hebrew	*Kor*	Korean	*Por*	Portuguese	*Tu*	Turkish
Cz	Czech	*Hin*	Hindi	*Lao*	Laotian	*Rom*	Romanian	*Vt*	Vietnamese
Dan	Danish	*Hun*	Hungarian	*Lat*	Latvian	*Rus*	Russian	*Wel*	Welsh

Glossary

A

Abar (*Ar*) – wells
Abyar (*Ar*) – wells
Adasi (*Tu*) – island
Adrar (*Ber*) – mountains
Ain (*Ar*) – spring, well
Akra (*Gr*) – cape, point
Alb (*Ger*) – mountains
Alpen (*Ger*) – mountains
Alpes (*Fr*) – mountains
Alpi (*It*) – mountains
Alto (*Por*) – high
-alv (*Swe*) – river
-alven (*Swe*) – river
Appenino (*It*) – mountain range
Aqabat (*Ar*) – pass
Archipielago (*Sp*) – archipelago
Arquipielago (*Por*) – archipelago
Arrecife (*Sp*) – reef
Ayia (*Gr*) – saint
Ayios (*Gr*) – saint
Ayn (*Ar*) – spring, well

B

Bab (*Ar*) – strait
Bad (*Ger*) – spa
Badiyah (*Ar*) – desert
Bælt (*Dan*) – strait
Baharu (*Mal*) – new
Bahia (*Sp*) – bay
Bahr (*Ar*) – bay, canal, lake, stream
Bahrat (*Ar*) – lake
Baia (*Por*) – bay
Baie (*Fr*) – bay
Baja (*Sp*) – lower
Ban (*Khm, Lao, Th*) – village
-bana (*Jap*) – cape, point
Banco (*Sp*) – bank
-bandao (*Ch*) – peninsula
Bandar (*Per*) – bay
Baraji (*Tu*) – reservoir
Barqa (*Ar*) – hill
Barragem (*Por*) – reservoir
Bassin (*Fr*) – basin, bay
Batin (*Ar*) – depression
Beinn (*Gae*) – mountain
Beloyy (*Rus*) – white
Ben (*Gae*) – mountain
Bereg (*Rus*) – bank, shore
Berg (*Ger*) – mountain
Berge (*Afr*) – mountains
Bheinn (*Gae*) – mountain
Biar (*Ar*) – wells
Bir (*Ar*) – well
Bi'r (*Ar*) – well
Birkat (*Ar*) – well
Birket (*Ar*) – well
Boca (*Sp*) – river mouth
Bocche (*It*) – mouths, estuary
Bodden (*Ger*) – bay
Bogazi (*Tu*) – strait
Boka (*S-C*) – gulf, inlet
Bol'shoy (*Rus*) – big
Bol'shoye (*Rus*) – big
Bory (*Pol*) – forest
Bratul (*Rom*) – river channel
Bucht (*Ger*) – bay
Bugt (*Dan*) – bay
Buhayrat (*Ar*) – lagoon, lake
Bukit (*Mal*) – hill, mountain
Bukt (*Nor*) – bay
Bulak (*Rus*) – spring
Burnu (*Tu*) – cape, point
Burun (*Tu*) – cape, point
Busen (*Ger*) – bay
Buyuk (*Tu*) – big

C

Cabo (*Por, Sp*) – cape, point
Cachoeira (*Sp*) – waterfall
Cap (*Fr*) – cape, point
Campos (*Sp*) – upland
Cao Nguyen (*Th*) – plateau, tableland
Cataratas (*Sp*) – waterfall
Cayi (*Tu*) – stream
Cayo (*Sp*) – islet, rock
Cerro (*Sp*) – hill
Chaco (*Sp*) – jungle
Chaine (*Fr*) – mountain chain
Chapada (*Por*) – hills
Ch'eng (*Ch*) – town
Chiang (*Ch*) – river
Chiang (*Th*) – town
Chott (*Ar*) – marsh, salt lake
Chute (*Fr*) – waterfall
Cienaga (*Sp*) – marshy lake
Ciudad (*Sp*) – city, town
Co (*Tib*) – lake
Col (*Fr*) – pass
Colinas (*Sp*) – hills
Cordillera (*Sp*) – mountain range
Costa (*Sp*) – coast, shore
Cote (*Fr*) – coast, slope
Coteau (*Fr*) – hill, slope
Coxilha (*Por*) – mountain pasture
Cuchillas (*Sp*) – hills

D

Dag (*Tu*) – mountain
Dagi (*Tu*) – mountain
Daglari (*Tu*) – mountains
-dake (*Jap*) – peak
-dal (*Nor*) – valley
Dao (*Ch*) – island
Darreh (*Per*) – valley
Daryacheh (*Per*) – lake
Dasht (*Per*) – desert
Denizi (*Tu*) – sea
Desierto (*Sp*) – desert
Djebel (*Ar*) – mountain
-djik (*Dut*) – dyke
Do (*Kor, Jap, Vt*) – island
Dolina (*Rus*) – valley
Dolok (*Ind*) – mountain
Dolna (*Bul*) – lower
Dolni (*Cz*) – lower
-dong (*Kor*) – village
-dorp (*Afr*) – village
Dur (*Ar*) – mountains

E

Eiland (*Dut*) – island
Eilanden (*Dut*) – islands
-elva (*Nor*) – river
Embalse (*Sp*) – reservoir
Erg (*Ar*) – sandy desert
Estero (*Sp*) – bay, estuary, inlet
Estrecho (*Sp*) – strait
Etang (*Fr*) – lagoon, pond
Ezers (*Lat*) – lake

F

Feng (*Ch*) – mountain, peak
Fels (*Ger*) – rock
Firth (*Gae*) – estuary
-fjall (*Swe*) – mountains
Fjeld (*Dan*) – mountain
-fjell (*Nor*) – mountain
-floi (*Ice*) – bay
-fjoraur (*Ice*) – fjord
Forde (*Ger*) – inlet
Foret (*Fr*) – forest
-foss (*Ice*) – waterfall

G

-gan (*Jap*) – rock
Gang (*Ch*) – harbour
Ganga (*Hin*) – river
Gata (*Jap*) – inlet, lagoon
Gave (*Fr*) – torrent
Gebel (*Ar*) – mountain
Gebirge (*Ger*) – mountains
Ghat (*Hin*) – range of hills
Ghubbat (*Ar*) – bay
Glen (*Gae*) – valley
Gletscher (*Ger*) – glacier
Gobi (*Mon*) – desert
Golfe (*Fr*) – bay, gulf
Golfo (*It, Sp*) – bay, gulf
Golu (*Tu*) – lake
Gora (*Bul*) – forest
Gora (*Pol, Rus*) – mountain
-gorod (*Rus*) – small town
Gory (*Pol, Rus*) – mountains
Grada (*Rus*) – mountain range
Grad (*Bul, Rus, S-C*) – city, town
Gross (*Ger*) – big
Gryada (*Rus*) – ridge
Guba (*Rus*) – bay
-gunto (*Jap*) – island group
Gunung (*Ind, Mal*) – mountain

H

Hadh (*Ar*) – sand dunes
Hafen (*Ger*) – harbour, port
Haff (*Ger*) – bay, lagoon
Hai (*Ch*) – sea
Haixia (*Ch*) – strait
-holm (*Dan*) – island
Halvo (*Dan*) – peninsula
-hama (*Jap*) – beach
Hamada (*Ar*) – plateau
-hamar (*Ice*) – mountain
Hammadah (*Ar*) – plain, stony desert
Hamun (*Per*) – marsh
-hanto (*Jap*) – peninsula
Harrat (*Ar*) – lava field
Hav (*Swe*) – gulf
Havet (*Nor*) – sea
-havn (*Dan, Nor*) – harbour
Hawr (*Ar*) – lake
He (*Ch*) – river
Heide (*Ger*) – heath, moor
-hisar (*Tu*) – castle
Ho (*Ch*) – river
Hohe (*Ger*) – hills
Horn (*Ger*) – peak, summit
Hu (*Ch*) – lake
-huk (*Swe*) – cape, point

I

Idd (*Ar*) – well
Idhan (*Ar*) – sand dunes
Ile (*Fr*) – island
Iles (*Fr*) – islands
Ilha (*Por*) – island
Ilhas (*Por*) – islands
Insel (*Ger*) – island
Inseln (*Ger*) – islands
Irq (*Ar*) – sand dunes
Irmak (*Tu*) – large river
Isfjord (*Dan*) – glacier
Iskappe (*Dan*) – icecap
Isla (*Sp*) – island
Islas (*Sp*) – islands
Isola (*It*) – island
Isole (*It*) – islands
Istmo (*Sp*) – isthmus

J

Jabal (*Ar*) – mountain
-jarvi (*Fin*) – lake
Jaza 'ir (*Ar*) – islands
Jazirat (*Ar*) – island
Jazovir (*Bul*) – reservoir
Jbel (*Ar*) – mountain
Jebel (*Ar*) – mountain
Jezero (*Alb, S-C*) – lake
Jezioro (*Pol*) – lagoon, lake
Jezirat (*Ar*) – island
-jiang (*Ch*) – river
Jibal (*Ar*) – mountain
Jiddat (*Ar*) – gravel plain
-jima (*Jap*) – island
-joki (*Fin*) – river
-jokull (*Ice*) – glacier

K

Kaap (*Afr*) – cape, point
-kai (*Jap*) – bay, sea
-kaikyo (*Jap*) – strait
Kanaal (*Dut*) – canal
Kap (*Ger*) – cape, point
-kapp (*Nor*) – cape, point
Kas (*Khm*) – island
Kavir (*Per*) – desert
-kawa (*Jap*) – river
Kenet (*Alb*) – inlet
Kep (*Alb*) – cape, point
Kepulauan (*Ind*) – archipelago, islands
Kereb (*Ar*) – hill, ridge
Khalij (*Ar*) – bay, gulf
Khawr (*Ar*) – wadi
Khrebet (*Ru*) – mountain range
Kiang (*Ch*) – river
Klein (*Afr, Ger*) – small
Ko (*Th*) – island
-ko (*Jap*) – inlet, lake
Koh (*Khm*) – island
Kolpos (*Gr*) – gulf
Kolymskoye (*Rus*) – mountain range
Korfezi (*Tu*) – bay, gulf
Kosa (*Rus*) – spit
Kotlina (*Cz, Pol*) – basin, depression
Kraj (*Cz, Pol, S-C*) – region
Krasnyy (*Rus*) – red
Kray (*Rus*) – region
Kreis (*Ger*) – district
Kryazh (*Rus*) – mountains
Kucuk (*Tu*) – small
Kuh (*Per*) – mountain
Kuhha (*Per*) – mountains
Kum (*Rus*) – sandy desert
Kyst (*Dan*) – coast
Kyun (*Bur*) – island
Kyunzu (*Bur*) – islands

L

La (*Tib*) – pass
Lac (*Fr*) – lake
Lacul (*Rom*) – lake
Laem (*Th*) – point
Lago (*It, Por, Sp*) – lake
Lagoa (*Por*) – lagoon
Laguna (*Sp*) – lagoon, lake
Lam (*Th*) – stream
Lande (*Fr*) – heath, sandy moor
Laut (*Ind*) – sea
Ling (*Ch*) – mountain range
Liman (*Rus*) – bay, gulf
Limni (*Gr*) – lagoon, lake
Llano (*Sp*) – plain, prairie
Llanos (*Sp*) – plains, prairies

M

Mae Nam (*Th*) – river
Mala (*S-C*) – small
Malaya (*Rus*) – small
Male (*Cz*) – small
Maloye (*Rus*) – small
Malyy (*Rus*) – small
Mar (*Por, Sp*) – sea
Mare (*It*) – sea
Masirah (*Ar*) – channel
Massif (*Fr*) – mountains
Mato (*Por*) – forest
Meer (*Afr, Dut, Ger*) – lake, sea
Menor (*Por, Sp*) – lesser, smaller
Mer (*Fr*) – sea
Mesa (*Sp*) – tableland
Minami (*Jap*) – south
-misaki (*Jap*) – cape, point
Mont (*Fr*) – mountain
Montagna (*It*) – mountain
Montagne (*Fr*) – mountain
Montagnes (*Fr*) – mountains
Montana (*Sp*) – mountain
Montanas (*Sp*) – mountains
Monte (*It, Por, Sp*) – mountain
Monti (*It*) – mountains
More (*Rus*) – sea
Mull (*Gae*) – cape, point, promontory
Munkhafad (*Ar*) – depression
Muntii (*Rom*) – mountains
Mynydd (*Wel*) – mountain
Mys (*Rus*) – cape, point

N

-nada (*Jap*) – gulf, sea
Nadrz (*Cz*) – reservoir
Nafud (*Ar*) – desert, dune
Nagor'ye (*Rus*) – highland, uplands
Nagy- (*Hun*) – great
Nahr (*Ar*) – river
Namakzar (*Per*) – desert, salt flat
Nei (*Ch*) – inner
Ness (*Gae*) – cape, promontory
Neu (*Ger*) – new
Nevada (*Sp*) – snow capped mountains
Nevado (*Sp*) – mountain
Ngoc (*Vt*) – mountain peak
-nisi (*Gr*) – island
Nisoi (*Gr*) – islands
Nisos (*Gr*) – island
Nizhnyaya (*Rus*) – lower
Nizina (*Pol*) – depression, lowland
Nizmennost' (*Rus*) – lowland
Noord (*Dut*) – north
Nord (*Dan, Fr, Ger*) – north
Norte (*Por, Sp*) – north
Nos (*Bul, Rus*) – point, spit
Nosy (*Mlg*) – island
Nova (*Bul*) – new
Nova (*Cz*) – new
Novaya (*Rus*) – new
Nove (*Cz*) – new
Novi (*Bul*) – new
Nudo (*Sp*) – mountain
Nuruu (*Mon*) – mountain range
Nuur (*Mon*) – lake

O

Ø (*Dan*) – island
Oblast' (*Rus*) – province

Llyn (*Wel*) – lake
Loch (*Gae*) – lake
Lough (*Gae*) – lake

Occidental (Fr, Rom, Sp) – western
Oki (Jap) – bay
-oog (Ger) – island
Ojo (Sp) – spring
Orasul (Rom) – city
Ori (Gr) – mountains
Oriental (Fr, Rom, Sp) – eastern
Ormos (Gr) – bay
Oros (Gr) – island
Ort (Ger) – cape, point
Ostrov (Rus) – island
Ostrova (Rus) – islands
Otok (S-C) – island
Otoki (S-C) – islands
Ouadi (Ar) – wadi, dry watercourse
Oued (Ar) – dry river bed, wadi
Ovasi (Tu) – plain
Ozero (Rus) – lake

P
Pampa (Sp) – plain
Paniai (Ind) – lake
Paso (Sp) – pass
Passage (Fr) – pass
Passo (It) – pass
Pasul (Rom) – pass
Pelagos (Gr) – sea
Pendi (Ch) – basin
Pengunungnan (Ind) – mountain range
Peninsola (It) – peninsula
Peninsule (Fr) – peninsula
Pereval (Rus) – pass
Peski (Rus) – desert, sands
Phnom (Khm) – hill, mountain
Phu (Vt) – mountain
Pic (Fr) – peak
Picacho (Sp) – peak
Pico (Sp) – peak
Pik (Rus) – peak
Pingyuan (Ch) – plain
Pizzo (It) – peak
Planalto (Por) – plateau
Plana (S-C, Sp) – plain
Planina (Bul, S-C) – mountains
Plato (Afr, Bul, Rus) – plateau
Ploskogor'ye (Rus) – plateau
Ploskogorje (Rus) – plateau
Poco (Ind) – peak

Pohorie (Cz) – mountain range
Pointe (Fr) – cape, point
Pojezierze (Pol) – plateau
Poluostrov (Rus) – peninsula
Polwysep (Pol) – peninsula
Ponta (Por) – cape, point
Presa (Sp) – reservoir
Proliv (Sp) – strait
Pueblo (Sp) – village
Puerto (Sp) – harbour, pass
Pulau (Ind, Mal) – island
Puna (Sp) – desert plateau
Puncak (Ind) – peak
Punta (It, Sp) – cape, point
Puy (Fr) – peak

Q
Qalamat (Ar) – well
Qalib (Ar) – well
Qararat (Ar) – depression
Qolleh (Per) – mountain
Qornet (Ar) – peak
Qundao (Ch) – archipelago

R
Ramlat (Ar) – dunes
Ra's (Ar, Per) – cape, point
Ras (Ar) – cape, point
Rass (Som) – cape, point
Ravnina (Rus) – plain
Recife (Por) – reef
Represa (Por) – dam
Reshteh (Per) – mountain range
-retto (Jap) – island chain
Rijeka (S-C) – river
Rio (Por, Sp) – river
Riviere (Fr) – river
Rt (S-C) – cape, point
Rubha (Gae) – cape, point
Ruck (Ger) – mountain
Rucken (Ger) – ridge
Rud (Per) – river
Rudohorie (Cz) – mountains
Rzeka (Pol) – river

S
Sabkhat (Ar) – salt flat
Sagar (Hin) – lake
Sahara (Ar) – desert

Sahl (Ar) – plain
Sahra (Ar) – desert
Sa'id (Ar) – highland
-saki (Jap) – cape, point
Salar (Sp) – salt pan
Salina (Sp) – salt pan
San (Sp) – saint
-san (Jap) – mountain
-sanchi (Jap) – mountainous area
Sankt (Ger, Swe) – saint
-sanmyaku (Jap) – mountain range
Santa (Sp) – saint
Sao (Por) – saint
Sar (Kur) – mountain
Satu (Rom) – village
Sawqirah (Ar) – bay
Se (I-C) – river
See (Ger) – lake
-sehir (Tu) – town
Selat (Ind) – channel, strait
-selka (Fin) – bay
Selva (Sp) – forest
Serra (Por) – mountain range
Serrania (Sp) – mountains
-seto (Jap) – channel, strait
Severnaya (Rus) – southern
Sfintu (Rom) – saint
Shamo (Ch) – desert
Shan (Ch) – mountains
Shandi (Ch) – mountainous area
Shatt (Ar) – river mouth, river
-shima (Jap) – islands
Shiqqat (Ar) – interdune trough
-shoto (Jap) – group of islands
Sierra (Sp) – mountain range
Sint (Afr, Dut) – saint
Slieve (Gae) – range of hills
So (Dan, Nor) – lake
Soder- (Swe) – southern
Sondre (Dan, Nor) – southern
Song (Vt) – river
Spitze (Ger) – peak
Sredne (Rus) – middle
Stadt (Ger) – town
Stara (Cz) – old
Staraya (Rus) – old
Stenon (Gr) – strait, pass
Step' (Rus) – plain, steppe
Strelka (Rus) – spit
Stretto (It) – strait

-suido (Jap) – channel, strait
Sund (Swe) – sound, strait
Szent- (Hun) – saint

T
-take (Jap) – peak
Tall (Ar) – hill
Tallat (Ar) – hills
Tanggula (Tib) – pass
Tanjong (Ind, Mal) – cape, point
Tanjon'i (Mlg) – cape, point
Tanjung (Ind, Mal) – cape, point
Tao (Ch) – island
Taraq (Ar) – hills
Tassili (Ber) – rocky plateau
Tau (Rus) – mountains
Taung (Bur) – mountain, south
Tekojarvi (Fin) – reservoir
Tell (Ar) – hill
Teluk (Ind) – bay
Tenere (Fr) – desert
Terre (Fr) – land
Thale (Th) – lake
Thamad (Ar) – well
Tirat (Ar) – canal
Tjarn (Swe) – lake
Tso (Tib) – lake
Tonle (Khm) – lake
Tutul (Ar) – hills

U
Ujung (Ind) – cape, point
-ura (Jap) – inlet
Urayq (Ar) – sand ridge
Uruq (Ar) – dunes
Ust (Rus) – river mouth
Uul (Mon) – mountain

V
Valea (Rom) – valley
-varos (Hun) – town
-varre (Nor) – mountain
-vatten (Swe) – lake
Vaux (Fr) – valleys
Velika (S-C) – big
Velikaya (Rus) – big
Verkhne (Rus) – upper
-vesi (Fin) – lake, water
Ville (Fr) – town
Vinh (Vt) – bay

Virful (Rom) – peak
Vodokhranilishche (Rus) – reservoir
Volcan (Sp) – volcano
Vorota (Rus) – strait
Vostochnyy (Rus) – eastern
Vozvyshennost' (Rus) hills, upland
Vpadina (Rus) – depression

W
Wadi (Ar) – river, stream
Wahat (Ar) – oasis
Wai (Ch) – outer
Wald (Ger) – forest
Wan (Ch) – bay
Wasser (Ger) – lake, water
Wenz (Ar) – river
Wielka (Pol) – big

X
Xan (Ch) – strait
Xi (Ch) – stream, west
Xia (Ch) – gorge, lower
Xian (Ch) – county
Xiao (Ch) – small
Xu (Ch) – island

Y
Yam (Heb) – lake
-yama (Jap) – mountain
Yarimadasi (Tu) – peninsula
Yazovir (Bul) – reservoir
Ye (Bur) – island
Yoma (Bur) – mountain range
Yugo- (Rus) – southern
Yuzhnyy (Rus) – southern

Z
Zaki (Jap) – cape, point
Zalew (Pol) – bay, inlet
Zaliv (Rus) – bay
-zan (Jap) – mountain
Zapadno (Rus) – western
Zatoka (Pol) – bay
Zee (Dut) – sea
Zemiya (Rus) – island, land
-zhen (Ch) – town

Abbreviations

A
A. – Alp, Alpen, Alpi
Akr. – Akra
And. – Andorra
Arch. – Archipelago
Arr. – Arrecife
Aust. – Australia
Ay. – Ayios

B
B. – Bahia, Baia, Baie, Bay, Bucht, Bukt
Ba. – Bahia
Bang. – Bangladesh
Bah. – Bahrain
Bel. – Belgium
Ben. – Benin
Bg. – Berg
Bhu. – Bhutan
Bk. – Bukit
Bol. – Bol'shoy, Bol'shoye
Bos. – Bosnia-Herzegovina
Br. – Burnu, Burun
Bru. – Brunei
Bt. – Bukit
Bu. – Burundi
Bü. – Büyük
Bulg. – Bulgaria
Bur. Faso – Burkina Faso

C
C. – Cabo, Cap, Cape, Cerro
Cam. – Cambodia
Can. – Canal, Canale
Cga. – Cienaga
Chan. – Channel
Co. – Cerro
Col. – Columbia
Cord. – Cordillera
Cr. – Creek
Czech. – Czech Rep.

D
D. – Dag, Dagi, Daglari, Daryacheh
D.C. – District of Columbia
Den. – Denmark
Djib. – Djibouti

E
E. – East
Eq. – Equatorial
Est. – Estrecho

F
Fd. – Fjord
Fk. – Fork
Fr. – France
Ft. – Fort

G
G. – Golfe, Golfo, Guba, Gulf, Gora, Gunung
Gd. – Grand
Gde – Grande
Geb. – Gebirge
Gen. – General
Geog. – Geographical
Ger. – Germany
Gh. – Ghana
Gl. – Glacier
Gr. – Grande, Gross
Gt. – Great
Guy. – Guyana

H
Har. – Harbor
Hd. – Head
Hung. – Hungary

I
I. – Ile, Ilha, Insel, Isla, Island, Isle, Isola, Isole

Is. – Ilhas, Iles, Islands, Islas, Isles
Isth. – Isthmus

J
J. – Jabal, Jbel, Jebel, Jezioro, Jezero, Jazair
Jor. – Jordan

K
K. – Kap, Kuh, Kuhha, Koh, Kolpos
Kan. – Kanal, Kanaal
Kep. – Kepulauan
Khr. – Khrebet
Kör. – Körfezi
Kuw. – Kuwait

L
L. – Lac, Lacul, Lago, Lake, Limni, Llyn, Loch, Lough
Lag. – Lagoon, Laguna
Leb. – Lebanon
Liech. – Liechtenstein
Lit. – Little
Lux. – Luxembourg

M
M. – Mys
Mal. – Malawi
Mex. – Mexico
Mgne. – Montagne
Mt. – Mont, Mount, Mountain
Mti. – Monti
Mtii. – Muntii
Mts. – Monts, Mounts, Mountains

N
N. – Nord, North, Nos
Neb.– Nebraska
Neth. – Netherlands

Nev. – Nevado
N.H. – New Hampshire
Nizh. – Nizhnyaya
Nizm. – Nizmennost
Nor. – Norway
N.Z. – New Zealand

O
O. – Ost, Ostrov
Os. – Ostova
Oz. – Ozero

P
P. – Point
Pass. – Passage
Penn. – Pennsylvania
Peg. – Peganungan
Pen. – Peninsola, Peninsula, Peninsule
Pk. – Peak, Puncak
Pl. – Planina
Pol. – Poluostrov
Port. – Portugal
Prom. – Promontory
Pt. – Point
Pta. – Ponta, Punta
Pte. – Pointe
Pto. – Puerto, Punto

Q
Qat. – Qatar

R
R. – Reshteh
Ra. – Range
Rep. – Republic
Res. – Reservoir
Rés. – Réservoir
Rom. – Romania
Rw. – Rwanda

S
S. – Shatt, South
Sa. – Serra, Sierra
S.A. – South Africa
Sd. – Sound, Sund
Sp. – Spain
Sprs. – Springs
St. – Saint, Sint
Sta. – Santa
Ste. – Sainte
Str. – Strait
Sur. – Suriname
Switz. – Switzerland

T
Tg. – Tanjong, Tanjung
Tk. – Teluk

U
U.A.E. – United Arab Emirates
U.K. – United Kingdom
U.S.A. – United States of America

V
V. – Volcano
Vdkhr. – Vodokhranilishche
Ven. – Venezuela
Verkh. – Verkhne
Vn. – Volcan
Vol. – Volcan, Volcano

W
W. – Wadi, Wald, West

Y
Y. – Yarimadasi

Z
Zal. – Zaliv

INDEX

The index includes an alphabetical list of all names appearing in the map section of the atlas. Names on the maps and in the index are generally in the local language. For names in languages not written in the Roman alphabet, the officially accepted transliteration system has been used.

Most features are indexed to the largest scale map on which they appear. Extensive features are usually indexed to maps that show the features completely or show them in their relationship to surrounding areas. For extensive regional features, locations are given for the approximate center of the feature, those for linear features are given at the position of the name.

Each entry in the index is located by a page number and an alphanumeric grid reference on that particular page. The grid is defined by letters, positioned at the top and at the bottom of the map spread, and numbers, shown at the sides of the spread. For example, Bandung in Indonesia has the reference 90 D7. It can thus be found on page 90 in the grid square D7.

Where two identical names are referenced to the same page and grid square, it should be noted that they relate to different adjacent features. For example, the name Avon appears twice in the index and in both cases it is referenced to 52 E3. These two entries locate firstly the county of Avon and secondly the River Avon.

A

A 62 E3
Aachen 70 B3
Aalst 64 F3
Aanekoski 62 L5
Aarau 68 B2
Aare 68 A2
Aareavaara 62 K3
Aarschot 64 F3
Aba *China* 93 K2
Aba *Nigeria* 105 G4
Abacaxis 136 F4
Abacka 62 G4
Abadan 94 J6
Abadeh 95 L6
Abaete 138 G3
Abaetetuba 137 H4
Abag Qi 87 M3
Abaid, Bahr el 103 F5
Abajo Mountains 127 H2
Abakaliki 105 G4
Abakan 84 E6
Abana 76 E2
Abancay 136 C6
Abarqu 95 L6
Abarqu, Kavir-e 95 L6
Abashiri 88 K3
Abashiri-wan 88 K4
Abatskiy 84 A5
Abau 114 D4
Abay 86 C2
Abay Wenz 103 G5
Abaza 84 E6
Abbadia San Salvatore 69 C4
Abbah 77 H4
Abberton Reservoir 53 H3
Abbeville *France* 64 D3
Abbeville *Louisiana* 128 F6
Abbeyfeale 59 D8
Abbey Head 54 F2
Abbeyleix 59 H7
Abbot Ice Shelf 141 T4
Abbot, Mount 113 K3
Abbotsbury 52 E4
Abbotsford 122 C3
Abbottabad 92 D2
Abd Al Aziz, Jbel 77 H4

Abd al Kuri 97 N10
Abdanan 94 H5
Abdulino 78 J5
Abeche 102 D5
Abelvaer 62 H4
Abengourou 104 E4
Abenra 63 C9
Abeokuta 105 F4
Aberaeron 52 C2
Abercarn 52 D3
Aberchirder 56 F3
Abercraf 52 D3
Aberdare 52 D3
Aberdaron 52 C2
Aberdeen *South Africa* 108 D6
Aberdeen *U.K.* 57 F3
Aberdeen *Maryland* 125 M7
Aberdeen *Mississippi* 128 H4
Aberdeen *Ohio* 124 J7
Aberdeen *S.Dakota* 123 Q5
Aberdeen *Washington* 122 C4
Aberdeen Lake 119 R3
Aberfoyle 57 D4
Abergavenny 52 D3
Abergele 55 F3
Abergwaun 52 C3
Abergwynft 52 D3
Aberhonddu 52 D3
Abermo 52 D2
Abersoch 52 C2
Abersychan 52 D3
Abertawe 52 D3
Aberteifi 52 C2
Abertillery 52 D3
Aberystwyth 52 C2
Abez 78 L2
Abha 96 F7
Abhar 94 J3
Abhar Rud 95 K4
Abide 76 B2
Abidjan 104 E4
Abilene *Kansas* 123 R8
Abilene *Texas* 127 N4
Abingdon 53 F3
Abingdon Island 136 A7
Abington 57 E5
Abisko 62 H2
Abitibi 125 K2
Abitibi, Lake 125 L2

Abiy Adi 96 D10
Ablaketka 86 E2
Abo 63 M6
Aboisso 104 E4
Abomey 105 F4
Abongabong, Gunung 90 B5
Abong Mbang 105 H5
Aborigen, Pik 85 R4
Aborlan 91 F4
Abou Deia 102 C5
Aboyne 57 F3
Abrad, Wadi 96 G9
Abraham's Bay 133 L3
Abrantes 66 B3
Abruzzese, Appennino 69 D4
Abu Ali 97 J3
Abu al Khasib 94 H6
Abu Arish 96 F8
Abu Dhabi 97 M4
Abu el Jir 77 K6
Abu Gamel 96 C9
Abu Hamed 96 A7
Abuja 105 G4
Abu Jifan 97 H4
Abu Kamal 94 E4
Abu Latt 96 E7
Abu Madd, Ra's 96 C4
Abu Musa 95 M9
Abu Qatur 77 G5
Abu Shagara, Ras 96 C6
Abut Head 115 C5
Abu Tig 102 F2
Abu Zabad 102 E5
Abu Zabi 97 M4
Abwong 103 F6
Aby 63 G7
Abyad, Ar Ra's al 96 D5
Abyalven 62 J4
Abybro 63 C8
Abyek 95 K3
Acalayong 105 G5
Acambaro 131 J7
Acambay 131 K8
Acandi 132 J10
Acaponeta 130 G6
Acapulco 131 K9
Acarai, Serra 136 F3
Acarau *Brazil* 137 J4
Acarau *Brazil* 137 J4

Acarigua 136 D2
Acatlan *Mexico* 130 H7
Acatlan *Mexico* 131 K8
Acatzingo 131 L8
Acayucan 131 M9
Acceglio 68 A3
Accra 104 E4
Accrington 55 G3
Achacachi 138 C3
Achavanich 56 E2
Acheng 88 A3
Achikouya, Plateau des 106 B3
Achill 58 C5
Achill Head 58 B5
Achill Island 58 B5
Achim 70 C2
Achinsk 84 E5
Achmore 56 B2
Achnacroish 57 C4
Achosnich 57 B4
Acigol 76 F3
Acipayam 76 C4
Acireale 69 E7
Acklins Island 133 K3
Acle 53 J2
Acomayo 136 C6
Aconcagua, Cerro 139 C6
Aconchi 127 G6
Acores 48 F3
Acoyapa 132 E9
Acqui Terme 68 B3
Acre *Brazil* 136 C5
Acre *Brazil* 136 D5
Acre *Israel* 94 B5
Actopan 131 K7
Acu 137 K5
Ada *Ghana* 104 F4
Ada *Oklahoma* 128 D3
Adair, Bahia de 126 F5
Adaja 66 D2
Adak Island 118 Ac9
Adaksu 77 K3
Adalia 76 D4
Adam 97 N5
Adaminaby 113 K6
Adan 96 G10
Adana 76 F4
Adapazari 76 D2
Adare 59 E7

146

Name	Page	Grid
Adda	68	B2
Adda	68	B3
Ad Dakhla	100	B4
Ad Dali	96	G10
Ad Dammam	97	K3
Ad Darb	96	F8
Ad Dawadimi	96	G4
Ad Dawhah	97	K4
Ad Dila	97	K7
Ad Dilam	96	H5
Ad Diriyah	96	H4
Ad Duwaniyah	94	G6
Ad Duwayd	96	F1
Adel	124	C6
Adelaide *Antarctic*	141	V5
Adelaide *Australia*	113	H5
Adelaide *Bahamas*	129	P8
Adelaide Island	141	V5
Adelaide Peninsula	120	G4
Aden	96	G10
Aden, Gulf of	103	J5
Adh Dhayd	97	M4
Adi	114	A2
Adi Ark'ay	96	C10
Adi Dairo	96	D9
Adige	68	C3
Adigrat	96	D9
Adiguzel Baraji	76	C3
Adi Keyah	96	D9
Adilabad	92	E5
Adilcevaz	77	K3
Adin	122	D7
Adirondack Mountains	125	N4
Adis Abeba	103	G6
Adi Ugri	96	D9
Adiyaman	77	H4
Adjud	73	J2
Adjuntas, Presa de las	131	K6
Adka	118	Ac9
Adlington	55	G3
Admello	68	C2
Admiralty Gulf	112	F1
Admiralty Inlet	120	J3
Admiralty Island *Canada*	119	Q2
Admiralty Island *U.S.A.*	118	J4
Admiralty Islands	114	D2
Admund Ringnes Island	120	G2
Ado-Ekiti	105	G4
Adonara	91	G7
Adoni	92	E5
Adorf	70	E3
Adoumaoua, Massif de l'	105	H4
Adour	65	C7
Adra	66	E4
Adrano	69	E7
Adrar	100	E3
Adre	102	D5
Adria	68	D3
Adrian *Michigan*	124	J6
Adrian *Texas*	127	L3
Adriatic Sea	68	E4
Adwa	96	D9
Adwick le Street	55	H3
Adycha	85	P3
Adzhima	88	G1
Adzvavom	78	K2
Aegean Sea	75	H3
Afafura, Laut	91	K7
Afanasevo	78	J4
Affobakka	137	F3
Affric	56	C3
Afghanistan	92	B2
Afgooye	107	J2
Afif	96	F5
Afikpo	105	G4
Afmadow	107	H2
Afognak Island	118	E4
Afon Efyrnwy	52	D2
Afrin	77	G4
Afsin	77	G3
Afyon	76	D3
Agadez	101	G5
Agadir	100	D2
Agadyr	86	C2
Agaie	105	G4
Agalta, Sierra de	132	E7
Agano	89	G7
Agapa *Russia*	84	D2
Agapa *Russia*	84	D2
Agapitovo	84	D3
Agartala	93	H4
Agaruut	87	K3
Agats	114	B3
Agatti	92	D6
Agattu Island	118	Aa9
Agbaja	105	G4
Agboville	104	E4
Agdam	94	H2
Agde	65	E7
Agematsu	89	F8
Agen	65	D6
Aghada	59	F9
Agha Jari	95	J6
Agiabampo, Estero de	130	E4
Agin	77	H3
Agira	69	E7
Aglasun	76	D4
Agnanda	75	F4
Agno	68	C3
Agnone	69	E5
Agout	65	D7
Agra	92	E3
Agram	72	C3
Agreda	67	F2
Agri	69	F5
Agri	77	K3
Agrigento	69	D7
Agrinion	75	F3
Agropoli	69	E5
Agua Clara	138	F4
Aguadas	136	B2
Aguadilla	133	P5
Aguanaval	130	H5
Agua Prieta	127	H5
Aguascalientes	130	H7
Agua, Volcan de	132	B7
Aguelhok	100	F5
Aguemour	101	F3
Aguilar de Campoo	66	D1
Aguilas	67	F4
Aguja, Cabo de la	133	K9
Aguja, Punta	136	A5
Agulhas, Kaap	108	D6
Agusan	91	H4
Ahar	94	H2
Aheim	62	A5
Ahimahasoa	109	J4
Ahipara Bay	115	D1
Ahititi	115	E3
Ahlat	77	K3
Ahmadabad	92	D4
Ahmadi	95	N8
Ahmadnagar	92	D5
Ahmadpur	92	D3
Ahmar Mountains	103	H6
Ahoskie	129	P2
Ahram	95	K7
Ahtari	62	L5
Ahtarinjarvi	62	L5
Ahuachapan	132	C8
Ahvaz	94	J6
Ahvenanmaa	63	H6
Ahwar	96	H10
Aiddejavrre	62	K2
Aidhipsos	75	G3
Aigen	68	D1
Aigues	65	F6
Aiken	129	M4
Ailao Shan	93	K4
Ailsa Craig	57	C5
Aim	85	N5
Aimores, Serra dos	138	H3
Ain	65	F5
Ain Beida	101	G1
Ain Bessem	67	H4
Ain Defla	67	G4
Ain El Hadjel	67	H5
Ain Oulmene	67	J5
Ain Sefra	100	E2
Ainsworth	123	Q6
Aioun el Atrouss	100	D5
Aiquile	138	C3
Air	101	G5
Airbangis	90	B5
Airdrie	57	E5
Aire *France*	64	F4
Aire *U.K.*	55	J3
Airedale	55	H3
Aire-sur-l'Adour	65	C7
Air Force Island	120	M4
Airgin Sum	87	L3
Airi-selka	62	L3
Aisne	64	E4
Aitape	114	C2
Aith	56	F1
Aix-en-Provence	65	F7
Aix-les-Bains	65	F6
Aiyina	75	G4
Aiyinion	75	G2
Aiyion	75	G3
Aizawl	93	H4
Aizpute	63	J8
Aizu-Wakamatsu	89	G7
Ajaccio	69	B5
Ajana	112	C4
Ajanta Range	92	E4
Ajdabiya	101	K2
Ajlun	94	B5
Ajman	97	M4
Ajmer	92	D3
Akaishi-sanchi	89	G8
Akalkot	92	E5
Akamkpa	105	G4
Akaroa Head	115	D5
Akbou	67	J4
Akbulak	79	K5
Akcaabat	77	H2
Akcaakale	77	H4
Akcadag	77	G3
Akcakoca	76	D2
Akcaova	76	C4
Akcay	76	C4
Akchatau	86	C2
Akdagmadeni	77	F3
Ak Dovurak	84	E6
Akershus	63	D6
Akeshir Golu	76	D3
Aketi	106	D2
Akgevir	77	J4
Akhalkalaki	77	K2
Akhaltsikhe	77	K2
Akhdar, Al Jabal al	101	K2
Akhdar, Jabal	97	N5
Akhdar, Wadi	96	C3
Akheloos	75	F3
Akhiok	118	E4
Akhisar	76	B3
Akhmim	103	F2
Akhtubinsk	79	H6
Akhtyrka	79	E5
Aki	89	D9
Akimiski Island	121	K7
Akincilar	77	H2
Akinkeen	59	D9
Akinli	77	J4
Akita	88	H6
Akjoujt	100	C5
Akkavare	62	J3
Akkeshi	88	K4
Akko	94	B5
Akkoy	76	B4
Akkus	77	G2
Aklavik	118	H2
Akmola	84	A6
Akniste	63	L8
Akola	92	E4
Akonolinga	105	H5
Akordat	96	C9
Akoren	76	E4
Akot	92	E4
Akpatok Island	121	N5
Akpinar	76	E3
Akqi	86	D3
Akranes	62	T12
Akron	125	K6
Aksar	77	K2
Aksaray	76	E3
Aksay *China*	86	G4
Aksay *Kazakhstan*	79	J5
Aksehir	76	D3
Akseki	76	D4
Aksenovo-Zilovskoye	85	K6
Aks-e Rostam	95	M7
Aksha	85	J6
Akshimrau	79	J7
Aksu *China*	86	E3
Aksu *Turkey*	76	D4
Aksu *Kazakhstan*	79	J5
Aksu-Ayuly	86	C2
Aksu Cayi	76	D4
Aksum	96	D9
Aksumbe	86	B3
Aktau *Kazakhstan*	84	A6
Aktau *Kazakhstan*	79	J7
Akti	75	H2
Aktogay	86	D2
Akulivik	120	L5
Akune	89	C9
Akun Island	118	Ae9
Akure	105	G4
Akureyri	62	V12
Akuse	104	F4
Akutan Island	118	Ae9
Akwanga	105	G4
Akyab	93	H4
Akyatan Golu	76	F4
Akyazi	76	D2
Akyurt	76	E2
Akzhar	86	C3
Al Aaiun	100	C3
Alabama *U.S.A.*	129	J4
Alabama *U.S.A.*	129	J4
Alaca	76	F2
Alacahan	77	G3
Alacam	77	F2
Alacam Daglari	76	C3
Alacran, Arrecife	131	Q6
Alagoas	137	K5
Alagoinhas	137	K6
Alagon *Spain*	66	C2
Alagon *Spain*	67	F2
Al Ahmadi	97	J2
Al Ajaiz	97	N7
Alajarvi	62	K5
Alajuela	132	E9
Alakanuk	118	C3
Alakol, Ozero	86	E2
Alakyla	62	L3
Al Amarah	94	H6
Alameda *California*	126	A2
Alameda *New Mexico*	127	J3
Alamicamba	132	E8
Alamo	126	E2
Alamogordo	127	K4
Ala, Monti di	69	B5
Alamos	127	H7
Alamosa	127	K2
Aland	63	H6
Alands hav	63	M6
Alanya	76	E4
Alaotra, Lake	109	J3
Alapayevsk	84	Ad5
Al Aqulah	97	J5
Alarcon, Embalse de	66	E3
Al Artawiyah	96	G3
Alasehir	76	C3
Al Ashkhirah	97	P6
Alaska, Gulf of	118	F4
Alaska Peninsula	118	Af8
Alaska Range	118	E3
Alassio	68	B4
Alatna	118	E2
Alatyr	78	H5
Alausi	136	B4
Alaverdi	77	L2
Alavus	62	K5
Al Ayn	97	M4
Alayor	67	J3
Alayskiy Khrebet	86	C4
Al Azamiyah	77	L6
Alazeya	85	S2
Alba	68	B3
Al Bab	77	G4
Albacete	67	F3
Alba de Tormes	66	D2
Al Badi	96	H5
Al Badi	77	J5
Alba Iulia	73	G2
Albak	63	D8
Alba, Mount	115	B6
Albanel, Lake	121	M7
Albania	74	E2
Albano	137	H4
Albany *Australia*	112	D5
Albany *Canada*	121	K7
Albany *Georgia*	129	K5
Albany *Kentucky*	124	H8
Albany *New York*	125	P5
Albany *Oregon*	122	C5
Albarracin	67	F2
Al Basrah	94	H6
Albatross Bay	113	J1
Albatross Point	115	E3
Al Bayda	96	G10
Albayrak	77	L3
Albemarle	129	M3
Albemarle Island	136	A7
Albemarle Sound	129	P2
Albenga	68	B3
Albentosa	67	F2
Alberche	66	D2
Alberga	113	G4
Albergaria-a-Velha	66	B2
Alberique	67	F3
Albert	64	E3
Alberta	119	M5
Albert Edward, Mount	114	D3
Albert Kanaal	64	F3
Albert, Lake	107	F2
Albert Lea	124	D5
Albert Nile	107	F2
Albertville *France*	65	G6
Albertville *Zaire*	107	F4
Albi	65	E7
Albina	137	G2
Al Bir	96	C2
Al Birk	96	E7
Albocacer	67	G2
Albo, Monti	69	B5
Alboran, Isla de	66	E5
Alborg	63	D8
Alborg Bugt	63	D8
Alborz, Reshteh-ye Kuhta ye	95	K3
Albro	113	K3
Albufeira	66	B4
Albu Gharz, Sabkhat	77	J5
Albuquerque	127	J3
Al Buraymi	97	M4
Albury	113	K6
Al Busayyah	94	H6
Al Buzun	97	K9
Alcacer do Sal	66	B3
Alcala de Henares	66	E2
Alcamo	69	D7
Alcanices	66	C2
Alcaniz	67	F2
Alcantara	66	C3
Alcantara	137	J4
Alcantara, Embalse de	66	C3
Alcaraz	66	E3
Alcaraz, Sierra de	66	E3
Alcaudete	66	D4
Alcazar de San Juan	66	E3
Alcester	53	F2
Alchevsk	79	F6
Alcolea del Pinar	66	E2
Alcoutim	66	C4
Alcoy	67	F3
Alcubierre, Sierra de	67	F2
Alcublas	67	F3
Alcudia	67	H3
Aldabra Islands	82	C7
Aldama	131	K6
Aldan *Russia*	85	M5
Aldan *Russia*	85	N4
Aldanskoye Nagorye	85	M5
Alde	53	J2
Aldeburgh	53	J2
Aldeia Nova	66	C4
Alderley Edge	55	G3
Alderney	53	M6
Aldershot	53	G3
Aldridge	53	F2
Aleg	100	C5
Alegrete	138	E5
Aleksandra, Mys	85	P6
Aleksandriya	79	E6
Aleksandrov	78	F4
Aleksandrovac	73	F4
Aleksandrov Gay	79	H5
Aleksandrovsk	78	K4
Aleksandrovskoye	79	G7
Aleksandrovsk-Sakhalinskiy	85	Q6
Aleksandry, Ostrov	80	F1
Alekseyevka *Kazakhstan*	84	A6
Alekseyevka *Russia*	79	F5
Aleksin	78	F5
Alem Paraiba	138	H4
Alencon	64	D4
Alenquer	137	G4
Alentejo	66	C3
Alenuihaha Channel	126	S10
Aleppo	77	G4

Name	Page	Grid
Aleria	69	B4
Alerta	136	C6
Ales	65	F6
Aleshki	78	H2
Alessandria	68	B3
Alessio	74	E2
Alesund	62	B5
Aleutian Islands	118	Ab9
Aleutian Range	118	D4
Aleutian Trench	143	H3
Alevina, Mys	85	S5
Alexander Archipelago	118	J4
Alexander Bay	108	C5
Alexander, Cape	119	P2
Alexander City	129	K4
Alexander Island	141	V4
Alexander, Kap	120	M2
Alexandra *Australia*	113	K6
Alexandra *New Zealand*	115	B6
Alexandretta	77	G4
Alexandria *Egypt*	102	E1
Alexandria *Romania*	73	H4
Alexandria *South Africa*	108	E6
Alexandria *U.K.*	57	D5
Alexandria *Louisiana*	128	F5
Alexandria *Minnesota*	124	C4
Alexandria *Virginia*	125	M7
Alexandroupolis	75	H2
Aleysk	84	C6
Al Fallujah	77	K6
Alfambra *Spain*	67	F2
Alfambra *Spain*	67	F2
Alfaro	136	B4
Alfatar	73	J4
Al Faw	94	J7
Alfeld	70	C3
Alfios	75	F4
Alford *Grampian, U.K.*	56	F3
Alford *Lincolnshire, U.K.*	55	K3
Alfreton	55	H3
Al Fuhayhil	97	J2
Al Fujayrah	97	N4
Al Fuqaha	101	J3
Al Furat	77	J5
Algard	63	A7
Algarrobo del Aguila	139	C7
Algarve	66	B4
Algatart	86	C3
Algeciras	66	D4
Algena	96	D8
Alger, Baie d	67	H4
Algeria	101	F3
Al Ghaydah	97	L8
Alghero	69	B5
Algiers	101	F1
Algoa Bay	108	E6
Algodoes	137	K5
Algodonales	66	D4
Algona	124	C5
Algonquin Park	125	L4
Algueirao	109	F4
Al Hadd	97	P5
Al Hadithah	94	F4
Al Hadr	77	K5
Al Halfayah	94	H6
Al Hallaniyah	97	N8
Al Hamar	96	H5
Alhambra	66	E3
Al Hanakiyah	96	E4
Al Hariq	96	H5
Al Hasa	97	J3
Al Hasakah	77	J4
Al Hashimiyah	94	G5
Al Hawtah	96	H9
Al Hayy	94	H5
Al Hillah *Iraq*	94	G5
Al Hillah *Saudi Arabia*	96	H5
Al Hilwah	96	H5
Al Hudaydah	96	F9
Al Hufuf	96	J4
Al Huraydah	97	J9
Aliabad	94	H4
Aliabad	95	M7
Aliaga	76	B3
Aliaga	67	F2
Aliakmon	75	G2
Ali al Gharbi	94	H5
Alibag	92	D5
Alibey, Ozero	73	L3
Alibunar	73	F3
Alicante	67	F3
Alice	128	C7
Alice, Punta	69	F6
Alice Springs	113	G3
Aligarh	92	E3
Aligudarz	95	J5
Alijuq, Kuh-e	95	K6
Al Ikhwan	97	N10
Alima	106	C3
Alindao	102	D6
Alingsas	63	E8
Alinskoye	84	D4
Alipka	84	D5
Al Isawiyah	94	C6
Alisos	126	G5
Alistati	75	G2
Aliwal North	108	E6
Al Jaghbub	101	K2
Al Jahrah	97	H2
Al Jawarah	97	N7
Al Jawf *Libya*	101	K4
Al Jawf *Saudi Arabia*	96	D2
Al Jazirah	77	J4
Al Jubayl	97	J3
Aljustrel	66	B4
Al Kalban	97	P6
Al Kamil	97	P5
Al Khaburah	97	N5
Al Khalis	94	G5
Al Khaluf	97	P6
Al Khasab	97	N3
Al Khatt	97	N4
Al Khawr	97	K4
Al Khubar	97	K3
Al Khufrah	101	K4
Al Khums	101	H2
Al Khuraybah	97	J9
Al Khuwayrah	97	K3
Al Khuwayr	97	K3
Alkmaar	64	F2
Al Kufah	94	G5
Al Kut	94	G5
Al Kuwayt	97	H2
Allada	105	F4
Al Ladhiqiyah	77	F5
Allahabad	92	F3
Allahuekber Daglari	77	K2
Allakh-Yun	85	P4
Allanmyo	93	J5
Allanridge	108	E5
Allaqi, Wadi	103	F3
Allariz	66	C1
Alldays	108	E4
Allegheny	125	L6
Allegheny Mountains	124	J8
Allegheny Plateau	125	K7
Allen *Philippines*	91	G3
Allen *U.K.*	52	C4
Allen, Bog of	59	H6
Allendale	129	M4
Allende	127	M6
Allen, Lough	58	F4
Allenstein	71	J2
Allentown	125	N6
Alleppey	92	E7
Aller	70	D2
Allerston	55	J2
Allevard	65	G6
Allgauer Alpen	68	C2
Alliance *Nebraska*	123	N6
Alliance *Ohio*	125	K6
Allier	65	E5
Allik	121	Q6
Al Lith	96	E6
Alloa	57	E4
Al Luhayyah	96	F9
Allur	92	F6
Alma *Canada*	125	Q2
Alma *Michigan*	124	H5
Alma *Nebraska*	123	Q7
Alma-Ata	86	D3
Almaciles	66	E4
Almada	66	B3
Al Maddah	96	F7
Almaden	66	D3
Al Madinah	96	D4
Almagro	66	E3
Al Mahmudiyah	94	G5
Al Majmaah	96	G4
Almalyk	86	B3
Al Manamah	97	K3
Almanor, Lake	122	D7
Almansa	67	F3
Al Mansuriyah	96	F9
Almanzor, Pic de	66	D2
Al Mariyah	97	L5
Al Marj	101	K2
Al Masnaah	97	N5
Al Mawsil	77	K4
Al Mayadin	77	J5
Al Mayyah	96	F3
Almazan	66	E2
Almeirim	137	G4
Almelo	64	G2
Almendra, Embalse de	66	C2
Almeria	66	E4
Almeria, Golfo de	66	E4
Almetyevsk	78	J5
Almhult	63	F8
Al Midhnab	96	G4
Almina, Punta	66	D5
Al Miqdadiyah	94	G5
Almiropotamos	75	H3
Almiros	75	G3
Almirou, Kolpos	75	H5
Al Mishab	96	J3
Almodovar	66	B4
Almond	57	E4
Almonte	66	D3
Almora	92	E3
Al Mubarraz	97	J4
Al Mudawwara	94	B7
Al Mudaybi	97	P5
Al Mudayrib	97	P5
Al Muharraq	97	K3
Al Mukalla	97	J9
Al Mukha	96	F10
Almuradiel	66	E3
Al Musaymir	96	G10
Al Musayyib	94	G5
Almus Baraji	77	G2
Al Muwayh	96	E5
Al Muwaylih	96	B3
Aln	57	G5
Alness	56	D3
Alnwick	55	H1
Alofi	111	T4
Alor	91	G7
Alora	66	D4
Alor, Kepulauan	91	G7
Alotau	114	K4
Alpe-d'Huez	65	G6
Alpena	124	J4
Alpercatas, Serra das	137	J5
Alpine *Arizona*	127	H4
Alpine *Texas*	127	L5
Alps	50	J6
Alpu	76	D3
Al Qaffay	97	K4
Al Qaim	77	J5
Al Qalibah	96	C2
Al Qamishli	94	E3
Al Qaryatayn	77	G5
Al Qatif	97	J3
Al Qatn	97	J9
Al Qaysumah	96	H2
Al Qubbah	101	K2
Alqueva, Barragem de	66	C3
Al Qunfudhah	96	E7
Al Qurayni	97	L6
Al Qurayyat	97	P5
Al Qurnah	94	H6
Al Qutayfah	94	C5
Al Quwayiyah	96	G4
Al Quzah	97	J9
Al Ramadi	77	K6
Als	70	C1
Alsace	64	G4
Alsask	123	K2
Alsasua	67	E1
Alsek	118	H4
Alsfeld	70	C3
Alsh, Loch	56	C3
Alsten	62	E4
Alstermo	63	F8
Alston	55	G2
Alta	62	P2
Altaelv	62	K2
Altafjord	62	K1
Alta Gracia	138	D6
Altagracia	133	M9
Altai	86	G2
Altamaha	129	M5
Altamira	137	G4
Altamura	69	F5
Altamura, Isla de	130	E5
Alta, Sierra	67	C2
Altay *Russia*	84	Ae4
Altay *China*	86	F2
Altay *Mongolia*	86	H2
Altdorf	68	B2
Altenburg	70	E3
Altinekin	76	E3
Altinhisar	76	F3
Altinkaya	76	D4
Altin Kopru	77	L5
Altinova	76	B3
Altinozu	77	G4
Altintas	76	D3
Altkirche	65	G5
Altmark	70	D2
Altmuhl	70	D4
Altnaharra	56	D2
Alto Araguaia	138	F3
Alto Coite	138	F3
Alto Molocue	109	G3
Alton *Hampshire, U.K.*	53	G3
Alton *Staffordshire, U.K.*	53	F2
Altoona	125	L6
Alto Sucuriu	138	F3
Altrincham	55	G3
Altun Shan	92	F1
Alturas	122	D7
Al Ubaylah	97	K6
Alucra	77	H2
Aluksne	63	M8
Al Ula	96	C3
Alumine	139	B7
Al Uqayr	97	K4
Alur Setar	90	C4
Al Uwayja	96	G5
Alva	128	C2
Alvarado	131	M8
Alvaro Obregon	131	N8
Alvdal	63	H5
Alvdalen	63	F6
Alvito	66	C3
Alvorada	137	H6
Alvsborg	63	E8
Alvsbyn	62	J4
Al Wajh	96	C3
Al Wakrah	97	K4
Alwar	92	E3
Alwen Reservoir	55	F3
Alwinton	57	F5
Al Wusayl	97	K4
Alyaskitovyy	85	Q4
Alyat	94	J2
Alyth, Forest of	57	E4
Alytus	71	L1
Alzamay	84	F5
Amadeus, Lake	112	G3
Amadiyah	77	K4
Amadjuak Lake	120	M5
Amagasaki	89	E8
Amager	63	E9
Amahai	91	H6
Amakusa-Shimo-shima	89	C9
Amal	63	E7
Amalfi	69	E5
Amalias	75	F4
Amalner	92	E4
Amami-O-shima	89	B11
Amami-shoto	89	J10
Amandola	69	D4
Amantea	69	F6
Amanzimtoti	108	F6
Amapa	137	G3
Amapa	137	G3
Amarante	66	B2
Amarapura	93	J4
Amargosa	126	D3
Amarillo	127	M3
Amaro	69	E4
Amasiya	77	K2
Amasra	76	E2
Amasya	77	F2
Amatignak Island	118	Ac9
Amatrice	69	D4
Amazon	137	G4
Amazonas	137	G4
Amazon, Mouths of the	137	G4
Ambala	92	E2
Ambalavao	109	J4
Ambanja	109	J2
Ambar	84	E3
Ambarchik	85	U3
Ambarnyy	78	E2
Ambato	136	B4
Ambato-Boeny	109	J3
Ambatolampy	109	J3
Amberg	70	D4
Ambergris Cay	132	D5
Amberieu-en-Bugey	65	F6
Ambert	65	E6
Ambikapur	92	F4
Ambilobe	109	J2
Amble-by-the-Sea	55	H1
Ambleside	55	G2
Ambodifototra	109	J3
Amboise	65	D5
Ambon *Indonesia*	91	H6
Ambon *Indonesia*	91	H6
Ambositra	109	J4
Ambovombe	109	J5
Ambriz	106	B4
Ambrym	114	U12
Amchitka Island	118	Ab9
Amchitka Pass	118	Ab9
Amdassa	91	J7
Amderma	84	Ad3
Amdo	93	H2
Ameca	130	G7
Amecameca	131	K8
Amendolara	69	F6
Ameralik	120	R5
American	122	D8
American Falls Reservoir	122	H6
American Samoa	111	U4
Americus	129	K4
Amersham	53	G3
Amery Ice Shelf	141	E5
Ames	124	D5
Amesbury	53	F3
Amfiklia	75	G3
Amfilokhia	75	F3
Amfipolis	75	G2
Amfissa	75	G3
Amga *Russia*	85	N4
Amga *Russia*	85	N4
Amgu	88	F3
Amguema	85	Y3
Amgun	85	P6
Amherst *Canada*	121	P8
Amherst *Virginia*	125	L8
Amiata, Monte	69	C4
Amiens	64	E4
Amikino	85	L6
Amilhayt, Wadi al	97	L7
Amindivi Islands	92	D6
Amirante Islands	82	D7
Amistad Reservoir	127	M6
Amitioke Peninsula	120	K4
Amka	85	Q5
Amland	64	F2
Amlia Island	118	Ad9
Amlwch	55	E3
Amman	94	B6
Ammanford	52	C3
Ammer	70	D4
Ammersee	70	D5
Amol	95	L3
Amorgos *Greece*	75	H4
Amorgos *Greece*	75	J4
Amos	125	L2
Amot *Buskerud, Norway*	63	C7
Amot *Telemark, Norway*	63	C7
Amotfors	63	E7
Ampana	91	G6
Ampanihy	109	H4
Ampato, Nevado de	138	B3
Amposta	67	G2
Ampthill	53	G2
Amqui	125	S2
Amran	96	F9
Amravati	92	E4
Amritsar	92	D2
Amroha	92	E3
Amrum	70	C1
Amsterdam *Netherlands*	64	F2
Amsterdam *U.S.A.*	125	N5
Am Timan	102	D5
Amuay	133	M9
Amundsen Glacier	141	P1
Amundsen-Scott	141	A1
Amundsen Sea	141	S5

Name	Page	Grid
Amuntai	90	F6
Amur *China*	87	N1
Amur *Russia*	85	Q6
Amuri Pass	115	D5
Amursk	85	P6
Amurskaya Oblast	85	M6
Amur, Wadi	103	F4
Amvrakikos Kolpos	75	F3
Amvrosiyevka	79	F6
Anabar	84	J2
Anaco	133	Q10
Anaconda	122	H4
Anadarko	128	C3
Anadyr *Russia*	85	W4
Anadyr *Russia*	85	X4
Anadyrskiy Khrebet	85	W3
Anafi *Greece*	75	H4
Anafi *Greece*	75	H4
Anafjallet	62	E5
Anah	77	J5
Anaheim	126	D4
Anahuac	128	B7
Anahuac	92	F5
Anaktuvuk	118	E2
Analalava	109	J2
Anamur	76	E4
Anamur Burun	76	E4
Anan	89	E9
Ananes	75	H4
Anantapur	92	E6
Anantnag	92	E2
Ananyev	73	K2
Ananyevo	86	D3
Anapolis	138	J3
Anapu	137	G4
Anar	95	M6
Anarak	95	L5
Anar Darreh	95	Q5
Anatuya	138	D5
Anaua	136	E3
Anavilhanas, Arquipielago das	136	E4
A Nazret	103	G6
Anbei	86	H3
Ancenis	65	C5
Ancha	85	P4
Anchi	105	G4
Anchorage	118	F3
Anchor Island	115	A6
Ancohuma, Nevado	138	C3
Ancona	68	D4
Ancrum	57	F4
Ancuabe	109	G2
Ancuaque	138	C3
Ancud	139	B8
Ancud, Golfo de	139	B8
Anda	87	P2
Andalgala	138	C5
Andalsnes	62	B5
Andalucia	66	D4
Andalusia	129	J5
Andaman Islands	93	H6
Andaman Sea	93	J6
Andamarca	136	C6
Andam, Wadi	97	P6
Andanga	78	H4
Andapa	109	J2
Andarai	137	J6
Andeba Ye Midir Zerf Chaf	96	E9
Andeg	78	J2
Andenes	62	G2
Andermatt	68	B2
Anderson *Canada*	118	K2
Anderson *Indiana*	124	H6
Anderson *Missouri*	124	C8
Anderson *S. Carolina*	129	L3
Anderson Bay	113	K7
Andes	136	B2
Andevoranto	109	J3
Andfjorden	62	G2
Andhra Pradesh	92	E5
Andikithira	75	G5
Andimeshk	94	J5
Andimilos	75	H4
Andiparos	75	H4
Andipaxoi	75	F3
Andirin	77	G4
Andizhan	86	C3
Andkhvoy	95	S3
Andoas	136	B4
Andong	89	B7
Andongwei	87	M4
Andorra	66	G1
Andorra la Vella	67	G1
Andover	53	F3
Andoya	62	F2
Andraitx	67	H3
Andrascoggin	125	Q4
Andravidha	75	F4
Andreafsky	118	C3
Andreanof Islands	118	Ac9
Andrews	127	L4
Andreyevka	79	J5
Andreyevo Ivanovka	73	L2
Andreyevsk	85	J5
Andria	69	F5
Andrijevica	72	E4
Andringitra	109	J4
Andros	132	H2
Andros *Greece*	75	H4
Andros *Greece*	75	H4
Androth	92	D6
Andujar	66	D3
Andulo	106	C5
Andyngda	85	K3
Anegada	133	Q5
Anegada, Bahia	139	D8
Aneho	105	F4
Aneityum	114	U13
Anelghowhat	114	U14
Aneto, Pic D'	67	G1
Angamos, Punta	138	B4
Angar	114	A2
Angara	84	E5
Angara Basin	140	A1
Angarsk	84	G6
Ange	62	F5
Angel de la Guarda, Isla	126	F6
Angeles	91	G2
Angel Falls	136	E2
Angelholm	63	E8
Angelino	128	E5
Angellala	113	K4
Angeson	62	J5
Angical	138	J6
Angicos	137	K5
Angikuni Lake	119	R3
Ango	106	E2
Angoche	109	G3
Angohran	95	N8
Angol	139	B7
Angola	106	C5
Angola *Indiana*	124	H6
Angoram	114	C2
Angostura, Presa de la	131	N9
Angouleme	65	D6
Angoumois	65	D6
Angren	86	B3
Anguila Islands	132	H3
Anguilla	133	R5
Angus, Braes of	57	E4
Anholt	63	D8
Anhua	93	M3
Anhui	93	N2
Anhumas	138	F3
Aniak	118	D3
Anidhros	75	H4
Anina	73	F3
Aniva	88	J2
Aniva, Mys	88	J2
Aniva, Zaliv	88	J2
Aniwa	114	U13
Anjalankoski	63	M6
Anjou	65	C5
Anjouan	109	H2
Anjozorobe	109	J3
Anju	87	P4
Ankacho	84	H4
Ankang	93	L2
Ankara	76	E3
Ankazoabo	109	H4
Ankazobe	109	J3
Ankiliabo	109	H4
Ankleshwar	92	D4
Ankober	103	G6
Ankpa	105	G4
Anlong	93	L3
Anlu	93	M2
Anna	79	G5
Annaba	101	G1
Annaberg-Buchholz	70	E3
An Nabk *Saudi Arabia*	94	C6
An Nabk *Syria*	94	C4
Anna Creek	113	H4
Annagh Bog	59	D8
Annagh Head	58	B4
Annagh Island	59	C5
An Najaf	94	G6
Annalong	58	L4
Annan *U.K.*	57	E5
Annan *U.K.*	57	F2
Annandale	57	E5
Anna Plains	112	E2
Annapolis	125	M7
Annapurna	92	F3
Ann Arbor	124	J5
An Nasiriyah	94	H6
Ann, Cape	125	Q5
Annecy	65	G6
Annenskiy-Most	78	F3
Annfield Plain	55	H2
An Nhon	93	L6
Anniston	129	K4
Annonay	65	F6
An Nuayriyah	97	J3
An Numan	96	B3
Ano Arkhanai	75	H5
Anosibe an Ala	109	J3
Ano Viannos	75	H5
Anoyia	75	H5
Anqing	87	M5
Ansbach	70	D4
Anse de Vauville	53	N6
Anserma	136	B2
Anshan	87	N3
Anshun	93	L3
Ansley	123	Q7
Anson	127	N4
Anson Bay	112	G1
Ansongo	100	F5
Anston	55	H3
Anstruther	57	F4
Ansudu	114	B2
Antabamba	136	C6
Antakya	77	G4
Antalaha	109	K2
Antalya	76	D4
Antalya Korfezi	76	D4
Antananarivo	109	J3
Antarctic Peninsula	141	W5
An Teallach	56	C3
Antequera	66	D4
Anti-Atlas	100	D3
Antibes	65	G7
Anticosti Island	121	P8
Antigo	124	F4
Antigua	133	S6
Antigua and Barbuda	133	S6
Antigua Guatemala	132	B7
Antioch	126	B2
Antipayuta	84	B3
Antipodes Islands	111	S11
Antlers	128	E3
Antofagasta	138	B4
Antofagasta de la Sierra	138	C5
Antofalla, Salar de	138	C5
Antofalla, Volcan	138	C5
Antonio, Ponta Santo	137	K7
Antonovo	73	J4
Antrain	64	C4
Antrim *U.K.*	58	K3
Antrim *U.K.*	58	K3
Antrim Mountains	58	K2
Antrim Plateau	112	F2
Antsalova	109	H3
Antseranana	109	J2
Antsirabe	109	J3
Antsohihy	109	J2
Antu	88	B4
Antufush	96	F9
Antwerp	64	F3
Antwerpen	64	F3
Anuchino	88	D4
Anugul	92	F4
Anundsjo	62	H5
Anupgarh	92	D3
Anuradhapura	92	F7
Anvers Island	141	V6
Anxi	86	H3
Anxious Bay	113	G5
Anyama	104	E4
Anyang	87	L4
Anyemaqen Shan	93	J2
Anyudin	78	K3
Anzhero-Sudzhensk	84	D5
Anzhu, Ostrova	85	Q1
Anzio	69	D5
Aoba	114	T11
Aola	114	K6
Aomori	88	H5
Aosta	68	A3
Aoukale	102	D5
Aouker	100	D5
Apalachee Bay	129	K6
Apalachicola	129	K6
Apaporis	136	D4
Aparri	91	G2
Apatity	62	Q3
Apatzingan	130	H8
Apeldoorn	64	F2
Apia	111	U4
Apiacas, Serra dos	137	F5
Apin-Apin	90	F4
Apio	114	K6
Apizaco	131	K8
Apolda	70	D3
Apollonia	75	H4
Apopka, Lake	129	M6
Apostle Islands	124	E3
Apostolou Andrea, Akra	76	F5
Apostolovo	79	E6
Appennino	68	C4
Appleby-in-Westmorland	55	G2
Appleton	124	F4
Apsheronsk	79	F7
Apt	65	F7
Apucarana	138	F4
Apure	136	D2
Apurimac	136	C6
Apuseni, Muntii	73	G2
Aq	77	L3
Aqaba	94	B7
Aqaba, Gulf of	103	F2
Aqabah, Khalij-al-	96	B2
Aqal	86	D3
Aqda	95	L5
Aqiq	96	D7
Aqrah	77	K4
Aqueda	66	C2
Aquidauana	138	E4
Ara	92	F3
Arababad	95	N5
Araban	77	G4
Arabatskaya Strelkha, Kosa	79	F6
Araba, Wadi	94	B6
Arab, Bahr el	102	E5
Arabelo	136	E3
Arabian Desert	103	F2
Arabian Sea	97	N8
Arab, Shatt al	94	H6
Arac	76	E2
Aracaju	137	K6
Aracati	137	K4
Aracatuba	138	F4
Aracena	66	C4
Aracena, Sierra de	66	C4
Aracuai *Brazil*	138	H3
Aracuai *Brazil*	137	H3
Arad	73	F2
Aradah	97	L5
Arafuli	96	D9
Aragats	77	L2
Aragon	67	F1
Araguacema	137	H5
Aragua de Barcelona	136	E2
Araguaia	137	H5
Araguaine	137	H5
Araguari	137	G3
Araioses	137	J4
Arak	95	L4
Arakamchechen, Ostrov	118	A3
Arakan Yoma	93	H5
Arakhthos	75	F3
Arakli	77	J2
Araks	77	K2
Aral	86	E3
Aralik	77	L3
Aralqi	86	F4
Aral Sea	98	J2
Aralsk	86	A2
Aralskoye More	80	G5
Aramah, Al	96	H4
Aranda de Duero	66	E2
Arandai	114	A2
Aran Island	58	E3
Aran Islands	59	C6
Aranjuez	66	E2
Aranlau	114	A3
Araouane	100	E5
Arapahoe	123	Q7
Arapawa Island	115	E4
Arapiraca	137	K5
Arapkir	77	H3
Arapongas	138	F4
Ar'ar	94	E6
Araracuara	136	C4
Araraquara	138	G4
Araras, Serra das *Maranhao, Brazil*	137	H5
Araras, Serra das *Mato Grosso do Sul, Brazil*	138	F3
Ararat	77	L3
Araripe, Chapada do	137	K5
Arar, Wadi	94	E6
Aras	77	K2
Arato	89	H6
Arauca *Colombia*	136	C2
Arauca *Venezuela*	136	D2
Aravalli Range	92	D3
Araxa	138	G3
Araya	88	H5
Araya, Peninsula de	136	E1
Arba	67	F1
Arbatax	69	B6
Arbil	77	L4
Arboga	63	F7
Arboleda, Punta	127	H7
Arborg	119	R5
Arbra	63	G6
Arbroath	57	F4
Arbus	69	B6
Arcachon	65	C6
Arcachon, Bassin d	65	C6
Arcadia	129	M7
Arcata	122	B7
Arc Dome	122	F8
Archidona	66	D4
Arcis-sur-Aube	64	F4
Arco	122	H6
Arcos de la Frontera	66	D4
Arctic Bay	120	J3
Arctic Ocean	140	A1
Arctic Red	118	J2
Arctic Red River	118	J2
Arctowski	141	W6
Arda	73	H5
Ardabil	94	J2
Ardahan	77	K2
Ardalstangen	63	B6
Ardanuc	77	K2
Ardara	58	F3
Ardarroch	56	C3
Ardee	58	J5
Ardennes	64	F3
Ardentinny	57	D4
Ardesen	77	J2
Ardestan	95	L5
Ardfert	59	C8
Ardglass	58	L4
Ardgour	57	C4
Ardh es Suwwan	94	C6
Ardila	66	C3
Ardino	73	H5
Ardivacher Point	56	A3
Ardlussa	57	C4
Ardminish	57	C5
Ardmore	128	D3
Ardnacross Bay	57	C5
Ardnamurchan	57	B4
Ardnamurchan Point	57	B4
Ardnave Point	57	B5
Ardrossan	57	D5
Ards Peninsula	58	L3
Ardtalla	57	B5
Ardvasar	57	C3
Ardvule, Rubha	56	A3
Areao	137	H4
Arecibo	133	P5

Name	Page	Grid
Areia Branca	137	K4
Arena de las Ventas, Punta	130	E5
Arena, Point	122	B8
Arena, Punta	130	E6
Arenas de San Pedro	66	D2
Arenas, Punta de	139	C10
Arendal	63	C7
Areopolis	75	G4
Arequipa	138	A3
Arevalo	66	D2
Arezzo	68	C4
Arfersiorfik	120	R4
Arga	67	F1
Argan	86	F3
Arganil	66	B2
Argeles-Gazost	65	C7
Argens	65	G7
Argent	65	E5
Argenta	68	C3
Argentan	64	C4
Argentat	65	D6
Argentera	68	A3
Argenteuil	64	E4
Argentina	139	C7
Argentino, Lago	139	B10
Argenton-sur-Creuse	65	D5
Arges	73	H3
Argo	102	F4
Argolikos Kolpos	75	G4
Argonne, Foret d'	64	F4
Argopuro, Gunung	90	E7
Argo Reefs	114	S9
Argos	75	G4
Argostolion	75	F3
Arguello, Point	126	B3
Argun	85	K6
Argungu	105	F3
Argunsk	85	L6
Arguvan	77	H3
Argyle, Lake	112	F2
Argyll	57	C4
Arhavi	77	J2
Ar Horqin Qi	87	M3
Arhus	63	D8
Ariano Irpino	69	E5
Arica	138	B3
Ariege	65	D7
Ariha	77	G5
Arilje	72	F4
Arima	136	E1
Arinagour	57	B4
Arinos	137	F6
Aripuana	136	E5
Arisaig, Sound of	57	C4
Aristazabal Island	118	K5
Arivonimamo	109	J3
Arivruaich	56	B2
Ariza	67	E2
Arizaro, Salar de	138	C4
Arizona *Argentina*	139	C7
Arizona *U.S.A.*	126	F3
Arjang	63	E7
Arjeplog	62	H3
Arjona	136	B1
Arkadak	79	G5
Arkadelphia	128	F3
Arkaig, Loch	57	B4
Arkalyk	84	Ae6
Arkansas *U.S.A.*	128	E3
Arkansas *U.S.A.*	128	F3
Arkansas City	128	D2
Arkhangelos	75	K4
Arkhangelsk	78	G3
Arkhipovka	88	D4
Arklow	59	K7
Arkoi	75	J4
Arkona, Kap	70	E1
Arkticheskogo Instituta, Ostrova	84	C1
Arlagnuk Point	120	K4
Arlanza	66	E1
Arlberg Pass	68	C2
Arles *France*	65	E7
Arles *France*	65	F7
Arlington *Oregon*	122	D5
Arlington *S. Dakota*	123	R5
Arlington *Virginia*	125	M7
Arlon	64	F4
Armadale	57	E5
Armagh *U.K.*	58	J4
Armagh *U.K.*	58	J4
Armagnac	65	D7
Armah, Wadi	97	K8
Arman	85	S4
Armancon	65	E5
Armathia	75	J5
Armavir	79	G6
Armenia	79	G7
Armenia *Colombia*	136	B3
Armenis	73	G3
Armidale	113	L5
Armori	92	E4
Armoy	58	K2
Armstrong	124	F1
Armthorpe	55	H3
Armu	88	F2
Armutlu	76	C2
Armutova	76	B3
Armyansk	79	E6
Arnaia	75	G2
Arnarfjordur	62	S12
Arnaud	121	M5
Arnauti, Akra	76	E5
Arnedo	67	E1
Arneiroz	137	J5
Arnhem	64	F2
Arnhem, Cape	113	H1
Arnhem Land	113	G1
Arno	68	C4
Arnold	53	F2
Arnon	65	E5
Arnoy	62	J1
Arnprior	125	M4
Aro	70	D1
Aroab	108	C5
Aroeira	138	F4
Arona	68	B3
Aroostook	125	R3
Arorae	111	S2
Aroroy	91	G3
Arosa	68	B2
Arpa	77	K2
Arpacay	77	K2
Arraias	137	H6
Ar Ramadi	94	F5
Arran	57	C5
Ar Raqqah	77	H5
Arras	64	E3
Ar Rass	96	F4
Ar Rawdah	96	F6
Ar Rawuk	97	J9
Arrecife	100	C3
Arree, Monts d'	64	B4
Ar Rifai	94	H6
Arrino	112	D4
Ar Riyad	96	H4
Arromanches	64	C4
Arroux	65	F5
Arrow	52	E2
Arrow, Lough	58	F4
Arrowtown	115	B6
Arroyo Verde	139	C8
Ar Ruays	97	L4
Ar Rub al Khali	97	L6
Ar Rumaytha	97	K4
Ar Rumaythah	94	G6
Ar Rusafah	77	H5
Ar Rustaq	97	N5
Ar Rutbah	94	E5
Ars	63	C8
Ars	94	H3
Arsaynshand	87	L3
Arsenajan	95	L7
Arsenyev	88	D3
Arsin	77	H2
Arsk	78	H4
Arslankoy	76	F4
Art	114	V15
Arta	75	F3
Arta	67	H3
Artashat	94	G2
Arteaga	130	H8
Artem	88	D4
Artemisa	132	F3
Artem-Ostrov	79	J7
Artemovsk	79	F6
Artemovskiy	84	Ad5
Artenay	65	D4
Artesia	127	K4
Arthur's Pass	115	C5
Arthur's Town	133	K2
Arti	78	K4
Artigas	138	E6
Artillery Lake	119	P3
Artois	64	E3
Artova	77	G2
Artrutx, Cabo 'd	67	H3
Artsiz	79	D6
Artux	86	D4
Artvin	77	J2
Artyk	85	R4
Arua	107	F2
Aruana	137	G6
Aruba	133	N8
Aru, Kepulauan	114	A3
Aruma	136	E4
Arun	53	G4
Arunachal Pradesh	93	H3
Arundel	53	G4
Arun Qi	87	N2
Aruppukkottai	92	E7
Arusha	107	G3
Arus, Tanjung	91	G5
Aru, Tanjung	90	F6
Aruwimi	106	E2
Arvayheer	87	J2
Arvidsjaur	62	M4
Arvika	63	E7
Arviksand	62	J1
Arxang	86	F3
Arys	86	B3
Arzamas	78	G4
Arzanah	97	L4
Arzew	100	E1
Arzew, Golfe 'd	67	F5
Arzua	66	B1
As	63	D7
Asadabad	94	J4
Asad, Buhayrat al	77	H5
Asagipinar	76	E3
Asahi-Dake	88	J4
Asahi Kawa	88	J4
Asalem	94	J3
Asamankese	104	E4
Asansk	84	F5
Asansol	92	G4
Asap	77	H2
Asarna	62	F5
Asbestos Mountains	108	D5
Asbury Park	125	P6
Ascencion	138	D3
Ascension	99	B7
Ascension, Bahia de la	131	R8
Aschaffenburg	70	C4
Aschersleben	70	D3
Asco	69	B4
Ascoli Piceno	69	D4
Ascot	53	G3
Aseb	103	H5
Aseda	63	F8
Asele	62	G4
Asenovgrad	73	H5
Asha	78	K4
Ashbourne *Ireland*	59	K5
Ashbourne *U.K.*	55	H3
Ashburton *Australia*	112	D3
Ashburton *New Zealand*	115	C5
Ashburton *U.K.*	52	D4
Ashbury	53	F3
Ashby-de-la-Zouch	53	F2
Ashcroft	122	D2
Ashdod	94	B6
Ashdown	128	E4
Asheboro	129	N3
Ashern	119	R5
Asheville	129	L3
Ashford *Ireland*	59	K6
Ashford *U.K.*	53	H3
Ashgabat	95	P3
Ashikaga	89	G7
Ashington	55	H1
Ashizuri-misaki	89	D9
Ashkazar	95	M6
Ashkinak	95	R6
Ashland *California*	122	C6
Ashland *Kentucky*	124	J7
Ashland *Montana*	123	L5
Ashland *Nebraska*	123	R7
Ashland *Ohio*	124	J6
Ashland *Wisconsin*	124	E3
Ashmore Reef	112	E1
Ashqelon	94	B6
Ash Shabakah	94	F6
Ash Shadadah	77	J4
Ash Shamiyah	94	G6
Ash Shariqah	97	M4
Ash Sharqat	77	K5
Ash Shatrah	94	H6
Ash Shaykh Uthman	96	G10
Ash Shihr	97	J9
Ash Shisar	97	L7
Ash Shuaybah	97	J2
Ash Shubah	96	G2
Ash Shumlul	96	H3
Ash Shuqayq	96	F8
Ash Shurayf	96	D4
Ashta	92	E4
Ashtabula	125	K6
Ashton-under-Lyne	55	G3
Ashuanipi Lake	121	N7
Asi	94	C4
Asika	92	F5
Asilah	100	D1
Asinara, Golfo dell	69	B5
Asinara, Isola	69	B5
Askale	77	J3
Askeaton	59	E7
Asker	63	H7
Askersund	63	F7
Askilje	62	G4
Askim	63	D7
Askiz	84	E6
Askja	62	W12
Askola	63	L6
Aslantas Baraji	77	G4
Asmera	96	D9
Asmera	103	G4
Asnen	63	F8
Asoteriba, Jebel	96	C6
Aspatria	55	F2
Aspermont	127	M4
Aspres-sur-Buech	65	F6
As Saan	77	G5
As Sadiyah	94	G4
As Salif	96	F9
As Sallum	101	L2
As Salman	94	G6
Assam	93	H3
As Samawah	94	G6
As Saquia al Hamra	100	C3
Assateague Island	125	N7
As Sawda	97	M8
Assen	64	G2
Assens	63	C9
Assers	63	D8
Assiniboia	123	A3
Assiniboine	123	Q3
Assiniboine, Mount	122	G2
Assis	138	F4
Assisi	69	D4
As Sukhnah	77	H5
As Sulaymaniyah	96	H4
As Sulaymi	96	E3
As Sulayyil	96	G6
As Suq	96	F6
As Suwayda	94	C5
As Suwayh	97	P5
As Suwayrah	94	G5
Astakidha	75	J5
Astara	94	J2
Asti	68	B3
Astin Tagh	92	G1
Astipalaia *Greece*	75	J4
Astipalaia *Greece*	75	J4
Astorga	66	C1
Astoria	122	C4
Astrakhan	79	H6
Astrakhan Bazar	94	J2
Astrolabe Bay	114	D3
Astros	75	G4
Astudillo	66	D1
Asturias	66	D1
Asuncion	138	E5
Asuncion, Bahia de	126	E7
Aswan	103	F3
Aswan High Dam	103	F3
Asyut	102	F2
Ata	111	T6
Atabey	76	D4
Atacama, Desierto do	138	C4
Atacama, Puna de	138	C4
Atacama, Salar de	138	C4
Atafu	111	U3
Atakora, Chaine de l	105	F3
Atakpame	104	F4
Atalandi	75	G3
Atar	100	C4
Atasu	86	C2
Ataturk Baraji	77	H4
Atauro	91	H7
Atbara *Sudan*	103	F4
Atbara *Sudan*	103	G4
Atbasar	84	Ae6
At-Bashi	86	D3
Atchafalaya	128	G5
Atchafalaya Bay	128	G6
Atchison	124	C7
Ateca	67	F2
Aterno	69	D4
Atesine, Alpi	68	C2
Ath	64	E3
Athabasca	119	N4
Athabasca, Lake	119	P4
Athboy	58	J5
Athenry	59	E6
Athens *Greece*	75	G3
Athens *Georgia*	129	L4
Athens *Ohio*	124	J7
Athens *Tennessee*	129	K3
Athens *Texas*	128	E4
Atherstone	53	F2
Atherton	113	K2
Athinai	75	G4
Athlone	59	G6
Athol	115	B6
Atholl, Forest of	57	E4
Atholl, Kap	120	N2
Athos	75	H2
Athy	59	J7
Ati	102	C5
Atiabad	95	P4
Atiamuri	115	F3
Atico	136	C7
Atienza	66	E2
Atikokan	124	E2
Atikonak Lake	121	P7
Atka *U.S.A.*	118	Ad9
Atka *Russia*	85	S4
Atka Island	118	Ad9
Atkarsk	79	H5
Atlacomulco	131	K8
Atlanta *Georgia*	129	K4
Atlanta *Texas*	128	E4
Atlantic	124	C6
Atlantic City	125	N7
Atlantic Ocean, North	48	E3
Atlantic Ocean, South	48	F5
Atlin, Lake	118	J4
Atlixco	131	K8
Atmakur	92	E6
Atofinandrahana	109	J4
Atoka	128	D3
Atomainty	109	J3
Atondrazaka	109	J3
Atotonilco	130	H7
Atoyac	131	J9
Atrak	95	N3
Atran	63	E8
Atrato	136	B2
Atrek	95	M3
Atsumi	88	G6
At Taif	96	E6
At Tall al Abyad	77	H4
Attawapiskat *Canada*	121	K7
Attawapiskat *Canada*	121	K7
Attemovsk	84	E6
Attila Line	76	E5
Attleboro	125	Q6
Attleborough	53	J2
Attopeu	93	L6
Attu	118	Ae9
Attu Island	118	Aa9
Attur	92	E6
At Turbah	96	G10
At Tuwayrifah	97	J6
Atuel	139	C7
Atura	107	F2
Atvidaberg	63	G7
Atyrau	79	J6
Aua Island	114	C2
Auas Mountains	108	C4
Aub	70	D4
Aubagne	65	F7

Balakhta	84 E5	Balotra	92 D3	Banika	114 J6	Bardneshorn	62 Y12
Balakleya	79 F6	Balrampur	92 F3	Bani Khatmah	96 G7	Bardney	55 J3
Balakovo	79 H5	Balranald	113 J5	Bani Maarid	96 H7	Bardsey Island	52 C2
Bala Lake	52 D2	Bals	73 H3	Bani Walid	101 H2	Bareilly	92 E3
Balama	109 G2	Balsas *Brazil*	137 H5	Baniyas	94 B5	Barentsevo More	78 F2
Balambangan	91 F4	Balsas *Mexico*	131 J8	Baniyas	94 B4	Barentsoya	80 D2
Bala Morghab	95 R4	Balsas *Peru*	136 B5	Bani Zaynan, Hadh	97 J6	Barents Sea	78 F2
Balangir	92 F4	Balsta	63 G7	Banja Luka	72 D3	Barentu	103 G4
Balashov	79 G5	Balta	79 D6	Banjarmasin	90 E6	Bareo	90 F5
Balassagyarmat	72 E1	Baltanas	66 D2	Banjul	104 B3	Barfleur, Point de	64 C4
Balaton	72 D2	Baltasound	56 A1	Banka Banka	113 G2	Barford	53 F2
Balatonszentgyorgy	72 D2	Balti	73 J2	Ban Kantang	93 J7	Bargrennan	57 D5
Balazote	66 E3	Baltic Sea	63 G9	Ban Keng Phao	93 L6	Barguzinskiy Khrebet	84 H6
Balbi, Mount	114 E3	Baltim	102 F1	Bankfoot	57 E4	Barh	92 G3
Balbriggan	58 K5	Baltimore	125 M7	Ban Khemmarat	93 L5	Barhaj	92 F3
Balcarce	139 E7	Baltinglass	59 J7	Ban Khok Kloi	93 J7	Barham	53 J3
Balchik	73 K4	Baluchistan	92 C3	Banks Island *Australia*	114 C4	Bar Harbor	125 R4
Balchrick	56 C2	Balurghat	93 G3	Banks Island *British Columbia, Canada*	118 J5	Bari	69 F5
Balclutha	115 B7	Balvicar	57 C4			Baridi, Ra's	96 C4
Bald Knob	128 G3	Balya	76 B3	Banks Island *NW.Territories, Canada*	119 L1	Barika	67 J5
Baldock	53 G3	Balykshi	79 J6	Banks Islands	111 Q4	Barinas	136 C2
Baleares, Islas	67 H3	Bam	95 N3	Banks Peninsula	115 D5	Baring, Cape	119 M1
Balearic Islands	67 H3	Bam	95 P7	Banks, Point	118 E4	Baripada	92 G4
Baleia, Ponta da	137 K7	Bama	105 H3	Banks Strait	113 K7	Bari Sadri	92 D4
Baleine, Grande Riviere de la	121 L6	Bamako	100 D6	Ban Kui Nua	93 J6	Barisal	93 H4
Baleine, Riviere a la	121 N6	Bamba	100 E5	Bankura	93 G4	Barisan, Pegunungan	90 C6
Baler	91 G2	Bambari	102 D6	Bankya	73 G4	Barito	90 E6
Balerno	57 E5	Bamberg *Germany*	70 D4	Ban Mae Sariang	93 J5	Barka	97 N5
Balestrand	63 B6	Bamberg *U.S.A.*	129 M4	Banmauk	93 J4	Barkan, Ra's-e	95 J7
Baley	85 K6	Bambesa	106 E2	Ban Me Thuot	93 L6	Barking	53 H3
Balfes Creek	113 K3	Bamenda	105 H4	Bann	58 K3	Barkley Sound	122 B3
Balfour	56 F1	Bami	95 N2	Ban Nabo	93 L5	Barkly East	108 E6
Balguntay	86 F3	Bamian	92 C2	Ban Na San	93 J7	Barkly Tableland	113 H2
Balhaf	97 J10	Bam Posht	95 R8	Bannockburn	108 E4	Barkol	86 F3
Bali	90 F7	Bampton	53 F3	Bannu	92 D2	Barkston	53 G2
Baligrod	71 K4	Bampur	95 Q8	Banolas	67 H1	Barle	52 D3
Balikesir	76 B3	Banaba	111 Q2	Banovce	71 H4	Bar-le-Duc	64 F4
Balik Golu	77 K3	Banadia	133 M11	Ban Pak Chan	93 J6	Barlee, Lake	112 D4
Balikpapan	90 F6	Banagher	59 G6	Ban Sao	93 K5	Barlestone	53 F2
Bali, Laut	90 F7	Banalia	106 E2	Banska Bystrica	71 H4	Barletta	69 F5
Balimbing	91 F4	Banam	93 L6	Banska Stiavnica	71 H4	Barmby Moor	55 J3
Balimo	114 C3	Bananal, Ilha do	137 G6	Bansko	73 G5	Barmer	92 D3
Balinqiao	87 M3	Ban Aranyaprathet	93 K6	Banstead	53 G3	Barmouth	52 D2
Balintang Channel	91 G2	Banas	92 E3	Banswara	92 D4	Barnard Castle	55 H2
Balkashino	84 Ae6	Banas, Ras	96 C5	Bantaeng	91 F7	Barnaul	84 C6
Balkh	92 C1	Bana, Wadi	96 G10	Ban Takua Pa	93 J7	Barnes Ice Cap	120 M3
Balkhash	86 C2	Banaz	76 C3	Ban Tan	93 K6	Barnet	53 G3
Balkhash, Ozero	86 C2	Banbridge	58 K4	Banteer	59 E8	Barnhart	127 M5
Balladonia	112 E5	Banbury	53 F2	Ban Tha Sala	93 J7	Barnoldswick	55 G3
Ballaghaderreen	58 E5	Banchory	57 F3	Bantry	59 D9	Barnsley	55 H3
Ballandean	113 L4	Bancroft	125 M4	Bantry Bay	59 C9	Barnstaple	52 C3
Ballangen	62 G2	Banda	92 F3	Banya	73 H4	Barnstaple Bay	52 C3
Ballantrae	57 C5	Banda Aceh	90 B4	Banyak, Kepulauan	90 B5	Baro	105 G4
Ballao	69 B6	Banda Elat	91 J7	Banyo	105 H4	Baroda	92 D4
Ballarat	113 J6	Banda, Kepulauan	91 H6	Banyuls	65 E7	Barony, The	56 E1
Ballard, Lake	112 E4	Banda, Laut	91 H7	Banyuwangi	90 E7	Barquilla	66 D3
Ballasalla	54 E2	Bandama Blanc	104 D4	Banzyville	106 D2	Barquinha	66 B3
Ballash	92 F4	Bandan Kuh	95 Q6	Baoding	87 M4	Barquisimeto	136 D1
Ballater	57 E3	Banda, Punta la	126 D5	Baofeng	93 M2	Barra *Brazil*	137 J6
Balle	100 D5	Bandar Abbas	95 N8	Baoji	93 L2	Barra *U.K.*	57 A4
Ballenas, Bahia de	126 F7	Bandar-e Anzali	94 J3	Baoqing	88 D2	Barra do Bugres	138 E3
Ballenas, Canal de las	126 F6	Bandar-e Deylam	95 K6	Baoshan	93 J4	Barra do Corda	137 H5
Balleny Islands	141 L5	Bandar-e Lengeh	95 M8	Baoting	93 L5	Barra Head	57 A4
Ballia	92 F3	Bandar e Mashur	94 J6	Baotou	87 L3	Barra Mansa	138 H4
Ballina	58 D4	Bandar-e Moghuyeh	95 M8	Baoxing	88 C1	Barranca *Peru*	136 B4
Ballinafad	58 F4	Bandar-e Rig	95 K7	Bapatla	92 F5	Barranca *Venezuela*	133 L10
Ballinamore	58 G4	Bandar-e Torkeman	95 M3	Bapaume	64 E3	Barrancabermeja	136 C2
Ballinasloe	59 F6	Bandar Khomeyni	94 J6	Baqubah	77 L6	Barrancas	133 R10
Ballincollig	59 E9	Bandar Seri Begawan	90 E5	Bar *Ukraine*	73 J1	Barrancos	66 C3
Ballindine	58 E5	Bande	66 C1	Bar *Yugoslavia*	77 E1	Barranqueras	138 E5
Ballineen	59 E9	Band-e-pay	95 L3	Bara	102 F5	Barranquilla	136 C1
Ballinhassig	59 E9	Bandiagara	100 E6	Baraawe	107 H2	Barra, Sound of	57 A3
Ballinluig	57 E4	Bandirma	76 B2	Barabai	90 F6	Barre	125 P4
Ballinskelligs Bay	59 B9	Bandol	65 F7	Bara Banki	92 F3	Barreiras	137 H6
Ball Peninsula	120 K5	Bandon *Ireland*	59 E9	Barabinsk	84 B5	Barreiro	66 B3
Ballsh	74 E2	Bandon *Ireland*	59 E9	Barabinskaya Step	84 B6	Barren Island, Cape	110 L10
Ballybay	58 J4	Bandundu	106 C3	Baracoa	133 K4	Barren Islands	118 E4
Ballybofey	58 G3	Bandung	90 D7	Baraganul	73 J3	Barren River Lake	124 H8
Ballybunion	59 C7	Baneh	94 G4	Barahona	133 M5	Barretos	138 G4
Ballycastle *Ireland*	58 D4	Banes	133 K4	Barail Range	93 H3	Barrhead *Canada*	119 N5
Ballycastle *U.K.*	58 K2	Banff *Canada*	122 G2	Baraka	96 C8	Barrhead *U.K.*	57 F4
Ballyclare	58 L3	Banff *U.K.*	56 F3	Barakkul	84 Ae6	Barrhill	57 D5
Ballycotton Bay	59 G9	Banfora	104 E3	Baram	90 E5	Barrie	125 L4
Ballycroy	58 C4	Bangalore	92 E6	Baran	92 E3	Barrier, Cape	115 E2
Ballydesmond	59 D8	Bangangte	105 H4	Baranavichy	71 L2	Barriere	122 D2
Ballyduff	59 C8	Bangassou	102 D7	Barang, Dasht-i-	95 Q5	Barrington Tops	113 L5
Ballygalley Head	58 L3	Bangeta, Mount	114 D3	Barankul	84 Ae6	Barrocao	138 H3
Ballygawley	58 H4	Banggai	91 G6	Baranof Island	118 H4	Barrow *Argentina*	139 D7
Ballygowan	58 L4	Banggai, Kepulauan	91 G6	Baraoltului, Muntii	73 H2	Barrow *Ireland*	59 H8
Ballyhaunis	58 E5	Banggi	91 F4	Barapasai	114 B2	Barrow *U.S.A.*	118 D1
Ballyheige	59 C8	Banghazi	101 K2	Barat Daya, Kepulauan	91 H7	Barrowford	55 G3
Ballyheige Bay	59 C8	Bangka	90 D6	Barbacena	138 H4	Barrow Islands	112 D3
Ballyhooly	59 F8	Bangkalan	90 E7	Barbados	133 T6	Barrow, Point	118 D1
Ballyjamesduff	58 H5	Bangkaru	90 B5	Barbas, Cap	100 B4	Barrow Range	112 F4
Ballykeel	58 H3	Bangka, Selat	90 D6	Barbastro	67 G1	Barrow Strait	120 G3
Ballylongford	59 D7	Bangko	90 D6	Barberton *South Africa*	108 F5	Barry	52 D3
Ballymahon	59 G5	Bangkok	93 K6	Barberton *U.S.A.*	125 K6	Barry's Bay	125 M4
Ballymena	58 K3	Bangkok, Bight of	93 K6	Barbezieux	65 C6	Barsalpur	92 D3
Ballymoe	58 F5	Bangladesh	93 G4	Barbuda	133 S6	Barsi	92 E5
Ballymoney	58 J2	Bangor *Down, U.K.*	58 L3	Barcaldine	113 K3	Barstow	126 D3
Ballymore Eustace	59 J6	Bangor *Gwynedd, U.K.*	54 E3	Barcelona *Spain*	67 H2	Bar-sur-Aube	64 F4
Ballymote	58 E4	Bangor *U.S.A.*	125 R4	Barcelona *Venezuela*	136 E2	Bar-sur-Seine	64 F4
Ballynahinch	58 L4	Bangor Erris	58 C4	Barcelonnette	65 G6	Barth	70 E1
Ballyquintin Point	58 M4	Bang Saphan Yai	93 J6	Barcelos *Brazil*	136 E4	Bartica	136 F2
Ballyragget	59 H7	Bangui *Central African Rep.*	102 C7	Barcelos *Portugal*	66 B2	Bartin	76 E2
Ballyshannon	58 F3	Bangui *Philippines*	91 G2	Barcin	71 G2	Bartle Frere, Mount	113 K2
Ballysitteragh	59 B8	Bangweulu, Lake	107 E5	Barcoo	113 J3	Bartlesville	128 D2
Ballyteige Bay	59 J8	Bangweulu Swamps	107 E5	Barcs	72 D3	Barton *Philippines*	91 F3
Ballyvaghan Bay	59 D6	Ban Hat Yai	93 K7	Barda	79 H7	Barton *U.S.A.*	125 P4
Ballyvourney	59 D9	Ban Houei Sai	93 K4	Bardai	102 C3	Barton-upon-Humber	55 J3
Ballywater	58 M3	Bani	100 D6	Bardas Blancas	139 C7	Bartoszyce	71 J1
Balmedie	56 F3	Bani	133 M5	Barddhaman	93 G4	Barumun	90 C5
Balonne	113 K4	Baniara	114 D3	Bardejov	71 J4	Barus	90 B5

Name	Page	Ref
Baruun Urt	87	L2
Barvas	56	B2
Barwani	92	D4
Barwon	113	K4
Barysaw	63	Q9
Barysh	79	H5
Basaidu	95	M8
Basankusu	106	C2
Basco	91	G1
Bascunan, Cabo	138	B5
Basel	68	A2
Basento	69	F5
Bashakerd, Kuhha-ye	95	P8
Bashi Haixia	87	N7
Basht	95	K6
Basilan *Philippines*	91	G4
Basilan *Philippines*	91	G4
Basildon	53	H3
Basingstoke	53	F3
Baskale	77	L3
Baskatong, Reservoir	125	N3
Baskil	77	H3
Baskoy	77	K2
Basle	68	A2
Basoko	106	D2
Bassano del Grappa	68	C3
Bassar	104	F4
Bassas da India	109	G4
Bassein	93	H5
Bassenthwaite	55	F2
Bassenthwaite Lake	55	F2
Basse Santa Su	104	C3
Basseterre	133	R6
Basse Terre	133	S6
Bassett	123	Q6
Bassila	105	F4
Bass Strait	113	K6
Bastad	63	E8
Bastak	95	M8
Bastam	95	M3
Basti	92	F3
Bastia	69	B4
Bastogne	64	F4
Bastrop *Louisiana*	128	G4
Bastrop *Texas*	128	D5
Basyurt	77	J3
Bata	105	G5
Batabano, Golfo de	132	F3
Batagay	85	N3
Batagay-Alyta	85	N3
Batakan	90	E6
Bataklik Golu	76	E4
Batala	92	E2
Batalha	66	B3
Batamay	85	M4
Batan	91	G1
Batang	93	J2
Batangafo	102	C6
Batangas	91	G3
Batanghari	90	C6
Batan Islands	91	G1
Batatais	138	G4
Batavia	125	L5
Bataysk	79	F6
Batchelor	112	G1
Batesville	128	G3
Bath *U.K.*	52	E3
Bath *U.S.A.*	125	M5
Batha	102	C5
Bathgate	57	E5
Bathurst *Australia*	113	K5
Bathurst *Canada*	125	T3
Bathurst *Gambia*	104	B3
Bathurst Inlet	119	P2
Bathurst Island	112	G1
Bathurst Islands	120	F2
Batie	104	E4
Batiki	114	R8
Batinah, Al	97	N4
Batin, Wadi al	96	H2
Batiscan	125	P3
Batitoroslar	76	D4
Batlaq-e Gavkhuni	95	L5
Batley	55	H3
Batman *Turkey*	77	J4
Batman *Turkey*	77	J4
Batna	101	G1
Baton Rouge	128	G5
Batouri	105	H5
Batroun	77	F5
Batsfjord	62	N1
Battambang	93	K6
Batticaloa	92	F7
Battle *Canada*	119	N5
Battle *U.K.*	53	H4
Battle Creek	124	H5
Battle Harbour	121	Q7
Battle Mountain	122	F7
Batu	103	G6
Batubetumbang	90	D6
Batum	77	J2
Batumi	77	J2
Batu Pahat	90	C5
Batuputih	91	G7
Baturaja	90	D6
Baturite	137	K4
Baubau	91	G7
Bauchi	105	G3
Bauda	92	F4
Baudette	124	C2
Baudo	136	B2
Baudouinville	107	E4
Bauge	65	C5
Bauhinia Downs	113	K3
Baukau	91	H7
Bauld, Cape	121	Q7
Baumann Fjord	120	J2
Baunie	113	L4
Baurtregaum	59	C8
Bauru	138	G4
Baus	138	F3
Bautzen	70	F3
Bawdeswell	53	J2
Bawdsey	53	J2
Bawean	90	E7
Bawiti	102	E2
Bawku	104	E3
Bawtry	55	H3
Baxley	129	L5
Bayamo	132	J4
Bayamon	133	P5
Bayan	88	A2
Bayan-Aul	84	B6
Bayandalay	87	J3
Bayanday	84	H6
Bayan Harshan	93	J2
Bayanhongor	86	J2
Bayan Mod	87	J3
Bayan Obo	87	K3
Bayano, Laguna	132	H10
Bayan-Ondor	86	H3
Bayan-Uul	86	H3
Bayantsagaan	87	K2
Bayantsogt	87	L2
Bayan-Uul	87	L2
Bayard *Nebraska*	123	N7
Bayard *New Mexico*	127	H4
Bayat *Turkey*	76	D3
Bayat *Turkey*	76	F2
Bayburt	77	J2
Bay City *Michigan*	124	J5
Bay City *Texas*	128	E6
Baydaratskaya Guba	84	Ae3
Baydhabo	107	H2
Baydon	53	F3
Bayerischer Wald	70	E4
Bayeux	64	C4
Bayfield	124	E3
Bayhan al Qasab	96	G9
Bayindir	76	B3
Bayir	94	C6
Baykadam	86	B3
Baykal	84	G6
Baykalovo	84	Ae5
Baykal, Ozero	84	H6
Baykan	77	J3
Bay-Khak	84	E6
Baykit	84	F4
Baynunah	97	L5
Bayombong	91	G2
Bayona	66	B1
Bayonne	65	C7
Bayo Point	91	G3
Bayram-Ali	95	R3
Bayramic	76	B3
Bayramiy	94	J2
Bayramtepe	76	C2
Bayreuth	70	D4
Bayrut	76	F6
Bay Saint Louis	128	H5
Bayt al Faqih	96	F9
Baytown	128	E6
Bayy al Kabir, Wadi	101	H2
Baza	66	E4
Bazaliya	71	M4
Bazar-Dyuzi	79	H7
Bazaruto, Ilha do	109	G4
Bazas	65	C6
Bazman	95	Q8
Bazman, Kuh-e-	95	Q7
Bcharre	77	F5
Beach	123	N4
Beachy Head	53	H4
Beaconsfield	53	G3
Beadnell Bay	55	H1
Beagh, Lough	58	G2
Beagle Gulf	112	G1
Beagle Reef	112	E2
Beal	57	G5
Bealanana	109	J2
Beaminster	52	E4
Beampingaratra	109	J4
Bear	122	J6
Beara Peninsula	59	C9
Beardmore	124	G2
Beardstown	124	E6
Bear Island *Canada*	121	K7
Bear Island *Ireland*	59	C9
Bear Lake	122	J7
Bearley	53	F2
Bearn	65	C7
Bear Paw Mount	122	K3
Bearsden	57	D5
Beartooth Range	123	K5
Beata, Cabo	133	M6
Beata, Isla	133	M6
Beatrice	123	R7
Beatty	126	D2
Beattyville	125	M2
Beau Basin	109	L7
Beaucaire	65	F7
Beaufort *Malaysia*	90	F4
Beaufort *U.S.A.*	129	M4
Beaufort Sea	118	H1
Beaufort West	108	D6
Beaugency	65	D5
Beauly *U.K.*	56	D3
Beauly *U.K.*	56	D3
Beauly Firth	56	D3
Beaumaris	54	E3
Beaumont *France*	64	E4
Beaumont *California*	126	D4
Beaumont *Texas*	128	E5
Beaune	65	F5
Beaurepaire	65	F6
Beauvais	64	E4
Beauvoir-sur-Mer	65	B5
Beaver *Saskatchewan, Canada*	119	P5
Beaver *Yukon, Canada*	118	K3
Beaver Dam *Kentucky*	124	G8
Beaver Dam *Wisconsin*	124	F5
Beaverhill Lake	119	N5
Beawar	92	D3
Beazley	139	C6
Bebedouro	138	G4
Bebington	55	F3
Beccles	53	J2
Becej	72	F3
Becerrea	66	C1
Bechar	100	E2
Becharof Lake	118	D4
Bechet	73	G4
Beckingham	55	J3
Beckley	125	K8
Beclean	73	H2
Bedale	55	H2
Bedarieux	65	E7
Bede, Point	118	E4
Bedford *U.K.*	53	G2
Bedford *U.S.A.*	124	G7
Bedford Level	53	H2
Bedfordshire	53	G2
Bedlington	55	H1
Bedwas	52	D3
Bedworth	53	F2
Beer Sheva	94	B6
Beeston	53	F2
Beeswing	57	E5
Beeville	128	D6
Befale	106	D2
Befandriana	109	J3
Begejska Kanal	72	F3
Begoml	63	N10
Behbehan	95	K6
Behraamkale	76	B3
Behshahr	95	L3
Beian	87	P2
Beibu Wan	93	L4
Beihai	93	L4
Beijing	100	B5
Beila	87	M4
Beinn a' Ghlo	57	E4
Beinn Bheigier	57	B5
Beinn Dearg *Highland, U.K.*	56	D3
Beinn Dearg *Tayside, U.K.*	57	E4
Beinn Dorain	57	D4
Beinn Eighe	56	C3
Beinn Fhada	56	C3
Beinn Ime	57	D4
Beinn Mhor	56	A3
Beinn na Caillich	57	C3
Beinn Resipol	57	C4
Beinn Sgritheall	57	C3
Beipiao	87	N3
Beira	109	F3
Beirut	76	F6
Bei Shan	86	H3
Beit Lahm	94	B6
Beius	73	G2
Beja	66	C3
Beja	101	G1
Bejaia	101	G1
Bejaia, Golfe de	67	J4
Bejar	66	D2
Bejestan	95	P4
Beji	92	C3
Bekdast	79	J7
Bekescsaba	73	F2
Bekily	109	J4
Bekopaka	109	H3
Bekwai	104	E4
Bela *India*	92	F3
Bela *Pakistan*	92	C3
Belabo	105	H5
Belaga	90	E5
Belang	91	G5
Bela Palanka	73	G4
Belarus	71	L2
Bela Vista	109	F5
Belawan	90	B5
Belaya *Russia*	78	K4
Belaya *Russia*	85	W3
Belaya-Kalitva	79	G6
Belaya Kholunitsa	78	J4
Belayan	90	F5
Belcher Channel	120	G2
Belcher Islands	121	L6
Belchiragh	94	S4
Belchite	67	F2
Belcoo	58	G4
Belderg	58	C4
Belebey	78	J5
Beledweyne	103	J7
Belem	137	H4
Belen *Turkey*	76	E4
Belen *U.S.A.*	127	J3
Belep, Iles	114	V15
Belesar, Embalse de	66	C1
Belev	79	F5
Belfast *New Zealand*	115	D5
Belfast *U.K.*	58	L3
Belfast Lough	58	L3
Belfield	123	N4
Belford	57	G5
Belfort	65	G5
Belgaum	92	D5
Belgium	64	E3
Belgorod	79	F5
Belgorod-Dnestrovskiy	79	E6
Belgrade	72	F3
Belgrano	141	X3
Belica	71	L2
Beli Lom	73	J4
Beli Manastir	72	E3
Belimbing	90	C7
Belin	65	C6
Belinskiy	79	G5
Belinyu	90	D6
Belitsa	73	G5
Belitung	90	D6
Belize	132	C6
Belkina, Mys	88	F3
Belknap, Mount	122	H8
Belkovskiy, Ostrov	85	P1
Bella Bella	118	K5
Bellac	65	D5
Bella Coola	118	K5
Bellaire	128	E6
Bellary	92	E5
Bella Vista *Argentina*	138	C5
Bella Vista *Argentina*	138	E5
Belleek	58	F4
Bellefontaine	124	J6
Belle Fourche *South Dakota*	123	N5
Belle Fourche *Wyoming*	123	M5
Belle Glade	129	M7
Belle Ile	65	B5
Belle Isle	121	Q7
Belleme	64	D4
Belleville *Canada*	125	M4
Belleville *Illinois*	124	F7
Belleville *Kansas*	123	R8
Bellevue *Idaho*	122	G6
Bellevue *Washington*	122	C4
Belley	65	F6
Bellingham *U.K.*	57	F5
Bellingham *U.S.A.*	122	C3
Bellinghaussen Sea	141	U5
Bellingshausen	141	W6
Bellinzona	68	B2
Bello	136	B2
Bellona Island	114	J7
Bellona Reefs	111	N6
Bellpuig	67	G2
Bellshill	57	D5
Belluno	68	D2
Bell Ville	138	D6
Belly	122	H3
Belmont	56	A1
Belmonte *Portugal*	66	C2
Belmonte *Spain*	66	E3
Belmopan	132	C6
Belmullet	58	B4
Belogorsk	79	E6
Belogorye	71	M4
Belogradchik	73	G4
Belo Horizonte	138	K4
Beloit	124	F5
Belokorovichi	79	D5
Belomorsk	78	E3
Belorado	66	E1
Belorechensk	79	F7
Beloren	76	E4
Belorusskaya Gryada	71	L2
Belot, Lac	118	K2
Belo-Tsiribihina	109	H3
Belousovka	84	C6
Belovo	84	D6
Beloye More	78	F2
Beloye Ozero	78	F3
Belozersk	78	F4
Belozerskoye	84	Ae5
Belper	55	H3
Belsay	57	G5
Belterra	137	F4
Belton	55	J3
Belturbet	58	H4
Belukha, Gora	86	F2
Belvedere Marittimo	69	E6
Belvidere	124	F5
Belvoir, Vale of	53	G2
Belyando, River	113	K3
Belyayevka	73	L2
Belyy, Ostrov	85	A2
Belyy Yar	84	D5
Belzyce	71	K3
Bemaraha, Plateau du	109	J3
Bembridge	53	F4
Bemidji	124	C3
Benabarre	67	G1
Ben Alder	57	D4
Benalla	113	K6
Benares	92	F3
Benavente	66	D2
Ben Avon	57	E3
Benbaun	59	C5
Ben Chonzie	57	E4
Bencorr	59	C5
Ben Cruachan	57	C4
Bend	122	D5
Bende	105	G4
Bender Qaasim	103	J5
Bendigo	113	J6
Benesov	70	F4
Benevento	69	E5
Bengbu	87	M5
Benghazi	101	K2

Name	Page	Ref
Biskra	101	G2
Biskupiec	71	J2
Bislig	91	H4
Bismarck Archipelago	114	D2
Bismarck Range	114	D3
Bismark	123	P4
Bismil	77	J4
Bismo	63	C6
Bisotun	94	H4
Bispfors	62	G5
Bissau	104	B3
Bissett	123	S2
Bistcho Lake	119	M4
Bistretu	73	G4
Bistrita *Romania*	73	H2
Bistrita *Romania*	73	J2
Bistritei, Muntii	73	H2
Bitburg	70	B3
Bitche	64	G4
Bitik	79	J5
Bitkine	102	C5
Bitlis	77	K3
Bitola	73	F5
Bitonto	69	F5
Bitterfontein	108	C6
Bitterroot	122	G4
Bitterroot Range	122	G4
Bitti	69	B5
Biu	105	H3
Bivolu	73	H2
Biwa-ko	89	E8
Biyad, Al	96	H5
Biyagundi	96	C9
Biysk	84	D6
Bizerta	69	B7
Bizerte	101	G1
Bjargtangar	62	S12
Bjelovar	72	D3
Bjerkvik	62	L2
Bjorklinge	63	G6
Bjorksele	62	H4
Bjorna	62	H5
Bjorneborg *Finland*	63	J6
Bjorneborg *Sweden*	63	F7
Bjornevatn	62	N2
Bjornoya	80	C2
Bjurholm	62	H5
Bjursas	63	F6
Bla Bheinn	56	B3
Black *Alaska*	118	G2
Black *Arizona*	127	H4
Black *Arkansas*	128	G3
Black *New York*	125	N5
Blackadder Water	57	F5
Blackall	113	K3
Black Bay	124	F2
Black Belt	129	J4
Blackburn	55	G3
Black Canyon City	126	F3
Blackdown Hills	52	D4
Blackfoot	122	H6
Blackford	57	E4
Black Head	59	D6
Blackhead Bay	59	D6
Blackhill	55	H3
Black Hills	123	N5
Black Isle	56	D3
Black Mesa	126	G2
Blackmill	52	D3
Black Mountain	52	D3
Black Mountains	52	D3
Blackpool	55	F3
Black Range	127	J4
Black River Falls	124	E4
Blackrock	58	K5
Black Rock Desert	122	E7
Black Sea	51	P7
Blacksod Bay	58	B4
Blackstairs Mount	59	J7
Blackstairs Mountains	59	J7
Blackthorn	53	F3
Black Volta	104	E4
Black Water	57	E4
Blackwater *Australia*	113	K3
Blackwater *Meath, Ireland*	58	J5
Blackwater *Waterford, Ireland*	59	F8
Blackwater *Essex, U.K.*	53	H3
Blackwater *Hampshire, U.K.*	53	G3
Blackwaterfoot	57	C5
Blackwater Lake	119	L3
Blackwater Reservoir *Highland, U.K.*	57	D4
Blackwater Reservoir *Tayside, U.K.*	57	E4
Blackwell	128	D2
Blackwood	112	D5
Blaenavon	52	D3
Blafjall	62	W12
Blagodarnyy	79	G6
Blagoevgrad	73	G4
Blagoveshchensk *Russia*	78	K4
Blagoveshchensk *Russia*	85	M6
Blagoyevo	78	H3
Blair Atholl	57	E4
Blairgowrie	57	E4
Blaka	101	H4
Blakely	129	K5
Blakeney	53	J2
Blakesley	53	F2
Blanca, Bahia	139	D7
Blanca, Costa	67	F3
Blanca Peak	127	K2
Blanca, Punta	126	E6
Blanca, Sierra	127	K4
Blanc, Cap	69	B7
Blanche Channel	114	H6
Blanche, Lake	113	H4
Blanchland	55	G2
Blanc, Mont	65	G6
Blanco	136	E7
Blanco, Cabo	139	C9
Blanco, Cape	122	B6
Blanda	62	V12
Blandford Forum	53	E4
Blanes	67	H2
Blangy	64	D4
Blankenberge	64	E3
Blanquilla, Isla	136	E1
Blantyre	107	G6
Blarney	59	E9
Blasket Islands	59	A8
Blavet	65	B5
Blaydon	55	H2
Blaye	65	C6
Bleadon	52	E3
Bleaklow Hill	55	H3
Bled	72	C2
Blekinge	63	F8
Bletchley	53	G3
Bleus, Monts	107	F2
Blida	101	F1
Bligh Water	114	R8
Blind River	124	J3
Blisworth	53	G2
Block Island	125	Q6
Bloemfontein	108	E5
Blois	65	D5
Blonduos	62	U12
Bloodvein	123	R2
Bloody Foreland	58	F2
Bloomfield	124	D6
Bloomington *Illinois*	124	F6
Bloomington *Indiana*	124	G7
Bloomington *Minnesota*	124	D4
Bloomsbury	113	K3
Blouberg	108	E4
Blubberhouses	55	H3
Bludenz	68	B2
Bluefield	125	K8
Bluefields	132	F9
Blue Mountain Lake	125	N5
Blue Mountain Peak	132	J5
Blue Mountains	122	E5
Bluemull Sound	56	A1
Bluenose Lake	119	M2
Blue Ridge	129	K3
Blue Ridge Mountains	129	L3
Blue Stack	58	F3
Blue Stack Mountains	58	F3
Bluff *New Zealand*	115	B7
Bluff *U.S.A.*	127	H2
Bluff Knoll	112	D5
Bluff Point	112	C4
Bluff, Punta	126	F6
Blumenau	138	G5
Blunt	123	Q5
Blyth *Northumberland, U.K.*	55	H1
Blyth *Nottinghamshire, U.K.*	55	H3
Blyth *Suffolk, U.K.*	53	J2
Blythe	126	E4
Blythe Bridge	53	E2
Blytheville	128	H3
Bo	104	C4
Boac	91	G3
Boa Fe	136	C5
Boa Vista *Cape Verde*	104	L7
Boa Vista *Amazonas, Brazil*	136	D4
Boa Vista *Roraima, Brazil*	136	E3
Bobai	93	M4
Bobaomby, Tanjoni	109	J2
Bobbili	92	F5
Bobbio	68	B3
Bobo Dioulasso	104	E3
Bobolice	71	G2
Bobr	70	F3
Bobrinents	79	E6
Bobrka	71	L4
Bobrov	79	G5
Bobures	133	M10
Boca del Pao	136	E2
Boca do Acre	136	D5
Boca Grande	136	E2
Bocaiuva	138	H3
Boca Mavaca	136	D3
Bocaranga	102	C6
Boca Raton	129	M7
Bochnia	71	J4
Bocholt	70	B3
Bochum	70	B3
Bodalla	113	L6
Boddam	56	A2
Boden	62	J4
Bodensee	70	C5
Bodhan	92	E5
Bodmin	52	C4
Bodmin Moor	52	C4
Bodo	62	F3
Bodrum	76	B4
Bodva	71	J4
Bodza, Pasul	73	J3
Boen	65	F6
Boende	106	D3
Boffa	104	C3
Bogalusa	128	H5
Bogan	113	K5
Bogaz	76	E2
Bogazkale	76	F2
Bogazkaya	77	F2
Bogazkopru	76	F3
Bogazliyan	76	F3
Bogbonga	106	C2
Bogen	62	L2
Boggeragh Mountains	59	E8
Boghar	67	H5
Bogia	114	D2
Bognes	62	G2
Bognor Regis	53	G4
Bogo	91	G3
Bogodukhov	79	F5
Bogong, Mount	113	K6
Bogor	90	D7
Bogorodchany	71	L4
Bogorodskoye *Russia*	78	J4
Bogorodskoye *Russia*	85	Q6
Bogota	136	C3
Bogotol	84	D5
Bogra	93	G4
Boguchany	84	F5
Boguchar	79	G6
Bogue	100	C5
Bogue Chitto	128	G5
Boguslav	79	E6
Bo Hai	87	K4
Bohemia	70	E4
Bohmer Wald	70	E4
Bohol	91	G4
Bohol Sea	91	G4
Boiano	69	E5
Boigul	114	C3
Boipeba, Ilha	137	K6
Bois Blanc Island	124	H4
Boisdale, Loch	57	A3
Boise *U.S.A.*	122	F6
Boise *U.S.A.*	122	F6
Boise City	127	L2
Bois, Lac des	118	K2
Boissevain	123	P3
Boizenburg	70	D2
Bojana	74	E2
Bojnurd	95	N3
Boka	73	F3
Boka Kotorska	72	E4
Boke	104	C3
Bokhara	113	K4
Boknafjord	63	A7
Bokol	107	G2
Bokoro	102	C5
Boksitogorsk	78	E4
Boktor	85	P6
Bokungu	106	D3
Bolama	104	B3
Bolanos	130	H7
Bolan Pass	92	C3
Bolbec	64	D4
Bolchary	84	Ae5
Bole	104	E4
Boleslawiec	70	F3
Bolgatanga	104	E3
Bolgrad	79	D6
Boli	88	C3
Bolia	106	C3
Boliden	62	J4
Bolinao	91	F2
Bol Irgiz	79	H5
Bolivar	139	D7
Bolivar *Missouri*	124	D8
Bolivar *Tennessee*	128	H3
Bolivar, Cerro	133	R11
Bolivar, Pico	133	M10
Bolivia	138	C3
Boljevac	73	F4
Bolkhov	79	F5
Bollington	55	G3
Bollnas	63	G6
Bollon	113	K4
Bollstabruk	62	G5
Bolmen	63	E8
Bolobo	106	C3
Bologna	68	C3
Bologoye	78	E4
Bolotnoye	84	C5
Boloven, Cao Nguyen	93	L5
Bolsena, Lago di	69	C4
Bolsherechye	84	A5
Bolsheretsk	85	T6
Bolshevik	85	R4
Bolshevik, Ostrov	81	M2
Bolshezemelskaya Tundra	78	K2
Bolshoy Anyuy	85	U3
Bolshoy Atlym	84	Ae4
Bolshoy Balkhan, Khrebet	95	M2
Bolshoy Begichev, Ostrov	84	J2
Bolshoy Chernigovka	79	J5
Bolshoy Kavkaz	77	L1
Bolshoy Kunyak	84	A5
Bolshoy Lyakhovskiy, Ostrov	85	Q2
Bolshoy Murta	84	E5
Bolshoy Pit	84	E5
Bolshoy Porog	84	E3
Bolshoy Shantar, Ostrov	85	P5
Bolshoy Usa	78	K4
Bolshoy Yenisey	84	E6
Bolshoy Yugan	84	A5
Bolsover	55	H3
Boltana	67	G1
Bolt Head	52	D4
Bolton *Greater Manchester, U.K.*	55	G3
Bolton *Northumberland, U.K.*	57	G5
Bolu	76	D2
Bolucan	77	G3
Bolus Head	59	B9
Bolvadin	76	D3
Bolyarovo	73	J4
Bolzano	68	C2
Bom	114	D3
Boma	106	B4
Bombala	113	K6
Bombay	92	D5
Bomili	106	E2
Bom Jesus	137	J5
Bom Jesus da Lapa	137	J6
Bomlafjord	63	A7
Bomlo	63	A7
Bomongo	106	C2
Bonab	94	H3
Bonaire	133	N8
Bonaire Trench	133	N9
Bona, Mount	118	G3
Bonar Bridge	56	D3
Bonavista	121	R8
Bonavista Bay	121	R8
Bon, Cap	101	H1
Bondo	106	D2
Bondokodi	91	F7
Bondoukou	104	E4
Bone	69	A7
Bo'ness	57	E4
Bonete, Cerro	138	C5
Bone, Teluk	91	G6
Bongabong	91	G3
Bongor	102	C5
Bonham	128	D4
Bonifacio	69	B5
Bonifacio, Strait of	69	B5
Bonn	70	B3
Bonners Ferry	122	F3
Bonnetable	64	D4
Bonneval	64	D4
Bonneville	65	G5
Bonneville Salt Flats	122	H7
Bonnie Rock	112	D5
Bonny *France*	65	E5
Bonny *Nigeria*	105	G5
Bonnyrigg	57	E5
Bono	69	B5
Bonobono	91	F4
Bonorva	69	B5
Bonthe	104	C4
Bontoc	91	G2
Booligal	113	J5
Boologooro	112	C3
Boone *Iowa*	124	D5
Boone *N. Carolina*	129	M2
Booneville *Mississippi*	128	H3
Booneville *New York*	125	N5
Booroorban	113	J5
Boosaaso	103	J5
Boothia, Gulf of	120	J4
Boothia Peninsula	120	H3
Bootle	55	F3
Boot Reefs	114	C3
Bopeechee	113	H4
Boquilla, Presa de la	127	K7
Boquillas del Carmen	127	L6
Bor *Sudan*	102	F6
Bor *Turkey*	76	F4
Bor *Yugoslavia*	73	G3
Boraha, Nosy	109	J3
Borah Peak	122	H5
Boras	63	E8
Borasambar	92	F4
Borazjan	95	K7
Borba	136	F4
Borborema, Planalto da	137	K5
Borca	73	H2
Borcka	77	J2
Bordeaux	65	C6
Borden Island	120	D2
Borden Peninsula	120	K3
Borders	57	F5
Bordertown	113	J6
Bordeyri	62	U12
Bordj-Bou-Arreridj	67	J4
Bordj Bounaama	67	G5
Bordj Omar Driss	101	G3
Borensberg	63	F7
Boreray	56	A3
Borga	63	L6
Borgarnes	62	U12
Borgefjellet	62	E4
Borger	127	M3
Borgholm	63	G8
Borgo San Lorenzo	68	C4
Borgosesia	68	B3
Borgo Val di Taro	68	B3
Borgo Valsugana	68	C2
Borislav	71	K4
Borisoglebsk	79	G5
Borispol	79	E5
Borja	67	F2
Borkovskaya	78	H2
Borkum	70	B2
Borlange	63	F6
Borlu	76	C3
Bormida	68	B3
Bormio	68	C2
Borneo	90	E5
Bornholm	70	F1
Bornholmsgattet	63	F9
Bornova	76	B3
Borohoro Shan	86	E3
Boroko	91	G5
Boromo	104	E3
Boronga Islands	93	H5
Borongan	91	H3

Borovichi	78	E4
Borovlyanka	84	C6
Borovsk	78	K4
Borovskoye	84	Ad6
Borrika	113	J6
Borris	59	J7
Borrisokane	59	F7
Borrisoleigh	59	G7
Borroloola	113	H2
Borrowdale	55	F2
Borshchev	73	J1
Borshchovochnyy Khrebet	85	J6
Borth	52	C2
Borujen	95	K6
Borujerd	94	J5
Borve	57	A4
Borzhomi	77	K2
Borzya	85	K7
Bosa	69	B5
Bosanski Brod	72	E3
Bosanski Novi	72	D3
Bosanski Petrovac	72	D3
Boscastle	52	C4
Bose	93	L4
Bos Gradiska	72	D3
Boshruyeh	95	N5
Bosilegrad	73	G4
Boskovice	71	G4
Bosna	72	E3
Bosnia-Herzegovina	72	D3
Bosnik	114	B2
Bosobolo	106	C2
Boso-hanto	89	H8
Bosphorus	76	C2
Bossambele	102	C6
Bossangoa	102	C6
Bossier City	128	F4
Bostan *Iran*	94	H6
Bostan *Pakistan*	92	C2
Bostanabad	94	H3
Bosten Bagrax Hu	86	F3
Boston *U.K.*	53	G2
Boston *U.S.A.*	125	Q5
Boston Mountains	128	E3
Botesdale	53	J2
Botev	73	H4
Botevgrad	73	G4
Bothel	55	F2
Bothnia, Gulf of	62	J5
Botna	73	K2
Botosani	73	J2
Botsmark	62	J4
Botswana	108	D4
Botte Donato	69	F6
Bottenhavet	63	H6
Bottenviken	62	K4
Bottesford	53	G2
Bottineau	123	P3
Bottisham	53	H2
Bottrop	70	B3
Botucatu	138	G4
Bouafle	104	D4
Bouake	104	D4
Bouar	102	C6
Bouarfa	100	E2
Boucant Bay	113	G1
Bouchegouf	69	A7
Bougainville	114	E3
Bougainville, Cape	112	F1
Bougainville Reef	113	K2
Bougainville Strait	114	J5
Bougaroun, Cap	101	G1
Bougie	67	J4
Bougouni	100	D6
Bougzdul	67	H5
Bouhalloufa	67	G4
Bouillon	64	F4
Bouira	67	H4
Bou Ismail	67	H4
Boujdour	100	C3
Bou Kadir	67	G4
Boulay	64	G4
Boulder	123	M8
Boulder City	126	E3
Boulogne-sur-Mer	64	D3
Boumbe I	102	C7
Boumbe II	102	C7
Boumo	102	C6
Bouna	104	E4
Boundiali	104	D4
Boung Long	93	L6
Boun Tai	93	K4
Bountiful	122	J7
Bounty Islands	111	S11
Bourail	114	W16
Bourbon-l'Archambault	65	E5
Bourbonnais *France*	65	E5
Bourbonnais *U.S.A.*	124	G6
Bourbonne-les-Bains	65	F5
Bourem	100	E5
Bourganeuf	65	D6
Bourg-en-Bresse	65	E5
Bourges	65	E5
Bourgogne	65	F5
Bourgogne, Canal de	65	E5
Bourg-Saint-Andeol	65	F6
Bourke	113	K5
Bourne	53	G2
Bournemouth	53	F4
Bou Saada	101	F1
Boussac	65	E5
Bousso	102	C5
Boutilimit	100	C5
Boves	68	A3
Bovey	52	D4
Bovey Tracy	52	D4
Bovingdon	53	G3
Bovino	69	E5
Bow	122	H2
Bowbells	123	N3
Bowen	113	K3
Bowers Bank	118	Ab9
Bowes	55	G2
Bowfell	55	F2
Bowie	128	D4
Bow Island	122	J3
Bowkan	94	H3
Bowland, Forest of	55	G2
Bowling Green *Kentucky*	124	G8
Bowling Green *Ohio*	124	J6
Bowman	123	N4
Bowman Bay	120	M4
Bowness	55	G2
Bowness-on-Solway	55	F2
Bowraville	113	L5
Boxford	53	H2
Bo Xian	93	N2
Boxing	87	M4
Box Tank	113	J5
Boyabat	76	F2
Boyang	87	M6
Boyarka	84	F2
Boyd Lake	119	Q3
Boyer	124	C6
Boyle	58	F5
Boyne	58	K5
Boynton Beach	129	M7
Boyuibe	138	D4
Bozburun	76	C4
Bozcaada	75	H3
Boz Daglari	76	B3
Bozdogan	76	C4
Bozeman	122	J5
Bozen	68	C2
Boze Pole	71	G1
Bozkir	76	E4
Bozoum	102	C6
Bozova	77	H4
Bozqush, Kuh-e	94	H3
Bozuyuk	76	D3
Bra	68	A3
Brabant Island	141	V6
Brabourne	53	H3
Brac	72	D4
Bracadale	56	B3
Bracadale, Loch	56	B3
Bracciano	69	D4
Bracke	62	F5
Brackley	53	F2
Bracknell	53	G3
Brad	73	G2
Bradano	69	F5
Bradda Head	54	E2
Bradenton	129	L7
Bradford *U.K.*	55	H3
Bradford *U.S.A.*	125	L6
Bradford-on-Avon	52	E3
Bradwell Waterside	53	H3
Brady	127	N5
Brady Mountains	127	N5
Brae	56	A1
Braemar	57	E3
Braemore	56	E2
Braeswick	56	F1
Braga	66	B2
Bragado	139	D7
Braganca	66	C2
Braganca Paulista	138	G4
Bragar	56	B2
Brahman Baria	93	H4
Brahmani	92	G4
Brahmapur	92	F5
Brahmaputra	93	H3
Braidwood	113	K6
Braila	73	J3
Brailsford	53	F2
Brainerd	124	C3
Braintree	53	H3
Braishfield	53	F3
Brake	70	C2
Brakel	70	C3
Brallos	75	G3
Bramdean	53	F3
Bramham	55	H3
Bramming	63	C9
Brampton *Canada*	125	L5
Brampton *U.K.*	55	G2
Bramsche	70	B2
Brancaster	53	H2
Brancaster Bay	53	H2
Branco	136	E3
Branco, Cabo	137	L5
Brandberg	108	B4
Brandbu	63	D6
Brande	63	C9
Brandenburg	70	E2
Brandesburton	55	J3
Brandon *Canada*	123	Q3
Brandon *U.S.A.*	125	P5
Brandon Bay	59	B8
Brandon Mount	59	B8
Brandon Point	59	B8
Brandval	63	E6
Branesti	73	J3
Braniewo	71	H1
Bran, Pasul	73	H3
Brantford	125	K5
Brantley	129	J5
Brantome	65	D6
Brasileia	136	D6
Brasilia *Distrito Federal, Brazil*	138	F3
Brasilia *Minas Gerais, Brazil*	138	H3
Braslav	63	M9
Brasov	73	H3
Brassey Range	91	F5
Brates, Lacul	73	K3
Bratislava	71	G4
Bratsk	84	G5
Bratslav	73	K1
Braunau	68	D1
Braunsberg	71	H1
Braunschweig	70	D2
Braunton	52	C3
Brava	104	L7
Brava, Costa	67	H2
Bravo del Norte, Rio	127	L6
Brawley	126	E4
Bray	59	K6
Bray Head	59	B9
Bray Island	120	L4
Brazil	137	G5
Brazos	128	D5
Brazzaville	106	C3
Brcko	72	E3
Brda	71	G2
Breadalbane	57	D4
Breaksea Sound	115	A6
Brean	52	D3
Brebes	90	D7
Brechfa	52	C3
Brechin	57	F4
Breckenridge *Texas*	128	C4
Breckenridge *Minnesota*	124	B3
Breckland	53	H2
Brecknock, Peninsula	139	B10
Breclav	71	G4
Brecon	52	D3
Brecon Beacons	52	D3
Breda	64	F3
Bredon Hill	53	F3
Bredstedt	70	C1
Breezewood	125	L7
Bregenz	68	B2
Bregovo	73	G3
Breidafjordur	62	T12
Brejo	137	J4
Brekken	62	D5
Brekstad	62	C5
Bremen *U.S.A.*	129	K4
Bremen *Germany*	70	C2
Bremerhaven	70	C2
Bremer Range	112	E5
Bremerton	122	C4
Bremervorde	70	C2
Brendon Hills	52	D3
Brenham	128	D5
Brenig, Llyn	55	F3
Brenish	56	A2
Brenner Pass	68	C2
Breno	68	C3
Brenta	68	C3
Brentford	53	G2
Brentwood *U.K.*	53	H3
Brentwood *U.S.A.*	125	P6
Brescia	68	C3
Breskens	64	E3
Breslau	71	G3
Bressanone	68	C2
Bressay	56	A2
Bressay Sound	56	A2
Bressuire	65	C5
Brest *France*	64	A4
Brest *Belorussia*	71	K2
Brestlitovsk	79	E5
Brest Litovsk	71	K2
Bretagne	64	B4
Bretcu	73	J2
Breteuil *France*	64	D4
Breteuil *France*	64	E4
Breton, Cape	121	Q8
Breton Sound	128	H6
Brett	53	H2
Brett, Cape	115	E1
Breueh	90	B4
Brevoort Island	120	P5
Brewer	125	R4
Brewster	122	E3
Brewton	129	J5
Breznice	70	E4
Brezo, Sierra del	66	D1
Bria	102	D6
Briancon	65	G6
Brianne, Llyn	52	D2
Briare	65	E5
Bribie Island	113	L4
Brichany	73	J1
Bricquebe	53	N7
Bride	54	E2
Bridestowe	52	C4
Bridgend *Mid Glamorgan, U.K.*	52	D3
Bridgend *Strathclyde, U.K.*	57	B5
Bridge of Allan	57	E4
Bridge of Gaur	57	D4
Bridge of Orchy	57	D4
Bridge of Weir	57	D5
Bridgeport *Alabama*	129	K3
Bridgeport *California*	126	C1
Bridgeport *Connecticut*	125	P6
Bridgeport *Nebraska*	123	N7
Bridgeton	125	N7
Bridgetown *Australia*	112	D5
Bridgetown *Barbados*	133	T8
Bridgetown *Canada*	121	N9
Bridgewater	121	P9
Bridgnorth	52	E2
Bridgwater	52	D3
Bridgwater Bay	52	D3
Bridlington	55	J2
Bridlington Bay	55	J2
Bridport	52	E4
Brieg	71	G3
Brienne-le-Chateau	64	F4
Brier Island	125	S4
Briey	64	F4
Brig	68	A2
Brigg	55	J3
Brighouse	55	H3
Brightlingsea	53	J3
Brighton	53	G4
Brignoles	65	G7
Brihuega	66	E2
Brikama	104	B3
Brindakit	85	P4
Brindisi	69	F5
Brinian	56	F1
Brinkley	128	G3
Brioude	65	E6
Brisbane	113	L4
Bristol *U.K.*	52	E3
Bristol *U.S.A*	125	P6
Bristol Bay	118	D4
Bristol Channel	52	D2
Bristol Lake	126	E3
Bristow	128	D3
British Columbia	118	L4
Brits	108	E5
Britstown	108	D6
Brittle, Lake	57	B3
Brive-la-Gaillarde	65	D6
Briviesca	66	E1
Brixham	52	D4
Brlik	86	C3
Brno	71	G4
Broad	129	M3
Broadback	121	L7
Broad Bay	56	B2
Broad Cairn	57	E4
Broad Haven	58	C3
Broad Hinton	53	F3
Broadhurst Range	112	E3
Broad Sound *Australia*	113	K3
Broad Sound *U.K.*	52	B3
Broadstairs	53	J3
Broads, The	53	J2
Broadus	123	M5
Broadway	53	F2
Brochel	56	B3
Brocken	70	D3
Brockenhurst	53	F4
Brock Island	120	D2
Brockman, Mount	112	D3
Brockton	125	Q5
Brod	73	F5
Broddanes	62	U12
Brodeur Peninsula	120	J3
Brodick	57	C5
Brodick Bay	57	C5
Brodnica	71	H2
Brodokalmak	84	Ad5
Brody	79	D5
Brok	71	J2
Broken Bay	113	L5
Broken Bow *Nebraska*	123	Q7
Broken Bow *Oklahoma*	128	E3
Broken Bow Lake	128	E3
Broken Hill *Australia*	113	J5
Broken Hill *Zambia*	107	E5
Bromberg	71	G2
Bromley	53	H3
Bromsgrove	53	E2
Bromyard	52	E2
Bronderslev	63	C8
Bronnoysund	62	E4
Bronte	69	E7
Brookfield	124	D7
Brookhaven	128	G5
Brookings *Oregon*	122	B6
Brookings *S. Dakota*	123	R5
Brookneal	125	L8
Brooks	122	H2
Brooks Range	118	D2
Brooksville	129	L6
Broome	112	E2
Broom, Loch	56	C3
Brora *U.K.*	56	D2
Brora *U.K.*	56	E2
Brosteni	73	G3
Broto	67	F1
Brotton	55	J2
Brou	64	D4
Brough	55	G2
Brough Head	56	E1
Brough Ness	58	F2
Broughshane	58	K3
Broughton	57	E5
Broughton in Furness	55	F2
Broughton Island	120	P4
Broughton Poggs	53	F3
Browerville	124	C3
Brow Head	59	C10
Brownfield	127	L4
Brownhills	53	F2
Browning	122	H3
Brownsville	128	D8
Brownwood	128	C5

Name	Page	Grid
Brownwood, Lake	127	N5
Bru	62	Y12
Bruar, The Falls of	57	E4
Bruay-en-Artois	64	E3
Bruce Bay	115	B5
Bruce, Mount	112	D3
Bruce Mountains	120	M3
Bruchsal	70	C4
Bruck	68	F1
Bruck an der Mur	68	E2
Brue	52	E3
Bruernish Point	57	A4
Bruges	64	E3
Brugg	68	B2
Brugge	64	E3
Bruhl	70	B3
Bruichladdich	57	B5
Brumado	137	J6
Brumunddal	63	D6
Brunei	90	E4
Brunette Downs	113	H2
Brunflo	62	F5
Brunico	68	C2
Brunkeberg	63	C7
Brunn	71	G4
Brunsbuttel	70	C2
Brunswick *Georgia*	129	M5
Brunswick *Maine*	121	N9
Brunswick *Maryland*	125	M7
Brunswick *Germany*	70	D2
Brunswick Bay	112	E2
Brunswick, Península	139	B10
Bruny Island	111	L10
Brusa	76	C2
Brush	123	N7
Brusilovka	79	J5
Brusovo	84	D4
Brussel	64	F3
Bruthen	113	K6
Bruton	52	E3
Bruxelles	64	F3
Bryan *Ohio*	124	H6
Bryan *Texas*	128	D5
Bryan, Mount	113	H5
Bryansk	79	E5
Bryanskoye	79	H7
Bryher	52	K5
Bryne	63	D6
Brynmawr	52	D3
Brynzeny	73	J1
Brza Palanka	73	G3
Brzava	73	F3
Brzeg	71	G3
Bua *Fiji*	114	R8
Bua *Sweden*	63	E8
Buala	114	J6
Bubanza	107	E3
Bubiyan	97	J2
Buca *Fiji*	114	R8
Buca *Turkey*	76	B3
Bucak	76	D4
Bucaramanga	136	C2
Buchach	79	D6
Buchan	56	F3
Buchanan	104	C4
Buchanan, Lake	127	N5
Buchan Gulf	120	M3
Buchannan Bay	120	L2
Bucharest	73	J3
Buchholz	70	C2
Buchlgvie	57	D4
Buchloe	70	D4
Buchon, Point	126	B3
Buchs	68	B2
Buckeye	126	F4
Buckfastleigh	52	D4
Buckhannon	125	K7
Buckhaven	57	E4
Buckie	56	F3
Buckingham	53	G3
Buckingham Bay	113	H1
Buckinghamshire	53	G3
Buckkisla	76	E4
Buckley	55	F3
Bucksburn	57	F3
Buck, The	56	F3
Bucuresti	73	J3
Bud	62	B5
Budapest	72	E2
Budardalur	62	U12
Budareyri	62	X12
Budaun	92	E3
Budduso	69	B5
Bude *U.K.*	52	C4
Bude *U.S.A.*	128	G5
Bude Bay	52	B4
Budennovsk	79	G7
Budingen	70	C3
Budir	62	Y12
Budjala	106	C2
Budleigh Salterton	52	E4
Budogoshch	78	E4
Budun	87	K1
Budungbudung	91	F6
Budu, Sabkhat al	97	J5
Buea	105	G5
Buenaventura *Colombia*	136	B3
Buenaventura *Mexico*	127	J6
Buenaventura, Bahia	136	B3
Buena Vista	125	L8
Buena Vista Lake Bed	126	C3
Buenos Aires	139	D6
Buenos Aires, Lago	139	B9
Buffalo *New York*	125	L5
Buffalo *S. Dakota*	123	N5
Buffalo *Texas*	128	D5
Buffalo *Wyoming*	123	L5
Buffalo Lake	119	M3
Buffalo Narrows	119	P4
Buftea	73	H3
Bug	71	K2
Buga	136	B3
Bugdayli	95	M2
Bugel, Tanjung	90	E7
Bugoynes	62	N2
Bugrino	78	H2
Bugsuk	91	F4
Bugulma	78	J5
Buguruslan	78	J5
Buhl	122	G6
Buhusi	73	J2
Buie, Loch	57	B4
Builth Wells	52	D2
Buin	114	G5
Buinsk	78	H5
Buin Zahra	95	K4
Buitrago del Lozoye	66	E2
Bujaraloz	67	F2
Buje	72	B3
Bujumbura	107	E3
Buk	72	D2
Buka	114	E3
Bukama	106	E4
Bukavu	107	E3
Bukhara	80	H6
Bukittinggi	90	D6
Bukk	72	F1
Bukoba	107	F3
Bukoloto	107	F2
Bula	114	A2
Bulanash	84	Ad5
Bulancak	77	H2
Bulandshahr	92	E3
Bulanik	77	K3
Bulanovo	79	K5
Bulawayo	108	E4
Buldan	76	C3
Buldana	92	E4
Buldir Island	118	Ab9
Buldurty	79	J6
Bulgan *Mongolia*	86	G2
Bulgan *Mongolia*	87	J2
Bulgaria	73	G4
Buliluyan, Cape	91	F4
Bulkeley	55	G3
Bulle	68	A2
Buller	115	C4
Bullhead City	126	E3
Bull Shoals Lake	128	F2
Bulolo	114	D3
Bulum	85	M2
Buma	114	K6
Bumba	106	D2
Buna	74	E2
Bunbeg	58	F2
Bunbury	112	D5
Bunclody	59	J7
Buncrana	58	H2
Bundaberg	113	L3
Bundoran	58	F4
Bungalaut, Selat	90	B6
Bungay	53	J2
Bungo-suido	89	D9
Bunguran Utara, Kepulauan	90	D5
Bunia	107	F2
Bunie	128	F5
Bunratty	59	E7
Buntingford	53	G3
Buntok	90	E6
Bunyan	77	F3
Buolkalakh	85	K2
Buol Kheyr	95	K7
Buorkhaya, Guba	85	N2
Buorkhaya, Mys	85	N2
Buqayq	97	J4
Buqum, Harrat al	96	F6
Buram	102	E5
Buran	86	F2
Buraydah	96	F3
Burbage	53	F3
Burbank	126	C3
Burco	103	J6
Burdalyk	95	S2
Burdekin	113	K3
Burdur	76	D4
Burdur Golu	76	D4
Bure	53	J2
Burea	62	J4
Burentsogt	87	L2
Bureya *Russia*	85	M7
Bureya *Russia*	85	N6
Burg	70	D2
Burgas	73	J4
Burgdorf	68	A2
Burgeo	121	Q8
Burgersdorp	108	E6
Burgess Hill	53	G4
Burghead	56	E3
Burghead Bay	56	E3
Burgh-le-Marsh	55	K3
Burgos	66	E1
Burgsteinfurt	70	B2
Burgsvik	63	H8
Burguete	67	F1
Burhan Budai Shan	93	J1
Burhaniye	76	B3
Burhanpur	92	E4
Burias	91	G3
Burica, Punta	132	F10
Burin Peninsula	121	Q8
Buri Peninsula	96	D9
Buriram	93	K5
Burj Safita	77	G5
Burke Island	141	S4
Burketown	113	H2
Burkhala	85	R4
Burley	122	H6
Burli	79	J5
Burlington *Canada*	125	L5
Burlington *Colorado*	123	N8
Burlington *Iowa*	124	E6
Burlington *N. Carolina*	129	N2
Burlington *Vermont*	125	P4
Burlington *Washington*	122	C3
Burlton	52	E2
Burlyu-Tobe	86	D2
Burma (see Myanmar)	93	J4
Burmantovo	78	L3
Burnaby	122	C3
Burneston	55	H2
Burnet	128	C5
Burnham-on-Crouch	53	H3
Burnham-on-Sea	52	E3
Burnie	113	K7
Burnley	55	G3
Burns	122	E6
Burntwood	119	R4
Burqan	97	H2
Burqin	86	F2
Burra	113	H5
Burravoe	56	A1
Burray	56	F2
Burren, The	59	D6
Burriana	67	F3
Burrow Head	54	E2
Burrs Junction	122	F6
Burrundie	112	G1
Burton Joyce	53	F2
Burton Lake	121	L7
Burton Latimer	53	G2
Burton upon Stather	55	J3
Burton-upon-Trent	53	F2
Burtrask	62	J4
Buru	91	H6
Burum	97	J9
Burundi	107	E3
Burunnoye	79	J5
Bururi	107	E3
Burwell	56	F2
Burwick	56	F2
Bury	55	G3
Burylbaytal	86	C2
Burynshik	79	J6
Bury Saint Edmunds	53	H2
Busayta, Al	96	D1
Bushat	74	E2
Bushehr	95	K7
Bushimaie	106	D4
Bushmills	58	J2
Businga	106	D2
Busira	106	C3
Busk	71	L4
Buskerud	63	C6
Busko	71	J3
Busselton	112	D5
Bussol , Proliv	85	S7
Bustakh, Ozero	85	Q2
Busto Arsizio	68	B3
Busuanga	91	G3
Buta	106	D2
Butang Group	93	J7
Butare	107	E3
Bute	57	C5
Bute, Sound of	57	C5
Butiaba	107	F2
Butler	125	L6
Butmah	77	K4
Butte	122	H5
Buttermere	55	F2
Butterworth *Malaysia*	90	C4
Butterworth *South Africa*	108	E6
Buttevant	59	E8
Button Islands	121	P5
Butuan	91	H4
Butung	91	G7
Buturlinovka	79	G5
Buulobarde	103	J7
Buurhakaba	107	H2
Buwatah	96	D4
Buxton	55	H3
Buy	78	G4
Buyba	84	E6
Buynaksk	79	H7
Buyr Nuur	87	M2
Buyuk Agri Dagi	77	L3
Buyuklacin	76	F2
Buyuk Menderes	76	C4
Buzancais	65	D5
Buzau *Romania*	73	J3
Buzau *Romania*	73	J3
Buzi	109	F3
Buzovyazy	78	K5
Buzuluk	84	Ae6
Buzuluk	79	J5
Byam Martin, Cape	120	L3
Byam Martin Island	120	F2
Byczyna	71	H3
Bydgoszcz	71	G2
Byers	123	M8
Byfleet	53	G3
Byglandsfjord	63	B7
Bykhov	79	E5
Bykovo *Russia*	79	H6
Bykovo *Russia*	78	H3
Byla Slatina	73	G4
Bylot Island	120	L3
Byrock	113	K5
Byron, Cape	113	L4
Byron, Isla	139	A9
Byrranga, Gory	84	E2
Byrum	63	D8
Byserovo	78	J4
Byske	62	J4
Byskealven	62	J4
Bystra	71	H4
Bystraya	85	T6
Bystrzyca Klodzka	71	G3
Bytantay	85	N3
Bytca	71	H4
Byten	71	L2
Bytom	71	H3
Bytow	71	G1
Byxelkrok	63	G8

C

Name	Page	Grid
Caala	106	C5
Caatingas	137	H5
Caballos Mestenos, Llano de los	127	K6
Caballeria, Cabo	67	J2
Cabanatuan	91	G2
Cabano	125	R3
Cabeza de Buey	66	D3
Cabeza Lagarto, Punta	136	B6
Cabezas	138	D3
Cabimas	136	C1
Cabinda *Angola*	106	B4
Cabinda *Angola*	106	B4
Cabo	137	L5
Cabo Colnet	126	D5
Cabo Gracias a Dios, Punta	132	F7
Cabonga, Reservoir	125	M3
Cabool	124	D8
Caboolture	113	L4
Cabora Bassa Dam	109	F3
Cabo Raso	139	C8
Caborca	126	F5
Cabot Strait	121	P8
Cabourg	64	C4
Cabourne	55	J3
Cabrach	56	E3
Cabra del Santo Cristo	66	E4
Cabrera	67	H3
Cabrera, Sierra	66	C1
Cabriel	67	F3
Cabrobo	137	K5
Cabruta	136	D2
Cacak	72	F4
Caceras *Spain*	66	C3
Caceres *Brazil*	138	E3
Caceres *Colombia*	136	B2
Cache Creek	122	C8
Cache Peak	122	H6
Cachimbo	137	G5
Cachimbo, Serra do	137	G5
Cachi, Nevado de	138	C4
Cachoeira	138	K6
Cachoeiro de Itapemirim	138	H4
Cachos, Punta de	138	B5
Cacinci	72	D3
Cacipore, Cabo	137	G3
Cacolo	106	C5
Caconda	106	C5
Cacula	106	B5
Cadadley	103	H6
Cadale	107	J2
Cadaques	67	H1
Cadereyta	128	C8
Cader Idris	52	D2
Cadibarrawirracana, Lake	113	H4
Cadillac *Canada*	123	L3
Cadillac *U.S.A.*	124	H4
Cadi, Sierra del	67	G1
Cadiz	66	C4
Cadiz	91	G3
Cadiz, Baia de	66	C4
Cadiz, Golfo de	66	C4
Caen	64	C4
Caerdydd	52	D3
Caerfyrddin	52	C3
Caergybi	54	E3
Caernarfon	54	E3
Caernarfon Bay	54	E3
Caerphilly	52	D3
Caersws	52	D2
Caetite	137	J6
Cafayate	138	C5
Cagayan	91	G2
Cagayan de Oro	91	G4
Cagayan Islands	91	G4
Cagayan Sulu	91	F4
Cagliari	69	B6
Cagliari, Golfo di	69	B6
Caguan	136	C3
Caguas	133	P5
Cahama	106	B6
Caha Mountains	59	C9
Caherbarnagh	59	D8

Carryduff	58	L3	Castro del Rio	66	D4	Celaya	131	J7	Chaibasa	92	G4
Carsamba	76	E4	Castropol	66	C1	Celebes	91	G6	Chai Buri	93	K5
Carsamba	77	G2	Castro Urdiales	66	E1	Celebi	76	E3	Chaiya	93	J7
Carsibasi	77	H2	Castro Verde	66	B4	Celestun	131	P7	Chaiyaphum	93	K5
Carson City	126	C1	Castrovillari	69	F6	Celikhan	77	H3	Chajari	138	E6
Carson Sink	122	E8	Castuera	66	D3	Celina	124	H6	Chala	136	C7
Carsphairn	57	D5	Cat	77	J3	Celje	72	C2	Chalais	65	D6
Cartagena Colombia	136	B1	Catacamas	132	E7	Celle	70	D2	Chalap Dalan	92	B2
Cartagena Spain	67	F4	Catacaos	136	A5	Celtik	76	D3	Chala, Punta	136	B7
Cartago Colombia	136	B3	Cataingan	91	G3	Celyn, Llyn	52	D2	Chalatenango	132	C7
Cartago Costa Rica	132	F10	Catak	77	K3	Cemaes Head	52	C2	Chaldonka	85	K6
Cartaret	53	N7	Catakkopru	77	J3	Cemilbey	76	F2	Chale	53	F4
Cartaxo	66	B3	Catalca	76	C2	Cemisgezek	77	H3	Chaleur, Baie de	121	N8
Cartaya	66	C4	Cataluna	67	G2	Cendrawasih, Teluk	91	K6	Chaleur Bay	125	T3
Carteret	64	C4	Catalzeytin	76	F2	Cenga	91	H6	Chalhuanca	136	C6
Carterton	115	E4	Catamarca	138	C5	Cenrana	91	F6	Chalisgaon	92	E4
Carthage Missouri	124	C8	Catanduanes	91	G3	Center	128	E5	Challaco	139	C7
Carthage Texas	128	E4	Catanduva	138	G4	Centinela, Picacho Del	127	L6	Challacombe	52	D3
Cartier Island	110	F4	Catania	69	E7	Cento	68	C3	Challans	65	C5
Cartwright	121	Q7	Catanzaro	69	F6	Central	57	D4	Challis	122	G5
Caruara	137	K5	Cataqueama	136	E6	Central African Republic	102	D6	Chalmny Varre	78	F2
Carumbo	106	C4	Catastrophe, Cape	113	H5	Central Brahui Range	92	C3	Chalna	93	G4
Carupano	136	E1	Catatumbo	133	L10	Central, Cordillera Colombia	136	B3	Chamba India	92	E2
Caruthersville	128	H2	Catbalogan	91	G3	Central, Cordillera Dominican Republic	133	M5	Chamba Russia	84	G4
Carvoeiro, Cabo	66	B3	Caterham	53	G3	Central, Cordillera Peru	136	B5	Chambal	92	E3
Cary	52	E3	Catete	106	B4	Central, Cordillera Philippines	91	G2	Chamberlain Australia	112	F2
Casablanca	100	D2	Cathcart	108	E6	Central Heights	126	G4	Chamberlain U.S.A.	123	Q6
Casa Grande	126	G4	Cat Island	133	K2	Centralia	122	C4	Chambersburg	125	M7
Casale Monferrato	68	B3	Cato	111	N6	Central Makran Range	92	B3	Chambery	65	F6
Casalmaggiore	68	C3	Catoche, Cabo	131	R7	Central, Massif	65	E6	Chamela	130	G8
Casamance	104	B3	Catria, Monte	68	D4	Central Range	114	C2	Chamical	138	C6
Casanare	136	C2	Catrimani Brazil	136	E3	Central Siberian Plateau	84	H3	Chamonix	65	G6
Casas Ibanez	67	F3	Catrimani Brazil	136	E3	Cephalonia	75	F3	Chamouchouane	125	P2
Cascade	122	F5	Catskill	125	P5	Cepu	90	E7	Champagne	64	F4
Cascade Mountains	122	D3	Catskill Mountains	125	N5	Ceram	91	H6	Champagnole	65	F5
Cascade Point	115	B5	Catwick Islands	93	L6	Cercal	66	B4	Champaign	124	F6
Cascade Range	122	C6	Cauca	133	K11	Cerchov	70	E4	Champflower	52	D3
Cascais	66	B3	Caucaia	137	K4	Ceres	138	G3	Champlaine, Lake	125	P4
Cascapedia	125	S2	Caucasia	133	K11	Ceret	65	E7	Champlitte	65	F5
Cascavel Ceara, Brazil	137	K4	Caucasus	77	L1	Cerignola	69	E5	Champoton	131	P8
Cascavel Parana, Brazil	138	F4	Cauit Point	91	H4	Cerigo	75	G4	Chamrajnagar	92	E6
Caschuil	138	C5	Caulkerbush	55	F1	Cerkes	76	E2	Chamusca	66	B3
Caserta	69	E5	Caungula	106	C4	Cerkeskoy	76	B2	Chanaral	138	B5
Casey	141	H5	Cauquenes	139	B7	Cermei	73	F2	Chanaran	95	P3
Cashel	59	G7	Caura	133	Q11	Cermik	77	H3	Chanca	66	C4
Casiguran	91	G2	Causapscal	125	S2	Cerna Romania	73	G3	Chandalar	118	F2
Casilda	138	D6	Caussade	65	D6	Cerna Romania	73	K3	Chandausi	92	E3
Casma	136	B5	Cauterets	65	C7	Cerne Abbas	52	E4	Chandeleur Islands	128	H6
Casnewydd	52	E3	Cauto	132	J4	Cerralvo	128	C7	Chandigarh	92	E2
Caspe	67	F2	Cauvery	92	E6	Cerralvo, Isla	130	E5	Chandler	121	P8
Casper	123	L6	Cavado	66	B2	Cerreto Sannita	69	E5	Chandmani Mongolia	86	G2
Caspian Sea	51	S7	Cavaillon	65	F7	Cerro Azul	136	B6	Chandmani Mongolia	86	H2
Cass	124	J5	Cavalcante	138	H6	Cerro de Pasco	136	B6	Chandpur	93	H4
Cassamba	106	D5	Cavally	104	D4	Cerro Machin	131	L9	Chandrapur	92	E5
Casse, Grande	65	G6	Cavan Ireland	58	H5	Cerro Manantiales	139	C10	Chandvad	92	D4
Cassiar Mountains	118	J3	Cavan Ireland	58	H5	Cerros Colorados, Embalse	139	C7	Chanf	95	Q8
Cassinga	106	C6	Cavdir	76	C4	Cervaro	69	E5	Changan	109	F4
Cassino	69	D5	Cavendish	53	H2	Cervati, Monte	69	E6	Changane	109	F4
Cass Lake U.S.A.	124	C3	Cavite	91	G3	Cervera	67	G2	Changbai	88	B5
Cass Lake U.S.A.	124	C3	Caxias	136	C4	Cervera de Pisuerga	66	D1	Changbai Shan	88	B4
Cassongue	106	B5	Caxias	137	J4	Cervia	68	D3	Changchun	87	P3
Casteljaloux	65	D6	Caxias do Sul	138	E5	Cervione	69	B4	Changde	93	M3
Castellammare del Golfo	69	D6	Caxito	106	B4	Cesar	133	L9	Chang-hua	87	N7
Castellammare, Golfo di	69	D6	Cay	76	D3	Cesena	68	D3	Chang Jiang	87	M5
Castellane	65	G7	Cayagzi	76	F2	Cesenatico	68	D3	Chang, Ko	93	K6
Castellar de Santiago	66	E3	Caycuma	76	E2	Cesis	63	L8	Changle	87	M4
Castellar de Santisteban	66	E3	Cayeli	77	J2	Ceske Budejovice	70	F4	Changling	87	N3
Castelli	139	E7	Cayenne	137	G3	Cesky Brod	70	F3	Changma	86	H4
Castellnedd	52	D3	Cayeux	64	D3	Cesme	76	B3	Changnyon	87	P4
Castellon de la Plana	67	F3	Caygoren Baraji	76	C3	Cessnock	113	L5	Changsan-got	87	N4
Castellote	67	F2	Cayiralan	77	F3	Cetate	73	G3	Changsha	93	M3
Castelnaudary	65	D7	Cayirli	77	H3	Cetinje	72	E4	Changshan	87	M6
Castelo Branco	66	C3	Caykara	77	J2	Cetinkaya	77	G3	Changtai	87	M7
Castelsarrasin	65	D6	Caylarbasi	77	H4	Cetraro	69	E6	Changting	87	M6
Casteltermini	69	D7	Cayman Brac	132	H5	Ceuta	66	D4	Changwu	93	L1
Castelvetrano	69	D7	Cayman Trench	132	F5	Ceva-i-Ra	111	R6	Changxing	87	M5
Castets	65	C7	Caynabo	103	J6	Cevennes	65	F6	Changyi	87	M4
Castilla la Nueva	66	E3	Cayuga Lake	125	M5	Cevherli	76	F4	Changzhi	87	L4
Castilla la Vieja	66	D2	Cayuga Lake	125	M5	Cevio	68	B2	Changzhou	87	M5
Castilletes	136	C1	Cazma Croatia	72	D3	Cevizli	76	D4	Channel Islands	53	M7
Castillo, Pampa del	139	C9	Cazma Croatia	72	D3	Ceyhan Turkey	76	F4	Channel-Port-aux-Basques	121	Q8
Castillos	139	F6	Cazombo	106	D5	Ceyhan Turkey	77	F4	Chantada	66	C1
Castlebar	58	D5	Cazorla	66	E4	Ceylanpinar	77	J4	Chanthaburi	93	K6
Castlebay	57	A4	Cea	66	D1	Chaadayevka	79	H5	Chantilly	64	E4
Castlebellingham	58	K5	Ceahlau	73	H2	Chablis	65	E5	Chantonnay	65	C5
Castleblayney	58	J4	Ceanannus Mor	58	J5	Chacabuco	139	D6	Chantrey Inlet	120	G4
Castle Bolton	55	H2	Ceara	137	K5	Chachani, Nevado de	138	B3	Chanute	128	E2
Castle Carrock	55	G2	Ceara-Mirim	137	K5	Chachapoyas	136	B5	Chany, Ozero	84	B6
Castleconnel	59	F7	Ceballos	127	K7	Chachoengsao	93	K6	Chao	136	B5
Castledawson	58	J3	Cebollera	66	E1	Chaco Austral	138	D5	Chao Hu	87	M5
Castlederg	58	G3	Cebu Philippines	91	G3	Chaco Boreal	138	E4	Chao Phraya	93	K6
Castledermot	59	J7	Cebu Philippines	91	G3	Chaco Central	138	D4	Chaor He	87	N2
Castle Douglas	54	F2	Cecina	68	C4	Chad	102	C5	Chaouen	100	D1
Castleellis	59	K8	Cedar	124	D5	Chad Russia	78	K4	Chaoyang China	87	N3
Castleford	55	H3	Cedar City	126	F2	Chadan	84	E6	Chaoyang China	87	N3
Castleisland	59	D8	Cedar Creek Lake	128	D4	Chadderton	55	G3	Chaozhou	87	M7
Castlemaine	113	J6	Cedar Falls	124	D5	Chaddesley Corbett	53	E2	Chapadinha	137	J4
Castlemartyr	59	F9	Cedar Lake	119	Q5	Chadileovu	139	C7	Chapala, Laguna de	130	H7
Castlepollard	58	H5	Cedar Rapids	124	E6	Chad, Lake	102	B5	Chapanda	85	N5
Castlerea	58	E5	Cedartown	129	K3	Chadobets	84	F5	Chapayevo	79	J5
Castle Rock	123	M8	Cedros, Isla de	126	E6	Chadron	123	N6	Chapayevsk	79	H5
Castleside	55	H2	Ceduna	113	G5	Chagai Hills	92	B3	Chapayev-Zheday	85	K4
Castleton	55	H3	Ceelbuur	103	J7	Chagda	85	N5	Chapchachi	79	H6
Castletown Highland, U.K.	56	E2	Ceeldheer	103	J7	Chaghcharan	95	S4	Chapeco	138	F5
Castletown Isle of Man, U.K.	54	E2	Ceerigaabo	103	J5	Chagny	65	F5	Chapel-en-le-Frith	55	H3
Castletownbere	59	C9	Cefalu	69	E6	Chagoda	78	F4	Chapel Hill	129	N3
Castletownshend	59	D9	Cega	66	D2	Chagos Archipelago	82	F7	Chapeltown Grampian, U.K.	56	E3
Castlewellan	58	L4	Cegled	72	E2	Chahah Burjah	95	R6			
Castonos	127	M7	Ceica	73	G2	Chah Bahar	95	Q9			
Castor	122	J1	Cekerek Turkey	77	F2	Chahbounia	67	H5			
Castres	65	E7	Cekerek Turkey	76	F2	Chaho	88	B5			
Castries	133	S7	Celalli	77	G3	Chahuites	131	M9			
Castro	139	B8	Celano	69	D4						
Castro Alves	137	K6									

Chugunash 84 D6
Chuguyevka 88 D3
Chukchi Sea 118 B2
Chuken 88 F2
Chukhloma 78 G4
Chukotat 121 L5
Chukotskiy Khrebet 85 W3
Chukotskiy Poluostrov 81 V3
Chulak-Kurgan 86 B3
Chula Vista 126 D4
Chulman 85 L5
Chulmleigh 52 D4
Chulym *Russia* 84 C5
Chulym *Russia* 84 C5
Chum 78 L2
Chumbicha 138 C5
Chumek 86 F2
Chumikan 85 P6
Chumphon 93 J6
Chuna 84 F5
Chunchon 87 P4
Chungju 87 P4
Chunhua 88 C4
Chunoyar 84 F5
Chunya 107 F4
Chunyang 88 B4
Chunyang 89 B7
Chuquibamba 138 B3
Chuquicamata 138 B4
Chur 68 B2
Churan 85 L4
Churapcha 85 N4
Churchill *Canada* 119 S4
Churchill *Canada* 119 S4
Churchill *Newfoundland, Canada* 121 P7
Churchill, Cape 119 S4
Churchill Falls 121 P7
Churchill Peak 118 L4
Church Stretton 52 E2
Churia Ghati Hills 92 G3
Churin 136 B6
Churu 92 D3
Churuguara 136 D1
Chushevitsy 78 G3
Chushul 92 E2
Chusovaya 78 K4
Chusovoy 78 K4
Chust 86 C3
Chute des Passes 125 Q2
Chuuronjang 88 B5
Chuxiong 93 K4
Chu Yang Sin 93 L6
Chwarta 94 G4
Chyulu Range 107 G3
Cianjur 90 D7
Cicekdagi 76 F3
Cicia 114 S8
Cide 76 E2
Cidones 66 E2
Ciechanow 71 J2
Ciego de Avila 132 H4
Cienaga 136 C1
Cienfuegos 132 G3
Cieszyn 71 H4
Cieza 67 F3
Ciftehan 76 F4
Cifteler 76 D3
Cifuentes 66 E2
Cihanbeyli 76 E3
Cijara, Embalse de 66 D3
Cilacap 90 D7
Cildir 77 K2
Cildir Golu 77 K2
Cilo Dagi 77 L4
Cimarron 128 A2
Cimone, Monte 68 C3
Cimpeni 73 G2
Cimpina 73 H3
Cimpulung 73 H3
Cimpuri 73 J2
Cinar 77 J4
Cinaruco 136 D2
Cina, Tanjung 90 C7
Cinca 67 G2
Cincer 72 D4
Cincinnati 124 H7
Cinderford 52 E3
Cine 76 C4
Cingus 77 H3
Cinto, Monte 69 B4
Circeo, Capo 69 D5
Circle *Alaska* 118 G2
Circle *Montana* 123 M4
Circular Reef 114 D2
Cirebon 90 D7
Cirencester 53 F3
Ciri 136 E5
Ciria 67 E2
Ciro 69 F6
Cisco 128 C4
Cislau 73 J3
Cisna 71 K4
Cisneros 136 B2
Cistierna 66 D1
Citac, Nevado 136 C6
Citlaltepetl, Volcan 131 L8
Citt a di Castello 68 D4
Cittanova 69 F6
Ciucului, Muntii 73 H2
Ciudad Acuna 127 M6
Ciudad Bolivar 136 E2
Ciudad Camargo 127 K7
Ciudad Cuauhtemoc 131 P10
Ciudad del Carmen 131 P8
Ciudad del Maiz 131 K6
Ciudad de Mexico 131 K8
Ciudadela 67 H3
Ciudad Guayana 136 E2
Ciudad Guzman 130 H8
Ciudad Ixtepec 131 M9
Ciudad Juarez 127 J5
Ciudad Lerdo 127 L8
Ciudad Madero 131 L6
Ciudad Mante 131 K6
Ciudad Mier 128 C7
Ciudad Obregon 127 H7
Ciudad Ojeda 133 M9
Ciudad Piar 133 R11
Ciudad Real 66 E3
Ciudad Rodrigo 66 C2
Ciudad Valles 131 K7
Ciudad Victoria 131 K6
Civa Burun 77 G2
Cividale del Friuli 68 D2
Civita Castellana 69 D4
Civitanova Marche 68 D4
Civitavecchia 69 C4
Civray 65 D5
Civril 76 C3
Cizre 77 K4
Clach Leathad 57 D4
Clacton-on-Sea 53 J3
Cladich 57 C4
Claerwen Reservoir 52 D2
Clain 65 D5
Claire, Lac a lEau 121 M6
Claire, Lake 119 N4
Clamecy 65 E5
Clane 59 J6
Clanton 129 J4
Clanwilliam 108 C6
Claonaig 57 C5
Clare *Australia* 113 H5
Clare *Ireland* 59 D7
Clare Island 58 B5
Claremont 125 P5
Claremorris 58 D5
Clarence *New Zealand* 115 D5
Clarence *New Zealand* 115 D5
Clarence, Cape 120 H3
Clarence Head 120 L2
Clarence Strait *Australia* 112 G1
Clarence Strait *U.S.A.* 118 J4
Clarence Town 133 K3
Clarinda 124 C6
Clarion 125 L6
Clark 123 K5
Clarke River 113 K2
Clark Fork *Montana* 122 H4
Clark Fork *Washington* 122 F3
Clark, Lake 118 E3
Clarksburg 125 K7
Clarksdale 128 G3
Clarks Hill Lake 129 L4
Clarkston 122 F4
Clarksville *Arkansas* 128 F3
Clarksville *Tennessee* 129 J2
Clar, Loch nan 56 D2
Clatteringshaws Loch 57 D5
Claughton 55 G2
Clavering O 120 X3
Claxton 129 M4
Clay Center 123 R8
Clay Cross 55 H3
Claydon 53 J2
Clayton *Georgia* 129 L3
Clayton *New Mexico* 127 L2
Clear, Cape 59 C10
Clearfield *Pennsylvania* 125 L6
Clearfield *Utah* 122 J7
Clear Fork 127 N4
Clear Hills 119 M4
Clear Island 59 D10
Clear Lake *California* 122 C8
Clear Lake *Iowa* 124 D5
Clear Lake Reservoir 122 D7
Clearwater *Canada* 122 G1
Clearwater *Canada* 119 P4
Clearwater *Florida* 129 L7
Clearwater *Idaho* 122 F4
Clearwater Mountains 122 G4
Cleethorpes 55 J3
Clerke Reef 112 D2
Clermont *Australia* 113 K3
Clermont *France* 64 E4
Clermont-Ferrand 65 E6
Clermont-l'Herault 65 E7
Clervaux 64 G3
Cleve 113 H5
Clevedon 52 E3
Cleveland *U.K.* 55 H2
Cleveland *Mississippi* 128 G4
Cleveland *Ohio* 125 K6
Cleveland *Tennessee* 129 K3
Cleveland *Texas* 128 E5
Cleveland, Cape 113 K2
Cleveland Hills 55 H2
Cleveland, Mount 122 H3
Cleveleys 55 F3
Clew Bay 58 C5
Clifden *Ireland* 59 B6
Clifden *New Zealand* 115 A7
Cliffe 53 H3
Cliffs of Moher 59 D7
Clifton 55 G2
Clincha Alta 136 B6
Clinch Mountains 129 L2
Clingmans Dome 129 L3
Clinton *Canada* 122 D2
Clinton *Illinois* 124 F6
Clinton *Iowa* 124 E6
Clinton *Mississippi* 128 G4
Clinton *Missouri* 124 D7
Clinton *N. Carolina* 129 N3
Clinton *Oklahoma* 128 C3
Clinton-Colden Lake 119 P3
Clipperton Island 117 J7
Clisham 56 B3
Clisson 65 C5
Clitheroe 55 G3
Cliza 138 C3
Cloates, Point 112 C3
Clogheen 59 G8
Clogherhead 58 K5
Clogher Head 58 K5
Clogh Mills 58 K3
Clonakilty 59 E9
Clonakilty Bay 59 E9
Cloncurry *Australia* 113 J3
Cloncurry *Australia* 113 J3
Clonmel 59 G8
Clonmult 59 F9
Clophill 53 G2
Cloppenburg 70 C2
Cloquet 124 D3
Cloud Peak 123 L5
Cloudy Bay 115 E4
Clough 58 L4
Cloughton 55 J2
Clovelly 52 C3
Clovis 127 L3
Cloyes 65 D4
Cluanie, Loch 57 C3
Cluj-Napoca 73 G2
Clun 52 E2
Cluny 65 F5
Cluses 65 G5
Clusone 68 B3
Clutha 115 B7
Clwyd *U.K.* 55 F3
Clwyd *U.K.* 55 F3
Clwydian Range 55 F3
Clyde *Canada* 120 N3
Clyde *U.K.* 57 E5
Clydebank 57 D5
Clyde, Firth of 57 D5
Clydesdale 57 E5
Clynnog-fawr 54 E3
Clywedog, Llyn 52 D2
Coa 66 C2
Coachella 126 D4
Coachella Canal 126 E4
Coaldale 126 D2
Coalinga 126 B2
Coalisland 58 J3
Coal River 118 K4
Coalville 53 F2
Coan, Cerro 136 B5
Coari *Brazil* 136 E4
Coari *Brazil* 136 E4
Coast Mountains 122 B2
Coast Range 122 C5
Coatbridge 57 D5
Coaticook 125 Q4
Coats Island 120 K5
Coats Land 141 Y3
Coatzacoalcos *Mexico* 131 M8
Coatzacoalcos *Mexico* 131 M9
Coban 132 B7
Cobar 113 K5
Cobh 59 F9
Cobija 136 D6
Cobourg 125 L5
Cobram 113 K6
Cobue 109 F2
Coburg 70 D3
Coburg Island 120 L2
Cochabamba 138 C3
Cochem 70 B3
Cochin 92 E7
Cochrane *Canada* 122 G2
Cochrane *Chile* 139 B9
Cock Bridge 57 E3
Cockburn 113 J5
Cockburnspath 57 F5
Cockenzie 57 F4
Cockerham 55 G3
Cockermouth 55 F2
Cockfield *Durham, U.K.* 55 H2
Cockfield *Suffolk, U.K.* 53 H2
Coco 132 E7
Cocoa 129 M6
Coco Channel 93 H6
Coco Islands 93 H6
Cocoparra Range 113 K5
Cocos 137 J6
Cocula 130 H7
Codajas 136 E4
Cod, Cape 125 R6
Codera, Cabo 136 D1
Codfish Island 115 A7
Codford 53 E3
Codigoro 68 D3
Cod Island 121 P6
Codo 137 J4
Codogno 68 B3
Cod's Head 59 B9
Coen 113 J1
Coeroeni 137 F3
Coesfeld 70 B3
Coeur d'Alene 122 F4
Coeur d'Alene Lake 122 F4
Coevorden 64 G2
Coffeyville 128 E2
Coffin Bay 113 H5
Coff's Harbour 113 L5
Cogealac 73 K3
Coghinas 69 B5
Cognac 65 C6
Cogo 105 G5
Cogolludo 66 E2
Cohuna 113 J6
Coiba, Isla 132 G11
Coigach 56 C2
Coigeach, Rubha 56 C2
Coihaique 139 B9
Coimbatore 92 E6
Coimbra 66 B2
Coipasa, Salar de 138 C3
Cokak 77 G4
Colac 113 J6
Colap 77 H4
Colatina 138 E3
Colby 123 P8
Colchester 53 H3
Cold Ashton 52 E3
Coldstream 57 F5
Coldwater *Kansas* 127 N2
Coldwater *Michigan* 124 H6
Colebrook 125 Q4
Coleman *Australia* 113 J1
Coleman *U.S.A.* 127 N5
Colemerick 77 K4
Coleraine *Australia* 113 J6
Coleraine *U.K.* 58 J2
Colesberg 108 E6
Coleshill 53 F2
Coles, Punta de 139 B3
Colfax 122 F4
Colgrave Sound 56 B1
Colhue Huapi, Lago 139 C9
Colima 130 H8
Colima, Nevado de 130 H8
Colinas 137 J5
Colintraive 57 C5
Coll 57 C4
Collatto 68 D2
College Park 129 K4
Collie 112 D5
Collier Bay 112 E2
Colliford Lake Reservoir 52 C4
Collingbourne Kingston 53 F3
Collingham 55 J3
Collingwood *Canada* 125 K4
Collingwood *New Zealand* 115 D4
Collins 128 H5
Collin Top 58 K3
Collooney 58 F4
Colmar 64 G4
Colmars 65 G6
Colmenar 66 D4
Colmenar Viejo 66 E2
Colne *Essex, U.K.* 53 H3
Colne *Lancashire, U.K.* 55 G3
Cologne 70 B3
Colombia 136 C3
Colombo 92 E7
Colomoncagua 132 C7
Colon *Cuba* 132 G3
Colon *Panama* 132 H10
Colonia Las Heras 139 C9
Colonna, Capo 69 F6
Colonsay 57 B4
Colorado *Argentina* 139 D7
Colorado *Arizona* 126 E4
Colorado *Texas* 127 M4
Colorado *U.S.A.* 123 L8
Colorado Canal 123 N8
Colorado, Cerro 126 E5
Colorado City 127 M4
Colorado River Aqueduct 126 D4
Colorado Springs 127 K1
Colsterworth 53 G2
Coluene 137 G6
Columbia *Missouri* 124 D7
Columbia *Pennsylvania* 125 M7
Columbia *S. Carolina* 129 M4
Columbia *Tennessee* 129 J3
Columbia *Washington* 122 D5
Columbia, District of 125 M7
Columbia Falls 122 G3
Columbia, Mount 119 M5
Columbine, Cape 108 C6
Columbus *Georgia* 129 K4
Columbus *Indiana* 124 H7
Columbus *Mississippi* 128 H4
Columbus *Montana* 123 K5
Columbus *Nebraska* 123 R7
Columbus *Ohio* 124 J7
Columbus *Texas* 128 D6
Colville *Alaska* 118 D2
Colville *Washington* 122 F3
Colville, Cape 115 E2
Colville Channel 115 E2
Colville Lake 118 K2
Colwyn Bay 54 F3
Comacchio 68 D3
Comana 73 J3
Comandante Ferraz 141 W6
Comandante Fontana 138 E5
Comayagua 132 D7
Combarbala 138 B6
Combe Martin 52 C3
Comber 58 L3
Combermere Bay 93 H5

162

Cuiaba *Brazil*	138	E3
Cuiaba *Brazil*	138	E3
Cuicatlan	131	L9
Cuilcagh	58	G4
Cuillin Hills	56	B3
Cuillin Sound	57	B3
Cuito	106	C6
Cuito Cuanavale	106	C6
Cuitzeo, Laguna de	131	J8
Cuiuni	136	E4
Cukai	90	C5
Cukurca	77	K4
Cu Lao Hon	93	L6
Culbertson	123	M3
Culebra Peak	127	K2
Culebra, Sierra de la	66	C2
Culiacan	130	F5
Culion	91	F3
Culiseui	137	G6
Culkein	56	C2
Cullera	67	F3
Cullin, Lough	58	D5
Cullman	129	J3
Cullybackey	58	K3
Culm	52	D4
Culmen	77	H4
Culpeper	125	L7
Cults	57	F3
Culverden	115	D5
Culworth	53	F2
Culzean Bay	57	D5
Cumacay	77	K3
Cumali	76	B2
Cumana	136	E1
Cumbal, Nevado de	136	B3
Cumberland *Kentucky*	124	H8
Cumberland *W. Virginia*	125	L7
Cumberland Bay	139	J10
Cumberland Mountains	129	K2
Cumberland Peninsula	120	P4
Cumberland Plateau	129	J3
Cumberland Sound	120	N4
Cumbernauld	57	E5
Cumbria	55	G2
Cumbrian Mountains	55	F2
Cumbum	92	E5
Cumina	137	F4
Cummings	122	C8
Cumnock	57	D5
Cumpas	127	H5
Cumra	76	E4
Cunderdin	112	D5
Cunene	106	B6
Cuneo	68	A3
Cunnamulla	113	K4
Cunningham	57	D5
Cuorgne	68	A3
Cupar	57	E4
Cupica	136	B2
Cuprija	73	F4
Cupula, Pico	130	D5
Curacao	133	N8
Curacautin	139	B7
Curaco	139	C7
Curaray	136	B4
Curepipe	109	L7
Curico	139	B7
Curitiba	138	F5
Curitibanos	138	F5
Currais Novos	137	K5
Curralinho	137	H4
Curra, Lough	59	E6
Currane, Lough	59	B9
Currelo	138	H3
Curtici	73	F2
Curtis *Canada*	120	J4
Curtis *U.S.A.*	123	P7
Curtis Channel	113	L3
Curtis Island *Australia*	113	L3
Curtis Island *New Zealand*	111	T8
Curua *Brazil*	137	G4
Curua *Brazil*	137	G5
Curuca	137	G4
Curupira	136	E4
Curupira, Sierra de	136	E3
Curuzu Cuatia	138	E5
Cushcamcarragh	58	C5
Cushendall	58	K2
Cushendun	58	K2
Cusiana	136	C3
Cut Bank	122	H3
Cuthbert	129	K5
Cutral-Co	139	B7
Cuttack	92	G4
Cuvelai	106	C6
Cuxhaven	70	C2
Cuyo Islands	91	G3
Cuyuni	136	F2
Cuzco	136	C6
Cvrsnica	72	D4
Cwmbran	52	D3
Cwmffrwd	52	C3
Cyclades	75	H4
Cynthiana	124	H7
Cypress Hills	123	K3
Cyprus	76	E5
Cyrene	101	K2
Czarna	71	J3
Czech Republic	70	F4
Czeremcha	71	K2
Czernowitz	73	H1
Czerwiensk	70	F2
Czestochowa	71	H3
Czluchow	71	G2

D

Dabakala	104	E4
Daban Shan	93	K1
Daba Shan	93	L2
Dabat	103	G5
Dabeiba	136	B2
Dabie Shan	93	N2
Dabola	104	C3
Daboya	104	E4
Dabrowa	71	K2
Dabrowa Gornicza	71	H3
Dabrowa Tarnowska	71	J3
Dabsan	86	G2
Da Cabreira, Sierra	66	B2
Dacca	93	G4
Dadale	114	J6
Daday	76	E2
Dadianzi	88	B4
Dadu	92	C3
Daeni	73	K3
Daer Reservoir	57	E5
Daet	91	G3
Dafla Hills	93	H3
Dafrah, Ad	97	L5
Dagana	104	B2
Dagardi	76	C3
Dagbasi	77	H2
Dagbeli	76	D4
Dagenham	53	H3
Daggs Sound	115	A6
Daglica	77	L4
Daglingworth	53	E3
Dagongcha	86	H4
Dagua	114	C2
Dagupan	91	G2
Dagyolu	77	H3
Dahab	96	B2
Dahanu	92	D5
Dahezhen	88	D2
Dahi, Nafud ad	96	G5
Da Hinggan Ling	87	N2
Dahlak Archipelago	96	E9
Dahlem	70	B3
Dahme	70	E3
Dahm, Ramlat	96	G8
Dahna, Ad *Saudi Arabia*	96	H6
Dahna, Ad *Saudi Arabia*	96	H4
Dahod	92	D4
Dahra	67	G4
Dahuk	77	K4
Dai	114	K5
Daia	73	J4
Daik	90	D6
Daimiel	66	E3
Daingean	59	H6
Dair, Jebel ed	102	F5
Dairut	102	F2
Daito-jima	83	M4
Dajarra	113	H3
Dakar	104	B3
Dakhla Oasis	102	E2
Dak Kon	93	L6
Dakoro	101	G6
Dakovica	72	F4
Dakovo	72	E3
Dakshin Gangotri	141	A5
Dala	114	K6
Dalaba	104	C3
Dalab, Chalp	95	S5
Dalad Qi	87	K3
Dala-Jarna	63	F6
Dalalven	63	G6
Dalaman	76	C4
Dalandzadgad	87	J3
Dalanganem Islands	91	G3
Dalaoba	86	E3
Da Lat	93	L6
Dalbandin	92	B3
Dalbeattie	54	F2
Dalby	113	L4
Dalch	52	D4
Dale *Norway*	63	A6
Dale *U.S.A.*	124	G7
Dalhalvaig	56	E2
Dalhart	127	L2
Dalhousie	125	S2
Dalhousie, Cape	118	K1
Dali	93	K3
Dalian	87	N4
Dalidag	94	H2
Dalkeith	57	E5
Dalkey	59	K6
Dallas	128	D4
Dalles, The	122	D5
Dall Island	118	J4
Dallol Bosso	101	F6
Dalma	97	L4
Dalmally	57	D4
Dalmatia	72	C3
Dalmellington	57	D5
Dalnaspidal	57	D4
Dalnegorsk	88	E3
Dalnerechensk	88	D3
Daloa	104	D4
Dalou Shan	93	L3
Dalrymple	57	D5
Dalrymple, Mount	113	K3
Dalsmynni	62	U12
Daltengani	92	F4
Dalton	129	K3
Daluolemi	88	B3
Dalupiri	91	G2
Dalvik	62	V12

Daly	112	G1
Daly Waters	113	G2
Damal	77	K2
Daman	92	D4
Damanhur	102	F1
Damar	91	H7
Damascus	77	G6
Damavand	95	L4
Damba	106	C4
Dame Marie	133	K5
Dame Marie, Cabo	133	K5
Damghan	95	M3
Damh, Loch	56	C3
Damietta	103	F1
Daming	87	M4
Damlacik	77	H4
Damodar	92	G4
Damoh	92	E4
Damongo	104	E4
Dampier	112	D3
Dampier Archipelago	112	D3
Dampier Land	112	E2
Dampier, Selat	91	J6
Dampier Strait	114	D3
Damqawt	97	L8
Da Nang	93	L5
Danau Toba	90	B5
Danba	93	K2
Danbury	125	P6
Danby Lake	126	E3
Dandong	87	N3
Daneborg	120	X3
Dangchang	93	K2
Dangori	93	J3
Dangrek, Phnom	93	K6
Dangshan	93	N2
Daniel	123	J6
Danilov	78	G4
Danilovgrad	72	E4
Dank	97	N5
Danli	132	D7
Dannenburg	70	D2
Dannevirke	115	F4
Danshui	87	L7
Dansville	125	M5
Danu	114	E2
Danube	71	H5
Danumparai	90	F5
Danville *Illinois*	124	G6
Danville *Kentucky*	124	H8
Danville *Virginia*	125	L8
Dan Xian	93	L5
Dany	113	J6
Danzig, Gulf of	71	H1
Dao	91	G3
Daoud	101	G1
Dao Xian	93	M3
Dapaong	104	F3
Dapiak, Mount	91	G4
Daqing	87	N2
Daqm	97	N7
Daqq-e-Patargan	95	Q5
Dara	94	C5
Darab	95	M7
Darabani	73	J1
Daran	95	K5
Dar Anjir, Kavir-e	95	M5
Darasun	85	J6
Daravica	74	F1
Darband	95	N6
Darbhanga	92	G3
Darby, Cape	118	C3
Dardanelle Lake	128	F3
Dardanelles	75	J2
Dar El Beida	100	D2
Darende	77	G3
Dar Es Salaam	107	G4
Dargaville	115	D1
Darica	76	C2
Darien, Golfo del	136	B2
Darija	77	K5
Darjeeling	93	G3
Darjiling	93	G3
Dar Lac, Cao Nguen	93	L6
Darlag	93	J2
Darling	113	J5
Darling Downs	113	K4
Darling Range	112	D5
Darlington *U.K.*	55	H2
Darlington *U.S.A.*	129	N3
Darmanesti	73	J2
Darmstadt	70	C4
Darnah	101	K2
Darnick	113	J5
Darnley Bay	118	L2
Darnley, Cape	141	E5
Daroca	67	F2
Darokhov	71	L4
Darovskoye	78	H4
Darreh Gaz	95	P3
Darsi	92	E5
Darsser Ort	70	E1
Dart	52	D4
Dartford	53	H3
Dartmoor	52	D4
Dartmouth *Canada*	121	P9
Dartmouth *U.K.*	52	D4
Darton	55	H3
Darty Mountains	58	F4
Daru	114	C3
Daruba	91	H5
Daruvar	72	D3
Darvel	57	D5

Darvi	86	G2
Darwen	55	G3
Darwin	112	G1
Darwin, Mount	126	C2
Daryacheh-ye Orumiyeh	77	L4
Darzin	95	P7
Das	97	L4
Dashitou	86	F3
Dashizhai	87	N2
Dashkhovuz	80	G5
Dasht *Iran*	95	N3
Dasht *Pakistan*	92	B3
Dashti-oburdon	86	B4
Da, Song	93	K4
Datca	76	B4
Datia	92	E3
Datong	87	L3
Datong Shan	93	J1
Datuk, Tanjung	90	D5
Datu Piang	91	G4
Daugava	63	M8
Daugavpils	63	P9
Daule *Ecuador*	136	B4
Daule *Ecuador*	136	B3
Daun	70	B3
Dauphin	119	Q5
Dauphine	65	F6
Dauphine, Alpes du	65	F6
Dauphin Lake	119	R5
Davangere	92	E6
Davao	91	H4
Davao Gulf	91	H4
Davarzan	95	N3
Dave Creek	127	H2
Davenport	124	E6
Daventry	53	F2
David	132	F10
David-Gorodok	79	D5
Davidson	123	L2
Davidson Mountains	118	G2
Davington	57	D7
Davis *Antarctic*	141	F5
Davis *Australia*	112	E3
Davis *U.S.A.*	126	K1
Davis Mountains	127	K5
Davis Sea	141	F6
Davis Strait	120	P4
Davlekanovo	78	K5
Davos	68	B2
Davulga	76	D3
Dawa	87	N3
Dawasir, Wadi al	96	G6
Dawa Wenz	103	H7
Dawhat Salwah	97	K4
Dawley	52	E2
Dawlish	52	D4
Dawna Range	93	J5
Dawqah	97	M7
Dawros Head	58	E3
Dawson *Australia*	113	K3
Dawson *Canada*	118	H3
Dawson *Georgia*	129	K5
Dawson *N. Dakota*	123	Q4
Dawson Creek	119	L4
Dawson, Mount	122	F2
Dawson Range	118	H3
Dawu	93	M2
Dawusi	93	H1
Dawwah	97	P6
Dax	65	C7
Da Xian	93	L2
Daxue Shan	93	K2
Dayr az Zawr	77	J5
Dayr Hafir	77	G4
Dayton *Ohio*	124	H7
Dayton *Tennessee*	129	K3
Dayton *Washington*	122	F4
Daytona Beach	129	M6
Dayu	93	M3
Da Yunhe	87	M4
Dayville	122	E5
Dazkiri	76	C4
De Aar	108	D6
Dead Sea	94	B6
Deakin	112	F5
Deal	53	J3
Dean	93	N3
Dean *Canada*	118	K5
Dean *U.K.*	55	G3
Dean, Forest of	52	E3
Dean Funes	138	D6
Dean Island	141	R4
Dearborn	124	J5
Dease Arm	119	L2
Dease Inlet	118	D1
Dease Lake	118	J4
Dease Strait	119	P2
Death Valley	126	D2
Deauville	64	D4
Deben	53	J2
Debin	85	S4
Deblin	71	J3
Deboyne Islands	114	E4
Debre Birhan	103	G6
Debrecen	73	F2
Debre Markos	103	G5
Debre Tabor	103	G5
Decatur *Alabama*	129	J3
Decatur *Georgia*	129	K4
Decatur *Illinois*	124	F7
Decatur *Indiana*	124	H6
Decatur *Texas*	128	D4
Decazeville	65	E6
Deccan	92	E5

Name	Page	Grid		Name	Page	Grid		Name	Page	Grid		Name	Page	Grid		Name	Page	Grid
Deception	108	D4		Dengkou	87	K3		Dewangiri	93	H3		Dinara Planina	72	D3
Deception	120	M5		Dengqen	93	J2		Dewas	92	H4		Dinard	64	B4
Dechang	93	K3		Den Haag	64	F2		De Witt	128	G3		Dinas Head	52	C2
Decize	65	E5		Den Helder	64	F2		Dewsbury	55	H3		Dinbych	55	F3
Decorah	124	E5		Denia	67	G3		Dey-Dey, Lake	112	G4		Dinbych-y-pysgod	52	C3
Deda	73	H2		Deniliquin	113	K6		Deyhuk	95	N5		Dinder	96	B10
Deddington	53	F3		Denio	122	E7		Deylaman	95	J3		Dindigul	92	E6
Dedeagach	75	H2		Denison *Iowa*	124	C6		Deyong, Tanjung	114	B3		Dinek	76	E4
Dedegol Daglari	76	D4		Denison *Texas*	128	D4		Deyyer	95	K8		Dinggye	93	G3
Dedekoy	76	E2		Denison, Mount	118	E4		Dez	94	J5		Dingle	59	B8
Dedougou	104	E3		Denizli	76	C4		Dezful	94	J5		Dingle Bay	59	B8
Dedu	87	P2		Denmark	63	B9		Dezhneva, Mys	118	B2		Dingle Peninsula	59	B8
Dee *Cheshire, U.K.*	55	G3		Denmark Strait	116	S2		Dezhou	87	M4		Dinguiraye	104	C3
Dee *Dumfries and*				Dennis Head	56	F1		Dhaka	93	G4		Dingwall	56	D3
Galloway, U.K.	54	F2		Denny	57	E4		Dhamar	96	G9		Dingxi	93	K1
Dee *Grampian, U.K.*	57	F3		Denpasar	90	F7		Dhampur	92	E3		Dingxin	86	H3
Dee, Linn of	57	E4		Densongi	91	G6		Dhamtari	92	F4		Dingxing	87	M4
Deep River	125	M3		Denta	73	F3		Dhanbad	92	G4		Dinh Lap	93	L4
Deeps, The	56	A2		Denton	128	D4		Dhandhuka	92	D4		Dinnington	55	H3
Deering, Mount	112	F4		D'Entrecasteaux Islands	114	E3		Dhang Range	92	F3		Dinosaur	123	K7
Deer Lake	121	Q8		D'Entrecasteaux, Point	112	D5		Dhankuta	93	G3		Dionard	56	D2
Deer Lodge	122	H4		Denver	123	M8		Dhar	92	E4		Diorbivol	104	C2
Defiance	124	H6		Deogarh	92	F4		Dharmapuri	92	E6		Diouloulou	104	B3
Defiance Plateau	127	H3		Deoghar	92	G4		Dharmavaram	92	E6		Diourbel	104	B3
Deflotte, Cape	114	X16		Deolali	92	D5		Dharmjaygarh	92	F4		Dipolog	91	G4
De Funiak Springs	129	J5		Deosai, Plains of	92	E2		Dharwad	92	D5		Dir	92	D1
Degeberga	63	F9		Dep	85	M6		Dhaulagiri	92	F3		Direction, Cape	113	J1
Degeh Bur	103	H6		Deqen	93	J3		Dhaulpur	92	E3		Dire Dawa	103	H6
Degelis	125	R3		Deqing	93	M4		Dhenkanal	92	G4		Direkli	77	G3
Degerhamn	63	G8		De Queen	128	E3		Dhenousa	75	H4		Dirk Hartogs Island	112	C4
Deggendorf	70	E4		Dera Bugti	92	C3		Dhermatas, Akra	75	G3		Dirra	102	E5
De Grey	112	E3		Dera Ghazikhan	92	D2		Dhermi	74	E2		Dirranbandi	113	K4
Dehaj	95	M6		Dera Ismail Khan	92	D2		Dheskati	75	F3		Disappointment, Cape	122	B4
Dehak	95	R8		Derajat	92	D2		Dhespotiko	75	H4		Disappointment, Lake	112	E3
Dehalak Deset	103	H4		Derazhno	71	M3		Dhialvos Zakinthou	75	F4		Discovery Bay	113	J6
Deh Bid	95	L6		Derazhnya	73	J1		Dhidhimotikhon	75	J2		Dishna *Egypt*	103	F2
Deh-Dasht	95	K6		Derbent	79	H7		Dhikti Ori	75	H5		Dishna *U.S.A.*	118	D3
Deheq	95	K5		Derby *Australia*	112	E2		Dhirfis	75	G3		Disko	120	R4
Dehiwala	92	E7		Derby *U.K.*	53	F2		Dhodhekanisos	75	J4		Disko Bay	120	R4
Dehkhvareqan	94	G3		Derbyshire	55	H3		Dhomokos	75	G3		Disna *Belarus*	63	M9
Dehloran	94	H5		Derekoy	76	B2		Dhoraji	92	D4		Disna *Belarus*	63	N9
Dehra Dun	92	E2		Dereli	77	H2		Dhoxaton	75	H2		Dispur	93	H3
Deh Salm	95	P6		Derg	58	G3		Dhrangadhra	92	D4		Diss	53	J2
Dehui	87	P3		Dergachi	79	F5		Dhrepanon, Akra	75	G3		Dissen	96	E8
Deim Zubeir	102	E6		Derg, Lough *Donegal, Ireland*	58	G3		Dhuburi	93	G3		Distrito Federal	138	G3
Dej	73	G2		Derg, Lough *Tipperary, Ireland*	59	F7		Dhule	92	D4		Ditchling Beacon	53	G4
De Kalb *Illinois*	124	F6		De Ridder	128	F5		Dia	75	H5		Ditinn	104	C3
De Kalb *Texas*	128	E4		Derik	77	J4		Diamante	138	D6		Dittaino	69	E7
Dekemhare	96	D9		Derinkuyu	76	F3		Diamantina *Australia*	113	H4		Ditton Priors	52	E2
Dekese	106	D3		Derna	101	K2		Diamantina *Brazil*	138	H3		Diu	92	D4
Delami	102	F5		Derong	93	J3		Diamantina, Chapada	137	J6		Divandarreh	94	H4
Delano	126	C3		Derravaragh, Lough	58	H5		Diamond Lake Junction	122	D6		Divinopolis	138	G4
Delaram	95	R5		Derry	58	H2		Diaoling	88	B3		Divi Point	92	F5
Delaware *Ohio*	124	J6		Derrynasaggart Mountains	59	D9		Diavata	75	G2		Divisor, Serra do	136	C5
Delaware *Pennsylvania*	125	N6		Derryveagh Mountains	58	F7		Diba al Hisn	97	N4		Divnoye	79	G6
Delaware *U.S.A.*	125	N7		Derudeb	103	G4		Dibaya	106	D4		Divrigi	77	H3
Delaware Bay	125	N7		Derveni	75	G3		Dibdibah, Ad	96	H2		Dixcove	104	E5
Delcevo	73	G5		Derventa	72	D3		Dibrugarh	93	H3		Dixon Entrance	118	J5
Delemont	68	A2		Derwent *Australia*	113	K7		Dickinson	123	N4		Diyadin	77	K3
Delft	64	F2		Derwent *Derbyshire, U.K.*	55	H3		Dickson	129	J2		Diyala	94	G4
Delfzijl	64	G2		Derwent *N. Yorkshire, U.K.*	55	J2		Dicle	77	J4		Diyarbakir	77	J4
Delgada, Punta	131	L8		Derwent Reservoir	55	H2		Didcot	53	F3		Diza	77	L3
Delgado, Cabo	109	H2		Derwent Water	54	E2		Dididnga Hills	103	F7		Dja	105	H5
Delgerhaan	87	J2		Derzhavinsk	84	Ae6		Didnovarre	62	K1		Djado	101	H4
Delgo	102	F3		Desaguadero *Argentina*	138	C6		Didwana	92	D3		Djambala	106	B3
Delhi *India*	92	E3		Desaguadero *Bolivia*	138	C3		Die	65	F6		Djanet	101	G4
Delhi *India*	92	E3		Descanso	126	D4		Diebougou	104	E3		Djelfa	101	F2
Delhi *Colorado*	127	L2		Deschambault Lake	119	Q5		Diefenbaker, Lake	123	L2		Djema	102	E6
Delhi *New York*	125	N5		Deschutes	122	D5		Diego-Suarez	109	J2		Djenne	100	E6
Delice *Turkey*	76	E3		Dese	103	G5		Dielette	53	N6		Djibouti	103	H5
Delice *Turkey*	76	F2		Deseado	139	C9		Dien Bien Phu	93	K4		Djibouti	103	H5
Delicias	127	K6		Desemboque	126	F5		Diepholz	70	C2		Djolu	106	D2
Delijan	95	K4		Desengano, Punta	139	C9		Dieppe	64	D4		Djougou	105	F4
Delingha	93	J1		Desert Center	126	E4		Dietfurt	70	D4		Djourab	102	C4
Delitzsch	70	E3		Desert Peak	122	H7		Diffa	101	H6		Djupivogur	62	X12
Delle	65	G5		Des Moines *U.S.A.*	124	D6		Digby	121	N9		Djurdjura	67	J4
Dellys	101	F1		Des Moines *U.S.A.*	124	D6		Digges Island	120	L5		Djursland	63	D8
Delmenhorst	70	C2		Desna	79	E5		Digne	65	G6		Dmitriya Lapteva, Proliv	85	Q2
Delnice	72	C3		Desolacion, Isla	139	B10		Digoin	65	F5		Dmitrov	78	F4
De Long Mountains	118	C2		Des Plaines	124	G5		Digor	77	K2		Dnepr	79	E6
Deloraine	113	K7		Dessau	70	E3		Digul	114	C3		Dneprovskaya Nizmennost	79	D5
Delray Beach	129	M7		Destna	71	G3		Diinsoor	107	H2		Dneprovsko-Bugskiy Kanal	71	L2
Del Rio	127	M6		Dete	108	E3		Dijlah, Nahr	77	K5		Dnestr	73	K2
Delsbo	63	G6		Detmold	70	C3		Dijon	65	F5		Dnestrovskiy Liman	73	L2
Delta *Colorado*	127	H1		Detour, Point	124	G4		Dikakah, Ad	97	K7		Dniprodzerzhynsk	79	E6
Delta *Utah*	126	F1		Detroit	124	J5		Dikanas	62	G4		Dnipropetrovsk	79	F6
Delta Junction	118	F3		Detroit Lakes	124	C3		Dikbiyik	77	G2		Dno	78	E4
Delvin	58	H5		Deutschlandsberg	68	E2		Dikili	76	B3		Doaktown	125	T3
Dema	78	J5		Deva	73	G3		Dikson	84	C2		Doba	102	C6
Demanda, Sierra de la	66	E1		Devakottai	92	E7		Dikwa	105	H3		Dobbiaco	68	D2
Demba	106	D4		Devdevdyak	84	H4		Dili	91	H7		Dobeln	70	E3
Dembi Dolo	103	F6		Devecikonagi	76	C3		Di Linh	93	L6		Dobiegniew	70	F2
Demer	64	F3		Devecser	72	D2		Dilizhan	77	L2		Dobo	114	A3
Demerara	136	F2		Devegedcidi Baraji	77	H3		Dillia	101	H5		Doboj	72	E3
Deming	127	J4		Develi	76	F3		Dilling	102	E5		Dobra	71	H3
Demini	136	E3		Deventer	64	G2		Dillingen	70	D4		Dobre Miasto	71	J2
Demirci	76	C3		Deveron	56	F3		Dillingham	118	D4		Dobric	73	J4
Demir Kazik	76	F4		Devils	127	M5		Dillon	122	H5		Dobrodzien	71	H3
Demirkoy	76	B2		Devil's Bridge	52	C2		Dilolo	106	D5		Dobrogea	73	K3
Demmin	70	E2		Devils Lake	123	Q3		Dimapur	93	H3		Dobrovolsk	71	K1
Demnate	100	D2		Devils Paw	118	J4		Dimashq	77	G6		Dobrush	79	E5
Demopolis	129	J4		Devils Tower	123	M5		Dimbelenge	106	D4		Dobryanka	78	K4
Dempo, Gunung	90	C6		Devin	73	H5		Dimbokro	104	E4		Dobsina	71	J4
Demyanskoye	84	Ae5		Devizes	53	F3		Dimbo vita	73	H3		Dobson	115	C5
Denakil	103	H5		Devli	92	E3		Dimitrovgrad *Bulgaria*	73	H4		Dochart	57	D4
Denan	103	H6		Devnya	73	J4		Dimitrovgrad *Russia*	78	H5		Docking	53	H2
Denau	86	B4		Devoll	75	F2		Dimona	94	B6		Dodecanese	75	J4
Denbigh	55	F3		Devon	52	D4		Dimovo	73	G4		Dodge City	127	M2
Denbigh, Cape	118	C3		Devon Island	120	J2		Dinagat	91	H3		Dodman Point	52	C4
Denby Dale	55	H3		Devonport	115	E2		Dinajpur	93	G3		Dodoma	107	G4
Dendang	90	D6		Devrek	76	D2		Dinan	64	B4		Doetinchem	64	G3
Dendermonde	64	F3		Devrekani	76	E2		Dinanagar	92	E2		Dofa	91	H6
Dendi	103	G6		Devrez	76	E2		Dinant	64	F3		Dogai Coring	93	G2
Denezhkino	84	D3		Devyatkova	84	Ae5		Dinar	76	D3		Doganbey	76	D4

Doganhisar **76** D3
Dogankent **76** F4
Dogansehir **77** G3
Doganyol **77** H3
Doganyurt **76** E2
Dog Creek **122** C2
Dogen Co **93** H2
Dog Lake **124** F2
Dogo **89** D7
Dogondoutchi **101** F6
Dogubeyazit **77** L3
Dogukardeniz Daglari **77** J2
Doha **97** K4
Doi Luang **93** K5
Dojran **73** G5
Dojransko Jezero **73** G5
Doka *Indonesia* **114** A3
Doka *Sudan* **96** B10
Dokkum **64** G2
Dokshitsy **63** M9
Dokurcun **76** D2
Dolak **114** B3
Dolak, Tanjung **91** K7
Dolanog **52** D2
Dolbeau **125** P2
Dol-de-Bretagne **64** C4
Dole **65** F5
Dolgellau **52** D2
Dolginovo **71** M1
Dolgiy, Ostrov **84** Ac3
Dolgoye **71** K4
Dolina **79** C6
Dolinsk **88** J2
Dolinskaya **79** E6
Dollar **57** E4
Dollar Law **57** E5
Dolni Kralovice **70** F4
Dolok, Tanjung **114** A3
Dolomitiche, Alpi **68** C2
Dolo Odo **103** H7
Dolores *Argentina* **139** E7
Dolores *Uruguay* **139** E6
Dolores *U.S.A.* **122** K8
Dolphin and Union Strait **119** N1
Dolphin, Cape **139** E10
Dolsk **71** G3
Domanic **76** C3
Dombas **63** C5
Dombe **109** F3
Dombe Grande **106** B5
Dombovar **72** E2
Dombrad **73** F1
Dome, Puy de **65** E6
Domett **115** D5
Domfront **64** C4
Dominica **133** S7
Dominical **132** F10
Dominican Republic **133** M5
Dominion, Cape **120** M4
Domo **103** J6
Domodossola **68** B2
Domuya, Cerro **139** B7
Don *Grampian, U.K.* **56** F3
Don *S. Yorkshire, U.K.* **55** H3
Don *Russia* **79** G6
Donaghadee **58** L3
Donaldsville **128** G5
Donau **68** E1
Donauworth **70** D4
Don Benito **66** D3
Doncaster **55** H3
Dondo **106** B4
Dondra Head **92** F7
Donegal *Ireland* **58** F3
Donegal *Ireland* **58** G3
Donegal Bay **58** F3
Donegal Point **59** C7
Donenbay **86** D2
Doneraile **59** E8
Donetsk **79** F6
Dongan *Heilongjiang, China* **88** E2
Dongan *Hunan, China* **93** M3
Dongara **112** C4
Dongbolhai Shan **93** G2
Dongchuan **93** K3
Dongfang **93** L5
Dongfanghong **88** D2
Donggala **91** F6
Dong Hoi **93** L5
Dongjingcheng **88** B3
Dongliu **87** M5
Dongluk **86** F4
Dongning **88** C3
Dongola **102** F4
Dongping **87** M4
Dongshan **87** N5
Dongsheng **87** K4
Dongtai **87** N5
Donguena **106** B6
Dong Ujimqin Qi **87** M2
Dongxi Lian Dao **87** M5
Donington **53** G2
Doniphan **124** E8
Donji Vakuf **72** D3
Donna **62** E3
Donner Pass **122** D8
Donnington **52** E2
Dooagh **58** B5
Doon **57** D5
Doonbeg **59** C7
Doonerak, Mount **118** E2
Doon, Loch **57** D5
Doorin Point **58** F3
Dor **95** R6
Dorada, Costa **67** G2
Dora, Lake **112** E3
Dora Riparia **68** A3
Dorbiljin **86** E2
Dorchester **52** E4
Dorchester, Cape **120** L4
Dordogne **65** C6
Dordrecht **64** F3
Dore **65** E6
Dore Lake **119** P5
Dore, Mont **65** E6
Dorgali **69** B5
Dori **104** E3
Dorking **53** G3
Dormo, Ras **96** F10
Dornbirn **68** B2
Dornie **56** C3
Dornoch **56** D3
Dornoch Firth **56** D3
Dorofeyevskaya **84** C2
Dorohoi **73** J2
Dorotea **62** G4
Dorovitsa **78** H4
Dorset **52** E4
Dortdivan **76** E2
Dortmund **70** B3
Dortyol **77** G4
Doruokha **84** J2
Dorutay **77** L3
Dosatuy **85** K7
Dosso **101** F6
Dossor **79** J6
Dothan **129** K5
Douai **64** E3
Douala **105** G5
Douarnenez **64** A4
Double Mountain Fork **127** M4
Doubs **65** F5
Doubtful Sound **115** A6
Doubtless Bay **115** D1
Doue-la-Fontaine **65** C5
Douentza **100** E5
Douglas *South Africa* **108** D5
Douglas *Isle of Man, U.K.* **54** D2
Douglas *Strathclyde, U.K.* **57** E5
Douglas *Arizona* **127** H5
Douglas *Georgia* **129** L5
Douglas *Wyoming* **123** M6
Doullens **64** E3
Doulus Head **59** B9
Doume **105** H5
Doune **57** D4
Dourada, Serra **137** H6
Dourados *Brazil* **138** E3
Dourados *Brazil* **138** F4
Dourados, Serra dos **138** F4
Douro **66** B2
Dove **55** H3
Dove Dale **55** H3
Dover *U.K.* **53** J3
Dover *Delaware* **125** N7
Dover *New Hampshire* **125** Q5
Dover *Ohio* **125** K6
Dover-Foxcroft **125** R4
Dover, Strait of **53** J4
Dovrefjell **62** C5
Dowa **107** F5
Dowlatabad *Afghanistan* **95** R5
Dowlatabad *Afghanistan* **95** S3
Dowlatabad *Iran* **95** N7
Dowlat Yar **92** C2
Down **58** L4
Downham Market **53** H2
Downpatrick **58** L4
Downpatrick Head **58** D4
Downs, The **53** J3
Downton **53** F4
Dow Rud **94** J5
Dowshi **92** C1
Dozen **89** D7
Draa, Oued **100** D3
Drac **65** F6
Dracevo **73** F5
Drachten **64** G2
Dragalina **73** J3
Dragasani **73** H3
Dragoman **73** G4
Dragonera, Isla **67** H3
Dragon's Mouth **133** S9
Dragsfjard **63** K6
Draguignan **65** G7
Dra, Hamada du **100** D3
Drake **123** P4
Drakensberg **108** E6
Drake Passage **141** V7
Drama **75** H2
Drammen **63** H7
Drangedal **63** C7
Draperstown **58** J3
Dras **92** E2
Drau **68** E2
Drava **72** E3
Dravograd **72** C2
Drawa **70** F2
Drawsko, Jezioro **71** G2
Drayton Valley **119** N5
Dren **73** G4
Drenewydd **52** D2
Dresden **70** E3
Dresvyanka **78** K2
Dreux **64** D4
Drin **75** F2
Drina **72** E3
Drin i zi **74** E1
Drobak **63** H7
Drobin **71** H2
Drogheda **58** K5
Drogichin **71** L2
Drogobych **79** C6
Drohiczyn **71** K2
Droichead Atha **58** K5
Droichead Nua **59** J6
Droitwich **53** E2
Drokiya **73** J1
Drome **65** F6
Dromedary, Cape **113** L6
Dromore **58** K4
Dronfield **55** H3
Dronne **65** D6
Dronning Maud Land **141** Z5
Dropt **65** D6
Drovyanaya **84** A2
Drumcollogher **59** E8
Drumheller **122** H2
Drummond **122** H4
Drummond Islands **124** J3
Drummond Range **113** K3
Drummondville **125** P4
Drummore **54** E2
Drumochter, Pass of **57** D4
Drumshanbo **58** F4
Druridge Bay **55** H1
Druskininkai **71** K1
Druzhba *Kazakhstan* **86** E2
Druzhba *Russia* **71** J1
Druzhina **85** R3
Drvar **72** D3
Drweca **71** H2
Dry **112** G2
Dry Bay *Canada* **121** N6
Dry Bay *U.S.A.* **118** H4
Dryden **124** D2
Drysdale, River **112** F2
Dschang **105** H4
Duab **94** J4
Dualo **91** G6
Duarte, Pico **133** M5
Duba **96** B3
Dubai **97** M4
Dubawnt Lake **119** Q3
Dubayy **97** M4
Dubbagh, Jambal Ad **96** B3
Dubbo **113** K5
Dubenskiy **79** K5
Dublin *Ireland* **59** K6
Dublin *Ireland* **59** K6
Dublin *U.S.A.* **129** L4
Dublin Bay **59** K6
Dubna **78** F4
Dubno **79** D5
Du Bois **125** L6
Dubois *Idaho* **122** H5
Dubois *Wyoming* **123** K6
Dubossary **79** D6
Dubreka **104** C4
Dubrovitsa **71** M3
Dubrovka *Russia* **79** E5
Dubrovka *Russia* **79** G6
Dubrovnik **72** E4
Dubrovskoye **84** J5
Dubuque **124** E5
Duchang **87** M6
Duchesne *U.S.A.* **123** J7
Duchesne *U.S.A.* **123** J7
Duchess **113** H3
Ducie Island **143** J5
Duck **129** J3
Ducklington **53** F3
Duck Mountain **119** Q5
Duddington **53** G2
Dudinka **84** D3
Dudley **53** E2
Duenas **66** D2
Duero **66** D2
Duffield **53** F2
Duff Islands **114** N6
Dufftown **56** E3
Dufton **55** G2
Duga Zapadnaya, Mys **85** R5
Dughaill, Loch **56** C3
Dugi Otok **72** C3
Duisburg **70** B3
Dukambiya **96** C9
Dukat **73** G4
Duk Fadiat **102** F6
Duk Faiwil **102** F6
Dukhan **97** K4
Duki Bolen **85** P6
Dukla **71** J4
Dukou **93** K3
Dulan **93** J1
Duldurga **85** J6
Duleek **58** K5
Dulga-Kyuyel **84** J4
Dulgalakh **85** N3
Dullingham **53** H2
Dull Lake **118** C3
Dulnain **56** E3
Dulovo **73** J4
Duluth **124** D3
Duma **77** G6
Dumaguete **91** G4
Dumai **90** C5
Dumaran **91** F3
Dumas *Arkansas* **128** G4
Dumas *Texas* **127** M3
Dumbarton **57** D5
Dumbea **114** X17
Dumbier **71** H4
Dumfries **55** F1
Dumfries and Galloway **57** E5
Dumitresti **73** J3
Dumka **93** G4
Dumlu **77** J2
Dumlupinar **76** C3
Dumoine **125** M3
Dumont d'Urville **141** K5
Dumont d'Urville Sea **141** J6
Dumyat **103** F1
Duna **72** E2
Dunaj **71** H5
Dunajec **71** J3
Dunany Point **58** K5
Dunarea **73** J3
Dunaujvaros **72** E2
Dunav **73** H4
Dunay *Moldova* **73** K3
Dunay *Russia* **88** D4
Dunayevtsy **73** J1
Dunay, Ostrov **85** L2
Dunbar *Australia* **113** J2
Dunbar *U.K.* **57** F4
Dunblane **57** E4
Dunboyne **59** K6
Duncan *Canada* **122** C3
Duncan *U.S.A.* **128** D3
Duncan Passage **93** H6
Duncansby Head **56** E2
Dunchurch **53** F2
Dundaga **63** K8
Dundalk *Ireland* **58** K4
Dundalk *U.S.A.* **125** M7
Dundalk Bay **58** K5
Dundas **120** M2
Dundas, Lake **112** E5
Dundas Peninsula **120** D3
Dundas Strait **112** G1
Dun Dealgan **58** K4
Dundee *South Africa* **108** F5
Dundee *U.K.* **57** F4
Dundonald **57** D5
Dundonnell **56** C3
Dundrennan **54** F2
Dundrod **58** K3
Dundrum **58** L4
Dundrum Bay **58** L4
Dundwa Range **92** F3
Dunecht **57** F3
Dunedin *New Zealand* **115** C6
Dunedin *U.S.A.* **129** L6
Dunfanaghy **58** G2
Dunfermline **57** E4
Dungannon **58** J3
Dungarpur **92** D4
Dungarvan **59** G8
Dungarvan Harbour **59** G8
Dungeness **53** H4
Dungiven **58** J3
Dungloe **58** F3
Dungu **107** E2
Dungun **90** C5
Dunholme **55** J3
Dunhua **88** B4
Dunhuang **86** F3
Dunkeld **113** J6
Dunkerque **64** E3
Dunkirk **125** L5
Dunkur **103** G5
Dunkwa **104** E4
Dun Laoghaire **59** K6
Dunlavin **59** J6
Dunleer **58** K5
Dunmanus Bay **59** C9
Dunmanway **59** D9
Dunmore Town **132** J2
Dunmurry **58** K3
Dunnet Bay **56** E2
Dunnet Head **56** E2
Dunoon **57** D5
Dunragit **54** E2
Duns **57** F4
Dunseith **123** P3
Dunsford **52** D4
Dunstable **53** G3
Dunstan Mountains **115** B6
Dunster **52** D3
Duntelchaig, Loch **56** D3
Duntroon **115** C6
Dunvegan **56** B3
Dunvegan Head **56** B3
Dupang Ling **93** M3
Dupree **123** P5
Duque de York, Isla **139** A10
Du Quoin **124** F7
Duragan **76** F2
Durance **65** F7
Durand, Recif **114** Y17
Durango *Mexico* **130** G5
Durango *U.S.A.* **127** J2
Durankulak **73** K4
Durant **128** D3
Durazno **138** E6
Durazzo **74** E2
Durban **108** F6
Durcal **66** E4
Durdevac **72** D2
Durelj **87** J4
Duren **70** B3
Durg **92** F4
Durgapur *Bangladesh* **93** H3
Durgapur *India* **93** G4
Durham *U.K.* **55** H2

Name	Page	Grid
El Sahuaro	126	F5
El Salado	139	C9
El Salto	130	G6
El Salvador	132	C8
El Sam'an de Apure	133	N11
El Sauzal	126	D5
Elsham	55	J3
El Socorro	126	F5
Elster	70	E3
Elsterwerda	70	E3
El Sueco	127	J6
El Suweis	103	F2
El Tambo	136	B4
Eltham	115	E3
El Thamad	96	B2
El Tigre	133	Q10
El Tih	96	A2
Eltisley	53	G2
El Tocuyo	133	N10
Elton *U.K.*	53	G2
Elton *Russia*	79	H6
El Tule	131	L9
El Tur	96	A2
Eluru	92	F5
Elvanfoot	57	E5
Elvas	66	C3
Elveden	53	H2
Elverum	63	D6
El Viejo	133	L11
El Vigia	136	C2
Elwy	55	F3
Ely *Cambridgeshire, U.K.*	53	H2
Ely *Mid Glamorgan, U.K.*	52	D3
Ely *Minnesota*	124	E3
Ely *Nevada*	126	E1
Elze	70	C2
Ema	63	M7
Emae	114	U12
Emamrud	95	M3
Emam Taqi	95	P4
Eman	63	G8
Emao	114	U12
Emba	79	K6
Embarcacion	138	D4
Embleton	55	H1
Embona	75	J4
Embrun	65	G6
Embu	107	G3
Emden	70	B2
Emerald	113	K3
Emerald Island	120	D2
Emerson	123	R3
Emet	76	C3
Emeti	114	C3
Emi	84	F6
Emigrant Pass	122	F7
Emin	86	E2
Emine, Nos	73	J4
Emirdag	76	D3
Emir Dagi	76	D3
Emita	113	K7
Emmaboda	63	F8
Emmaste	63	K7
Emmen	64	G2
Emory Peak	127	L6
Empalme	126	G7
Empangeni	109	F5
Empedrado	138	E5
Empingham	53	G2
Empoli	68	C4
Emporia *Kansas*	128	D1
Emporia *Virginia*	125	M8
Ems	70	B2
Emu	88	B4
Enard Bay	56	C2
Encantada, Cerro Del La	126	E5
Encarnacion	138	E5
Enchi	104	E4
Encinal	128	C6
Encontrados	136	C2
Encounter Bay	113	H6
Endau	90	C5
Ende	91	G7
Endeavour Strait	113	J1
Enderbury Island	111	U2
Enderby Land	141	D5
Endicott Mountains	118	C2
Ene	136	C6
Enez	76	B2
Enfield *Ireland*	59	J6
Enfield *U.K.*	53	G3
Engano, Cabo	133	N5
Engano, Cape	91	G2
Engaru	88	J3
Engels	79	H5
Enggano	90	C7
Engger Us	87	J3
Engineer Group	114	E4
Englehart	125	L3
Englewood	123	M8
English Channel	50	G5
Enguera	67	F3
Enguera, Sierra de	67	F3
Enid	128	D2
Enkhuizen	64	F2
Enkoping	63	G7
Enna	69	E7
Ennadai Lake	119	Q3
En Nahud	102	E5
Ennedi	102	D4
Ennell, Lough	59	H6
Ennerdale Water	55	F2
Enning	123	N5
Ennis *Ireland*	59	E7
Ennis *U.S.A.*	128	D4
Enniscorthy	59	J7
Enniskillen	58	G4
Ennistymon	59	D7
Enns	68	E1
Enonkoski	62	N5
Enontekio	62	K2
Enrekang	91	F6
Enschede	64	G2
Ensenada	126	D5
Enshi	93	L2
Enstone	53	F3
Entebbe	107	F2
Enterprise	129	K5
Entinas, Punta de las	66	E4
Entraygues	65	E6
Entrecasteaux, Recifs d'	111	N5
Enugu	105	G4
Enurmino	118	A2
Enz	70	C4
Eo	66	C1
Eolie	69	E6
Epano Fellos	75	H4
Epanomi	75	G2
Epernay	64	E4
Ephrata	122	E4
Epi	114	U12
Epinal	64	G4
Epping	53	H3
Eppynt, Mynydd	52	D2
Epsi	77	J4
Epsom	53	G3
Eqlid	95	L6
Equatorial Guinea	105	G5
Equeipa	136	E2
Erap	114	D3
Erbaa	77	G2
Erba, Jebel	96	C6
Ercek	77	K3
Ercis	77	K3
Ercsi	72	E2
Erdek	76	B2
Erdemli	76	F4
Erdenet	87	J2
Erdre	65	C5
Erechim	138	F5
Ereenstav	87	M2
Eregli *Turkey*	76	D2
Eregli *Turkey*	76	F4
Erek Dagi	77	K3
Erenhot	87	L3
Erentepe	77	K3
Eresma	66	D2
Eressos	75	H3
Erfelek	76	F2
Erfurt	70	D3
Ergani	77	H3
Ergene	76	B2
Ergli	63	L8
Ergun He	85	K6
Ergun Zuoqi	87	N1
Eriboll, Loch	56	D2
Ericht, Loch	57	D4
Ericiyas Dagi	76	F3
Erie	125	K5
Erie, Lake	125	K5
Erikousa	74	E3
Erimanthos	75	F4
Erimo-misaki	88	J5
Eriskay	57	A3
Erkelenz	70	B3
Erkilet	76	F3
Erkowit	96	C7
Erlandson Lake	121	N6
Erlangen	70	D4
Erldunda	113	G4
Erme	52	D4
Ermelo	108	F5
Ermenak	76	E4
Ernakulam	92	E7
Erne	58	H5
Erne, Lower Lough	58	G4
Erne, Upper Lough	58	G4
Erode	92	E6
Eromanga	113	J4
Eromango	114	U13
Errego	109	G3
Errigal	58	F2
Erris Head	58	B4
Errochty, Loch	57	D4
Errogie	56	D3
Erromango	114	U13
Erseke	75	F2
Erskine	124	C3
Ertai	86	G2
Eruh	77	K4
Erwigol	86	F3
Eryuan	93	J3
Erzen	74	E2
Erzgebirge	70	E3
Erzin	84	F6
Erzincan	77	H3
Erzurum	77	J3
Esa-Ala	114	E3
Esan-misaki	88	H5
Esashi *Japan*	88	H5
Esashi *Japan*	88	J3
Esbjerg	63	C9
Esbo	63	N6
Escalona	66	D2
Escambia	129	J5
Escanaba	124	G4
Escarpe, Cape	114	X16
Escocesa, Bahia de	133	N5
Escondido *Brazil*	138	J3
Escondido *U.S.A.*	126	D4
Escrick	55	H3
Escuintla	132	B7
Ese-Khayya	85	N3
Esemer	77	K3
Esen	76	C4
Esendere	77	L4
Esfahan	95	K5
Esfarayen, Reshteh ye	95	N3
Eshan	93	K4
Esha Ness	56	A1
Esh Sheikh, Jbel	77	G6
Esino	68	D4
Esk	57	E5
Eskdale	57	E5
Eske, Lough	58	F3
Eskifjordur	62	Y12
Eskilstuna	63	G7
Eskimalatya	77	H3
Eskimo Lakes	118	J2
Eskimo Point	119	S3
Eskipazar	76	E2
Eskishir	76	D3
Esla	66	D1
Eslamabad-e Gharb	94	H4
Eslam Qaleh	95	Q4
Esme	76	C3
Esmeralda, Isla	139	A9
Esmeraldas	136	B3
Espalion	65	E6
Espanola *Canada*	125	K3
Espanola *U.S.A.*	127	J3
Espanola, Isla	136	A7
Espenberg, Cape	118	C2
Esperance	112	E5
Esperance Bay	112	E5
Esperanza *Antarctic*	141	W6
Esperanza *Argentina*	139	B10
Esperanza *Argentina*	138	D6
Espiel	66	D3
Espinhaco, Serra da	138	H3
Espinho	66	B2
Espinosa de los Monteros	66	E1
Espirito Santo	138	H3
Espiritu Santo	114	T11
Espiritu Santo, Cape	91	H3
Espiritu Santo, Isla	130	D5
Espiye	77	H2
Espoo	63	N6
Esposende	66	B2
Espot	67	G1
Espungabera	109	F4
Esquel	139	B8
Es Sahra en Nubiya	96	B6
Essaouira	100	D2
Es Semara	100	C3
Essen	70	B3
Essex	53	H3
Essex, Punta	136	A7
Esslingen	70	C4
Esso	85	T5
Estacado, Llanos	127	L4
Estados, Isla de los	139	D10
Estahbanat	95	M7
Estancia	138	K6
Estcourt	108	E5
Este	68	C3
Esteli	132	D8
Estella	67	E1
Estepona	66	D4
Este, Punta del	139	F6
Esterhazy	123	N2
Esternay	64	E4
Estes Park	123	M7
Estevan	123	N3
Estherville	124	C5
Eston	55	H2
Estonia	63	L7
Estrela, Sierra da	66	C2
Estrella, Punta	126	E5
Estremadura	66	B3
Estremoz	66	C3
Estrondo, Serra do	137	H5
Esztergom	72	E2
Etah	92	E3
Etain	64	F4
Etampes	64	E4
Etaples	64	D3
Etawah	92	E3
Ethiopia	103	G6
Etive, Loch	57	C4
Etna, Monte	69	E7
Eton	53	G3
Etosha Pan	108	C3
Etretat	64	D4
Ettington	53	F2
Ettlingen	70	C4
Ettrick	57	E5
Ettrick Forest	57	E5
Etwall	53	F2
Eu	64	D3
Eua	111	U6
Euboea	75	H3
Euclid	125	K6
Euclides da Cunha	137	K6
Eufaula	129	K5
Eufaula Lake	128	E3
Eugene	122	C5
Eugenia, Punta	126	E7
Eunice	128	E5
Euphrates	94	G6
Eupora	128	H4
Eure	64	D4
Eureka *California*	122	B7
Eureka *Montana*	122	G3
Eureka *Nevada*	126	D1
Eureka Sound	120	J2
Europa, Ile de l	109	H4
Europa, Picos de	66	D1
Europa Point	66	D4
Eutaw	129	J4
Evans, Lake	121	L7
Evans, Mount	123	M8
Evans Strait	120	K5
Evanston *Illinois*	124	G5
Evanston *Wyoming*	122	J7
Evansville	124	G7
Evaux-les-Bains	65	E5
Evaz	95	L8
Evenlode	53	F3
Everard, Cape	113	K6
Everard, Lake	113	G5
Everest, Mount	92	G3
Everett	122	C4
Everett Mountains	120	N5
Everglades, The	129	M7
Evesham	53	F2
Evesham, Vale of	53	F2
Evigheds Fjord	120	R4
Evisa	69	B4
Evje	63	B7
Evora	66	C3
Evreux	64	D4
Evropos	75	G2
Evros	75	J2
Evrotas	75	G4
Evvoia	75	H3
Evvoikos Kolpos	75	G3
Ewasse	114	E3
Ewe, Loch	56	C3
Ewes	57	E5
Exbourne	52	D4
Exe	52	D4
Exeter	52	D4
Exford	52	D3
Exmoor	52	D3
Exmouth	52	D4
Exmouth Gulf	112	C3
Exo Hora	75	F4
Expedition Range	113	K3
Exploits	121	Q8
Exton	52	D3
Extremadura	66	C3
Exuma Sound	132	J2
Eyakit-Terde	85	J3
Eyam	55	H3
Eyasi, Lake	107	F3
Eyemouth	57	F4
Eye Peninsula	56	B2
Eyjafjallajokull	62	U13
Eyjafjordur	62	V11
Eyl	103	J6
Eynesil	77	H2
Eynsham	53	F3
Eyre	112	F5
Eyre Creek	113	H4
Eyre Mountains	115	B6
Eyre North, Lake	113	H4
Eyre Peninsula	113	H5
Eyre South, Lake	113	H4
Eysturoy	62	Z14
Eyvanaki	95	L4
Ezequil Ramos Mexia, Embalse	139	C7
Ezine	76	B3

F

Name	Page	Grid
Faber Lake	119	M3
Faborg	63	D9
Fabriano	68	D4
Facatativa	136	C3
Facundo	139	C9
Fada	102	D4
Fada NGourma	104	F3
Faddeya, Zaliv	84	H2
Faddeyevskiy, Ostrov	85	Q1
Faenza	68	C3
Faeros	62	Z14
Fafen Shet	103	H6
Fagaras	73	H3
Fagersta	63	F6
Faget	73	G3
Fagnano, Lago	139	C10
Fagnes	64	F3
Faguibine, Lac	100	E5
Fagurholsmyri	62	**W**13
Fahraj	95	P7
Fairbanks	118	F3
Fairborn	124	J7
Fairfield	126	A1
Fair Isle	56	A2
Fairlie	115	C6
Fairlight *Australia*	113	J2
Fairlight *U.K.*	53	H4
Fairmont *Minnesota*	124	C5
Fairmont *W. Virginia*	125	K7
Fair Ness	120	M5
Fairview	128	C2
Fairweather, Mount	118	H4
Faisalabad	92	D2
Faith	123	N5
Faither, The	56	A1
Faizabad	92	F3
Fajr, Wadi	96	D2

Gobabis 108 C4
Gobi 87 K3
Gobo 89 E9
Gochas 108 C4
Godafoss 62 W12
Godalming 53 G3
Godavari 92 F5
Godbout 125 S2
Goderich 125 K5
Godhavn 120 R4
Godhra 92 D4
Godollo 72 E2
Gods 119 S4
Godshill 53 F4
Gods Lake 119 S5
Godthab 120 R5
Godwin Austen 92 E1
Goeland, Lac au 121 L8
Goes 64 E3
Gogama 125 K3
Goginan 52 D2
Gogland, Ostrov 63 M6
Gogolin 71 H3
Goiana 137 L5
Goiania 138 G3
Goias *Brazil* 138 F3
Goias *Brazil* 137 H6
Gojome 88 H6
Gokceada 76 A2
Gokcekaya Baraji 76 D2
Gokdere 77 G2
Gokirmak 76 F2
Gokova Korfezi 76 B4
Goksu *Turkey* 76 E4
Goksu *Turkey* 77 F4
Goksun 77 G3
Goktas 77 J2
Goktepe 76 E4
Gol 63 C6
Golaghat 93 H3
Golam Head 59 C6
Golashkerd 95 N8
Golbasi *Turkey* 76 E3
Golbasi *Turkey* 77 G4
Golcar 55 H3
Golchikha 84 C2
Golconda 122 F7
Golcuk 76 C2
Golcuk Daglari 76 B3
Goldap 71 K1
Gold Coast 113 L4
Golden 122 F2
Golden Bay 115 D4
Goldendale 122 D5
Golden Hinde 122 B3
Goldsboro 129 P3
Goldsworthy 112 D3
Gole 77 K2
Golebert 77 K2
Goleniow 70 F2
Golfito 132 F10
Golfo Aranci 69 B5
Golgeli Daglari 76 C4
Golhisar 76 C4
Golija Planina 72 F4
Golkoy 77 G2
Golmarmara 76 B3
Golmud 93 H1
Golo 69 B4
Golova 76 D4
Golovanevsk 73 L1
Golovnino 88 K4
Golpayegan 95 K5
Golpazari 76 D2
Goma 107 E3
Gombe 105 H3
Gombi 105 H3
Gomera 100 B3
Gomez Palacio 127 L8
Gomishan 95 M3
Gonaives 133 L5
Gonam *Russia* 85 M5
Gonam *Russia* 85 N5
Gonave, Golfe de la 133 L5
Gonave, Ile de la 133 L5
Gonbad-e Kavus 95 M3
Gonda 92 F3
Gondal 92 D4
Gonder 103 G5
Gondia 92 F4
Gonen *Turkey* 76 B2
Gonen *Turkey* 76 B3
Gongbogyamda 93 H3
Gongolo 105 H3
Gongpoquan 86 H3
Goniadz 71 K2
Gonumillo 139 C8
Gonzales *California* 126 B2
Gonzales *Texas* 128 D6
Gonzales Chaves 139 D7
Goob Weyn 107 H3
Goodenough, Cape 141 J5
Goodenough Island 114 E3
Good Hope, Cape of 108 C6
Gooding 122 G6
Goodland 123 P8
Goole 55 J3
Goolgowi 113 K5
Goomen 113 L4
Goondiwindi 113 L4
Goose Bay 121 P7
Goose Creek 129 M4
Goose Lake 122 D7
Goplo, Jezioro 71 H2
Goppingen 70 C4
Gora Kalwaria 71 J3
Gorakhpur 92 F3
Gorazde 72 E4
Gorda, Punta 138 B3
Gordes 76 C3
Gordonsville 125 L7
Gore 115 B7
Gore 103 G6
Gorele 77 H2
Goresbridge 59 J7
Gorey *Ireland* 59 K7
Gorey *U.K.* 53 M7
Gorgan 95 M3
Gorgan, Rud-e 95 M3
Gorgona, Isola di 68 B4
Gorgoram 105 H3
Gori 77 L1
Gorice 75 F2
Gorinchem 64 F3
Goris 94 H2
Gorizia 68 D3
Gorka 78 H3
Gorkha 92 F3
Gorki *Belarus* 78 E5
Gorki *Russia* 84 Ae3
Gorki *Russia* 78 H4
Gorkovskoye Vodokhranilishche 78 G4
Gorlev 63 D9
Gorlice 71 J4
Gorlitz 70 F3
Gornji Milanovac 72 F3
Gornji Vakuf 72 D4
Gorno-Altaysk 84 D6
Gornozavodsk 88 H2
Gornyak 84 C6
Gornyy *Russia* 79 H5
Gornyy *Russia* 85 P6
Gorodenka 73 H1
Gorodets 78 G4
Gorodok 71 K4
Gorodovikovsk 79 G6
Goroka 114 D3
Gorokhov 71 L3
Gorong, Kepulauan 91 J6
Gorongoza 109 F3
Gorontalo 91 G5
Goroshikha 84 D3
Gorran Haven 52 C4
Gorseinon 52 C3
Gort 59 E6
Gortaclare 58 H3
Gortahork 58 F2
Gorumna Island 59 C6
Goryn 79 D5
Gorzow Wielkopolski 70 F2
Goschen Strait 114 E4
Gosforth 55 H1
Goshogawara 88 H5
Gospic 72 C3
Gosport 53 F4
Gostivar 73 F5
Gota 62 Z14
Gota Kanal 63 G7
Gotaland 63 E8
Goteborg 63 H8
Goteborg Och Bohus 63 D7
Gotene 63 E7
Gotha 70 D3
Gothenburg 63 D8
Gotland 63 H8
Goto-retto 89 B9
Gotse Delchev 73 G5
Gotska Sandon 63 H7
Gotsu 89 D8
Gottingen 70 C3
Gottwaldov 71 G4
Gouda 64 F2
Goudhurst 53 H3
Gough Island 48 F6
Gouin, Reservoir 125 N2
Goulais 124 J3
Goulburn 113 K5
Goulburn Islands 113 G1
Goundam 100 E5
Gourdon 65 D6
Goure 101 H6
Gourma-Rharous 100 E5
Gournay 64 D4
Gourock 57 D5
Govena, Mys 85 V5
Goverla 71 L4
Governador Valadares 138 H3
Governor's Harbour 132 J2
Govind Pant Sagar 92 F4
Govorovo 85 M2
Gowanbridge 115 D4
Gowanda 125 L5
Gower 52 C3
Gowna, Lough 58 G5
Goya 138 E5
Goynucek 77 F2
Goynuk *Turkey* 76 D2
Goynuk *Turkey* 77 J3
Goz Beida 102 D5
Gozne 76 F4
Gozo 74 C4
Goz Regeb 96 B8
Graaff Reinet 108 D6
Gracac 72 C3
Gradaus, Serra dos 137 G5
Grado *Italy* 68 D3
Grado *Spain* 66 C1
Gradoli 69 C4
Gradsko 73 F5
Grafham Water 53 G2
Grafton *Australia* 113 L4
Grafton *N. Dakota* 123 R3
Grafton *W. Virginia* 125 K7
Grafton, Islas 139 B10
Graham 128 C4
Graham Island *British Columbia, Canada* 118 J5
Graham Island *NW. Territories, Canada* 120 H2
Graham Land 141 V5
Grahamstown 108 E6
Graie, Alpi 68 A3
Graiguenamanagh 59 J7
Grain 53 H3
Grajau 137 H4
Grajewo 71 K2
Grampian 56 E3
Grampian Mountains 57 D4
Grampound 52 C4
Gramsh 75 F2
Gran 137 F3
Granada *Nicaragua* 132 E9
Granada *Spain* 66 E4
Granard 58 H5
Gran Bajo 139 C9
Granby *Canada* 125 P4
Granby *U.S.A.* 123 L7
Gran Canaria 100 B3
Gran Chaco 138 D4
Grand *Canada* 125 K5
Grand *Michigan* 124 H5
Grand *Missouri* 124 C6
Grand *S. Dakota* 123 P5
Grand Bahama 132 H1
Grand Bois, Coteau de 124 C3
Grand Canal *China* 87 M5
Grand Canal *Ireland* 59 H6
Grand Canyon *U.S.A.* 126 F2
Grand Canyon *U.S.A.* 126 F2
Grand Cayman 132 G5
Grand Coulee 122 E4
Grand Coulee Dam 122 E4
Grande *Brazil* 138 G4
Grande *Mexico* 131 L9
Grande *Nicaragua* 132 E8
Grande, Bahia 139 C10
Grande Cache 119 M5
Grande, Cienaga 133 K10
Grande Comore 109 H2
Grande Miquelon 121 Q8
Grande O'Guapay 138 D3
Grande Prairie 119 M4
Grande, Punta 137 G3
Grande, Rio 127 M6
Grande Ronde 122 F5
Gran Desierto 126 E5
Grandes Rocques 53 M7
Grand Falls *New Brunswick, Canada* 125 S3
Grand Falls *Newfoundland, Canada* 121 Q8
Grand Forks 123 R4
Grand Island 123 Q7
Grand Isle 128 H6
Grand Junction 127 H1
Grand Lahou 104 E4
Grand Lake *New Brunswick, Canada* 128 G6
Grand Lake *Newfoundland, Canada* 121 Q8
Grand Lake *U.S.A.* 125 S3
Grand Lake O' the Cherokees 128 E2
Grand-Lieu, Lac de 65 C5
Grand Manan Island 125 S4
Grand Marais *Michigan* 124 H3
Grand Marais *Minnesota* 124 E3
Grand-Mere 125 P3
Grandola 66 B3
Grand Popo 105 F4
Grand Prairie 128 D4
Grand Rapids *Canada* 119 R5
Grand Rapids *Michigan* 124 H5
Grand Rapids *Minnesota* 124 D3
Grandrieu 65 E6
Grand Saint Bernard, Col du 68 A3
Grand Santi 137 G3
Graney, Lough 59 E7
Grangemouth 57 E4
Grange-over-Sands 55 G2
Grangesberg 63 F6
Grangeville 122 F5
Granite Peak 123 K5
Granitola, Capo 69 D7
Granna 63 F7
Granollers 67 H2
Gran Pajonal 136 C6
Gran Paradiso 68 A3
Grantham 53 G2
Grant Island 141 R4
Grant, Mount 122 E8
Grantown-on-Spey 56 E3
Grants 127 J3
Grantshouse 57 F4
Grants Pass 122 C6
Granville 64 C4
Granville Lake 119 Q4
Grasby 55 J3
Gras, Lac de 119 N3
Grasmere 55 F2
Graso 63 H6
Grasse 65 G7
Grassrange 123 K4
Grass Valley 122 D8
Grassy 113 J7
Grassy Knob 125 K7
Gratens 65 D7
Graus 67 G1
Gravatai 138 F5
Gravdal 62 E2
Gravelines 64 E3
Grave, Pointe de 65 C6
Gravesend 53 H3
Gravois, Pointe-a- 133 L5
Gray 65 F5
Grayling 124 H4
Grays 53 H3
Grays Harbor 122 B4
Graz 68 E2
Great Abaco 132 J1
Great Artesian Basin 113 J4
Great Astrolabe Reef 114 R9
Great Australian Bight 112 F5
Great Ayton 55 H2
Great Baddow 53 H3
Great Bahama Bank 132 H2
Great Bardfield 53 H3
Great Barrier Island 115 E2
Great Barrier Reef 113 K2
Great Basin 122 F7
Great Bear Lake 119 L2
Great Bend 127 N1
Great Blasket Island 59 A8
Great Budworth 55 G3
Great Cumbrae 57 D5
Great Dividing Range 113 K3
Great Driffield 55 J2
Great Dunmow 53 H3
Greater Antarctica 141 D2
Greater Antilles 132 G4
Greater Khingan Range 87 N2
Greater London 53 G3
Greater Manchester 55 G3
Great Exuma Island 132 K3
Great Falls 122 J4
Great Fish 108 E6
Great Gable 55 F2
Great Guana Cay 132 J2
Great Harwood 55 G3
Great Inagua 133 L4
Great Indian Desert 92 D3
Great Island 59 F9
Great Karas Berg 108 C5
Great Karoo 108 D6
Great Lakes 143 L3
Great Longton 55 H2
Great Malvern 52 E2
Great Mercury Island 115 E2
Great Nicobar 93 H7
Great North East Channel 114 C3
Great Ormes Head 54 F3
Great Ouse 53 H2
Great Papuan Plateau 114 C3
Great Plains 123 J2
Great Ruaha 107 G4
Great Sacandaga Lake 125 N5
Great Salt Lake 122 H7
Great Salt Lake Desert 122 H7
Great Sand Hills 123 K2
Great Sandy Desert 112 E3
Great Sankey 55 G3
Great Sea Reef 114 R8
Great Sitkin Island 118 Ac9
Great Slave Lake 119 N2
Great Smeaton 55 H2
Great Stour 53 J3
Great Sugar Loaf 59 K6
Great Torrington 52 C4
Great Victoria Desert 112 F4
Great Wall of China, The 87 L4
Great Whernside 55 H2
Great Witley 52 E2
Great Yarmouth 53 J2
Great Yeldham 53 H2
Great Zab 94 F3
Gredos, Sierra de 66 D2
Greece 75 F3
Greeley 123 M7
Greely Fjord 120 K1
Green *Kentucky* 124 G8
Green *Wyoming* 123 J6
Green Bay *U.S.A.* 124 G4
Green Bay *U.S.A.* 124 G4
Green Bell, Ostrov 80 H1
Greenbrier 125 K8
Greencastle 58 K4
Greeneville 129 L2
Greenfield 125 P5
Green Hammerton 55 H2
Greenhead 55 G2
Green Island 115 C6
Greenisland 58 L3
Green Islands 114 E2
Greenland 116 Q1
Greenlaw 57 F4
Greenlough 112 D4
Greenlowther 57 D5
Green Mountains 125 P5
Greenock 57 D5
Green River *Papua New Guinea* 114 C2
Green River *Utah* 127 G1
Green River *Wyoming* 123 K7
Greensboro 129 N2
Greensburg 125 L6
Greenstone Point 56 C3
Green Valley 126 G5

Name	Page	Grid
Greenville *Alabama*	129	J5
Greenville *Liberia*	104	D4
Greenville *Mississippi*	128	G4
Greenville *N. Carolina*	129	P3
Greenville *S. Carolina*	129	L3
Greenville *Texas*	128	D4
Greenwood *Mississippi*	128	G4
Greenwood *S. Carolina*	129	L3
Greers Ferry Lake	128	F3
Gregorio	136	C5
Gregory, Lake	113	H4
Gregory Range	113	J2
Greian Head	57	A3
Greifswald	70	E1
Grein	68	E1
Greipstad	62	H2
Greiz	70	E3
Gremikha	78	F2
Gremyachinsk	78	K4
Grena	63	D8
Grenada	133	S8
Grenada *U.S.A.*	128	H4
Grenadines, The	133	S8
Grenen	63	D8
Grenfell	123	N2
Grenivik	62	V12
Grenoble	65	F6
Grenville, Cape	113	J1
Gresford	55	G3
Gresham	122	C5
Grevena	75	F2
Greybull	123	K5
Grey Island	121	Q7
Grey Mare's Tail	57	E5
Greymouth	115	C5
Grey Range	113	J4
Greysteel	58	H2
Greystones	59	K6
Greytown	115	E4
Griefswald Bodden	70	E1
Griffin	129	K4
Griffith	113	K5
Griffith Island	120	G3
Grigoriopol	73	K2
Grimailov	71	M4
Grim, Cape	113	J7
Grimsby	55	J3
Grimsey	62	W11
Grimshaw	119	M4
Grimstad	63	C7
Grindavik	62	T13
Grindsted	63	C9
Gringley on the Hill	55	J3
Grinnell	124	D6
Grinnell Peninsula	120	G2
Grintavec	68	E2
Gris-Nez, Cap	64	D3
Griva	78	J3
Grmec Planina	72	D3
Grobming	68	D2
Grodekovo	88	C3
Groix, Ile de	65	B5
Grombalia	69	C7
Grong	62	E4
Groningen *Netherlands*	64	G2
Groningen *Suriname*	137	F2
Groot	108	D6
Groote Eylandt	113	H1
Grootfontein	108	C3
Grossa, Ponta	137	H3
Grosseto	69	C4
Grossevichi	88	G1
Gros Ventre Mountains	123	J6
Grottaglie	69	F5
Groundhog	124	J2
Grove	53	J3
Grove City	125	K6
Grove Hill	129	J5
Grover City	126	B3
Groznyy	79	H7
Grudovo	73	J4
Grudziadz	71	H2
Gruinard Bay	56	C3
Gruinart, Loch	57	B5
Grums	63	E7
Grunaw	108	C5
Grunberg	70	F3
Grund	62	U12
Grundarfjordur	62	T12
Grundy	124	J8
Gruznovka	84	H5
Gryazi	79	F5
Gryazovets	78	G4
Gryfice	70	F2
Gryfino	70	F2
Guabito	136	A2
Guacanayabo, Golfo de	132	J4
Guadajoz	66	D4
Guadalajara *Mexico*	130	H7
Guadalajara *Spain*	66	E2
Guadalcanal *Solomon Is.*	114	J6
Guadalcanal *Spain*	66	D3
Guadalete	66	D4
Guadalimar	66	E3
Guadalmez	66	D3
Guadalope	67	F2
Guadalquivir	66	D4
Guadalupe *Mexico*	128	B8
Guadalupe *Mexico*	127	J5
Guadalupe *Spain*	66	D3
Guadalupe *Texas*	128	D6
Guadalupe Mountains	127	K5
Guadalupe, Sierra de	66	D3
Guadalupe Victoria	130	G5
Guadarrama *Spain*	66	D2
Guadarrama *Spain*	66	D2
Guadarrama, Sierra de	66	E2
Guadeloupe	133	S6
Guadeloupe Passage	133	S6
Guadelupe	126	D4
Guadiana	66	C4
Guadiana, Bahia de	132	E3
Guadiana Menor	66	E4
Guadix	66	E4
Guafo, Isla	139	B8
Guainia	136	D3
Guaiquinima, Cerro	136	E2
Guajira, Peninsula de	136	C1
Gualachulian	57	C4
Gualaquiza	136	B4
Gualeguay *Argentina*	138	E6
Gualeguay *Argentina*	138	E6
Gualeguaychu	138	E6
Guam	83	N5
Guama	137	H4
Guamblin, Isla	139	A8
Guampi, Sierra de	136	D2
Guamuchil	130	E5
Gua Musang	90	C5
Guanare *Venezuela*	136	D2
Guanare *Venezuela*	136	D2
Guanay, Sierra	136	D2
Guandi	88	B4
Guangan	93	L2
Guangdong	93	M4
Guanghua	93	M2
Guangnan	93	L4
Guangning	93	M4
Guangping	87	M4
Guangxi	93	L4
Guangyuan	93	L2
Guangze	87	M6
Guangzhou	93	M4
Guanhaes	138	H3
Guanipa	133	R10
Guanoca	136	E1
Guantanamo	133	K4
Guan Xian	93	K2
Guapi	136	B3
Guapiles	132	F9
Guapore	136	E6
Guaqui	138	C3
Guarabira	137	K5
Guarapuava	138	F5
Guara, Sierra de	67	F1
Guarda *Portugal*	66	C2
Guarda *Portugal*	66	C2
Guardo	66	D1
Guarenas	136	D1
Guaribas, Cachoeira	137	G4
Guarico	136	D2
Guasave	130	E5
Guasdualito	136	C2
Guasipati	136	E2
Guastalla	68	C3
Guatemala	132	B7
Guatemala	132	B7
Guaviare	136	D3
Guaxupe	138	G4
Guayaquil	136	B4
Guayaquil, Golfo de	136	A4
Guaymas	126	G7
Guazacapan	132	B7
Guba	103	G5
Guba Dolgaya	84	Ac2
Gubakha	78	K4
Gubbio	68	D4
Gubdor	78	K3
Guben	70	F3
Gucuk	77	G3
Gudar, Sierra de	67	F2
Gudbrandsdalen	63	D6
Gudena	63	C8
Gudur	92	E6
Gudvangen	62	B6
Guekedou	104	C4
Guelma	101	G1
Guelph	125	K5
Guereda	102	D5
Gueret	65	D5
Guernsey *U.K.*	53	M7
Guernsey *U.S.A.*	123	M6
Guerrero Negro	126	E6
Gugu	73	G3
Guhakolak, Tanjung	90	D7
Guia	138	E3
Guide	93	K1
Guider	105	H4
Guidong	93	M3
Guiglo	104	D4
Gui Jiang	93	M4
Guildford	53	G3
Guildtown	57	E4
Guilin	93	M3
Guillestre	65	G6
Guimaraes	66	B2
Guinea	104	C3
Guinea Bissau	104	C3
Guinea, Gulf of	105	F5
Guines	132	F3
Guingamp	64	B4
Guiratinga	138	F3
Guiria	136	E1
Guisanbourg	137	G3
Guisborough	55	H2
Guise	64	E4
Guiseley	55	H3
Guiting Power	53	F3
Guiuan	91	H3
Guixi	87	M6
Gui Xian	93	L4
Guiyang	93	L3
Guizhou	93	L3
Gujarat	92	D4
Gujranwala	92	D2
Gujrat	92	D2
Gulbarga	92	E5
Gulbene	63	M8
Gulcayir	76	D3
Gulcha	86	C3
Gulfport	128	H5
Gulian	87	N1
Gullane	57	F4
Gullfoss	62	V12
Gull Lake	123	K2
Gullspang	63	F7
Gulluk	76	B4
Gulnar	76	E4
Gulpinar	76	B3
Gulsehir	76	F3
Gulyantsi	73	H4
Gumbaz	95	R6
Gummi	105	G3
Gumushacikoy	76	F2
Gumushane	77	H2
Guna	92	E4
Gundagi	113	K6
Gundogmus	76	L2
Gunedidalem	91	H6
Guney	76	C3
Guneydogutoroslar	77	H3
Gungu	106	C4
Gunnedah	113	L5
Gunning	113	K5
Gunnison *Colorado*	127	J1
Gunnison *Colorado*	123	K8
Gunnison *Utah*	126	G1
Guntakal	92	E5
Guntersville	129	J3
Guntersville Lake	129	J3
Guntur	92	F5
Gunungsitoli	90	B5
Gunungsugih	90	D6
Gunzenhausen	70	D4
Gurban Obo	87	L3
Gurbulak	77	L3
Gurdim	95	Q9
Gurdzhaani	79	H7
Gure	76	C3
Gurgaon	92	E3
Gurgei, Jebel	102	D5
Gurghiului, Muntii	73	H2
Gurgueia	137	J5
Gur I Topit	75	F2
Gurpinar	77	K3
Gurue	109	G3
Gurun	77	G3
Gurupa	137	G4
Gurupa, Ilha Grande do	137	G4
Gurupi	137	H4
Gurupi, Serra do	137	H4
Guruzala	92	E5
Gusau	105	G3
Gusev	71	K1
Gushgy	95	R4
Gusinoozersk	84	H6
Gus-Khrustalnyy	78	G4
Gustrow	70	E2
Gusyatin	73	J1
Gutcher	56	A1
Guthrie *Oklahoma*	128	D3
Guthrie *Texas*	127	M4
Gutian	87	M6
Guttenberg	124	E5
Guvem	76	E2
Guyana	136	F2
Guyenne	65	D6
Guymon	127	M2
Guyuan	93	L1
Guzelbag	76	D4
Guzeloluk	76	F4
Guzelsu	77	K3
Guzelyurt	76	F3
Guzman, Laguna de	127	J5
Gvardeysk	71	J1
Gvardeyskoye	73	J1
Gwa	93	H5
Gwabegar	113	K5
Gwadar	92	B3
Gwalior	92	E3
Gwanda	108	E4
Gweebarra Bay	58	F3
Gwelo	108	E3
Gwent	52	E3
Gweru	108	E3
Gwoza	105	H3
Gwydir,	113	K4
Gwynedd	52	D2
Gyandzha	79	H7
Gyangze	93	G3
Gyaring Hu	93	J2
Gydanskaya Guba	84	B2
Gydanskiy Poluostrov	84	B2
Gydnia	71	H1
Gympie	113	L4
Gynymskaya	85	N5
Gyongyos	72	E2
Gyonk	72	E2
Gyor	72	D2
Guise	64	E4
Gypsumville	123	Q2
Gyueshevo	73	G4
Gyula	73	F5
Gyumri	77	K2

H

Name	Page	Grid
Haabunga	62	W12
Haapai Group	111	U5
Haapajarvi	62	L5
Haapamaki	63	L5
Haapsalu	63	K7
Haardt	70	B4
Haarlem	64	F2
Haast *New Zealand*	115	B5
Haast *New Zealand*	115	B5
Haast Passage	115	B6
Hab	92	C3
Habawnah, Wadi	96	G8
Habban	96	H9
Habbaniyah	94	F5
Habbaniyah, Hawr al	94	F5
Haberli	77	J4
Habirag	87	M3
Haboro	88	H3
Hachenburg	70	B3
Hachijo-jima	89	G9
Hachiman	89	F8
Hachinohe	88	H5
Hachioji	89	G8
Hacibektas	76	F3
Hacihalil Dagi	77	K2
Haciomer	77	J3
Hackas	62	F5
Hadan, Harrat	96	E6
Hadarah	96	E7
Hadarba, Ras	96	C5
Haddenham	53	H2
Haddington	57	F5
Hadd, Ra's al	97	P5
Hadejia	105	G3
Hadera	94	B5
Haderslev	63	E9
Hadhalil, Al	96	G2
Hadhramawt	97	J9
Hadiboh	97	P10
Hadim	76	E4
Hadleigh	53	H2
Hadley Bay	119	P1
Hadong	93	L4
Hadrian's Wall	57	F5
Hadsund	63	D8
Haeju	87	P4
Hafar al Batin	96	H2
Hafik	77	G3
Hafit	97	M5
Hafnarfjordur	62	U12
Hafratindur	62	U12
Haft Gel	94	J6
Haftqala	95	R4
Hag Abdullah	103	F5
Hagemeister Island	118	A3
Hagen	70	B3
Hagen, Mount	114	C3
Hagerstown	125	M7
Hagfors	63	E6
Haggenas	62	F5
Hagi	89	C8
Ha Giang	93	K4
Hagimas	73	H2
Hagley	53	E2
Hagondange	64	G4
Hags Head	59	D7
Hague, Cap de la	64	C4
Haguenau	64	G4
Haian	93	M4
Haibei	88	A2
Haicheng	87	N3
Hai Duong	93	L4
Haifa	94	B5
Haifeng	87	M7
Haikang	93	M4
Haikou	93	M5
Hail	96	E3
Hailar	87	M2
Hailar He	87	M2
Hailsham	53	H4
Hailun	88	A2
Hailuoto *Finland*	62	L4
Hailuoto *Finland*	63	L2
Hainan Dao	93	M5
Haines	118	H4
Haines City	129	M6
Haiphong	93	L4
Haiti	133	L5
Haivare	114	C3
Haiya	96	C7
Hajarah, Al	96	F2
Hajduboszormeny	73	F2
Hajdunanas	73	F2
Hajiki-saki	89	G6
Hajipur	92	G3
Hajjah	96	F9
Hajjiabad	95	M7
Hajmah	97	N7
Hajr, Wadi	97	J9
Hakataramea	115	C6
Hakkari	77	K4
Hakkas	62	J3
Hakkibey	76	F4
Hakodate	88	H5
Haku-san	89	F7
Hala	92	C3

Name	Page	Grid
Halab	94	C3
Halaban	96	G5
Halabja	94	G4
Halaib	103	G3
Halat Ammar	96	C2
Halaveden	63	F7
Halawa *Hawaii*	126	S10
Halawa *Hawaii*	126	T10
Halba	77	G5
Halberstadt	70	D3
Halcon, Mount	91	G3
Halden	63	D7
Haldensleben	70	D2
Halesowen	53	E2
Halesworth	53	J2
Halfeti	77	G4
Halfin, Wadi	97	N6
Halfmoon Bay	115	B7
Halfway	119	L4
Hali	96	E7
Haliburton Highlands	125	L4
Halifax *Canada*	121	P9
Halifax *U.K.*	55	H3
Halifax Bay	113	K2
Halikarnassos	76	B4
Halileh, Ra's-e	95	K7
Halin	88	B3
Halisah	77	G4
Halitpasa	76	B3
Halkapinar	76	F4
Halkett, Cape	118	E1
Halla	62	G5
Halladale	56	E2
Hallanca	136	B5
Halland	63	E8
Hallandsas	63	E8
Halle	70	C3
Hallefors	63	F7
Hallen	62	F5
Halley	141	Y3
Hallingdal	63	C6
Hallingskarvet	63	B6
Hall Peninsula	120	N5
Halls Creek	112	F2
Hallstavik	63	H6
Hallum	64	F2
Halmahera	91	H5
Halmahera, Laut	91	H6
Halmstad	63	E8
Hals	63	D8
Halsinge-skogen	63	F6
Halsingland	63	G6
Halstead	53	H3
Halton Lea Gate	55	G2
Halul	97	L4
Ham *France*	64	E4
Ham *U.K.*	56	A2
Hamada	89	D8
Hamad, Al	94	D6
Hamadan	94	J4
Hamah	94	C4
Hamam	77	G4
Hamamatsu	89	F8
Hamar	63	D6
Hamata, Gebel	96	B4
Hama-Tombetsu	88	J3
Hambantota	92	F7
Hambleton	55	G3
Hamburg *U.S.A.*	124	C6
Hamburg *Germany*	70	D2
Hamdaman, Dasht-i	95	Q4
Hamd, Wadi al	96	C4
Hame	63	L6
Hameln	70	C2
Hamhung	87	P4
Hami	86	F3
Hamilton	113	H3
Hamilton *Bermuda*	117	N5
Hamilton *Canada*	125	L5
Hamilton *New Zealand*	115	E2
Hamilton *U.K.*	57	D5
Hamilton *Alabama*	129	J3
Hamilton *Montana*	122	G4
Hamilton *Ohio*	124	H7
Hamilton Inlet	121	Q7
Hamim, Wadi al	101	K2
Hamina	63	M6
Hamitabat	76	D4
Hamm	70	B2
Hammar, Hawr al	94	H6
Hammarstrand	62	G5
Hammeenlinna	63	L6
Hammerdal	62	F5
Hammerfest	62	K1
Hammersley Range	112	D3
Hammond *Indiana*	124	G6
Hammond *Louisiana*	128	G5
Hammond *Montana*	123	M5
Hamnavoe	56	A1
Hampden	115	C6
Hampshire	53	F3
Hampshire Downs	53	F3
Hampton *Arkansas*	128	F4
Hampton *S. Carolina*	129	M4
Hampton *Virginia*	125	M8
Hamra , Al Hammadah al	101	H3
Hamrange	63	G6
Hamrin, Jebel	77	L5
Hamun-i Mashkel	92	B3
Hamur	77	K3
Hanahan	114	E3
Hanak	77	K2
Hanalei	126	R9
Hanamaki	88	H6

Name	Page	Grid
Hancheng	93	M1
Hancock	125	L7
Handa	89	F7
Handan	87	L4
Handeni	107	G4
Handlova	71	H4
Hanford	126	C2
Hangang	87	P4
Hangayn Nuruu	86	H2
Hanggin Houqi	87	K3
Hanggin Qi	87	K4
Hango	63	K7
Hangzhou	87	N5
Hangzhou Wan	87	N5
Hanhongor	87	J3
Hani	77	J3
Hanifah, Wadi	96	H4
Hanish al Kabir	96	F10
Haniyah, Al	94	H7
Han Jiang	87	M7
Hanko	63	K7
Hanksville	126	G1
Hanna	122	H2
Hannah Bay	121	L7
Hannibal	124	E7
Hann, Mount	112	F2
Hannover	70	C2
Hano-bukten	63	F9
Hanoi	93	L4
Hanover *Canada*	125	K4
Hanover *South Africa*	108	D6
Hanover *U.S.A.*	125	P5
Hanover, Isla	139	B10
Hanpan, Cape	114	E2
Han Pijesak	72	E3
Han Shui	93	M2
Hansbo Bay	115	F6
Hanstholm	63	C8
Hantay	86	J2
Hanyuan	93	K3
Hanzhong	93	L2
Haparanda	62	L4
Happisburgh	53	J2
Hapsu	88	B5
Hapur	92	E3
Haql	96	B2
Hara	87	K2
Harad *Saudi Arabia*	97	J4
Harad *Yemen*	96	F8
Harads	62	J3
Haramachi	89	H7
Harare	108	F3
Harasis, Jiddat al	97	N7
Harbin	87	P2
Harbiye	77	G4
Harbour Breton	121	Q8
Harby	53	G2
Hardangerfjord	63	B6
Hardanger-Jokulen	63	B6
Hardangervidda	63	B6
Hardin	123	L5
Hardoi	92	F3
Hardy	128	G2
Hare Bay	121	Q7
Harer	103	H6
Harewood	55	H3
Hargeysa	103	H6
Hargigo	96	D9
Har Hu	93	J1
Harib	96	G9
Haridwar	92	E3
Harihari	115	C5
Harima-nada	89	E8
Harim, Jambal Al	97	N4
Hari-Rud	95	S4
Harjedalen	62	E5
Harlan	124	C6
Harlem	123	K3
Harleston	53	J2
Harlingen	64	F2
Harlow	53	H3
Harlowton	123	K4
Harmancik	76	C3
Harmil	96	E8
Harney Basin	122	D6
Harney Lake	122	E6
Harnosand	62	G5
Haro	66	E1
Haro, Cabo	126	G7
Haroldswick	56	A1
Harpanahalli	92	E6
Harpenden	53	G3
Harper	104	D5
Harper Passage	115	C5
Harpstedt	70	C2
Harrah, Ad	94	D6
Harran	77	H4
Harray, Loch of	56	E1
Harricanaw	125	M2
Harrietsham	53	H3
Harrington	55	F2
Harris	56	B3
Harrisburg *Illinois*	124	F8
Harrisburg *Pennsylvania*	125	M6
Harrismith	108	E5
Harrison	128	F2
Harrison Bay	118	E1
Harrisonburg	125	L7
Harrison, Cape	121	Q7
Harrison Lake	122	D3
Harrisonville	124	C7
Harris Ridge	140	A1
Harris, Sound of	56	A3
Harrogate	55	H3

Name	Page	Grid
Harrow	53	G3
Harsit	77	H2
Harstad	62	G2
Harsvik	62	D4
Hart	118	H2
Hartbees	108	D5
Hartberg	68	E2
Harteigen	63	B6
Hartford	125	P6
Harthill	57	E5
Hartkjolen	62	E4
Hartland	52	C4
Hartland Point	52	C3
Hartlepool	55	H2
Hartley	127	L3
Hartola	63	M6
Hartsville	129	M3
Hartwell Reservoir	129	L3
Hartz	108	E5
Harut	97	L8
Harvey *Australia*	112	D5
Harvey *U.S.A.*	124	G6
Harwich	53	J3
Haryana	92	E3
Harz	70	D3
Hasan Dagi	76	F3
Hashish, Ghubbat	97	P6
Haskoy	77	K2
Haslemere	53	G3
Haslingden	55	G3
Hassa	77	G4
Hassan	92	E6
Hassankeyf	77	J4
Hassela	63	L5
Hassi Habadra	101	F3
Hassleholm	63	E8
Hastings *Australia*	113	K7
Hastings *New Zealand*	115	F3
Hastings *U.K.*	53	H4
Hastings *Michigan*	124	H5
Hastings *Nebraska*	123	Q7
Hastveda	63	E8
Hasvik	62	K1
Haswell	55	H2
Hatanbulag	87	K3
Hatchie	128	H3
Hatfield *Hertfordshire, U.K.*	53	G3
Hatfield *S. Yorkshire, U.K.*	55	H3
Hatfield Peverel	53	H3
Hatgal	86	J1
Hathras	92	E3
Hatibah, Ra's	96	D6
Ha Tien	93	K6
Ha Tinh	93	L5
Hatip	76	E4
Hat Island	120	G4
Hato	136	A2
Hatohudo	91	H7
Hatskiy	84	D5
Hatteras, Cape	129	Q3
Hattiesburg	128	H5
Hatton	56	G3
Hattras Passage	93	J6
Hatunsaray	76	E4
Hatuoto	91	H6
Haugesund	63	A7
Haughton	53	E2
Hauhui	114	K6
Haukivesi	62	N5
Haukivuori	63	M5
Hauraha	114	K7
Hauraki Gulf	115	E2
Haut Atlas	100	D2
Hauts Plateaux	100	E2
Havana	124	E6
Havant	53	F4
Havasu, Lake	126	E3
Havel	70	E2
Havelock North	115	F3
Haverfordwest	52	C2
Haverhill *U.K.*	53	H2
Haverhill *U.S.A.*	125	Q5
Havoysund	62	L1
Havran	76	B3
Havre	123	K3
Havre-Saint-Pierre	121	P7
Havsa	76	B2
Havza	77	F2
Hawaii *U.S.A.*	126	R10
Hawaii *U.S.A.*	126	T11
Hawaya, Al	97	J6
Hawea, Lake	115	B6
Hawera	115	E3
Hawes	55	G2
Haweswater Reservoir	55	G2
Hawick	57	F5
Hawke	121	Q7
Hawke Bay	115	F3
Hawke, Cape	113	L5
Hawkesbury	125	N4
Hawkhurst	53	H3
Hawkinge	53	J3
Hawknest Point	133	K2
Hawnby	55	H2
Hawng Luk	93	J4
Hawra	97	J9
Hawran, Wadi	94	E5
Hawsker	55	J2
Hawthorne	126	C1
Haxby	55	H2
Hay *New South Wales, Australia*	113	J5
Hay *Northern Territory,*		

Name	Page	Grid
Australia	113	H3
Hay *Canada*	119	M3
Hayden	123	L7
Hayes	119	R4
Hayes Halvo	120	N2
Hayes, Mount	118	F3
Hayjan	96	G8
Hayl	97	N4
Hayl, Wadi al	77	H5
Haymana	76	E3
Hayrabolu	76	B2
Hay River	119	M3
Hays	96	F10
Hays	123	Q8
Haywards Heath	53	G4
Hazaran, Kuh-e	95	N7
Hazard	124	J8
Hazar Golu	77	H3
Hazaribag	92	G4
Hazaribagh Range	92	F4
Hazar Masjed, Kuh-e	95	P3
Hazel Grove	55	G3
Hazelton *Canada*	118	K4
Hazelton *U.S.A.*	125	N6
Hazen Bay	118	B3
Hazlehurst	128	G5
Hazro	77	J3
Headcorn	53	H3
Head of Bight	112	G5
Healdsburg	126	A1
Healesville	113	K6
Heanor	55	H3
Heard Islands	142	D6
Hearst	124	J2
Hearst Island	141	V5
Heart	123	P4
Heathfield	53	H4
Heathrow	53	G3
Hebbronville	128	C7
Hebden Bridge	55	G3
Hebei	87	M4
Hebel	113	K4
Heber City	122	J7
Hebi	87	L4
Hebrides, Sea of the	57	A4
Hebron *Canada*	121	P6
Hebron *Israel*	94	B6
Hebron *N. Dakota*	123	N4
Hebron *Nebraska*	123	R7
Hecate Strait	118	J5
Hechi	93	L4
Hechuan	93	L2
Heckington	53	G2
Hecla and Griper Bay	120	D2
Hector, Mount	115	E4
Hede	62	E5
Hedland, Port	112	D3
Hedmark	63	D6
Heerenveen	64	F2
Heerlen	64	F3
Hefa	94	B5
Hefei	87	M5
Hefeng	93	M3
Hegang	87	Q2
Hegura-jima	89	F7
Heiban	102	F5
Heide	70	C1
Heidelberg	70	C4
Heidharhorn	62	U12
Heighington	55	H2
Heilbron	108	E5
Heilbronn	70	C4
Heiligenhafen	70	D1
Heiligenstadt	70	D3
Heilong Jiang *China*	88	B2
Heilongjiang *China*	88	D1
Heimaey	62	U13
Heimdal	62	D5
Heinavesi	62	N5
Heinola	63	M6
Heinze Islands	93	J6
Hejing	86	F3
Hekimhan	77	G3
Hel	71	H1
Helagsfjallet	62	E5
Helena *Arkansas*	128	G3
Helena *Montana*	122	J4
Helen Island	91	J5
Helensburgh	57	D4
Helensville	115	E2
Helgoland	70	B1
Helgolander Bucht	70	B1
Heli	88	C2
Heligenblut	68	D2
Helleh	95	K7
Hellin	67	F3
Hell's Mouth	52	C2
Hell-Ville	109	J2
Helmand	95	R6
Helmond	64	F3
Helmsdale *U.K.*	56	E2
Helmsdale *U.K.*	56	E2
Helong	88	B4
Hel, Polwysep	71	H1
Helsingborg	63	E8
Helsingfors	63	L6
Helsingor	63	E8
Helsinki	63	K6
Helston	52	B4
Helvecia	137	K7
Helvellyn	55	F2
Hemel Hempstead	53	G3
Hempstead	128	D5
Hemsworth	55	H3

Name	Page	Grid
Henan	93	M2
Henares	66	E2
Henashi-zaki	88	G5
Henbury	113	G3
Hendek	76	D2
Henderson *Kentucky*	124	G8
Henderson *N. Carolina*	129	N2
Henderson *Nevada*	126	E3
Henderson *Texas*	128	E4
Hendersonville	129	L3
Hendorabi	95	L8
Hendota	124	F6
Hendrik Verwoerd Dam	108	E6
Hengdaohezi	88	B3
Hengduan Shan	93	J3
Hengelo	64	G2
Hengshan *Hunan, China*	93	M3
Hengshan *Shanxi, China*	87	K4
Hengshui	87	M4
Heng Xian	93	L4
Hengyang	93	M3
Henley-on-Thames	53	G3
Hennebont	65	B5
Henqam	95	M8
Henrietta Maria, Cape	121	K6
Henryetta	128	E3
Henry Ice Rise	141	W2
Henry Mountains	126	G1
Henry Point	112	D5
Henslow, Cape	114	K6
Hentiyn Nuruu	87	K2
Henty	113	K6
Henzada	93	J5
Heppner	122	E5
Hepu	93	L4
Hequ	87	L4
Heradsfloi	62	X12
Herat	95	R4
Herault	65	E7
Herbertville	115	F4
Herby	71	H3
Heredia	132	E9
Hereford *U.K.*	52	E2
Hereford *U.S.A.*	127	L3
Hereford and Worcester	52	E2
Hereke	76	C2
Heretaniwha Point	115	B5
Herford	70	C2
Herington	123	R8
Herisau	68	B2
Herlen Gol	87	L2
Herm	53	M7
Hermanas	127	M7
Herma Ness	56	B1
Hermanus	108	C6
Hermel	94	C4
Hermiston	122	E5
Hermitage	53	F3
Hermitage Bay	121	Q8
Hermit Islands	114	D2
Hermon, Mount	77	G6
Hermosillo	126	G6
Hernad	73	F1
Herne	70	B3
Herne Bay	53	J3
Herning	63	C8
Herrera del Duque	66	D3
Herriard	53	F3
Herrick	113	K7
Herroro, Punta	131	R8
Hersbruck	70	D4
Herschel Island	118	H2
Hertford	53	G3
Hertfordshire	53	G3
Hervey Bay	113	L3
Herzberg	70	D3
Hesdin	64	E3
Hessfjord	62	M2
Hesteyri	63	T11
Hestra	63	E8
Heswall	55	F3
Hethersett	53	J2
Hetton-le-Hole	55	H2
Heuru	114	K7
Heversham	55	G2
Hexham	55	G2
He Xian *Anhui, China*	87	M5
He Xian *Guangxi, China*	93	M4
Heydalir	62	X12
Heysham	55	G2
Heyuan	87	L7
Heywood	55	G3
Heze	93	N1
Hialeah	129	M8
Hibak, Al	97	L6
Hibaldstow	55	J3
Hibbing	124	D3
Hibernia Reef	110	F4
Hickory	129	M3
Hicks Cays	132	C6
Hico	128	C4
Hidaka-sammyaku	88	J4
Hidalgo del Parral	127	K7
Hiddensee	70	E1
Hidrolandia	138	G3
Hieflau	68	E2
Hienghene	114	W16
Hierro	100	B3
Higashi-suido	89	B8
Higham Ferrers	53	G2
Highampton	52	C4
Highbury	113	J2
Highclere	53	F3
High Force	55	G2
High Hesket	55	G2
Highland	56	C3
Highland Park	124	G5
High Level	119	M4
High Point	129	N3
High River	122	H2
High Street	55	G2
High Wycombe	53	G3
Higuera de Zaragozao	127	H8
Higuey	133	N5
Hiiumaa	63	K7
Hijar	67	F2
Hijaz	96	E6
Hikman, Barr al	97	P6
Hikone	89	F8
Hikurangi	115	E1
Hildesheim	70	C2
Hill City	123	Q8
Hillingdon	53	G3
Hillington	53	H2
Hill Island Lake	119	N3
Hillsboro *N. Dakota*	123	R4
Hillsboro *Ohio*	124	J7
Hillsboro *Texas*	128	D5
Hillsborough	58	M4
Hilo	126	T11
Hilpsford Point	55	F2
Hilton Head Island	129	M4
Hilvan	77	H4
Hilversum	64	F2
Hima	96	G7
Himachal Pradesh	92	E2
Himalaya	92	E3
Himare	74	E2
Himatnagar	92	D4
Himeji	89	E8
Himmerland	63	C8
Himmetdede	76	F3
Hims	94	C4
Hinche	133	L5
Hinchinbrook Island	118	F3
Hinckley	53	F2
Hinderwell	55	J2
Hindhead	53	G3
Hindley	55	G3
Hindmarsh, Lake	113	J6
Hindon	53	E3
Hindubagh	92	C2
Hindu Kush	92	D1
Hindupur	92	E6
Hinganghat	92	E4
Hingoli	92	E5
Hinis	77	J3
Hinnoya	62	F2
Hinojosa del Duque	66	D3
Hintlesham	53	J2
Hinton	119	M5
Hinzir Burun	77	F4
Hirado-shima	89	B9
Hirakud Reservoir	92	F4
Hirara	89	G11
Hiratsuka	89	G8
Hirfanli Baraji	76	E3
Hirlau	73	J2
Hiroo	88	J4
Hirosaki	88	H5
Hiroshima	89	D8
Hirschberg	70	F3
Hirsova	73	J3
Hirtshals	63	C8
Hirwaun	52	D3
Hisar	92	E3
Hisma	96	C2
Hissjon	62	J5
Hit	94	F5
Hitachi	89	H7
Hitchin	53	G3
Hitoyoshi	89	C9
Hitra	62	C5
Hiu	114	T10
Hiuchi-nada	89	D8
Hiz	53	G2
Hizan	77	K3
Hjalmaren	63	G7
Hjalmer Lake	119	P3
Hjelmeland	63	B7
Hjorring	63	C8
Ho	104	F4
Hoa Binh	93	L4
Hobara	89	H7
Hobart	113	K7
Hobbs	127	L4
Hoboksar	86	F2
Hobro	63	C8
Hobyo	103	J6
Hocalar	76	C3
Hochalm Spitze	68	D2
Ho Chi Minh	93	L6
Hochstadt	70	D4
Hockley	53	H3
Hockley Heath	53	F2
Hodal	92	E3
Hodder	55	G3
Hoddesdon	53	G3
Hodge Beck	55	H2
Hodmezovasarhely	72	F2
Hodna, Monts du	67	J5
Hodnet	52	E2
Hodonin	71	G4
Hoea	126	T10
Hoeryong	88	B4
Hof	70	D3
Hofdakaupstadur	62	U12
Hofmeyr	108	E6
Hofn *Iceland*	62	T11
Hofn *Iceland*	62	X12
Hofors	63	G6
Hofsjokull	62	V12
Hofu	89	C8
Hoganas	63	E8
Hoggar	101	G4
Hogsby	63	G8
Hogsty Reef	133	L4
Hohe Rhon	70	C3
Hohe Tauern	68	D2
Hohhot	87	L3
Hoh Xil Shan	92	G1
Hoi An	93	L5
Hoima	107	F2
Hokensas	63	F7
Hokianga Harbour	115	D1
Hokitika	115	C5
Hokkaido	88	H3
Hokksund	63	C7
Hokota	89	H7
Hokou	93	K4
Hokuno	89	F8
Holarfjall	62	V12
Holbeach	53	H4
Holbrook	127	G3
Holdenville	128	D3
Holderness	55	J3
Holdrege	123	Q7
Holguin	132	J4
Holic	71	G4
Holitna	118	D3
Holjes	63	E6
Hollabrunn	68	F1
Holland	124	G5
Hollandstoun	56	F1
Hollis	128	C3
Hollywood	129	M7
Holm	62	E4
Holman Island	119	M1
Holmavik	62	U12
Holme-on-Spalding-Moor	55	J3
Holmes Chapel	55	G3
Holmes Reef	113	K2
Holmfirth	55	H3
Holms O	120	Q3
Holmsund	62	J5
Holoin Gun	86	J3
Holstebro	63	C8
Holsteinsborg	120	R4
Holsworthy	52	C4
Holt	53	J2
Holton *Canada*	121	Q7
Holton *U.S.A.*	124	C7
Holy Cross	118	D3
Holyhead	54	E3
Holyhead Bay	54	E3
Holy Island *Gwynedd, U.K.*	54	E3
Holy Island *Northumberland, U.K.*	55	H1
Holy Island *Strathclyde, U.K.*	57	C5
Holyoke *Colorado*	123	N7
Holyoke *Massachusetts*	125	P5
Holywell	55	F3
Holywood *Dumfries and Galloway, U.K.*	57	E5
Holywood *Down, U.K.*	58	L3
Homalin	93	H4
Hombre Muerto, Salar de	138	C5
Home Bay	120	N4
Home Hill	113	K2
Home Point	115	E1
Homer	128	F4
Homer Tunnel	115	A6
Hommelvik	62	D5
Hommersak	63	D6
Homoine	109	G4
Homs	77	G5
Homyel	79	E5
Honavar	92	D6
Honaz Dagi	76	C3
Hon Chong	93	K6
Hondo *Mexico*	131	Q8
Hondo *U.S.A.*	128	C6
Honduras	132	C7
Honduras, Golfo de	132	C6
Honefoss	63	D6
Honesdale	125	N6
Honey Lake	122	D7
Hong Kong	87	L7
Hongliuyuan	86	H3
Hongo	86	G2
Hongor *Mongolia*	87	L2
Hongor *Mongolia*	87	L2
Hongshui He	93	L4
Hong, Song	87	K4
Hongsong	87	P4
Honguedo Strait	121	P8
Hongxing Sichang	86	F3
Hongze	87	M5
Hongze Hu	87	M5
Honiara	114	J6
Honingham	53	J2
Honiton	52	D4
Honjo	88	G6
Hon Khoai	93	K7
Honningsvag	62	L1
Honohina	126	T11
Honokaa	126	T10
Honolulu	126	S10
Honshu	89	E7
Hood	119	N2
Hood Canal	122	C4
Hood Island	136	A7
Hood, Mount	122	D5
Hood Point	114	D4
Hood River	122	D5
Hoogeveen	64	G2
Hooghly	93	G4
Hook	53	G3
Hooker	127	M2
Hook Head	59	J8
Hook Norton	53	F3
Hooper, Cape	120	N4
Hoor	63	E9
Hoorn	64	F2
Hoover Dam	126	E2
Hopa	77	J2
Hope *Canada*	122	D3
Hope *U.K.*	55	H3
Hope *U.S.A.*	128	F4
Hopedale	121	P6
Hopelchen	131	Q8
Hope, Loch	56	D2
Hopen	80	D2
Hope Pass	115	C5
Hope, Point	118	B2
Hopes Advance, Cape	121	N5
Hopetown	108	D5
Hopewell	125	M8
Hopkins Lake	112	F3
Hopkinsville	124	G8
Hoquiam	122	C4
Horasan	77	K2
Horby	63	E9
Hordaland	63	B6
Horezu	73	G3
Horley	53	G3
Horlick Mountains	141	R1
Horlivka	79	F6
Hormoz	95	N8
Hormuz, Strait of	97	N3
Horn *Austria*	68	E1
Horn *Iceland*	62	T11
Hornavan	62	G3
Horn, Cape	139	C10
Horncastle	55	J3
Horndal	63	G6
Horndean	53	F4
Hornefors	62	H5
Hornepayne	124	H2
Horn Head	58	G2
Horn, Iles de	111	T4
Horningsham	52	E3
Horn Mountains	119	L3
Hornos, Cabo de	139	C11
Hornsea	55	J3
Horovice	70	E4
Horqin Youyi Qianqi	87	N2
Horqin Zuoyi Houqi	87	N3
Horqueta	138	E4
Horsehoe Bend	122	F6
Horsens	63	C9
Horsey	53	J2
Horsforth	55	H3
Horsham *Australia*	113	J6
Horsham *U.K.*	53	G3
Horsham Saint Faith	53	J2
Horsley	53	G3
Horsovsky Tyn	70	E4
Horten	63	D7
Horton	118	L2
Horwich	55	G3
Hosaina	103	G6
Hosap	77	K3
Hose Mountains	90	E5
Hoseynabad	94	H4
Hoshangabad	92	E4
Hoshiarpur	92	E2
Hospet	92	E5
Hospitalet	67	H2
Hossegor	65	C7
Hoste, Isla	139	C11
Hotamis	76	E4
Hotan	92	F1
Hotazel	108	D5
Hoti	91	J6
Hoting	62	G4
Hot Springs *Arkansas*	128	F3
Hot Springs *S. Dakota*	123	N6
Hottah Lake	119	M2
Hotte, Massif de la	133	K5
Houailou	114	W16
Houdan	64	D4
Houghton	124	F3
Houghton-le-Spring	55	H2
Houlton	125	S3
Houma *China*	93	M1
Houma *U.S.A.*	128	G6
Houmt Souk	101	H2
Hounde	104	E3
Hounslow	53	G3
Houston *Mississippi*	128	H4
Houston *Texas*	128	E6
Houtman Rocks	112	C4
Hova	63	F7
Hovd	86	G2
Hovd Gol	86	G2
Hove	53	G4
Hoveyzeh	94	J6
Hovingham	55	J2
Hovlya	79	G6
Hovsgol	87	K3
Hovsgol Nuur	86	J1
Howa	102	E4
Howakil	96	E9
Howard City	124	H5

Name	Page	Grid
Howard Lake	119	P3
Howden Moor	55	H3
Howden Reservoir	55	H3
Howe, Cape	113	K6
Howe of the Mearns	57	F4
Howitt, Mount	113	K6
Howland Island	111	T1
Howrah	93	G4
Hoxtolgay	86	F2
Hoxud	86	F3
Hoy	56	E2
Hoyanger	63	B6
Hoyerswerda	70	F3
Hoylake	55	F3
Hoyos	66	C2
Hoy Sound	56	E2
Hradeckralove	70	F3
Hrodna	71	K2
Hron	71	H4
Hrubieszow	71	K3
Hsin-cheng	87	N7
Hsin-chu	87	N7
Hsipaw	93	J4
Huab	108	B4
Huacho	136	B6
Huachuan	88	C2
Huacrachuco	136	B5
Huade	87	L3
Huadian	87	P3
Huaibei	93	N2
Huaide	87	N3
Huai He	93	M2
Huaihua	93	M3
Huaiji	93	M4
Huainan	87	M5
Huairou	87	M3
Huaiyin	87	M5
Huajuapan de Leon	131	L9
Huallaga	136	B5
Huallanca	136	B5
Huama	88	C2
Huamachuco	136	B5
Huambo	106	C5
Huampusirpi	132	E7
Huanan	88	C2
Huancane	138	C3
Huancavelica	136	B6
Huancayo	136	B6
Huangehuan	93	N2
Huang Hai	87	N4
Huang He	87	L4
Huanghua	87	M4
Huangling	93	L1
Huangpi	93	M2
Huangshi	93	M2
Huang Xian	87	N4
Huangyan	87	N6
Huangyuan	93	K1
Huanren	87	P3
Huanta	136	C6
Huanuco	136	B5
Huan Xian	93	L1
Huanzo, Cordillera	136	C6
Huara	138	C3
Huaral	136	B6
Huaraz	136	B5
Huarmey	136	B6
Huascaran, Nevado	127	H7
Huatabampo	127	H7
Huayin	93	M2
Huayuan	93	L3
Hubei	93	M2
Hubli	92	E5
Hucknall	55	H3
Huddersfield	55	H3
Hudiksvall	63	G6
Hudson *Florida*	129	L6
Hudson *New York*	125	P5
Hudson *New York*	125	P5
Hudson Bay	116	L3
Hudson, Cape	141	L5
Hudson Land	120	X3
Hudson Strait	120	M5
Hue	93	L5
Huebra	66	C2
Huedin	73	G2
Huehuento, Cerro	130	G5
Huehuetenango	132	B7
Huelgoat	64	B4
Huelva *Spain*	66	C4
Huelva *Spain*	66	C4
Huercal Overa	67	F4
Huesca	67	F1
Huescar	66	E4
Huetamo	131	J8
Huete	66	E2
Hufrah, Al	96	D2
Hughenden	113	J3
Hugh Town	52	K5
Hugo	128	E4
Hugo Reservoir	128	E3
Hugoton	127	M2
Huhehot	87	L3
Huiarau Range	115	F3
Huichapan	131	K7
Huicholes, Sierra de los	130	G6
Huichon	87	P3
Huila, Nevado del	136	B3
Huimin	87	M4
Huisne	65	N4
Huitong	93	L3
Huittinen	63	K6
Huixtla	131	N10
Huize	93	K3
Huizhou	87	L7
Huj, Al	96	D2
Huka Falls	115	E3
Hukou	87	M6
Hula	114	D4
Hulan He	88	A2
Hulayfah	96	E4
Huld	87	K3
Hulin	88	D3
Hull *Canada*	125	N4
Hull *U.K.*	55	J3
Hultsfred	63	F8
Hulun	87	M2
Hulun Nur	87	M2
Huma	87	P1
Humahuaca	138	B4
Humaita	136	E5
Humarklo	62	X12
Humaya	130	F5
Humber	55	J3
Humber, Mouth of the	55	K3
Humberside	55	J3
Humboldt *Canada*	123	M1
Humboldt *Nevada*	122	E7
Humboldt *Tennessee*	128	H3
Humboldt, Mount	114	X16
Humbolt Gletscher	120	P2
Humedan	95	P9
Humphreys Peak	126	G3
Humpolec	70	F4
Hunan	93	M3
Hunchun	88	C4
Hunfeld	70	C3
Hungary	72	D2
Hungerford	53	F3
Hunghae	89	B7
Hungnam	87	P4
Hungry Hill	59	C9
Hunjiang	87	P3
Huns Mountains	108	C5
Hunsruck	70	B4
Hunstanton	53	H2
Hunsur	92	E6
Hunte	70	C2
Hunter	113	L5
Hunter, Cape	120	M3
Hunter Islands	113	J7
Huntingdon *U.K.*	53	G2
Huntingdon *U.S.A.*	125	M6
Huntington *Indiana*	124	H6
Huntington *W. Virginia,*	124	J7
Huntington Beach	126	C4
Huntley	52	E3
Huntly *New Zealand*	115	E2
Huntly *U.K.*	56	F3
Huntsville *Canada*	125	L4
Huntsville *Alabama*	129	J3
Huntsville *Texas*	128	E5
Huolongmen	87	P2
Huon Gulf	114	D3
Huon Peninsula	114	D3
Hurd, Cape	125	K4
Hurdiyo	103	K5
Hure Qi	87	N3
Hurghada	103	F2
Hurimta	87	K2
Hurliness	56	E2
Hurn	53	F4
Huron	123	Q5
Huron, Lake	124	J4
Hurricane	126	F2
Hurrungane	63	B6
Hurunui	115	D5
Husavik *Denmark*	62	Z14
Husavik *Iceland*	62	W11
Husbands Bosworth	53	F2
Husbondliden	62	H4
Hushan	88	C3
Hushinish	56	A3
Husi	73	K2
Huskvarna	63	F8
Husn Al Abr	96	H8
Husum *Sweden*	62	H5
Husum *Germany*	70	C1
Hutag	86	J2
Hutaym, Harrat	96	E3
Hutchinson *Kansas*	128	D1
Hutchinson *Minnesota*	124	C4
Hutou	88	D2
Huttenberg	68	E2
Huttoft	55	K3
Hutton, Mount	113	K4
Hutubi	86	F3
Huwar	97	K4
Huxley, Mount	115	B6
Huyuk	76	D4
Huzhou	87	N5
Hvallatur	62	S12
Hvammstangi	62	U12
Hvar	72	D4
Hveragerdi	62	U13
Hvita	62	U12
Hwange	108	E3
Hwlffordd	52	C2
Hyannis *Massachusetts*	125	Q6
Hyannis *Nebraska*	123	P7
Hyargas Nuur	86	G2
Hyde *New Zealand*	115	C6
Hyde *U.K.*	55	G3
Hyderabad *India*	92	E5
Hyderabad *Pakistan*	92	C3
Hyeres	65	G7
Hyeres, Iles d'	65	G7
Hyesan	88	B5
Hyltebruk	63	E8
Hyndman Peak	122	G6
Hynish Bay	57	B4
Hyrynsalmi	62	N4
Hythe *Hampshire, U.K.*	53	F4
Hythe *Kent, U.K.*	53	J3
Hyuga	89	C9
Hyvinkaa	63	L6

I

Name	Page	Grid
Iaco	136	D5
Iacobeni	73	H2
Ialomita	73	J3
Iapala	109	G2
Iar Connaught	59	D6
Iasi	73	J2
Ib	78	J3
Iba	91	F2
Ibadan	105	F4
Ibague	136	B3
Ibarra	136	B3
Ibb	96	G10
Ibi	105	G4
Ibiapaba, Serra da	137	J4
Ibiza *Spain*	67	G3
Ibiza *Spain*	67	G3
Ibn Suaydan, Ramlat	97	M6
Ibo	109	H2
Ibonma	91	J6
Ibotirama	138	J6
Ibra	97	P5
Ibra, Wadi	102	D5
Ibri	97	N5
Ibriktepe	76	B2
Ibsley	53	F4
Ibusuki	89	C10
Ica	136	B6
Ica	136	D4
Icabaru	136	E3
Icana *Brazil*	136	D3
Icana *Brazil*	136	D3
Icel	76	F4
Iceland	62	V12
Ichalkaranji	92	D5
Ichchapuram	92	F5
Ichera	84	H5
Ichilo	138	D3
Ichinomiya	89	F8
Ichinoseki	88	H6
Ichnya	79	E5
Ichoa	138	C3
Icy Bay	118	G4
Icy Cape	118	C1
Icy Strait	118	H4
Idabel	128	E4
Idah	105	G4
Idaho	122	G5
Idaho Falls	122	H6
Idanha-a-Nova	66	C3
Idar-Oberstein	70	B4
Ider	86	H2
Idfu	103	F3
Idhi Oros	75	H5
Idhra	75	G4
Idil	77	J4
Idiofa	106	C3
Idiouia	67	G5
Idlib	94	C4
Idre	63	E6
Idrigill Point	56	B3
Ieper	64	E3
Ierapetra	75	H5
Ierissos	75	G2
Iesi	68	D4
Ifanadiana	109	J4
Ife	105	F4
Iforas, Adrar des	100	F5
Igara Parana	136	C4
Igarape Miri	137	H4
Igarka	84	D3
Igdir	76	E2
Igdir	77	L3
Igdir Dagi	77	H2
Iggesund	63	G6
Iglesia	139	C6
Iglesias	69	B6
Igloolik	120	K4
Igluligarjuk	119	S3
Ignace	124	E2
Igneada	76	B2
Igneada Burun	76	C2
Igoumenitsa	75	F3
Igra	78	J4
Iguala	131	K8
Igualada	67	G2
Iguape	138	G4
Iguatu	137	K5
Iguazu, Cataratas del	138	F5
Iguazu Falls	138	F5
Iguidi, Erg	100	D3
Iheya-retto	89	H10
Ih-Hayrhaan	87	K2
Ihlara	76	F3
Ihosy	109	J4
Ihsaniye	76	D3
Iida	89	F8
Iide-san	89	G7
Iisalmi	62	M5
Ijebu Ode	105	F4
IJmuiden	64	F2
IJssel	64	F2
IJsselmeer	64	F2
Ijzer	64	E3
Ik	78	J4
Ika	84	H5
Ikaalinen	63	K6
Ikaria	75	J4
Ikast	63	C8
Iked	89	D8
Ikeda	88	J4
Ikela	106	D3
Iki-shima	89	B9
Ikizce	76	E3
Ikizdere	77	J2
Ikom	105	G4
Ikomba	107	F4
Ikongo	109	J4
Ikpikpuk	118	E1
Ikuno	89	E8
Ila	105	F4
Ilagan	91	G2
Ilam	94	H5
Ilanskiy	84	F5
Ilaro	105	F4
Ilawa	71	H2
Ilbenge	85	L4
Ileanda	73	G2
Ilebo	106	D3
Ilek	79	J5
Ilesha	105	F4
Ilfracombe	52	C3
Ilgaz	76	E2
Ilgaz Daglari	76	F2
Ilgin	76	D3
Ilheus	137	K6
Ili	86	D3
Ilia	73	G3
Iliamna Lake	118	D4
Ilic	77	H3
Iligan	91	G4
Ilikurangi	115	G2
Ilinskiy	88	J1
Ilintsy	73	K1
Iliodhromia	75	G3
Iliomar	91	H7
Ilja	71	M1
Ilkeston	53	F2
Ilkley	55	H3
Ilkley Moor	55	H3
Illampu, Nevado de	138	C3
Illapel	138	B6
Illbille, Mount	112	G4
Iller	70	D4
Illescas	66	E2
Illimani, Nevado	138	C3
Illinois *U.S.A.*	124	E6
Illinois *U.S.A.*	124	E6
Illizi	101	G3
Illo	105	F3
Illote, Punta	136	A4
Ilm	70	D3
Ilmen , Ozero	78	E4
Ilminster	52	E4
Iloilo	91	G3
Ilorin	105	F4
Ilpyrskiy	85	U5
Ilsin-dong	88	B5
Ilwaki	91	H7
Ilych	78	K3
Ilza	71	J3
Ilzanka	71	J3
Ima	85	K5
Imabari	89	D8
Imamoglu	77	F4
Iman	88	E3
Imandra, Ozero	62	Q3
Imari	89	B9
Imataca, Serrania de	136	E2
Imatra	63	N6
Imese	106	C2
Imishli	94	J2
Immenstadt	70	D5
Immingham	55	J3
Imola	68	C3
Imotski	72	D4
Imperatriz	137	H5
Imperia	68	A4
Imperial	123	P7
Imperieuse Reef	112	D2
Impfondo	106	C2
Imphal	93	H4
Imrali	76	C2
Imst	68	C2
Imundsen Gulf	118	L1
Imuris	126	G5
Ina	89	F8
Inagh	59	D7
Inakona	114	K6
In Amenas	101	G3
Inangahua Junction	115	C4
Inanwatan	91	J6
Inapari	136	D6
Inari	62	M2
Inarijarvi	62	M2
Inawashiro-ko	89	H7
Inca	67	H3
Incebel Daglari	77	G3
Ince Burun	76	F1
Incekum Burun	76	E4
Incesu	76	F3
Inchard, Loch	56	C2
Inchon	87	P4
Inchope	109	F3
Indalsalven	62	G5
Inda Silase	96	D9

Jague	138	C5	Jauja	136	B6	Jijel	101	G1	Jordan	94 B5
Jahmah	94	G7	Jaunpur	92	F3	Jijia	73	J2	Jordan U.S.A.	123 L4
Jahrom	95	L7	Java	90	E7	Jijiga	103	H6	Jordanow	71 H4
Jaicos	137	J5	Java Trench	142	E5	Jijihu	86	F3	Jordan Valley	122 F6
Jailolo	91	H5	Javier, Isla	139	B9	Jilava	73	J3	Jorhat	93 H3
Jailolo, Selat	91	H5	Javor	72	E3	Jilin China	87	P3	Jorn	62 J4
Jaipur	92	E3	Javorniky	71	H4	Jilin China	87	P3	Jorong	90 E6
Jaisalmer	92	D3	Jawa	90	D7	Jiloca	67	F2	Jorpeland	63 B7
Jajarm	95	N3	Jawa, Laut	90	E7	Jilove	70	F4	Jos	105 G3
Jajce	72	D3	Jawb, Al	97	K5	Jima	103	G6	Jose de San Martin	139 B8
Jajpur	92	G4	Jawhar	107	J2	Jimba Jimba	112	D4	Joseph Bonaparte Gulf	112 F1
Jakarta	90	D7	Jawor	71	G3	Jimena de la Frontera	66	D4	Joseph, Lac	121 N7
Jakhau	92	C4	Jayanca	136	B5	Jimenez	127	M6	Josselin	65 B5
Jakobstad	62	K5	Jaya, Puncak	91	K6	Jimenez Mexico	128	C8	Jos Sodarso, Pulau	91 K7
Jakupica	73	F5	Jayapura	91	L6	Jimenez Mexico	127	K7	Jostedalsbreen	63 B6
Jalaid Qi	87	N2	Jayawijaya, Pegunungan	91	K6	Jimo	87	N4	Jotunheimen	63 C6
Jalalabad	92	D3	Jayena	66	E4	Jinan	87	M4	Jounie	94 B5
Jalalpur Pirwala	92	D3	Jaypur	92	F5	Jincheng	93	M1	Joutsa	63 M6
Jalapa Mexico	131	L8	Jayrud	94	C5	Jingbian	87	K4	Joyces Country	59 C5
Jalapa Mexico	131	N9	Jazirah, Al	94	E4	Jingchuan	93	L1	J. Percy Priest Lake	129 J2
Jalasjarvi	62	K5	Jaz Murian, Hamun-e	95	P8	Jingdezhen	87	M6	Juan Aldama	130 H5
Jalgaon	92	E4	Jebal Barez, Kuh-e	95	P7	Jinghai	87	M4	Juan de Fuca Strait	122 B3
Jalingo	105	H4	Jebba	105	F4	Jinghe	86	E3	Juan de Nova	109 H3
Jalna	92	E5	Jebel, Bahr el	102	F6	Jinghong	93	K4	Juan Fernandez, Islas de	135 A6
Jalon	67	F2	Jech Doab	92	D2	Jingle	87	L4	Juanjui	136 B5
Jalor	92	D3	Jedburgh	57	F5	Jingmen	93	M2	Juarez, Sierra	126 D4
Jalostotitlan	130	H7	Jedeida	69	B7	Jingpo	88	B3	Juazeiro	137 J5
Jalpa	130	H7	Jefferson	122	H5	Jingpo Hu	88	B4	Juazeiro do Norte	137 K5
Jalpaiguri	93	G3	Jefferson City Missouri	124	D7	Jingtai	93	K1	Juba	103 F7
Jalpan	131	K7	Jefferson City Tennessee	129	L2	Jingxi	93	L4	Jubany	141 W6
Jalu	101	K2	Jefferson, Mount Nevada	122	F8	Jing Xian	93	L3	Jubba	107 H2
Jam	95	Q4	Jefferson, Mount Oregon	122	D5	Jinhua	87	M6	Juby, Cap	100 C3
Jamaica	132	J5	Jef Jef el Kebir	102	D3	Jining Nei Mongol Zizhiqu, China	87	L3	Jucar	67 F3
Jamaica Channel	133	K5	Jehile Puzak	95	Q6	Jining Shandong, China	87	M4	Juchitan	131 M9
Jamalpur Bangladesh	93	G4	Jekabpils	63	L8	Jinja	107	F2	Judenburg	68 E2
Jamalpur India	92	G3	Jeldesa	103	H6	Jinkou	87	N4	Juigalpa	132 E8
Jamanxim	137	F5	Jelenia Gora	70	F3	Jinning	93	K4	Juist	70 B2
Jamari	136	E5	Jelgava	63	K8	Jinotepe	132	D9	Juiz de Fora	138 H4
Jambi	90	C6	Jelow Gir	94	H5	Jinsha Jiang	93	J3	Juklegga	63 E6
James	123	R6	Jemaja	90	D5	Jinta	86	H4	Julia	136 D4
James Bay	121	K7	Jember	90	E7	Jinxi	87	N3	Juliaca	138 B3
James Island	136	A7	Jeminay	86	F2	Jin Xian	87	N4	Julia Creek	113 J3
James Ross, Cape	120	D3	Jemnice	70	F4	Jinzhou	87	N3	Julianhab	116 Q2
James Ross Island	141	W6	Jena	70	D3	Jinzhou Wan	87	N4	Julijske Alpe	72 B2
James Ross Strait	120	G4	Jendouba	69	B7	Jiparana	136	E5	Julio de Castilhos	138 F5
Jamestown South Africa	108	E6	Jenin	94	B5	Jipijapa	136	A4	Jullundur	92 E2
Jamestown N. Dakota	123	Q4	Jenkins	124	J8	Jiquilpan	130	H8	Jumilla	67 F3
Jamestown New York	125	L5	Jennings	128	F5	Jirriiban	103	J6	Jumla	92 F3
Jamjo	63	F8	Jenny Lind Island	119	Q2	Jirueque	66	E2	Junagadh	92 D4
Jamkhandi	92	E5	Jens Munk Island	120	L4	Jirwan	97	K5	Junction	127 N5
Jamkhed	92	E5	Jequie	137	J6	Jishou	93	L3	Junction City	123 R8
Jammerbugten	63	C8	Jequitinhonha Brazil	138	H3	Jisr ash Shughur	94	C4	Jundiai	138 G4
Jammu	92	D2	Jequitinhonha Brazil	138	H3	Jiu	73	G3	Juneau	118 J4
Jammu and Kashmir	92	E2	Jerada	100	E2	Jiujiang	93	N3	Junee	113 K5
Jamnagar	92	D4	Jerba, Ile de	101	H2	Jiuling Shan	93	M3	Jungfrau	68 A2
Jampur	92	D3	Jeremie	133	K5	Jiutai	87	P3	Junggar Pendi	86 F2
Jamsa	63	L6	Jeremoabo	137	K6	Jiwa , Al	97	M5	Junin	139 D6
Jamshedpur	92	G4	Jerevan	77	L2	Jiwani	92	B3	Junin de los Andes	139 B7
Jamtland	62	F5	Jerez	130	H6	Jiwani, Ras	92	B4	Junosuando	62 K3
Jamuna	93	G3	Jerez de la Frontera	66	C4	Jixi Anhui, China	87	M5	Junsele	62 G5
Janda, Laguna de la	66	D4	Jericho Australia	113	K3	Jixi Heilongjiang, China	87	Q2	Jun Xian	93 M2
Jandaq	95	M4	Jericho Israel	94	B6	Jixian	88	C2	Jura France	65 G5
Jandiatuba	136	D4	Jerome	122	G6	Jizan	96	F8	Jura U.K.	57 C5
Janesville	124	F5	Jersey	53	M7	Jizl, Wadi	96	C3	Jura, Sound of	57 C5
Janjira	92	D5	Jersey City	125	N6	Jiz, Wadi al	97	K8	Juratishki	71 L1
Jan Mayen	48	F2	Jerseyville	124	F7	Joao Pessoa	137	L5	Juriti	137 F4
Jannatabad	95	Q4	Jerusalem	94	B6	Joaquin V. Gonzalez	138	D5	Jurua Brazil	136 D4
Janos	127	H5	Jervis Inlet	122	C2	Joban	89	H7	Jurua Brazil	136 D4
Januaria	138	H3	Jeseniky	71	G3	Jodar	66	E4	Juruena	136 F6
Janubiyah, Al Badiyah al	94	H6	Jessheim	63	D6	Jodhpur	92	D3	Jussey	65 F5
Jaora	92	E4	Jessore	92	G4	Joensuu	62	N5	Jutai Brazil	136 D4
Japan	89	G7	Jesup	129	M5	Joetsu	89	G7	Jutai Brazil	136 D5
Japan, Sea of	88	D6	Jevnaker	63	D6	Jofane	109	F4	Juterbog	70 E3
Japan Trench	142	F3	Jezerce	74	E1	Joffre, Mount	122	G2	Juticalpa	132 D7
Japaratuba	137	K6	Jeziorak, Jezioro	71	H2	Jogeva	63	M7	Jutland	63 C8
Japura	136	D4	Jeznas	71	L1	Joghatay	95	N3	Juuka	62 N5
Jarabulus	94	D3	Jezzine	94	B5	Johannesburg	108	E5	Juva	63 M6
Jaragua	138	G3	Jhang Maghiana	92	D2	John Day U.S.A.	122	D5	Juventud, Isla de la	132 F4
Jaraguari	138	F4	Jhansi	92	E3	John Day U.S.A.	122	E5	Ju Xian	87 M4
Jarama	66	E2	Jhelum Pakistan	92	D2	John H. Kerr Reservoir	129	N2	Juymand	95 P4
Jarandilla	66	D2	Jhelum Pakistan	92	D2	John O'Groats	56	E2	Juyom	95 M7
Jarash	94	B5	Jialing Jiang	93	L2	Johnshaven	57	F4	Juzna Morava	73 H4
Jardee	112	D5	Jiamusi	88	C2	Johnson City	129	L2	Jylland	63 C8
Jardines de la Reina	132	H4	Jian	93	N3	Johnston U.K.	52	B3	Jyvaskyla	62 L5
Jari	137	G3	Jianchuan	93	J3	Johnston U.S.A.	129	M4		
Jarir, Wadi al	96	F4	Jiande	87	M6	Johnstone	57	D5		
Jarna	63	G7	Jiange	93	L2	Johnston Lakes, The	112	E5		
Jarnac	65	C6	Jiangjin	93	L3	Johnstown	125	L6		
Jaromer	70	F3	Jiangjunmiao	86	F3	Johor Baharu	90	C5		
Jaroslaw	71	K3	Jiangmen	93	M4	Joigny	65	E5		
Jarpen	62	E5	Jiangsu	87	M5	Joinville Brazil	138	G5		
Jarrow	55	H2	Jiangxi	93	M3	Joinville France	64	F4		
Jarruhi	94	J6	Jianning	87	M6	Joinville Island	141	W6		
Jartai	87	K4	Jianou	87	M6	Jokkmokk	62	H3		
Jarvso	63	G6	Jianquanzi	86	H3	Jokulbunga	62	T11		
Jashpurnagar	92	F4	Jianshi	93	L2	Jokulsa a Bru	62	X12		
Jask	95	N9	Jiaohe	87	P3	Jokulsa-a Fjollum	62	W12		
Jasper Canada	119	M5	Jiaoling	87	M7	Jolfa	94	G2		
Jasper Alabama	129	J4	Jiaozuo	93	M1	Joliet	124	G6		
Jasper Florida	129	L5	Jia Xian	87	L4	Joliette	125	P3		
Jasper Texas	128	F5	Jiaxing	87	N5	Jolo Philippines	91	G4		
Jassy	73	J2	Jiayin	88	C1	Jolo Philippines	91	G4		
Jastrebarsko	72	C3	Jiayuguan	86	H4	Jonava	63	N9		
Jastrowie	71	G2	Jiboia	136	D3	Jonesboro	128	G3		
Jastrzebie-Zdroj	71	H4	Jibou	73	G2	Jones Sound	120	J2		
Jaszbereny	72	E2	Jibsh, Ra's	97	P6	Jonglei Canal	102	F6		
Jatai	138	F3	Jicatuyo	132	C7	Joniskis	63	K8		
Jatapu	136	F4	Jiddah	96	D6	Jonkoping Sweden	63	F8		
Jath	92	E5	Jidong	88	C3	Jonkoping Sweden	63	F8		
Jativa	67	F3	Jiekkevarre	62	H2	Jonquiere	125	Q2		
Jatoba	137	G6	Jieknaffo	62	G3	Jonzac	65	C6		
Jau	136	E4	Jiesavrre	62	L2	Joplin	124	C8		
Jau	138	G4	Jihlava Czech Rep.	70	F4	Jordan	94	B6		
Jauaperi	136	E4	Jihlava Czech Rep.	71	G4					

K

Kaala-Gomen	114	W16
Kaamanen	62	M2
Kaavi	62	N5
Kaba	104	C4
Kabaena	91	G7
Kabala	104	C4
Kabale	107	E3
Kabalega Falls	107	F2
Kabalo	106	E4
Kabambare	107	E3
Kabara	114	S9
Kabba	105	G4
Kabinatagami	124	H1
Kabirkuh	94	H5
Kabompo	106	D5
Kabongo	106	E4
Kabud Gonbad	95	P3
Kabul Afghanistan	92	C2
Kabuli	114	D2
Kaburuang	91	H5
Kabwe	107	E5
Kabyrdak	84	A5
Kachchh, Gulf of	92	C4
Kachchh, Rann of	92	C4
Kachemak Bay	118	E4

Name	Page	Grid
Kariba, Lake	108	E3
Karibib	108	C4
Kaributo	88	H4
Karigasniemi	62	L2
Karikari, Cape	115	D1
Karima	103	F4
Karimata, Kepulauan	90	D6
Karimata, Selat	90	D6
Karimganj	93	H4
Karimnagar	92	E5
Karimunjawa, Kepulauan	90	E7
Karin	103	J5
Karistos	75	H3
Kariz	95	Q4
Karkaralinsk	86	D2
Karkaralong, Kepulauan	91	H5
Karkar Island	114	D2
Karkas, Kuh-e	95	L5
Karkkila	63	L6
Karlino	70	F1
Karliova	77	J3
Karl-Marx-Stadt	70	E3
Karlobag	72	C3
Karlovac	72	C3
Karlovo	73	H4
Karlovy Vary	70	E3
Karlsborg	63	F7
Karlskoga	63	F7
Karlskrona	63	F8
Karlsruhe	70	C4
Karlstad *Sweden*	63	E7
Karlstad *U.S.A.*	124	B2
Karlstadt	70	C4
Karmanovka	79	J6
Karmoy	63	A7
Karnafuli Reservoir	93	H4
Karnal	92	E3
Karnali	92	F3
Karnataka	92	E6
Karnobat	73	J4
Karonie	112	E5
Karora	103	G4
Karossa, Tanjung	91	F7
Karousadhes	74	E3
Karoy	86	D2
Karpathos *Greece*	75	J5
Karpathos *Greece*	75	J5
Karpathos Straits	75	J5
Karpathou, Stenon	75	J5
Karpenision	75	F3
Karpinsk	84	Ad5
Karpogory	78	G3
Karratha	112	D3
Karrats Fjord	120	R3
Karree Berge	108	D6
Kars *Turkey*	77	K2
Kars *Turkey*	77	K2
Karsakpay	86	B2
Karsamaki	62	L5
Karsanti	76	F4
Karshi *Kazakhstan*	79	J7
Karshi *Uzbekistan*	80	H6
Karsiyaka	76	B3
Karskoye More	84	A2
Karsun	78	H5
Kartal	76	C2
Kartayel	78	J3
Kartuni	133	T11
Kartuzy	71	H1
Karufa	91	J6
Karun	94	J6
Karvina	71	H4
Karwar	92	D6
Karym	84	Ae4
Karymskoye	85	J6
Kas	76	C4
Kasai	106	C3
Kasaji	106	D5
Kasama	107	F5
Kasane	108	E3
Kasanga	107	F4
Kasangulu	106	C3
Kasaragod	92	D6
Kasar, Ras	96	D7
Kasba Lake	119	Q3
Kasba Tadla	100	D2
Kasempa	106	E5
Kasese	107	F2
Kashaf	95	Q3
Kashan	95	K5
Kashary	79	G6
Kashgar	86	D4
Kashi	86	D4
Kashima	89	C9
Kashin	78	F4
Kashipur	92	E3
Kashira	78	F5
Kashiwazaki	89	G7
Kashkanteniz	86	C2
Kashkarantsy	78	F2
Kashmar	95	P4
Kasimov	78	G5
Kasin	92	D2
Kasiruta	91	H6
Kaskinen	62	J5
Kasko	62	J5
Kas Kong	93	K6
Kasli	84	Ad5
Kasmere Lake	119	Q4
Kasongo	106	D3
Kasongo-Lunda	106	C4
Kasos	75	J5
Kasos, Stenon	75	J5
Kaspiyskiy	79	H6
Kassala	103	G4
Kassandra	75	G4
Kassel	70	C3
Kasserine	101	G1
Kastamonu	76	E2
Kastaneai	75	J2
Kastelli	75	G5
Kastellorizon	76	C4
Kastoria	75	F2
Kastorias, Limni	75	F2
Kastron	75	H3
Kasulu	107	F3
Kasumi	89	E8
Kasumiga-ura	89	H7
Kasungu	107	F5
Kata	84	G5
Kataba	106	E6
Katagum	105	H3
Katahdin, Mount	125	R4
Katako Kombe	106	D3
Katanning	112	D5
Katastari	75	F4
Katav Ivanovsk	78	K5
Katchall	93	H7
Katen	88	F2
Katerini	75	G2
Katha	93	J4
Katherina, Gebel	103	F2
Katherine	112	G1
Kathmandu	92	G3
Kati	100	D6
Katihar	93	G3
Katikati	115	E2
Katiola	104	D4
Katla	62	V13
Katlabukh, Ozero	73	K3
Katmai Volcano	118	E4
Kato Nevrokopion	75	G2
Katoomba	113	L5
Kato Stavros	75	G2
Katowice	71	H3
Katrineholm	63	G7
Katrine, Loch	57	D4
Katsina	105	G3
Katsina Ala	105	G4
Katsuura	89	H8
Katsuyama	89	F7
Kattavia	75	J5
Kattegat	63	D8
Kauai	126	R9
Kauai Channel	126	R10
Kauhajoki	62	K5
Kauiki Head	126	S10
Kaujuitok	120	H3
Kaulakahi Channel	126	Q9
Kaunakakai	126	S10
Kaunas	71	K1
Kaura Namoda	105	G3
Kaushany	73	K2
Kautokeino	62	K2
Kavacha	85	V4
Kavaje	74	E2
Kavak	77	G2
Kavaklidere	76	C4
Kavalerovo	88	E3
Kavali	92	E6
Kavalla	75	H2
Kavar	95	L7
Kavarna	73	K4
Kavgamis	77	H4
Kavieng	114	E2
Kavir, Dasht-e	95	M4
Kavir-e Namak	95	N4
Kavungo	106	D5
Kavusshap Daglari	77	K3
Kaw	137	G3
Kawagoe	89	G8
Kawaguchi	89	G8
Kawaihae	126	T10
Kawakawa	115	E1
Kawambwa	107	E4
Kawardha	92	F4
Kawasaki	89	G8
Kawerau	115	F3
Kawhia	115	E3
Kawhia Harbour	115	E3
Kawimbe	107	F4
Kawkareik	93	J5
Kawthaung	93	J7
Kayak Island	118	G4
Kayan	91	F5
Kaydak, Sor	79	J7
Kaye, Cape	120	H3
Kayenta	127	G2
Kayes	100	C6
Kaymaz	76	D3
Kaynar	86	D2
Kaynarca	76	D2
Kayseri	76	F3
Kayuagung	90	C6
Kazachinskoye	84	H5
Kazachye	85	P2
Kazakh	77	L2
Kazakhskiy Melkosopochnik	86	C2
Kazakhskiy Zaliv	79	J2
Kazakhstan	79	J6
Kazan	78	H4
Kazan *Turkey*	76	E2
Kazan	119	R3
Kazandzhik	95	M2
Kazan Lake	119	R3
Kazanluk	73	H4
Kazan-retto	83	N4
Kazatin	79	D6
Kazbek	77	L1
Kazerun	95	K7
Kazgorodok	84	Ae6
Kazhim	78	J3
Kazi Magomed	94	J1
Kazim Barekir	76	E4
Kaztalovka	79	H6
Kazumba	106	D4
Kazy	95	N2
Kazym	84	Ae4
Kazymskaya	84	Ae4
Kazymskiy Mys	84	Ae4
Kea *Greece*	75	H4
Kea *Greece*	75	H4
Keady	58	J4
Keal, Loch na	57	B4
Kearny	126	G4
Keaukaha	126	T11
Keban	77	H3
Keban Baraji	77	H3
Kebemer	104	B2
Kebezen	84	D6
Kebnekaise	62	H3
Kebock Head	56	B2
Kebri Dehar	103	H6
Kech a Terara	103	G6
Kechika	118	K4
Keciborlu	76	D4
Kecil, Kai	91	J7
Kecskemet	72	E2
Kedainiai	63	K9
Kedgwick	125	S3
Kediri	90	E7
Kedong	87	P2
Kedougou	104	C3
Kedva	78	J3
Keel	58	B5
Keelby	55	J3
Keele	118	K3
Keele Peak	118	J3
Keeler	126	D2
Keene	125	P5
Keeper Hill	59	F7
Keetmanshoop	108	C5
Keewatin *N.W. Territories, Canada*	119	R3
Keewatin *Ontario, Canada*	124	C2
Kefallinia	75	F3
Kefamenanu	91	G7
Kefken	76	D2
Keflavik	62	T12
Keglo Bay	121	N6
Kegulta	79	G6
Keighley	55	H3
Keitele *Kaskisuomi, Finland*	62	L5
Keitele *Kuopio, Finland*	62	M5
Keith	56	F3
Keith Arm	119	L2
Keiyasi	114	Q8
Kekertaluk Island	120	N4
Keketa	114	C3
Kel	85	M3
Kelang	90	C5
Keld	55	G2
Keles	76	C3
Kelibia	101	H1
Kelkit *Turkey*	77	G2
Kelkit *Turkey*	77	H2
Keller Lake	119	L3
Kellett, Cape	118	K1
Kellog	84	D4
Kellogg	122	F4
Kelloselka	62	N3
Kells	58	J5
Kelme	63	K9
Kelmentsy	73	J1
Kelo	102	C6
Kelolokan	91	F5
Kelowna	122	E3
Kelsey Bay	122	B2
Kelso *New Zealand*	115	B6
Kelso *U.K.*	57	F5
Keluang	90	C5
Kelvedon	53	H3
Kem	78	E3
Kemah	77	H3
Kemaliye	77	H3
Kemalpasa	77	J2
Kemalpasar	76	B3
Kemano	118	K5
Kemer *Turkey*	76	C4
Kemer *Turkey*	76	C4
Kemer *Turkey*	76	D4
Kemerovo	84	D5
Kemi	62	L4
Kemijarvi *Finland*	62	L3
Kemijarvi *Finland*	62	M3
Kemijoki	62	L3
Kemmerer	123	J7
Kempen	64	F3
Kempendyayi	85	K4
Kemp, Lake	127	N4
Kemps Bay	132	H2
Kempsey	113	L5
Kempten	70	D5
Kempt, Lac	125	N3
Kempton	113	K7
Ken	92	F3
Kenadsa	100	E2
Kenai	118	E3
Kenai Mountains	118	E4
Kenai Peninsula	118	F3
Kendal	55	G2
Kendall, Cape	120	J5
Kendari	91	G6
Kendawangan	90	E6
Kendraparha	92	G4
Kendyrliki	86	F2
Kenema	104	C4
Kenete Karavastas	74	E2
Kenge	106	C3
Kengtung	93	J4
Kenhardt	108	D5
Kenilworth	53	F2
Kenitra	100	D2
Keniut	85	X4
Kenli	87	M4
Kenmare *Ireland*	59	C9
Kenmare *Ireland*	59	C9
Kenmore	57	D4
Kennacraig	57	C5
Kennebec	125	R4
Kenner	128	G5
Kennet	53	F3
Kennewick	122	E4
Kenninghall	53	J2
Kenn Reef	113	M3
Kenogami	121	K7
Keno Hill	118	H3
Kenora	124	C2
Kenosha	124	G5
Kent *U.K.*	53	H3
Kent *U.S.A.*	127	K5
Kentau	86	B3
Kentford	53	H2
Kentmere	55	G2
Kent Peninsula	119	P2
Kentucky *U.S.A.*	124	G8
Kentucky *U.S.A.*	124	H8
Kentucky Lake	124	F8
Kentwood	128	G5
Kenya	107	G2
Keokea	126	S10
Keokuk	124	E6
Keos	75	H4
Kepi	91	K7
Kepno	71	G3
Keppel Bay	113	L3
Kepsut	76	C3
Kerala	92	E6
Kerama-retto	89	H10
Keravat	114	E2
Kerch	79	F6
Kerchenskiy Proliv	79	F6
Kerema	114	D3
Keremeos	122	E3
Keren	103	G4
Kerguelen, Ile	142	D6
Keri	75	F4
Kericho	107	G3
Kerinci, Gunung	90	C6
Keriya He	92	F1
Kerki	95	S3
Kerkinitis, Limni	75	G2
Kerkira *Greece*	74	E3
Kerkira *Greece*	74	E3
Kerma	102	F4
Kermadec Islands	111	T8
Kermadec Trench	143	H6
Kerman	95	N6
Kerman Desert	95	P7
Kermen	73	J4
Kermit	127	L5
Kern	126	C2
Keros	78	J3
Kerpineny	73	K2
Kerrera	57	C4
Kerrville	127	N5
Kerry	59	C8
Kerry Head	59	C8
Kerrykeel	58	G2
Keruh	90	C4
Kerulen	87	L2
Kesalahti	63	N6
Kesan	76	B2
Kesap	77	H2
Kesennuma	88	H6
Keshvar	94	J5
Keskin	76	E3
Keski-Suomi	62	K5
Keskozero	78	E3
Keswick	55	F2
Keszthely	72	D2
Ket	84	D5
Keta	104	F4
Keta, Ozero	84	E3
Ketapang	90	D6
Ketchikan	118	J4
Kete	104	E4
Ketmen, Khrebet	86	E3
Ketoy, Ostrov	85	S7
Ketrzyn	71	J1
Kettering	53	G2
Kettle Ness	55	J2
Kettle River Range	122	E3
Kettlewell	55	G2
Kettusoja	62	N3
Keurus-selka	63	L5
Keushki	84	Ae4
Kew	133	M4
Kewanee	124	F6
Keweenaw	124	G3
Keweenaw Bay	124	G3
Keweenaw Point	124	G3
Keyano	121	M7
Keyaygyr	86	D3

Name	Page	Ref
Keyi	86	E3
Key Largo	129	M8
Key, Lough	58	F4
Keynsham	52	E3
Key West	129	M8
Keyworth	53	F2
Kez	78	J4
Kezhma	84	G5
Khabarovo	84	Ad3
Khabarovsk	88	E1
Khabarovsk Kray	85	P6
Khabur	94	E4
Khadki	92	D5
Khairagarh	92	F4
Khairpur *Pakistan*	92	C3
Khairpur *Pakistan*	92	D3
Khakhar	85	P5
Khalafabad	94	J6
Khalili	95	L8
Khalkhal	94	J3
Khalki	75	J4
Khalkis	75	G3
Khalmer-Yu	84	Ad3
Khalturin	78	H4
Khamar Daban, Khrebet	84	G6
Khambhat	92	D4
Khambhat, Gulf of	92	D4
Khamili	75	J5
Khamir	96	F8
Khamis Mushayt	96	F7
Kham Keut	93	K5
Khammam	92	F5
Khamra	85	J4
Khanabad	92	C1
Khan al Baghdadi	94	F5
Khanaqin	94	G4
Khanda	84	H6
Khandela	92	E3
Khandra	75	J5
Khandwa	92	E4
Khandyga	85	P4
Khangokurt	84	Ad4
Khanh Hoa	93	L6
Khanh Hung	93	L7
Khani	85	L5
Khania	75	H5
Khaniadhana	92	E4
Khanion Kolpos	75	G5
Khanka, Ozero	88	D3
Khankendi	92	H2
Khanpur	92	D3
Khan Shaykhun	94	C4
Khantau	86	C3
Khantayka	84	D3
Khantayskoye, Ozero	84	E3
Khanty-Mansiysk	84	Ae4
Khan Yunis	94	B6
Kharabali	79	H6
Kharagpur	93	G4
Kharalakh	85	L3
Kharan	95	N7
Kharanaq	95	M5
Kharaulakhskiy Khrebet	85	M2
Kharbur	77	J5
Kharga, El Wahat el	102	F3
Kharg Island	97	K2
Kharitah, Shiqqat al	96	H8
Khark	97	K2
Kharkiv	79	F6
Kharku	97	K2
Khar Kuh	95	L6
Kharlovka	78	F2
Kharsawan	92	G4
Kharstan	85	Q2
Khartoum	103	F4
Khartoum North	103	F4
Kharutayuvam	78	K2
Khasalakh	85	M2
Khasan	88	C4
Khasavyurt	79	H7
Khash	95	Q7
Khash	95	R6
Khash, Dasht-i-	92	B2
Khashm el Girba	96	B9
Khash Rud	95	R6
Khashuri	77	K2
Khasi Hills	93	H3
Khaskovo	73	H5
Khatanga *Russia*	84	G2
Khatanga *Russia*	84	G2
Khatangskiy Zaliv	84	H2
Khatayakha	78	K2
Khatyrka	85	X4
Khaybar, Harrat	96	E4
Khaypudyrskaya Guba	78	K2
Khayran, Ra's al	97	P5
Khaysardakh	85	M4
Khe Bo	93	K5
Kheisia	77	J5
Khemis Miliana	67	H4
Khemisset	100	D2
Khenchela	101	G1
Khenifra	100	D2
Kherrata	67	J4
Khersan	95	K6
Kherson	79	E6
Khe Sanh	93	L5
Kheta	84	G2
Khiitola	63	N6
Khilok	85	J6
Khios *Greece*	75	H3
Khios *Greece*	75	J3
Khirbat Isriyah	77	G5
Khiva	80	H5

Name	Page	Ref
Khlebarovo	73	J4
Khmelnik	79	D6
Khmelnytskyy	79	D6
Khodzhakala	95	N2
Kholm *Afghanistan*	92	C1
Kholm *Russia*	78	E4
Kholmogory	78	G3
Kholmsk	88	J2
Khomas Highland	108	C4
Khomeyn	95	K5
Khomeynishahr	95	K5
Khong	93	L6
Khongkhoyuku	85	N4
Khonj	95	L8
Khoper	79	G5
Khor *Russia*	88	E2
Khor *Russia*	88	E2
Khora Sfakion	75	H5
Khorat, Cao Nguyen	93	K5
Khordha	92	G4
Khordogoy	85	K4
Khoreyver	78	K2
Khorgo	84	J2
Khorinsk	84	H6
Khorod	79	E6
Khorol	88	C3
Khorovaya	84	A3
Khorramabad *Iran*	94	J5
Khorramabad *Iran*	95	N4
Khorramshahr	94	J6
Khosf	95	P5
Khosheutovo	79	H6
Khosk	95	R4
Khosrowabad	94	J6
Khotin	73	J1
Khouribga	100	D2
Khoyniki	79	D5
Khrístiana	75	H4
Khroma	85	Q2
Khudzhand	86	B3
Khuff	96	G4
Khulna	93	G4
Khulo	77	K2
Khunjerab Pass	92	E1
Khunsar	95	K5
Khunti	92	G4
Khur	95	P4
Khurays	97	J4
Khurja	92	E3
Khuryan Munjan, Jazair	97	N8
Khust	79	C6
Khutu Datta	85	Q7
Khuzdar	92	C3
Khvaf	95	Q4
Khvalynsk	79	H5
Khvor	95	M5
Khvormuj	95	K7
Khvoy	94	G2
Khvoynaya	78	E4
Khwaja Muhammad, Koh-i-	92	D1
Khyber Pass	92	D2
Khyrov	71	K4
Kiamba	91	G4
Kiantajarvi	62	N4
Kiaton	75	G3
Kiberg	62	P1
Kibombo	106	E3
Kibondo	107	F3
Kibwezi	107	G3
Kibworth Harcourt	53	G2
Kicevo	73	F5
Kicking Horse Pass	119	M5
Kidal	100	F5
Kidan, Al	97	M5
Kidderminster	52	E2
Kidnappers, Cape	115	F3
Kidsgrove	55	G3
Kidwelly	52	C3
Kidyut, Wadi	97	K8
Kiel	70	D1
Kielce	71	J3
Kielder	57	F5
Kielder Forest	57	F5
Kielder Water	57	F5
Kieler Bucht	70	D1
Kieta	114	F3
Kiev	79	E5
Kiffa	100	C5
Kifissos	75	G3
Kifri	94	G4
Kigali	107	F3
Kigi	77	J3
Kiglapait, Cape	121	P6
Kigoma	107	E3
Kiholo	126	T11
Kii-sanchi	89	E9
Kii-suido	89	E9
Kikai-jima	89	B11
Kikiakki	84	C4
Kikinda	72	F3
Kikladhes	75	H4
Kikonai	88	H5
Kikori	114	C3
Kikwit	106	C3
Kil	63	E7
Kilafors	63	G6
Kilakh	97	K5
Kilauea	126	R9
Kilauea Crater	126	T11
Kilbasan	76	E4
Kilbeggan	59	H6
Kilberry	58	J2
Kilbirnie	57	D5
Kilbrannan Sound	57	C5

Name	Page	Ref
Kilbride *Ireland*	59	K7
Kilbride *U.K.*	57	A3
Kilbuck Mountains	118	D3
Kilchu	88	B5
Kilcock	59	J6
Kilcolgan	59	E6
Kilcormac	59	G6
Kilcoy	113	L4
Kilcullen	59	J6
Kildare *Ireland*	59	J6
Kildare *Ireland*	59	J6
Kildin, Ostrov	62	R2
Kildinstroy	62	Q2
Kilfinnane	59	F8
Kilgore	128	E4
Kilham	57	F5
Kilickaya	77	J2
Kilifi	107	G3
Kilimanjaro	107	G3
Kilinailau Islands	114	F2
Kilis	77	G4
Kiliya	79	D6
Kilkee	59	C7
Kilkeel	58	L4
Kilkelly	58	E5
Kilkenny *Ireland*	59	H7
Kilkenny *Ireland*	59	H7
Kilkhampton	52	C4
Kilkieran Bay	59	C6
Killadysert	59	D7
Killala	58	D4
Killala Bay	58	D4
Killaloe	59	F7
Killarney	59	C8
Killashandra	58	G4
Killeen	128	D5
Killenaule	59	G7
Killiecrankie	57	E4
Killiecrankie, Pass of	57	E4
Killin	57	D4
Killinek Island	121	P5
Killini	75	G4
Killorglin	59	C8
Killybegs	58	F3
Killylea	58	J4
Kilmacthomas	59	H8
Kilmallock	59	E8
Kilmaluag	56	B3
Kilmarnock	57	D5
Kilmaurs	57	D5
Kilmelford	57	C4
Kilmez	78	J4
Kilmurry	59	D7
Kilnsea	55	K3
Kiloran	57	B4
Kilosa	107	G4
Kilpisjarvi	62	J2
Kilrea	58	J3
Kilrush	59	D7
Kilsyth	57	D5
Kiltan	92	D6
Kilwa Masoko	107	G4
Kilwinning	57	F4
Kilyos	76	C2
Kimbal, Mount	118	G3
Kimbe Bay	114	E3
Kimberley *Canada*	122	G3
Kimberley *South Africa*	108	D5
Kimberley Plateau	112	F2
Kimi	75	H3
Kimito	63	K6
Kimmeridge	53	E4
Kimolos	75	H4
Kimry	78	F4
Kimvula	106	C4
Kimzha	78	G2
Kinabalu, Gunung	90	F4
Kinbasket Lake	122	F2
Kinbrace	56	E2
Kincardine *Canada*	125	K4
Kincardine *U.K.*	57	E4
Kindat	93	H4
Kinder	128	F5
Kinder Scout	55	H3
Kindersley	123	K2
Kindia	104	C3
Kindu	106	E3
Kinel	79	J5
Kinel-Cherkasy	78	J5
Kineshma	78	G4
Kingaroy	113	L4
Kingarth	57	C5
King Christian Island	120	F2
King City	126	B2
King George Island	141	W6
King George Sound	112	E3
Kinghorn	57	E4
Kingiseppa	63	K7
King Island	113	J6
King, Lake	112	D5
King Leopold Ranges	112	F2
Kingman	126	E3
Kingoonya	113	H5
Kings	126	B2
King Salmon	118	D4
Kingsbarns	57	F4
Kingsbridge	52	D4
King's Bromley	53	F2
Kingsclere	53	F3
Kingscote	113	H6
Kingscourt	58	J5
Kingsford	124	F4
Kingsley	55	H3
King's Lynn	53	H2

Name	Page	Ref
Kingsmill Group	111	R2
King Sound	112	E2
Kings Peak	123	J7
Kingsport	129	L2
Kingston *Australia*	113	H6
Kingston *Canada*	125	M4
Kingston *Jamaica*	132	J5
Kingston *New Zealand*	115	B6
Kingston *U.S.A.*	125	P6
Kingston Bagpuize	53	F3
Kingston-upon-Hull	55	J3
Kingston-upon-Thames	53	G3
Kingstown	133	S8
Kingsville	128	D7
Kingswood	52	E3
Kington	52	D2
Kingussie	57	D3
King William Island	120	G3
King William's Town	108	E6
Kiniama	107	E5
Kinik	76	B3
Kinloch	57	B3
Kinlochewe	56	C3
Kinloch Hourn	57	C3
Kinna	63	E8
Kinnaird Head	56	F3
Kinnegad	59	H6
Kinnerley	52	E2
Kinnert, Yam	94	B5
Kinoosao	119	Q4
Kinross	57	E4
Kinsale	59	E9
Kinsalebeg	59	G9
Kinsarvik	63	B6
Kinshasa	106	C3
Kinsley	127	N2
Kinston	129	P3
Kintampo	104	E4
Kintore	56	F3
Kintyre	57	C5
Kintyre, Mull of	57	C5
Kinuachdrachd	57	C4
Kiparissia	75	F4
Kiparissiakos Kolpos	75	F4
Kipawa, Lac	125	L3
Kipengere Range	107	F4
Kipili	107	F4
Kipini	107	H3
Kipnuk	118	C4
Kipseli	75	G3
Kirakira	114	K7
Kiraz	76	C3
Kirazli	76	B2
Kirbasi	76	D2
Kirbey	84	H3
Kirbey	57	B4
Kircubbin	58	L4
Kirec	76	C3
Kirenga	84	H5
Kirenis	76	C4
Kirensk	84	H5
Kirgizskiy Khrebet	86	C3
Kirgiz Step	79	J6
Kiri	106	C3
Kiribati	111	S2
Kirik	77	J2
Kirikhan	77	G4
Kirikkale	76	E3
Kirillo	78	F4
Kirin	87	P3
Kirinyaga	107	G3
Kirka	76	D3
Kirkagac	76	B3
Kirk Bulag Dag	94	H3
Kirkburton	55	H3
Kirkby	55	G3
Kirkby in Ashfield	55	H3
Kirkby Lonsdale	55	G2
Kirkby Stephen	55	G2
Kirkcaldy	57	E4
Kirkcambeck	57	F5
Kirkcolm	54	D2
Kirkcudbright	54	E2
Kirkcudbright Bay	54	E2
Kirkenes	62	P2
Kirkestinden	62	H2
Kirkheaton	57	G5
Kirkintilloch	57	D5
Kirkland Lake	125	K2
Kirk Langley	53	F2
Kirklareli	76	B2
Kirklington	55	J3
Kirk Michael	54	E2
Kirkoswald	55	G2
Kirk Smeaton	55	H3
Kirksville	124	D6
Kirkton	57	F4
Kirkton of Culsalmond	56	F3
Kirkton of Largo	57	F4
Kirkuk	94	G4
Kirkwall	56	F2
Kirkwhelpington	57	F5
Kirkwood	108	E6
Kirlangic Burun	76	D4
Kirmir	76	E2
Kirov *Russia*	78	E5
Kirov *Russia*	78	H4
Kirova	86	D2
Kirovhrad	79	E6
Kirovo-Chepetsk	78	H4
Kirovsk *Russia*	62	Q3
Kirovsk *Turkmenistan*	95	Q3
Kirovskiy	88	D3
Kirriemuir	57	F4
Kirs	78	J4

Name	Page	Grid
Kirsanov	79	G5
Kirsehir	76	F3
Kirtgecit	77	K3
Kirthar Range	92	C3
Kirtlington	53	F3
Kirton	55	J3
Kiruna	62	J3
Kiryu	89	G7
Kisa	63	F8
Kisamou, Kolpos	75	G5
Kisangani	106	E2
Kisar	91	H7
Kisarazu	89	G8
Kiselevsk	84	D6
Kishanganj	93	G3
Kishangarh	92	D3
Kishb, Harrat	96	E5
Kishika-zaki	89	C10
Kishiwada	89	E8
Kishorganj	93	H4
Kishorn, Loch	56	C3
Kisii	107	F3
Kiska Island	118	Ab9
Kiskunfelegyhaza	72	E2
Kiskunhalas	72	E2
Kislovodsk	79	G7
Kismaayo	107	H3
Kiso-Fukushima	89	F8
Kiso-sammyaku	89	F8
Kispest	72	E2
Kissidougou	104	C4
Kissimmee	129	M7
Kisumu	107	F3
Kita	100	D6
Kitajaur	62	J3
Kitakami Japan	88	H6
Kitakami Japan	88	H6
Kitakami-sanmyaku	88	J3
Kita-kyushu	89	C9
Kitale	107	G2
Kitami	88	J4
Kitami-sammyaku	88	H6
Kitangari	107	G5
Kitay, Ozero	73	K3
Kit Carson	127	L1
Kitchener	125	K5
Kitee	62	P5
Kitgum	107	F2
Kithira Greece	75	G4
Kithira Greece	75	G4
Kithnos Greece	75	H4
Kithnos Greece	75	H4
Kitikmeot	119	N1
Kitimat	118	K5
Kitinen	62	M3
Kitkiojoki	62	K3
Kitsuki	89	C9
Kittanning	125	L6
Kittila	62	L3
Kitui	107	G3
Kitunda	107	F4
Kitwe	107	E5
Kitzbuhel	68	D2
Kitzbuheler Alpen	68	D2
Kitzingen	70	D4
Kivalo	62	L3
Kivijarvi	62	L5
Kivu, Lake	107	E3
Kiyevka	88	D4
Kiyevskoye Vodokhranilishche	79	E5
Kiyikoy	76	C2
Kizel	78	K4
Kizema	78	H3
Kizilagac	77	J3
Kizilcaboluk	76	C4
Kizilcadag	76	C4
Kizilhisar	76	C4
Kizilirmak	76	E2
Kizil Irmak	77	F2
Kizilkaya	76	D4
Kiziloren	76	E4
Kiziltepe	77	J4
Kizlyar	79	H7
Kizyl-Arvat	95	N2
Kizyl-Atrek	95	M3
Kizyl Ayak	95	S3
Kizyl-Su	95	L2
Kjollefjord	62	M1
Kjopsvick	62	L2
Kladanj	72	E3
Kladno	70	F3
Kladovo	73	G3
Klagenfurt	68	E2
Klaipeda	63	L9
Klamath U.S.A.	122	B7
Klamath U.S.A.	122	C7
Klamath Falls	122	D6
Klamath Mountains	122	C6
Klamono	91	J6
Klaralven	63	J6
Klatovy	70	E4
Klekovaca	72	D3
Klenak	72	E3
Klerksdorp	108	E5
Klichka	85	K7
Klimovichi	79	E5
Klin	78	F4
Klinovec	70	E3
Klintsovka	79	H5
Klintsy	79	E5
Klisura	73	H4
Kljuc	72	D3
Klobuck	71	H3
Klodzka Poland	71	G3
Klodzko Poland	71	G3
Klos	75	F2
Klosterneuberg	68	F1
Klosters	68	B2
Klrovskiy	79	H6
Kluane	118	H3
Kluane Lake	118	H3
Kluczbork	71	H3
Klyevka	84	A6
Klyuchevskaya Sopka	85	U5
Klyuchi	85	U5
Klyukvinka	84	D5
Kmagta	114	J6
Kmanjab	108	B3
K2, Mount	92	E1
Knapdale	57	C5
Knaresborough	55	H2
Knife	123	N4
Knight Island	118	F3
Knighton	52	D2
Knin	72	D3
Knjazevac	73	G4
Knockadoon Head	59	G9
Knockalla Mount	58	G2
Knockanaffrin	59	G8
Knockaunapeebra	59	G8
Knocklayd	58	K2
Knockmealdown Mountains	59	G8
Knocknaskagh	59	F8
Knottingley	55	H3
Knox, Cape	118	J5
Knoxville Iowa	124	D6
Knoxville Tennessee	129	L3
Knoydart	57	C3
Knud Rasmussen Land	120	P2
Knutholstind	63	C6
Knutsford	55	G3
Knyazhaya Guba	62	Q3
Knyazhevo	78	G4
Knysna	108	D6
Knyszyn	71	K2
Koba	90	D6
Kobarid	72	B2
Kobayashi	89	C10
Kobberminebugt	120	R5
Kobelyaki	79	E6
Kobenhavn	63	E9
Koblenz	70	B3
Kobowre, Pegunungan	91	K6
Kobrin	71	L2
Kobroor	91	J7
Kobuk	118	D2
Kobya	85	M4
Koca Turkey	76	B3
Koca Turkey	76	C3
Koca Turkey	76	E2
Kocapinar	77	K3
Kocarli	76	B4
Koceljevo	72	E3
Koch Bihar	93	G3
Kochechum	84	G3
Kochegarovo	85	K5
Kocher	70	C4
Kochi	89	D9
Koch Island	120	L4
Kochkorka	86	D3
Koch Peak	122	J5
Kochumdek	84	E4
Koden	71	K3
Kodiak	118	E4
Kodiak Island	118	E4
Kodima	78	G3
Kodinar	92	D4
Kodok	103	F6
Kodomari	88	H5
Kodyma	73	L2
Kofcaz	76	B2
Koffiefontein	108	D5
Koflach	68	E2
Koforidua	104	E4
Kofu	89	G8
Koge	63	E9
Kogilnik	73	K2
Ko, Gora	88	F2
Kohat	92	D2
Kohima	93	H3
Koh-i Qaisar	95	S5
Kohtla-Jarve	63	M7
Koide	89	G7
Koi Sanjaq	94	G3
Koitere	62	P5
Koivu	62	L3
Koje	89	B8
Kojonup	112	D5
Kokand	86	B3
Kokas	91	J6
Kokchetav	84	Ae6
Kokemaenjoki	63	K6
Kokenau	91	K6
Kokkola	62	K5
Koko	105	G4
Kokoda	114	D3
Kokomo	124	G6
Kokpekty	86	E2
Koksoak	121	N6
Kokstad	108	E6
Koktas	86	C2
Kokubu	89	C10
Kokuora	85	R2
Kokura	89	C9
Kokuy	85	K6
Kok-Yangak	86	C3
Kola	62	Q2
Kolaka	91	G6
Kolar	92	E6
Kolari	62	K3
Kolarovgrad	73	J4
Kolasin	72	E4
Kolay	77	F2
Kolberg	70	F1
Kolbuszowa	71	J3
Kolchugino	78	F4
Kolda	104	C3
Kolding	63	C9
Kole	106	D3
Kolguyev, Ostrov	78	H2
Kolhapur	92	D5
Kolin	70	F3
Kolki	71	L3
Kolkuskull	62	V12
Kollabudur	62	T12
Koln	70	B3
Kolno	71	J2
Koloa	126	R10
Kolobrzeg	70	F1
Kologriv	78	G4
Kolombangara	114	H5
Kolomna	78	F4
Kolono	91	G6
Koloubara	72	F3
Kolozsvar	73	G2
Kolpashevo	84	C5
Kolpino	78	E4
Kolskiy Poluostrov	78	F2
Koltubanovskiy	79	J5
Koluszki	71	H3
Kolva Russia	78	K3
Kolva Russia	78	K3
Kolwezi	106	E5
Kolyma	85	U3
Kolymskaya Nizmennost	85	T3
Kolymskiy, Khrebet	85	T4
Komadugu Gana	105	H3
Komandorskiye Ostrova	81	T4
Komarno	71	H5
Komarom	72	E2
Komatsu	89	F7
Komering	90	C6
Komodo	91	F7
Komoe	104	E4
Kom Ombo	103	F3
Komoran	91	K7
Komosomolets, Ostrov	81	L1
Komotini	75	H2
Komovi	74	E1
Kompong Cham	93	L6
Kompong Chhnang	93	K6
Kompong Som	93	K6
Kompong Speu	93	K6
Kompong Sralao	93	L6
Kompong Thom	93	K6
Komrat	79	D6
Komsomolets, Zaliv	79	J6
Komsomolsk	79	E6
Komsomolskiy	79	J6
Komsomolsk-na-Amure	85	P6
Konakovo	78	F4
Koncanica	72	D3
Konch	92	E3
Konda Indonesia	91	J6
Konda Russia	84	Ae4
Kondagaon	92	F5
Kondinin	112	D5
Kondinskoye	84	Ae5
Kondoa	107	G3
Kondon	85	P6
Kondoponga	78	E3
Konduz	92	C1
Kone	114	W16
Konevo	78	F3
Kong	104	E4
Kongan	89	J10
Kong Christian den X Land	120	W3
Kong Karls Land	80	D2
Kongolo	106	E4
Kongsberg	63	C7
Kongsvinger	63	E6
Kong Wilhelms Land	120	X2
Koniecpol	71	H3
Konigsberg	71	J4
Konigs Wusterhausen	70	E2
Konin	71	H2
Konitsa	75	F2
Koniya	89	B11
Konkamaalv	62	J2
Konkoure	104	C3
Konnern	70	D3
Konnevesi	62	M5
Konosha	78	G3
Konotop	79	E5
Konqi He	86	F3
Konskie	71	J3
Konstantinovsk	79	G6
Konstanz	68	B2
Konstyantynivka	79	F6
Kontagora	105	G3
Kontcha	105	H4
Kontiomaki	62	N4
Kontum	93	L6
Kontum, Plateau du	93	L6
Konya	76	E4
Konya Ovasi	76	E3
Konzhakovskiy Kamen , Gora	78	K4
Kootenai	122	G3
Kootenay	122	F3
Kootenay Lake	122	F3
Kopaonik	73	F4
Kopasker	62	W11
Kopavogur	62	U12
Koper	72	B3
Kopervik	63	A7
Kopet Dag, Khrebet	95	N2
Kopeysk	84	Ad5
Koping	63	F7
Kopka	124	F1
Kopmanholmen	62	H5
Koppang	63	D6
Kopparberg Sweden	63	F7
Kopparberg Sweden	63	F6
Koppi Russia	88	G1
Koppi Russia	88	H1
Kopru	76	D4
Koprubasi	76	C3
Kopruoren	76	C3
Kopychintsy	73	H1
Kor	95	L6
Kora	77	K2
Korab	72	F5
Korahe	103	H6
Koraluk	121	P6
Korana	72	C3
Korba	69	C7
Korbach	70	C3
Korbu, Gunung	90	C5
Korce	75	F2
Korcula	72	D4
Korda	84	F4
Kord Kuv	95	M3
Korea Bay	87	N4
Korea, North	87	P4
Korea, South	87	P4
Korea Strait	89	B8
Korennoye	84	H2
Korenovsk	79	F6
Korf	85	V4
Korforskiy	88	E1
Korgan	77	G2
Korgen	62	E3
Korhogo	104	D4
Korido	91	K6
Korim	91	K6
Korinthiakos Kolpos	75	G3
Korinthos	75	G4
Koriyama	89	H7
Korkinitskiy Zaliv	79	E6
Korkodon	85	T4
Korkuteli	76	D4
Korla	86	F3
Kormakiti, Akra	76	E5
Kornat	72	C4
Koro	114	R8
Korocha	79	F5
Koroglu Daglari	76	E2
Koronia, Limni	75	G2
Koronowo	71	G2
Koros	72	F2
Korosten	79	D5
Korostyshev	79	D5
Korotaikha	78	L2
Korovin Volcano	118	Ad9
Korpilombolo	62	K3
Korsakov	88	J2
Korsnas	62	J5
Korsor	63	D9
Korti	103	F4
Kortrijk	64	E3
Korucu	76	B3
Koryakskaya Sopka	85	U6
Koryanskiy Khrebet	85	Z5
Koryazhma	78	H3
Korzybie	71	G1
Kos Greece	75	J4
Kos Greece	75	J4
Koschagyl	79	J6
Koscian	71	G2
Koscierzyna	71	G1
Kosciusco, Mount	113	K6
Kosciusko	128	H4
Kose	77	H2
Kos Golu	76	B2
Koshiki-retto	89	B10
Kosice	71	J4
Koski	63	K6
Koslan	78	H3
Koslin	71	G1
Kosma	78	H2
Kosong	88	B6
Kosong-ni	88	B5
Kossou, Lac de	104	D4
Kossovo	71	L2
Kostajnica	72	D3
Kosti	103	F5
Kostino	84	D3
Kostomuksha	62	P4
Kostopol	71	M3
Kostroma Russia	78	G4
Kostroma Russia	78	G4
Kostrzyn	70	F2
Kosu-dong	89	B8
Kosva	78	K4
Kosyu	78	K2
Kosyuvom	78	K2
Koszalin	71	G1
Kota	92	E3
Kotaagung	90	C7
Kota Baharu	90	C4
Kotabaru Indonesia	90	F6
Kotabaru Indonesia	90	F6
Kota Belud	90	F4
Kotabumi	90	C5

Name	Page	Grid	Name	Page	Grid	Name	Page	Grid	Name	Page	Grid
Kota Kinabalu	90	F4	Krasnousolskiy	78	K5	Kucevo	73	F3	Kuqa	86	E3
Kotala	62	N3	Krasnovishersk	78	K3	Kuching	90	E5	Kura	77	L2
Kotamubagu	91	G5	Krasnovodsk	95	L2	Kuchinoerabu-jima	89	C10	Kurashasayskiy	79	K5
Kota Tinggi	90	C5	Krasnovodskiy Poluostrov	79	J7	Kuchinotsu	89	C9	Kurashiki	89	D8
Kotel	73	J4	Krasnoyarsk	84	E5	Kuchurgan	73	K2	Kurday	86	D3
Kotelnich	78	H4	Krasnoyarskiy Kray	84	E3	Kucuk	76	B3	Kurdzhali	73	H5
Kotelnikovo	79	G6	Krasnoye	78	G4	Kucukcekmece	76	C2	Kure	89	D8
Kotelnyy, Ostrov	85	P1	Krasnstaw	71	K3	Kucuk Kuyu	76	B3	Kure	76	E2
Kotikovo	88	E2	Krasnyy Chikoy	84	H6	Kudat	90	F4	Kurecik	77	G3
Kotka	63	M6	Krasnyye Okny	73	K2	Kudirkos-Naumiestis	71	K1	Kure Daglari	76	F2
Kot Kapura	92	D2	Krasnyy Kholm	79	J5	Kudus	90	E7	Kuresaare	63	M7
Kotlas	78	H3	Krasnyy Kut	79	H5	Kudymkar	78	J4	Kureyka	84	D3
Kotli	92	D2	Krasnyy Luch	79	F6	Kufi	76	C3	Kurgan	84	Ae5
Kotlik	118	C3	Krasnyy Yar *Russia*	79	G5	Kufstein	68	D2	Kurganinsk	79	G7
Koto	85	P7	Krasnyy Yar *Russia*	79	H6	Kugaly	86	D3	Kurgan-Tyube	86	B4
Kotor	72	E4	Kratie	93	L6	Kugi	84	Ad4	Kurikka	62	N4
Kotovo	79	G5	Kraulshavn	120	Q3	Kugmallit Bay	118	J2	Kurilskiye Ostrova	85	S7
Kotovsk *Russia*	79	G5	Kravanh, Chuor Phnum	93	K6	Kuhdasht	94	H5	Kuril Trench	142	G3
Kotovsk *Ukraine*	79	D6	Krefeld	70	B3	Kuh-e Bul	95	L6	Kurkcu	76	E4
Kotri	92	C3	Kremenchugskoye Vodokhranilishche	79	E6	Kuh-e Garbosh	95	K5	Kurlek	84	C5
Kottagudem	92	F5	Kremenchuk	79	E6	Kuh Lab, Ra's	95	Q9	Kurmuk	103	F5
Kottayam	92	E7	Kremnets	79	D5	Kuhmo	62	N4	Kurnool	92	E5
Kotto	102	D6	Krems	68	E1	Kuhpayeh *Iran*	95	L5	Kuroi	89	E8
Kotuy	84	G2	Krenitzin Islands	118	Ae9	Kuhpayeh *Iran*	95	N6	Kuroiso	89	G7
Kotyuzhany	73	K2	Kresevo	72	E4	Kuhran, Kuh-e	95	P8	Kurow	71	K3
Kotzebue	118	C2	Kresttsy	78	E4	Kuh, Ra's-al-	95	N9	Kursk	79	F5
Kotzebue Sound	118	C2	Kresty	84	D2	Kuito	106	C5	Kursumlija	73	F4
Kouango	102	C6	Krestyakh	85	K4	Kuji	88	H5	Kursunlu	76	E2
Koudougou	104	E3	Krestyanka	84	C2	Kuju-san	89	C9	Kurtalan	77	J4
Koufonisi	75	J5	Kretinga	63	J9	Kukalar, Kuh-e	95	K6	Kurtamysh	84	Ad6
Koukajuak, Great Plain of the	120	M4	Kribi	105	G5	Kukes	75	F1	Kurtun	77	H2
Kouki	102	C6	Krichev	79	E5	Kukhomskaya Volya	71	L3	Kuru	63	K6
Koumac	114	W16	Krichim	73	H4	Kukmor	78	J4	Kurucasile	76	E2
Koumenzi	86	F3	Krieza	75	H3	Kukpowruk	118	C2	Kuruman *South Africa*	108	D5
Koumra	102	C6	Krifovon	75	F3	Kukudu	114	H6	Kuruman *South Africa*	108	D5
Koundara	104	C3	Krilon, Mys	88	J3	Kukup	90	C5	Kurume	89	C9
Koungou Mountains	106	B3	Krios, Akra	75	G5	Kukushka	85	M6	Kurunegala	92	F7
Kounradskiy	86	D2	Krishna	92	E5	Kula *Turkey*	76	C3	Kurzeme	63	K8
Kourou	137	G2	Krishnagiri	92	E6	Kula *Yugoslavia*	72	E3	Kusadasi	76	B4
Kouroussa	104	D3	Krishnanagar	93	G4	Kulagino	79	J6	Kusadasi Korfezi	76	B4
Kousseri	105	J3	Kristdala	63	G8	Kulakshi	79	K6	Kusel	70	B4
Koutiala	100	D6	Kristel	67	F5	Kulal, Mont	107	G2	Kusey Andolu Daglari	77	H2
Kouvola	63	M6	Kristiansand	63	B7	Kulata	73	G5	Kushchevskaya	79	F6
Kova	84	G5	Kristianstad *Sweden*	63	E8	Kuldiga	63	N8	Kushima	89	C10
Kovachevo	73	J4	Kristianstad *Sweden*	63	F8	Kule	108	D4	Kushimoto	89	E9
Kovanlik	77	H2	Kristiansund	62	B5	Kulebaki	78	G4	Kushiro	88	K4
Kovdor	62	P3	Kristiinankaupunki	63	J5	Kulgera	113	G6	Kushka *Russia*	85	U4
Kovdozero, Ozero	62	Q3	Kristinestad	63	J5	Kulikov	71	L4	Kushmurun	84	Ad6
Kovel	71	L3	Kristinovka	73	K1	Kulinda *Russia*	84	G4	Kushtia	93	G4
Kovernino	78	G4	Kriti	75	H5	Kulinda *Russia*	84	H4	Kushva	78	K4
Kovero	62	P5	Kritikon Pelagos	75	H5	Kulmac Daglari	77	G3	Kuskokwim	118	C3
Kovik Bay	121	L5	Kriulyany	73	K2	Kulmbach	70	D3	Kuskokwim Bay	118	C4
Kovno	71	K1	Kriva Palanka	73	G4	Kuloy *Russia*	78	G3	Kuskokwim Mountains	118	D3
Kovrov	78	G4	Krivoye Ozero	73	L2	Kuloy *Russia*	78	G2	Kusma	92	F3
Kovylkino	78	G5	Krk	72	C3	Kulp	77	J3	Kussharo-ko	88	K4
Kowalewo	71	H2	Krnov	71	G3	Kulsary	79	J6	Kustanay	84	Ad6
Kowloon	87	L7	Krokodil	108	E4	Kultay	79	J6	Kustrin	70	F2
Koycegiz	76	C4	Krokom	62	F5	Kultuk	84	G6	Kuta	105	G4
Koyda	78	G2	Krokong	90	E5	Kulu	76	E3	Kutahya	76	C3
Koyuk	118	C3	Krokowa	71	H1	Kulu Island	118	J4	Kutaisi	77	K1
Koyukuk	118	D3	Krolevets	79	E5	Kulul	96	E9	Kutchan	88	H4
Koyulhisar	77	G2	Kromy	79	F5	Kulunda	84	B6	Kutima	84	H5
Koza	89	E9	Kronach	70	D3	Kulundinskoye, Ozero	84	B6	Kut, Ko	93	K6
Kozakli	76	F3	Krononberg	63	F8	Kulyab	86	B4	Kutna Hora	70	F4
Kozan	77	F4	Kronshtadt	63	N7	Kuma	79	H7	Kutno	71	H2
Kozani	75	F2	Kroonstad	108	E5	Kumagaya	89	G7	Kutu	106	C3
Kozekovo	71	M1	Kropotkin	79	G6	Kumakh-Surt	85	M2	Kutubdia	93	H4
Kozelsk	78	F5	Krosno	71	J4	Kumamoto	89	C9	Kutum	102	D5
Kozhevnikovo	84	B5	Krotoszyn	71	G3	Kumano	89	F9	Kuujjuaq	121	N6
Kozhikode	92	E6	Krsko	72	C3	Kumanovo	73	F4	Kuujjuarapik	121	L6
Kozhim	78	K2	Krugersdorp	108	E5	Kumara	115	C5	Kuuli-Mayak	79	J7
Kozhposelok	78	F3	Krui	90	C7	Kumasi	104	E4	Kuusamo	62	N4
Kozhva	78	K2	Kruje	74	E2	Kumba	105	G5	Kuvango	106	C5
Kozlu	76	D2	Krumbach	70	D4	Kumbakonam	92	E6	Kuvet	85	X3
Kozludere	77	G4	Krumovgrad	73	H5	Kum-Dag	95	M2	Kuwait	94	H7
Kozluk	77	J3	Krung Thep	93	K6	Kumertau	79	K5	Kuwait	97	J2
Kozmodemyansk	78	H4	Krusenstern, Cape	118	C2	Kuminki	62	L4	Kuwana	89	F8
Kozu-shima	89	G8	Krusevac	73	F4	Kuminskiy	84	Ae5	Kuya	78	G2
Kpalime	104	F4	Krusevo	73	F5	Kumkuduk	86	F3	Kuybyshev *Russia*	84	B5
Krabi	93	J7	Krustpils	63	M8	Kumluca	76	D4	Kuybyshevskoye Vodokhranilishche	78	H4
Kragero	63	C7	Kruzenshterna, Proliv	85	S7	Kummerower See	70	E2	Kuyeda	78	K4
Kragujevac	73	F3	Kruzof Island	118	H4	Kumnyong	87	P5	Kuygan	86	C2
Krakow	71	H3	Krym	79	E6	Kumon Bum	93	J3	Kuytun	86	F3
Krakowska, Jura	71	H3	Krymsk	79	F7	Kumru	77	G2	Kuyucak	76	C4
Kral Chlmec	71	K4	Krynki	71	K2	Kumsong	87	P4	Kuyumba	84	F4
Kralendijk	133	N8	Kryry	70	E3	Kumta	92	D6	Kuyus	84	D6
Kraljevo	72	F4	Kryvyy Rih	79	E6	Kumyr	86	C3	Kuzino	78	K4
Kramfors	62	G5	Krzeszowice	71	H3	Kunas	86	E3	Kuzitrin	118	C2
Krania	75	F3	Ksabi	100	E3	Kunas Chang	86	E3	Kuzmovka	84	E4
Kranidhion	75	G4	Ksar El Boukhari	101	F1	Kunashir, Ostrov	88	L3	Kuznetsk	79	H5
Kranj	72	C2	Ksarel Kebir	100	D2	Kundelungu Mountains	107	E5	Kuznetsovo	88	G2
Kranskop	108	F5	Ksar es Souk	100	E2	Kunduz	92	C1	Kuzomen	78	F2
Krasavino	78	H3	Ksenofontova	78	K3	Kungalv	63	H8	Kuzucubelen	76	F4
Krasino	84	Ab2	Ksour Essaf	101	H1	Kungar	78	K4	Kvaloy	62	H2
Kraskino	88	C4	Kstovo	78	G4	Kunghit Island	118	J5	Kvaloya	62	K1
Krasneno	85	X4	Kualakapuas	90	E6	Kungrad	51	U7	Kvalsund	62	L1
Krasnoarmeyesk	84	Ae6	Kuala Kerai	90	C4	Kungsor	63	G7	Kvarner	72	C3
Krasnoarmeyskiy	85	W3	Kuala Lipis	90	C5	Kungu	106	C2	Kvarneric	72	C3
Krasnoborsk	78	H3	Kuala Lumpur	90	C5	Kunlun Shan	92	F1	Kvichak Bay	118	D4
Krasnodar	79	F6	Kualapembuang	90	E6	Kunmadaras	72	F2	Kvidinge	63	E8
Krasnogorsk	88	J1	Kuala Penyu	90	F4	Kunming	93	K4	Kvigtind	62	E4
Krasnograd	79	F6	Kuala Terengganu	90	C4	Kunsan	87	P4	Kvikkjokk	62	G3
Krasnokamsk	78	K4	Kuandian	87	N3	Kununurra	112	F2	Kvina	63	B7
Krasnokutskoye	84	B6	Kuantan	90	C5	Kunu-ri	87	P4	Kvorning	63	C8
Krasnolesnyy	79	F5	Kuba	89	D8	Kuolayarvi	62	N3	Kwa	106	C3
Krasnorechenskiy	88	E3	Kuban	79	G6	Kuopio *Sweden*	62	M5	Kwale	105	G4
Krasnoselkup	84	C3	Kubenskoye Ozero	78	F4	Kuopio *Sweden*	62	M5	Kwamouth	106	C3
Krasnoslobodsk	78	G5	Kubkain	114	C2	Kupa	72	C3	Kwangju	87	P4
Krasnoturinsk	84	Ad5	Kubokawa	89	D9	Kupang	91	G7	Kwango	106	C3
Krasnoufimsk	78	K4	Kubonitu, Mount	114	J6	Kuparuk	118	E2	Kwanso-ri	88	B5
			Kubor, Mount	114	C3	Kupino	84	B6	Kwatisore	91	J6
			Kubrat	73	J4	Kupreanof Island	118	J4	Kwekwe	108	E3
			Kubuang	90	F5	Kupreanof Point	118	Ag8			
						Kupyansk	79	F6			

Name	No.	Ref.
Liddesdale	57	F5
Liden	62	G5
Lidingo	63	H7
Lidkoping	63	E7
Lidzbark Warminski	71	J1
Liebling	73	F3
Liechtenstein	70	C5
Liege	64	F3
Liegnitz	71	G3
Lielope	63	L8
Lienz	68	D2
Liepaja	63	L8
Lier	64	F3
Liestal	68	A2
Liezen	68	E2
Liffey	59	J6
Lifford	58	H3
Lifi Mahuida	139	C8
Lifou	114	X16
Ligger Bay	52	B4
Lighthouse Reef	132	D6
Ligonha	109	G3
Ligui	126	G8
Ligure, Appennino	68	B3
Ligurian Sea	68	B4
Lihir Group	114	E2
Lihou Reefs	113	L2
Lihue	126	R10
Lihula	63	K7
Lijiang	93	K3
Likasi	106	E5
Likhoslavl	78	F4
Liku	90	D5
Likupang	91	H5
L'Ile-Rousse	69	B4
Lille	64	E3
Lille Balt	63	C8
Lillebonne	64	D4
Lillehammer	63	D6
Lillesand	63	C7
Lillestrom	63	H7
Lillhamra	63	F6
Lillhardal	63	F6
Lillholmsjon	62	F5
Lillo	66	E3
Lillviken	62	G3
Lilongwe	107	F5
Liloy	91	G4
Lima *Paraguay*	138	E4
Lima *Peru*	136	B6
Lima *Portugal*	66	B2
Lima *Montana*	122	H5
Lima *Ohio*	124	H6
Limah	97	N4
Limankoy	76	C2
Limavady	58	J2
Limay	139	C7
Limbang	90	E5
Limbani	136	D6
Limbe *Cameroon*	105	G5
Limbe *Malawi*	107	G6
Limburg	70	C3
Limeira	138	G4
Limenaria	75	H2
Limen Vatheos	75	J4
Limerick *Ireland*	59	E8
Limerick *Ireland*	59	E7
Limfjorden	63	C8
Limin	75	H2
Limmen Bight	113	H1
Limni	75	G3
Limnos	75	H3
Limoeiro *Ceara, Brazil*	137	K5
Limoeiro *Pernambuco, Brazil*	137	K5
Limoges	65	D6
Limon	132	F9
Limon	123	N8
Limousin	65	D6
Limoux	65	E7
Limpopo	109	F4
Linaalv	62	J3
Linah	96	F2
Linapacan Strait	91	F3
Linares *Chile*	139	B7
Linares *Mexico*	128	C8
Linares *Spain*	66	E3
Lincang	93	K4
Lincoln *New Zealand*	115	D5
Lincoln *U.K.*	55	J3
Lincoln *Illinois*	124	F6
Lincoln *Maine*	125	R4
Lincoln *Nebraska*	123	R7
Lincoln City	122	M5
Lincoln Sea	140	R2
Lincolnshire	55	J3
Lincolnton	129	M3
Lindau	70	C5
Linde	85	L3
Linden *Guyana*	136	F2
Linden *U.S.A.*	129	J3
Linderodsasen	63	G9
Lindesberg	63	F7
Lindi	107	G4
Lindley	108	E5
Lindos	75	K4
Lindsay *Canada*	125	L4
Lindsay *California*	126	C2
Lindsay *Montana*	123	M4
Lindu Point	114	S8
Linfen	93	M1
Lingao	93	L5
Lingayen	91	G2
Lingen	70	B2
Lingfield	53	G3
Lingga	90	C6
Lingga, Kepulauan	90	C6
Lingle	123	M6
Lingling	93	M3
Lingshi	87	L4
Lingshui	93	M5
Lingsugur	92	E5
Ling Xian	93	M3
Linguere	104	B2
Lingyuan	87	M3
Lingyun	93	L4
Linhai	87	N6
Linhares	138	H3
Linhe	87	K3
Linh, Ngoc	93	L5
Linkoping	63	F7
Linkou	88	C3
Linlithgow	57	E5
Linnhe, Loch	57	C4
Linosa	74	B5
Linru	93	M2
Lins	138	G4
Linsell	63	E5
Linslade	53	G3
Lintao	93	K1
Linton *U.K.*	53	H2
Linton *U.S.A.*	123	P4
Linwu	93	M3
Linxi	87	M3
Linxia	93	K1
Linyi *China*	87	M4
Linyi *China*	87	M4
Linz *Austria*	68	E1
Linz *Germany*	70	B3
Linze	86	J4
Lion, Golfe du	65	F7
Liouesso	106	C2
Lipa *Philippines*	91	G3
Lipa *Bos.*	72	D3
Lipari, Isola	69	E6
Lipari, Isole	69	E6
Lipenska nadrz	70	F4
Lipetsk	79	F5
Lipiany	70	F2
Lipin Bor	78	F3
Liping	93	L3
Lipkany	79	D6
Lipljan	73	F4
Lipnishki	71	L2
Lipno	71	H2
Lippe	70	C3
Lipsoi	75	J4
Lipson	75	F3
Lipu	93	M4
Lipusz	71	G1
Lira	107	F2
Lircay	136	C6
Liri	69	D5
Lisabata	91	H6
Lisala	106	D2
Lisboa	66	B3
Lisbon *Portugal*	66	B3
Lisbon *U.S.A.*	123	R4
Lisburn	58	K3
Lisburne, Cape	118	B2
Liscannor Bay	59	D7
Lisdoonvarna	59	D6
Lishi	87	L4
Lishui	87	M6
Lisieux	64	D4
Liskeard	52	C4
Liski	79	F5
L'Isle-Jourdain	65	D7
Lismore *Australia*	113	L4
Lismore *Ireland*	59	G8
Lismore *U.K.*	57	C4
Liss	53	G3
Listowel	59	D8
Lit	62	F5
Litang	93	K3
Litani	137	G3
Litchfield	124	F7
Litherland	55	G3
Lithgow	113	L5
Lithinon, Akra	75	H5
Litos	66	C2
Lithuania	63	K9
Litovko	85	P7
Little	128	E4
Little Abaco	132	J1
Little Aden	96	G10
Little Andaman	93	H6
Little Bahama Bank	132	H1
Little Barrier Island	115	E2
Little Belt Mountains	122	J4
Littleborough	55	G3
Little Bow	122	H2
Little Cayman	132	G5
Little Colorado	126	G3
Little Falls *Minnesota*	124	C3
Little Falls *New York*	125	N5
Littlefield	127	L4
Littlehampton	53	G4
Little Inagua Island	133	L4
Little Karoo	108	D6
Little Minch, The	56	B3
Little Missouri	123	M5
Little Nicobar	93	H7
Little Ouse	53	H2
Little Pamir	92	D1
Littleport	53	H2
Little Red	128	G3
Little Rock	128	F3
Little Rocky Mountains	123	K3
Little Scarcies	104	C4
Little Sitkin Island	118	Ab9
Little Smoky	119	M5
Little Snake	123	K7
Little South-west Miramichi	125	S3
Little Strickland	55	G2
Littleton *Colorado*	123	M8
Littleton *New Hampshire*	125	Q4
Little Wabash	124	F7
Little Waltham	53	H3
Liulin	87	L4
Liupan Shan	93	L1
Liuyang	93	M3
Liuzhou	93	L4
Livani	63	M8
Live Oak	129	L5
Livermore	126	B2
Livermore, Mount	127	K5
Liverpool *Australia*	113	L5
Liverpool *U.K.*	55	G3
Liverpool Bay *Canada*	118	K1
Liverpool Bay *U.K.*	55	F3
Livingston *Canada*	121	N7
Livingston *U.K.*	57	E5
Livingston *Montana*	123	J5
Livingston *Texas*	128	E5
Livingstone	106	E6
Livingstone, Chutes de	106	B4
Livingstone Falls	106	B4
Livingstone Mountains	107	F4
Livingston Island	141	V6
Livingston, Lake	128	E5
Livno	72	D4
Livny	79	F5
Livojoki	62	M4
Livonia	124	J5
Livorno	68	C4
Liwiec	71	J2
Liwonde	107	G6
Li Xian	93	M3
Lizard	52	B4
Lizardo	137	H5
Lizard Point	52	B4
Ljosavatn	62	W12
Ljubinje	72	E4
Ljubisnja	72	E4
Ljubljana	72	C2
Ljungan	62	G5
Ljungby	63	E8
Ljusdal	63	G6
Ljusnan	63	F5
Llanarmon Dyffryn Ceiriog	52	D2
Llanbadarn Fynydd	52	D2
Llanbedr	52	C2
Llanberis	54	E3
Llanbrynmair	52	D2
Llandeilo	52	D3
Llandovery	52	D3
Llandrindod Wells	52	D2
Llandudno	54	F3
Llanelli	52	C3
Llanerchymedd	54	E3
Llanes	66	D1
Llanfaethlu	54	E3
Llanfair Caereinion	52	D2
Llanfairfechan	54	F3
Llanfair Talhaiarn	55	F3
Llanfyllin	52	D2
Llangefni	55	E3
Llanglydwen	52	C3
Llangollen	52	D2
Llangranog	52	C2
Llangurig	52	D2
Llanidloes	52	D2
Llanilar	52	C2
Llanos	136	D2
Llanquihue, Lago	139	B8
Llanrhystud	52	C2
Llanrwst	54	F3
Llantrisant	52	D3
Llanwenog	52	C2
Llanwrtyd Wells	52	D2
Llawhaden	52	C3
Llerena	66	C3
Lleyn Peninsula	52	C2
Lliria	67	F3
Llivia	67	G1
Llobregat	67	G2
Lloydminster	119	P5
Lluchmayor	67	H3
Llyswen	52	D2
Loa	138	C4
Loanhead	57	E5
Lobatse	108	E5
Lobau	70	F3
Loberia	139	E7
Lobez	70	F2
Lobito	106	B5
Lobos	139	E7
Lobos, Island	126	G7
Locarno	68	B2
Lochaber	57	D4
Lochailort	57	C4
Lochan Fada	56	C3
Loch Ard Forest	57	D4
Lochboisdale	57	A3
Lochearnhead	57	D4
Loches	65	D5
Lochgelly	57	E4
Lochgilphead	57	C4
Lochinver	56	C2
Lochmaben	57	E5
Lochmaddy	56	A3
Lochnagar	57	E4
Lochranza	57	C5
Loch Shin	56	D2
Lochy, Loch	57	D4
Lock	113	H5
Lockerbie	57	E5
Lockhart	128	D6
Lock Haven	125	M6
Lockport	125	L5
Locri	69	F6
Loddekopinge	63	E9
Loddon *Australia*	113	J6
Loddon *U.K.*	53	J2
Lodeve	65	E7
Lodeynoye Pole	78	E3
Lodge Grass	123	L5
Lodgepole	123	M7
Lodi *Italy*	68	B3
Lodi *U.S.A.*	126	B1
Lodingen	62	F2
Lodja	106	D3
Lodwar	107	G2
Lodz	71	H3
Loeriesfontein	108	C6
Lofoten	62	E2
Loftus	55	J2
Logan	122	J7
Logan, Mount	118	G3
Logansport *Indiana*	124	G6
Logansport *Louisiana*	128	F5
Loge	106	B4
Logishin	71	M2
Logone	102	C5
Logrono	66	E1
Logrosan	66	D3
Loh	114	T10
Lohardaga	92	F4
Loharu	92	E3
Lohit	93	J3
Lohja	63	L6
Lohtaja	62	K4
Loikaw	93	J5
Loimaa	63	K6
Loimijoki	63	K6
Loing	65	E5
Loi, Phu	93	K4
Loir	65	C5
Loire	65	B5
Loja *Ecuador*	136	B4
Loja *Spain*	66	D4
Lokantekojarvi	62	M3
Lokhpodgort	78	M2
Lokhvitsa	79	E5
Lokichokio	107	F2
Lokilalaki, Gunung	91	G6
Lokka	62	M3
Loknya	78	E4
Lokoja	105	G4
Lokshak	85	N6
Lokuru	114	H6
Lol	102	E6
Lola	104	D4
Lolland	63	D9
Lolo	122	G4
Loloda	91	H5
Lolo Pass	122	G4
Lolvavana, Passage	114	U11
Lom *Bulgaria*	73	G4
Lom *Norway*	63	C6
Lomami	106	D3
Lomas Coloradas	139	C3
Lomazy	71	K3
Lombarda, Serra	137	G3
Lombe	107	G4
Lombez	65	D7
Lomblen	91	G7
Lombok	90	F7
Lome	104	F4
Lomela	106	D3
Lomir	94	J2
Lomond Hills	57	E4
Lomond, Loch	57	D4
Lomonosov Ridge	140	A1
Lompobattang, Gunung	91	F7
Lompoc	126	B3
Lomza	71	K2
London *Canada*	125	K5
London *U.K.*	53	G3
Londonderry *U.K.*	58	H2
Londonderry *U.K.*	58	J3
Londonderry, Cape	112	F1
Londonderry, Isla	139	B11
Londoni	114	R8
Londrina	138	F4
Lone Pine	126	C2
Longa *Angola*	106	C5
Longa *Angola*	106	C6
Longa Island	56	C3
Long Akah	90	E5
Longa, Ostrova de	81	S2
Long Bay	129	N6
Long Beach *California*	126	C4
Long Beach *New York*	125	P6
Long Branch	125	P6
Longchang	93	L3
Longchuan	87	M7
Longde	93	L1
Long Eaton	53	F2
Longford *Ireland*	58	G5
Longford *Ireland*	58	G5
Longformacus	57	F5
Longframlington	57	G5
Longhoughton	55	H1
Longhua	87	M3

Longhui 93 M3
Long Island *Bahamas* 133 K3
Long Island *Canada* 121 L7
Long Island *New Zealand* 115 A7
Long Island *Papua New Guinea* 114 D3
Long Island *U.S.A.* 125 P6
Long Island Sound 125 P6
Longjiang 87 N2
Longjing 88 B4
Longlac 124 G2
Long Lake 124 G2
Longli 93 L3
Long, Loch 57 D4
Long Melford 53 H2
Longmen 87 L7
Long Mynd, The 52 E2
Longnan 87 L7
Longnawan 90 E5
Longney 52 E3
Long Point *Canada* 125 K5
Long Point *New Zealand* 115 B7
Long Preston 55 G2
Long Range 121 Q8
Long Range Mountains 121 Q7
Longreach 113 J3
Long Reef 114 E4
Longridge 55 G3
Longshan 93 L3
Longsheng 93 M3
Longs Peak 123 M7
Long Stratton 53 J2
Longton 55 G3
Longtown 57 F5
Longuyon 64 F4
Longview *Texas* 128 E4
Longview *Washington* 122 C4
Longwy 64 F4
Longxi 93 K2
Long Xuyen 93 L6
Longyan 87 M6
Longyao 87 L4
Lons-le-Saunier 65 F5
Looe 52 C4
Lookout, Cape 129 P3
Loongana 112 F5
Loop Head 59 C7
Lopatin 79 H7
Lopatino 79 H5
Lopatka 85 T6
Lopatka, Mys 85 T6
Lop Buri 93 K6
Lopevi 114 U12
Lopez, Cap 106 A3
Lop Nur 86 G3
Lopphavet 62 J1
Lopra 62 Z14
Lopydino 78 J3
Lora del Rio 66 D4
Lorain 124 J6
Loralai 92 C2
Lorca 67 F4
Lordegan 95 K6
Lord Howe Island 113 M5
Lordsburg 127 H4
Lore 91 H7
Lorengau 114 D2
Lorentz 91 K7
Lorenzo 136 B3
Loreto *Brazil* 137 H5
Loreto *Colombia* 136 C4
Loreto *Mexico* 126 G7
Lorica 133 K10
Lorient 65 B5
Lorillard 119 S3
Lorinci 72 E2
Lorn 57 C4
Lorne 113 J6
Lorn, Firth of 57 C4
Lorrach 70 B5
Lorraine 64 F4
Los 63 F6
Los Alamos 127 J3
Los Andes 139 B6
Los Angeles *Chile* 139 B7
Los Angeles *U.S.A.* 126 C4
Los Angeles Aqueduct 126 C3
Los Banos 126 B2
Los Blancos 138 D4
Los Filabres, Sierra de 66 E4
Losinj 72 C3
Los Mochis 127 H8
Los Pedraches 66 D3
Los Roques 136 D1
Lossie 56 E3
Lossiemouth 56 E3
Los Teques 136 D1
Los Testigos 133 R9
Lost Trail Pass 122 H5
Lostwithiel 52 C4
Lot 65 D6
Lota 139 B7
Lotfahad 95 P3
Lothian 57 E5
Lotta 62 N2
Lottorp 63 G8
Lo-tung 87 N7
Lotzen 71 J1
Loudeac 64 B4
Loudun 65 D5
Louga 104 B2
Loughborough 53 F2
Loughbrickland 58 K4
Lougheed Island 120 E2
Loughor 52 C3

Loughrea 59 E6
Loughsalt Mount 58 G2
Lough Swilly 58 G2
Louhans 65 F5
Louisa 124 J7
Louisiade Archipelago 114 T10
Louisiana 128 F5
Lou Island 114 D2
Louis Trichardt 108 E4
Louisville *Kentucky* 124 H7
Louisville *Mississippi* 128 H4
Loukhi 62 Q3
Loule 66 B4
Loup 123 Q7
Lourdes 65 C7
Louth *Ireland* 58 K5
Louth *U.K.* 55 K1
Louvain 64 F3
Louviers 64 D4
Lovanger 62 J4
Lovat 78 E4
Lovberga 62 F5
Lovech 73 H4
Loveland 123 M7
Lovell 123 K5
Lovere 68 C3
Loviisa 63 M6
Lovington 127 L4
Lovisa 63 M6
Lovnas 62 F4
Lovosice 70 F3
Lovua 106 D5
Low, Cape 120 J5
Lower Arrow Lake 122 E3
Lower Hut 115 E4
Lowestoft 53 J2
Lowicz 71 H2
Lowther Hills 57 E5
Lowther Island 120 G3
Loyal, Loch 56 D2
Loyaute, Iles 114 X16
Loyma 78 H3
Loyne, Loch 57 C3
Lozarevo 73 J4
Lozere, Mont 65 E6
Loznica 72 E3
Lozovaya 79 F6
Lualaba 106 E3
Luan 93 N2
Luanda 106 B4
Luang Prabang 93 K5
Luangwa 107 F5
Luan He 87 M4
Luanjing 87 K4
Luanping 87 M3
Luanshya 107 E5
Luapula 107 E5
Luarca 66 C1
Luashi 106 D5
Luau 106 D5
Lubalo 106 C4
Lubanas Ezers 62 M8
Lubang Islands 91 G3
Lubango 106 B5
Lubartow 71 K3
Lubawa 71 H2
Lubben 70 E3
Lubbock 127 M4
Lubeck 70 D2
Lubefu 106 D3
Lubenka 79 J5
Lubero 107 E3
Lubie, Jezioro 70 F2
Lubien 71 H2
Lublin 71 K3
Lubny 79 E5
Lubosalma 62 P5
Lubsko 70 F3
Lubtheen 70 D2
Lubudi 106 E4
Lubuklinggau 90 C6
Lubumbashi 107 E5
Lubutu 106 E3
Lucan 59 K6
Lucano, Appennino 69 E5
Lucaya 129 N7
Lucca 68 C4
Lucea 132 H5
Luce Bay 54 E2
Lucedale 128 H5
Lucena *Philippines* 91 G3
Lucena *Spain* 66 D4
Lucena del Cid 67 F2
Lucenec 71 H4
Lucera 69 E5
Lucerne 68 B2
Luchow 70 D2
Luckau 70 E3
Luckenwalde 70 E2
Lucknow 92 F3
Lucon 65 C5
Lucrecia, Cabo 133 K4
Lucusse 106 D5
Luda 87 N4
Ludensheid 70 B3
Luderitz 108 C5
Ludford 55 J3
Ludgvan 52 B4
Ludhiana 92 E2
Ludington 124 G5
Ludlow *U.K.* 52 E2
Ludlow *U.S.A.* 126 D3
Ludogorie 73 J4
Ludus 73 H2

Ludvika 63 F6
Ludwigsburg 70 C4
Ludwigshafen 70 B4
Ludwigslust 70 D2
Ludza 63 M8
Luebo 106 D4
Luena 106 C5
Luepa 136 E2
Lueyang 93 L2
Lufeng 87 M7
Lufkin 128 E5
Luga 63 N7
Lugano 68 B2
Lugano, Lago di 68 B3
Luganville 114 T11
Lugela 109 G3
Lugenda 109 G2
Lugg 52 E2
Lugnaquilla 59 K7
Lugo *Italy* 68 C3
Lugo *Spain* 66 C1
Lugoj 73 F3
Lugovoy 86 C3
Lugton 57 D5
Luhansk 79 F6
Luiana 106 D6
Luichart, Loch 56 D3
Luik 64 F3
Luimneach 59 E7
Luing 57 D4
Luinne Bheinn 57 C3
Luiro 62 M3
Luiza 106 D4
Lujan 139 C6
Lujiang 87 M5
Lukashkin Yar 84 B4
Lukeville 126 F5
Lukovit 73 H4
Lukovo 72 F5
Lukow 71 K3
Lukoyanov 78 G4
Lukulu 106 D5
Lulea 62 K4
Lulealven 62 J3
Luleburgaz 76 B2
Lulo 106 C4
Lulong 87 M4
Lulonga 106 C2
Luluabourg 106 D4
Lulworth Cove 53 E4
Lumbala Nguimbo 106 D5
Lumberton 129 N3
Lumbovka 78 G2
Lumbrales 66 C2
Lumbreras 66 E1
Lumbres 64 E3
Lumijoki 62 L4
Lumphanan 57 F3
Lumsden 115 B6
Lumut, Tanjung 90 D6
Lunan 93 K4
Lunan Bay 57 F4
Lunayyir, Harrat 96 C4
Lunberger Heide 70 C2
Lund 63 E9
Lundar 123 Q2
Lundazi 107 F5
Lundy 52 C3
Lune 55 G2
Luneburg 70 D2
Lunel 65 F7
Luneville 64 G4
Lungga 114 K6
Lungwebungu 106 D5
Luni 92 D3
Luninets 71 M2
Lunsar 104 C4
Lunsemfwa 107 E5
Luntai 86 E3
Luobei 88 C2
Luobuzhuang 86 F4
Luocheng 93 L4
Luodian 93 L3
Luoding 93 M4
Luo He 93 L1
Luohe 93 M2
Luotian 93 N2
Luoyang 93 M2
Luqu 93 K2
Lure 65 G5
Lurgan 58 K4
Lurio *Mozambique* 109 G2
Lurio *Mozambique* 109 H2
Lusaka 107 E6
Lusambo 106 D3
Lusancay Islands 114 K6
Lushi 93 M2
Lush, Mountain 112 F2
Lushoto 107 G3
Lushui 93 J3
Lusignan 65 D5
Lusk 123 M6
Luspebryggan 62 H3
Lussac-les-Chateaux 65 D5
Lut, Bahrat 94 B6
Lut, Dasht-e 95 P6
Lut-e Zangi Ahmad 95 P7
Luthrie 57 E4
Luton 53 G3
Lutong 90 E5
Lutsk 79 D5
Lutterworth 53 F2
Luukkonen 63 N6
Luuq 107 H2

Luverne 124 B5
Luwingu 107 E5
Luwuk 91 G6
Luxembourg 64 F4
Luxembourg 64 G4
Luxeuil 65 G5
Luxi 93 J4
Luxor 103 F2
Luza *Russia* 78 H3
Luza *Russia* 78 H3
Luzern 68 B2
Luzhou 93 L3
Luziania 138 G3
Luzilandia 137 J4
Luzon 91 G2
Luzon Strait 91 G1
Lviv 71 L4
Lvovka 84 B5
Lwowek 71 G2
Lyadova 73 J1
Lyakhovskiye Ostrova 85 Q2
Lyall, Mount 122 G3
Lyallpur 92 D2
Lyapin 78 L3
Lybster 56 E2
Lyck 71 K2
Lycksele 62 H4
Lydd 53 H4
Lyddan Ice Rise 141 Y4
Lydenburg 108 F5
Lydford 52 C4
Lydney 52 E3
Lyell Range 115 D4
Lyman 123 J7
Lyme Bay 52 D4
Lyme Regis 52 E4
Lymington 53 F4
Lymm 55 G3
Lyna 71 J1
Lynchburg 125 L8
Lynd 113 J2
Lyndon 112 D3
Lyne 57 F5
Lyness 56 E2
Lyngdal 63 B7
Lyngseidet 62 J1
Lynher 52 C4
Lynn 125 Q5
Lynn Canal 118 H4
Lynn Lake 119 Q4
Lynton 52 D3
Lynx Lake 119 P3
Lyon *France* 65 F6
Lyon *U.K.* 57 D4
Lyon Inlet 120 K4
Lyon, Loch 57 D4
Lyonnais, Monts du 65 F6
Lyra Reef 114 E2
Lyskovo 78 H4
Lysva 78 K4
Lysychansk 79 F6
Lytham Saint Annes 55 F3
Lythe 55 J2
Lyttelton 115 D5
Lytton 122 D2
Lyubashevka 73 L2
Lyubcha 71 M2
Lyubertsy 78 F4
Lyubeshov 71 L3
Lyubimets 73 J5
Lyuboml 71 L3
Lyubotin 79 F6
Lyudinovo 79 E5
Lyushcha 71 M2

M

Maaia 109 H2
Maam Cross 59 C6
Maan 94 B6
Maanqiao 86 F3
Maanselka 62 N5
Maanshan 87 M5
Maarianhamina 63 G6
Maarrat an Numan 94 C4
Maas 64 F3
Maaseik 64 F3
Maasin 91 G3
Maastricht 64 F3
Maba 91 H5
Mabalane 109 F4
Mabar 96 G9
Mablethorpe 55 K3
Macachin 139 D7
McAdam 125 S4
Macedonia 73 F5
Macae 138 H4
McAlester 128 E3
McAllen 128 C7
McAllister, Mount 113 K5
MacAlpine Lake 119 Q2
Macapa 137 G3
Macara 136 B4
McArthur 113 H2
Macau 137 K5
Macaubas 138 J6
Macauley Islands 111 T8
McBeth Fjord 120 N4
McBride 119 L5
McCamey 127 L5
McCammon 122 H6
McCarthy 118 G5
Macclesfield 55 G3

Manadir, Al **97** M5
Manado **91** G5
Managua **132** D8
Managua, Laguna de **132** D8
Manakara **109** J4
Manakhah **96** F9
Manambolo **109** H3
Manam Island **114** D2
Mananara *Madagascar* **109** J4
Mananara *Madagascar* **109** J3
Mananjary **109** J4
Manantavadi **92** E6
Manaoba **114** K6
Manapire **136** D2
Manapouri **115** A6
Manapouri, Lake **115** A6
Manas **93** H3
Manau **114** D3
Manaus **136** F4
Manavgat **76** D4
Manbij **94** C3
Mancha Real **66** E4
Manchester *U.K.* **55** G3
Manchester *Connecticut* **125** P6
Manchester *Kentucky* **124** J8
Manchester *New Hampshire,* **125** Q5
Manchester *Tennessee* **129** J3
Mancora **136** A4
Mand **95** K7
Mandab, Bab el **103** H5
Mandal *Afghanistan* **95** Q5
Mandal *Norway* **63** B7
Mandala, Puncak **91** L6
Mandalay **93** J4
Mandalgovi **87** K2
Mandali **94** G5
Mandal-Ovoo **87** J3
Mandan **123** P4
Mandaon **91** G3
Mandar, Teluk **91** F6
Mandasawu, Poco **91** G7
Mandav Hills **92** D4
Mandeville **132** J5
Mandi **92** E2
Mandiore, Lago **138** E3
Mandla **92** F4
Mandoudhion **75** G3
Mandurah **112** D5
Manduria **69** F5
Mandvi **92** C4
Mandya **92** E6
Manea **53** H2
Manevichi **71** L3
Manfredonia **69** E5
Manfredonia, Golfo di **69** F5
Manga **138** J6
Mangakino **115** E3
Mangalia **73** K4
Mangalore **92** D6
Mangaon **92** D5
Mangapehi **115** E3
Manggautu **114** J7
Mangin Range **93** J4
Mangkalihat, Tanjung **91** F5
Manglares, Punta **136** B3
Mangochi **107** G5
Mangoky **109** H4
Mangole **91** H6
Mangonui **115** D1
Mangoro **109** J3
Mangotsfield **52** E3
Mangral **92** D4
Manguari **136** D4
Mangueira, Lagoa **138** F6
Mangui **87** N1
Manguinha, Pontal do **137** K6
Mangut **85** J7
Mangyshlak **79** J7
Mangyshlak, Poluostrov **79** J7
Mangyshlakskiy Zaliv **79** J7
Manhan **86** G2
Manhattan **123** R8
Manhica **109** F5
Manicore **136** E5
Manicouagan **121** N7
Manicouagan, Reservoir **121** N7
Manifah **97** J3
Manika, Plateau de la **106** E4
Manila **91** G3
Manipa, Selat **91** H6
Manipur **93** H4
Manisa **76** B3
Man, Isle of **54** E2
Manistee *U.S.A.* **124** G4
Manistee *U.S.A.* **124** H4
Manistique **124** G4
Manitoba **119** R4
Manitoba, Lake **123** Q2
Manitou Falls **123** T2
Manitou Island **124** G4
Manitoulin **124** J4
Manitowoc **124** G4
Maniwaki **125** N3
Manizales **136** B2
Manja **109** H4
Manjra **92** E5
Mankato **124** C4
Mankono **104** D4
Mankovka **73** L1
Manna **90** C6
Mannar **92** E7
Mannar, Gulf of **92** E7
Mannheim **70** C4
Manning, Cape **120** B2
Manning Strait **114** J5
Manningtree **53** J3
Mannu **69** B6
Manoa Abuna **136** D5
Manokwari **91** J6
Manolas **75** F3
Manonga **107** F3
Manono **107** E4
Manorbier **52** C3
Manorcunningham **58** G3
Manorhamilton **58** F4
Manoron **93** J6
Manosque **65** F7
Manouane, Reservoir **121** M7
Mano-wan **89** G7
Manpojin **87** P3
Manra **111** U2
Manresa **67** G2
Mansa **107** E5
Mansehra **92** D2
Mansel Island **120** L5
Mansfield *U.K.* **55** H3
Mansfield *Louisiana* **128** F5
Mansfield *Ohio* **124** J6
Mansfield *Pennsylvania* **125** M6
Mansfield Woodhouse **55** H3
Mansle **65** D6
Manson Creek **118** L4
Mansoura **67** J4
Manston **53** J3
Mansurlu **77** F4
Manta **136** A4
Mantalingajan, Mount **91** F4
Mantaro **136** B6
Mantecal **136** D2
Mantes **64** D4
Mantiqueira, Serra da **138** G4
Mantova **68** C3
Mantsala **63** L6
Mantta **63** L5
Mantua **68** C3
Mantyharju **63** M6
Manua **111** V4
Manuel **131** K6
Manui **91** G6
Manu Island **114** C2
Manujan **95** N8
Manukau **115** E2
Manukau Harbour **115** E2
Manulla **58** D5
Manus Islands **114** D2
Manya **78** L3
Manyas **76** B2
Manych Gudilo, Ozero **79** G6
Manyoni **107** F4
Manzanares **66** E3
Manzanillo *Cuba* **132** J4
Manzanillo *Mexico* **130** G8
Manzanillo, Punta **136** B2
Manzariyeh **95** K4
Manzhouli **87** M2
Manzini **109** F5
Manzya **84** F5
Mao **102** C5
Maoershan **88** A3
Maoke, Pegunungan **91** K6
Maoming **93** M4
Mapai **109** F4
Mapam Yumco **92** F2
Mapire **133** Q11
Maple Creek **123** K3
Mappi *Indonesia* **91** K7
Mappi *Indonesia* **91** K7
Maprik **114** C2
Mapuera **136** F4
Maputo **109** F5
Maqdam, Ras **96** C7
Maqna **96** B2
Maqueda **66** D2
Maquinchao **139** C8
Maraba **137** H5
Maracaibo **136** C1
Maracaibo, Lago de **136** C2
Maraca, Ilha de **137** G3
Maracay **136** D1
Maradah **101** J3
Maradi **101** G6
Maragheh **94** H3
Marajo, Baia de **137** H4
Marajo, Ilha de **137** H4
Maralal **107** G2
Maramasike **114** K6
Maramba **106** E6
Maran **90** C5
Marand **94** G2
Maranguape **137** K4
Maranhao **137** H5
Maranhao Grande, Cachoeira **137** F4
Maran, Koh-i- **92** C3
Maranon **136** C4
Marans **65** C5
Marari **136** D5
Marasesti **73** J3
Marassume **137** H4
Marateca **66** B3
Marathokambos **75** J4
Marathon *Canada* **124** G2
Marathon *Florida* **129** M8
Marathon *Texas* **127** L5
Marau **90** E6
Marau Point **115** G3
Maravovo **114** J6
Marbella **66** D4
Marble Bar **112** D3
Marble Canyon **126** G2
Marburg **70** C3
Marcelino **136** D4
March **53** H2
Marche *Belgium* **64** F3
Marche *France* **65** D5
Marchena **66** D4
Marchena, Isla **136** A7
Mar Chiquita, Lago **138** D6
Marcigny **65** F5
Marcus Baker, Mount **118** F3
Marcus Island **83** P4
Mardan **92** D2
Mar del Plata **139** E7
Mardin **77** J4
Mare **114** Y16
Mareeba **113** K2
Maree, Loch **56** C3
Mareeq **103** J7
Mareuil **65** D6
Margai Caka **92** G1
Marganets **79** E6
Margaret, Cape **120** H3
Margaret River **112** F2
Margarita, Isla de **136** E1
Margaritovo **88** E4
Margate **53** J3
Margeride, Monts de la **65** E6
Margita **73** F3
Margo, Dasht-i **95** R6
Marguerite **121** N7
Marguerite Bay **141** V5
Mari **114** C3
Maria Elena **138** C4
Maria, Golfo de Ana **132** H4
Maria Madre, Isla **130** F7
Maria Magdalena, Isla **130** F7
Mariampole **71** K1
Marianas Islands **83** N5
Marianas Trench **142** F4
Marian Lake **119** M3
Marianna *Arkansas* **128** G3
Marianna *Florida* **129** K5
Marianske Lazne **70** E4
Marias **122** J3
Marias, Islas **130** F7
Mariato, Punta **132** G11
Maria van Diemen, Cape **115** D1
Mariazell **68** E2
Marib **96** G9
Maribor **72** C2
Maridi **102** E7
Marie Byrd Land **141** S3
Marie Galante **133** S7
Mariehamn **63** H6
Marienbad **70** E4
Marienburg **71** H1
Mariental **108** C4
Marienwerder **71** H2
Mariestad **63** E7
Marietta *Georgia* **129** K4
Marietta *Ohio* **125** K7
Marigot **133** S7
Mariinsk **84** D5
Marina di Carrara **68** C3
Marina di Leuca **69** G6
Marina di Monasterace **69** F6
Marinette **124** G4
Maringa **106** D2
Maringa **138** F4
Marion *Illinois* **124** F8
Marion *Indiana* **124** H6
Marion *Ohio* **124** J6
Marion *S. Carolina* **129** N3
Marion *Virginia* **125** K8
Marion, Lake **129** M4
Marion Reefs **113** L2
Maripa **136** D2
Marisa **91** G5
Mariscal Estigarribia **138** D4
Maritimes, Alpes **65** G6
Maritsa **73** H4
Mariupol **79** F6
Marivan **94** H4
Marjamaa **63** L7
Marjayoun **94** B5
Marka **96** E7
Marka **107** H2
Markam **93** J3
Market Deeping **53** G2
Market Drayton **52** E2
Market Harborough **53** G2
Markethill **58** J4
Market Rasen **55** J3
Market Weighton **55** J3
Markha **85** K4
Markham **114** D3
Marlborough *Australia* **113** K3
Marlborough *Guyana* **136** F2
Marlborough *U.K.* **53** F3
Marlin **128** D5
Marlinton **125** K7
Marlow **53** G3
Marmagao **92** D5
Marmande **65** D6
Marmara *Turkey* **76** B2
Marmara *Turkey* **76** B2
Marmara Denizi **76** C2
Marmaraereglisi **76** B2
Marmara Golu **76** C3
Marmara, Sea of **76** C2
Marmaris **76** C4
Marmblada **68** C2
Marmelos **136** E5
Marne **64** E4
Maro **102** C3
Maroantsetra **109** J3
Marolambo **109** J4
Marondera **109** F3
Maroni **137** G3
Maros **91** F6
Marotiri Islands **115** E1
Maroua **105** H3
Marovoay **109** J3
Marowyne **137** G3
Marple **55** G3
Marquette **124** G3
Marquise **64** D3
Marquises, Iles **143** J5
Marra, Jebel **102** D5
Marrakech **100** D2
Marrakesh **100** D2
Marrak Point **120** R5
Marrawah **113** J7
Marree **113** H4
Marresale **84** Ae3
Marrupa **109** G2
Marsa Alam **96** B4
Marsabit **107** G2
Marsala **69** D7
Marsden *Australia* **113** K5
Marsden *U.K.* **55** H3
Marseille **65** F7
Mar, Serra do **138** G5
Marsfjallet **62** G3
Marshall *Minnesota* **124** C4
Marshall *Missouri* **124** D7
Marshall *Texas* **128** E4
Marshall Bennett Islands **114** E3
Marshall Islands **143** G4
Marshalltown **124** D5
Marshchapel **55** K3
Marshfield **124** E4
Marsh Island **128** G6
Marske-by-the-Sea **55** H2
Marsta **63** G7
Martaban **93** J5
Martaban, Gulf of **93** J5
Martapura **90** E6
Martes, Sierra **67** F3
Marthaguy **113** K5
Martha's Vineyard **125** Q6
Martigny **68** A2
Martigues **65** F7
Martin *Poland* **71** H4
Martin *Spain* **67** F2
Martin *S. Dakota* **123** P6
Martin *Tennessee* **128** H2
Martinavas **53** N6
Martinborough **115** E4
Martinique **133** S7
Martinique Passage **133** S7
Martin Lake **129** K4
Martin Point **118** G1
Martinsberg **68** E1
Martinsville **125** L8
Martock **52** E4
Marton *New Zealand* **115** E4
Marton *U.K.* **55** J3
Martorell **67** G2
Martos **66** E4
Martre, Lac La **119** M3
Martuk **79** K5
Martuni **79** H7
Martyn **78** K2
Martze **136** D4
Marudi **90** E5
Marugame **89** D8
Marum, Mount **114** U12
Marunga **114** E2
Marungu **107** E4
Marv Dasht **95** L7
Marvejols **65** E6
Marvine, Mount **122** J8
Marwar **92** D3
Mary **95** Q3
Maryborough **113** L4
Maryevka **84** Ae6
Maryland **125** M7
Maryport **55** F2
Mary, Puy **65** E6
Marystown **121** Q8
Marysville *California* **126** B1
Marysville *Kansas* **123** R8
Maryvale **113** L4
Maryville *Missouri* **124** C6
Maryville *Tennessee* **129** L3
Marzo, Cabo **132** J11
Masagua **132** B7
Masai Steppe **107** G3
Masaka **107** F3
Masally **94** J2
Masan **89** B8
Masasi **107** G5
Masaya **132** D8
Masbate *Philippines* **91** G3
Masbate *Philippines* **91** G3
Mascara **100** F1
Mascarene Islands **109** L7
Masela **91** H7
Maseru **108** E5
Mashabih **96** C4
Masham **55** H2
Mashan *Guangxi, China* **93** L4
Mashan *Heilongjiang, China* **88** C3
Mashhad **95** P3
Mashike **88** H4
Mashiz **95** N7

Name	Page	Grid
Mashkid	95	R8
Masi	62	K2
Masilah, Wadi al	97	J9
Masi-Manimba	106	C3
Masindi	107	F2
Masirah	97	P6
Masirah, Khalij	97	N7
Masirah, Khawr al	97	P6
Masiri	95	K6
Masisi	107	E3
Masjed Soleyman	94	J6
Mask, Lough	58	D5
Maskutan	95	P8
Maslen Nos	73	J4
Masoala, Cap	109	K3
Mason Bay	115	A7
Mason City	124	D5
Ma, Song	93	K4
Masqat	97	P5
Massa	68	C3
Massachusetts	125	P5
Massachusetts Bay	125	Q5
Massakori	102	C5
Massa Marittima	68	C4
Massangena	109	F4
Massape	137	J4
Massava	84	Ad4
Massenya	102	C5
Massigui	100	D6
Massillon	124	K6
Massinga	109	G4
Massingir	109	F4
Masteksay	79	H6
Masterton	115	E4
Mastikho, Akra	75	J3
Mastuj	92	D1
Masturah	96	D5
Masuda	89	C8
Masulch	94	J3
Masurai, Bukit	90	C6
Masvingo	108	F4
Masyaf	94	C4
Mat	74	F2
Mataboor	91	K6
Mataca	109	G2
Matachel	66	C3
Matad	87	M2
Matadi	106	B4
Matafome	66	B3
Matagalpa	132	E8
Matagami *Ontario, Canada*	125	M2
Matagami *Quebec, Canada*	125	M2
Matagami, Lac	125	M1
Matagorda Bay	128	D6
Matagorda Island	128	D6
Matakana Island	115	F2
Matakaoa Point	115	G2
Matala	106	C5
Matale	92	F7
Matam	104	C2
Matamata	115	E2
Matamoros *Mexico*	128	D8
Matamoros *Mexico*	127	L8
Matane	125	S2
Mata Negra	136	E2
Matanzas	132	G3
Matapan, Cape	75	G4
Matapedia	125	S2
Matara	92	F7
Mataram	90	F7
Matarani	138	B3
Mataranka	112	G1
Mataro	67	H2
Matata	115	F2
Matatiele	108	E6
Mataura *New Zealand*	115	B6
Mataura *New Zealand*	115	B7
Matawai	115	F3
Matay	86	D2
Matcha	86	B4
Matehuala	131	J6
Matera	69	F5
Mateszalka	73	G2
Mateur	101	G1
Matfors	62	G5
Matheson	125	K2
Mathis	128	D6
Mathry	52	B3
Mathura	92	E3
Mati	91	H4
Matlock	55	H3
Mato, Cerro	133	Q11
Mato Grosso	136	F6
Mato Grosso do Sul	138	E3
Mato Grosso, Planalto do	138	E3
Matra	72	E2
Matrah	97	P5
Matrosovo	71	J1
Matruh	102	E1
Matsubara	89	J10
Matsue	89	D8
Ma-tsu Lieh-tao	87	M6
Matsumae	88	H5
Matsumoto	89	F7
Matsusaka	89	F8
Matsuyama	89	D9
Mattagami	121	K8
Mattancheri	92	E7
Mattawa	125	L3
Matterhorn *Switzerland*	68	A3
Matterhorn *U.S.A.*	122	G7
Matthews Peak	107	G2
Matthew Town	133	L4
Matti, Sabkhat	97	K10
Mattoon	124	F7
Matty Island	120	G3
Matua, Ostrov	85	S7
Matuku	114	R9
Maturin	136	E2
Matyushkinskaya	84	B5
Mau	92	F3
Maua	109	G2
Maubara	91	H7
Maubeuge	64	E3
Maubin	93	J5
Maubourguet	65	D7
Mauchline	57	D5
Maud	56	F3
Maues	136	F4
Mauganj	92	F4
Maui	126	S10
Maula	62	L4
Maule	139	B7
Mauleon-Licharre	65	C7
Maumere	91	G7
Maumtrasna	58	C5
Maumturk Mountains	59	C5
Maun	108	D4
Mauna Kea	126	T11
Mauna Loa	126	T11
Maungmagan Islands	93	J6
Maunoir, Lac	118	L2
Maures	65	G7
Mauriac	65	E6
Maurice, Lake	112	G4
Mauritania	100	C5
Mauritius	109	L7
Mauron	64	B4
Mauston	124	E5
Mautern	68	E2
Mavinga	106	D6
Mawbray	55	F2
Mawhai Point	115	G3
Mawlaik	93	H4
Mawson	141	E5
Maxaila	109	F4
Maxmo	62	K5
Maya	85	N5
Mayaguana Island	133	L3
Mayaguana Passage	133	L3
Mayaguez	133	P5
Mayak *China*	86	F2
Mayak *Russia*	71	H1
Mayak *Russia*	79	K5
Mayamey	95	M3
Mayas, Montanas	132	C6
Maybole	57	D5
May, Cape	125	N7
Maychew	96	D10
Maydh	103	J5
Mayenne *France*	64	C4
Mayenne *France*	65	C5
Mayero	84	G3
Mayfaah	97	H9
Mayfield *U.K.*	53	H3
Mayfield *U.S.A.*	124	F8
May, Isle of	57	F4
Maykop	79	G7
Maykor	78	K4
Maymakan *Russia*	85	N5
Maymakan *Russia*	85	P5
Maymyo	93	J4
Mayn	85	W4
Maynooth	59	J6
Mayo *Argentina*	139	B9
Mayo *Canada*	118	H3
Mayo *Ireland*	58	D5
Mayo *Mexico*	130	E4
Mayor Island	115	F2
Mayor, Pic	67	H4
Mayotte	109	J2
May Pen	132	J6
Mayraira Point	91	G2
Mayrata	75	F3
Maysville	124	J7
Mayumba	106	A3
Mayuram	92	E6
Mayville	123	R4
Mayyun Island	96	F10
Mazalat	73	H4
Mazamari	136	C6
Mazamet	65	E7
Mazar	92	E1
Mazar-e Sharif	92	C1
Mazarete	67	E2
Mazarredo	139	C9
Mazarron	67	F4
Mazarsu	86	C3
Mazaruni	136	F2
Mazatenango	132	B7
Mazatlan	130	F6
Mazdaj	95	K5
Mazeikiai	63	K8
Mazgirt	77	H3
Mazhur, Irq al	96	G3
Mazidagi	77	J4
Mazinan	95	N3
Mazirbe	63	K8
Mazury	71	J2
Mbabane	108	F5
Mbaiki	102	C7
Mbala	107	F4
Mbalavu	114	S8
Mbale	107	F2
Mbalmayo	105	H5
Mbalo	114	K6
Mbandaka	106	C2
MBanza Congo	106	B4
Mbanza-Ngungu	106	B4
Mbarara	107	F3
Mbengwi	105	G4
Mbeya	107	F4
Mbouda	105	H4
Mbour	104	B3
Mbout	100	C5
Mbuji-Mayi	106	D4
Mchinji	107	F5
MClintock	119	S4
Meade *Alaska*	118	D1
Meade *Kansas*	127	M2
Meadie, Loch	56	D2
Mead, Lake	126	E2
Meadow Lake	119	P5
Meadville	125	K6
Mealhada	66	B2
Meana	95	Q3
Meath	58	J5
Meaux	64	E4
Mebula	91	G7
Mecca	96	D6
Mechelen	64	F3
Mecheria	100	E2
Mechigmen	118	A2
Mechigmen Zaliv	118	A2
Mecidie	76	B2
Mecitozu	76	F2
Mecklenburger Bucht	70	D1
Mecsek	72	E2
Mecufi	109	H2
Mecula	109	G2
Medak	92	E5
Medan	90	B5
Medanos	139	D7
Medanosa, Punta	139	C9
Medea	101	F1
Medellin	136	B2
Medelpad	62	G5
Medenine	101	H2
Mederdra	100	B5
Medford	122	C6
Medgidia	73	K3
Medicine Bow Mountains	123	L7
Medicine Bow Peak	123	L7
Medicine Hat	123	J3
Medicine Lodge	127	N2
Medina *Saudi Arabia*	96	D4
Medina *N. Dakota*	123	Q4
Medina *New York*	125	L5
Medinaceli	66	E2
Medina del Campo	66	D2
Medina de Rioseco	66	D2
Medina Sidonia	66	D4
Medina Terminal Canal	125	L5
Medinipur	93	G4
Mediterranean Sea	98	D3
Medjerda, Monts de la	69	B7
Medkovets	73	G4
Mednyy, Ostrov	81	T4
Medoc	65	C6
Medole	68	C3
Medvezhl, Ostrova	85	U2
Medvezhyegorsk	78	E3
Medvyeditsa	78	F4
Medway	53	H3
Medyn	78	F5
Medynskiy Zavorot, Poluostrov	78	K2
Meeberrie	112	D4
Meechkyn, Kosa	85	Y3
Meekatharra	112	D4
Meeker	123	L7
Meerut	92	E3
Meeteetse	123	K5
Mega	91	J6
Megalo Khorio	75	J4
Megalopolis	75	G4
Megara	75	G3
Megeve	65	G6
Megget Reservoir	57	E5
Meghalaya	93	H3
Megion	84	B4
Megisti	76	C4
Megra *Russia*	78	F3
Megra *Russia*	78	G2
Mehamn	62	M1
Mehndawal	92	F3
Mehran	94	H5
Meig	56	D3
Meighen Island	120	G2
Meiktila	93	J4
Meiningen	70	D3
Meira	66	C1
Meissen	70	E3
Mei Xian	87	M7
Mejez El Bab	69	B7
Mejillones	138	B4
Mekambo	106	B2
Mekele	103	G5
Meknes	100	D2
Mekong	93	L6
Mekong, Mouths of the	93	L7
Mela	62	U12
Melaka	90	C5
Melambes	75	H5
Melanesia	142	F4
Melawi	90	E6
Melbourne *Australia*	113	J6
Melbourne *U.S.A.*	129	M6
Melbourne Island	119	Q2
Melbu	62	F2
Melchor Muzquiz	127	M7
Melenki	78	G4
Meleuz	78	K5
Melfi *Chad*	102	C5
Melfi *Italy*	69	E5
Melfort	119	Q5
Melgaco	137	G4
Melhus	62	D4
Melilla	100	E1
Melipilla	139	B6
Melita	123	P3
Melito di Porto Salvo	69	E7
Melitopol	79	F6
Melk	68	E1
Melksham	53	E3
Mellegue, Oued	101	G1
Mellerud	63	E7
Melle-sur-Bretonne	65	C5
Melling	55	G2
Mellish Reef	113	M2
Mellte	52	D3
Melnik	70	F3
Melo	138	F6
Melolo	91	G7
Melozitna	118	E2
Melrhir, Chott	101	G2
Melrose	124	C4
Melsungen	70	C3
Meltaus	62	L3
Melton Mowbray	53	G2
Melun	64	E4
Melut	103	F5
Melvern Lake	124	C7
Melville	123	N2
Melville Bugt	120	P2
Melville, Cape	113	J1
Melville Hills	118	L2
Melville Island *Australia*	112	G1
Melville Island *Canada*	120	D2
Melville, Kap	120	P2
Melville, Lake	121	Q7
Melville Peninsula	120	K4
Melvin, Lough	58	F4
Melykut	72	E2
Melyuveyem	85	W4
Memba	109	H2
Memberamo	91	K6
Memboro	91	F7
Memel	63	L9
Memmingen	70	D4
Mempawah	90	D5
Memphis *Tennessee*	128	H3
Memphis *Texas*	127	M3
Mena	128	E3
Menai Bridge	55	E3
Menaka	101	F5
Mendawai	90	E6
Mende	65	E6
Mendi	114	C3
Mendip Hills	52	E3
Mendocino, Cape	122	B7
Mendoza	138	C6
Menemen	76	B3
Menen	64	E3
Menfi	69	D7
Mengcheng	93	N2
Mengcun	87	M4
Mengen	76	E2
Mengene Dagi	77	L3
Menggala	90	D6
Menghai	93	K4
Mengjiagang	88	C2
Mengjiawan	87	K4
Mengla	93	K4
Mengshan	93	M4
Mengyin	87	M4
Meniet	101	F3
Menihek, Lac	121	N7
Meningie	113	H6
Menkya	78	L3
Menominee *U.S.A.*	124	G4
Menominee *U.S.A.*	124	G4
Menomonee Falls	124	F5
Menongue	106	C5
Menorca	67	J3
Mentawai, Kepulauan	90	B6
Mentawai, Selat	90	B6
Mentok	90	D6
Menton	68	A4
Mentor	125	K6
Menyamya	114	D3
Menzel Bourguiba	69	B7
Meon	53	F4
Meppel	64	G2
Meppen	70	B2
Mequinenza	67	G2
Merabellou, Kolpos	75	H5
Merak	90	D7
Merano	68	C2
Merauke	91	L7
Mercan Dagi	77	H3
Mercato Saraceno	68	D4
Merced	126	B2
Mercedario, Cerro	138	B6
Mercedes *Argentina*	139	C6
Mercedes *Argentina*	139	E5
Mercedes *Argentina*	138	E5
Mercedes *Uruguay*	138	E6
Mercimek	77	F4
Mercimekkale	77	J3
Mercurea	73	G3
Mercury Bay	115	E2
Mercy, Cape	120	P5
Mere	52	E3
Meredith, Cape	139	D10
Meredoua	100	F3

Name	Page	Grid
Mere Lava	114	U11
Mereworth	53	H3
Mergenovo	79	J6
Mergui	93	J6
Mergui Archipelago	93	J6
Meribah	113	J5
Meric	76	B2
Merida *Mexico*	131	Q7
Merida *Spain*	66	C3
Merida *Venezuela*	136	C2
Merida, Cordillera de	136	C2
Meriden	125	P6
Meridian	128	H4
Merig	114	T11
Merir	91	J5
Meriruma	137	G3
Merkys	63	L9
Mermaid Reef	112	D2
Merowe	103	F4
Merredin	112	D5
Merrick	57	D5
Merrill	124	F4
Merrillville	124	G6
Merrimack	125	Q5
Merritt	122	D2
Merritt Island	129	M6
Merriwa	113	L5
Mersa Fatma	96	E9
Mersea Island	53	H3
Merseburg	70	D3
Merse, The	57	F5
Mersey	55	G3
Merseyside	55	G3
Mersin	76	F4
Mersing	90	C5
Mersrags	63	K8
Merthyr Tydfil	52	D3
Mertola	66	C4
Mertvyy Kultuk, Sor	79	J6
Mertz Glacier	141	K5
Merzifon	76	F2
Merzig	70	B4
Mesa	126	G4
Mesaras, Kolpos	75	H5
Meschede	70	C3
Meselefors	62	G4
Meshik	118	D4
Meshraer Req	102	E6
Mesolongion	75	F3
Messina *Italy*	69	E6
Messina *South Africa*	108	F4
Messina, Stretto di	69	E6
Messingham	55	J3
Messini	75	F4
Messiniakos Kolpos	75	F4
Messo	84	B3
Messoyakha	84	B3
Mesta	75	H2
Mestiya	77	K1
Mestre	68	D3
Mesudiye	77	G2
Meta	136	D2
Metan	138	D5
Metapan	132	C7
Metaponto	69	F5
Metema	103	G5
Meteran	114	E2
Methven *New Zealand*	115	C5
Methven *U.K.*	57	E4
Methwin, Mount	112	E4
Metkovic	72	D4
Metlika	72	C3
Metropolis	124	F8
Metsovon	75	F3
Metu	103	G6
Metz	64	G4
Meulaboh	90	B5
Meureudu	90	B4
Meurthe	64	G4
Meuse	64	F3
Mexborough	55	H3
Mexia	128	D5
Mexicali	126	E4
Mexico	130	H6
Mexico *U.S.A.*	124	E7
Mexico City	131	K8
Mexico, Gulf of	117	K6
Meydancik	77	K2
Meydan e Gel	95	M7
Meydani, Ra's e	95	P9
Meymaneh	94	S4
Meymeh	95	K5
Meynypilgyno	85	X4
Meyrueis	65	E6
Mezdra	73	G4
Mezen *Russia*	78	G2
Mezen *Russia*	78	H2
Mezenc, Mont	65	F6
Mezenskaya Guba	78	G2
Mezenskiy	84	F2
Mezhdurechensk	84	D6
Mezhdusharskiy, Ostrov	80	G2
Mezhgorye	71	K4
Mezotur	72	F2
Mezquital	130	G6
Mezzana	68	C2
Mhangura	108	F3
Mhow	92	E4
Miahuatlan	131	L9
Miajadas	66	D3
Miami *Arizona*	126	G4
Miami *Florida*	129	M8
Miami *Ohio*	124	H7
Miami Beach	129	M8
Mianabad	95	N3
Miandowab	94	H3
Mianeh	94	H3
Miang, Pou	93	K5
Mianwali	92	D2
Mianyang	93	K2
Miarinarivo *Madagascar*	109	J3
Miarinarivo *Madagascar*	109	J3
Miass	84	Ad5
Miastko	71	G1
Micang Shan	93	L2
Michalovce	71	J4
Michelson, Mount	118	G2
Michigan	124	H5
Michigan City	124	G6
Michigan, Lake	124	G5
Michipicoten	124	H3
Michipicoten Island	124	H3
Michurinsk	79	G5
Mickle Fell	55	G2
Mickleton	53	F2
Micronesia	142	F4
Micurin	73	J4
Middelburg *Netherlands*	64	E3
Middelburg *South Africa*	108	E5
Middelburg *South Africa*	108	E6
Middle Andaman	93	H6
Middle Barton	53	F3
Middlebury	125	P4
Middlefart	63	C9
Middlemarch	115	C6
Middlesboro	124	J8
Middlesbrough	55	H2
Middleton *Greater Manchester, U.K.*	55	G3
Middleton *Strathclyde, U.K.*	57	B4
Middleton Cheney	53	F2
Middle Tongue	55	G2
Middleton-on-the-Wolds	55	J3
Middleton Reef	113	M4
Middletown *U.K.*	52	D2
Middletown *New York*	125	N6
Middletown *Ohio*	124	H7
Middlewich	55	G3
Mid Glamorgan	52	D3
Midhurst	53	G4
Midi	96	F8
Midland *Canada*	125	L4
Midland *Michigan*	124	H5
Midland *Texas*	127	M5
Midleton	59	F9
Midongy Atsimo	109	J4
Midsomer Norton	52	E3
Midwest	123	L6
Midwest City	128	D3
Midyan	96	B3
Midyat	77	J4
Mid Yell	56	A1
Midzor	73	G4
Miechow	71	J3
Miedwie, Jezioro	70	F2
Miedzyrzecz	70	F2
Mielec	71	J3
Miena	113	K7
Mieres	66	D1
Mieso	103	H6
Mieszkowice	70	F2
Miford Sound	115	A6
Mighan	95	P6
Miguel Aleman, Presa	131	L8
Miguel Alves	137	J4
Miguel Hidalgo, Presa	127	H7
Mihaliccik	76	D3
Mihara	89	D8
Miharu	89	H7
Mihrad, Al	97	L6
Miida	96	E9
Mijares	67	F2
Mikha Tskhakaya	77	J1
Mikhaylova	84	D1
Mikhaylovgrad	73	G4
Mikhaylov Island	141	F6
Mikhaylovka *Russia*	88	C4
Mikhaylovka *Russia*	79	G5
Mikindani	107	G5
Mikkeli *Finland*	63	M6
Mikkeli *Finland*	63	M6
Mikolajki	71	J2
Mikonos	75	H4
Mikri Prespa, Limni	75	F2
Mikulov	71	G4
Mikun	78	J3
Mikuni	89	F7
Mikuni-sammyaku	89	G7
Mikura-jima	89	G9
Milaca	124	D4
Milagro	136	B4
Milan *Italy*	68	B3
Milan *U.S.A.*	128	H3
Milano	68	B3
Milas	76	B4
Milazzo	69	E6
Milbank	123	R5
Mildenhall	53	H2
Mildurra	113	J5
Mile	93	K4
Mileh Tharthar	94	F5
Miles	113	L4
Miles City	123	M4
Milford *U.K.*	58	G2
Milford *U.S.A.*	125	N7
Milford Haven	52	B3
Milford Sound	115	A6
Milgun	112	D4
Milh, Bahr al	94	F5
Miliana	101	F1
Miliane, Oued	69	C7
Milk	123	L3
Millas	65	E7
Millau	65	E6
Milledgeville	129	L4
Mille Lacs, Lac des	124	E2
Mille Lacs Lake	124	D3
Miller	123	Q5
Millerovo	79	G6
Millers Flat	115	B6
Millford	58	J4
Millington	128	H3
Mill Island *Antarctic*	141	G5
Mill Island *Canada*	120	L5
Millisle	58	L3
Millnocket	125	R4
Millom	55	F2
Millport	57	D5
Mills Lake	119	M3
Milltown	58	K2
Milltown Malbay	59	D7
Millville	125	N7
Millwood Lake	128	F4
Milngavie	57	D5
Milogradovo	88	E4
Milolii	126	T11
Milos *Greece*	75	H4
Milos *Greece*	75	H4
Milowka	71	H4
Milparinka	113	J4
Milpillas	131	K9
Milton *New Zealand*	115	B7
Milton *Florida*	129	J5
Milton *Pennsylvania*	125	M6
Milton Abbot	52	C4
Milton Ernest	53	G2
Milton Keynes	53	G2
Miluo	93	M3
Milwaukee	124	G5
Mimizan	65	C6
Mimon	70	F3
Mina Abd Allah	97	J2
Minab	95	N8
Mina de San Domingos	66	C4
Minahassa Peninsula	91	G5
Minamata	89	C9
Minas *Indonesia*	90	C5
Minas *Uruguay*	139	E6
Mina Saud	97	J2
Minas Gerais	138	G3
Minas, Sierra de las	132	C7
Minatitlan	131	M8
Minbu	93	H4
Minch, The	56	C2
Mincio	68	C3
Mindanao	91	G4
Mindelo	104	L7
Minden *U.S.A.*	128	F4
Minden *Germany*	70	C2
Mindoro	91	G3
Mindoro Strait	91	G3
Mindra	73	G3
Minehead	52	D3
Mine Head	59	G9
Mineola	128	E4
Mineral Wells	128	C4
Minerva Reefs	111	T6
Minervino Murge	69	F5
Minfeng	92	F1
Mingechaur	79	H7
Mingela	113	K2
Minglanilla	67	F3
Mingshui *Gansu, China*	86	H3
Mingshui *Heilongjiang, China*	87	P2
Mingulay	57	A4
Minicoy	92	D7
Minigwal	112	E4
Min Jiang	93	K3
Minle	86	J4
Minna	105	G4
Minneapolis	124	D4
Minnedosa	123	Q2
Minnesota *U.S.A.*	124	C3
Minnesota *U.S.A.*	124	C4
Minnitaki Lake	124	E1
Mino	66	B1
Minorca	67	J3
Minot	123	P3
Minsk	78	D5
Minsk Mazowiecki	71	J2
Minsterley	52	E2
Mintlaw	56	F3
Minto	125	S3
Minto Inlet	119	M1
Minto, Lac	121	L6
Minturn	123	L8
Minusinsk	84	E6
Minwakh	97	J8
Min Xian	93	K2
Minyar	78	K4
Miquelon	125	M2
Mira *Italy*	68	D3
Mira *Portugal*	66	B4
Mirabad	95	Q6
Miracema do Norte	137	H5
Miraflores	136	C2
Miraj	92	D5
Miramichi Bay	121	N8
Miramont	65	D6
Miram Shah	92	D2
Miranda *Brazil*	138	E4
Miranda *Brazil*	138	E4
Miranda de Ebro	66	E1
Miranda do Douro	66	C2
Mirande	65	D7
Mirandela	66	C2
Mirandola	68	C3
Mirapinima	136	E4
Miravci	73	G5
Mirbat, Ra's	97	M8
Mirbut	97	M8
Mirear Island	96	B5
Mirebeau	65	D5
Mirgorod	79	E6
Miri	90	E5
Miri Hills	93	H3
Mirimire	136	D1
Mirim, Lagoa	138	F6
Mirjaveh	95	Q7
Mirnyy *Antarctic*	141	G5
Mirnyy *Russia*	85	J4
Mironovo	84	H5
Mirpur Khas	92	C3
Mirriam Vale	113	L3
Mirtoan Sea	75	G4
Mirtoon Pelagos	75	G4
Miryang	89	B8
Mirzapur	92	F3
Misgar	92	D1
Mishan	88	C3
Mi-shima	89	C8
Mishkino	78	K4
Misima Island	114	T10
Miskolc	73	F1
Misool	91	J6
Misratah	101	J2
Missinaibi	121	K7
Mission *Canada*	122	C3
Mission *U.S.A.*	123	P6
Mission Viejo	126	D4
Mississauga	125	L5
Mississippi *U.S.A.*	128	G4
Mississippi *U.S.A.*	128	G5
Mississippi Delta	128	H6
Missoula	122	G4
Missouri *U.S.A.*	124	D7
Missouri *U.S.A.*	124	E7
Missouri, Coteau de	123	P4
Mistassibi	121	M8
Mistassini *Canada*	125	P2
Mistassini *Canada*	125	P2
Mistassini, Lac	121	M7
Mistelbach	68	F1
Mistretta	69	E7
Mitatib	96	C9
Mitchell *Australia*	113	J2
Mitchell *Australia*	113	K4
Mitchell *U.S.A.*	123	Q6
Mitchell, Mount	129	L3
Mitchelstown	59	F8
Mithankot	92	D3
Mithimna	75	J3
Mitilini	75	J3
Mito	89	H7
Mitre	111	R4
Mitrofanovskaya	78	K3
Mitsio, Nosy	109	J2
Mitsiwa	103	G4
Mitsiwa Channel	96	D9
Mittelland Kanal	70	B2
Mittelmark	70	E2
Mitumba, Chaine des	107	E4
Mitwaba	107	E4
Mitzic	106	B2
Mixteco	131	K8
Miyah, Wadi al	77	H5
Miyake-jima	89	G8
Miyake-shoto	89	G11
Miyako	88	H6
Miyako-jima	89	G11
Miyakonojo	89	C10
Miyaly	79	J6
Miyazaki	89	C10
Miyazu	89	E8
Miyoshi	89	D8
Mizdah	101	H2
Mizen Head *Cork, Ireland*	59	C10
Mizen Head *Wicklow, Ireland*	59	K7
Mizhi	87	L4
Mizil	73	J3
Mizoram	93	H4
Mizpe Ramon	94	B6
Mjolby	63	F7
Mjosa	63	D6
Mlada Boleslav	70	F3
Mladenovac	72	F3
Mlawa	71	J2
Mljet	72	D4
Moa *Cuba*	133	K4
Moa *Indonesia*	91	H7
Moab	127	H1
Moa Island	114	C4
Moala	114	R9
Moate	59	G6
Moatize	109	F3
Moba	107	E4
Mobaye	102	D7
Mobayi-Mbongo	106	D2
Moberly	124	D7
Mobile	129	H5
Mobile Bay	129	H5
Mobridge	123	P5
Mobutu Sese Seko, Lake	107	F2
Moca	114	S9
Mocajuba	137	G4
Mocambique	109	H3

Name	Page	Grid
Nags Head	129	Q3
Nagykanizsa	72	D2
Nagykata	72	E2
Nagykoros	72	E2
Naha	89	H10
Nahariya	94	B5
Nahavand	94	J4
Nahe	70	B4
Nahoi, Cap	114	T11
Nahuel Huapi, Lago	139	B8
Naikliu	91	G7
Nailsea	52	E3
Nailsworth	52	E3
Naiman Qi	87	N3
Nain	95	L5
Nain	121	P6
Naini Tal	92	E3
Nairai	114	R8
Nairn	56	E3
Nairobi	107	G3
Najafabad	95	K5
Najd	96	E4
Najibabad	92	E3
Najin	88	C4
N Ajjer, Tassili	101	G3
Najran	96	G8
Najran, Wadi	96	G8
Nakadori-shima	89	B9
Nakajo	89	G6
Nakamura	89	D9
Nakano	89	G7
Nakano-shima	89	B11
Nakatay	84	Ad5
Nakatsu	89	C9
Nakatsugawa	89	F8
Nakfa	103	G4
Nakhichevan	77	L3
Nakhl *Eygpt*	96	A2
Nakhl *Oman*	97	N5
Nakhodka *Russia*	84	B3
Nakhodka *Russia*	88	D4
Nakhon Pathom	93	J6
Nakhon Phanom	93	K5
Nakhon Ratchasima	93	K6
Nakhon Sawan	93	K5
Nakhon Si Thammarat	93	J7
Nakina	121	J7
Nakiri	89	F8
Naknek Lake	118	D4
Nakskov	63	F9
Naktong	87	P4
Nakuru	107	G3
Nakusp	122	F2
Nalchik	79	G7
Nalgonda	92	E5
Nallamala Hills	92	E5
Nallihan	76	D2
Nalut	101	H2
Namaa, Tanjung	91	H6
Namacunde	106	C6
Namacurra	109	G3
Namak, Daryacheh-ye	95	K4
Namaki	95	M6
Namakzar	95	Q5
Namakzar, Daryacheh-ye	95	Q5
Namangan	86	C3
Namapa	109	G2
Namaponda	109	G3
Namarroi	109	G3
Namasagali	107	F2
Namatanai	114	E2
Nambour	113	L4
Nam Can	93	K7
Nam Co	93	H2
Nam Dinh	93	L4
Nametil	109	G3
Namib Desert	108	B4
Namibe	106	B6
Namibia	108	C4
Namlea	91	H6
Namoi	113	L5
Namosi Peak	114	R8
Nampa	122	F6
Nampula	109	G3
Namse La	92	F3
Namsen	62	E4
Namsos	62	D4
Namti	93	J3
Namtok	93	J5
Namuka-i-Lau	114	S9
Namuli	109	G3
Namur	64	F3
Namutoni	108	C3
Namwala	106	E6
Nana Barya	102	C6
Nanaimo	122	C3
Nanam	88	B5
Nanao	89	F7
Nancha	88	B2
Nanchang	87	M6
Nanchong	93	L2
Nancowry	93	H7
Nancy	64	G4
Nanda Devi	92	E2
Nandan	93	L3
Nanded	92	E5
Nandurbar	92	D4
Nandyal	92	E5
Nanfeng	87	M6
Nanga Eboko	105	H5
Nangahpinoh	90	E6
Nanga Parbat	92	D1
Nangatayap	90	E6
Nangong	87	M4
Nan Hai	83	K5
Nanjing	87	M5
Nanking	87	M5
Nan, Mae Nam	93	K5
Nanning	93	L4
Nanortalik	116	Q2
Nanpan Jiang	93	K4
Nanpara	92	F3
Nanpi	87	M4
Nanping	87	M6
Nansei-shoto	89	H10
Nansen Sound	120	H1
Nanshan Islands	90	E4
Nansha Qundao	90	E4
Nantais, Lac	121	M5
Nantes	65	C5
Nantong	87	N5
Nantua	65	F5
Nantucket Island	125	Q6
Nantucket Sound	125	Q6
Nantwich	55	G3
Nant-y-moch Reservoir	52	D2
Nanuku Passage	114	S8
Nanuku Reef	114	S8
Nanumanga	111	S3
Nanumea	111	S3
Nanusa, Kepulauan	91	H5
Nanyang	93	M2
Nanyuki	107	G2
Nao, Cabo de la	67	G3
Naococane, Lake	121	M7
Naousa	75	G2
Napa	126	A1
Napabalana	91	G6
Napalkovo	84	A2
Napas	84	C5
Nape	93	L5
Napier	115	F3
Naples *Italy*	69	E5
Naples *U.S.A.*	129	M7
Napo	136	C4
Napoleon	124	H6
Napoletano, Appennino	69	E5
Napoli	69	E5
Napoli, Golfo di	69	E5
Naqadeh	94	G3
Nar	53	H2
Nara *Japan*	89	E8
Nara *Mali*	100	H3
Nara *Pakistan*	92	C4
Naracoorte	113	J6
Naran	87	L2
Narasapur	92	F5
Narat	86	E3
Narathiwat	93	K7
Narayanganj	93	H4
Narberth	52	C3
Narbonne	65	E7
Narborough Island	136	A7
Narcea	66	C1
Nardin	95	M3
Narew *Poland*	71	J2
Narew *Poland*	71	K2
Narince	77	H4
Narken	62	K3
Narkher	92	E4
Narli	77	G4
Narmada	92	E4
Narman	77	J2
Narnaul	92	E3
Narodnaya, Gora	84	Ad3
Naro-Fominsk	78	F4
Narowal	92	D2
Narpes	62	J5
Narrabi	113	K5
Narrandera	113	K5
Narrogin	112	D5
Narromine	113	K5
Narsimhapur	92	E4
Narsinghgarh	92	E4
Nart	87	M3
Nartabu	91	J6
Naruko	88	H6
Narva	63	N7
Narvik	62	G2
Naryan Mar	78	J2
Narymskiy Khrebet	86	E2
Naryn *Russia*	84	F6
Naryn *Kyrgyzstan*	86	C3
Naryn *Kyrgyzstan*	86	D3
Nasarawa	105	G4
Naseby	115	C6
Nashua	125	Q5
Nashville	129	J2
Nasice	72	E3
Nasielsk	71	J2
Nasijarvi	63	K6
Nasik	92	D5
Nasir	103	F6
Nasir, Buhayrat	103	F3
Nasorolevu	114	R8
Nass	118	K4
Nassau	129	P8
Nasser, Lake	103	F3
Nassjo	63	F8
Nastapoka Islands	121	L6
Nastved	63	D9
Nata	108	E4
Natagaima	136	B3
Natal *Brazil*	137	K5
Natal *Indonesia*	90	B5
Natara	85	L3
Natashquan	121	P7
Natchez	128	G5
Natchitoches	128	F5
Natewa Bay	114	R8
National City	126	D4
Natitingou	105	F3
Natividade	137	H6
Natori	89	H6
Natron, Lake	107	G3
Nattavaara	62	J3
Natuna Besar	90	D5
Natuna, Kepulauan	90	D5
Naturaliste, Cape	112	D5
Naturaliste Channel	112	C4
Nauen	70	E2
Naueyi Akmyane	63	K8
Naujoji Vilnia	71	L1
Naul	58	K5
Naumburg	70	D3
Naungpale	93	J5
Nauru	111	Q2
Naurzum	84	Ad6
Nausori	114	R9
Nautanwa	92	F3
Nautla	131	L7
Nauzad	95	S5
Navadwip	93	G4
Navahermosa	66	D3
Naval	91	G3
Navalcarnero	66	D2
Navalmoral de la Mata	66	D3
Navalpino	66	D3
Navan	58	J5
Navarin, Mys	85	X4
Navarino, Isla	139	C11
Navarra	67	F1
Navars	67	G2
Navasota	128	G5
Navassa Island	133	K5
Navax Point	52	B4
Navenby	55	J3
Naver, Loch	56	D2
Navia *Spain*	66	C1
Navia *Spain*	66	C1
Naviti	114	Q8
Navlya	79	E5
Navojoa	127	H7
Navolato	130	F5
Navpaktos	75	F3
Navplion	75	G4
Navrongo	104	E3
Navsari	92	D4
Navua	114	R9
Nawabshah	92	C3
Nawada	92	G4
Nawah	92	C2
Nawasif, Harrat	96	F6
Naws, Ra's	97	M8
Nawton	55	J2
Naxos *Greece*	75	H4
Naxos *Greece*	75	H4
Nayagarh	92	G4
Nayau	114	S8
Nay Band	95	L8
Nay Band	95	N5
Nayoro	88	J3
Nazare	137	K6
Nazareth *Israel*	94	B3
Nazareth *Peru*	136	B5
Nazarovo	84	E5
Nazas	130	G5
Nazca	136	C6
Naze	89	B11
Nazerat	94	B5
Naze, The	53	J3
Nazik	94	G2
Nazik Golu	77	K3
Nazilli	76	C4
Nazmiye	77	H3
Nazwa	97	N5
Nazyvayevsk	84	A5
Ncheu	107	F5
Ndalatando	106	B4
Ndele	102	D6
Ndeni	114	N7
Ndjamena	102	C5
Ndjote	106	B3
Ndola	107	E5
Nea	62	D5
Nea Filippias	75	F3
Neagh, Lough	58	K3
Neah Bay	122	B3
Neale, Lake	112	G3
Nea Moudhania	75	G2
Neapolis *Greece*	75	F2
Neapolis *Greece*	75	H5
Nea Psara	75	G3
Near Islands	118	Aa9
Neath	52	D3
Nebine	113	K4
Nebit Dag	95	M2
Neblina, Pico da	136	D3
Nebraska	123	N7
Nebraska City	124	C6
Nebrodi, Monti	69	E7
Nechako	118	L5
Nechi	133	K11
Neckar	70	C4
Necochea	139	E7
Nedong	93	H3
Nedstrand	63	A7
Needles *Canada*	122	E3
Needles *U.S.A.*	126	E3
Needles Point	115	E2
Needles, The	53	F4
Neepawa	123	Q2
Neergaard Lake	120	L3
Nefedovo	84	A5
Nefta	101	G2
Neftechala	94	J2
Neftegorsk	79	J5
Neftekamsk	78	J4
Nefyn	52	C2
Nefza	69	B7
Negele	103	G6
Negev	94	B6
Negoiu	73	H3
Negombo	92	E7
Negotin	73	G3
Negrais, Cape	93	H5
Negra, Punta	136	A5
Negritos	136	A4
Negro *Argentina*	139	C7
Negro *Amazonas, Brazil*	136	E4
Negro *Santa Catarina, Brazil*	138	F5
Negro *Uruguay*	138	F6
Negros	91	G3
Negru Voda	73	K4
Nehavand	94	J4
Nehbandan	95	Q6
Nehe	87	N2
Nehoiasu	73	J3
Neijiang	93	K3
Nei Mongol Zizhiqu	87	L3
Neisse *Poland*	70	F3
Neisse *Poland*	71	G3
Neiteyugansk	84	A4
Neiva	136	B3
Neixiang	93	M2
Nekemte	103	G6
Neksikan	85	R4
Nekso	63	H9
Nelidovo	78	E4
Neligh	123	Q6
Nelkan	85	P5
Nellore	92	E6
Nelma	88	G2
Nelson *Canada*	122	F2
Nelson *New Zealand*	115	D4
Nelson *U.K.*	55	G3
Nelson, Cape *Australia*	113	J6
Nelson, Cape *Papua New Guinea*	114	D3
Nelson Lagoon	118	Af8
Nelspruit	108	F5
Nema	100	D5
Neman	78	C4
Neman	71	K1
Nemira	73	J2
Nemirov	73	K1
Nemiscau	121	L7
Nemours	64	E4
Nemun	63	J9
Nemuro	88	K4
Nemuro-kaikyo	88	K4
Nemuy	85	P5
Nenagh	59	F7
Nenana	118	F3
Nene	53	G2
Nen Jiang	87	P1
Nenjiang	87	P2
Nenthead	55	G2
Neokhorion	75	J4
Neon Karlovasi	75	J4
Neosho *Kansas*	124	C7
Neosho *Missouri*	124	C8
Nepa *Russia*	84	H5
Nepa *Russia*	84	H5
Nepal	92	F3
Nephi	126	G1
Nephin Beg Range	58	C4
Nera	69	D4
Nerac	65	D6
Nerchinsk	85	K6
Neretva	72	D4
Neriquinha	106	D6
Neris	63	L9
Nermete, Punta	136	A5
Neryuktey-l-y	85	K4
Neryuvom	84	Ad3
Nes	63	C6
Nesbyen	63	C6
Neskaupstadur	62	Y12
Nesna	62	E3
Nesscliffe	52	E2
Nesterov *Russia*	71	K3
Nesterov *Ukraine*	71	K1
Nesterovo	84	H6
Neston	55	F3
Nestos	75	H2
Nesvizh	71	M2
Netanya	94	B5
Netherlands	64	F2
Neto	69	F6
Nettilling Lake	120	M4
Nettleham	55	J3
Netzahualcoyotl, Presa	131	N9
Neubrandenburg	70	E2
Neuchatel	68	A2
Neuchatel, Lac de	68	A2
Neufchateau *Belgium*	64	F4
Neufchateau *France*	64	F4
Neufchatel	64	D4
Neufelden	68	D1
Neumunster	70	C1
Neunkirchen *Austria*	68	F2
Neunkirchen *Germany*	70	B4

Name	Page	Ref
Ormos	75	H4
Ormskirk	55	G3
Ornain	64	F4
Orne	64	C4
Ornskoldsvik	62	H5
Oro	130	G4
Orobi, Alpi	68	B3
Orocue	136	C3
Orofino	122	F4
Oromocto	125	S4
Oron	85	K5
Orona	111	U2
Oronsay	57	B5
Oronsay, Passage of	57	B5
Orontes	77	G5
Oropesa	66	D3
Oroqen Zizhiqi	87	N1
Oroquieta	91	G4
Orosei, Golfo di	69	B5
Oroshaza	72	F2
Orotukan	85	S4
Oroville *California*	122	D8
Oroville *Washington*	122	E3
Oroville, Lake	122	D8
Orrin Reservoir	56	D3
Orsa	63	F6
Orsa Finnmark	63	F6
Orsaro, Monte	68	C3
Orsha	78	E5
Orsta	62	B5
Orta	76	E2
Ortabag	77	K4
Ortaca	76	C4
Ortakoy *Turkey*	76	F2
Ortakoy *Turkey*	76	F3
Ortatoroslar	76	F4
Ortega	136	B3
Ortegal, Cabo	66	C1
Ortelsburg	71	J2
Orthez	65	C7
Ortigueira	66	C1
Ortiz	133	P10
Ortles	68	C2
Ortona	69	E4
Orto-Tokoy	86	D3
Orumiyeh	77	L4
Orumiyeh, Daryacheh-ye	94	G3
Oruro	138	C3
Orvieto	69	D4
Orwell	53	J3
Oryakhovo	73	G4
Os	62	D5
Osa	78	K4
Osage	124	D7
Osaka *Japan*	89	E8
Osaka *Japan*	89	F8
Osaka-wan	89	E8
Osa, Peninsula de	132	F10
Osceola *Arkansas*	128	H3
Osceola *Iowa*	124	D6
Osh	86	B3
Oshamambe	88	H4
Oshawa	125	L5
O-shima	89	G8
Oshkosh	124	F4
Oshkurya	84	Ac3
Oshmarino	84	C2
Oshmyanskaya Vozvyshennost	71	M1
Oshmyany	71	L1
Oshnoviyeh	94	G3
Oshogbo	105	F4
Oshtoran Kuh	94	J5
Oshtorinan	94	J4
Oshwe	106	C3
Osijek	72	E3
Osimo	68	D4
Osinniki	84	D6
Osipovichi	79	D5
Oskaloosa	124	D6
Oskamull	57	B4
Oskara, Mys	84	F1
Oskarshamn	63	G8
Oskarstrom	63	E8
Oskoba	84	G4
Oskol	79	F5
Oslo *Norway*	63	D7
Oslo *Norway*	63	D7
Oslob	91	G4
Oslofjorden	63	H7
Osmanabad	92	E5
Osmancik	76	F2
Osmaneli	76	C2
Osmaniye	77	G4
Osmington	52	E4
Osmino	63	N7
Osmo	63	G7
Osnabruck	70	C2
Osogovska Planina	73	G4
Osorno *Chile*	139	B8
Osorno *Spain*	66	D1
Osoyro	63	A6
Osprey Reef	113	K1
Oss	64	F3
Ossa	75	G3
Ossa, Mount	110	L10
Ossett	55	H3
Ossian, Loch	57	D4
Ossokmanuan Lake	121	P7
Ostashkov	78	E4
Ostavall	62	F5
Ostby	63	E6
Oste	70	C2
Osterburken	70	C4
Osterdala!ven	63	E6
Osterdalen	63	D5
Ostergotland	63	F7
Osterode	71	H2
Ostersund	62	F5
Ostfold	63	D7
Ost Friesische Inseln	70	B2
Ostfriesland	70	B2
Osthammar	63	H6
Ostiglia	68	C3
Ostra	68	D4
Ostrava	71	H4
Ostroda	71	H2
Ostrog	79	D5
Ostrogozhsk	79	F5
Ostroleka	71	J2
Ostrov	63	N8
Ostrovnoy, Mys	88	D4
Ostrow	71	G3
Ostrowiec	71	J3
Ostrow Mazowiecki	71	J2
Ostuni	69	F5
Osum	75	F2
Osum	73	H4
Osumi-kaikyo	89	C10
Osumi-shoto	89	C10
Osuna	66	D4
OsVan	78	K2
Oswaldtwistle	55	G3
Oswego	125	M5
Oswestry	52	D2
Otaki	115	E4
Otaru	88	H4
Otava	70	E4
Otavi	108	C3
Otawara	89	G7
Otchinjau	106	B6
Otelec	73	F3
Otelu Rosu	73	G3
Otematata	115	C6
Othe, Foret d'	65	E4
Othonoi	74	E3
Othris	75	G3
Oti	104	F4
Otira	115	C5
Otis	123	N7
Otish, Monts	121	M7
Otjiwarongo	108	C4
Otley	55	H3
Otlukbeli Daglari	77	J2
Otnes	63	D6
Otocac	72	C3
Otorohanga	115	E3
Otoskwin	121	H7
Otra	63	B7
Otranto	69	G5
Otranto, Capo d	69	G5
Otranto, Strait of	74	E2
Otsu	89	E8
Otsu	89	H7
Otta *Norway*	63	C6
Otta *Norway*	63	C6
Ottawa *Canada*	125	L3
Ottawa *Canada*	125	N4
Ottawa Islands	121	K6
Otter	52	D4
Otterburn	57	F5
Otter Rapids	125	K1
Otterup	63	D9
Ottery	52	C4
Ottery Saint Mary	52	D4
Ottumwa	124	D6
Oturkpo	105	G4
Otway, Bahia	139	B10
Otway, Cape	113	J6
Otway, Seno	139	B10
Otwock	71	J2
Otynya	71	L4
Otztaler Alpen	68	C2
Ouachita	128	F4
Ouachita, Lake	128	F3
Ouachita Mountains	128	E3
Ouadda	102	D6
Ouagadougou	104	E3
Ouahigouya	104	E3
Oualata	100	D5
Oua-n Ahagar, Tassili	101	G4
Ouanda Djaile	102	D6
Ouarane	100	D4
Ouargla	101	G2
Ouarra	102	E6
Ouarsenis, Massif de l'	67	G5
Ouarzazate	100	D2
Ouatoais	125	M4
Oubangui	106	C3
Oudenaarde	64	E3
Oude Rijn	64	F2
Oudtshoorn	108	D6
Oued Zem	100	D2
Oueme	105	F4
Ouen	114	X17
Ouessant, Ile d'	64	A4
Ouesso	106	C2
Ouezzane	100	D2
Oughterard	59	D6
Oughter, Lough	58	H4
Ouidah	105	F4
Oujda	100	E2
Oulainen	62	L4
Oulmes	100	D2
Oulu *Finland*	62	L4
Oulu *Finland*	62	M4
Oulujarvi	62	M4
Oulujoki	62	M4
Oulx	68	A3
Oum Chalouba	102	D4
Oum El Bouaghi	101	G1
Oum er Rbia, Oued	100	D2
Ou, Nam	93	K4
Ounasjoki	62	L3
Oundle	53	G2
Ounianga Kebir	102	D4
Oupu	87	P1
Ouricuri	137	J5
Ourinhos	138	G4
Ouro Preto	138	H4
Ourthe	64	F3
Ouse *Australia*	113	K7
Ouse *U.K.*	55	H3
Oust	65	B5
Outardes, Reservoir	121	N7
Outer Hebrides	56	A3
Outokumpu	62	N5
Out Skerries	56	B1
Outwell	53	H2
Ouvea	114	X16
Ouyen	113	J6
Ovacik *Turkey*	77	H4
Ovacik *Turkey*	77	J2
Ovada	68	B3
Ovalau Batiki	114	R8
Ovalle	138	B6
Ovau	114	H5
Ovejo	66	D3
Oven	115	X17
Overbister	56	F1
Overbygd	62	H2
Overkalix	62	K3
Overnas	62	G3
Overtornea	62	K3
Oviedo	66	D1
Ovinishche	78	F4
Ovre Ardal	63	B6
Ovruch	79	D5
Owahanga	115	F4
Owaka	115	B7
Owando	106	C3
Owase	89	F8
Owatonna	124	D4
Owbeh	95	R4
Owel, Lough	58	H5
Owenbeg	58	E4
Owenkillew	58	H3
Owenmore	58	C4
Owens	126	C2
Owensboro	124	G8
Owens Lake	126	D2
Owen Sound	125	K4
Owen Stanley Range	114	D3
Owerri	105	G4
Owo	105	G4
Owosso	124	H5
Owyhee *Nevada*	122	F7
Owyhee *Oregon*	122	F6
Oxbow	123	N3
Oxelosund	63	G7
Oxenholme	55	G2
Oxenhope	55	H3
Oxford *New Zealand*	115	D5
Oxford *U.K.*	53	F3
Oxford *U.S.A.*	128	H3
Oxfordshire	53	F3
Ox Mountains	58	E4
Oxnard	126	C3
Oxton	55	H3
Oyaca	76	E3
Oyali	77	J4
Oyapock	137	G3
Oyem	106	B2
Oykel	56	D3
Oykel Bridge	56	D3
Oymyakon	85	Q4
Oyo	105	F4
Ozalp	77	L3
Ozamiz	91	G4
Ozark Plateau	124	D8
Ozarks, Lake of the	124	D7
Ozd	72	F1
Ozernovskiy	85	T6
Ozernoye	84	A5
Ozersk	71	K1
Ozhogina	85	R3
Ozieri	69	B5
Ozinki	79	H5
Ozona	127	M5
Ozora	72	E2
Ozyurt	76	F3

P

Name	Page	Ref
Paama	114	U12
Paarl	108	C6
Pabbay *U.K.*	56	A3
Pabbay *U.K.*	57	A4
Pabellon de Arteaga	130	H6
Pabjanice	71	H3
Pabna	92	G4
Pabrade	63	L9
Pacaas Novos, Serra dos	136	E6
Pacaraima, Sierra	136	E3
Pacasmayo	136	B5
Pachino	69	E7
Pachora	92	E4
Pachuca	131	K7
Pacifica	126	A2
Pacific Ocean	87	P7
Pacific Ocean, North	143	H3
Pacific Ocean, South	143	J5
Pacitan	90	E7
Packwood	122	D4
Padang *Indonesia*	90	C6
Padang *Indonesia*	90	C5
Padangpanjang	90	D6
Padangsidimpuan	90	B5
Padasjoki	63	L6
Padauiri	136	E3
Paderborn	70	C3
Pades	73	G3
Padiham	55	G3
Padilla *Bolivia*	138	D3
Padilla *Mexico*	131	K5
Padina	73	J3
Padje-Ianta	62	G3
Padloping Island	120	P4
Padova	68	C3
Padrao, Pointa do	106	B4
Padron	66	B1
Padstow	52	C4
Padstow Bay	52	C4
Padua	68	C3
Paducah *Kentucky*	124	F8
Paducah *Texas*	127	M4
Padunskoye More	62	P2
Paekariki	115	E4
Paengnyong-do	87	N4
Paeroa	115	E2
Pag *Croatia*	72	C3
Pag *Croatia*	72	C3
Pagadian	91	G4
Pagasitikos Kolpos	75	G3
Pagatan	90	F6
Page	126	G2
Pagosa Springs	127	J2
Pagwa River	124	H2
Pagwi	114	C2
Pahala	126	T11
Pahang	90	C5
Pahia Point	115	A7
Pahiatua	115	E4
Pahlavi Dezh	95	M3
Pahoa	126	T11
Pahokee	129	M7
Pahra Kariz	95	Q4
Paia	126	S10
Paide	63	L7
Paignton	52	D4
Paijanne	63	L6
Pailolo Chan	126	S10
Paimpol	64	B4
Painswick	53	E3
Painted Desert	126	G2
Paisley	57	D5
Paita	136	A5
Paita	114	X17
Paittasjarvi	62	K2
Pajala	62	K3
Pakaraima Mountains	136	E2
Pakistan	92	C3
Pak Lay	93	K5
Pakokku	93	H4
Pakpattan	92	D2
Pakrac	72	D3
Paks	72	E2
Pakse	93	L5
Pala	102	B6
Palabuhanratu	90	D7
Palafrugell	67	H2
Palagruza	72	D4
Palaiokastron	75	J5
Palaiokhora	75	G5
Pala Laharha	92	G4
Palamos	67	H2
Palana	85	T5
Palanan Point	91	G2
Palanga	63	J9
Palangan, Kuh-e-	95	Q6
Palangkaraya	90	E6
Palanpur	92	D4
Palapye	108	E4
Palar	92	E6
Palata	69	E5
Palatka *U.S.A.*	129	M6
Palatka *Russia*	85	S4
Palau	69	B5
Palau Islands	91	J4
Palawan	91	F4
Palawan Passage	91	F4
Palayankottai	92	E7
Palazzola Acreide	69	E7
Paldiski	63	L7
Palembang	90	C6
Palena, Lago	139	B8
Palencia	66	D1
Palermo	69	D6
Palestine	128	E5
Paletwa	93	H4
Palghat	92	E6
Palgrave Point	108	B4
Palhoca	138	G5
Pali	92	D3
Palisade	127	H1
Palit, Kep i	74	E2
Palkane	63	L6
Palk Strait	92	E7
Pallaresa	67	G1
Pallas Green	59	F7
Pallasovka	79	H5
Pallastunturi	62	K2
Palliser Bay	115	E4
Palliser, Cape	115	E4
Palma *Mozambique*	109	H2

Name	Pg	Grid	Name	Pg	Grid	Name	Pg	Grid	Name	Pg	Grid
Penas, Cabode	66	C1	Pervomaysk *Ukraine*	79	E6	Pibor Post	103	F6	Pioner, Ostrov	81	L2
Penasco, Puerto	126	F5	Pervouralsk	84	Ac5	Pic	124	G2	Pionerskiy *Russia*	84	Ad4
Pena, Sierra de la	67	F1	Pesaro	68	D4	Picardie	64	E4	Pionerskiy *Russia*	71	J1
Pencader	52	C3	Pescara	69	E4	Picayune	128	H5	Piotrkow Trybunalski	71	H3
Pencaitland	57	F5	Peschanyy, Mys	79	J7	Pichilemu	139	B6	Piove di Sacco	68	D3
Pendalofon	75	F2	Pesha	78	H2	Pickering	55	J2	Piperi	75	H3
Pendembu	104	C4	Peshanjan	95	Q5	Pickering, Vale of	55	J2	Pipestone	124	B5
Pendine	52	C3	Peshawar	92	D2	Pickle Lake	121	J7	Pipmudcan, Reservoir	125	Q2
Pendleton	122	E5	Peshkopi	75	F2	Pico	69	D5	Piracicaba	138	G4
Pend Oreille Lake	122	F3	Peski *Belarus*	71	L2	Picos	137	J5	Piracuruca	137	J4
Pendra	92	F4	Peski *Kazakhstan*	84	Ae6	Pico Truncado	139	C9	Piraeus	75	G4
Penedo	138	K6	Pesqueira *Brazil*	137	K5	Picton	115	E4	Pirahmet	77	H2
Penfro	52	C3	Pesqueria *Mexico*	127	N8	Picun-Leufu	139	C7	Piraievs	75	G4
Penganga	92	E5	Pestovo	78	F4	Pidalion, Akra	76	F5	Piranhas *Amazonas, Brazil*	136	E5
Pengkou	87	M6	Petah Tiqwa	94	B5	Pidurutalagala	92	F7	Piranhas *Sergipe, Brazil*	137	K5
Pengze	87	M5	Petajavesi	62	L5	Piedecuesta	136	C2	Piranshahr	77	L4
Peniche	66	B3	Petalcalco, Bahia	130	H9	Piedrabuena	66	D3	Pirapora	138	H3
Penicuik	57	E5	Petalioi	75	H4	Piedrahita	66	D2	Pirara	136	F3
Peniscola	67	G2	Petalion, Kolpos	75	H4	Piedralaves	66	D2	Pirgos *Greece*	75	F4
Penistone	55	H3	Petaluma	126	A1	Piedras Negras	127	M6	Pirgos *Greece*	75	H5
Penitentes, Serra do	137	H5	Petatlan	131	J9	Piedra Sola	138	E6	Pirimapun	114	B3
Penmaenmawr	54	F3	Petauke	107	F5	Pielavesi	62	M5	Pirineos	67	F1
Penmarch, Pointe de	65	A5	Peterborough *Australia*	113	H5	Pielinen	62	N5	Pirin Planina	73	G5
Penne	69	D4	Peterborough *Canada*	125	L4	Pierowall	56	F1	Piripiri	137	J4
Penner	92	E6	Peterborough *U.K.*	53	G2	Pierre	123	P5	Pirmasens	70	B4
Penneshaw	113	H6	Peterhead	56	G3	Pietarsaari	62	K5	Pirna	70	E3
Pennine, Alpi	68	A2	Peterlee	55	H2	Pietermaritzburg	108	F5	Piro do Rio	138	G3
Pennines	55	G2	Petermann Ranges	112	F3	Pietersburg	108	E4	Pirot	73	G4
Pennsylvania	125	L6	Peter Pond Lake	119	P4	Pietrosu	73	H2	Pir Panjal Range	92	D2
Penny Highlands	120	N4	Petersburg *Alaska*	118	J4	Pieve di Cadore	68	D2	Piru	91	H6
Peno	78	E4	Petersburg *Virginia*	125	M8	Pigadhia	75	J5	Piryatin	79	E5
Penobscot	125	R4	Petersfield	53	G3	Piggott	128	G2	Piryi	75	H3
Penobscot Bay	125	R4	Peterstow	52	E3	Pihtipudas	62	L5	Pisa	68	C4
Penonome	132	G10	Petite Kabylie	67	J4	Pijijiapan	131	N10	Pisco	136	B6
Penrith	55	G2	Petite Miquelon	121	Q8	Pikes Peak	123	M8	Piscopi	75	J4
Penryn	52	B4	Petit Mecatina, Riviere du	121	P7	Pikeville	124	J8	Pisek	70	F4
Pensacola	129	J5	Petitot	119	L4	Pikhtovka	84	C5	Pishan	92	E1
Pensamiento	136	E6	Petkula	62	M3	Pila	71	G2	Pishin	95	Q8
Pentecost Island	114	U11	Peto	131	Q7	Pilar	138	E5	Pishin-Lora	92	C3
Pentire Head	52	C4	Petoskey	124	H4	Pilaya	138	D4	Pistayarvi, Ozero	62	P4
Pentland Firth	56	E2	Petra Velikogo, Zaliv	88	C4	Pilcaniyeu	139	B8	Pisticci	69	F5
Pentland Hills	57	E5	Petre Bay	115	F6	Pilcomayo	138	D4	Pistilfjordur	62	X11
Pen-y-ghent	55	G2	Petrila	73	G3	Pili	75	J4	Pistoia	68	C4
Penza	79	H5	Petrodvorets	63	N7	Pilibhit	92	E3	Pisuerga	66	D1
Penzance	52	B4	Petrolandia	137	K5	Pilica	71	H3	Pit	122	D7
Penzhina	85	V4	Petrolina *Amazonas, Brazil*	136	D4	Pilion	75	G3	Pita	104	C3
Penzhinskaya Guba	85	U4	Petrolina *Pernambuco, Brazil*	137	J5	Pilos	75	F4	Pitanga	138	E4
Peoria	124	F6	Petropavlovsk	84	Ae6	Pilot Point	118	D4	Pitcairn Island	143	J5
Peqin	74	E2	Petropavlovsk-Kamchatskiy	85	T6	Pilsen	70	E4	Pitea	62	J4
Perak	90	C5	Petropolis	138	H4	Pimenta Bueno	136	E6	Pitealven	62	H4
Perama	75	F3	Petrovac	72	E4	Pimentel	137	G4	Pitesti	73	H3
Percival Lakes	112	E3	Petrovsk	79	H5	Pina	67	F2	Pithiviers	64	E4
Perdido, Monte	67	G1	Petrovskoye	78	K5	Pinang *Malaysia*	90	C4	Pitkyaranta	78	E3
Peregrebnoye	84	Ae4	Petrovsk-Zabaykalskiy	84	H6	Pinang *Malaysia*	90	C4	Pitlochry	57	E4
Pereira	136	B3	Petrozavodsk	78	E3	Pinarbasi *Turkey*	76	E2	Pitlyar	84	Ae3
Perelazovskiy	79	G6	Petsamo	62	P2	Pinarbasi *Turkey*	77	G3	Pitt Island *Canada*	118	K5
Perello	67	G2	Petteril	55	G2	Pinar del Rio	132	F3	Pitt Island *New Zealand*	115	F7
Peremyshlyany	71	L4	Petukhovo	84	Ae5	Pinarhisar	76	B2	Pittsburg	124	C8
Perenjori	112	D4	Petworth	53	G4	Pinawa	123	S2	Pittsburgh	125	K6
PereslavlZalesskiy	78	F4	Peureula	90	B5	Pincher Creek	122	H3	Pittsfield	124	E7
Perevolotskiy	79	J5	Pevek	85	W3	Pindare	137	H4	Pitt Strait	115	F7
Pereyaslavka	88	E2	Pewsey, Vale of	52	F3	Pindhos Oros	75	F3	Piui	138	G4
Pergamino	139	D6	Peza	78	H2	Pindi Gheb	92	D2	Piura	136	A5
Pergamum	76	B3	Pezenas	65	E7	Pine Bluff	128	F3	Pjorsa	62	N2
Perhojoki	62	K5	Pezinok	71	G4	Pine Bluffs	123	M7	Pjorsa	62	V12
Peri	77	J3	Pezmog	78	J3	Pine City	124	D4	Placentia Bay	121	Q8
Peribonca	121	M8	Pfaffenhofen	70	D4	Pine Creek	112	G1	Placer	91	G3
Peribonca	125	Q2	Pfarrkirchen	70	E4	Pine Creek Lake	128	E3	Placerville	126	B1
Perigueux	65	D6	Pforzheim	70	C4	Pinedale	123	K6	Placido do Castro	136	D6
Perija, Sierra de	136	C2	Phalaborwa	108	F4	Pine Falls	119	R5	Plackoviea	73	G5
Perim	96	F10	Phalodi	92	D3	Pinega *Russia*	78	G3	Plainview	127	M3
Peris	73	J3	Phaltan	92	D5	Pinega *Russia*	78	G3	Plaka	75	H2
Peristrema	76	F3	Phangan, Ko	93	K6	Pine Island Bay	141	T4	Plakenska Planina	73	F5
Perito Moreno	139	B9	Phangnga	93	J7	Pine Pass	119	L5	Plampang	91	F7
Peritoro	137	J4	Phan Rang	93	L6	Pine Point	119	N3	Plana	70	E4
Perlas, Punta de	132	F8	Phan Thiet	93	L6	Pine Ridge	123	N6	Planeta Rica	133	K10
Perlez	72	F3	Phatthalung	93	K7	Pinerolo	68	A3	Plankinton	123	Q6
Perm	78	K4	Phenix City	129	K4	Pines, Lake O' the	128	E4	Plant City	129	L7
Pernambuca	137	K5	Phet Buri	93	J6	Pinetop-Lakeside	127	H3	Plaquemine	128	G5
Pernik	73	G4	Phetchabun, Thiu Khao	93	K5	Pineville	124	J8	Plasencia	66	C2
Peronne	64	E4	Philadelphia *Mississippi*	128	H4	Pingbian	93	K4	Plastun	88	F3
Perote	131	L8	Philadelphia *Pennsylvania*	125	N6	Pingdingshan	93	M2	Platani	69	D7
Perote, Cofre de	131	L8	Philip	123	P5	Pingelly	112	D5	Plata, Rio de la	139	E6
Perouse Strait, La	88	J3	Philip Island	111	Q7	Pingguo	93	L4	Plati	75	G2
Perpignan	65	E7	Philippeville	64	F3	Pingjiang	93	M3	Plato	136	C2
Perran Bay	52	B4	Philippines	91	G2	Ping, Mae Nam	93	J5	Platte	123	R7
Perranporth	52	B4	Philippine Sea	91	G1	Pingquan	93	L1	Platteville	124	E5
Perros-Guirec	64	B4	Philipstown	108	D6	Pingtan Dao	87	M6	Plattling	70	E4
Perry *Canada*	119	Q2	Phillipsburg	123	Q8	Ping-tung	87	N7	Plattsburgh	125	P4
Perry *Florida*	129	L5	Philpots Island	120	L2	Pingwu	93	K2	Plattsmouth	124	C6
Perry *Oklahoma*	128	D2	Phnom Penh	93	K6	Pingxiang *Guangxi, China*	93	L4	Plauen	70	E3
Perryton	127	M2	Phoenix	126	F4	Pingxiang *Jiangxi, China*	93	M3	Plav	72	E4
Perryville *Alaska*	118	D4	Phoenix Islands	111	U2	Pingyang	87	N6	Playa Azul	130	H8
Perryville *Missouri*	124	F8	Phong Saly	93	K4	Pingyao	87	L4	Pleasanton	128	C6
Persembe	77	G2	Phong Tho	93	K4	Pingyi	87	M4	Pleihari	90	E6
Perseverancia	136	E6	Phu Cuong	93	L6	Pingyin	87	M4	Pleiku	93	L6
Persian Gulf	97	K3	Phu Dien Chau	93	L5	Pinhao	66	C2	Plenty, Bay of	115	F2
Pertek	77	H3	Phuket	93	J7	Pinhel	66	C2	Plentywood	123	M3
Perth *Australia*	112	D5	Phuket, Ko	93	J7	Pini	90	B5	Plesetsk	78	G3
Perth *Canada*	125	M4	Phulabani	92	F4	Pinios *Greece*	75	F4	Plessisville	125	Q3
Perth *U.K.*	57	E4	Phu Ly	93	L4	Pinios *Greece*	75	F3	Pleszew	71	G3
Perth-Andover	125	S3	Phuoc Le	93	L6	Pinnes, Akra	75	H2	Pletipi Lake	121	M7
Pertominsk	78	F3	Phu Tho	93	L4	Pinos, Point	126	B2	Pleven	73	H4
Pertugskiy	78	H4	Phyajoki	62	L4	Pinotepa Nacional	131	L9	Plitra	75	G4
Pertuis Breton	65	C5	Piacenza	68	B3	Pinrang	91	F6	Pljevlja	72	E4
Peru	136	B5	Piana	69	B4	Pins, Ile des	114	X17	Plock	71	H2
Peru *Illinois*	124	F6	Pianosa, Isola	69	C4	Pinsk	71	M2	Plockenstein	70	E4
Peru *Indiana*	124	G6	Piatra Neamt	73	J2	Pintados	138	C4	Ploermel	65	B5
Peru-Chile Trench	143	L5	Piaui	137	J5	Pinta, Isla	136	A7	Ploiesti	73	J3
Perugia	68	D4	Piaui, Serra do	137	J5	Pinto	138	D5	Plomb du Cantal	65	E6
Perushtitsa	73	H4	Piave	68	D3	Pinyug	78	H3	Plombieres	65	G5
Pervari	77	K4	Piaya	90	F7	Pioche	126	E2	Ploner See	70	D1
Pervomaskiy	79	K5	Piazza Armerina	69	E7	Piombino	69	C4	Plonsk	71	J2
Pervomaysk *Russia*	78	G5	Pibor	103	F6				Ploty	70	F2

Prasto 63 E9
Prata 138 G3
Prato 68 C4
Pratt 127 N2
Pravets 73 G4
Pravia 66 C1
Predazzo 68 C2
Predcal 73 H3
Predeal, Pasul 73 H3
Predivinsk 84 E5
Predlitz 68 D2
Premer 113 K5
Premuda 72 C3
Prenai 71 K1
Prentice 124 E4
Prenzlau 70 E2
Preobrazhenka 84 H5
Preparis 93 H6
Preparis North Channel 93 H5
Preparis South Channel 93 H6
Prerov 71 G4
Prescot 55 G3
Prescott *Arizona* 126 F3
Prescott *Arkansas* 128 F4
Prescott Island 120 G3
Preseli, Mynydd 52 C3
Preservation Inlet 115 A7
Presevo 73 F4
Presho 123 Q6
Presidencia Roque Saenz Pena 138 D5
Presidente Dutra 137 J4
Presidente Epitacio 138 F4
Presidente Prudente 138 E4
Presidio 127 K6
Preslav 73 J4
Presnovka 84 Ae6
Presov 71 J4
Prespansko Jezero 75 F2
Presque Isle 125 S3
Pressburg 71 G4
Prestatyn 55 F3
Presteigne 52 D2
Preston *U.K.* 55 G3
Preston *Minnesota* 124 D5
Preston *Missouri* 124 D8
Prestonburg 124 J8
Prestonpans 57 F5
Prestwick 57 F4
Pretoria 108 E5
Preveza 75 F3
Prey Veng 93 L6
Pribilof Islands 118 Ad8
Pribinic 72 D3
Pribram 70 F4
Price 126 G1
Price, Cape 93 H6
Prichard 129 H5
Priego 66 E2
Priego de Cordoba 66 D4
Prieska 108 D5
Priest Lake 122 F3
Priest River 122 F3
Prievidza 71 H4
Prignitz 70 D2
Prijedor 72 D3
Prikaspiyskaya Nizmennost 79 J6
Prilep 73 F5
Priluki *Russia* 78 G3
Priluki *Ukraine* 79 E5
Primavera 141 V6
Primorsk *Azerbaijan* 79 H7
Primorsk *Ukraine* 79 F6
Primorsk *Russia* 79 H6
Primorsk *Russia* 63 N6
Primorskiy Kray 88 E3
Primorsko 73 J4
Primorsko-Akhtarsk 79 F6
Primrose Lake 119 P5
Prince Albert *Canada* 119 P5
Prince Albert *South Africa* 108 D6
Prince Albert Peninsula 119 N1
Prince Albert Road 108 D6
Prince Albert Sound 119 N1
Prince Alfred, Cape 120 B3
Prince Charles Island 120 L4
Prince Charles Mountains 141 E4
Prince Edward Island 121 P8
Prince Edward Islands 142 C6
Prince George 119 L5
Prince Gustav Adolph Sea 120 E2
Prince of Wales, Cape *Canada* 121 M5
Prince of Wales, Cape *U.S.A.* 118 B2
Prince of Wales Island *Australia* 114 C4
Prince of Wales Island *Canada* 120 G3
Prince of Wales Island *U.S.A.* 118 J4
Prince of Wales Strait 119 M1
Prince Patrick Island 120 B2
Prince Regent Inlet 120 H3
Prince Rupert 118 J5
Princes Risborough 53 G3
Princess Astrid Coast 141 A4
Princess Charlotte Bay 113 J1
Princess Elizabeth Land 141 F4
Princess Marie Bay 120 L2
Princethorpe 53 F2
Princeton *Canada* 122 D3
Princeton *Illinois* 124 F6
Princeton *Kentucky* 124 G8
Princeton *Missouri* 124 D6
Princeton *W. Virginia* 125 K8
Prince William Sound 118 F3
Principe 105 G5
Prineville 122 D5
Prins Karls Forland 80 C2
Prinzapolca 132 E8
Priozersk 63 P6
Pripet Marshes 79 D5
Pripyat 71 M2
Pristina 73 F4
Pritzwalk 70 E2
Privas 65 F6
Privolzhskaya Vozvyshennost 79 H5
Prizzi 69 D7
Prnjavor 72 D3
Probolinggo 90 E7
Proddatur 92 E6
Progreso 131 Q7
Prokhladnyy 79 G7
Prokletije 74 E1
Prokopyevsk 84 D6
Prokuplje 73 F4
Proletarsk 79 G6
Prome 93 J5
Proprad 71 J4
Propria 137 K6
Propriano 69 B5
Prorva 79 J6
Prosna 71 G3
Prospect 122 C6
Prosperous 59 J6
Prostejov 71 G4
Provence 65 G7
Providence *Seychelles* 82 D7
Providence *U.S.A.* 125 Q6
Providence, Cape *Canada* 120 D3
Providence, Cape *New Zealand* 115 A7
Providencia 136 B4
Providencia, Isla de 132 G8
Provideniya 81 V3
Provincetown 125 Q5
Provins 64 E4
Provo 122 J7
Prudhoe 55 H2
Prudhoe Bay 118 F1
Prum 70 B3
Pruszkow 71 J2
Prut 73 K2
Prutul 73 J2
Pruzhany 71 L2
Pryazha 78 E3
Prydz Bay 141 F5
Pryor 128 E2
Przechlewo 71 G2
Przemysl 71 K4
Przeworsk 71 K3
Przhevalsk 86 D3
Przysucha 71 J3
Psakhna 75 G3
Psara 75 H3
Pskov 63 Q8
Pskovskoye, Ozero 63 M7
Ptolemais 75 F2
Ptuj 72 C2
Puan 87 P4
Pucallpa 136 C5
Pucarani 138 C3
Pudai 95 R6
Pudasjarvi 62 M4
Puddletown 52 E4
Pudnya 63 N8
Pudozh 78 F3
Pudsey 55 H3
Puduchcheri 92 E6
Pudukkottai 92 E6
Puebla 131 K8
Puebla de Don Rodrigo 66 D3
Puebla de Sanabria 66 C1
Puebla de Trives 66 C1
Pueblo 127 K1
Pueblo Hundido 138 B5
Pueblo Nuevo 136 D1
Puelen 139 C7
Puente Alto 139 C6
Puerto Acosta 138 C3
Puerto Aisen 139 B9
Puerto Asis 136 B3
Puerto Ayacucho 136 D2
Puerto Ayora 136 A7
Puerto Barrios 132 C7
Puerto Cabello 136 D1
Puerto Cabezas 132 F7
Puerto Carreno 136 D2
Puerto Casado 138 E4
Puerto Coig 139 C10
Puerto Cortes *Costa Rica* 132 F10
Puerto Cortes *Honduras* 132 D7
Puerto Cumarebo 136 D1
Puerto del Rosario 100 C3
Puerto de Pollensa 67 H3
Puerto Deseado 139 C9
Puerto Escondido 131 L10
Puerto Estrella 136 C1
Puerto Eten 136 B5
Puerto Guarani 138 E4
Puerto Juarez 131 R7
Puerto La Cruz 136 E1
Puerto-Lapice 66 E3
Puerto Leguizamo 136 C4
Puerto Libertad 126 F6
Puertollano 66 D3
Puerto Lobos 139 C8
Puerto Madryn 139 C8
Puerto Maldonado 136 D6
Puerto Merazan 132 D8
Puerto Montt 139 B8
Puerto Natales 139 B10
Puerto Ordaz 133 R10
Puerto Paez 136 D2
Puerto Penasco 126 F5
Puerto Pico 138 E5
Puerto Plata 133 M5
Puerto Portillo 136 C5
Puerto Princesa 91 F4
Puerto Rey 132 J10
Puerto Rico *Bolivia* 136 D6
Puerto Rico *U.S.A.* 133 P5
Puerto Rico Trench 133 P5
Puerto San Antonio Oeste 139 C8
Puerto Santa Cruz 139 C10
Puerto Sastre 138 E4
Puerto Siles 136 D6
Puerto Suarez 138 E3
Puerto Tejado 136 B3
Puerto Vallarta 130 G7
Puerto Varas 139 B8
Puerto Villazon 136 E6
Puesto Arturo 136 C4
Pueyrredan, Lago 139 B9
Pugachev 79 H5
Pugachevo 88 J1
Pugal 92 D3
Puger 90 E7
Puget-Theniers 65 G7
Pui 73 G3
Puigcerda 67 G1
Pujehun 104 C4
Pukaki, Lake 115 C6
Pukchong 88 B5
Puke 74 E1
Pukekohe 115 E2
Pukeuri 115 C6
Puksa 78 F3
Pula 72 B3
Pular, Cerro 138 C4
Pulaski *New York* 125 M5
Pulaski *Tennessee* 129 J3
Pulaski *Virginia* 125 K8
Pulau Jos Sodarso 114 B3
Pulaupunjung 90 D6
Pulborough 53 G4
Pu-li 87 N7
Pulicat Lake 92 F6
Pulkkila 62 L4
Pullman 122 F4
Pulo Anna 91 J5
Pulog, Mount 91 G2
Pulonga 78 G2
Pulpito, Punta 126 G7
Pultusk 71 J2
Pulumur 77 H3
Pumasillo, Cerro 136 C6
Pumsaint 52 D2
Puna, Isla 136 A4
Punakha 93 G3
Pune 92 D5
Pungsan 88 B5
Punjab 92 E2
Puno 138 B3
Punta Alta 139 D7
Punta Arenas 139 B10
Punta, Cerro de 133 P5
Punta de Diaz 138 B5
Punta Delgada 139 D8
Punta Delgado 139 C10
Punta Gorda 132 C6
Punta Prieta 126 E6
Puntarenas 132 E9
Punta Saavedra 139 B7
Punto Fijo 136 C1
Puolanka 62 M4
Puquio 136 C6
Puquios 138 C5
Pur 84 B3
Pura 84 D2
Purari 114 D3
Purbeck, Isle of 53 E4
Purchena 66 E4
Purdy Islands 114 D2
Purepero 130 J8
Puri 92 G5
Purnia 93 G3
Pursat 93 K6
Purtuniq 120 M5
Puruliya 92 G4
Purus 136 E4
Puruvesi 63 N6
Purwakarta 90 D7
Purwokert 90 D7
Puryong 88 B4
Pusa 63 M8
Pusan 89 B8
Pushkino 94 J2
Pushlakhta 78 F3
Pusht-i-Rud 95 R6
Pustoshka 63 N8
Putao 93 J3
Putaruru 115 E3
Putian 87 M6
Putila 71 L5
Puting, Tanjung 90 E6
Putnok 72 F1
Putorana, Gory 84 F3
Putorino 115 F3
Puttalam 92 E7
Puttgarden 70 D1
Putumayo 136 C4
Putusibau 90 E5
Puulavesi 63 M6
Puuwai 126 Q10
Pu Xian 93 M1
Puyko 84 Ae3
Puyo 136 B4
Puzla 78 J3
Pweto 107 E4
Pwllheli 52 C2
Pyaozero, Ozero 62 P3
Pyapon 93 J5
Pyasina 84 D2
Pyasinado 84 B3
Pyasino, Ozero 84 D3
Pyatigorsk 79 G7
Pygmalion Point 93 H7
Pyhajarvi *Finland* 62 L5
Pyhajarvi *Finland* 62 L5
Pyhajarvi *Turku-Pori, Finland* 63 K6
Pyhajoki 62 L4
Pyhaselka 62 N5
Pyinmana 93 J5
Pylkaram 84 C4
Pyonggok-tong 89 B7
Pyonghae-ri 89 B7
Pyongyang 87 P4
Pyramid Lake 122 E7
Pyrenees 65 D7
Pyrzyce 70 F2
Pytalovo 63 M8

Q

Qaamiyat, Al 97 J7
Qabr Hud 97 J8
Qadimah 96 D5
Qadub 97 P10
Qaemshahr 95 L3
Qagan Tolgoi 87 K4
Qaidam Pendi 93 H1
Qaidam Shan 93 J1
Qaisar 94 S4
Qala Adras Kand 95 R5
Qalaen Nahl 96 B10
Qalamat ar Rakabah 97 L6
Qalamat Faris 97 K6
Qalansiyah 97 P10
Qalat 92 C2
Qalat Bishah 96 F6
Qalat Salih 94 H6
Qalat Sukkar 94 H6
Qala Vali 95 R4
Qaleh-ye Now 95 R4
Qamar, Ghubbat al 97 L8
Qamar, Jabal al 97 L8
Qaminis 101 K2
Qamsar 95 K5
Qandala 103 J5
Qapqal 86 E3
Qarabagh 95 Q4
Qara, Jabal al 97 M8
Qaratshuk 94 F3
Qardho 103 J6
Qareh Aqaj 94 H3
Qareh Su 94 H2
Qareh Su 94 H5
Qarqan He 86 F4
Qarqi 86 F3
Qaryat al Ulya 97 H3
Qasab 77 K4
Qasa Murg 95 S4
Qasr Amij 77 J6
Qasr-e-Qand 95 Q8
Qasr-e-Shirin 94 G4
Qatabah 96 G10
Qatah 77 J5
Qatana 94 C5
Qatar 97 K4
Qatrana 94 C6
Qattara Depression 102 E2
Qattara, Munkhafed el 102 E2
Qayen 95 P5
Qazvin 95 K3
Qeisum 96 A3
Qena 103 F2
Qeshm *Iran* 95 N8
Qeshm *Iran* 95 N8
Qeydar 94 J3
Qeys 95 L8
Qezel Owzan 94 J3
Qeziot 94 B6
Qianan 87 N2
Qianjiang 93 L3
Qianwei 87 N3
Qianxi 93 L3
Qianxinan 93 K3
Qiaowan 86 H3
Qidong *Hunan, China* 93 M3
Qidong *Jiangsu, China* 87 N5
Qiemo 92 G1
Qihe 87 M4
Qihreg 87 L3
Qijiaojing 86 F3
Qikou 87 M4
Qila Ladgasht 92 B3
Qila Saifullah 92 C2
Qilian Shan 86 H4
Qinab, Wadi 97 J8
Qingan 88 A2
Qingdao 87 N4
Qinggang 87 P2
Qinghai 93 J2
Qinghai Hu 93 K1
Qinghai Nanshan 93 J1
Qinghe 88 B2
Qing Xian 87 M4
Qingyang 93 L1
Qingyuan *Liaoning, China* 87 N3
Qingyuan *Zhejiang, China* 87 M6

Rebrovo	**73**	G4
Rebun-to	**88**	H3
Recanati	**68**	D4
Recea	**73**	G3
Recherche, Archipelago of the	**112**	E5
Rechitsa	**79**	E5
Rechna Doab	**92**	D2
Recife	**137**	L5
Recklinghausen	**70**	B3
Recknitz	**70**	E2
Reconquista	**138**	E5
Recreio	**136**	F5
Red *Canada*	**123**	R2
Red *U.S.A.*	**128**	F5
Redalen	**63**	D6
Red Bay	**121**	Q7
Redbird	**123**	M6
Red Bluff	**122**	C7
Red Bluff Lake	**127**	L5
Redcar	**55**	H2
Redcliffe	**113**	L4
Red Cloud	**123**	Q7
Red Deer *Canada*	**122**	G2
Red Deer *Canada*	**122**	H1
Red Deer *Canada*	**123**	J2
Red Deer *Saskatchewan, Canada*	**119**	Q5
Redding	**122**	C7
Redditch	**53**	F2
Redencao	**137**	J5
Redfield	**123**	Q5
Redhakhol	**92**	F4
Redhill	**53**	G3
Red Hills	**127**	N2
Red Lake *Canada*	**123**	S2
Red Lake *Canada*	**123**	T2
Red Lake *U.S.A.*	**124**	C3
Red Lake *U.S.A.*	**123**	R4
Red Lodge	**123**	K5
Redmond	**122**	D5
Redon	**65**	B5
Redondela	**66**	B1
Redondo	**66**	C3
Red Rock	**124**	F2
Redruth	**52**	B4
Red Sea	**103**	G3
Red Tank	**113**	K5
Red Wharf Bay	**54**	E3
Red Wing	**124**	D4
Redwood City	**126**	A2
Reed City	**124**	H5
Reedsport	**122**	B6
Ree, Lough	**58**	G5
Reetton	**115**	C5
Refahiye	**77**	H3
Refresco	**138**	C5
Rega	**70**	F2
Regen	**70**	E4
Regensburg	**70**	E4
Reggane	**100**	F3
Reggio di Calabria	**69**	E6
Reggio nell Amelia	**68**	C3
Regina *Brazil*	**137**	G3
Regina *Canada*	**123**	M2
Reguengos de Monsaraz	**66**	C3
Rehna	**70**	D2
Rehoboth	**108**	C4
Rehoboth Beach	**125**	N7
Rehovot	**94**	B6
Reidh, Rubha	**56**	C3
Reidsville	**129**	N2
Reiff	**56**	C2
Reigate	**53**	G3
Reighton	**55**	J2
Re, Ile de	**65**	C5
Reims	**64**	F4
Reina Adelaida, Archipielago de la	**139**	B10
Reindeer Lake	**119**	Q4
Reine	**62**	E3
Reinga, Cape	**115**	D1
Reinheimen	**62**	B5
Reinosa	**66**	D1
Reitz	**108**	E5
Relizane	**100**	F1
Remada	**101**	H2
Rembang	**90**	E7
Remeshk	**95**	P8
Remiremont	**65**	G4
Remontnoye	**79**	G6
Remoulins	**65**	F7
Remscheid	**70**	B3
Rena *Norway*	**63**	D6
Rena *Norway*	**63**	D6
Renaix	**64**	E3
Renard Islands	**114**	E4
Rendova Island	**114**	H6
Rendsburg	**70**	C1
Renfrew *Canada*	**125**	M4
Renfrew *U.K.*	**57**	D5
Rengat	**90**	D6
Rengo	**139**	B6
Renish Point	**56**	B3
Renk	**103**	F5
Renmark	**113**	J5
Renmin	**87**	P2
Rennell Island	**114**	K7
Rennes	**64**	C4
Reno *Italy*	**68**	C3
Reno *U.S.A.*	**122**	E8
Reo	**91**	G7
Repetek	**95**	R2
Repolovo	**84**	Ae4
Republican	**123**	R7
Repulse Bay *Australia*	**113**	K3
Repulse Bay *Canada*	**120**	J4
Requena *Peru*	**136**	C5
Requena *Spain*	**67**	F3
Rere	**114**	K6
Resadiye *Turkey*	**76**	B4
Resadiye *Turkey*	**77**	G2
Resen	**73**	F5
Resia, Passo de	**68**	C2
Resistencia	**138**	E5
Resita	**73**	F3
Resolution Island *Canada*	**121**	P5
Resolution Island *New Zealand*	**115**	A6
Resolution Lake	**121**	P6
Restigouche	**125**	S3
Retalhuleu	**132**	B7
Rethel	**64**	F4
Rethimnon	**75**	H5
Retiche, Alpi	**68**	C2
Retsag	**72**	E2
Retuerta de Bullaque	**66**	D3
Reunion	**109**	L7
Reus	**67**	G2
Reuss	**68**	B2
Reut	**73**	J2
Reutlingen	**70**	C4
Revel	**65**	D7
Revelstoke	**122**	E2
Reventador, Volcan	**136**	B4
Revillagigedo Island	**118**	J5
Revillagigedo, Islas	**130**	D8
Rewa	**92**	F4
Rewari	**92**	E3
Rexburg	**122**	J6
Reyes, Point	**122**	C9
Reyhanli	**77**	G4
Rey, Isla del	**132**	H10
Reykjaheidi	**62**	W12
Reykjahhd	**62**	W12
Reykjanesta	**62**	T13
Reykjavik	**62**	U12
Reynivellir *Iceland*	**62**	U12
Reynivellir *Iceland*	**62**	W12
Reynosa	**128**	C7
Rezekne	**63**	M8
Rhatikon Pratigau	**68**	B2
Rhayader	**52**	D2
Rheda-Wiedenbruck	**70**	C3
Rhee	**53**	G2
Rhein	**70**	B3
Rheine	**70**	B2
Rhewl	**55**	F3
Rhiconich	**56**	D2
Rhine	**64**	G4
Rhinelander	**124**	F4
Rhino Camp	**107**	F2
Rhir, Cap	**100**	D2
Rho	**68**	B3
Rhode Island	**125**	Q6
Rhodes	**75**	J4
Rhodopi Planina	**73**	G4
Rhondda	**52**	D3
Rhone	**65**	F7
Rhoose	**52**	D3
Rhosneigr	**55**	E3
Rhuddlan	**55**	F3
Rhum	**57**	B3
Rhum, Sound of	**57**	B4
Rhydaman	**52**	C3
Rhyl	**55**	F3
Rhynie	**56**	F3
Riachao do Jacuipe	**138**	K6
Riacho de Santana	**138**	J6
Riano	**66**	D1
Riansares	**66**	E3
Riau, Kepulauan	**90**	C5
Riaza	**66**	E2
Ribadeo	**66**	C1
Ribadesella	**66**	D1
Ribas do Rio Pardo	**138**	F4
Ribat	**95**	R5
Ribatejo	**66**	B3
Ribble	**55**	G2
Ribe	**63**	C9
Ribeirao Preto	**138**	G4
Ribeiro do Pombal	**137**	K6
Riberac	**65**	D6
Riberalta	**136**	D6
Ribnica	**72**	C3
Ribnitz-Damgarten	**70**	E1
Riccall	**55**	H3
Rice Lake *Canada*	**125**	L4
Rice Lake *U.S.A.*	**124**	E4
Richard Collinson Inlet	**119**	N1
Richards Island	**118**	H2
Richardson	**128**	D4
Richardson Mountains	**118**	H2
Richelieu	**125**	P4
Richfield	**126**	F1
Richland	**122**	E4
Richlands	**125**	K8
Richmond *Australia*	**113**	J3
Richmond *New Zealand*	**115**	D4
Richmond *South Africa*	**108**	D6
Richmond *Greater London, U.K.*	**53**	G3
Richmond *North Yorkshire, U.K.*	**55**	H2
Richmond *Indiana*	**124**	H7
Richmond *Kentucky*	**124**	H8
Richmond *Virginia*	**125**	M8
Richmond Range	**115**	D4
Rickmansworth	**53**	G3
Ricla	**67**	F2
Ricobayo, Embalse de	**66**	D2
Ridgecrest	**126**	D3
Ridgeland	**129**	M4
Ridgway	**125**	L6
Riding Mountain	**123**	P2
Ridsdale	**57**	F5
Ried	**68**	D1
Rienza	**68**	C2
Riesa	**70**	E3
Riesco, Isla	**139**	B10
Rietfontein	**108**	D4
Rieti	**69**	D4
Rifle	**123**	L8
Rifstangi	**62**	W11
Riga	**63**	L8
Riga, Gulf of	**63**	K8
Rigan	**95**	P7
Rigistan	**92**	B2
Rigolet	**121**	Q7
Rihab, Ar	**94**	G6
Rihand	**92**	F4
Riiser-Larsen Sea	**141**	B5
Rijeka	**72**	C3
Rika	**71**	K4
Rika, Wadi al	**96**	G5
Rimah, Wadi al	**96**	E3
Rimal, Ar	**97**	L6
Rimavska Sobota	**71**	J4
Rimbo	**63**	H7
Rimini	**68**	D3
Rimna	**73**	J3
Rimnicu Sarat	**73**	J3
Rimnicu Vilcea	**73**	H3
Rimouski	**125**	R2
Rinca	**91**	F7
Rinchinlhumbe	**86**	H1
Ringe	**63**	D9
Ringebu	**63**	D6
Ringgold Isles	**114**	S8
Ringkobing	**63**	C8
Ringkobing Fjord	**63**	C9
Ringmer	**53**	H4
Ringselet	**62**	L3
Ringvassoy	**62**	H2
Ringwood	**53**	F4
Rinia	**75**	H4
Rinjani, Gunung	**90**	F7
Rinns Point	**57**	B5
Riobamba	**136**	B4
Rio Branco *Brazil*	**136**	D5
Rio Branco *Uruguay*	**138**	F6
Rio Bravo	**128**	D8
Rio Bueno	**139**	B8
Rio Caribe	**136**	E1
Rio Claro	**136**	E1
Rio Colorado	**139**	D7
Rio Cuarto	**138**	D6
Rio de Janeiro *Brazil*	**138**	H4
Rio de Janeiro *Brazil*	**138**	H4
Rio de Oro, Baie de	**100**	B4
Rio Gallegos	**139**	C10
Rio Grande *Argentina*	**139**	C10
Rio Grande *Brazil*	**138**	F6
Rio Grande *U.S.A.*	**130**	H6
Rio Grande City	**128**	C7
Rio Grande de Santiago	**130**	G7
Rio Grande do Norte	**137**	K5
Rio Grande do Sul	**138**	F5
Riohacha	**136**	C1
Rio Hato	**132**	G10
Rio Lagartos	**131**	Q7
Riom	**65**	E6
Riom-es-Montagnes	**65**	E6
Rio Mulatos	**138**	C3
Rionegro	**136**	C2
Rio Negro *Brazil*	**138**	G5
Rio Negro *Spain*	**66**	C1
Rio Negro, Embalse del	**138**	E6
Rio Negro, Pantanal do	**138**	E3
Rioni	**77**	J1
Rio Pardo de Minas	**138**	H3
Rio Primero	**138**	D6
Rio Sao Goncalo	**138**	H4
Riosucio *Colombia*	**136**	B2
Riosucio *Colombia*	**136**	B2
Rio Verde	**138**	F3
Ripley *Ohio*	**124**	J7
Ripley *Tennessee*	**128**	H3
Ripley *W. Virginia*	**125**	K7
Ripoll	**67**	H1
Ripon	**55**	H2
Ripponden	**55**	H3
Risca	**52**	D3
Rishiri-to	**88**	H3
Rishon le Zion	**94**	B6
Risle	**64**	D4
Risor	**63**	C7
Risoyhamn	**62**	F2
Ritchie's Archipelago	**93**	H6
Ritter, Mount	**122**	E9
Ritzville	**122**	E4
Riva	**68**	C3
Rivas	**132**	E9
Rivera	**138**	E6
River Falls	**124**	D4
Riverina	**113**	K5
Riversdale	**108**	D6
Riverside	**126**	D4
Riverton *Australia*	**113**	H5
Riverton *Canada*	**123**	R2
Riverton *New Zealand*	**115**	B7
Riverton *U.S.A.*	**123**	K6
Riviere-du-Loup	**125**	R3
Rivne	**79**	D5
Rivoli	**68**	A3
Riwaka	**115**	D4
Riwoqe	**93**	J2
Riyan	**97**	J9
Rize	**77**	J2
Rizhskiy Zaliv	**63**	K8
Rizokarpaso	**76**	F5
Rjukan	**63**	C7
Rjuven	**63**	B7
Roa	**66**	E2
Road Town	**133**	Q5
Roan Fell	**57**	F5
Roanne	**65**	F5
Roanoke *N. Carolina*	**129**	P2
Roanoke *Virginia*	**125**	L8
Roanoke Rapids	**129**	P2
Roan Plateau	**123**	K8
Robat	**95**	R6
Robat Karim	**95**	K4
Robat Thand	**95**	Q7
Robel	**70**	E2
Robert Brown, Cape	**120**	K4
Roberton	**57**	E5
Robertsbridge	**53**	H4
Robertsfors	**62**	J4
Robert S. Kerr Reservoir	**128**	E3
Robertson Range	**112**	E3
Robertsport	**104**	C4
Roberval	**125**	P2
Robinson	**124**	G7
Robinson Ranges	**112**	D4
Robleda	**66**	C2
Robledollano	**66**	D3
Robles La Paz	**136**	C1
Roblin	**123**	P2
Robore	**138**	E3
Rob Roy Island	**114**	H5
Robson, Mount	**119**	M5
Roca, Cabo da	**66**	B3
Roca Partida, Isla	**130**	C8
Roca Partida, Punta	**131**	M8
Roccella Ionica	**69**	F6
Rocha	**139**	F6
Rocha da Gale, Barragem	**66**	C4
Rochdale	**55**	G3
Rochechouart	**65**	D6
Rochefort	**65**	C6
Rochelle	**124**	F6
Rochester *Kent, U.K.*	**53**	H3
Rochester *Northumberland, U.K.*	**57**	F5
Rochester *New Hamshire*	**125**	Q5
Rochester *New York*	**125**	M5
Rochester *Winconsin*	**124**	D4
Rochford	**53**	H3
Rochfortbridge	**59**	H6
Rock	**124**	F5
Rockefeller Plateau	**141**	R3
Rock Falls	**124**	F6
Rockford	**124**	F5
Rockglen	**123**	L3
Rockhampton	**113**	L3
Rockingham *Australia*	**112**	D5
Rockingham *U.S.A.*	**129**	N3
Rockingham Bay	**113**	K2
Rock Island	**124**	E6
Rockland *Maine*	**125**	R4
Rockland *Michigan*	**124**	F3
Rock Springs *Montana*	**123**	L4
Rock Springs *Wyoming*	**123**	K7
Rockwood	**125**	R4
Rocky Ford	**127**	L1
Rocky Mount	**129**	P3
Rocky Mountain House	**119**	N5
Rocky Mountains	**116**	G3
Rocroi	**64**	F4
Rodberg	**63**	C6
Rodby	**63**	D9
Rodeby	**63**	F8
Rodel	**56**	B3
Roden	**52**	E2
Rodez	**65**	E6
Rodhos *Greece*	**75**	J4
Rodhos *Greece*	**75**	K4
Rodi Garganico	**69**	E5
Roding	**53**	H3
Rodinga	**113**	G3
Rodna	**73**	H2
Rodnei, Muntii	**73**	H2
Rodney, Cape *New Zealand*	**115**	E2
Rodney, Cape *U.S.A.*	**118**	B3
Rodonit, Kep i	**74**	E2
Rodosto	**76**	B2
Roebuck Bay	**112**	E2
Roermond	**64**	F3
Roeselare	**64**	E3
Roes Welcome Sound	**120**	J5
Rogachev	**79**	E5
Rogaland	**63**	B7
Rogatin	**71**	L4
Rogers	**128**	E2
Rogers, Mount	**125**	K8
Roggeveld Berge	**108**	D6
Rogliano	**68**	B4
Rognan	**62**	F3
Rogozno	**71**	G2
Rohri	**92**	C3
Rohtak	**92**	E3
Rois Bheinn	**57**	C3
Rojas	**139**	D6
Rojo, Cabo *Mexico*	**131**	L7
Rojo, Cabo *U.S.A.*	**133**	P6
Rokan	**90**	C5

Saginaw Bay **124** J5
Sagiz *Kazakhstan* **79** J6
Sagiz *Kazakhstan* **79** J6
Sagiz *Kazakhstan* **79** J6
Sagkaya **77** F4
Saglek Bay **121** P6
Sagone, Golfe de **69** B4
Sagres **66** B4
Saguache **127** J1
Sagua la Grande **132** G3
Saguenay **121** M8
Sagunto **67** F3
Sahagun **66** D1
Sahand, Kuh-e **94** H3
Sahara **98** C4
Saharanpur **92** E3
Sahin **76** B2
Sahiwal *Pakistan* **92** D2
Sahiwal *Pakistan* **92** D2
Sahm **97** N4
Sahra al Hijarah **94** G6
Sahuaripa **127** H6
Sahuayo **130** H7
Sa Huynh **93** L6
Sahy **71** H4
Saibai Island **114** C3
Saicla **94** B5
Saida *Algeria* **100** F2
Saida *Lebanon* **76** F6
Saidabad **95** M7
Saidapet **92** F6
Saidor **114** D3
Saidpur **93** G3
Saigon **93** L6
Saijo **89** D9
Saimaa **63** M6
Saimbeyli **77** G3
Saindak **95** Q7
Saindezh **94** H3
Saint Abb's Head **57** B5
Saint-Affrique **65** E7
Saint-Agathe-des-Monts **125** N3
Saint Agnes *U.K.* **52** B4
Saint Agnes *U.K.* **52** K5
Saint-Agreve **65** F6
Saint Albans *U.K.* **53** G3
Saint Albans *Vermont* **125** P4
Saint Albans *W. Virginia* **124** K7
Saint Alban's Head **53** E4
Saint Aldhelm's **53** E4
Saint-Amand-Montrond **65** E5
Saint-Ambroix **65** F6
Saint Andre, Cap **109** H3
Saint Andrew **53** M7
Saint Andrews *New Zealand* **115** C6
Saint Andrews *U.K.* **57** F4
Saint Andrews Bay **57** F4
Saint-Anne-des-Monts **125** S2
Saint Annes **53** M6
Saint Ann's Bay **132** J5
Saint Ann's Head **52** B3
Saint Anthony *Canada* **121** Q7
Saint Anthony *U.S.A.* **122** J6
Saint Arnaud **115** D4
Saint Asaph **55** F3
Saint Aubin **53** M7
Saint Augustin **121** Q7
Saint Augustine **129** M6
Saint Augustin Saguenay **121** Q7
Saint Austell **52** C4
Saint Austell Bay **52** C4
Saint Bees **55** F2
Saint Bees Head **55** F2
Saint Benoit **109** L7
Saint Blazey **52** C4
Saint Brides **52** B3
Saint Brides Bay **52** B3
Saint-Brieuc **64** B4
Saint-Calais **65** D5
Saint Catherines **125** L5
Saint Catherines Island **129** M5
Saint Catherine's Point **53** F4
Saint-Cere **65** D6
Saint-Chamond **65** F6
Saint Charles **124** E7
Saint Clair, Lake **124** J5
Saint-Claude **65** F5
Saint Clears **52** C3
Saint Cloud *Florida* **129** M6
Saint Cloud *Minnesota* **124** C4
Saint Columb Major **52** C4
Saint Croix *Canada* **125** S4
Saint Croix *Minnesota* **124** D4
Saint Croix *U.S.A.* **133** Q6
Saint Croix Falls **124** D4
Saint David's **52** B3
Saint David's Head **52** B3
Saint-Denis **64** E4
Saint Denis **109** L7
Sainte-Foy-la-Grande **65** D6
Saint Elias, Mount **118** G3
Saint Elias Mountains **118** H3
Sainte-Marie **109** J3
Sainte-Marie-aux-Mines **64** G4
Sainte Marie, Cap **109** J5
Sainte-Maxime **65** G7
Sainte-Menehould **64** F4
Sainte Nazaire **65** B5
Saintes **65** C6
Saintes, Iles des **133** S7
Saintes-Maries-de-la-Mer **65** F7
Saint Etienne **65** F6
Saint Eustatius **133** R6
Saint-Fargeau **65** E5
Saintfield **58** L4
Saint Finan's Bay **59** B9
Saint-Florent, Golfe de **69** B4
Saint-Florentin **65** E4
Saint-Flour **65** E6
Saint Francis *Canada* **125** P4
Saint Francis *Arkansas* **128** G3
Saint Francis *Kansas* **123** P8
Saint Francis, Cape **108** D6
Saint Gallen **68** B2
Saint-Gaudens **65** D7
Saint George *Australia* **113** K4
Saint George *U.S.A.* **126** F2
Saint George, Cape *Canada* **121** Q8
Saint George, Cape *Papua New Guinea* **114** E2
Saint George Head **113** L6
Saint George Island *Alaska* **118** Ae8
Saint George Island *Florida* **129** K6
Saint Georges **125** Q3
Saint George's **133** S8
Saint Georges Bay **121** Q8
Saint George's Channel *Papua New Guinea* **114** E2
Saint George's Channel *U.K.* **52** B3
Saint-Germain **64** D4
Saint-Gildas-de-Rhuys **65** B5
Saint-Gilles-Croix-de-Vie **65** C5
Saint-Girons **65** D7
Saint Gotthard Pass **68** B2
Saint Govan's Head **52** C3
Saint Helena **99** C8
Saint Helena Bay **108** C6
Saint Helens *Australia* **113** K7
Saint Helens *U.K.* **55** G3
Saint Helens, Mount **122** C4
Saint Helens Point **113** K7
Saint Helier **53** M4
Saint Ignace **124** H4
Saint Ignatius **122** G4
Saint Ives *Cambridgeshire, U.K.* **53** G2
Saint Ives *Cornwall, U.K.* **52** B4
Saint Ives Bay **52** B4
Saint James, Cape **118** J5
Saint-Jean-d'Angely **65** C6
Saint-Jean-de-Luz **65** C7
Saint-Jean-de-Maurienne **65** G6
Saint-Jean-de-Monts **65** B5
Saint-Jean, Lac **125** P2
Saint-Jean-Pied-de-Port **65** C7
Saint-Jean-Sur-Richelieu **125** P4
Saint Jerome **125** P4
Saint John *Canada* **121** N8
Saint John *Canada* **121** N8
Saint John *U.K.* **53** M7
Saint John *U.S.A.* **133** Q5
Saint John Bay **121** Q7
Saint John's *Antigua* **133** S6
Saint Johns *Canada* **121** R8
Saint Johns *Arizona* **127** H3
Saint Johns *Florida* **129** M6
Saint Johns *Michigan* **124** H5
Saint Johnsbury **125** Q4
Saint John's Point *Ireland* **58** F3
Saint John's Point *U.K.* **58** L4
Saint Joseph *Arkansas* **128** G5
Saint Joseph *Missouri* **124** C7
Saint Joseph Island **128** D7
Saint-Junien **65** D6
Saint Just **52** B4
Saint Keverne **52** B4
Saint Kitts-Nevis **133** R6
Saint Laurent **137** G2
Saint Lawrence *Australia* **113** K3
Saint Lawrence *Canada* **121** N8
Saint Lawrence *Canada* **121** Q8
Saint Lawrence, Gulf of **121** P8
Saint Lawrence Island **118** B3
Saint Lawrence Seaway **125** N4
Saint Leonard **125** S3
Saint-Leonard-de-Noblat **65** D6
Saint Lewis **121** Q7
Saint Lo **64** C4
Saint Louis *Minnesota* **124** D3
Saint Louis *Missouri* **124** E7
Saint Louis *Senegal* **104** B2
Saint Lucia **133** S6
Saint Lucia, Cape **109** F5
Saint Lucia Channel **133** S7
Saint Lucia, Lake **109** F5
Saint Magnus Bay **56** A1
Saint-Maixent-l'Ecole **65** C5
Saint Malo **64** B4
Saint-Malo, Golfe de **64** C4
Saint Marc **133** L5
Saint-Marcellin **65** F6
Saint Margaret's-at-Cliffe **53** J3
Saint Maries **122** F4
Saint Martin *France* **133** R5
Saint Martin *U.K.* **53** M7
Saint Martin, Lake **123** Q2
Saint Martin's **52** L5
Saint-Martin-Vesubie **65** G6
Saint Mary Peak **113** H5
Saint Marys *Australia* **113** K7
Saint Mary's *Cornwall, U.K.* **52** L5
Saint Mary's *Orkney Islands, U.K.* **56** F2
Saint Marys *Florida* **129** M5
Saint Marys *Pennsylvania* **125** L6
Saint Mary's Loch **57** E5
Saint Matthias Group **114** D2
Saint-Maurice **121** M8
Saint Maurice **125** P3
Saint Mawes **52** B4
Saint-Maximin **65** F7
Saint Michael **118** C3
Saint-Mihiel **64** F4
Saint Monance **57** F4
Saint Moritz **68** B2
Saint Neots **53** G2
Saint Niklaas **64** F3
Saint Ninian's Island **56** A2
Saintogne **65** C6
Saint Omer **64** E3
Saint Pamphile **125** R3
Saint Pascal **125** R3
Saint Paul *Alberta, Canada* **119** N5
Saint Paul *Quebec, Canada* **121** Q7
Saint Paul *Liberia* **104** C4
Saint Paul *U.S.A.* **124** D4
Saint Paul Island **118** Ad8
Saint Peter **124** D4
Saint Peter Port **53** M7
Saint Petersburg *U.S.A.* **129** L7
Saint Petersburg *Russia* **78** E4
Saint Pierre *Canada* **121** Q8
Saint Pierre *France* **109** L7
Saint Pierre Bank **121** Q8
Saint Pol **64** E3
Saint-Pol-de-Leon **64** B4
Saint Polten **68** E1
Saint-Pons **65** E7
Saint-Pourcain **65** E5
Saint Queens Bay **53** M7
Saint-Quentin **64** E4
Saint-Raphael **65** G7
Saint Sampson **53** M7
Saint Sebastian Bay **108** D6
Saint-Seine-l'Abbaye **65** F5
Saint-Sever **65** C7
Saint Simeon **125** R3
Saint Stephen *Canada* **125** S4
Saint Stephen *U.S.A.* **129** N4
Saint Thomas *Canada* **125** K5
Saint Thomas *U.S.A.* **133** Q5
Saint-Tropez **65** G7
Saint-Valery-en-Caux **64** D4
Saint Veit **68** E2
Saint Vincent **133** S6
Saint Vincent, Gulf of **113** H6
Saint Vincent Island **129** K6
Saint Vincent Passage **133** S8
Saint Vith **64** G3
Saint-Yrieix **65** D6
Sajama **138** C3
Sajama, Nevado de **138** C3
Saji-dong **88** B5
Sajir, Ra's **97** L8
Sak **108** D6
Sakai **89** E8
Sakai-Minato **89** D8
Sakakah **96** E2
Sakakawea, Lake **123** P4
Sakami **121** L7
Sakami, Lake **121** L7
Sakania **107** E5
Sakarya *Turkey* **76** D2
Sakarya *Turkey* **76** D2
Sakata **88** G6
Sakete **105** F4
Sakhalin **85** Q6
Sakht-Sar **95** K3
Sakiai **71** K1
Sakmara **79** K5
Sakon Nakhon **93** K5
Sak-shima-shoto **89** G11
Sakti **92** F4
Sal *Cape Verde* **104** L7
Sal *Russia* **79** G6
Sala **63** G7
Salaberry-De-Valleyfield **125** N4
Salaca **63** L8
Salacgriva **63** L8
Sala Consilina **69** E5
Saladillo **139** E7
Salado *Argentina* **139** C6
Salado *Argentina* **138** D5
Salaga **104** E4
Salalah **97** M8
Salama **132** B7
Salamanca *Mexico* **131** J7
Salamanca *Spain* **66** D2
Salamanca *U.S.A.* **125** L5
Salamina **136** B2
Salamis **75** G4
Salamiyah **77** G5
Salard **73** G2
Salas **73** G3
Salas de los Infantes **66** E1
Salat **77** J4
Salavat **78** K5
Salawati **91** J6
Salba **84** E6
Salbris **65** E5
Salcha **118** F3
Salcia **73** H4
Salcombe **52** D4
Salda Golu **76** C4
Saldana **66** D1
Saldanha **108** C6
Saldus **63** K8
Sale **100** D2
Sale *Australia* **113** K6
Sale *U.K.* **55** G3
Salebabu **91** H5
Salekhard **84** Ae3
Salem *India* **92** E6
Salem *Illinois* **124** F7
Salem *Oregon* **122** C5
Salemi **69** D7
Salen *Highland, U.K.* **57** C4
Salen *Strathclyde, U.K.* **57** C4
Saiernes **65** G7
Salerno **69** E5
Salerno, Golfo di **69** E5
Salford **55** G3
Salgotarjan **72** E1
Salgueiro **137** K5
Salida **127** J1
Salies-de-Bearn **65** C7
Salihli **76** C3
Salima **107** F5
Salina *Kansas* **123** R8
Salina *Utah* **126** G1
Salina, Isola **69** E6
Salinas *Ecuador* **136** A4
Salinas *U.S.A.* **126** B2
Salinas, Cabo de **67** H3
Salinas Grandes **138** C4
Salinas O'Lachay, Punta de **136** B6
Salinas, Pampa de la **138** C6
Saline **123** Q8
Salinopolis **137** H4
Salins **65** F5
Salisbury *Maryland* **125** N7
Salisbury *N. Carolina* **129** M3
Salisbury *U.K.* **53** F3
Salisbury *Zimbabwe* **108** F3
Salisbury Island **120** L5
Salisbury Plain **52** F3
Saliste **73** G3
Salkhad **94** C5
Salla **62** N3
Sallisaw **128** E3
Sallvit **120** L5
Sallybrook **59** F9
Salmas **77** L3
Salmi **78** E3
Salmon *Canada* **119** L5
Salmon *U.S.A.* **122** F5
Salmon *U.S.A.* **122** H5
Salmon Arm **122** E2
Salmon Falls Creek **122** G6
Salmon River Mountains **122** G5
Salo **68** C3
Salo **63** K6
Salon-de-Provence **65** F7
Saloniki **75** G2
Salonta **73** F2
Salor **66** C3
Sal, Punta **132** D7
Salsacate **139** C6
Salsbruket **62** H4
Salsipuedes, Punta **126** D4
Salsk **79** G6
Salso **69** D7
Salsomaggiore Terme **68** B3
Salt *Jordan* **94** B5
Salt *Kentucky* **124** H8
Salt *Missouri* **124** D7
Salt *Oklahoma* **128** D2
Salta **138** C4
Saltash **52** C4
Saltburn-by-the-Sea **55** J2
Salt Cay **133** M4
Saltcoats **57** D5
Saltfjellet **62** F3
Saltfjord **62** F3
Saltfleet **55** K3
Saltillo **127** M8
Salt Lake City **122** J7
Salto *Italy* **69** D4
Salto *Uruguay* **138** E6
Salto da Divisa **138** G3
Salton Sea **126** E4
Saltpond **104** E4
Saluda *U.S.A.* **129** L3
Saluda *U.S.A.* **129** M3
Salumbar **92** D4
Saluzzo **68** A3
Salvador **137** K6
Salvatierra **131** J7
Salwah **97** K4
Salween **93** J5
Salyany **94** J2
Salyersville **124** J8
Salzach **68** D2
Salzburg **68** D2
Salzgitter **70** D2
Salzwedel **70** D2
Samah **96** G2
Samaipata **138** D3
Samak, Tanjung **90** D6
Samales Group **91** G4
Samana, Bahia de **133** N5
Samana, Cabo **133** N5
Samana Cay **133** L3
Samandag **77** F4
Samani **88** J4
Samanli Daglari **76** D2
Samanskoye **86** C2
Samar **91** H3
Samara **79** J5
Samarga *Russia* **88** G2
Samarga *Russia* **88** G2
Samariapo **136** D2
Samarina **75** F2
Samarinda **91** F6
Samarka **88** E3
Samarkand **86** B4
Samarra **77** K5
Samarskoye **86** F2

Seiling	128	C2	Sepik	114	C2	Seville	66	D4	Sharqi, Jebel esh	77	G6
Seille *France*	65	F5	Sepolno	71	G2	Sevola	71	L4	Sharqiyah, Ash	97	P5
Seille *France*	64	G4	Sept-Iles	121	N7	Sevre Nantaise	65	C5	Sharqiya, Sahra Esh	103	F2
Seinajoki	62	N4	Sepulveda	66	E2	Sevre Niortaise	65	C5	Sharurah	96	H8
Seine	64	D4	Sequeros	66	C2	Sevsk	79	E5	Sharwayn, Ra's	97	K9
Seine, Baie de la	64	C4	Sequillo	66	D2	Sewa	104	C4	Sharya	78	H4
Seini	73	G2	Serafimovich	79	G6	Seward *Alaska*	118	F3	Shashe	108	E4
Sekondi Takoradi	104	E4	Serakhs	95	Q3	Seward *Nebraska*	123	R7	Shashemene	103	G6
Se Kong	93	L6	Seram	91	H6	Seward Peninsula	118	C2	Shashi	93	M2
Sekota	103	G5	Seram, Laut	91	H6	Seyah Kuh, Kavir-e	95	L5	Shasta Lake	122	C7
Selaru	91	J7	Serang	90	D7	Seyakha	84	A2	Shasta, Mount	122	C7
Selatan	90	C6	Serasan, Selat	90	D5	Seychelles	82	D7	Shatsk	78	G5
Selatan, Tanjung	90	E6	Serba	96	E10	Seydisehir	76	D4	Shatura	78	F4
Selawik Lake	118	C2	Serbia	72	F3	Seydisfjordur	62	Y12	Shaubak	94	B6
Selayar	91	G7	Sercaia	73	H3	Seyhan	76	F4	Shaunavon	123	K3
Selayar, Selat	91	G7	Serchio	68	C4	Seyitgazi	76	D3	Shaw	55	G3
Selby *U.K.*	55	H3	Serdobsk	79	G5	Seym	79	E5	Shawano	124	F4
Selby *U.S.A.*	123	P5	Serdtse Karmen, Mys	118	A2	Seymchan	85	S4	Shawbury	52	E2
Selcuk	76	B4	Serebryansk	86	E2	Seymour *Australia*	113	K6	Shawinigan	125	P3
Selde	63	C8	Sered	71	G4	Seymour *Indiana*	124	H7	Shawnce	128	D3
Selebi-Phikwe	108	E4	Seredka	63	N7	Seymour *Texas*	127	N4	Sha Xi	87	M6
Selemdzha	85	N6	Sereflikochisar	76	E3	Sezanne	64	E4	Sha Xian	87	M6
Selendi	76	C3	Serein	65	E5	Sfax	101	H2	Shaybara	96	C4
Selenduma	84	H6	Seremban	90	C5	Sfintu Gheorghe	73	H3	Shaytanovka	78	K3
Selenge	87	J2	Serengeti Plain	107	F3	Sfintu Gheorghe, Bratul	73	K3	Shchara	71	L2
Selenge Moron	87	K2	Serenje	107	F5	s'Gravenhage	64	F2	Shchekino	78	F5
Selennyakh	85	Q3	Seret	71	L4	Sgurr na Lapaich	56	C3	Shchelyayur	78	J2
Selenter See	70	D1	Sergach	78	H4	Shaam	97	N4	Shcherbakovo	85	U3
Selestat	64	G4	Sergelen	87	K2	Shaanxi	93	L2	Shchigry	79	F5
Seletyteniz, Ozero	84	A6	Sergeyevka	88	D4	Shabunda	106	E3	Shchirets	71	K4
Selfoss	62	U13	Sergino	84	Ae4	Shadad, Namakzar-e	95	P6	Shchors	79	E5
Selgon	85	P7	Sergipe	137	K6	Shadrinsk	84	Ad5	Shchuchin	71	L2
Selibabi	100	C5	Sergiyev Posad	78	F4	Shadwan	96	A3	Shchuchinsk	84	A6
Seligman	126	F3	Seria	90	E5	Shaftesbury	53	E3	Shchuchye	84	Ad5
Selijord	63	C7	Serian	90	E5	Shagany, Ozero	73	K3	Shebalino	84	D6
Selim	77	K2	Serifos *Greece*	75	H4	Shagonar	84	E6	Shebekino	79	F5
Selimiye	76	B4	Serifos *Greece*	75	H4	Shag Point	115	C6	Sheberghan	92	C1
Selizharovo	78	E4	Serik	76	D4	Shahabad	92	E3	Sheboygan	124	G5
Seljaland	62	V13	Seringapatum Reef	112	E1	Shahbandar	92	C4	Shebshi Mountains	105	H4
Selkirk *Canada*	123	R2	Serio	68	B3	Shahdab	95	N6	Shebunino	88	H2
Selkirk *U.K.*	57	F5	Sermata, Kepulauan	91	H7	Shahdol	92	F4	Sheelin, Lough	58	H5
Selkirk Mountains	122	F2	Sermiligaarsuk	120	S5	Shah Fuladi	92	C2	Sheenjek	118	G2
Sellafirth	56	A1	Sernovodsk *Russia*	78	J5	Shahgarh	92	C3	Sheep Haven	58	G2
Selma	129	J4	Sernovodsk *Russia*	88	K4	Shahhat	101	K2	Sheep's Head	59	C9
Selseleh-ye- Pir Shuran	95	Q7	Sernur	78	H4	Shahjahanpur	92	E3	Sheerness	53	H3
Selsey	53	G4	Seroglazovka	79	H6	Shahpur	92	D2	Sheffield *Alabama*	129	J3
Selsey Bill	53	G4	Serov	84	Ad5	Shahpura *Madhya Pradesh, India*	92	F4	Sheffield *Texas*	127	M5
Selsviken	62	F5	Serpa	66	C4	Shahpura *Rajasthan, India*	92	D3	Sheffield *U.K.*	55	H3
Selva	138	D5	Serpent's Mouth	136	E2	Shahrabad	95	N3	Shegmas	78	H3
Selvagens, Ilhas	100	B2	Serpukhov	78	F5	Shahrak	95	S5	Shekhupura	92	D2
Selvas	136	D5	Serra Bonita	138	G3	Shahr-e Babak	95	M6	Sheki	79	H7
Selwyn Lake	119	Q3	Serracapriola	69	E5	Shahr-e Kord	95	K5	Shelagskiy	85	W2
Selwyn Range	113	J3	Serra do Navio	137	G3	Shahr Rey	95	K4	Shelagskiy, Mys	85	V2
Selyatin	71	L5	Serra Talhada	137	K5	Shah Rud	95	J3	Shelburne	121	N9
Seman	74	E2	Serrat, Cap	69	B7	Shajapur	92	E4	Shelburne Bay	113	J1
Semarang	90	E7	Serres	65	F6	Shakhauz	94	G2	Shelby *Montana*	122	J3
Sematan	90	D5	Serrinha	137	K6	Shakhs, Ras	96	E9	Shelby *N. Carolina*	129	M3
Semau	91	G8	Serta	66	B3	Shakhty	79	G6	Shelbyville *Indiana*	124	H7
Sembakung	91	F5	Sertania	137	K5	Shakhunya	78	H4	Shelbyville *Tennessee*	129	J3
Sembe	106	B2	Serui	91	K6	Shaki	105	F4	Shelikhova, Zaliv	85	T5
Semdinli	77	L4	Seruyan	90	E6	Shakotan-misaki	88	H4	Shelikof Strait	118	E4
Semenov	78	G4	Servia	75	G2	Shaktoolik	118	C3	Shell Creek Range	122	G8
Semenovka	79	E6	Serxu	93	J2	Shalamzar	95	K5	Shelly	122	H6
Seminoe Reservoir	123	L6	Se San	93	L6	Shaler Mountains	119	N1	Shelton	122	C4
Seminole *Oklahoma*	128	D3	Sese Island	107	F3	Shalfleet	53	F4	Sheltozero	78	F3
Seminole *Texas*	127	L4	Seshachalam Hills	92	E6	Shalkhar, Ozero	79	J5	Shemakha	79	H7
Seminole, Lake	129	K5	Sesheke	106	D6	Shaluli Shan	93	J2	Shemonaikha	84	C6
Semipalatinsk	84	C6	Sesia	68	B3	Shama, Ash	94	D6	Shenandoah *Iowa*	124	C6
Semirara Islands	91	G3	Se Srepok	93	L6	Shamary	78	K4	Shenandoah *Virginia*	125	L7
Semirom	95	K6	Sessa	106	D5	Shambe	102	F6	Shendam	105	G4
Semisopochnoi Island	118	Ab9	Sestri Levante	68	B3	Shamil	95	N8	Shendi	103	F4
Semitau	90	E5	Sestroretsk	63	N6	Shamiyah	94	D4	Shenge	104	C4
Semiyarka	84	B6	Sesupe	71	K1	Sham, Jambal	97	N5	Shenkursk	78	G3
Semnan	95	L4	Set	93	L5	Shammar	96	E3	Shenton, Mount	112	E4
Semois	64	F4	Setana	88	G4	Shand	95	R6	Shenyang	87	N3
Semporna	91	F5	Sete	65	E7	Shandan	86	J4	Shepetovka	79	D5
Senador Pompeu	137	K5	Sete Lagoas	138	H3	Shandong	87	M4	Shepherd Bay	120	H4
Sena Madureira	136	D5	Setermoen	62	H2	Shangani	108	E3	Shepherd Islands	114	U12
Senanga	106	D6	Setesdal	63	C7	Shanghang	87	M7	Shepparton	113	K6
Senatobia	128	H3	Setif	101	G1	Shangqiu	93	N2	Sheppey, Isle of	53	H3
Sendai *Japan*	89	C10	Seto	89	F8	Shangrao	87	M6	Shepshed	53	F2
Sendai *Japan*	89	H6	Settat	100	D2	Shang Xian	93	L2	Shepton Mallet	52	E3
Senec	71	G4	Settle	55	G2	Shangzhi	87	P2	Sheragul	84	G6
Seneca Lake	125	M5	Setubal	66	B3	Shanklin	53	F4	Sherard, Cape	120	K3
Senegal	104	B2	Setubal, Baia de	66	B3	Shannon *Ireland*	59	E7	Sherborne	52	E4
Senegal	100	C5	Seul, Lac	119	S5	Shannon *New Zealand*	115	E4	Sherbro	104	C4
Senekal	108	E5	Seumayan	90	B5	Shannon, Mouth of the	59	C7	Sherbro Island	104	C4
Sengata	91	F5	Seurre	65	F5	Shantarskiye Ostrova	85	P5	Sherbrooke	125	Q4
Sengiley	78	H5	Sevan, Ozero	77	L2	Shantou	87	M7	Sherburne Reef	114	D2
Senhor do Bonfim	137	J6	Sevastopol	79	E7	Shanxi	93	M1	Sherburn in Elmet	55	H3
Senigallia	68	D4	Seven	55	J2	Shan Xian	93	N2	Shereik	96	A7
Senirkent	76	D3	Seven Heads	59	E9	Shanyin	87	L4	Sheridan *Arkansas*	128	F3
Senise	69	F5	Seven Hogs, The	59	B8	Shaoguan	93	M4	Sheridan *Wyoming*	123	L5
Senj	72	C3	Sevenoaks	53	H3	Shaowu	87	M6	Sheringham	53	J2
Senja	62	H2	Seven Sisters	118	K4	Shaoxing	87	N6	Sherlovaya Gora	85	K6
Senjahopen	62	L2	Severac-le-Chateau	65	E6	Shaoyang	93	M3	Sherman	128	D4
Senkaku-shoto	89	F11	Severn *Canada*	121	J6	Shap	55	G2	's-Hertogenbosch	64	F3
Senkaya	77	K2	Severn *U.K.*	52	E3	Shapinsay	56	F1	Shetland	56	A1
Senkyabasa	84	J3	Severnaya Dvina	78	G3	Shapkina	78	J2	Shetland Islands	56	A1
Senlin Shan	88	C4	Severnaya Sosva	84	Ad4	Shaqra	96	G4	Shetpe	79	J7
Senlis	64	E4	Severnaya Zemlya	81	M1	Sharanga	78	H4	Shevchenko	79	J7
Sennar	103	F5	Severn, Mouth of the	52	E3	Sharbithat, Ra's	97	N8	Shewa Gimira	103	G6
Sennen	52	B4	Severnyy	78	H2	Shari	88	K4	Sheya	85	K4
Senno	78	D5	Severodvinsk	78	F3	Shari, Buhayrat	77	L5	Sheyang	87	N5
Sennybridge	52	D3	Severomorsk	62	Q2	Shark Bay	112	C4	Sheyenne	123	Q4
Senquerr	139	C9	Severouralsk	84	Ad4	Sharlauk	95	M2	Shiant Islands	56	B3
Sens	64	E4	Severskiy Donets	79	G6	Sharlyk	79	J5	Shiant, Sound of	56	B3
Senta	72	F3	Sevier	122	H8	Sharmah	96	B2	Shiashkotan, Ostrov	85	S7
Senyurt	77	J4	Sevier Lake	122	H8	Sharm el Sheikh	96	B3	Shibam	97	J9
Seoni	92	E4	Sevilla *Colombia*	136	B3	Sharon	125	K6	Shibata	89	G7
Seoul	87	P4	Sevilla *Spain*	66	D4	Sharon Springs	127	M1	Shibecha	88	K4
Sepanjang	90	F7				Sharqi, Al Hajar ash	97	P5	Shibetsu *Japan*	88	J3
Separation Point	115	D4				Sharqi, Jazair esh	94	C5	Shibetsu *Japan*	88	K4
Sepidan	95	L6							Shibin el Kom	102	F1

Name	Page	Grid
Shibotsu-jima	88	L4
Shibushi	89	C10
Shickshock Mountains	125	S2
Shiel Bridge	56	C3
Shieldaig	56	C3
Shiel, Loch	57	C4
Shihan, Wadi	97	L8
Shihezi	86	F3
Shiikh	103	J6
Shijiazhuang	87	L4
Shikarpur	92	C3
Shikoku	89	D9
Shikoku-sanchi	89	D9
Shikong	87	K4
Shikotan-to	88	L4
Shikotsu-ko	88	H4
Shildon	55	H2
Shilega	78	G3
Shiliguri	93	G3
Shilka *Russia*	85	K6
Shilka *Russia*	85	L6
Shillingstone	52	E4
Shillong	93	H3
Shilovo	78	G5
Shimabara	89	C9
Shimada	89	G8
Shimanovsk	85	M6
Shimian	93	K3
Shimizu	89	G8
Shimoda	89	G8
Shimoga	92	E6
Shimonoseki	89	C9
Shinano	89	G7
Shinas	97	N4
Shindand	95	R5
Shin Falls	56	D3
Shingu	89	E9
Shinjo	88	H6
Shinness	56	D2
Shinshar	77	G5
Shinyanga	107	F3
Shiogama	89	H6
Shiono-misaki	89	E9
Shiosawa	89	G7
Shiping	93	K4
Shipley	55	H3
Shippensburg	125	M6
Shippigan Island	121	P8
Shipston-on-Stour	53	F2
Shipton	55	H2
Shipton-under-Wychwood	53	F3
Shipunovo	84	C6
Shirakawa	89	H7
Shirane-san *Japan*	89	G8
Shirane-san *Japan*	89	G7
Shiraz	95	L7
Shire	107	F6
Shirebrook	55	H3
Shiretoko-misaki	88	K3
Shiriya-saki	88	H5
Shir Kuh	95	M6
Shirten Holoy Gobi	86	H3
Shirvan	95	N3
Shishaldin Volcano	118	Af9
Shivpuri	92	E3
Shivwits Plateau	126	F2
Shiwan Dashan	93	L4
Shiyan	93	M2
Shizhu	93	L3
Shizugawa	88	H6
Shizuishan	87	K4
Shizuoka	89	G8
Shkoder	74	E1
Shkumbin	74	E2
Shmidta, Ostrov	81	L1
Shobara	89	D8
Shokalskogo, Ostrov	84	A2
Shorapur	92	E5
Shorawak	95	S6
Shoreham-by-Sea	53	G4
Shorkot	92	D2
Shoshone	122	G6
Shoshone Mountains	122	F8
Shoshoni	123	K6
Shostka	79	E5
Shouguang	87	M4
Shouning	87	M6
Showa	141	C5
Showak	96	B9
Shozhma	78	G3
Shpikov	73	K1
Shpola	79	E6
Shrankogl	68	C2
Shreveport	128	F4
Shrewsbury	52	E2
Shrewton	53	F3
Shrigonda	92	D5
Shropshire	52	E2
Shrule	59	D5
Shuab, Ra's	97	P9
Shuanghezhen	87	P3
Shuangliao	87	N3
Shuangyashan	87	Q2
Shubar-Kuduk	79	K6
Shubra el-Khema	102	F1
Shucheng	87	M5
Shuga	84	B6
Shuicheng	93	K3
Shuikou	87	M6
Shujaabad	92	D3
Shulan	87	P3
Shumagin Islands	118	Af9
Shumen	73	J4
Shumerlya	78	H4
Shungnak	118	D2
Shuqrah	96	G10
Shura	77	K4
Shurab	95	K5
Shurab	95	N5
Shusf	95	Q6
Shush	94	J5
Shushenskoye	84	E6
Shushtar	94	J5
Shuswap Lake	122	E2
Shuya	78	G4
Shuya	89	G7
Shwebo	93	J4
Shwegyin	93	J5
Shweli	93	J4
Shyok	92	E2
Siahan Range	92	B3
Siah Koh	95	S5
Sialkot	92	D2
Siargao	91	H4
Siau	91	H5
Siauliai	63	K9
Sibenik	72	C4
Siberut	90	B6
Siberut, Selat	90	B6
Sibi	92	C3
Sibirskaya Nizmennost	84	G2
Sibirtsevo	88	D3
Sibiryakovo, Ostrov	84	B2
Sibiti	106	B3
Sibiu	73	H3
Sibolga	90	B5
Sibsagar	93	H3
Sibsey	55	K3
Sibu	90	E5
Sibut	102	C6
Sibutu	91	F5
Sibutu Passage	91	F5
Sibuyan	91	G3
Sibuyan Sea	91	G3
Sicasica	138	C3
Sichuan	93	K2
Sichuan Pendi	93	L3
Sicie, Cap	65	F7
Sicilia	69	D7
Sicilian Channel	69	C7
Sicily	69	D7
Sicuani	136	C6
Sidatun	88	E3
Sideby	63	J5
Sidheros, Akra	75	J5
Sidhirokastron	75	G2
Sidi Akacha	67	G4
Sidi Barram	102	E1
Sidi Bel Abbes	100	E1
Sidi Ifni	100	C3
Sidi Kacem	100	D2
Sidima	88	E1
Sidlaw Hills	57	E4
Sidmouth	52	D4
Sidmouth, Cape	113	J1
Sidney *Canada*	122	C3
Sidney *Montana*	123	M4
Sidney *Ohio*	124	H6
Sidon	94	B5
Sidorovsk	84	C3
Siedlce	71	K2
Siegen	70	C3
Siemiatycze	71	K2
Siem Reap	93	K6
Siena	68	C4
Sieniawa	71	K3
Sierpc	71	H2
Sierra Colorada	139	C8
Sierra Leone	104	C4
Sierra Vista	127	G5
Sierre	68	A2
Sifnos	75	H4
Sifton Pass	118	K4
Sigatoka *Fiji*	114	Q8
Sigatoka *Fiji*	114	Q9
Sigean	65	E7
Sighetu Marmatiei	73	G2
Sighisoara	73	H2
Sigli	90	B4
Siglufjordur	62	V11
Sigmaringen	70	C4
Signy	141	W6
Sigovo	84	D4
Sigtuna	63	G7
Siguenza	66	E2
Siguiri	104	D3
Sigulda	63	L8
Siikajoki	62	L4
Siikavuopio	62	J2
Siilinjarvi	62	M5
Siin	88	E2
Siipyy	63	J5
Siirt	77	J4
Sikar	92	E3
Sikasso	100	D6
Sikeston	124	F8
Sikhote Alin	88	E3
Sikinos	75	H4
Sikkim	93	G3
Sil	66	C1
Sila	97	K4
Silchar	93	H4
Sile	76	C2
Silesia	71	G3
Silgarhi	92	F3
Silifke	76	E4
Siligir	84	J3
Siling Co	93	G2
Silistra	73	J3
Silivri	76	C2
Siljan	63	F6
Silkeborg	63	C8
Sillajhuay	138	C3
Sillan, Lough	58	J4
Sillon de Talbert	64	B4
Siloam Springs	128	E2
Silom	114	E2
Silopi	77	K4
Silovsayakha	78	L2
Silsbee	128	E5
Silute	63	J9
Silvan	77	J3
Silver Bay	124	E3
Silver City	127	H4
Silvermines Mountains	59	F7
Silver Spring	125	M7
Silverstone	53	F2
Silverton *U.K.*	52	D4
Silverton *U.S.A.*	127	J2
Simanggang	90	E5
Simard, Lac	125	L3
Simareh Karkheh	94	H5
Simav *Turkey*	76	C3
Simav *Turkey*	76	C2
Simayr	96	E8
Simcoe	125	K5
Simcoe, Lake	125	L4
Simeonovgrad	73	H4
Simeulue	90	B5
Simferopol	79	E7
Simi	75	J4
Simiti	136	C2
Simitli	73	G5
Simla	92	E2
Simleu Silvaniei	73	G2
Simmern	70	B3
Simojarvi	62	M3
Simojoki	62	L4
Simonka	71	J4
Simplicio Mendes	137	J5
Simplon Pass	68	B2
Simpson Bay	119	N2
Simpson Desert	113	H3
Simpson Peninsula	120	J4
Simrishamn	63	F9
Simsor	77	J3
Simushir, Ostrov	85	S7
Sinabang	90	B5
Sinabung	90	B5
Sinac	72	C3
Sinafir	96	B3
Sinaia	73	H3
Sinai Peninsula	103	F2
Sinaloa	130	F4
Sinanaj	74	E2
Sinaxtla	131	L9
Sincan *Turkey*	76	E3
Sincan *Turkey*	77	G3
Since	133	K10
Sincelejo	136	B2
Sinclair's Bay	56	E2
Sind	92	E3
Sinda	88	F1
Sindal	63	D8
Sindangbarang	90	D7
Sindel	73	J4
Sindhuli Garhi	92	G3
Sindirgi	76	C3
Sindominic	73	H2
Sindor	78	J3
Sind Sagar Doab	92	D2
Sinegorye	78	J4
Sinelnikovo	79	F6
Sines	66	B4
Sines, Cabo de	66	B4
Sinetta	62	L3
Sinfra	104	D4
Singa	103	F5
Singapore	90	C5
Singaraja	90	F7
Sing Buri	93	K6
Singida	107	F3
Singitikos, Kolpos	75	G2
Singkang	91	G6
Singkawang	90	D5
Singkep	90	C6
Singleton	53	G4
Singleton, Mount	112	G3
Singosan	87	P4
Siniatsikon	75	F2
Siniscola	69	B5
Sinj	72	D4
Sinjai	91	G7
Sinjajevina	72	E4
Sinjar	77	J4
Sinkat	103	G4
Sinnamary	137	G2
Sinnes	63	B7
Sinni	69	F5
Sinnicolau Mare	72	F2
Sinoe	104	D4
Sinoe, Lacul	73	K3
Sinop	76	F2
Sinpo	88	B5
Sinpung-dong	88	B5
Sintang	90	E5
Sint Maarten	133	R5
Sinton	128	D6
Sintra	66	B3
Sinu	136	B2
Sinuiju	87	N4
Sinyavka	71	M2
Sinyaya	63	N8
Siocon	91	G4
Siofok	72	E2
Sion	68	A2
Sionascaig, Loch	56	C2
Sion Mills	58	H3
Sioule	65	E5
Sioux City	124	B5
Sioux Falls	123	R6
Sioux Lookout	119	S5
Sipalay	91	G4
Siping	87	N3
Sip Song Chau Thai	93	K4
Sipul	114	D3
Sipura	90	B6
Siquia	132	E8
Siquijor	91	G4
Sira *India*	92	E6
Sira *Norway*	63	B7
Sir Abu Nuayr	97	M4
Siracusa	69	E7
Sirajganj	93	G4
Sir Alexander, Mount	119	M5
Siran	77	H2
Sir Bani Yas	97	L4
Sir Edward Pellew Group	113	H2
Siret *Romania*	73	J2
Siret *Romania*	73	J2
Sirhan, Wadi	94	D6
Siri Kit Dam	93	K5
Sirik, Tanjung	90	E5
Sir James McBrien, Mount	118	R3
Sirjan, Kavir-e	95	L6
Sirk	95	N8
Sirna	75	J4
Sirnal	77	K4
Sirohi	92	D4
Siros *Greece*	75	H4
Siros *Greece*	75	H4
Sirri	95	M9
Sirr, Nafud as	96	G4
Sirsa	92	D3
Sir Sanford, Mount	122	F2
Sirsi	92	D6
Sirte	101	J2
Sirte, Gulf of	101	J2
Sirvan	77	K3
Sisak	72	D3
Sisaket	93	K5
Sisophon	93	K6
Sisseton	123	R5
Sissonne	64	E4
Sistan	95	P8
Sistan, Daryacheh-ye-	95	Q6
Sisteron	65	F6
Sistig-Khem	84	F6
Sistranda	62	C5
Sitamau	92	E4
Sitapur	92	F3
Sitges	67	G2
Sithonia	75	G2
Sitia	75	J5
Sitian	86	F3
Sitidgi Lake	118	J2
Sitio da Abadia	138	H6
Sitka	118	H4
Sittang	93	J5
Sittingbourne	53	H3
Sittwe	93	H4
Situbondo	90	E7
Siuri	93	G4
Siuruanjoki	62	M4
Sivas	77	G3
Sivasli	76	C3
Siverek	77	H4
Siverskiy	63	P7
Sivrice	77	H3
Sivrihisar	76	D3
Sivrihisar Daglari	76	D3
Sivuk	85	Q6
Siwa	102	E2
Siwalik Range	92	F3
Siwan	92	F3
Si Xian	87	M5
Sixmilebridge	59	E7
Sixpenny Handley	53	E4
Siya	78	G3
Siyal Islands	96	C5
Sizin	84	F6
Sjælland	63	D9
Sjorup	63	C8
Skadarsko Jezero	74	E1
Skadovsk	79	E6
Skafta	62	V13
Skagafjordur	62	V12
Skagaflos	62	T12
Skagen	63	D8
Skagerrak	63	C8
Skagit	122	D3
Skagway	118	H4
Skaill	56	F2
Skala-Podolskaya	73	J1
Skanderborg	63	C8
Skanor	63	E9
Skansholm	62	G4
Skantzoura	75	H3
Skara	63	E7
Skaraborg	63	E7
Skarbak	63	C9
Skard	62	V12
Skardu	92	E1
Skarnes	63	D6
Skattkarr	63	E7
Skaudvile	63	K9

Name	Page	Grid
Skaulo	62	J3
Skawina	71	H4
Skeena	118	K5
Skeena Mountains	118	K4
Skegness	55	K1
Skeidararsandur	62	W13
Skelda Ness	56	A2
Skelleftea	62	J4
Skelleftealven	62	H4
Skelmersdale	55	G3
Skelton	55	J2
Skerpioenpunt	108	D5
Skerries	58	K5
Skerries, The	54	E3
Skhiza	75	F4
Ski	63	D7
Skiathos	75	G3
Skibbereen	59	D9
Skiddaw	55	F2
Skidegate	118	J5
Skidel	71	L2
Skien	63	C7
Skierniewice	71	J3
Skiftet Kihti	63	J6
Skikda	101	G1
Skipton	55	G3
Skiropoula	75	H3
Skiros *Greece*	75	H3
Skiros *Greece*	75	H3
Skive	63	C8
Skjakerhatten	62	E4
Skjalfandafljot	62	W12
Skjalfandi	62	W11
Skjern	63	C9
Skjervoy	62	J1
Sklad	85	L2
Skoghall	63	E7
Skole	71	K4
Skomer Island	53	B3
Skopelos *Greece*	75	G3
Skopelos *Greece*	75	G3
Skopelos Kaloyeroi	75	H3
Skopin	79	F5
Skopje	73	F4
Skopun	62	Z14
Skorodum	84	A5
Skorovatn	62	E4
Skoruvik	62	X11
Skovde	63	E7
Skovorodino	85	L6
Skowhegan	125	R4
Skreia	63	D6
Skudenshavn	63	D6
Skulgam	62	H2
Skull	59	C9
Skulyany	73	J2
Skuodas	63	J8
Skutec	70	F4
Skutskar	63	G6
Skvira	79	D6
Skwierzyna	70	F2
Skye	56	B3
Skyring, Peninsula	139	B9
Skyring, Seno	139	B10
Slagelse	63	D9
Slagnas	62	H4
Slamannan	57	E5
Slamet, Gunung	90	D7
Slane	58	J5
Slaney	59	J8
Slany	70	F3
Slapin, Loch	57	B3
Slatina	73	H3
Slave	119	N4
Slave Lake	119	N4
Slavgorod *Russia*	84	B6
Slavgorod *Ukraine*	79	F6
Slavo	85	Q6
Slavyanka	88	C4
Slavyansk-na-Kubani	79	F6
Slawno	71	G1
Slawoborze	70	F2
Slea	55	J3
Sleaford	53	G2
Sleat, Sound of	57	C3
Sleetmute	118	D3
Sleights	55	J2
Slidell	128	H5
Slieve Anieren	58	G4
Slieveanorra	58	K2
Slieveardagh Hills	59	G7
Slieve Aughty Mountains	59	E6
Slieve Beagh	58	H4
Slieve Bloom Mountains	59	G6
Slieve Callan	59	D7
Slieve Car	58	C4
Slieve Donard	58	L4
Slieve Elva	59	D6
Slieve Gamph	58	E4
Slieve Kimalta	59	F7
Slieve League	58	E3
Slieve Mish Mountains	59	C8
Slieve Miskish	58	C9
Slieve Na Calliagh	58	H5
Slieve Rushen	58	G4
Slieve Snaght	58	H2
Sligo *Ireland*	58	E4
Sligo *Ireland*	58	F4
Sligo Bay	58	E4
Slioch	56	C3
Slipper Island	115	E2
Sliven	73	J4
Slobodchikovo	78	H3
Slobodka	73	K2
Slobodskoy	78	J4
Slobodzeya	73	K2
Slobozia *Romania*	73	H3
Slobozia *Romania*	73	J3
Slonim	71	L2
Slot, The	114	H6
Slough	53	G3
Slovak Republic	70	H4
Slovenia	72	C2
Slovyansk	79	F6
Sluch	79	D5
Slunj	72	C3
Slupsk	71	G1
Slussfors	62	G4
Slutsk	79	D5
Slyne Head	59	B6
Slyudyanka	84	G6
Smaland	63	F8
Smallwood Reservoir	121	P7
Smcanli	76	D3
Smederevo	73	F3
Smela	79	E6
Smethwick	53	E2
Smidovich	88	D1
Smiltene	63	M8
Smirnykh	85	Q7
Smith Arm	118	L2
Smith Bay *Canada*	120	L2
Smith Bay *U.S.A.*	118	E1
Smithfield *N. Carolina*	129	N3
Smithfield *Utah*	122	J7
Smith Island	121	L5
Smith Mount Lake	125	L8
Smiths Falls	125	N4
Smith Sound	120	M2
Smithton	113	K7
Smjorfjoll	62	X12
Smoky	119	M4
Smoky Cape	113	L5
Smoky Falls	121	K7
Smoky Hill	123	R8
Smoky Hills	123	Q8
Smola	62	C5
Smolenka	79	H5
Smolensk	78	E5
Smolikas	75	F2
Smolyan	73	H5
Smolyaninovo	88	D4
Smooth Rock Falls	125	K2
Smorgon	71	M1
Smotrich	73	J1
Smyrna	76	B3
Snaefell	54	E2
Snafell	62	X12
Snafellsjokull	62	T12
Snaith	55	H3
Snake	122	E4
Snake Range	122	G8
Snake River Plain	122	H6
Snap Point	132	J3
Snap, The	56	B1
Snares Islands	111	Q11
Snasa	62	E4
Snasavatn	62	E4
Sndre Isortoq	120	R4
Sndre Strmfjord	120	R4
Sndre Sund	120	Q3
Sneek	64	F2
Sneem	59	C9
Snettisham	53	H2
Snezka	70	F3
Sneznik	72	C3
Sniardwy, Jezioro	71	J2
Snina	71	K4
Snizort, Loch	56	B3
Snodland	53	H3
Snohetta	62	C5
Snoqualmie Pass	122	D4
Snoul	93	L6
Snowdon	54	E3
Snowtown	113	H5
Snowville	122	H7
Snowy, Mount	122	G3
Snug Corner	133	L3
Snyatyn	73	H1
Snyder	127	M4
Soalala	109	J3
Soalara	109	H4
Soan Kundo	87	P5
Soa Pan	108	E4
Soar	53	F2
Soa-Siu	91	H5
Soavinandriana	109	J3
Soay	57	B3
Soay Sound	57	B3
Sobat	103	F6
Sobinka	78	F4
Sobopol	85	M3
Sobradinho, Barragem de	137	J5
Sobrado	137	G5
Sobral *Acre, Brazil*	136	C5
Sobral *Ceara, Brazil*	137	J4
Sobv'yevsk	85	K7
Soca	72	B2
Socha	136	C2
Sochi	79	F7
Societe, Iles de la	143	H5
Socorro *Colombia*	136	C2
Socorro *U.S.A.*	127	J4
Socorro, Isla	130	D8
Socotra	97	P10
Soda Lake	126	D3
Sodankyla	62	M3
Soda Springs	122	J6
Soderala	63	G6
Soderhamn	63	G6
Soderkoping	63	G7
Sodermanland	63	G7
Sodertalje	63	G7
Sodra Ratansbyn	62	F5
Soe	91	G7
Soest	70	C3
Sofia *Bulgaria*	73	G4
Sofia *Madagascar*	109	J3
Sofiya	73	G4
Sofiysk	85	P6
Sogamoso *Colombia*	136	C2
Sogamoso *Colombia*	136	C2
Sogndalsfjora	63	B6
Sognefjorden	63	A6
Sogn og Fjordan	63	B6
Sogod	91	G3
Sogut *Turkey*	76	C4
Sogut *Turkey*	76	D2
Sogutlu	76	D2
Sog Xian	93	H2
Sohag	103	F2
Sohano	114	E3
Sohela	92	F4
Sohuksan	87	P5
Soissons	64	E4
Sojat	92	D3
Sojotan Point	91	G4
Sokal	71	L3
Soke	76	B4
Sokhumi	79	G7
Soko Banja	73	F4
Sokode	104	F4
Sokol	78	G4
Sokolo	100	D6
Sokolovka	88	D4
Sokolow Podlaski	71	K2
Sokoto *Nigeria*	105	F3
Sokoto *Nigeria*	105	G3
Sola	71	H4
Solander Island	115	A7
Solapur	92	E5
Sol, Costa del	66	D4
Soledad	133	K9
Soledade	136	D5
Solen	63	D6
Solent, The	52	F4
Solhan	77	J3
Soligorsk	79	D5
Solihull	53	F2
Solikamsk	78	K4
Sollletsk	79	J5
Solimoes	136	E4
Solingen	70	B3
Solleftea	62	G5
Soller	67	H3
Solnechnogorsk	78	F4
Solo	90	E7
Solobkovtsy	73	J1
Solok	90	D6
Solomon	123	Q8
Solomon Islands	114	J5
Solon Springs	124	E3
Solontsovo	85	K6
Solor, Kepulauan	91	G7
Solothurn	68	A2
Solotobe	86	B3
Solovyevsk	85	L6
Solta	72	D4
Soltanabad	95	P3
Soltaniyeh	94	J3
Soltau	70	C2
Soltsy	78	E4
Solvesborg	63	F8
Solway Firth	55	F2
Solwezi	106	E5
Soma	76	B3
Soma	89	H7
Somalia	103	J6
Sombor	72	E3
Sombrerete	130	H6
Sombrero Channel	93	H7
Somerset *Kentucky*	124	H8
Somerset *Pennsylvania*	125	L6
Somerset *U.K.*	52	D3
Somerset East	108	E6
Somerset Island	120	H3
Somerton	52	E3
Somerville Reservoir	128	D5
Somes	73	G2
Somes Point	115	F6
Somme	64	D3
Sommerda	70	D3
Somosomo	114	S8
Sompolno	71	H2
Somport, Puerto de	67	F1
Somuncura, Meseta de	139	C8
Son	92	F4
Sonakh	85	P6
Sonapur	92	F4
Sonara	127	M5
Sonderborg	63	C9
Sondre Strmfjord	120	R4
Sondrio	68	B2
Songea	107	G5
Songhua	88	B2
Songhua Jiang	87	P2
Songjin	88	B5
Songkhla	93	K7
Songololo	106	B4
Sonhat	92	F4
Sonid-Youqi	87	L3
Sonid Zuoqi	87	L3
Sonipat	92	E3
Sonkajarvi	62	M5
Sonkovo	78	F4
Son La	93	K4
Sonmiani	92	C3
Sonmiani Bay	92	C3
Sonoita	126	F5
Sonora	126	G6
Sonoran Desert	126	F4
Sonsonate	132	C8
Sonsorol Island	91	J4
Sooghemeghat	118	B3
Sopi, Tanjung	91	H5
Sopot	71	H1
Sopron	72	D2
Sopur	92	D2
Sor	66	B3
Sora	69	D5
Sorada	92	F5
Soraker	62	G5
Sorata	138	C3
Sorbas	67	E4
Sore	65	C6
Sorel	125	P3
Sorgun	76	F3
Soria	66	E2
Sorisdale	57	B4
Sorka	78	F4
Sorkh, Kuh-e	95	M5
Sormjole	62	J5
Sorocaba	138	G4
Sorochinsk	79	J5
Soroki	79	D6
Sorong	91	J6
Sorot	63	N7
Soroti	107	F2
Soroya	62	K1
Soroysundet	62	K1
Sorraia	66	B3
Sorrento	69	E5
Sorsele	62	G4
Sorso	69	B5
Sorsogon	91	G3
Sortavala	63	P6
Sortland	62	F2
Sor-Trondelag	62	D6
Sorvagsvatn	62	Z14
Sorvagur	62	Z14
Sorvar	62	K1
Sorvattnet	63	E5
Sos del Rey-Catolico	67	F1
Sosnogorsk	78	J3
Sosnovka	84	H6
Sosnovo	63	P6
Sosnovo-Ozerskoye	85	J6
Sosnowiec	71	H3
Sosunova, Mys	88	G2
Sosva	84	Ad5
Sotik	107	G3
Sotra	63	A6
Sotuelamos	66	E3
Soubre	104	D4
Soudan	113	H3
Souflion	75	J2
Souk Ahras	101	G1
Soumntam	67	J4
Sour	94	B5
Sour al Ghozlane	67	H4
Soure	137	H4
Souris *Manitoba, Canada*	123	P3
Souris *Prince Edward Island, Canada*	121	P8
Sousse	101	H1
South Africa, Republic of	108	D6
Southampton *U.K.*	53	F4
Southampton *U.S.A.*	125	P6
Southampton Island	120	K5
Southampton Water	53	F4
South Andaman	93	H6
South Baldy	127	J4
South Baymouth	124	J4
South Bend *Indiana*	124	G6
South Bend *Washington*	122	C4
South Benfleet	53	H3
Southborough	53	H3
South Boston	125	L8
South Canadian	128	D3
South Cape *Fiji*	114	R8
South Cape *U.S.A.*	126	T11
South Carolina	129	M3
South China Sea	87	L7
South Creake	53	H2
South Dakota	123	N5
South Dorset Downs	52	E4
South Downs	53	G4
Southeast Cape	118	B3
South East Cape	113	K6
Southend	119	Q4
Southend-on-Sea	53	H3
Southern Alps	115	C5
Southern Cross	112	D5
Southern Indian Lake	119	R4
Southern Pine Hills	128	H5
Southern Pines	129	N3
Southern Uplands	57	E5
Southery	53	H2
South Esk	57	E4
South Foreland	53	J3
South Forty Foot Drain	53	G2
South Geomagnetic Pole	141	H3
South Georgia	139	J10
South Glamorgan	52	D3
South Harbour	56	A2

Name	Page	Grid
Taganrog	79	F6
Taganrogskiy Zaliv	79	F6
Tagbilaran	91	G4
Taghmon	59	J8
Tagliamento	68	D3
Tagolo Point	91	G4
Tagounite	100	D3
Tagu	73	H2
Taguatinga	138	H6
Tagudin	91	G2
Tagula	114	E4
Tagula Island	114	E4
Tagum	91	H4
Tagus	66	C3
Tahan, Gunung	90	C5
Tahat, Mont	101	G4
Ta He	87	N1
Tahe	87	N1
Taheri	95	L8
Tahiryuak Lake	119	N1
Tahiti	143	J5
Tahlab, Dasht-i-	92	B3
Tahlequah	128	E3
Tahoe Lake *Canada*	119	P1
Tahoe, Lake *U.S.A.*	122	E8
Tahoka	127	M4
Tahoua	101	G6
Tahrud	95	N7
Tahta	102	F2
Tahtali Daglari	77	G3
Tahuamanu	136	D6
Tahulandang	91	H5
Taian	87	M4
Taibai Shan	93	L2
Taibus Qi	87	M3
Tai-chung	87	N7
Taier	115	C6
Taieri	115	C6
Taigu	87	L4
Taihape	115	E3
Taihe *Anhui, China*	93	N2
Taihe *Jiangxi, China*	93	M3
Tai Hu	87	N5
Taimba	84	F4
Tain	56	D3
Tai-nan	87	N7
Tainaron, Akra	75	G4
Taining	87	M6
Taipale	62	N5
Tai-pei	87	N6
Taiping	90	C5
Taipingbao	86	J4
Taipinggou	88	C1
Taira	89	H7
Taisei	88	G4
Taisha	89	D8
Taitao, Peninsula de	139	B9
Tai-tung	87	N7
Taivalkoski	62	N4
Taiwan	87	N7
Taiwan Haixia	87	M7
Taiyetos Oros	75	G4
Taiyuan	87	L4
Taiza	89	E8
Taizhou	87	M5
Taizz	96	G10
Tajabad	95	M6
Tajikistan	86	B4
Tajima	89	G7
Tajin-dong	88	B5
Tajito	126	F5
Tajo	66	D3
Tajrish	95	K4
Tajumuclo, Volcan de	132	B7
Tajuna	66	E2
Tak	93	J5
Takab	94	H3
Takada	89	G7
Takaka	115	D4
Takamatsu	89	E8
Takanabe	89	C9
Takaoka	89	F7
Takapuna	115	E2
Takasaki	89	G7
Takatshwane	108	D4
Takaungu	107	G3
Takayama	89	F7
Takefu	89	F8
Takengon	90	B5
Takeo	93	K6
Takestan	95	J3
Takhadid	94	G7
Takhi-i-Suleiman	95	K3
Takhta Bazar	95	R4
Takhtabrod	84	Ae6
Takikawa	88	H4
Takinoue	88	J3
Taklimakan Shamo	92	F1
Taku	118	J4
Takum	105	G4
Takwa	114	K6
Talagang	92	D2
Talamanca, Cordillera de	132	F10
Talangbetutu	90	C6
Talara	136	A4
Talar-i-Band	92	B3
Talas	86	C3
Talasea	114	E3
Talaton	52	D4
Talaud, Kepulauan	91	H5
Talavera de la Reina	66	D3
Talayuelas	67	F3
Talbot Inlet	120	L2
Talca	139	B7
Talcahuano	139	B7
Talcher	92	G4
Taldy-Kurgan	86	D2
Talgarth	52	D3
Taliabu	91	G6
Talihina	128	E3
Tali Post	102	F6
Talisay	91	G3
Taliwang	91	F7
Talkeetna	118	E3
Talkeetna Mountains	118	F3
Talladega	129	J4
Tall Afar	77	K4
Tallahassee	129	K5
Tallinn	63	L7
Tall Kalakh	77	G5
Tall Kayf	77	K4
Tall Kujik	77	K4
Tallow	59	F8
Tall Tamir	77	J4
Talmenka	84	C6
Talnoye	79	E6
Taloda	92	D4
Talodi	102	F5
Talok	91	F5
Talovka	84	E5
Taloye	85	M4
Talsi	63	K8
Taltal	138	B5
Taltson	119	N3
Talu	114	F3
Taluma	85	L5
Talvik	62	K1
Tama	124	D6
Tamabo Range	90	F5
Tamale	104	E4
Tamames	66	C2
Tamana	111	S2
Tamano	89	D8
Tamanrasset *Algeria*	100	F4
Tamanrasset *Algeria*	101	G4
Tamar *Australia*	113	K7
Tamar *U.K.*	52	C4
Tamar, Alto de	133	K11
Tamarite de Litera	67	G2
Tamatave	109	J3
Tamaulipas, Llanos de	128	C8
Tamazunchale	131	K7
Tambacounda	104	C3
Tambangsawah	90	C6
Tambelan, Kepulauan	90	D5
Tambey	84	A2
Tambo	113	K3
Tambora, Gunung	91	F7
Tamboril	137	J4
Tambov	79	G5
Tambre	66	B1
Tambura	102	E6
Tamchaket	100	C5
Tame	136	C2
Tamega	66	C2
Tamiahua, Laguna de	131	L7
Tamil Nadu	92	E6
Tamis	72	F3
Tamit, Wadi	101	J2
Tammerfors	63	M6
Tammisaari	63	K6
Tampa	129	L7
Tampa Bay	129	L7
Tampere	63	M6
Tampico	131	L6
Tamsagbulag	87	M2
Tamuin	131	K7
Tamworth *Australia*	113	L5
Tamworth *U.K.*	53	F2
Tana *Chile*	138	C3
Tana *Kenya*	107	H3
Tana *Norway*	62	M1
Tanabe	89	E9
Tana bru	62	N2
Tanafjorden	62	N1
Tana Hayk	103	G5
Tanahbala	90	B6
Tanahgrogot	90	F6
Tanahjampea	91	G7
Tanahmasa	90	B6
Tanahmerah	114	C3
Tanah Merah	90	C4
Tanami	112	F3
Tanana	118	E2
Tananarive	109	J3
Tanchon	88	B5
Tandag	91	H4
Tandek	91	F4
Tandil	139	E7
Tando Adam	92	C3
Tandragee	58	K4
Taneatua	115	F3
Tanega-shima	89	C10
Tan Emellel	101	G3
Tanen Tong Dan	93	J5
Tanew	71	K3
Tanezrouft	100	E4
Tanf, Jbel al	77	H6
Tanga *Tanzania*	107	G4
Tanga *Russia*	85	J6
Tanga Islands	114	E2
Tanganyika, Lake	107	F4
Tangarare	114	J6
Tanger	100	D1
Tanggula Shan	92	G3
Tanggula Shankou	93	H2
Tangra Yumco	92	G2
Tangshan	87	M4
Tangwang He	88	B2
Tangwanghe	88	B1
Tangyuan	88	B2
Tan Hill	53	F3
Tanhua	62	M3
Taiuantaweng Shan	93	J2
Tanimbar, Kepulauan	114	A3
Tanjung	90	F6
Tanjungbalai	90	B5
Tanjungkarang Telukbetung	90	D7
Tanjungpandan	90	D6
Tanjungpura	90	B5
Tanjungredeb	91	F5
Tanjungselor	91	F5
Tankapirtti	62	M2
Tankovo	84	D4
Tankse	92	E2
Tanlovo	84	A3
Tanna	114	U13
Tannu Ola	84	E6
Tannurah, Ra's	97	K3
Tanout	101	G6
Tan-shui	87	N6
Tanta	102	F1
Tan-Tan	100	C3
Tantoyuca	131	K7
Tanumshede	63	D7
Tanzania	107	G4
Taoan	87	N2
Tao He	93	K2
Tao, Ko	93	J6
Taolanaro	109	J5
Taormina	69	E7
Taos	127	K2
Taoudenni	100	E4
Taourirt	100	E2
Tapa	63	L7
Tapachula	131	N10
Tapah	90	C5
Tapajos	137	F4
Tapaktuan	90	B5
Tapan	90	D6
Tapanahoni	137	F3
Tapaua	136	D5
Taperoa	137	K6
Tappahannock	125	M8
Tappi-saki	88	H5
Tapsuy	78	L3
Tapti	92	D4
Tapuaenuku	115	D4
Tapul Group	91	G4
Taqah	97	M8
Taqtaq	94	G4
Taquari	138	E3
Taquari, Pantanal do	138	E3
Tara	84	A5
Tarabulus	101	H2
Taradale	115	F3
Tara, Hill of	58	J5
Tarakan	91	F5
Tarakli	76	D2
Tarakliya	73	K3
Taramana	91	G7
Taramo-jima	89	G11
Taran	84	A2
Tarancon	66	E2
Taransay	56	A3
Taransay, Sound of	56	A3
Taranto	69	F5
Taranto, Golfo di	69	F5
Tarapoto	136	B5
Tararua Range	115	E4
Tarascon	65	F7
Tarasovo	78	H2
Tarauaca *Brazil*	136	C5
Tarauaca *Brazil*	136	C5
Taravo	69	B5
Tarazona	67	F2
Tarazona de la Mancha	67	F3
Tarbagatay, Khrebet	86	E2
Tarbert *Ireland*	59	D7
Tarbert *Strathclyde, U.K.*	57	C5
Tarbert *Western Isles, U.K.*	56	B3
Tarbes	65	D7
Tarbet	57	D4
Tarbolton	57	D5
Tarboro	129	P3
Tarcaului, Muntii	73	J2
Tarcoola	113	G5
Tardienta	67	F2
Tardoki-yani, Gora	88	F1
Taree	113	L5
Tarendo	62	K3
Tareya	84	E2
Tarfa, Ra's at	96	F8
Tarfa, Wadi el	103	F2
Tarfaya	100	C3
Tarfside	57	F4
Targhee Pass	122	J5
Tarhunah	101	H2
Tarif	97	L4
Tarifa	66	D4
Tarija	138	D4
Tariku	114	B2
Tarim	97	J8
Tarim He	86	E3
Tarim Basin	86	E3
Tarim Pendi	86	E3
Taritatu	114	B2
Tarkasale	84	A3
Tarkastad	108	E6
Tarkhankut, Mys	79	E6
Tarkio	124	C6
Tarkwa	104	E4
Tarlac	91	G2
Tarlak	86	E3
Tarleton	55	G3
Tarma	136	B6
Tarn	65	D7
Tarna	72	F2
Tarnaby	62	F4
Tarnobrzeg	71	J3
Tarnow	71	J4
Tarnsjo	63	G6
Taro	68	B3
Taron	114	E2
Taroom	113	K4
Taroudannt	100	D2
Tarporley	55	G3
Tarragona	67	G2
Tarrasa	67	H2
Tarrega	67	G2
Tarsus	76	F4
Tartagal	138	D4
Tartas	65	C7
Tartu	63	P7
Tartung	90	B5
Tartus	94	B4
Tartus	77	F5
Tarutino	73	K2
Tarzout	67	G4
Tasci	77	F3
Tashakta	86	F2
Tashigang	93	H3
Tashk, Daryacheh-ye	95	L7
Tashkent	86	B3
Tashkepri	95	R3
Tashla	79	J5
Tashtagol	84	D6
Tasikmalaya	90	D7
Tasiujaq	121	N6
Taskesken	86	E2
Taskopru	76	F2
Tas-Kumsa	85	N3
Taslicay	77	K3
Tasman Bay	115	D4
Tasmania	113	K7
Tasman Mountains	115	D4
Tasnad	73	G2
Tasova	77	G2
Tas-Tumus	85	N2
Tasty	86	B3
Tasucu	76	E4
Tasuj	77	L3
Tataba	91	G6
Tatabanya	72	E2
Tatarbunary	73	K3
Tatarka	84	B6
Tatarsk	84	B5
Tataurovo	85	J6
Tateyama	89	G8
Tathlina Lake	119	M3
Tathlith	96	F7
Tathlith, Wadi	96	F6
Tatnam, Cape	119	S4
Tatry	71	H4
Tatsinskiy	79	G6
Tatsuno	89	E8
Tatta	92	C4
Tatum	127	L4
Tatvan	77	K3
Tau	111	V4
Tauari	137	F4
Taubate	138	G4
Tauchik	79	J7
Taumarunui	115	E3
Taunton *U.K.*	52	D3
Taunton *U.S.A.*	125	Q6
Taunus	70	C3
Taupo	115	F3
Taupo, Lake	115	E3
Tauq	94	G4
Tauq	77	L5
Taurage	63	K9
Tauranga	115	F2
Tauroa Point	115	D1
Taurus	76	E4
Tauste	67	F2
Tauu Islands	114	F2
Tavalesh, Kuhha-ye	94	J3
Tavana-i-Tholo	111	T6
Tavas	76	C4
Tavda *Russia*	84	Ad5
Tavda *Russia*	84	Ae5
Taverner Bay	120	M4
Taveuni	114	S8
Tavira	66	C4
Tavistock	52	C4
Tavolara, Isola di	69	B5
Tavoy	93	J6
Tavrichanka	88	C4
Tavsanli	76	C3
Tavua	114	Q8
Tavuna-i-Ra	111	T6
Tavy	52	C4
Taw	52	D4
Tawakoni, Lake	128	E4
Tawau	91	F5
Tawe	52	D3
Taweisha	102	E5
Tawila	96	A3
Tawil, At	96	D2
Tawitawi Group	91	G4
Ta-wu	87	N7
Tawurgha, Sabkhat	101	J2

Name	No.	Ref.
Till	57	F5
Tillaberi	100	F6
Tillanchang	93	H7
Tillicoultry	57	E4
Tilomar	91	H7
Tilos	75	J4
Tilsit	71	J1
Tilt	57	E4
Timanskiy Kryazh	78	H3
Timar	77	K3
Timaru	115	C6
Timashevsk	79	F6
Timbakion	75	H5
Timbedra	100	D5
Timbo *Guinea*	104	C3
Timbo *Liberia*	104	D4
Timbuktu	100	E5
Timfristos	75	F3
Timimoun	100	F3
Timiris, Cap	100	B5
Timis	73	G3
Timisoara	73	F3
Timkapaul	84	Ad4
Timmernabben	63	G8
Timmins	125	K2
Timok	73	G3
Timolin	59	J7
Timor	91	H7
Timor, Laut	91	H7
Timoshino	78	F3
Timsher	78	J3
Tinaca Point	91	H4
Tinaco	133	N10
Tinahely	59	K7
Tinakula	114	M7
Tindivanam	92	E6
Tindouf	100	D3
Tineo	66	C1
Tinglev	63	C9
Tingo Maria	136	B5
Tingsryd	63	F8
Tingvoll	62	C5
Tinhare, Ilha de	137	K6
Tinogasta	138	C5
Tinompo	91	G5
Tinos *Greece*	75	H4
Tinos *Greece*	75	H4
Tintinara	113	J6
Tinto *Spain*	66	C4
Tinto *U.K.*	57	E5
Tinto Hills	57	E5
Tinwald	115	C5
Tiomilaskogen	63	E6
Tipaza	67	H4
Tipitapa	132	D8
Tippecanoe	124	G6
Tipperary *Ireland*	59	F8
Tipperary *Ireland*	59	G7
Tipton	124	H6
Tiptree	53	H3
Tiquicheo	131	J8
Tiracambu, Serra do	137	H4
Tiran	96	B3
Tirana	74	E2
Tirane	74	E2
Tirano	68	C2
Tiraspol	79	D6
Tire	76	B3
Tirebolu	77	H2
Tiree	57	C4
Tirga Mor	56	B3
Tirgoviste	73	H3
Tirgu Bujor	73	J3
Tirgu Carbunesti	73	G3
Tirgu Frumos	73	J2
Tirgu Jiu	73	G3
Tirgu Mures	73	H2
Tirgu Neamt	73	J2
Tirgu Ocna	73	J2
Tirich Mir	92	D1
Tirnava Mare	73	H2
Tirnava Mica	73	H2
Tirnavos	75	G3
Tirol	68	C2
Tirpul	95	Q4
Tirso	69	B6
Tirua Point	115	E3
Tiruchchirappalli	92	E6
Tirumangalam	92	E7
Tirunelveli	92	E7
Tirupati	92	E6
Tiruppur	92	E6
Tiruvannamalai	92	E6
Tisa	72	F3
Tisisat Falls	103	G5
Tissa	71	K4
Tissington	55	H3
Tista	93	G3
Tisza	72	F2
Tit-Ary	85	M2
Titchfield	53	F4
Titicaca, Lago	138	C3
Titograd	72	E4
Titova Mitrovica	73	F4
Titovo Uzice	72	E4
Titovo Velenje	72	C2
Titov Veles	73	F5
Titran	62	C5
Tittmoning	70	E4
Titu	73	H3
Titusville	129	M6
Tiumpan Head	56	B2
Tivaouane	104	B2
Tiveden	63	F7
Tiverton	52	D4
Tivoli	69	D5
Tiwi	97	P5
Tiyas	77	G5
Tizimin	131	Q7
Tizi Ouzou	101	F1
Tiznit	100	D3
Tjamotis	62	H3
Tjornuvik	62	Z14
Tjotta	62	E4
Tlaltenango	130	H7
Tlapa	131	K9
Tlapehuala	131	J8
Tlaxiaco	131	L9
Tlemcen	100	E2
Toad River	118	K4
Toamasina	109	J3
Tobago	133	S9
Toba Kakar Ranges	92	C2
Tobercurry	58	E4
Tobermory *Canada*	125	K4
Tobermory *U.K.*	57	B4
Toberonochy	57	C4
Tobi	91	J5
Tobin Lake	112	F3
Tobi-shima	88	G6
Toboali	90	D6
Tobol	84	Ae5
Tobolsk	84	Ae5
Tobseda	78	J2
Tobysh	78	J3
Tocache Nuevo	136	B5
Tocantins	137	H4
Toccoa	129	L3
Toco	133	S9
Toconao	138	C4
Tocopilla	138	B4
Tocuyo	133	N9
Todeli	91	G6
Todi	68	B2
Todi	69	D4
Todmorden	55	G3
Todog	86	E3
Todos os Santos, Baia de	137	K6
Todos Santos *Bolivia*	138	C3
Todos Santos *Mexico*	130	D6
Todos Santos, Bahia de	126	D5
Toe Head *Ireland*	59	D10
Toe Head *U.K.*	56	A3
Toetoes Bay	115	B7
Tofino	122	B3
Toft	56	A1
Tofte	63	D7
Tofua	111	T5
Toga	114	T10
Togi	89	F7
Togiak	118	C4
Togian, Kepulauan	91	G6
Togni	96	B7
Togo	104	F4
Togtoh	87	L3
Toguchi	89	H10
Togur	84	C5
Tohamiyam	103	G4
Tohatchi	127	H3
Tohma	77	G3
Toi-misaki	89	C10
Tojo	89	D8
Tok	118	G3
Tokachi	88	J4
Tokachi-Dake	88	J4
Tokaj	73	F1
Tokanui	115	B7
Tokar	103	G4
Tokara-kaikyo	89	C10
Tokara-retto	89	B11
Tokat	77	G2
Tokelau	111	U3
Tokiwa	88	J3
Tokke	63	C7
Toklar	77	G3
Tokmak	86	D3
Tokolon	84	H5
Tokoro	88	K3
Tokoroa	115	E3
Toksun	86	F3
Tok-to	89	C7
Toktogul	86	C3
Tokuno-shima	89	J10
Tokushima	89	E8
Tokuyama	89	C8
Tokyo	89	G8
Tolar, Cerro	138	C5
Tolbonuur	86	G2
Tolbukhin	73	J4
Toledo *Spain*	66	D3
Toledo *U.S.A.*	124	J6
Toledo Bend Reservoir	128	F5
Toledo, Montes de	66	D3
Tolentino	68	D4
Toliara	109	H4
Tolitoli	91	G5
Tolka	84	C4
Tolmezzo	68	D2
Tolmin	72	B2
Tolochin	78	D5
Tolosa	67	E1
Tolo, Teluk	91	G6
Tolsta Head	56	B2
Tolstoye	73	H1
Tolstoy, Mys	85	T5
Toluca	131	K8
Toluca, Nevado de	131	K8
Tolyatti	79	H5
Tomah	124	E4
Tomahawk	124	F4
Tomakomai	88	H4
Tomani	90	F5
Tomaniivi	114	R8
Tomar *Portugal*	66	B3
Tomar *Kazakhstan*	86	D2
Tomari	88	J2
Tomarza	77	F3
Tomasevo	72	E4
Tomashevka	71	K3
Tomaszow Lubelski	71	K3
Tomaszow Mazowiecka	71	J3
Tombador, Serra do	136	F6
Tombe	103	F6
Tombigbee	129	H5
Tomboco	106	B4
Tombouctou	100	E5
Tombua	106	B6
Tomelilla	63	E9
Tomelloso	66	E3
Tomini, Teluk	91	G6
Tomioka	89	H7
Tomkinson Ranges	112	F4
Tomma	62	E3
Tommot	85	M5
Tomo	136	D2
Tomochic	84	H5
Tompa	85	P4
Tompo	84	D5
Tomsk	84	D5
Tonbridge	53	H3
Tondano	91	G5
Tonder	70	C1
Tone	52	E3
Tonelagee	59	K6
Tonga	111	U6
Tonga *Sudan*	102	F6
Tongariro	115	E3
Tongatapu	111	U6
Tongatapu Group	111	T6
Tonga Trench	143	H5
Tongcheng	93	M3
Tongchuan	93	L1
Tongdao	93	L3
Tonggu	93	M3
Tongguan	93	M2
Tonghai	93	K4
Tonghe	88	B2
Tonghua	87	P3
Tongjiang	88	D2
Tongking, Gulf of	93	L5
Tongliao	87	N3
Tongling	87	M5
Tonglu	87	M6
Tongnae	89	B8
Tongoa	114	U12
Tongren	93	L3
Tongtianheyan	93	H2
Tongue *U.K.*	56	D2
Tongue *U.S.A.*	123	L5
Tongue, Kyle of	56	D2
Tongue of the Ocean	132	J2
Tong Xian	87	M4
Tongxin	93	L1
Tongyu	87	N3
Tongzi	93	L3
Tonichi	127	H6
Tonk	92	E3
Tonkabon	95	K3
Tonle Sap	93	K6
Tonneins	65	D6
Tonnerre	65	E5
Tono	88	H6
Tonopah	126	D2
Tonosi	132	G11
Tonsberg	63	D7
Tonstad	63	B7
Tonya	77	H2
Tooele	122	H7
Toowoomba	113	L4
Topeka	124	C7
Toplane	74	E1
Toplica	73	F4
Toplita	73	H2
Topocalma, Punta	138	B6
Topola	72	F3
Topolcani	73	F5
Topoli	79	J6
Topolkki	63	N6
Topolovgrad	73	J4
Topozero, Ozero	62	P4
Toppenish	122	D4
Toprakli	76	F3
Toraka Vestale	109	H3
Tora-Khem	84	F6
Torbali	76	B3
Torbat-e-Heydariyeh	95	P4
Torbat-e Jam	95	Q4
Tor Bay *Australia*	112	D5
Tor Bay *U.K.*	52	D4
Tordesillas	66	D2
Tore	56	D3
Tore	62	K4
Torfastadir	62	U12
Torgau	70	E3
Torgo	85	K5
Torhout	64	E3
Torino	68	A3
Torkaman	94	H3
Tormes	66	D2
Tornealven	62	K3
Tor Ness	56	E2
Torne-trask	62	H2
Torngat Mountains	121	P6
Tornio	62	L4
Toro, Cerro de	138	C5
Toroiaga	73	H2
Torokina	114	F3
Torokszentmiklos	72	F2
Toronaios, Kolpos	75	G2
Toronto	125	L5
Toropets	78	E4
Tororo	107	F2
Toros Dagi	76	F4
Toros Daglari	76	F4
Torpoint	52	C4
Torquay	52	D4
Torrance	126	C4
Torrao	66	B3
Torre Annunziata	69	E5
Torre Baja	67	F2
Torreblanca	67	G2
Torrecilla en Cameros	66	E1
Torre del Greco	69	E5
Torrelaguna	66	E2
Torrelavega	66	D1
Torremolinos	66	D4
Torrens Creek	113	K3
Torrens, Lake	113	H5
Torrente	67	F3
Torreon	127	L8
Torres Island	114	T10
Torres Novas	66	B3
Torres Strait	114	C4
Torres Vedras	66	B3
Torrevieja	67	F4
Torr Head	58	K2
Torridge	52	C4
Torridon, Loch	56	C3
Torrijos	66	D3
Torrington *Connecticut*	125	P6
Torrington *Wyoming*	123	M6
Torrox	66	E4
Torsas	63	F8
Torsby	63	E6
Torshavn	62	Z14
Torsken	62	L2
Tortkuduk	84	Ae5
Tortola	133	Q5
Tortona	68	B3
Tortosa	67	G2
Tortosa, Cabo de	67	G2
Tortue, Ile de la	133	L4
Tortuga, Isla	126	G7
Tortuga, Isla la	136	D1
Tortum	77	J2
Torul	77	H2
Torun	71	H2
Tory Island	58	F2
Torysa	71	J4
Tory Sound	58	F2
Torzhok	78	F4
Torzym	70	F2
Tosa-shimizu	89	D9
Tosa-wan	89	D9
Toscaig	56	C3
Tosco-Emiliano, Appennino	68	C3
Tostado	138	D5
Tosya	76	F2
Totana	67	F4
Totes	64	D4
Totma	78	G4
Totnes	52	D4
Totness	137	F2
Totora	138	C3
Totota	104	C4
Totoya	114	S9
Totton	53	F4
Tottori	89	E8
Touba	104	D4
Toubkal, Jebel	100	D2
Tougan	104	E3
Touggourt	101	G2
Touho Ouegoa	114	W16
Toul	64	F4
Toulon	65	F7
Toulouse	65	D7
Toummo	101	H4
Toumodi	104	D4
Toungoo	93	J5
Touraine	65	D5
Tourcoing	64	E3
Tournai	64	E3
Tournon *France*	65	D5
Tournon *France*	65	F6
Tournus	65	F5
Touros	137	K5
Tours	65	D5
Tousside, Pic	102	C3
Touws River	108	D6
Tovarkovskiy	79	F5
Towada	88	H5
Towanda	125	M6
Towcester	53	G2
Tower Island	136	B7
Towie	56	F3
Townsend	122	J4
Townshend Island	113	L3
Townsville	113	K2
Towson	125	M7
Toxkan He	86	D3
Toya-ko	88	H4
Toyama	89	F7
Toyama-wan	89	F7
Toyohashi	89	F8
Toyonaka	89	E8
Toyooka	89	E8

Name	Page	Ref
Tyanya	85	K5
Tychany	84	F4
Tychy	71	H3
Tygda	85	M6
Tyler	128	E4
Tyloskog	63	F7
Tym	84	C5
Tymovskoye	85	Q6
Tynda	85	L5
Tyndall, Mount	115	C5
Tyndrum	57	D4
Tyne	55	H2
Tyne and Wear	55	H2
Tynemouth	55	H1
Tynset	62	D5
Tyr	85	P6
Tyre	94	B5
Tyret	84	G6
Tyrma	85	N6
Tyrone *U.K.*	58	H3
Tyrone *U.S.A.*	125	L6
Tyrrhenian Sea	69	D5
Tysnesoy	63	A7
Tyukalinsk	84	A5
Tyulgan	79	K5
Tyuli	84	Ae4
Tyung	85	L4
Tywi	52	C3
Tywyn	52	C2
Tzaneen	108	F4
Tzoumerka	75	F3

U

Name	Page	Ref
Uainambi	136	C3
Uapao, Cape	114	X16
Uapes	136	D4
Uatuma	136	F4
Uaupes	136	D3
Uava	137	K5
Uba	138	H4
Ubaitaba	137	K6
Ube	89	C9
Ubeda	66	E3
Ubekendt O	120	R3
Uberaba	138	J3
Uberaba, Laguna	138	E3
Uberlandia	138	G3
Ubinskoye	84	B5
Ubolratna Reservoir	93	K5
Ubombo	109	F5
Ubon Ratchathani	93	K5
Ubundu	106	E3
Ucayali	136	C4
Ucdam	77	J3
Uch Adzhi	95	R2
Uchami	84	F4
Ucharal	86	F2
Uchiura-wan	88	H4
Uchte	70	C2
Uchur	85	N5
Uckermark	70	E2
Uckfield	53	H4
Ucluelet	122	B3
Uda	85	N6
Udachnyy	84	J3
Udaipur	92	D4
Udayd, Ra's al	97	K4
Udbina	72	C3
Uddevalla	63	D7
Uddjaur	62	G4
Udine	68	D2
Udon Thani	93	K5
Udskoye	85	N6
Udupi	92	D6
Ueckermunde	70	F2
Ueda	89	G7
Uele *Russia*	84	J2
Uele *Zaire*	106	D2
Uelen	81	V3
Uelkal	85	Y3
Uelzen	70	D2
Ufa *Russia*	78	K4
Ufa *Russia*	78	K5
Ugab	108	B4
Uganda	107	F2
Ugashik Bay	118	D4
Ugashik Lakes	118	D4
Ughelli	105	G4
Ugijar	66	E4
Uglich	78	F4
Ugljane	72	D4
Ugra	78	E5
Ugun	85	M5
Ugurlu	77	J2
Ugurludag	76	F2
Ugut	84	A4
Uherske Hradiste	71	G4
Uhlava	70	E4
Uhrusk	71	K3
Uig	56	B3
Uige	106	C2
Uil *Kazakhstan*	79	J6
Uil *Kazakhstan*	79	J6
Uinskoye	78	K4
Uinta Mountains	122	J7
Uisong	89	B7
Uitenhage	108	E6
Ujiji	107	E3
Uji-shoto	89	B10
Ujjain	92	E4
Ujpest	72	E2
Ujscie	71	G2
Ujung Pandang	91	F7
Uka	85	U5
Ukholovo	79	G5
Ukhta	78	J3
Ukhunku	85	L3
Uki	114	K7
Ukiah	122	C8
Ukmerge	63	L9
Ukraine	79	D6
Ukta	71	J2
Uku	106	B5
Uku-jima	89	B9
Ukuma	106	C5
Ula	76	C4
Ulaangom	86	G2
Ulan Bator	87	K2
Ulan-Erge	79	G6
Ulanhad	87	M3
Ulan-Khol	79	H6
Ulan Tohoi	86	J3
Ulan-Ude	84	H6
Ulan Ula	93	H2
Ulas	77	G3
Ulawa	114	K6
Ulchin	89	B7
Ulcinj	74	E2
Uled Saidan	101	J3
Ulfborg	63	C8
Ulgumdzha	85	K4
Ulhasnagar	92	D5
Uliastay	86	H2
Ulithi Atoll	91	K4
Uljan	72	C3
Uljma	73	F3
Ulla	66	B1
Ullaanbaatar	87	K2
Ullanger	62	H5
Ullapool	56	C3
Ullock	55	F2
Ullswater	55	G2
Ullung-do	89	C7
Ulm	70	C4
Ulog	72	E4
Ulongue	109	F2
Ulricehamn	63	E8
Ulsan	89	B8
Ulsta	56	A1
Ulsteinvik	62	A5
Ulster	58	H3
Ulster Canal	58	H4
Ulubat Golu	76	C2
Ulubey *Turkey*	76	C3
Ulubey *Turkey*	77	G2
Uluborlu	76	D3
Ulucinar	77	F4
Uludag	76	C2
Ulu Dagi	76	C2
Uludere	77	K4
Uluguru Mountains	107	G4
Ulukisla	76	F4
Ulunkhan	85	J6
Ulus	76	E2
Ulva	57	B4
Ulverston	55	F2
Ulyanovsk	78	H5
Ulysses	127	M2
Ulzburg	70	C2
Umala	138	C3
Uman	79	E6
Uman	131	Q7
Umanak Fjord	120	R3
Umari	114	B2
Umarkot	92	C3
Umba	78	E2
Umbertide	68	D4
Umboi Island	114	D3
Umbro-Marchigiano, Appennino	68	D4
Umea	62	J5
Umealven	62	H4
Umm al Qaywayn	97	M4
Umm as Samim	97	M6
Umm Bel	102	E5
Umm Keddada	102	E5
Umm Lajj	96	C4
Umm Ruwaba	102	F5
Umm Said	97	K4
Umm Urumah	96	C4
Umnak Island	118	Ae9
Umred	92	E4
Umtali	109	F3
Umtata	108	E6
Umzingwani	108	E4
Una *Brazil*	137	K7
Una *Bosnia-Herzegovina*	72	C3
Unalaska Island	118	Ae9
Unare	133	Q10
Unayzah	96	F3
Uncia	138	C3
Uncompahgre Peak	123	L8
Uncompahgre Plateau	122	K8
Underwood	123	P4
Unecha	79	E5
Uneiuxi	136	D4
Ungava Bay	121	N6
Ungava, Peninsule d'	121	L5
Unggi	88	C4
Uniao dos Palmares	137	K5
Uniao do Vitoria	138	E5
Unije	72	C3
Unimak Island	118	Af9
Unimak Pass	118	Ae9
Unini	136	E4
Union	129	M3
Union City	128	H2
Uniondale	108	D6
Union Springs	129	K4
Uniontown	125	L7
United Arab Emirates	97	L5
United States of America	116	H4
Unity	122	E5
Universales, Montes	67	F2
University Park	127	J4
Unnao	92	F3
Unst	56	B1
Untaek	88	A5
Unye	77	G2
Unzha	78	G4
Uodgan	96	D8
Uoyan	85	J5
Upata	133	R10
Upavon	53	F3
Upemba, Lake	106	E4
Upernavik	120	Q3
Upernavik Isfjord	120	R3
Upington	108	D5
Upolu	111	U4
Upolu Point	126	T10
Upper Arrow Lake	122	F2
Upper Broughton	53	G2
Upper Hutt	115	E4
Upper Klamath Lake	122	D6
Upper Seal Lake	121	M6
Uppingham	53	G2
Uppsala *Sweden*	63	G6
Uppsala *Sweden*	63	L7
Upsala	124	E2
Upstart Bay	113	K2
Uqla Sawab	77	J6
Urad Qianqi	87	K3
Urad Zhongqi	87	K3
Urak	85	Q5
Urakan	84	H5
Urakawa	88	J4
Ural	79	J6
Uralsk	79	J5
Uralskiy Khrebet	78	K3
Urandangi	113	H3
Urandi	137	J6
Uranium City	119	P4
Uraricoera	136	E3
Urawa	89	G8
Urayirah	97	J4
Urayq, Al	96	D2
Urayq, Nafud al	96	F4
Urbana	124	J6
Urbino	68	D4
Urda	79	H6
Urdzhar	86	F2
Uren	78	H4
Urengoy	84	B3
Ureparapara	114	T10
Ures	126	G6
Urfa	77	H4
Urgal	85	N6
Urgel, Llanos de	67	G2
Urgench	80	G5
Urgup	76	F3
Urho	86	F2
Uritskiy	84	Ae6
Urkan	85	M6
Urla	76	B3
Urlingford	59	G7
Urmi	88	D1
Urosevac	73	F4
Urr Water	57	E5
Ursatyevskaya	86	B3
Uruacu	137	H6
Uruapan	130	H8
Urubamba	136	C6
Urubu	136	F4
Urucui	137	J5
Urucuia	138	G3
Urucui, Serra do	137	J5
Uruguaiana	138	E5
Uruguay	138	E6
Urumchi	86	F3
Urumqi	86	F3
Urupadi	137	F4
Urup, Ostrov	85	S7
Uruti Point	115	F4
Urville, Tanjung d'	114	B2
Uryupinsk	79	G5
Urzhum	78	H4
Urziceni	73	J3
Usa	78	K2
Usak	76	C3
Usambara Mountains	107	G3
Usedom	70	F1
Ushant	64	A4
Ushitsa	73	J1
Ushtobe	86	D2
Ushuaia	139	C10
Usk *Gwent, U.K.*	52	E3
Usk *Powys, U.K.*	52	D3
Usk Reservoir	52	D3
Uskudar	76	C2
Uslar	70	C3
Usman	79	F5
Usolye	78	K4
Usolye-Sibirskoye	84	G6
Uspenka	84	B6
Ussel	65	E6
Ussuri	88	E2
Ussuriysk	88	C4
Ust-Barguzin	84	H6
Ust-Belaya	85	W3
Ust-Chara	85	L4
UstChizhapka	84	B5
Ustica, Isola di	69	D6
UstIlimsk	84	G5
Ust-Ilych	84	Ac4
Usti nad Lebem	70	F3
Ustka	71	G1
UstKamchatsk	85	U5
Ust-Kamenogorsk	86	E2
Ust-Kamo	84	F4
Ust-Kan	84	E5
Ust-Kara	84	Ad3
Ust-Karenga	85	K6
Ust-Katav	78	K5
Ust-Kulom	78	J3
Ust-Kut	84	H5
Ust-Kuyga	85	P3
Ust-Labinsk	79	F6
UstLuga	63	N7
UstMaya	85	N4
Ust-Mayn	85	W3
Ust-Mil	85	N5
Ust-Muya	85	K5
UstNem	78	J3
Ust-Nera	85	Q4
UstNiman	85	N6
UstOmchug	85	R4
Ust-Ordynskiy	84	G6
Ustovo	73	H5
Ust-Ozernoye	84	D5
UstPenzhino	85	V4
Ust-Pit	84	E5
Ust-Port	84	C3
UstReka	78	H3
UstSara	78	E3
UstTapsuy	78	L3
Ust-Tatta	85	N4
Ust-Tsilma	78	J2
Ust-Tym	84	C5
UstTyrma	85	N6
UstUra	78	G3
UstUsa	78	K2
UstVaga	78	G3
UstVyyskaya	78	H3
UstYuribey	84	Ae3
Ustyurt, Plato	51	T7
Usuki	89	C9
Usulatan	132	C8
Usumacinta	131	P9
Utah	122	H8
Utah Lake	122	J7
Utajarvi	62	M4
Utara	90	C6
Ute Creek	127	L2
Utena	63	N9
Uthal	92	C3
Utiariti	136	F6
Utica	125	N5
Utiel	67	F3
Utikuma Lake	119	M4
Utkholok	85	T5
Utrecht	64	F2
Utrera	66	D4
Utsera	77	K1
Utsjoki	62	M2
Utsonomiya	89	G7
Utta	79	H6
Uttaradit	93	K5
Uttar Pradesh	92	F3
Uttoxeter	53	F2
Uttyakh	85	N3
Utubulak	86	F2
Utukok	118	C2
Utupua	114	N7
Uuldza	87	L2
Uummannaq	120	R3
Uusikaarlepyy	62	K5
Uusikaupunki	63	J6
Uusimaa	63	L6
Uvac	72	E4
Uvalde	127	N6
Uvarovo	79	G5
Uvea	111	T4
Uvinza	107	F4
Uvira	107	E3
Uvol	114	E3
Uvs Nuur	86	G1
Uwajima	89	D9
Uwayrid, Harrat al	96	C3
Uy	84	Ad6
Uyak	118	E4
Uyandina	85	Q3
Uyeg	78	J2
Uyuni	138	C4
Uyuni, Salar de	138	C4
Uz	71	K4
Uzaym, Nahr al	94	G4
Uzbekistan	86	B3
Uzda	71	M2
Uzen	79	J7
Uzerche	65	D6
Uzes	65	F6
Uzhgorod	79	C6
Uzhok	71	K4
Uzlovaya	78	F5
Uzumlu	76	D4
Uzun	84	D6
Uzundere	77	J2
Uzungol	77	J2
Uzunisa	77	G2
Uzunkopru	76	B2
Uzunkuyu	76	B3

V

Name	Page	Ref
Vaajakoski	62	L5
Vaal	108	E5
Vaala	62	M4
Vaal Dam	108	E5
Vaasa *Finland*	62	J5
Vaasa *Finland*	62	K5
Vacaria	138	F5
Vacha	70	D3
Vache, Ile-a-	133	L5
Vadodara	92	D4
Vadso	62	N1
Vadu	73	K3
Vaduz	68	B2
Vaga	78	G3
Vagar	62	Z14
Vagay *Russia*	84	Ae5
Vagay *Russia*	84	Ae5
Vage	63	A6
Vaghena	114	H5
Vagnharad	63	G7
Vah	71	G5
Vaich, Loch	56	D3
Vainikkala	63	N6
Vaitupu	111	S3
Vakarel	73	G4
Vakfikebir	77	H2
Valaam, Ostrov	63	P6
Valandovo	73	G5
Valcheta	139	C8
Valday *Russia*	78	E4
Valday *Russia*	78	F3
Valdayskaya Vozvyshennost	78	E4
Valdemarsvik	63	G7
Valdepenas	66	E3
Valderaduey	66	D2
Valderrobres	67	G2
Valdes, Peninsula	139	D8
Valdez	118	F3
Valdivia	139	B7
Val-d'Or	125	M2
Valdosta	129	L5
Valdres	63	C6
Valea Lui Mihai	73	G2
Valenca	66	B2
Valenca	138	K6
Valenca do Piaui	137	J5
Valencay	65	D5
Valence	65	F6
Valencia *Spain*	67	F3
Valencia *Venezuela*	136	D1
Valencia de Alcantara	66	C3
Valencia de Don Juan	66	D1
Valencia, Golfo de	67	G3
Valencia Island	59	B9
Valencia, Lago de	133	P9
Valenciennes	64	E3
Valentim, Serra do	137	J5
Valentin	88	E4
Valentine	123	P6
Valenzuela	91	G3
Valera	136	C2
Valga	63	M8
Valiente, Peninsula	132	G10
Valjevo	72	E3
Valkininkay	71	L1
Valladolid *Mexico*	131	Q7
Valladolid *Spain*	66	D2
Vallasana de Mena	66	E1
Vallay	56	A3
Valle de la Pascua	136	D2
Valle de Santiago	131	J7
Valledupar	136	C1
Valle Grande	138	D3
Valle Hermosa	128	D8
Vallejo	126	A1
Vallenar	138	B5
Valletta	74	C5
Valley Falls	122	D6
Valleyview	119	M4
Vallgrund	62	J5
Vallimanca	139	D7
Vallo di Lucania	69	E5
Valls	67	G2
Valmiera	63	L8
Valognes	64	C4
Val-Paradis	125	L2
Valparaiso	129	J5
Valparaiso *Chile*	139	B6
Valparaiso *Mexico*	130	H6
Valpovo	72	E3
Valsjobyn	62	F4
Vals, Tanjung	114	B3
Valtos	56	B2
Valurfossen	63	B6
Valuyki	79	F5
Valverde	100	B3
Valverde de Jucar	66	E3
Valverde del Camino	66	C4
Van	77	K3
Vanadzor	77	L2
Vanajanselka	63	L6
Vanavona	114	H6
Van Buren *Arkansas*	128	E3
Van Buren *Maine*	125	S3
Van Canh	93	L6
Vancouver *Canada*	122	C3
Vancouver *U.S.A.*	122	C5
Vancouver Island	122	A2
Vanda	63	N6
Vandalia	124	F7
Vanderhoof	118	L5
Van Diemen, Cape	112	G1
Van Diemen Gulf	112	G1
Vanern	63	E7
Vanersborg	63	E7
Vanga	107	G3
Vangaindrano	109	J4
Van Golu	77	K3
Vangou	88	D4
Vangunu	114	J6
Van Horn	127	K5
Vanikoro Islands	114	N7
Vanimo	114	C2
Vanna	62	H1
Vannas	62	H5
Vannes	65	B5
Van Rees, Pegunungan	114	B2
Vanrhynsdorp	108	C6
Vanrock	113	J2
Vansbro	63	F6
Vanset	77	K4
Vansittart Island	120	K4
Vantaa	63	N6
Vanua Balavu	114	S8
Vanua Lava	114	T10
Vanua Levu	114	R8
Vanua Levu Barrier Reef	114	R8
Vanuatu	114	T12
Vanwyksvlei	108	D6
Vanzevat	84	Ae4
Vapnyarka	73	K1
Varallo	68	B3
Varamin	95	K4
Varanasi	92	F3
Varandey	78	K2
Varangerfjorden	62	P1
Varangerhalvoya	62	N1
Varazdin	72	D2
Varazze	68	B3
Varberg	63	E8
Vardar	73	F5
Varde	63	C9
Vardo	62	P1
Varena	71	L1
Varennes	65	E5
Varese	68	B3
Varfolomeyevka	88	D3
Vargarda	63	E7
Vargas Guerra	136	B4
Varginha	138	G4
Varilla	138	B4
Varkaus	63	L5
Varmland	63	E7
Varmlands-nas	63	E7
Varna	73	J4
Varnamo	63	F8
Varnek	84	Ad3
Varnya	84	A3
Varoy	62	E3
Varto	77	J3
Vartry Reservoir	59	K6
Varzea Grande	137	J5
Varzino	78	F2
Varzuga	78	F2
Varzy	65	E5
Vasa	62	J5
Vascao	66	C4
Vascongadas	66	E1
Vashkovtsy	73	H1
Vasilishki	71	L2
Vasilkov	79	E5
Vasilyevka	79	F6
Vaskha	78	H3
Vaslui	73	J2
Vassdalsegga	63	B7
Vasteras	63	G7
Vasterbotten	62	G4
Vasterdalalven	63	E6
Vastergotland	63	E7
Vasterhaninge	63	H7
Vasternorrland	62	G5
Vastervik	63	G8
Vastmanland	63	G7
Vasto	69	E4
Vasyugan	84	B5
Vatersay	57	A4
Vathi *Greece*	75	F3
Vathi *Greece*	75	J4
Vaticano, Capo	69	E6
Vatilau	114	J6
Vatnajokull	62	W12
Vatneyri	62	A2
Vatoa	111	T5
Vatomandry	109	J3
Vatra Dornei	73	H2
Vattern	63	F7
Vatu-i-Ra Channel	114	R8
Vatulele	114	Q9
Vaughn	127	K3
Vaupes	136	C3
Vavatenina	109	J3
Vavau Group	111	U5
Vavuniya	92	F7
Vaxholm	63	H7
Vaxjo	63	F8
Vayalpad	92	E6
Vaygach	84	Ac2
Vaygach, Ostrov	84	Ac2
Veberod	63	E9
Vebomark	62	J4
Vecht	64	G2
Vechta	70	C2
Vechte	70	B2
Veddige	63	E8
Vega *Norway*	62	D4
Vega *U.S.A.*	127	L3
Vegorritis, Limni	75	F2
Vegreville	119	N5
Veidholmen	62	B5
Veinge	63	E8
Vejen	63	C9
Vejer de la Frontera	66	D4
Vejle	63	C9
Velanidhia	75	G4
Velas, Cabo	132	E9
Velasco, Sierra de	138	C5
Velay, Monts du	65	E6
Velebit Planina	72	C3
Velestinon	75	G3
Velez Malaga	66	D4
Velez Rubio	67	E4
Velhas	138	H3
Velichayevskoye	79	H7
Velika Gorica	72	D3
Velika Kapela	72	C3
Velikaya *Russia*	78	H2
Velikaya *Russia*	85	W4
Velikaya Kema	88	F3
Veliki Kanal	72	E3
Velikiy Bereznyy	71	K4
Velikiye Luki	78	E4
Velikonda Range	92	E6
Veliko Turnovo	73	H4
Veliky Ustyug	78	H3
Velingara	104	C3
Velingrad	73	H4
Velizh	78	E4
Vella Gulf	114	H5
Vella Lavella	114	H5
Velletri	69	D5
Vellore	92	E6
Velsk	78	G3
Velt	78	J2
Velvestad	62	E4
Venado Tuerto	139	D6
Venafro	69	E5
Venaria	68	A3
Venda Nova	66	C2
Venda Novas	66	B3
Vendome	65	D5
Vendsyssel	63	D8
Venecia	136	D6
Venezia	68	D3
Venezia, Golfo di	68	D3
Venezuela	136	D2
Venezuela Basin	134	C1
Venezuela, Golfo de	136	C1
Vengurla	92	D5
Veniaminof Volcano	118	Ag8
Venice *Italy*	68	D3
Venice *U.S.A.*	128	H6
Venkatapuram	92	F5
Venlo	64	G3
Vennesla	63	C7
Venta	63	J8
Ventimiglia	68	A4
Ventnor	53	F4
Ventry	59	B8
Ventspils	63	N8
Ventuari	136	D3
Ventura	126	C3
Venus Bay	113	K6
Venustiano Carranza *Mexico*	130	G5
Venustiano Carranza *Mexico*	131	N9
Vera *Argentina*	138	D5
Vera *Spain*	67	F4
Veracruz	131	L8
Veranopolis	138	F5
Veraval	92	D4
Verbania	68	B3
Vercelli	68	B3
Verdalsora	62	D5
Verde *Mexico*	131	L9
Verde *U.S.A.*	126	G3
Verden	70	C2
Verdigris	124	C8
Verdinho, Serra do	138	F3
Verdon	65	G7
Verdun	64	F4
Vereeniging	108	E5
Vereshchagino	78	J4
Verga, Cap	104	C3
Verin	66	C2
Verin Talin	77	K2
Verkhne-Avzyar	78	K5
Verkhnedvinsk	63	M9
Verkhne-Imanskiy	88	E3
Verkhneimbatskoye	84	D4
Verkhne Matur	84	D6
Verkhne Nildino	84	Ad4
Verkhne Skoblino	84	D5
Verkhnetulomskiy	62	P2
Verkhne Tura	78	K4
Verkhnevilyuysk	85	L4
Verkhniy Baskunchak	79	H6
Verkhniy Shar	78	J2
Verkhnyaya Amga	85	M5
Verkhnyaya Inta	78	L2
Verkhnyaya Toyma	78	H3
Verkhoturye	84	Ad5
Verkhovye	79	F5
Verkhoyansk	85	N3
Verkhoyanskiy Khrebet	85	M3
Verkhyaya Nildino	78	L3
Vermilion	119	N5
Vermilion Bay	128	G6
Vermilion Lake	124	D3
Vermillion	123	R6
Vermillion Bay	124	D2
Vermont	125	P5
Vernal	123	K7
Vernon *Canada*	122	E2
Vernon *France*	64	D4
Vernon *U.S.A.*	127	N3
Veroia	75	G2
Verona	68	C3
Versailles	64	E4
Vert, Cape	104	B3
Verviers	64	F3
Vervins	64	E4
Veryan Bay	52	C4
Veryuvom	78	L2
Veshenskaya	79	G6
Veslos	63	C8
Veslyana	78	J3
Vesoul	65	G5
Vest-Agder	63	B7
Vesteralen	62	F2
Vestfjorden	62	F2
Vest-Fold	63	D7
Vestre Jakobselv	62	N1
Vestvagoy	62	E2
Vesuvio	69	E5
Vesyegonsk	78	F4
Veszprem	72	D2
Vetekhtina	85	K5
Vetlanda	63	F8
Vetluga *Russia*	78	H4
Vetluga *Russia*	78	H4
Vetluzskiy	78	H4
Vettore, Monte	69	D4
Veun Kham	93	L6
Veurne	64	E3
Vevey	68	A2
Veyatie, Loch	56	C2
Vezelay	65	E5
Vezere	65	D6
Vezirkopru	76	F2
Viacha	138	C3
Viamao	138	F6
Viana	137	J4
Viana do Castelo	66	B2
Viangchan	93	K5
Viareggio	68	C4
Viaur	65	E6
Viborg	63	C8
Vibo Valentia	69	F6
Vicecomodoro Marambio	141	W6
Vicente Guerrero	130	H6
Vicenza	68	C3
Vich	67	H2
Vichada	136	D3
Vichuga	78	G4
Vichy	65	E5
Vicksburg	128	G4
Vico	69	B4
Vicosa	137	K5
Victor Emanuel Range	114	C3
Victor Harbor	113	H6
Victoria *Argentina*	138	D6
Victoria *Northern Territory, Australia*	112	G2
Victoria *Victoria, Australia*	113	J6
Victoria *Cameroon*	105	G5
Victoria *Canada*	122	C3
Victoria *Chile*	139	B7
Victoria *Hong Kong*	90	E1
Victoria *Malaysia*	90	F4
Victoria *Seychelles*	82	D7
Victoria *U.S.A.*	128	D6
Victoria de las Tunas	132	J4
Victoria Falls	108	E3
Victoria Island	119	P1
Victoria, Lake	107	F3
Victoria Land	141	L4
Victoria, Mount *Myanmar*	93	H4
Victoria, Mount *Papua New Guinea*	114	D3
Victoria Nile	107	F2
Victoria Peak	118	K5
Victoria Strait	119	Q2
Victoriaville	125	Q3
Victoria West	108	D6
Victorica	139	C7
Victorville	126	D3
Vicuna	138	B6
Vidago	66	C2
Vidalia	129	L4
Vidareidi	62	Z14
Vididalur	62	X12
Vidim	84	G5
Vidimyri	62	V12
Vidin	92	G4
Vidisha	92	E4
Vidivellir	62	X12
Vidomlya	71	K2
Vidsel	62	J4
Viedma	139	D8
Viedma, Lago	139	B9
Viella	67	G1
Vienna *Austria*	68	F1
Vienna *Illinois*	124	F8
Vienna *Ohio*	125	K7
Vienne *France*	65	D5
Vienne *France*	65	F6
Vientiane	93	K5
Vieques	133	Q5
Vierwaldstatter See	68	B2
Vierzon	65	E5
Vieste	69	F5
Vietnam	93	L5
Vif	65	F6

Name	Map	Grid
Vigan	91	G2
Vigevano	68	B3
Viggiano	69	E5
Vigia	137	G4
Viglio, Monte	69	D5
Vigo	66	B1
Vigrestad	63	A7
Viiala	63	K6
Vijayawada	92	F5
Vijose	74	E2
Vik	62	E4
Vik	62	V13
Vikajarvi	62	M3
Vikersund	63	D7
Vikhorevka	84	G5
Vikna	62	D4
Viksoyri	63	B6
Vila	114	U12
Viladikars	77	K2
Vila Franca	66	B3
Vilaine	65	C5
Vilaller	67	G1
Vilanculos	109	G4
Vila Nova	137	F4
Vila Nova de Famalicao	66	B2
Vila Pouca de Aguiar	66	C2
Vila Real	66	C2
Vila Real de Santo Antonio	66	C4
Vila Velha	138	H4
Vila Velha de Rodao	66	C3
Vila Vicosa	66	C3
Vilcheka, Zemlya	80	H1
Viled	78	H3
Vileyka	71	M1
Vilhelmina	62	G4
Vilhena	136	E6
Viliga-Kushka	85	T4
Viljandi	63	L7
Vilkitskogo, Proliv	81	M2
Vilkovo	73	K3
Villa Abecia	138	C4
Villa Angela	138	D5
Villa Aroma	138	C3
Villa Bella	136	D6
Villa Bens	100	C3
Villablino	66	C1
Villacarrillo	66	E3
Villacastin	66	D2
Villach	68	D2
Villa Cisneros	100	B4
Villa Constitucion	138	D6
Villa de Cura	136	D2
Villadiego	66	D1
Villa Dolores	139	C6
Villafranca del Bierzo	66	C1
Villafranca de los Barros	66	C3
Villafranca del Penedes	67	G2
Villafranca di Verona	68	C3
Villaguay	138	E6
Villa Hayes	138	E5
Villahermosa	131	N9
Villa Huidobro	139	D6
Villa Iris	139	D7
Villajoyosa	67	F3
Villalba	66	C1
Villalon de Campos	66	D1
Villalpando	66	D2
Villa Maria	138	D6
Villamayor de Santiago	66	E3
Villa Montes	138	D4
Villanueva	130	H6
Villanueva de Cordoba	66	D3
Villanueva del Fresno	66	C3
Villanueva de los Castillejos	66	C4
Villanueva de los Infantes	66	E3
Villanueva y Geltru	67	G2
Villaputzu	69	B6
Villarcayo	66	E1
Villarejo	66	E2
Villarrica	138	E5
Villarrobledo	66	E3
Villasandino	66	D1
Villa Union *Argentina*	138	C5
Villa Union *Mexico*	127	M6
Villavicencio	136	C3
Villaviciosa	66	D1
Villazon	138	C4
Villedieu	64	C4
Villefort	65	E6
Villefranche-de-Rouergue	65	E6
Villefranche-sur-Saone	65	F6
Villena	67	F3
Villeneuve-sur-Lot	65	D6
Villeneuve-sur-Yonne	65	E4
Ville Platte	128	F5
Villers-Bocago	64	C4
Villers-Cotterets	64	E4
Villeurbanne	65	F6
Villodrigo	66	D1
Vilna	71	L1
Vilnius	71	L1
Vilnya	71	L1
Vilshofen	70	E4
Vilyuy	85	M4
Vilyuysk	85	L4
Vilyuyskoye Plato	84	H3
Vimmerby	63	F8
Vimperk	70	E4
Vina del Mar	139	B6
Vinaroz	67	G2
Vinas	63	F6
Vincennes	124	G7
Vincennes Bay	141	H5
Vinchina	138	C5
Vindelalven	62	J4
Vindeln	62	H4
Vindhya Range	92	E4
Vineland	125	N7
Vinga	73	F3
Vinh	93	L5
Vinh Loi	93	L7
Vinh Long	93	L6
Vinh Yen	93	L4
Vinica	73	G5
Vinkovci	72	E3
Vinnytsya	79	D6
Vinogradov	71	K4
Vipiteno	68	C2
Vir	72	C3
Virac	91	G3
Viramgam	92	D4
Virandozero	78	F3
Viransehir	77	H4
Virarajendrapet	92	E6
Virden	123	P3
Vire *France*	64	C4
Vire *France*	64	C4
Virfurile	73	G2
Virgenes, Cabo	139	C10
Virgin	126	E2
Virgin Gorda	133	Q5
Virginia *Ireland*	58	H5
Virginia *Minnesota*	124	D3
Virginia *U.S.A.*	125	L8
Virginia Beach	125	N8
Virginia Falls	118	L3
Virgin Islands	133	Q5
Virmasvesi	62	M5
Virovitica	72	D3
Virrat	63	K5
Virudunagar	92	E7
Vis	72	D4
Visalia	126	C2
Visayan Sea	91	G3
Visby	63	H8
Viscount Melville Sound	120	E3
Visegrad	72	E4
Viseu *Brazil*	137	H4
Viseu *Portugal*	66	C2
Vishakhapatnam	92	F5
Vishera	78	K3
Vishnevets	71	L4
Vislanda	63	F8
Visoko	72	E4
Viso, Monte	68	A3
Vista	126	D4
Vistonis, Limni	75	H2
Vit	73	H4
Vitava	70	F4
Viterbo	69	D4
Viterog Planina	72	D3
Vitiaz Strait	114	C3
Vitichi	138	C4
Vitigudino	66	C2
Viti Levu	114	Q9
Vitim *Russia*	85	J5
Vitim *Russia*	85	J5
Vitina	75	G4
Vitoria	66	E1
Vitoria	138	H4
Vitoria da Conquista	137	J6
Vitoria de Santa Antao	137	K5
Vitre	64	C4
Vitry-le-Francois	64	F4
Vitsyebsk	78	E4
Vittangi	62	J3
Vittel	64	F4
Vittoria	69	E7
Vittorio Veneto	68	D3
Vivarais, Monts du	65	F6
Viver	67	F3
Vivero	66	C1
Vivi *Russia*	84	F4
Vivi *Russia*	84	F4
Vizcaino, Desierto de	126	F7
Vizcaino, Sierra	126	E7
Vize	76	B2
Vizhas	78	H2
Vizianagaram	92	F5
Vizinga	78	J3
Vizzavona	69	B4
Vladicin Han	73	G4
Vladikavkaz	77	L1
Vladimir	78	G4
Vladimirets	71	M3
Vladimirovka	79	J5
Vladimir Volynskiy	71	L3
Vladivostok	88	C4
Vlakherna	75	G4
Vlasenica	72	E3
Vlieland	64	F2
Vlissingen	64	E3
Vlore	74	E2
Vodice	72	C4
Vodlozero, Ozero	78	F3
Vogan	105	F4
Voghera	68	B3
Voh	114	W16
Vohemar	109	J2
Vohilava	109	J4
Vohimarina	109	J2
Vohipeno	109	J4
Voi	107	G3
Voiron	65	F6
Vojens	63	C9
Vojmsjon	62	G4
Vojnic	72	C3
Volary	70	E4
Volborg	123	M5
Volchansk	79	F5
Volda	62	B5
Volga	79	H6
Volgodonsk	79	G6
Volgograd	79	G6
Volgogradskoye Vodokhranilishche	79	H6
Volgsele	62	G4
Volissos	75	H3
Volkhov *Russia*	78	E4
Volkhov *Russia*	78	E4
Volklingen	70	B4
Volkovysk	71	L2
Volksrust	108	E5
Volnovakha	79	F6
Volochankao	84	E2
Volochayevka	88	E1
Volochisk	71	M4
Volodskaya	78	G3
Vologda	78	F4
Volokon	84	H5
Volonga	78	H2
Volos	75	G3
Voloshka	78	F3
Volovets	71	K4
Volozhin	71	M1
Volpa	71	L2
Volsk	79	H5
Volta	104	F4
Volta, Lake	104	E4
Volta Redonda	138	H4
Volterra	68	C4
Volteva	78	G3
Volturno	69	E5
Volvi, Limni	75	G2
Volynskaya Vozvyshennost	71	L3
Volynskoje Polesje	71	L3
Volzhskiy	79	G6
Von Martius, Cachoeira	137	G6
Vopnafjordur	62	X12
Voras Oros	75	F2
Vordingborg	63	D9
Voriai Sporadhes	75	H3
Vorkuta	78	L2
Vormsi	62	K7
Voronezh	79	F5
Voronovo	71	L1
Vorontsovo	63	N8
Voronya	78	F2
Voroshno	78	H4
Vortsjarv	63	M7
Voru	63	M8
Vosges	64	G4
Voskresensk	78	F4
Voss *Norway*	63	B6
Voss *Norway*	63	B6
Vostochno-Sibirskoye More	85	T2
Vostochnyy *Russia*	88	D4
Vostochnyy *Russia*	88	J1
Vostock	141	H3
Vostretsovo	88	E3
Votice	70	F4
Votkinsk	78	J4
Votkinskoye Vodokhranilishche	78	K4
Vot Tande	114	T10
Vouga	66	C2
Vouziers	64	F4
Vowchurch	52	E2
Voxnan *Sweden*	63	F6
Voxnan *Sweden*	63	F6
Voynitsa	62	P4
Voy Vozh	78	J3
Voyvozh	78	K3
Voza	114	H5
Vozhayel	78	H3
Vozhega	78	G3
Vozhe, Ozero	78	F3
Voznesensk	79	E6
Voznesenye	78	F3
Vozvyshennost Karabil	95	R3
Vrancei, Muntii	73	J3
Vrangelya, Mys	85	P6
Vrangelya, Ostrov	81	U2
Vranje	73	F4
Vranov	71	J4
Vratsa	73	G4
Vrbas	72	D3
Vrbovsko	72	C3
Vrede	108	E5
Vrhnika	72	C3
Vrindavan	92	E3
Vrlika	72	D4
Vrondadhes	75	J3
Vrsac	73	F3
Vrsacki Kanal	73	F3
Vryburg	108	D5
Vryheid	108	F5
Vucitrn	73	F4
Vukovar	72	E3
Vulavu	114	J6
Vulcan	73	G3
Vulcano, Isola	69	E6
Vung Tau	93	L6
Vunisea	114	R9
Vuokatti	62	N4
Vuollerim	62	J3
Vyartsilya	62	P5
Vyatka	78	J4
Vyatskiye Polyany	78	J4
Vyazemskiy	88	E2
Vyazma	78	E4
Vyazniki	78	G4
Vyborg	63	N6
Vychegda	78	H3
Vydrino	84	F5
Vygoda	73	L2
Vygozero, Ozero	78	F3
Vyhorlat	71	K4
Vyksa	78	G4
Vym	78	J3
Vyrnwy	52	D2
Vyshniy-Volochek	78	E4
Vysokoye	71	K2
Vytegra	78	F3
Vyzhva	71	L3

W

Name	Map	Grid
Wa	104	E3
Waal	64	F3
Waat	103	F6
Wabana	121	R8
Wabasca	119	N4
Wabash	124	G7
Wabe Gestro Wenz	103	H6
Wabe Shabele Wenz	103	H6
Wabigoon Lake	124	D2
Wabowden	119	R4
Wabush	121	N7
Waccasassa Bay	129	L6
Waco	128	D5
Wad Banda	102	E5
Waddan	101	J3
Waddeneilanden	64	F2
Waddenzee	64	F2
Waddesdon	53	G3
Waddington, Mount	118	K5
Wadebridge	52	C4
Wadena	124	C3
Wadi Gimal	96	B4
Wadi Halfa	102	F3
Wad Medani	103	F5
Wadomari	89	J10
Wad Rawa	103	F4
Wafra	97	H2
Wager Bay	120	J4
Wagga Wagga	113	K6
Wagin	112	D5
Wahai	91	H6
Waharoa	115	E2
Wahiawa	126	R10
Wahibah, Ramlat ahl	97	P6
Wahidi	96	H9
Wahoo	123	R7
Wahpeton	123	R4
Waialua	126	R10
Waianae	126	R10
Waiau *New Zealand*	115	A6
Waiau *New zealand*	115	D5
Waiau *New Zealand*	115	D5
Waibeem	91	J6
Waidhofen *Austria*	68	E2
Waidhofen *Austria*	68	E1
Waigeo	91	J6
Waiheke Island	115	E2
Waihi	115	E2
Waikabubak	91	F7
Waikato	115	E3
Waikerie	113	H5
Waikouaiti	115	C6
Wailuku	126	S10
Waimakariri	115	D5
Waimamaku	115	D1
Waimate	115	C6
Wainganga	92	E4
Waingapu	91	G7
Waini Point	136	F2
Wainwright	118	D1
Waiotapu	115	F3
Waiouru	115	E3
Waipa	115	E2
Waipahi	115	B7
Waipara	115	D5
Waipawa	115	F3
Waipiro	115	G3
Waipu	115	E1
Waipukurau	115	F3
Wairau	115	D4
Wairau Valley	115	D4
Wairio	115	B7
Wairoa	115	F3
Waitaki	115	C6
Waitangi	115	F6
Waitara	115	E3
Waitoa	115	E2
Waiuku	115	E2
Wajima	89	F7
Wajir	107	H2
Wakasa-wan	89	E8
Waka, Tanjung	91	H6
Wakatipu, Lake	115	B6
Wakaya	114	R8
Wakayama	89	E8
Wake	89	E8
Wakeeny	123	Q8
Wakefield	55	H3
Wakkanai	88	H3
Wakool *Australia*	113	J6
Wakool *Australia*	113	J6
Waku Kungo	106	C5
Walachia	73	H3
Walade	114	K6
Walagan	87	N1
Walbrzych	71	G3
Walcha	113	L5

Name	Pg	Grid
Yagan	86	J3
Yagodnoye	85	R4
Yagodnyy	84	Ae5
Yahuma	106	D2
Yahyali	76	F3
Yaizu	89	G8
Yakacik	77	G4
Yakapinar	77	F4
Yako	104	E3
Yakoruda	73	G4
Yakovlevka	88	D3
Yakrik	86	E3
Yaksha	78	K3
Yakumo	88	H4
Yaku-shima	89	C10
Yakutat	118	H4
Yakutsk	85	M4
Yala	93	K7
Yalak	77	G3
Yalcizcam	77	K2
Yalinca	77	K4
Yalinga	102	D6
Yalkubul, Punta	131	Q7
Yallourn	113	K6
Yalong Jiang	93	K3
Yalova	76	C2
Yalpug	73	K2
Yalpug, Ozero	73	K3
Yalta	79	E7
Yaltushkov	73	J1
Yalu	87	P3
Yalu He	87	N2
Yalutorovsk	84	Ae5
Yalvac	76	D3
Yamagata	89	H6
Yamaguchi	89	C8
Yamal, Poluostrov	84	Ae2
Yaman Dagi	77	G3
Yambering	104	C3
Yambio	102	E7
Yambol	73	J4
Yamdena	91	J7
Yamethin	93	J4
Yamgort	78	L3
Yamin, Puncak	91	K6
Yamma Yamma, Lake	113	J4
Yamoussoukro	104	D4
Yampa	123	L7
Yamparaez	138	D3
Yampol	73	K1
Yam, Ramlat	96	G8
Yamsk	85	S5
Yamuna	92	E3
Yamunanagar	92	E2
Yamyshevo	84	B6
Yamzho Yumco	93	H3
Yana	85	P2
Yanam	92	F5
Yanan	93	L1
Yanaul	78	J4
Yanbual Bahr	96	D4
Yancheng	87	N5
Yanchi	87	K4
Yanchuan	87	L4
Yande	114	V16
Yandrakinot	118	A3
Yandun	86	F3
Yangarey	78	L2
Yangchun	93	M4
Yanghe	87	M5
Yangjiang	93	M4
Yangon (Rangoon)	93	J5
Yangquan	87	L4
Yangshan	93	M4
Yangshuo	93	M4
Yangtze	93	L2
Yangyang	88	B6
Yangzhou	87	M5
Yanina	75	F3
Yanisyarvi, Ozero	62	P6
Yanji	88	B4
Yankton	123	R6
Yanqi	86	F3
Yanshou	88	B3
Yantai	87	N4
Yantra	73	H4
Yanxing	88	C2
Yanzhou	87	M4
Yao	102	C5
Yaoquanzi	86	H4
Yaounde	105	H5
Yaoxiaolong	88	A1
Yapen	91	K6
Yapen, Selat	91	K6
Yap Islands	91	K4
Yaprakali	76	E2
Yaqui	127	H6
Yar *U.K.*	53	F4
Yar *Russia*	78	J4
Yaraka	113	J3
Yaransk	78	H4
Yarashev	73	J1
Yardley Hastings	53	G2
Yare	53	J2
Yarenga	78	H3
Yarensk	78	H3
Yariga-take	89	F7
Yarim	96	G9
Yarimca	76	C2
Yaritagua	136	D2
Yarkant He	92	E1
Yarkovo	84	Ae5
Yarlung Zangbo Jiang	93	H3
Yarma	76	K3
Yarmolintsy	73	J1
Yarmouth	121	N9
Yarongo	84	Ae3
Yaroslavl	78	F4
Yarraloola	112	D3
Yarra Yarra Lakes	112	D4
Yarroto	84	A3
Yarrow	57	E5
Yar Sale	84	A3
Yarsomovy	84	A4
Yartsevo *Russia*	84	D4
Yartsevo *Russia*	78	E4
Yarty	52	D4
Yarumal	136	B2
Yary	84	Ae3
Yasawa	114	Q8
Yasawa Group	114	Q8
Yaselda	71	L2
Yashbum	96	H9
Yashiro-jima	89	D9
Yashkul	79	H6
Yasin	92	D1
Yasinya	71	L4
Yasnaya Polyana	88	F3
Yass	113	K5
Yasuj	95	K6
Yasun Burun	77	G2
Yata	136	D6
Yatagan	76	C4
Yate	114	X17
Yates Center	128	E2
Yates Point	115	A6
Yathkyed Lake	119	R3
Yatsushiro	89	C9
Yatta Plateau	107	G3
Yatton	52	E3
Yauri Espinar	136	C6
Yavatmal	92	E4
Yavi, Cerro	136	D2
Yavlenka	84	Ae6
Yavorov	71	K4
Yavr	62	N2
Yavu	77	G3
Yavuzeli	77	G4
Yawatahama	89	D9
Yawng-hwe	93	J4
Yawri Bay	104	C4
Ya Xian	93	L5
Yaxley	53	G2
Yaya	84	D5
Yaygin	77	J3
Yayla	77	J3
Yayladagi	77	G5
Yazd	95	M6
Yazd-e Khvast	95	L6
Yazihan	77	H3
Yazoo City	128	G4
Yazovir Dimitrov	73	H4
Ybbs	68	E1
Ydseram	105	H3
Ye	93	J5
Yealmpton	52	C4
Yecheng	92	E1
Yecla	67	F3
Yedinka	88	G2
Yedinsty	79	D6
Yedoma *Russia*	78	G3
Yedoma *Russia*	78	J2
Yedondin	85	J6
Yeeda River	112	E2
Yefira	75	G3
Yefremov	79	F5
Yegorova, Mys	88	F3
Yegoryevsk	78	F4
Yei	102	F7
Yeijo, Cerro	136	B4
Yekaterinburg	84	Ad5
Yekaterininka	78	L3
Yekaterinoslavka	85	M6
Yekhegnadzor	77	L3
Yelabuga	78	J4
Yelantsy	84	H6
Yelets	79	F5
Yeletskiy	78	L2
Yelizarovo	84	Ae4
Yelizavety, Mys	85	Q6
Yelkenli	77	K3
Yell	56	A1
Yellandu	92	F5
Yellel	67	G5
Yellowhead Pass	119	M5
Yellowknife *Canada*	119	N3
Yellowknife *Canada*	119	N3
Yellow River	87	M4
Yellow Sea	87	N4
Yellowstone	123	M4
Yellowstone Lake	123	J5
Yell Sound	56	A1
Yelnya	78	E5
Yemen, *Republic of*	96	G9
Yemetsk	78	G3
Yemtsa	78	G3
Yen Bai	93	K4
Yendi	104	E4
Yengisar *China*	86	D4
Yengisar *China*	86	E3
Yengue	105	G5
Yenice *Turkey*	76	B3
Yenice *Turkey*	77	F3
Yenice *Turkey*	76	F4
Yeniceoba	76	E3
Yenikem	76	E3
Yenikoy *Turkey*	77	G4
Yenikoy *Turkey*	77	K2
Yenipazar	76	C4
Yenisarbademli	76	D4
Yenisehir	76	C2
Yenisey	84	D3
Yeniseysk	84	E5
Yeniseyskiy Zaliv	84	C2
Yenotayevka	79	H6
Yeoryios	75	G4
Yeovil	52	E4
Yeraliyev	79	J7
Yerbent	95	P2
Yerbogachen	84	H4
Yerema	84	H4
Yerevan	77	L2
Yergeni	79	G6
Yerkoy	76	F3
Yermak	84	B6
Yermaki	84	H5
Yermakovo	84	D3
Yermitsa	78	J2
Yermolayevo	79	K5
Yerofey-Pavlovich	85	L6
Yerolimin	75	G4
Yershov	79	H5
Yerupaja, Cerro	136	B6
Yerushalayim	94	B6
Yesil	77	G2
Yesilcay	76	C2
Yesilgolcuk	76	F3
Yesilhisar	76	F3
Yesilkent	77	G4
Yesilova	76	C4
Yesilova	76	E3
Yesilyurt	77	G3
Yessey	84	G3
Yeste	66	E3
Yeu, Ile d'	65	B5
Yevlakh	79	H7
Yevpatoriya	79	E6
Yevreyskaya Ao	88	D1
Ye Xian	87	M4
Yeysk	79	F6
Y-Fenni	52	D3
Yhu	138	E5
Yian	87	P2
Yiannitsa	75	G2
Yibin	93	K3
Yichang	93	M2
Yicheng	93	M2
Yichun	87	P2
Yidu	93	M2
Yidun	93	J2
Yigilca	76	D2
Yilan	88	B2
Yildizeli	77	G3
Yimianpo	88	A3
Yimuhe	87	N1
Yinchuan	87	K4
Yindarlgooda, Lake	112	E5
Yingde	93	M4
Ying He	93	M2
Yingkou	87	N3
Yining	86	E3
Yin Shan	87	K3
Yinxian	87	N6
Yioura *Greece*	75	H4
Yioura *Greece*	75	H3
Yirga Alem	103	G6
Yirol	102	F6
Yishui	87	M4
Yithion	75	G4
Yitong	87	P3
Yi Xian	87	N3
Yixing	87	M5
Yiyang	93	M3
Yliharma	62	N4
Yli-kitka	62	N3
Yli-li	62	L4
Ylitornio	62	K3
Ylivieska	62	L4
Y Llethr	52	C2
Yntaly	86	C2
Yoakum	128	D6
Yogope Yaveo	131	M9
Yogyakarta	90	E7
Yojoa, Laguna de	132	D7
Yokadouma	105	J5
Yokkaichi	89	F8
Yokohama *Japan*	89	G8
Yokohama *Japan*	88	H5
Yokosuka	89	G8
Yokote	88	H6
Yola	105	H4
Yolaina, Cordillera de	132	E9
Yom, Mae Nam	93	J5
Yonabaru	89	H10
Yonago	89	D8
Yon dok	88	B5
Yonezawa	89	H7
Yong-an	88	B5
Yongan	87	M6
Yongchang	86	J4
Yongchuan	93	L3
Yongdeng	93	K1
Yongfeng	87	M6
Yongfu	93	L4
Yonghe	87	L4
Yonghung	87	P4
Yongju	89	B7
Yongkang	87	N6
Yongren	93	K3
Yongsanpo	87	P4
Yongsheng	93	K3
Yonkers	125	P6
Yonne	65	E5
York *U.K.*	55	H3
York *Nebraska*	123	R7
York *Pennsylvania*	125	M7
York, Cape *Australia*	113	J1
York, Cape *Papua New Guinea*	114	C4
Yorke Peninsula	113	H6
Yorketown	113	H6
York Factory	119	S4
York, Kap	120	N2
Yorkshire Moors	55	J2
Yorkshire Wolds	55	J3
Yorkton	123	N2
York, Vale of	55	H2
Yoro	132	D7
Yosemite Valley	126	C2
Yosemite Village	126	C2
Yoshioka	88	H6
Yoshkar-Ola	78	H4
Yosu	87	P5
Yotsukura	89	H7
Youghal	59	G9
Youghal Bay	59	G9
Youhao	88	B2
You Jiang	93	L4
Youkounkoun	104	C3
Young	113	K5
Young, Cape	115	F6
Youngstown	125	K6
Youssoufia	100	D2
You Xian	93	M3
Youyang	93	L3
Yozgat	76	F3
Ypres	64	E3
Yreka	122	C7
Ysabel Channel	114	C2
Ysbyty Ifan	54	F3
Ysgubor-y-coed	52	D2
Yssingeaux	65	F6
Ystad	63	E9
Ythan	56	F3
Ytterbyn	62	K4
Ytterhogdal	63	F5
Yuanjiang	93	K4
Yuan Jiang	93	M3
Yuanling	93	M3
Yuanmou	93	K3
Yuanping	87	L4
Yuba City	126	B1
Yubari	88	H4
Yucatan Channel	132	E4
Yucebag	77	J3
Yuci	87	L4
Yudaokou	87	M3
Yudoma	85	P5
Yudu	87	M6
Yuendumu	112	G3
Yueqing	87	N6
Yuexi	93	N2
Yuexi He	93	K3
Yueyang	93	M3
Yug	78	H3
Yugorskiy Poluostrov	84	Ad3
Yugoslavia	72	F3
Yuhebu	87	K4
Yuhuan	87	N6
Yuilsk	84	Ae4
Yu Jiang	93	L4
Yukon	118	D3
Yukon Delta	118	C3
Yuksekova	77	L4
Yukta	84	H4
Yukutat Bay	118	H4
Yula	78	G3
Yuli	86	F3
Yulin *Guangxi, China*	93	M4
Yulin *Shaanxi, China*	87	K4
Yuma	126	E4
Yumen	86	H4
Yumenzhen	86	H3
Yumurtalik	77	F4
Yuna	133	N5
Yunak	76	D3
Yunaska Island	118	Ad9
Yuncheng	93	M2
Yungay	136	B5
Yunnan	93	K4
Yunotsu	89	D8
Yunta	113	H5
Yunxiao	87	M7
Yurga	84	C5
Yurgamysh	84	Ad5
Yuribey *Russia*	84	A3
Yuribey *Russia*	84	B2
Yurimaguas	136	B5
Yurla	78	J4
Yurya	78	H4
Yuryevets	78	G4
Yuryev Polskiy	78	F4
Yusef, Bahr	102	F2
Yushan	87	M6
Yushino	78	J2
Yushkozero	62	Q4
Yushu *Jilin, China*	87	P3
Yushu *Qinghai, China*	93	J2
Yushugou	86	F3
Yusta	79	H6
Yusufeli	77	J2
Yutian	92	F1
Yuty	138	E5
Yuxi	93	K4